COMPARATIVE
PSYCHOLOGY

COMPARATIVE PSYCHOLOGY

Third Edition

CALVIN P. STONE, *Editor*

CONTRIBUTORS

CALVIN P. STONE, *Stanford University*
R. H. WATERS, *The College of Wooster*
PAUL THOMAS YOUNG, *University of Illinois*
WILLIAM C. YOUNG, *University of Kansas.*
W. T. HERON, *University of Minnesota*
HARRY F. HARLOW, *University of Wisconsin*
K. W. SPENCE, *State University of Iowa*
DONALD G. MARQUIS, *University of Michigan.*
K. U. SMITH, *University of Wisconsin*
CALVIN S. HALL, *Western Reserve University*
NICHOLAS E. COLLIAS, *University of Wisconsin*
HENRY W. NISSEN, *Yale University*
ROBERT A. PATTON, *University of Pittsburgh*

GREENWOOD PRESS, PUBLISHERS
WESTPORT, CONNECTICUT

Preface to the Third Edition

During the decade since *Comparative Psychology* underwent its first revision, new requests from users of this well-known textbook have been voiced in many quarters. These reflect a growing interest in studies of social and abnormal psychology, and in the more specialized aspects of genetics, neurophysiology, and endocrinology as related to behavior. To meet these needs in particular, but also to keep in touch with recent advances in genetic psychology, sense perception, motivation, anthropoid learning, individual differences, and learning theory as it bears on animal studies, the third edition of *Comparative Psychology* was undertaken.

Space requirements for the new chapter on "Abnormal Behavior in Animals" and for more extensive treatments of anthropoid learning and problem solving necessitated omitting the special chapter on "The Conditioned Reflex," which appeared in each of the previous editions. This seemed reasonable because coverage of this topic has been relatively complete in other publications.

New authors appearing for the first time in *Comparative Psychology* will be introduced, along with those who have written for previous editions, in the section entitled "Introducing the Authors."

CALVIN P. STONE
Editor

Preface to the First Edition

The increasing number of courses offered in Comparative Psychology gives some indication of the importance of the subject. Realizing the need for a satisfactory textbook in this field, a number of men who had been working in Animal Psychology convened at the Cornell meeting of the American Psychological Association and planned an introductory textbook. Each of them prepared independently a suggestive outline for the book as a whole. After studying this outline, a committee selected what appeared to be the most important topics and allocated the assignments among the men according to their specializations. Thereafter each contributor developed his topic in his own way and assumed full responsibility for content, for interpretation of data, and for placement of emphasis. The book is thoroughly documented, so that anyone wishing to go back to the original sources will have no difficulty in so doing.

The editor wishes to commend the contributors for their systematic teamwork in attempting to reduce or eliminate needless repetition of closely related subject matter. Perhaps still more along this line, as well as along the line of unification, could have been done had not the time and transport factors rendered personal consultations among the contributors impossible. There was no effort whatever to curb or to eliminate diverse opinions on controversial subjects; such opinions are omnipresent in rapidly changing subjects, and no student is any the worse for encountering them in his reading at the very outset.

Through cooperative efforts, singularly free from the secretive reserve sometimes found among specialists, a book more representative of Comparative Psychology as it is today has been obtained than could reasonably be expected from the hand of a single contributor in this varied and ever-expanding field. Breadth of view and wealth of subject matter more than compensate for a certain lack of unification inevitably present in a work of this kind.

F. A. Moss
Editor

Introducing the Authors

CALVIN P. STONE is Professor of Psychology at Stanford University. He received his A.B. from Valparaiso University, his M.A. from Indiana University, and his Ph.D. from the University of Minnesota. In 1916, he was Director of the Psychological Laboratory at the Indiana State Reformatory. Although Professor Stone has taught or held research appointments at several institutions, between 1915 and the present time, his major academic connection has been with Stanford University, where he began teaching in 1922. His chief research projects have been in the field of comparative psychology, with special emphasis on sex behavior, learning, abnormal behavior, and the effects of brain lesions and electroconvulsive shocks on innate and learned responses. He has been Editor of the *Journal of Comparative and Physiological Psychology* and is now Editor of the *Annual Review of Psychology*.

ROLLAND HAYS WATERS is a graduate of Baker University and completed his graduate studies at the University of Chicago. He has been a Professor of Psychology at the University of Arizona, University of Arkansas, and The College of Wooster, where he is Director of the Psychology Department. His research and publications have been chiefly in comparative psychology, learning, and psychological theory. Professor Waters was on leave during the year 1950-51, working as a Research Associate with Dunlap & Associates, Inc., New York City.

PAUL THOMAS YOUNG has served on the teaching staff of Cornell University, the University of Minnesota, and the University of Illinois, where he has been Professor of Psychology since 1934. He is the author of two standard works, *Motivation of Behavior* (1936), and *Emotion in Man and Animal* (1943). He has published several encyclopedia articles upon motivation and numerous papers reporting experiments upon motivation, affectivity, social behavior, and other topics. In 1926-27, as National Research Council Fellow at the University of Berlin, he commenced his studies of food preference and also did a well-known experiment upon sound localization with the pseudophone. At the present, Professor Young is on the editorial board of the *Comparative Psychology Monographs* and the *Journal of Social Psychology.*

WILLIAM CALDWELL YOUNG is Professor of Anatomy in the University of Kansas School of Medicine. Prior to going to Kansas, he was at Brown University and at the Yerkes Laboratories of Primate Biology in Orange Park, Florida. His research interests are in the microscopic anatomy and physiology of reproduction. Early in his work he was attracted by the close relationship between the structural changes associated with reproduction and the patterns of reproductive behavior. The articles that he and his students have published have dealt largely with these relationships in guinea pigs, rats and chimpanzees. Professor Young is currently at work on a monographic treatment of the relationship between the thyroid gland and reproduction in mammals.

WILLIAM T. HERON is Professor of Psychology at the University of Minnesota. He was previously connected with the Department of Psychology at the University of Kansas, the University of Texas, and the University of Chicago. His special interests are animal psychology, the theory of learning, and hypnosis. His writings include chapters on "Learning and Complex Learning Processes," in *Comparative Psychology* (1942), *"Clinical Applications of Suggestion and Hypnosis"* (1950), and various papers in the *Journal of Comparative and Physiological Psychology.* He is presently engaged in teaching and research on the theory of learning.

HARRY F. HARLOW, Ph.D., Stanford University, has been a member of the Department of Psychology at the University of Wisconsin since 1930, and was Chairman of the Department in 1949-50. He was a Carnegie Fellow in Anthropology at Columbia University in 1939-40. Professor Harlow was granted a leave of absence from the University of Wisconsin for the 1950-51 academic year to serve as Scientific Advisor to the Research and Development Division of the Army. His primary fields of interest are comparative and physiological psychology. He founded the Primate Laboratory at the University of Wisconsin and has conducted systematic studies on the social behavior, sensory capacities, learning, and thinking of old world and new world monkeys.

KENNETH W. SPENCE was born in Chicago, Illinois and educated in Montreal, Canada, obtaining the B.A. and M.A. degrees at McGill

University. After receiving the Ph.D. degree from Yale University, he was a National Research Council Fellow at the Yale Laboratories of Primate Biology. Since 1942 he has been Professor and Head of the Department of Psychology at the State University of Iowa. His main research interests are in the fields of learning, motivation, and scientific methodology. His writings include "Theoretical Interpretations of Learning," in Moss, *Comparative Psychology* (1942); "Theories of Learning," in Stevens, *Handbook of Experimental Psychology* (1951); and various monographs and articles that have appeared in such periodicals as *The Psychological Review, Journal of Comparative Psychology,* and *Journal of Experimental Psychology.* During World War II he was engaged in research projects with the Civil Aeronautics Administration on pilot aptitude tests and with the Navy Department on gunnery training devices.

DONALD G. MARQUIS is Professor of Psychology and Chairman of the Department at the University of Michigan. In his training and experience he has combined anatomical and physiological study of the nervous system with psychological study of behavior. After receiving his Ph.D. degree from Yale, he spent a year as a National Research Council Fellow in J. F. Fulton's laboratory of neurophysiology, and later a year as Rockefeller Fellow at Queen's Square Hospital for nervous diseases in London. He is the author, with Ernest R. Hilgard, of "Conditioning and Learning" (1940). During World War II he was on leave from his position as Chairman of the Psychology Department at Yale University to organize the Army-Navy-OSRD Vision Committee. Subsequently he has served as Chairman of the Committee on Human Resources of the Defense Department's Research and Development Board.

KARL U. SMITH, Department of Psychology, University of Wisconsin, received his Ph.D. degree from Brown University in 1936. He has done his initial graduate research and later research in the field of animal and physiological psychology, mainly on problems of the neurophysiology of discrimination and learning. His major research writings have dealt with studies of the cortical relations of animal vision, role of the cortex in learning, sidedness and visual perception in man, and analysis of optically controlled eye movements in animals. Professor Smith is presently engaged in studies of analysis of movements in the human individual, the phenomena of human motor coordination, and the systematic study of human thinking.

CALVIN S. HALL has been Chairman of the Division of Psychology of Western Reserve University, Cleveland, Ohio, since 1937. After attending the University of Washington and ᵥthe University of California (Berkeley), where he received his A.B. and Ph.D., he taught for three years at the University of Oregon before moving to Cleveland. During the war years, Professor Hall was a public panel member for the War Labor Board in Cleveland. He has published a number of articles in his special field of interest of temperament and personality, and he has contributed chapters to several recent books. Professor Hall's most recent interest is the study of dreams, which he hopes will provide a method of investigating temperament and personality in people.

NICHOLAS E. COLLIAS, Ph.D., University of Chicago, is on the staff of the Department of Zoology at the University of Wisconsin. His special fields are animal ecology and animal behavior, with special reference to birds. He has written various articles on social behavior of vertebrate animals, particularly on dominance relations and on physiological control of social behavior. He has worked in the field of animal sociology with W. C. Allee at the University of Chicago, N. Tinbergen at the University of Leiden, David Lack at Oxford University, and as a summer fellow at the New York Zoological Park. During World War II Professor Collias was an Aviation Physiologist with the United States Army Air Corps.

HENRY W. NISSEN, Ph.D., Columbia University, is Research Associate at Yale University and Assistant Director of the Yerkes Laboratories of Primate Biology at Orange Park, Florida. He began his studies of anthropoid behavior with a field study of chimpanzees in their native habitat in Africa. Since 1939 he has been in charge of the chimpanzee research and breeding colony at Orange Park, and has organized a program of developmental studies in which physical, physiological, and behavioral changes are studied intensively from birth to maturity. During this time he participated, also, in military research and in studies of human psychopathology. His contributions to the professional journals and reference works are mainly in the field of comparative psychobiology, and deal especially with behavior analysis of the chimpanzee.

ROBERT A. PATTON, Ph.D., is Director of Research and Associate Professor of Psychology at the University of Pittsburgh, Psychiatric

Institute and Clinic. He was a Research Fellow at the University of Pittsburgh from 1940 to 1944 under grants from the Buhl Foundation and the Williams-Waterman Fund of the Research Corporation, New York. His research papers have included studies of the relationship of nutritional deficiencies to abnormal behavior, studies of convulsive behavior in animals, and evaluation of the effects of electroshock convulsions on animal behavior. His present work includes teaching and research in areas related to the field of mental disorders.

Table of Contents

CHAPTER 1

Introduction

CALVIN P. STONE

Stanford University

Comparative Psychology, as a term, is applied to the study of behavior of diverse animals—chiefly studies that are intended to bring out differences and similarities.

They are analogous to the comparative studies of Anatomy and Physiology undertaken during the seventeenth and eighteenth centuries that led zoologists to the discovery that all animals may be placed into a few great groups or phyla, distinguishable from one another by readily seen differences in structure or body conformation. Such studies may also deal with relatively small differences between animals of a single race or species; in that case one speaks of individual, rather than group, differences.

Crude methods of comparison were applied to natural groupings of animals in ancient times; however, it is only within the past 100 years that Comparative Psychology has deserved a place in the hierarchy of biological sciences. Fragmentary records handed down from ancient civilizations indicate that fanciers and practical animal breeders took account of prominent differences and similarities in the behavior of animals. They brought together individual animals that appealed to their sense of esthetic or economic values in order better to compare and test them. Gradually those that surpassed the others in respect to beauty, tamability, educability, agility, fleetness, strength, endurance, fecundity, and so on, were identified. In time, knowledge arose as to which of these had attributes that persisted when representatives were taken from their native habitats and maintained through successive generations under novel conditions or in competition with local breeds.

Using rule-of-thumb methods of isolation and restricted mating, pioneer husbandmen achieved noteworthy progress along three lines: (*a*) elimination of undesirable characteristics, (*b*) strengthening of desirable traits, and (*c*) production of novel attributes by cross breed-

1

ing. During many centuries of slow progress, the fanciers and practical animal husbandmen, using crude comparative methods, standardized the behavioral characters of many of the ancestral breeds of domestic animals with which civilized peoples of this day are acquainted. Some of them are the ancestors of such well-known varieties as the pouter, tumbler, and carrier pigeon; the nonbroody leghorn, broody brahma, and bellicose gamecock; the rat terrier, fox hound, and Pekinese lap dog; the Arabian running horse, English hackney, and powerful clydesdale; the jersey, polled shorthorn, and Texas longhorn; the hampshire, duroc-jersey, and poland china pig; and so on.

The Animal Mind

Despite a good beginning on the part of practical breeders in the use of objective methods, few of the early writers can be considered exemplary in their attempts to describe and understand the animal mind. There was a well-nigh universal disposition to solve this problem at one fell swoop by attributing to animals many, if not all, of the attributes and processes of mind that traditional folk psychology had ascribed to man. An inordinate desire to humanize or to debase the brute usually prevailed; this gave rise to widely circulated collections of animal lore, such as the Physiologus, Aesop Fables, Bestiaries and other admixtures of fact and fiction. Exemplifying some of the absurdities perpetrated by men of the Middle Ages, who sometimes used animal lore to highlight interpretations of scriptural passages, is the following quotation from the Physiologus [(1), p. 178].

The Ape

This animal is very mischievous and fond of imitation. Whatever it sees men do, it immediately does the same. Hence he who wishes to catch an Ape takes a kind of lime which is called bird-lime, and pretends to anoint his eyes with the lime; then he goes away from that place and leaves the lime there. When now the hunter is quite gone away from the place where he left the lime and has hidden himself in a particular spot, then the Ape comes out of his nest and anoints his eyes as the hunter did, and he becomes blind and knows not where he is. As soon as the hunter sees that the Ape has anointed his eyes with the lime and has become blind, he runs up with a cord which he has ready, and ties the cord round the Ape's neck, and fastens the end of the cord to a tree. And the Ape steps up and down and becomes tame by force.

In this manner does the Devil, the great hunter, chase us. He comes into the world and brings with him the lime of sin, for sin is like bird-lime.

And he shows man how to blind his eyes and darken his mind, and draws him on from sin to sin and from evil to evil, and he makes a great snare of rope, for sin is insatiable, and the man becomes spotted with it, body and soul . . . I warn you, listen not to that Evil one lest he triumph over you through his cunning. So as often as we sin so often let us repent and hasten to God and cry with holy Paul: "Shall not the fallen one stand up again?" As often as thou fallest so often stand up again, and forthwith thou seest clearly the love of God and his mercy vouchsafed to us penitents.

Well spake Physiologus of the Ape.

A human-centered viewpoint, in which animals were endowed with the mental processes ascribed to man, was relatively unfruitful for the development of scientific Comparative Psychology. The unbridled desire of popular authors to humanize, of theologians to debase, of raconteurs to embellish, together with the lack of any powerful incentive for systematic observation and experiment, contributed to the almost universal disesteem with which Comparative Psychology was regarded prior to the last 25 years of the nineteenth century.

Kinship With Comparative Anatomy

Comparative studies of Anatomy, first actively pursued by zoologists during the seventeenth and eighteenth centuries, inevitably provided a wealth of factual information on the "habits" of living animals and also of conjectures about the "habits" of extinct species, which at that time were major concerns of paleontologists. Having discovered that vertebrates were fundamentally alike in the plan of their axial skeletons, they could offer plausible explanations for the rise of obvious diversities. Behavioral adaptations, they reasoned, had played an effective role in producing diversities through the principle of use and disuse. For example, the forelimb of the horse could be regarded as homologous to the forearm of the ape. Through differential use and consequent adaptations, and also because of atrophy that accompanies disuse, the forelimbs of primitive horses gradually lost their two outermost digits, and the second and fourth digits became mere vestiges. Only the third digit, which continued to grow in prominence, remained functional. Thus it came about that the horse eventually walked on a structure that is homologous to the third finger of a monkey or chimpanzee. Similar comparisons could be made with the wings of birds and forelegs of flying reptiles. This theory of gradual modification of homologous parts through use and disuse gave rise to the concepts of behavioral "archetypes," "vestigial habits," and atavisms or "throwbacks" of various kinds, all of which had structural counterparts.

As was true in Comparative Anatomy, interest in origins ultimately led to ontogenetic studies of behavioral development. While Embryology was splitting off as a special division within the broader field of Morphology, there accumulated, with increasing knowledge of tissue and organ formation, a vast fund of information about the earliest activities of organs or of behavioral systems. This was the forerunner of detailed information on the developmental schedules of embryos, fetuses, and new-born young, which will be described in Chapter 3. By analogy, comparative psychologists regarded these data as the foundations of an embryology of mind.

Steady progress in the correlation of behavior and structures, particularly receptors, effectors, and central nervous structures, during the eighteenth century set the stage for the cordial reception given to the early theories of evolution by Lamarck, Buffon, and Erasmus Darwin appearing about 1800; and later on, to the epoch-making treatise on mental evolution by Charles Darwin, first developed in *The Origin of Species,* and later expanded in *The Descent of Man* and in *The Expression of Emotions in Man and Animals* (see Chapter 2).

Kinship With Comparative Physiology

Many zoologists of the eighteenth and nineteenth centuries regarded Anatomy as the handmaid of Physiology. It was another way of saying that the ultimate goal of biology is that of understanding function, rather than describing form and structure. Thus a powerful stimulus to the pursuit of Comparative Psychology in its own right was received from Comparative Physiology, where objective, experimental methods were being developed to investigate a multitude of dynamic processes, such as those relating to the ingestion of food, consumption of fluids, concealment, defense, aggression, reproduction, migration, hibernation, and so on. All of these are problems that have a common psychobiological significance for diverse species of animals.

Early kinship with Comparative Physiology kindled the latter's interest in behavior of the lower classes of animals. This was of inestimable value because it provided an occasion for tracing phylogenetic advances in development from the lowest to the highest phyla, thereby giving a unified conception of the organic bases of all behavior. It also fostered the detached objectivity that is of paramount value in studies of social processes, temperaments, emotions, animal lust, parental solicitude, fraternal attachment, effects of brain lesions, and neurotic behavior, to name only a few of the fields of research in which an objective viewpoint is particularly helpful in studies of intricate bio-social problems. Physiological studies by Jacques Loeb at the end of the nineteenth century were epoch-making not only in Comparative Physiology but also in Comparative Psychology, where they highlighted advantages to be gained from the description of behavior of sea urchins, starfish, insects, amphibians, and higher vertebrates, with minimal recourse to the older mentalistic terms, such as sensation, perception, apperception, intuition, attention, reasoning, judgment, and so forth. Thanks to his example, a generation of able, behaviorally-minded zoologists developed comparative methods for correlating changes in behavior with man-made alterations in function of the nervous system, sense organs, endocrine glands, blood stream, and so on. These provided effective reasons why young, experimental psychologists at the turn of the twentieth century should depend less and less upon subjective approaches in studies of the animal mind, and should adopt an objective, behavioristic approach.

Psychological Levels

Comparative Psychology is still lacking an adequate rationale for the arrangement of its facts. The problem was sensed by Romanes when in the preface to his *Animal Intelligence* (2), he wrote:

It is almost needless to say that if the animal kingdom were classified with reference to Psychology instead of with reference to Anatomy, we should have a very different kind of zoological tree from that which is now given in our diagrams. There is, indeed, a general and, philosophically considered, most important parallelism running through the whole animal kingdom between structural affinity and mental development; but this parallelism is exceedingly rough, and to be traced only in broad outlines, so that although it is convenient for the purpose of definite arrangement to take the animal kingdom in the order presented by zoological classification, it would be absurd to restrict an inquiry into Animal Psychology by considerations of the apparently disproportionate length and minute subdivisions with which it is necessary to treat of the groups. Anatomically, an ant or a bee does not require more consideration than a beetle or a fly;

but psychologically there is need for as great a difference of treatment as there is in the not very dissimilar case of a monkey and a man (p. ix-x).

In the chapters that follow no attempt will be made to deal with behavioral problems with equal attention to representatives of the different phyla. Most of the subject matter pertains to vertebrates of the class mammalia. It is doubtful whether the science of Comparative Psychology is sufficiently far advanced to justify undertaking detailed comparative studies of all the behavioral systems of even one or two well-chosen species, as is the custom in Comparative Anatomy where structural systems are contrasted and compared in great detail.

Recurrent Problems

Although barely 100 years of concerted effort have been directed to the development of Comparative Phychology as a science, it already has a host of persistent, unsolved problems. Some of those that have received considerable attention are as follows:

1. Where in the animal kingdom does mind or consciousness first appear? Some would drop this question, on the ground that it is unfruitful or insoluble; however, there still are eminent biologists, philosophers, and psychologists who believe that a solution should be sought.
2. What, at a neurological level, is correlated in a causal sense with conscious behavior? Gross brain structures? Amount of cerebral cortex, relative to body size or to noncortical portions of the central nervous system? Cytoarchitecture of the cortex? Interconnections between cortical areas, between cortex and subcortical areas, or between cell layers of the cortex?
3. What, phylogenetically speaking, is the origin of the most clear-cut human mental traits? This essentially is the problem of determining *what* in lower species of mammals is *homologous* to *what* in man, as opposed merely to being *analogous*.
4. How account for hereditary diversity within a given race or species of animals? Do principles of continuous variation in the Darwinian sense or of mutation in the sense of DeVries apply to behavior? May one speak of unit characters in respect to behavior as is done in respect to structural attributes?
5. Is the Lamarck hypothesis totally disproved with respect to behavior? If not, how account for what is learned becoming fixed in the germ plasm, as opposed to being organized only in the somatoplasm? Is it possible that at times a mechanism, analogous to that of "pangenesis," as described by Darwin, becomes effective, causing certain habits that

are automatized in succeeding generations to be fixed finally as hereditary characters?

6. What from the standpoint of ultimate behavioral capacity is the significance of prolonged "infancy" in the anthropoids? In answering this
question should one lean more heavily on the growth and differentiation of structures, or give more thought to the role of experience, particularly infantile experiences that can form the warp and woof of
later, complicated acts?

7. Which animals, practically speaking, are most suitable for the solution
of particular problems of behavior? And what degree of parsimony
shall be observed in generalizing from "best animal for the problem"
to animals that, according to the phylogenetic scale, are either lower
or higher?

In the chapters that follow, the reader will be introduced to a
host of additional problems and experimental methods that someone
has considered trialworthy for a solution. To the extent that these,
or analogous methods, have been applied to different species of
animals, comparative data have been compiled; and to the extent
that the accumulated data have been applied to the solution of persistent problems, the broader aims of Comparative Psychology have
been partially realized.

Here and there a chief objective of animal research has been that
of satisfying individual curiosity. This was particularly true of John
Lubbuck. Nonetheless, data so accumulated have been applied by
others to elucidate persistent scientific problems in psycho-biology
and also to solve immediately practical problems, such as the control
of predatory animals, poisoning of insects, breeding of fur-bearing
animals, accelerating growth of meat animals, developing earlier-
laying hens, improvement of song in canaries, enhancing the speed
and endurance of thoroughbred race horses, offsetting the debility
of aging, and so on. Generally speaking, however, the most fundamental contributions to the solution of persistent problems in
animals behavior have come from scientists who pursue these topics
as a part of their vocational obligations, rather than from men who
have toyed with them as avocational hobbies. Because of this fact
authors of the following chapters have taken the pains to document
a great deal of literature brought to the reader's attention. The absence of documentation, however, does not mean that the topic under
discussion is any less credible or worthy of consideration than the
topics for which one or more citations appear.

8 INTRODUCTION

Bibliography

1. *Physiologus* (Translated by James Carlill), in the *History of Reynard the Fox,* translated by William Caxton. New York: E. P. Dutton & Co., pp. 278.
2. Romanes, George J., *Animal Intelligence.* New York: D. Appleton & Co., 1906, p. 520.

CHAPTER 2

Historical Background of Comparative Psychology

R. H. Waters

The College of Wooster

In the caves of prehistoric man the archaeologist has found numerous paintings, drawings, and sculptures of animals. The fact that animals rather than plants were selected as models by the artist is taken to mean that man of from 25,000 to 30,000 years ago was more interested in the former.

What is the meaning of these primitive works of art? It has been suggested that they had religious or superstitious significance. May it not be that our ancestors were trying by these means to invoke the aid or placate the anger of the gods of the chase? A less romantic interpretation of their meaning would be that these primitive artists turned to nature for their subjects and simply selected those that were a more prominent feature of their culture. Catching animals to replenish the food supply was, if not more vital, at least more exciting than gathering plants for the same purpose. We might also guess that, as an outgrowth of the hunt, the behavior of animals rather than their form and structure would arouse an added interest.

In ancient Egypt, Greece, and Rome the behavior of animals, especially of birds, was thought to be prophetic. Important undertakings such as wars, voyages, marriages, and induction into public office were undertaken only when the behavior of the animals of augury was favorable. Caesar was warned against going to the Senate on the Ides of March. According to the play this warning was based in part on just such auguries. These magical and superstitious practices were the beginning of modern Comparative Psychology with its laboratories and experimental techniques, its problems and theories.

The aim of a historical introduction is to trace the rise of new theories, new methods, and new experimental procedures as new problems were raised or old ones reformulated. By acquainting ourselves with its heritage and the men who have fashioned it we arrive at a deeper appreciation and a more intelligent understanding of the status of present-day Comparative Psychology. A short chapter can furnish but the skeleton of such a perspective. The bibliographic materials at the end of this chapter must be consulted to give it body and substance.

The customary procedure in presenting a brief history of the subject is to carve the fabric into appropriate units. This method recommends itself because it follows the general pattern set by other studies of historical thought and because it is possible by so doing to show rather sharp and critical changes in theories, methods, or problems that in successive periods have entered to mold the study. Such a cross-sectional analysis has the disadvantage of destroying in part the continuity that exists between present and past strands of the structure. The choice seems to be between a chronology of events and the genetic development of such characteristics as experimental methods and accompanying theories. By presenting as adequately as possible the chief features of the cross-sections the student can retrace his steps and complete the genetic picture. In what follows, the history of the entire movement is divided into chronological periods. In treating each, the attempt is made to present the major types of philosophical and theoretical thought that furnishes its background, the types of problems with which the workers in the field were engaged, and the methods and techniques that characterize the period.

The Grecian Period

It was in the era commonly called Grecian, since it was dominated by Grecian philosopher-scientists, that man began to deal in a serious fashion with the problems presented him by his universe. For the Greeks the chief interest was cosmology, the problem of the structure and laws of this universe. Their treatment of animal and human behavior, with the possible exception of the work of Aristotle (384-322 B.C.), was but incidental to this major program. It formed only one aspect of their more general philosophical inquiries into all natural phenomena.

The solution of two problems still current may be used to illustrate the work of the early Greek scientists. The first of these had to do with the conditions or causes of behavior. The general solution was in agreement with their broader interpretation of the universe as dualistic or monistic in nature. The dualistic conception was introduced by Empedocles (c. 500-430 B.C.) and somewhat modified by Anaxagoras (500-428 B.C.). According to this view material objects of the universe were reducible to physical elements—fire, earth, air, and water. To account for the organization of these elements into concrete objects, and to account for the movement of both the elements and the objects, nonphysical principles were assumed. For Empedocles these nonphysical principles were attraction and repulsion, or love and hate. Anaxagoras substituted for these two a single principle, Mind.

Opposed to this dualism was the belief, advanced by Leucippus and Democritus (460-370 B.C.), in material monism. In this belief the atoms composing matter were endowed with the power of movement. Hence no use was made of any nonphysical principle, soul, mind, or world-ordering Intelligence. Organization of atoms into objects and movement of bodies were to be explained in terms of physical principles only.

Plato (427-347 B.C.) continued the dualistic argument and offered a theory of the soul that provided a basis for distinguishing the behavior of man, animals, and plants from each other. He held that the soul was divisible into an irrational and a rational part. The irrational soul was further divided into a passionate and a nutritive part. Plants possessed only the lowest of these three, the nutritive soul. Animals had the two lower souls, the passionate in addition to the nutritive, and man possessed all three souls or parts of the single soul located in different areas of the body. The rational soul was located in the head, the passionate soul in the heart, and the nutritive soul in the abdomen. The observable differences in the behavior of plants, lower animals, and man were the result of the different souls possessed by each.

A second problem raised by the Greeks had to do with the development of different forms of life. A theory of evolution was proposed by Empedocles. He taught that life came from lifeless matter, the doctrine of abiogenesis, or in modern phraseology, spontaneous generation. Plants were believed to have been the first to appear, and from plants, animals were supposed to have developed. According to his theory, apparently, parts rather than complete animals were first formed. These parts, a head without a body, arms with no shoulders, and so on, were subject to the operation of the two principles, attraction and repulsion, and the parts attracted were joined. Any number of grotesque combinations could have resulted. Combinations that were not adapted to their environment or were incapable of reproducing disappeared. Nature may be supposed to have tried a variety of combinations, finally succeeding in perfecting types that fitted their surroundings and were capable of reproducing their kind. This conception of higher forms succeeding lower forms is an important feature of more modern evolutionary theories. It is in opposition to any theory of special creation, such as that found in Biblical literature, according to which each distinct species is unrelated to any other and incapable of giving rise to new forms.

The views of these early Greek philosophers were highly speculative. They were presented in the absence of what would be considered careful and accurate observation. Only rarely were experimental tests as we know them today undertaken. They are, nonetheless, forerunners of contemporary problems and theories.

A distinctly different trend was introduced by Aristotle, to whom, more than to any other of these pioneers, Comparative Psychology owes its greatest debt. The general temper of his work is so dominated by a new attitude toward scientific study that we might with some justification refer to the Aristotelian Period. He was discontented with the prevailing speculative approach to problems of nature. He proposed that careful investigation, observation, and gathering of facts be made the basis upon which theories were formulated. This strictly inductive method was an ideal that he approached but did not reach since he brought to his studies of animal behavior certain philosophical assumptions that colored his interpretation of all natural phenomena. Of these, the assumption of a teleological sequence present in the universe was perhaps the most important: "Nature creates nothing without a purpose, but always the best possible in each kind of living creature by reference to its essential constitution" [(2), p. 704^{b}]. This teleological sequence was governed by an ultimate principle, Reason, which, in cooperation with other minor principles, caused every object to appear in the form it possessed. This point of view was reflected in his defense of the study of animals. Animals should be studied for the sake of a better understanding of that part of man's environment, a modern notion, but more particularly such a study would help man to detect nature's plan and to discover the principles in harmony with which this plan was carried out. Aristotle says:

In certitude and in completeness our knowledge of terrestrial things has the advantage ... For if some (animals) have no graces to charm the sense, yet even these, by disclosing to intellectual perception the artistic spirit that designed them, give immense pleasure to all who can trace links of causation, and are inclined to philosophy ... If any person thinks the examination of the rest of the animal kingdom an unworthy task, he must hold in like disesteem the study of man. For no one can look at the primordia of the human frame—blood, flesh, bones, vessels, and the like— without much repugnance. Moreover, when any one of the parts or structures, be it which it may, is under discussion, it must not be supposed that it is its material composition to which attention is being directed or which is the object of the discussion, but the relation of such part to the total form [(3), p. 645ª].

Although Aristotle's interpretation of animal behavior was thus colored by his cosmological interest, he was the first to make what approached scientific observation. His *Historia Animalium* is essentially a natural history of animals. In it are discussed in considerable detail the differences between animals of different species in certain physical traits, habits of locomotion, breeding and mating, nesting, care of young by animals and man, and puberty and childbearing in man. Departing from strict adherence to the scientific procedure, animals are credited by him as exhibiting personality traits similar to those found in man.

In the great majority of animals there are traces of psychical qualities or attitudes which qualities are more markedly differentiated in the case of human beings. For, just as we pointed out resemblances in the physical organs, so in a number of animals we observe gentleness or fierceness, mildness or cross temper, courage or timidity, fear or confidence, high spirit or low cunning, and, with regard to intelligence something equivalent to sagacity ... The truth of this statement will be the more clearly apprehended if we have regard to the phenomena of childhood: for in children may be observed traces and seeds of what will one day be settled psychological habits, though psychologically a child hardly differs for the time being from an animal [(1), Book 8, Part 1, p. 588ª].

There are, by modern standards, some other obvious defects in Aristotle's work. It is difficult to determine how much of the factual material was the result of his own personal observation, how much was done by others under his direction, how much was borrowed from other writers, and, more importantly, what the conditions of observation were. There is, also a disconcerting mixture of really fine observational data with anecdotal material. As examples of the first we have his careful study of the habits of the bee, the behavior of certain fish, and the development of chick embryos. At the same time he seems to accept dubious anecdotes such as these: The sleeping dog's bark shows that he is dreaming; wolves tear fishermen's nets unless the fishermen share their catch with them; and sheep, if bred while north winds are blowing, will bear males, but if bred during a south wind, the offspring will be females. (A zoologist facetiously asked what Aristotle would have predicted in the event of a calm or a cyclone.)

Some of Aristotle's physiological conceptions are interesting when compared with our present knowledge. He argued that the heart is the seat of all the higher psychical processes because it is the first organ to manifest life (based on his study of the chick embryo) and because the most important organ would be found in the center of the body, just as the earth is at the center of the universe. He taught that the brain is not connected with any sense modality or psychical function. This, he argued, is true because observation revealed it, and also because no sensation is produced when the brain is touched (an observation in harmony with present-day beliefs). The function of the brain is that of a cooling mechanism for the heart—a kind of refrigerating apparatus—and tears were considered to be the result of the cooling action of the brain by which the vapors of the blood are condensed. The lack of flesh on the head is a provision for keeping the brain cool, permitting the readier radiation of heat.

But Aristotle did formulate some principles of importance for Comparative Psychology. In the first place, as has been mentioned, he argued for the necessity of accurate observation prior to the formulation of theories. Secondly, he tried, as had others before him, to account for the differences in behavior between plants, animals, and man. To this end he developed a theory of evolution that applied his philosophical conception of Reason to many classes of animals. He argued that the animals formed one continuous series from the lowest to the highest species but that the highest did not evolve from the lowest. Rather, all organisms were subjected to an "internal perfecting principle" that constantly strove for a perfect type. For him, it has been said, evolution worked from above downward rather than from below upward. His specific doctrine of the soul or souls possessed by various living forms was in many respects a refinement of Plato's teaching. Three souls were distinguished: the nutritive soul, which rules over nutrition and reproduction in all animals and plants; the sensitive soul, not found in plants, which is the arbiter of sensations and, in some of the higher animals, of locomotion as well; and the rational soul, peculiar to man. The higher forms possess the souls of the lower forms and, especially in man, the lower are subject to the rational soul to such an extent that the three are essentially a single soul with three subdivisions or parts.

It has been argued by certain writers that Aristotle, by assuming a close and intimate tie between the rational soul and the bodily form of man, made an approach to an abandonment of the earlier dualism and to the adoption of a somewhat modern view of man as a psychophysical organism. A number of other special doctrines are found in Aristotle that indicate his advanced type of thinking. He taught that animals have memory and can be trained. Only man, however, can voluntarily recall the past. He also formulated the laws of contiguity, of similarity, and of contrast. The law of effect is suggested in his statement that all animals seek pleasure in accordance with that which nature holds appropriate for them.

The development of scientific thought during the Grecian period reached its peak in Aristotle. Later contributions by other Grecian scholars include a return to the monistic position as developed by Democritus, the introduction of the concept of instinct as the basis for animal behavior, and the accumulation of considerable anecdotal data. Although the latter have little scientific merit, we shouldn't be too critical of these early philosopher-scientists. The fact is that until the latter part of the nineteenth century similar material was soberly proposed as evidence of the intellectual achievements of the brute. We must remind ourselves that the value of a given method can frequently be determined only on the basis of later scientific advances.

The Middle Ages

One of the most barren periods, as far as scientific investigation of natural phenomena is concerned, was that known as the Middle Ages. During that time the Church dominated all forms of intellectual endeavor and maintained a dictatorship over what man should believe and investigate. In so doing the Church Fathers claimed not only the authority of the Bible, but, strange as it may seem from the foregoing survey, the authority of Aristotle as well. The Biblical and Aristotelian philosophies were accepted as containing an adequate account of nature and life. So well satisfied were they with the accounts thus given that they frowned upon original investigation and refused to accept any statement of fact unless it was contained in one of these two sources. For example, "There is a well-known story of how the learned ecclesiastics disputed as to how many teeth the horse has according to Aristotle instead of looking into the mouth of a live horse to see for themselves" [(12), p. 78]. By this constant refusal to countenance any form of unbiased observational study, the most important feature of Aristotle's teaching was overlooked. Such an attitude meant a decline in scientific interest and research. Only in Arabia and through Arabian workers was interest in science kept alive. Their interest centered chiefly in medicine and physiology. From their work an indirect benefit resulted for Comparative Psychology, since they held that natural laws controlled physiological mechanisms. The fact that they did so quite possibly served to stimulate similar views for more complex forms of behavior.

The Renaissance and Early Evolution Period

The reawakening of the scientific spirit and the drive to empirical investigation of natural phenomena during the Renaissance was brought about by philosophers as well as by scientists proper. Francis Bacon (1561-1626) decried the natural science of the Greeks and championed the inductive method in science. René Descartes (1596-1650) also argued for the right to investigate every phenomenon of nature and proposed the application of mathematics to such studies. He was credited with the notion that animals were automata and that perhaps man was not the wholly rational animal he was thought to be. This suggestion may have been anticipated or made possible by the earlier work in physiology, especially the work of Harvey, who, about that time, demonstrated the circulation of the blood. But Descartes did not flout the authority of the Church too openly. He pointed out that it might be entirely possible to reach an intelligible solution of the order of the universe on the basis of rational hypotheses. He hastily added that of course everyone knew that the universe did not actually develop according to such principles. Thus he escaped the Inquisition. He went further and assumed that the soul played a role in the behavior of man. The soul was supposed to have its point of contact with the rest of the body in the pineal body, a small structure that has direct connection with both hemispheres of the brain. Here, he said, the soul directed the flow of animal spirits into this or that channel. In this way Descartes kept alive the tradition of a qualitative, not merely quantitative, difference in the behavior and nature of man and animal. So far as is known Descartes did not make any particular use of the soul after he had assigned it this channel of communication. He proceeded to account for behavior in terms of physical principles. The fact that he had included the soul in his system of explanation, although not necessarily in his system of belief, gave rise to the interactionistic interpretation of the relation of mind to body.

Leibnitz (1646-1716), Spinoza (1632-1677), Hume (1711-1776), and Kant (1724-1804) joined in the chorus for a naturalistic interpretation of nature as opposed to the interpretation stemming from philosophical speculation only. Kant, although arguing for the desirability of a naturalistic explanation, felt that such an attempt did not lie within the power of man. Man, he held, was simply not capable of envisaging principles of sufficient generality to account for the development of the various animal species. It was "absurd for man . . . to hope that a Newton may one day arise even to make the production of a blade of grass comprehensible, according to natural laws ordained by no intention." However, as Osborn points out (13), Darwin was Kant's Newton who did just that thing.

Thus through philosophy the way was being cleared for a return of the scientific investigation of animal behavior, the type of study that Aristotle years earlier had advocated. Other forces contributory to the same end were also developing. Aided by the new microscopic techniques, studies in physiology were revealing more and more of the *modus operandi* of neurophysiological processes. The works of Buffon (1717-1788) in natural history and of Bonnet (1720-1793) on insect forms, to mention but two of a considerable number of important men, were stimulating the interest of scientific workers toward more refined studies. It was almost inevitable that man's curiosity would lead him to make studies of animal behavior. But the most potent force impelling toward animal study was still to come, the theory of evolution as proposed by Darwin. As will be shown later, the nature of this theory was such that it led beyond the zoological to the psychological study of animal life.

The Darwinian Period

Charles Darwin (1809-1882) and his theory of evolution had such a profound influence on all the sciences in the period following the Renaissance that it is properly designated the Darwinian Period. Darwin grew up in an atmosphere that was charged with the general problem of the development of the species. Lamarck's theory, making the assumption of the inheritance of acquired characteristics, had been presented in 1802 and was being debated by prominent biologists of the time. Studies in embryology were showing the startling similarity of the embryonic forms of different species. Naturalists in France and Germany were contributing relevant materials. Darwin's grandfather, Erasmus Darwin (1731-1802), had been interested in the general problem and had presented a theory similar to Lamarck's. From every side, as Osborn says, "A storehouse of facts was fairly bursting for want of a generalization."

Darwin's first interests were geology and natural history. In part because of these interests he obtained the post of naturalist aboard the ship *Beagle* for a round-the-world cruise during the years 1831-1836. His observations and the questions raised during this voyage led him to undertake the formulation of his theory of evolutionary development embodying the familiar principles of variation, struggle for existence, and natural selection or survival of the fittest. His complete statement appeared in his *Origin of the Species* (1859). More important for the study of animal behavior, however, were two later books, *The Descent of Man* (1871) and *The Expressions of the Emotions in Man and Animals* (1872).

The latter two books represent Darwin's attempt to apply the general principles developed in the *Origin of the Species* to the physical, mental, and emotional development of man. In *The Descent of Man* he first stated and defended the case for the physical development of man and then turned to the more important and difficult task of explaining human mental development. He argued that differences in all animals present a series of fine gradations and that all differences are quantitative rather than qualitative in nature. In support of this claim he presented the following general theses: Man and the animals possess similar senses, similar instinctive action, the same fundamental emotions, and higher mental processes of attention, memory, imagination, deliberation, and choice. He even argued that animals show a trace of what, if the animal's intelligence equaled that of man, would be language, a sense of beauty, a belief in spirits. Almost all of the evidence he cited in support of these claims was anecdotal in nature. Precise experimental investigations were not made to obtain crucial and definitive data—the world was still lacking its Lloyd Morgan.

In *The Expressions of the Emotions in Man and Animals* Darwin argued that an adequate explanation of emotional expression as exhibited in the animal kingdom could be had only through an application of his evolutionary hypothesis. In this connection, he presented those principles that are now so well known to every student of emotion: the principle of serviceable associated habits, the principle of antithesis, and the principle of the direct action of the nervous system. Much of the evidence and argument that Darwin gives in defense of the validity of these principles would not be considered sound according to modern standards. The evidence collected came from a number of different sources. He made some observations on infants and common animals, studied (with little profit, he says) photographs and engravings, and tested the ability of untrained observers to judge emotions depicted in a number of specially-prepared photographs. In addition to the investigations of his own, he relied on the reports of others concerning the facial and emotional expressions of primitive peoples and the insane. Here again he runs into the dangers inherent in the anecdotal method. Furthermore, much of his argument assumes the validity of ascribing the same emotions to man and lower animals, which involves a form of circular reasoning as well as the fallacy of anthropomorphizing.

For the foregoing reasons the evidence given by Darwin does not measure up to contemporary standards of scientific exactness. Nevertheless his claims abundantly stimulated other scientists to devise experimental situations to test his hypotheses. In addition, the developmental course of Comparative Psychology was influenced in the direction of placing more emphasis on employment of the genetic method. As a result it was felt by some who followed Darwin that an adequate account of any type of behavior should be based on its phylogenetic and genetic history, a doctrine still in high favor among contemporary comparative psychologists. The most characteristic aspect of the period immediately following Darwin was the vigorous search for and the claim to have found higher mental traits in animals below man. It was here that the chief problem lay for those who would accept Darwin's theories. Little objection was made when man

was said to have instinctive and emotional traits in common with the
lower animals, but to say that both man and lower animals alike
possess higher mental processes was to deny a long line of historical
belief in a sharp dividing line between man and the lower animals.
This denial had the effect of raising the brute to the level of man
or, possibly worse, of lowering man to the level of the brute. Accordingly it behooved investigators to establish the fact of these higher
processes being present in animals.

The most prominent of the immediate followers of Darwin was
G. J. Romanes (1848-1894). So important were his writings that
Boring describes him as being Darwin's apostle in Comparative
Psychology. Romanes continued the plan outlined by Darwin and
argued for the continuity of the animal and human mind. But once
again the anecdotal method was employed to solve the problems.
Therefore many of his contributions to animal study lack really good
experimental support. A typical instance contributed by Romanes
may be given [(14), p. 56]:

Watch is a collie dog . . . a very remarkable dog . . . very intelligent,
understands many words, and can perform tricks. What I mention him
for, however, is that he is the only dog I ever met with a dramatic faculty.
His favourite drama is chasing imaginary pigs. He used now and then to
be sent to chase real pigs out of a field, and after a time it became a custom . . . to open the door for him after dinner in the evening, and say,
"Pigs!", when he always ran about wildly chasing imaginary pigs. If no
one opened the door, he went to it himself wagging his tail, asking for his
customary drama. He now reaches a further stage, for as soon as we get
up after our last meal he begins to bark violently, and if the door is open
he rushes out to chase imaginary pigs with no one saying the word "pigs"
at all. He usually used to be sent out to chase pigs after prayers in the
evening and when he came to my small house it was amusing to see that he
recognized the function of prayers performed with totally different accompaniments to be the same as prayers performed in an episcopal chapel, so
far as he expected "pigs" to be the end of both. The word "pigs" uttered
in any tone, will always set him off playing the same drama.

The dangers and limitations of the anecdotal method were made
so apparent by Romanes' publications that it is no longer employed
by scientists. It is therefore pertinent to ask, What is the anecdotal
method and what is wrong with it? One answer is, in effect, that the
anecdotal method is being employed whenever an individual's report
of some item of animal behavior is accepted as valid if the controls
surrounding the observation and report do not measure up to modern

scientific standards. The lack of such controls may vitiate the report in any of the following ways: The individual does not distinguish between what he observes and what he reads into the act or performance; he does not know the habits and past training of the animal observed nor those of the species to which it belongs and therefore reports an incident lifted out of its proper context; lastly, he is biased by what he believes concerning animal intelligence in general and the intelligence of the animal observed in particular.

The chief significance of the Darwinian period for the later development of Comparative Psychology lies in what may be called its theoretical contributions, in the fact that in this period a new spirit was injected into the study of animal behavior and that Comparative Psychology finally won independence from its philosophical parent. Since the time of Darwin, Comparative Psychology has taken its place as a definitely biological science and has developed as a strictly experimental rather than a speculative branch of knowledge. Naturalistic explanations of animal behavior are the only type now proposed. Before Darwin's time, studies of animal behavior were secondary to some larger interest. Among the Greeks it was secondary to their more general philosophical interest in the nature of the universe—to their cosmology; later it was secondary to the belief that man was the product of special creation; during the Darwinian period it was secondary to the general interest in the establishment of the theory of evolution. In the post Darwinian period, Comparative Psychology becomes an independent science. Animal behavior is studied as a legitimate scientific interest in itself as well as for the purpose of making comparative analyses and discovering principles applicable to human behavior. It is for these reasons that writers sometimes refer to Darwin as the founder of modern Comparative Psychology.

The First Half of the Twentieth Century

The development of Comparative Psychology since the time of Darwin is characterized by changes in methodology, in controversy over theory, and in scope of problems attacked. As we have said the anecdotal method is no longer countenanced. In its stead there developed during the last of the nineteenth and opening of the twentieth century distinctly experimental and laboratory methodologies. Interest began to shift from the study of the similarities in the behavior of man and animals to the study of what animals can or will do under controlled conditions. In response to this change in interest new methods and techniques for the laboratory study of higher animal forms were developed and applied. The investigator has striven to perfect those that will permit precise control of the living and training conditions of the animal, those to which quantitative analyses may be applied, and those in which control of stimuli and accurate record of the animal's reaction can be obtained so that the dependence of the behavior exhibited upon the stimulating conditions can be demonstrated. The succeeding chapters of this book will describe some of these methods. Our present purpose requires only a brief mention of their origin.

Sir John Lubbock (1834-1913) of England is credited with being the first to employ modern laboratory techniques to the study of insects. In so doing he exerted considerable influence in shaping the program of Comparative Psychology as it has developed in the United States. The American contributions to Comparative Psychology were initiated by the genius of E. L. Thorndike (1874-1949) who, in 1898, began publication of data from his studies on the learning behavior of chicks, cats, dogs, and monkeys. For these experiments he employed the problem box, which later became a standard piece of apparatus in many laboratories. But in addition to the introduction of this method, Thorndike's work was of major significance because of his demonstration of the possibiltiy of laboratory work on these higher animal forms, because of the light shed on problems that have furnished continual stimulation to others following him, and because of his negative conclusions as to the presence of ideas, reasoning, and imitation in animal learning. From these and other studies he formulated three important laws of learning—use, disuse, and effect— the application and validity of which have been lively controversial issues ever since.

In the same year, 1898, L. W. Kline (1866—) of Clark University gave impetus to Comparative Psychology as a subject of college study through the publication of two papers, one a sketch of methods in Comparative Psychology and the second, an outline for such a course. From the same laboratory, in 1900, W. S. Small (1870-1943) introduced the maze as an instrument for studying animal learning. Such an instrument had been anticipated by Thorndike, who had used a crude type of maze, but the pattern introduced by Small is the prototype of those that have since become standard equipment.

Another important figure in American Comparative Psychology is R. M. Yerkes (1876-), the founder and until recently, director of the Primate Laboratory of Yale University. His researches, beginning about 1900, have run the scale from invertebrates and the lower forms of vertebrates to the higher apes and man. Among his best-known contributions to methodology are the Yerkes-Watson discrimination box for studying visual discrimination (but easily adapted to testing other senses) and the multiple-choice methods for studying complex mental processes with the higher animals, especially the primates.

The widely-used conditioning method, first developed by Ivan Petrovich Pavlov (1849-1935), found an early champion in Watson at The Johns Hopkins University. Another general method, the *Umweg* or detour experiment, was developed by Wolfgang Köhler (1887-), a leader of the Gestalt movement in Germany, for the study of Chimpanzees. Köhler's book, *The Mentality of Apes* (1924), describes his methods and the theoretical interpretation of results obtained through their application from about 1914 to 1916.

The application of extirpation techniques to problems of cerebral function in habit formation was fostered in America by S. I. Franz (1874-1933) and K. S. Lashley (1890-). It constitutes another important chapter in the history of Comparative Psychology. Implications important for both Comparative and General Psychology have resulted from their work. These implications will be indicated more fully in later chapters. Anticipating a bit, the results from the extirpation method have well-nigh revolutionized our conceptions of neural action not only with respect to problems relating to cerebral localization of functions but also to laws of learning as well.

Within the past few years Comparative Psychology has witnessed the introduction of methods that promise to further our understanding of abnormalities of behavior. For many years interest has centered on the causes and cures of such behavior abnormalities. The genetic origin and development of these conditions in the human subject is extremely difficult to study experimentally. N. R. F. Maier and H. S. Liddell, among others, are pioneering in the field of "experimental neuroses." These conditions are being induced in such animals as the rat, cat, dog, pig, and sheep under laboratory conditions. At the same time the therapeutic efficacy of various procedures is being tested. In this way considerable light is being thrown by analogy on the conditions of human maladjustment.

Many of the methods already enumerated and also others especially designed for the purpose are being employed in the genetic study of animal development. These special procedures will be described in those portions of the text devoted to the role of maturation in the development of behavior. Another fertile area of research in Comparative Psychology is that in which animals are studied in their natural habitats but under conditions of systematic and objective observation. Mating, nesting, parental care, grouping, and other aspects of social behavior are the major foci of these field studies. Pioneering work was done in this area by C. Lloyd Morgan (1852-1936) on his pet dog, by Fabre on wasps and bees, and by the Peckhams on solitary wasps.

Concomitantly with these experimental and methodological changes, interpretative and theoretical issues were raised. The anthropomorphic interpretations by Charles Darwin and other earlier writers, which were carried to extremes by Romanes, were vigorously opposed by a few of their contemporaries. However, some of the criticisms could well be ignored as merely dogmatic, emotional outbursts. Others were well-reasoned, serious opinions of scientifically trained men, and had to be taken into account. The most significant of these criticisms were given by C. Lloyd Morgan in his *Introduction to Comparative Psychology* (1894). He recognized the fact that the interpretation of the animal mind rested on analogy with the mind of man and that such an interpretation might ascribe too much to the animal. He, therefore, proposed what has since been known as Lloyd Morgan's "canon," a form of the law of parsimony, as a guide against this error. This canon reads: *"In no case may we interpret an action as the outcome of the exercise of a higher psychical faculty, if it can be interpreted as the outcome of the exercise of one which stands lower in the psychological scale"* [(11), p. 53]. This principle has exerted a continuing influence on the explanations of animal behavior. In time, "the term 'anthropomorphic' acquired a peculiar significance in certain quarters. It became a choice epithet which you could hurl at an antagonist with telling effect when you wished to damn him in genteel terms. The word as used in this way seemed to convey the somewhat delicate suggestion that the individual in question was obtuse in intellect, a logical pervert, and an insipid sentimentalist." [1] Gestalt psychologists vigorously disagreed with the

---

[1] H. A. Carr. "The Interpretation of the Animal Mind," *Psychol. Rev.*, 1927, Vol. 34, p. 88.

rigid application of Morgan's canon. They argued that in human psychology there is need, and in Comparative Psychology still greater need, for qualitative descriptions that are not allowed on the basis of this canon. There is some justification for their position. Guiding principles should be sufficiently broad and elastic to serve as guides only, and not as masters. Such protests had relatively little effect. The power of the canon continued. It was indirectly responsible for the rise of our present-day behavioristic psychologies and thus led to the paradoxical situation in which human behavior could not be explained in mental terms.[2]

Joining forces with the anti-anthropomorphists, or mechano-morphists, Jacques Loeb (1859-1924) proposed a tropism theory. According to this theory animal behavior is satisfactorily explained in terms of the same physico-chemical principles as those that apply to the orientation of plants to external forces. He refused to use the expression "trial and error" or to employ descriptions suggestive of mental processes. Loeb's ambition was to explain animal behavior from the standpoint of the physical chemist. Any other type of explanation, he argued, was incapable of leading to quantitative experimentation. Animals were automata, and, like lifeless matter, were the puppets of external forces. Most of his work was done on plants and invertebrates. That the tropistic theory was applicable to the behavior of higher forms, including man, was nonetheless clearly implied. He did admit "associative memory" in higher forms, but this was a poor symbol for the changes left in neural structures by previous behavior. Loeb's work constituted a thoroughgoing application of Lloyd Morgan's canon. We are reminded of Descartes and the early Grecian materialists, Democritus and Leucippus. The logical climax of the mechanical argument has been reached.

In opposition to Loeb's tropism theory, H. S. Jennings (1868-1947) proposed and defended the "trial-and-error" theory. Working with protozoan forms, he was able to show that their behavior was not harmonious with the tropistic theory. His experiments showed that when these animals oriented themselves to various stimuli, several preliminary movements or "attempts" occurred before the response in its final form took place. There was no immediate tropistic response as Loeb's theory would predict. Jennings held that the phrase "trial and error" more accurately described the behavior than did the term

---

2 R. H. Waters, "Morgan's Canon and Anthropomorphism," *Psychol. Rev.*, 1939, Vol. 46, pp. 534-540.

"tropism." This suggestion was not merely for the sake of a change in terminology. It called for a distinctly different theoretical explanation. It implied that behavior is not adequately explained in terms of physical and chemical principles. It meant that principles of a different sort are needed, principles that do not assume animals to be only simple automata.

The contemporary student will study the conflict between what are today called stimulus-response and field theories in later chapters. These rival theories are the modern counterparts of the older theories sketched above.

Accompanying the introduction of new methods, experimental techniques, and theories there has been an increase in the variety of problems studied. Prior to the twentieth century, studies of instinctive or unlearned behavior *outside* the laboratory were typical. Now such studies are being continued both outside and inside the laboratory. They are, however, no longer representative of the total range of contemporary problems. This has already been indicated in our survey. Current volumes of the *Psychological Abstracts* will be found to carry annually the titles of some 400 or more studies of animal behavior and closely related topics. There are abstracts of studies on all forms of animal life from the protozoa to man. These studies include such topics as neural function, motivation, learning, glandular and drug effects, sensory and perceptual processes, food preferences, neurotic behavior, and social activities such as dominance, submission, cooperation, and competition. The foregoing classification is rough and scarcely does justice to the wealth of experimental data being collected.

The rise of Comparative Psychology has stimulated interest in neighboring fields. The introduction of the genetic or developmental mode of study by Darwin gave impetus to the field of child and adolescent psychology. A similar impetus was given behavioristic psychology as developed by J. B. Watson (1878-   ), one of the earliest experimentalists in the field of Comparative Psychology in America. His text, *Behavior: An Introduction to Comparative Psychology* (1914), is an excellent presentation of the methodological and theoretical status of the subject at that time. Impressed by the results obtained by strictly objective methods, he later published *Psychology from the Standpoint of a Behaviorist* (1919). In it Watson advocated the application of the same objective methods used in Comparative Psychology for the analysis of human behavior. The extreme position advocated in this text has been repudiated to some extent by Watson's successors. Nonetheless an objective and mechanistic psychology is still popular among many present-day psychologists.

One historically interesting phase of Comparative Psychology is represented by the work of Margaret Floy Washburn (1871-1939). Her chief book, *The Animal Mind,* went through four editions from 1908 to 1936. The book is a frank attempt to investigate the nature and structure of consciousness in animals, as opposed to a study of learning, discrimination, imitation and so on, *per se.* The movement represented by this book, never a very popular one in America, has practically disappeared. Such a study is confronted with the task of determining the criteria, in terms of which, mind in animals can be inferred and described. Many such criteria have been suggested. Aristotle implied that the degree of structural and behavioral similarity between man and the animal was a valid criterion. Darwin apparently agreed with Aristotle. Ability to learn was proposed by C. Lloyd Morgan and Romanes. Loeb offered "associative memory" as the primary criterion. Yerkes submitted the foregoing criteria to a searching analysis in 1905, showing, among other things, that no animal so far studied has been found unable to profit by experience. As a result of this analysis he proposed six criteria, grouped under two main types as follows:

I. Structural Criteria
    A. General form of the organism (organization).
    B. Nervous system (neural-organization).
    C. Specialization in the nervous system (neural-specialization).

II. Functional Criteria
    A. General form of reaction (discrimination).
    B. Modifiability of reaction (docility).
    C. Variableness of reaction (initiative).

Nevertheless, and in spite of these criteria, the difficulties in, and possibly the lack of practical value of, arriving at a knowledge of the animal mind as evidenced by arbitrary criteria have turned the psychologist's interest to other and more promising channels.

Summary

In closing this survey it will be valuable to bring together briefly the chief trends in the history of Comparative Psychology.

1. In the first place, the field of Comparative Psychology has come

to occupy an important place in its own right. It has come of age. Until the Darwinian period the treatment of animal behavior formed only one phase of a more general treatment and interpretation of nature. It is now a special and independent field of study.

2. The evolutionary doctrine with its implications is now almost universally accepted. As a general principle this doctrine stimulated the application of the genetic method in the field of child psychology and justified the development of functional and behavioristic psychologies.

3. A significant trend is the change in methods of study. The anecdotal method is no longer accepted. The natural history methods are still employed, but with more adequate controls. Experimental and quantitative methods are now in use. A history of the change in methodology mirrors the development of the scientific method and scientific attitude in general.

4. Another highly significant feature is the incessant warfare carried on by the proponents of rival theories.

5. Correlated with these trends is an increase in the types of problems investigated. It would be safe to say that every basic or important question that has been asked concerning human behavior is now being asked of animal behavior.

6. Two motives have been at work in the study of Comparative Psychology. The first has for its aim a better understanding of the animal; the second, the discovery of principles that will lead to a better understanding of human behavior.

Bibliography

1. Aristotle, *Historia Animalium* (translated by D. W. Thompson), in *Works,* ed. by J. A. Smith and W. K. Ross. Oxford: Clarendon Press, 1912, Vol. IV.
2. —— *De Motu* and *De Incessu Animalium* (translated by A. S. I. Farquharson), in *Works,* ed. by J. A. Smith and W. K. Ross. Oxford: Clarendon Press, 1912, Vol. V.
3. —— *De Partibus Animalium* (translated by William Ogle), in *Works,* ed. by J. A. Smith and W. K. Ross. Oxford: Clarendon Press, 1912, Vol. V.
4. Boring, E. G., *A History of Experimental Psychology.* New York: D. Appleton-Century Company, Inc., 1929.
5. Darwin, C., *The Descent of Man.* New York: Hurst & Co., 1874.
6. Huxley, T. H., On the Hypothesis That Animals Are Automata, and Its History, fifth essay in *Method and Results: Essays.* New York: D. Appleton & Company, 1911.

7. Jennings, H. S., *Contributions to the Study of the Behavior of Lower Organisms*. Washington: Carnegie Institution, 1904.

8. Loeb, J., *Forced Movements, Tropisms, and Animal Conduct*. Philadelphia: J. B. Lippincott Company, 1918.

9. MacCurdy, G. G., *Human Origins: A Manual of Prehistory* (2 vols.). New York: D. Appleton & Company, 1924, 1926.

10. Maier, N. R. F., *Studies of Abnormal Behavior in the Rat*. New York: Harper and Brothers, 1939.

11. Morgan, C. L., *An Introduction to Comparative Psychology*. New York: Charles Scribner's Sons, 1901.

12. Nordenskiöld, Erik, *The History of Biology*. New York: Alfred A. Knopf, 1928.

13. Osborn, H. F., *From the Greeks to Darwin*. New York: The Macmillan Company, 1913.

14. Romanes, G. J., *Mental Evolution in Man*. New York: D. Appleton & Company, 1888.

15. Warden, C. J., The Historical Development of Comparative Psychology, *Psychological Review*, 1927, **34**, 57-85, 135-168.

16. ———— Jenkins, T. N., and Warner, L. H. *Comparative Psychology*, Vol. I, Principles and Methods. New York: The Ronald Press Company, 1935.

17. ———— and Warner, L. H., The Development of Animal Psychology in the United States During the Past Three Decades, *Psychological Review*, 1927, **34**, 196-205.

18. Washburn, M. F., *The Animal Mind* (2nd ed.). New York: The Macmillan Company, 1917.

19. Wilm, E. C., *The Theories of Instinct*. New Haven: Yale University Press, 1925.

20. Yerkes, R. M., Animal Psychology and the Criteria of the Psychic, *Journal of Philosophy, Psychology, and Scientific Methods*, 1905, **2**, 141-149.

CHAPTER 3

Maturation and "Instinctive" Functions

CALVIN P. STONE
Stanford University

Introduction

In a flower pot on my window ledge there appeared a half a dozen varieties of seedlings, each of which could be distinguished from the others by the spread of its branches, its leaves, color, and rate of growth. In an experimental garden of the university is a grafted fruit tree that, in season, will put forth three kinds of blossoms. From them will come three varieties of plums—Satsuma, Santa Rosa, and Blue Gage—ripening approximately three weeks apart.

Since there are no observable differences in the external surroundings of these seedlings or of the branches of the plum tree, we shall assume, as a working hypothesis, that metabolic agencies peculiar to the cells of each species or variety have played the dominant roles in bringing about the gross differential features of structure and behavior. Moreover, it will be assumed that these characteristic features were determined by original differences in their genetic constitutions that initiated and regulated a succession of intraorganic controls of cellular activities. The latter, in turn contributed to or actually became effective directing agencies of ontogenetic development.

Our assumption is not without foundation. Experimental biologists assure us that there is a hierarchy of internal regulatory factors that control cellular growth and functional organization from the moment the ovum is fertilized until adult status is reached and, possibly, even until life is terminated by death from natural causes.

To development that *primarily* is so regulated, the name *maturation* is given in order to set it off from other processes by which response mechanisms are acquired, particularly those traditionally designated by the term *learning*. Since different opinions are to be found as to which behavioral acquisitions may properly be accredited to *maturation* and which to *learning,* our present purposes will best be served by avoiding distinctions that are too complicated or finely drawn. Accordingly, let us say that the term *learning* will be used in typical instances to designate behavioral mechanisms that, in very young animals, are developed chiefly by modifying or by adapting total responses that previously had been acquired by the process of *maturation*. With advancing age, this type of learning continues, but, more and more, learning, especially in the higher phyla, involves the modification or adaptation of habits that originally were acquired by several different ways of *learning*. The following illustrations will help to make this distinction clear.

Through *maturational* development all puppy dogs acquire the necessary physiological mechanisms for urination and defecation prior to the time of birth. But only a few of the dogs in the world, and these at different ages and in response to quite variable patterns of stimulation or coercion by man, *learn* where upon the premises elimination may proceed with impunity. Similarly, as a result of *maturational* development, a fetal lamb acquires the sucking mechanism which enables it, after birth, to take milk from the mammary gland or from other nipple-like containers. At this time, it makes no distinctions between mothers, but within a few days, by *learning*, it can distinguish between several lactating sheep with a fair degree of accuracy and will pick out and follow its own mother as she moves in and out of the flock during the day. Still later many of the offspring-parent habits gradually weaken and ultimately disappear.

From the beginning of individual life, maturational development proceeds simultaneously along structural and functional lines on many frontages. Having somewhat specialized interests, however, an anatomist may be attracted only by form or mass at any given time, a physiologist by acceleration and deceleration of cell division, and a psychologist by overt behavior. However, this apparent separateness of vital processes is an artifact, and to the degree that one projects it upon an animal, to that same degree one is likely to suffer handicap in obtaining an accurate conception of the way in which development in an intact organism proceeds.

Ontogeny

Soon after reduction divisions of a fertilized egg have been completed it becomes apparent that aggregates of cells, similarly for all of a given race or species, help themselves to oxygen, water, minerals, and foodstuffs from their surrounding media with characteristic liberality and persistence. Normal fission and differentiation of embryonal cells depend upon the availability of these materials and upon a relatively stable physio-chemical environment, which biologists speak of as the standard internal environment. Presumably, at the outset, the genes are primary regulators of cell differentiation and organogenesis, but later on they are assisted by organizers, as described by Spemann, and by enzymes or other hormone-like substances.

Among the earliest actions of newly-formed organs are responses to internal stimuli, which often are related in some way to procurement, distribution, and utilization of oxygen, water, foods, inorganic salts, and other substances surrounding the embryo (for example, in the yolk of the egg, or the maternal circulation). Later on, through properly timed maturative processes, the embryo acquires reflexes and other innate mechanisms that directly or indirectly have to do with procurement, storage, and utilization of "tissue needs," or with the maintenance of specific relationships between the organism and its physical and social environment that are essential for growth, health, defense, and so forth. Throughout the pre-adult period new behavior mechanisms continue to appear at characteristic times, and these, along with the old ones, constantly undergo adaptive changes, the better to serve the expanding needs of the individual or the social group. During the pre-activity stage, there is only scanty evidence of *learning* as we have defined this term. Therefore, by inference, we may look upon development prior to bodily movement as primarily *maturational* in type.

On the Trail of Development Controls

If we are to discover agencies that direct maturational developments, it is necessary to observe cases in which one or more agencies suspected of having a regulatory influence are inoperative or effectively controlled.

1. **The yucca moth.** Perhaps no instance more dramatically illustrates the operation of intra- and extraorganic controls in maturational development than that of the yucca moth, so beautifully described by Lloyd Morgan [(28), p. 14].

The silvery, straw-colored insects emerge from their chrysalis cases just when the large, yellowish-white, bell-shaped flowers of the yucca open, each for a single night. From the antlers of one of these flowers the female moth collects the golden pollen and kneads the adhesive material into a little pellet, which she holds beneath her head by means of the greatly enlarged bristly palps. Thus laden, she flies off and seeks another flower. Having found one, she pierces with the sharp lancets of her ovipositor the tissue of the pistil, lays her eggs among the ovules, and then, darting to the top of the stigma, stuffs the fertilizing pollen-pellet into its funnel-shaped opening.

These visits of the insects are necessary for the pollination of the flower, which is accomplished by no other insect and by no other method. And, reciprocally, the fertilized ovules are necessary for the growth of yucca larvae when they emerge from the eggs in four or five days. After eating some of the tender ovules, the larvae cut holes through the ovary, spin webs, descend to the ground, burrow beneath its surface, and pass the winter there in the pupal state, from which they emerge at the time the yucca is in flower. The adult does not partake of the pollen it has gathered, and probably obtains no nourishment at all from the plant while performing this round of complicated activities. Finding the flower is itself an unlearned response, a type of chemotropism common among insects. The adult insect does not learn this complicated series of acts through imitation of its parents, long since dead, or from contemporaries, for its visual receptors do not provide the kind of vision necessary to the human concept of visual guidance. Most action systems of larvae are totally unlike those of adults, and the activities are even performed with different appendages; the body of the larva that descends the silken thread to bury itself in the ground is dedifferentiated and resynthesized during the resting state; and a prolonged interval of time, the winter season, intervenes between the last act of the larva and the first of the adult. In view of these facts, no concept of memory or transfer of training supported by experimental evidence can be invoked to account for the behavior of the yucca moth. Until evidence is at hand that will enable us to be still more explicit, we must continue to overlook great gaps in the life cycle of the yucca moth, and, for the present, assume that intraorganic controls are responsible for the organization and energizing of this cluster of ordered responses, appearing as they do only after a prolonged resting period near the end of the individual's life span, functionally similar in all members of the species, and differing in essential ways from the reproductive behavior of other species of moths.

Examples of similar unlearned responses could be gathered by the hundreds from the writings of entomologists to illustrate the marvelous aptitudes for complex responses first displayed by moths, bees, wasps, and other insects immediately after their last molt. Different species of insects, sheltered and nourished by the same plant or animal, may lay their eggs in the same sheltered nook; but each egg, in its own time, yields a larva that selects food, responds characteristically to light, shadow, odors, and tactile qualities of surface, molts at specific times, and eventually emerges as an adult—crawling, hopping, or flying.

Neither larvae nor adults of the class insecta acquire their entire repertoires of responses by the process of maturation. Under certain conditions many species have displayed remarkable capacities for reorganization of innate responses or habits previously acquired.

2. "Synthetic" queens among the honey bees. Variations in developmental trends are sometimes initiated by factors outside of the organism. However, most typically these factors are productive of inconstant, reversible *individual* differences, rather than differences between species. They are not transmitted as heritable characters. The following will illustrate the idea.

As is well known, one of the chief duties of young honey bees is that of feeding the larvae. The eggs hatch in about three days, leaving at the bottom of the cell a worm-like creature so helpless that food must be forced into its mouth by the "nursemaid" workers. At first all the larvae receive a predigested substance forced from the stomachs of the workers, known as "royal jelly." After about three days, most of them are given beebread, which is a mixture of honey and pollen, but a few, put into an enlarged cell, are fed on "royal jelly" throughout the larval period. These bees become queens and the former, workers. Should accident befall the developing queens, the "nursemaids" will enlarge the cells of worker-larvae, which just shortly before had been put on the diet of beebread, and restore their menu of "royal jelly." If development has not already progressed too far, these larvae will undergo a change in the course of development and become normal, fertile queens, like those that were never fed anything but "royal jelly."

Queen bees, differ from the workers in size, in form, and in primary and secondary sexual characters. Upon reaching the age of sexual maturity, they perform reproductive functions rather than diverse menial tasks like the workers. These facts indicate that, during the first three or four days of life, a female larva has the capacity of developing into either a queen or a worker, the course of somatic and behavioral development being regulated by nutritional factors and indirectly determined by adult members of the hive.

The males, or drones, have only half as many chromosomes as the workers and queens. This constitutes a potent regulatory factor in sex determination and also in sexual differentiation of structures and behavior of males and females.

3. Correlated neuromuscular development and behavior in amphibia. Numerous highly technical studies by Coghill (12) have correlated neuromuscular growth with integration of behavior patterns in amphibian larvae. Only by referring to his original papers can one obtain a correct impression of the great wealth of evidence he has provided to show how intricately behavioral growth is linked with neuromuscular growth, and how the *integration of action systems is primarily regulated by factors inherent within the organism from the very beginning of its development.* Coghill (11) says,

The growth of the nervous system, insofar as it has been definitely correlated with the development of the behavior pattern, demonstrates that fractional patterns (reflexes) arise by a process of individuation within a primarily integrated total pattern, and that the latter does not arise by an integration of independent reflexes. The form of the behavior pattern in Amblystoma up to and including locomotion is determined by specific neural counterparts that acquire their specificity in functional value through laws of growth in the nervous system. There is evidence also that mechanisms that condition the performance of such a behavior pattern as locomotion in mammals are determined in the same manner. It is important, therefore, to know how far growth, in the sense of the differentiation of new functional parts of cells, is projected into the life-history of the vertebrate, for so long as it continues it must participate in the function of the nervous system as a whole and, therefore, in the development of the behavior pattern. (p. 136)

The comprehensive study of Tracy (48) on the toadfish is a continuation and expansion of the work of Coghill. He observed patterns of bodily movement from their initial appearance in embryos through successive stages until the animals became free-swimming. His correlated studies of neuromuscular development and behavior led to the belief that differences in reactions displayed at different stages of development arose from temporal differences in the establishment of effective connections between various elements of the embryonal nervous system (primitive bilateral motor system, commissural elements, spinal ganglion cells, Rohn Beard cells, and receptors). He concurs with the view of Coghill that integration of behavior patterns is primarily regulated by intraorganic factors acting on bodily structures long before the initial movements of the embryo are seen.

4. Reproductive cycles in pigeons and rodents after cortical lesions. Rogers (33) studied the reproductive cycles of decorticated pigeons for the purpose of determining the ability of birds with large brain lesions to integrate the separate elements that make up the complete sexual cycle. He says,

The following cycles of reactions were observed in adult birds before and after various cerebral lesions were made: . . . mating, nesting, incubation, and rearing the young birds. A few observations of the development of the behavior cycles were made in birds in which cerebral lesions were made in the first month of life. Loss of all but traces of the cerebral cortex but leaving the major part of the hyperstriatum intact is followed by no characteristic behavior deficiencies . . . After loss of cortex and hyperstriatum there ensues a long period of helplessness, but the bird may regain the ability to feed itself, but does not go through the mating or nesting cycles of behavior. (p. 49)

In primiparous albino rats Stone (44) found apparently normal copulation, gestation, parturition, and maternal behavior (nesting, cleaning of young, retrieving, removal of the young from a cold draft or from excessive heat, and so forth) after they had been deprived of as much as 25 per cent of the cerebral cortex. With larger lesions maternal behavior showed less and less integration, and totally disappeared before 50 per cent destruction was reached. Breeding and parturition continued beyond that point. A more extensive, quantitative study of the same kind has been reported by Beach (5), who observed reproductive cycles in female rats subjected to lesions as large as those described by Stone. His quantitative study shows, however, that bilateral cortical destructions as low as 10 per cent reduce maternal efficiency. With lesions varying from 1 to 50 per cent of the total cerebral cortex, the rated maternal efficiency dropped progressively by amounts that were roughly proportional to the size of the lesions. This study clearly indicates that cortical destruction interferes with the arousal and integration of maternal responses, although as yet the precise manner is not known. The destruction may interfere with the production of hormones causally associated with maternal behavior or it may break up neural mechanisms that are responsible for complex innate behavior patterns. In the case of male rabbits, the work of Brooks (7) supports and extends earlier investigations that demonstrated that all of the cerebral cortex may be removed without suppressing the "copulatory instinct." He also found that female rabbits can mate and ovulate after removal of all of the cerebral cortex. Their maternal behavior after lesions was not fully reported.

5. **Hastening metamorphosis in amphibians.** Alterations of time relations in development as well as in sequential order of responses can be produced by varying the environments in which specific potentialities of the genes are realized. The following quotation from a study by Jennings (21) beautifully illustrates the point.

In that group of the Amphibia which includes the toads and frogs, at a certain period the tail and gills are lost, legs develop, there is an internal and external transformation, and the tadpole metamorphoses into the four-legged frog or toad. What brings about this metamorphosis? J. F. Gudernatsch found that if very young tadpoles are fed pieces of the thyroid gland, they quickly metamorphose into frogs, even though as yet extremely small. In this way frogs as small as flies were produced. Tadpoles of the bullfrog, that usually do not metamorphose till two or three years old, were thus caused to metamorphose during the first season of this existence, and within two weeks of the time that the feeding of the thyroid was begun. . . . The thyroid gland produces an inner secretion, or hormone, that contains iodine, and that passes into the blood and so circulates through the body. The iodine that it contains is united with certain organic compounds, and some of the effects of its secretions are not producible by iodine alone; this is particularly true of its effects in higher animals. The thyroid, like other parts of the body, develops gradually, and in the early stages of its development it does not produce its secretion. It remains thus inactive even past the time when the remainder of the body has become capable of reacting to its secretion. But at a certain period it begins to produce its characteristic secretion, and to pour it into the blood. And as a result the tadpole transforms into the frog or toad. (p. 113)

Needless to say, functional metamorphosis goes hand in hand with the structural metamorphosis that Jennings is chiefly discussing in the foregoing quotation. Further on, Jennings says,

The effect of the thyroid hormone thus differs greatly in different animals. The cells in different species have different constitutions, diverse genes; and they react diversely to the same hormone, just as diverse parts of the same individual react diversely to the same hormone. The effect produced depends as much on the constitution of the cells acted on as it does on the nature of the hormone. (p. 117)

6. Puberal behavior may be precociously awakened, delayed, or suppressed. It is well known that superior diets tend to hasten sexual maturity in animals. as compared with the diets ordinarily provided by unschooled animal caretakers. Also, deficiency diets retard the first manifestations of puberal behavior in young animals and suppress the vigor of that in adults, the degree varying somewhat with the nature, amount, and duration of the dietary deficiency. (20).

Marked accelerations and delays in the awakening of sexual libido can be caused in young animals by altering the amount of certain hormones in their blood streams. Domm and van Dyke (16) showed that male chicks from 9 to 13 days of age, which received subcu-

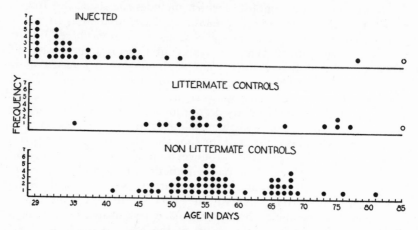

Fig. 1. **Frequency Distributions of the Ages of First Copulations of Young Male Albino Rats.** The experimental animals received a daily injection of 0.62 mg. of testosterone propionate, some beginning with the age of 22 days, some at 25 days, and some at 26 days. Their littermate controls and a group of non-littermate controls were similarly tested but received no injections of the male hormone.

taneous injections of a substance from the anterior lobe of the pituitary, began within a few days to crow, to tread, and in other ways to display sexual aggressiveness normally appearing in cockerels several weeks older. Similar results have been obtained by Hamilton (18) with young chicks, following subcutaneous injections of testosterone propionate. Behavior that is homologous to this, though differing in specific details, can be induced in any laboratory or domestic animal. Figure 1 illustrates the precocious awakening of copulatory activity in young male rats that received subcutaneous injections of testosterone propionate (45). Even in young boys who are treated with this substance to normalize somatic sexual development there may be deepening of the voice, sensitization of the sexual reflexes, and premature awakening of sexual desire (19). Young animals when deprived of the anterior pituitary lobe or gonads begin to show retardation of sexual development at once, and only if subjected to the appropriate hormonal therapy will again begin to develop along normal lines. So far as we know *there is no type of training which, if given to these young animals, will bring out anything even remotely like the typical sexual responses in males or females normally appearing at puberty.* Fundamentally, the foregoing are innate responses, acquired primarily by *maturation.*

As yet we do not know whether exactly the same factors that instigate and regulate the process of somatic sexual differentiation also give rise to the different patterns of behavior that characterize the two sexes, that is, masculinity and femininity. In nature there occur, in rare instances, fowls in which behavioral masculinization is associated with degeneration of the ovary and development of testicular tissue (13). Also, there are striking instances in which reversal of sex behavior follows transplantation of gonadal tissues from the opposite sex (1). These data suggest that different sex hormones are primarily responsible for sex differences in behavior within a given species. In support of this thesis, experiments by Kun (24) showed that sex reversal as well as bisexual behavior could be induced in adult male rats by injecting appropriate amounts of ovarian hormone. Ball (4) and others have induced masculine behavior in female rats by injections of testosterone propionate. (See Chapter 5.) In certain instances, however, both in animals and man, the behavior patterns are not perfectly coordinated with the bodily characteristics of sex, a condition sometimes appropriately called sex inversion or homosexuality (5).

7. **Temperamental traits in relation to genetic constitutions.** If one breeds albino rats of a strain known for its gentleness, and within a few minutes breeds the same females to wild males, a certain number of mixed litters may be expected. The pure albinos are readily distinguished from the half-breeds because all of them are white whereas the latter have brown hair. Even when the albino mothers are allowed to suckle the young in the usual way, and if, after weaning, all are treated alike and finally tested by the same person without reference to coat color, quantitative differences in wildness

and savageness will be readily seen. The manner of siring the litters as well as the subsequent treatment of the young point to the genetic constitution of the males as the primary cause of temperamental differences developing in the offspring. Had wild mothers been used instead of tame albinos, the absolute differences in wildness and savageness might have varied somewhat from those obtained in the experiment described above, for it is possible that the blood content of the mother and/or her attitude toward the young contribute something to their temperaments. However, a positive finding of this kind would not negate the substance of our original conclusion that the *difference* between the albinos and half-breeds is to be attributed primarily to intraorganic factors. These factors caused the albinos and half-breeds to utilize differently the maternal environment in which they were nurtured.

Extensive studies by Hall (17), in which hereditary differences in emotionality were brought out by selective breeding of rats, support the foregoing thesis in a general way. These important studies deserve more intensive consideration than is possible in this chapter. (See Chapter 11.)

8. Causal versus temporal relationships. The determinative agencies in the complex processes of histogenesis and organogenesis in embryos are known to act very early in the course of ontogenetic development, as is demonstrated by studies of homeo- and hetero-transplantation of tissues, limb buds, sections of the central nervous system, and receptors in living embryos (15). In all probability this generalization applies, with certain reservations, to behavior patterns as well, because behavior is so intimately correlated with cerebral and endocrine development. Probably the *anlagen* of the earliest behavioral patterns are laid down even before some of the essential organs or appendages required for their execution make their first appearance.

This point of view provides us with a proper basis for understanding the acquisition of adult behavior mechanisms in insects during the pupal stage, and also for understanding the results of experiments such as those reported by Carmichael (8, 9), who brought eggs of the frog and salamander into the laboratory to develop under conditions suitable for special observation. A number of embryos in their early head-bud and tail-bud stages were divided into control and experimental groups. The controls were allowed to develop in tap water, a satisfactory medium for normal growth and activity, whereas the experimental group was put into a chloreton solution of just sufficient concentration to keep the young larvae in a state of general anaesthesia without injury to developing structures. When the controls had reached a free-swimming stage, the anaesthetized individuals were transferred to tap water to recover from the narcotic. In addition some of the controls were anesthetized just prior to the testing of the experimentals, and then released into fresh water for comparison with the experimentals. The net result of this experiment is indicated in the following quotation (8):

In fact a number of the eighteen *amblystoma* embryos swam so well in less than one-half hour after they had shown the first sign of movement, that they could with difficulty, if at all, be distinguished from members of the control group who had been free-swimmers for five days. (p. 55)

The rate of recovery of the experimentals and the narcotized controls was said to be the same. Taken together, the results are presumptive evidence that maturational development, rather than learning, as we have used that term, accounts for the free-swimming responses of these amblystoma. Furthermore, it may be assumed that *use* of the locomotor equipment, gradually acquired by the control group, was not an *effective variable* so far as maturation of the locomotor system was concerned.

In many instances it is difficult to differentiate purely coincidental or temporal relationships from fundamental causal relationships in development. In the beginning responses may be inconstant, crude, or weak, but in time become strong, precise, and specific in direction. How to credit this improvement—whether to maturation, to learning, or to both, and if the latter, in what proportion—is a difficult problem, one that has provoked incessant controversy.

Developmental Schedules

Like organs of the body, initial responses in embryos, fetuses, and postnatal young make their advent in a sequential order and with temporal spacing that is highly characteristic of the species. For instance, chickens, ducks, turkeys, and quails pick up small seeds by pecking soon after they are hatched; but at this age sparrows, robins, and pigeons can only extend their necks and hold their mouths agape to receive soft foods from their parents' bills.

1. **Fetal and newborn rats.** By breeding receptive rats, it is possible to date the time of conception with only a few hours' experi-

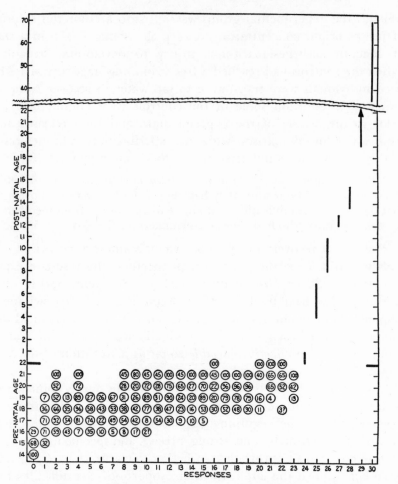

Fig. 2. Illustrating the Growth of Responses in the Prenatal and Postnatal Albino Rats. Data for the prenatal period, 14 to 22 days, are based on the extensive observations of Angulo, (2) who observed the following numbers of fœtuses of the ages 14 to 21 days respectively: 59, 63, 150, 93, 70, 90, 98, 20. (Gestation period, 22 days.) Data for the postnatal period are based on observations by Small (37) and the present author. The numbers enclosed in circles indicate the percentage of each group displaying the response indicated by the code numbers on the abscissa. Vertical lines at right of the diagram indicate the approximate age ranges at which postnatal responses, indicated by code numbers at the bottom of the diagram, are first manifested. Percentages for each age can be given only for the reproductive responses, and these vary somewhat according to the diet used. Numbers at the bottom of the diagram refer to the following responses:

0. Non-motile.
1. Lateral flexion of trunk.
2. Lateral flexion of trunk with movement of fore limbs.
3. Lateral flexion of rump.
4. Extension of head.

5. Extension of head with opening of mouth.
6. Extension of head with opening of mouth and protrusion of tongue.
7. Lateral flexion of rump with movements of hind limbs.

(*Continued on bottom of Page 43*)

mental error. Counting from the hour of breeding, the first movement of fetuses appears shortly after they are 14 days old, and if at this time a pregnant female is properly anaesthetized, the fetuses may be removed from the amniotic cavity and immersed in a saline solution of approximately the same temperature as the amniotic fluid, still obtaining their oxygen and food supply through the placentae, which, in this type of experiment, should not be detached. One may observe or stimulate the fetuses to determine when spontaneous movements or responses to external stimulation make their appearance. Taking the work of Angulo (2) as our source of information, we have constructed a chart of the rat's developmental schedule up to birth. Studies by Small (37) and others have provided additional data for the period of postnatal development.

Referring to Fig. 2, the reader will see that the occurrence of new responses in the fetus is very gradual and that behavioral growth continues well out into postnatal life without any significant change to mark the time of birth. Although individual differences are clearly evident at all stages of development, so small are they in amount, as compared with those between different species, that one may liken them to mere ripples appearing on the crests of giant ocean waves.

A survey of initial responses, in relation to the animal's postnatal needs for independent existence, indicates that functional utility (not always functional maturity) appears in behavior mechanisms somewhat in advance of the needs they are destined to serve. At first, responses may be weak, erratic, and nonspecific, but with further aging, specificity, precision, and strength are attained, even though opportunity for practice, in the usual sense of that term, is relatively meager. The order of appearance of responses in vertebrates seems

---

8. Ventroflexion of trunk and rump.
9. Independent movement of fore limbs.
10. Maintained contractions.
11. Contraction of abdominal muscles.
12. Extension of rump.
13. Attempts to assume *"the optimum physiological posture."*
14. Independent movement of hind limbs.
15. Extension of head and rump with kicking of hind limbs.
16. Independent opening of mouth.
17. Independent extension of hands.
18. Independent flexion of hands.
19. Specific reflexes.
20. Movement of tail.
21. Independent movement of feet.
22. Independent movement of tongue.
23. Independent closing of mouth.
24. Rolls from back to belly.
25. Crawls rapidly.
26. Washes face; sits on haunches.
27. Responds to noises.
28. Eyes open.
29. Eats solid foods.
30. Initial sexual responses.

For a discussion of the fact that some responses appearing early are not observed in the older fœtuses, see the original paper by Angulo. (2)

to run in a head-to-foot direction and from central axis to periphery, so far as the trunk and the appendages are concerned.

2. Fetal responses of guinea pigs. The following items roughly depict behavioral growth in prenatal guinea pigs, experimentally removed and detached from their mothers when they are between 50 and 68 days of age, the latter being the end of the gestation period. At or near the 50th day irregular breathing appears, but by the 64th day regular and continuous breathing is found. The upper and lower eyelids separate between the 55th and 57th days, but reflex movements indicate that the retina is sensitive to light prior to that time. Weak vocalizations are made by fetuses at 58 days and quite vigorous scratch reflexes with forepaws applied to the sides of the face appear on or before the 59th day. By the 60th day, the guinea pig crawls and rolls from back to side or even from back to feet. At about this time it displays a reflex twitch of the ear to auditory stimuli. On the 63rd day it stands well and even walks about. On or before the 62nd day vigorous sucking responses to the mother's nipple appear. Individuals of this age can be reared if placed with a willing, lactating mother.

Avery (3) inquired whether postures assumed by the mother during the latter part of the gravid period provided the adequate stimulus for young pigs of 63 days or more to shift their positions continually so that their backs were up and their feet toward the surface of the earth. To test this point, radiographs of pregnant females, held in various positions, were made with back down, back up, on right side, and on left side. In one series of tests pregnant females were shifted at five-minute intervals during a 30-minute period, and radiographs were made before each shift. The radiographs showed fetuses of the same litter in various positions, which strongly suggests that prior to birth they do not practice spatial orientation in response to shifts of the mother's position.

Since the time of Avery's study much better-controlled and thoroughgoing studies of fetal behavior in guinea pigs have been made by Carmichael (10), whose methods assured the continuance of circulation and temperature regulation similar to those obtaining under normal conditions. The first "spontaneous" movement occurred 28 days after insemination of the mother. At 31 days the first exteroceptively aroused reaction appeared, the response involving the neck and forelimb. Many new facts concerning receptor-effector mechanisms and patterns of sensorimotor behavior were brought out by this study. Concerning the adaptive nature of fetal responses he reached the following conclusions:

While strictly maintaining the scientific or "mechanistic" point of view, it is possible for the external observer to recognize many of the responses of the foetus as "adaptive." A number of such responses are considered in detail in regard to their origin and developmental change during foetal life. Among those considered are: (*a*) activity of the vibrissae; (*b*) eyeball movement; (*c*) iris responses; (*d*) eye-winking; (*e*) ear-muscle responses; (*f*) nostril dilation; (*g*) tongue movements; (*h*) changes in neck and body posture in relation to vestibular stimulation; (*i*) general subcutaneous muscle responses; (*j*) behavior acts concerned in feeding, air-breathing, excretion, locomotion, defense, expression, and emotional responses; and (*k*) adaptive responses of the total integrated organisms showing the sort of behavior which had been called "persistence by varied means toward the achievement of a goal" or "docility." (p. 480)

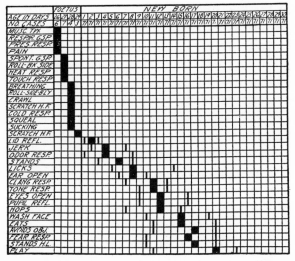

Fig. 3. Development of Responses in Foetal and Newborn Rabbits (the breed is known to the trade as "Dutch"). Heavy black lines or squares indicate the average ages at which responses or developmental characteristics were manifested; thin lines at the left and right of the heavy lines or squares indicate the earliest and the latest ages upon appearances of these responses. Each newborn rabbit was examined daily, following a standardized experimental program. [After Kao (22).]

3. Fetal and newborn rabbits. The rabbit, having a relatively short gestation period (30 days), provides an excellent contrast for rats and guinea pigs. If fetuses are removed from the mother from three to four days before the end of the gestation period, they will move the trunk and limbs spontaneously or in response to mechanical stimuli applied at various points on the body. At 26 days, respiratory movements are not yet adequate to support life for more than a few seconds, if at all, but with each succeeding day of intra-uterine life they become more and more serviceable. Within a day or two of birth, the fetus is capable of crawling, righting itself, and sucking from the mothers' nipple. None of these responses, how-ever, is as vigorous or precise as those of the newborn, a fact showing that functional maturation proceeds at a rapid rate during the later days of gestation. Figure 3, based on work of Kao (22), illustrates the ages at which other responses of postnatal life appear. Further study of rabbits in their native habitat provides supporting evidence for our earlier claim that serviceable maturity in each action system, acquired primarily by maturation, anticipates the biological need that that action system eventually will serve.

4. **Pouch-young opossums.** The first two months of postnatal de-velopment of the opossum, as described by Langworthy (25), corre-spond roughly to well-known stages of intra-uterine development in other mammals, because its gestation period is only from 12 to 14 days, one of the shortest known in mammals. At birth the young opossum is able to crawl from the region of the mother's cloaca to her pouch by grasping abdominal hair between the toes of its fore-legs. Wide, lateral sweeping movements of the head enable it to contact a nipple in the pouch to which it will hold with great tenacity. So close is the junction of mouth and breast that at one time it was believed that young opossums grew from the breast of the mother.

At birth the young will respond to cutaneous stimuli applied to various parts of the body, but most specifically to those applied on the face. At this stage they cannot right themselves when placed on side or back and make few if any of the defensive movements ex-hibited by young guinea pigs from seven to eight days before birth. They cannot perform any of the more complex acts exhibited by newborn sheep, calves, colts, and dozens of other well-known animals. (See Figs. 2, 3, 4.)

At one week of age, the forelegs beat in such a manner as to insure progression if the claws catch onto solid objects, but the hind legs are still more or less useless. The tail responds to cutaneous stimula-tion and acts as a prehensile, grasping organ, although it lacks sufficient strength to support the weight of the young. Thermal and tactile stimuli arouse local responses in any part of the trunk, and at this time the animal will crawl away from cold and toward warm objects. The eyes are not yet open and there is no response to auditory stimuli.

At approximately one month of age, the young opossum still lies upon its side because the righting reflexes are not yet functionally mature. The hind limbs move more than during the first week, but these movements are not well coordinated with those of the forelimbs. It can grasp a suspended thread with the foretoes but circles rather than climbs it.

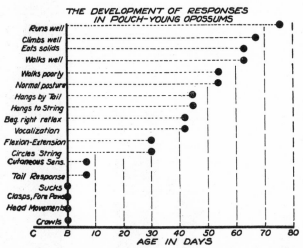

Fig. 4. **Development of Responses in Pouch-young Opossums.** The heavy dots indicate the approximate ages at which responses at the left are manifested. More extensive investigations will cause these dots to shift slightly to the right or to the left, but the general trend of results will probably stand as given in this pioneer study, based on only a small number of cases. [After Langworthy (25).]

By the end of six weeks, many responses previously crude have become more precise, and some that appeared to be uncoordinated with others have now become an integral part of fairly complex sequential movements. Immature righting reflexes appear at this time; when put on its feet, the animal can take two or three steps before falling on its side. Vocalizations now are made. At the age of 46 days, the animal can support its weight by grasping objects with its tail. At 54 days, it assumes the normal standing posture. Now it climbs a rope and can crawl quite well, but with legs sprawled out. At the end of nine weeks, the young opossum can walk and eat solid food. Climbing and running are efficient by the age of ten weeks, when, for the first time, one can say that the motor abilities are on a par with those of young guinea pigs or rats in their second or third week of postnatal life.

5. The human fetus and infant. Probably no animal has a more highly standardized or longer course of prenatal and postnatal development than the human infant. The philosopher Fisk has remarked, interestingly, that man has a longer period of infancy than the lower animals because he has a higher destiny to fulfill. No animals surpass man in all-round psychomotor development.

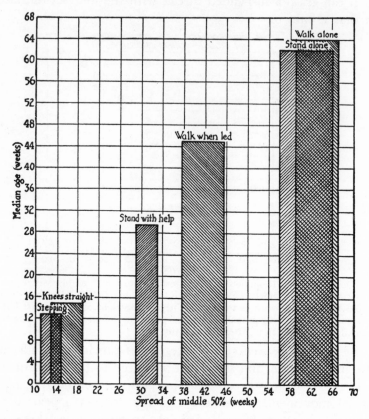

Fig. 5. Progress Toward Walking. [After Shirley (66).] Reproduced by permission of the University of Minnesota Press.

A small number of selected items will serve to illustrate the detail with which modern experimentalists have worked out schedules of development in the human infant. In Fig. 5 are illustrated certain stages of locomotor development as observed by Shirley (36). This and other diagrams provided by her, but not reproduced, indicate that the earliest responses pertaining to locomotion, such as chin movements, chest rising, sitting, knee pushing, and so on, make their appearance long before sitting alone, creeping, standing alone. and walking without support. Shirley states that locomotor development:

> ... follows a pattern that has five major orders. They may be described more or less adequately as: (*a*) development of passive postural control; (*b*) development of active postural control; (*c*) active efforts toward locomotion; (*d*) locomotion by creeping and walking with support; (*e*) walking alone. Each major order of development has several stages. There is some shifting in sequence of stages within an order, but there is no transposition of a stage from one order to another. (p. 193)

Intensive studies of developmental schedules in the human fetus, infant, and child clearly suggest that man will be found to differ from all other mammals even more radically in respect to personality, wants, and interests than in respect to the more externalized morphological and sensorimotor characters.

6. Common characteristics. Comparative studies of the development of several species of animals enable one to make certain observations that are common to all:

(*a*) As in the case of structural development, maturation of action systems in early life is contingent upon an animal's being surrounded by a standard *ensemble* of physical forces and social agencies. Acting together, the individual's genetic constitution, its relatively constant *milieu interne,* and its standard *milieu externe* determine the course of its development. Similarities in these three factors are presumably responsible for gross resemblances of behavior of all individuals of the same species.

(*b*) The order and temporal interval between initial appearances of responses are as characteristic of a species as the morphological characteristics on which our present classifications of animals are based.

(*c*) Orderly integration of responses in organisms occurs simultaneously on many frontiers, and serviceable maturity of action systems is attained before the time they come into the service of fundamental tissue needs. Without benefit of practice, as that term is ordinarily understood, behavioral mechanisms become integrated in immobile embryos; later on additional mechanisms appear without necessary practice or training. Immature young animals, developing homologous behavior mechanisms, tend to exhibit developmental schedules by which those of one species are distinct, irrespective of their associations with animals of other species.

Interdependent Relationships Between Maturation and Learning

Although one cannot say positively that development of behavior mechanisms by maturation and by learning are altogether different biological processes, in this chapter we have followed the tradition of making distinctions between them. Now it is our intention to point out certain dependent relationships between maturation and learning.

1. Modifiability in relation to age. Stoltenberg (39) rotated young pigeons on a turntable at the ages of 5, 10, 20, 35, and 90-120 days. Each bird was tested on 10 different occasions, with the direction of turning alternated on successive trials. Each complete trial consisted of 10 turns of the table during a 20-second interval, and successive trials were administered every 2 minutes. In Table 1

TABLE 1

AVERAGE NUMBER OF POSTROTATIONAL NYSTAGMIC MOVEMENTS IN DIFFERENT AGE GROUPS OF SQUABS

From 14 to 16 birds were in each group.

	Ages of Groups				
Rotations	5 Days	10 Days	20 Days	35 Days	90–120 Days
1 and 2	4.29	14.35	24.89	33.20	32.95
9 and 10	4.65	10.53	17.33	20.97	21.85
Decrease	−.36	3.82	7.56	12.23	11.10
% Decrease	−8.40	26.60	30.30	36.90	33.80

will be found the average number of nystagmic movements made by birds of each age group on the first and last pairs of trials. Table 2 gives similar data for the duration of nystagmic movements

TABLE 2

AVERAGE OF THE TIME INTERVALS IN WHICH POSTROTATIONAL NYSTAGMIC MOVEMENTS WERE OBSERVED IN DIFFERENT AGE GROUPS OF SQUABS

From 14 to 16 birds in each group.

	Ages of Groups				
Rotations	5 Days	10 Days	20 Days	35 Days	90–120 Days
1 and 2	3.66	10.75	19.11	23.59	23.56
9 and 10	3.67	8.07	13.68	16.20	17.13
Decrease	−.01	2.68	5.43	7.39	6.43
% Decrease	−.27	25.80	28.40	31.40	27.30

following each trial. From a consideration of these tables, it will be seen that there is an increase in both the number and the duration of movements up to the age of 35 days, or the approximate time young squabs leave the nest; also, and what is more important for our present discussion, there is a gradual decrease in both the frequency and the duration of movements associated with training on the turntable up to the age of 35 days, after which age differences are not found. The cause of this differential modifiability with age is by no means fully understood as yet, but it seems probable that it is brought about almost wholly by maturational factors. Opportunities to profit by experience similar or equivalent to that provided by the turntable are certainly very meager if not totally absent in nestling squabs.

2. **Quantitative study of improvement.** Bird (6) has repeated and greatly extended the classical experiment of Shepard and Breed (35) on the improvement of feeding reactions in chicks with age and with practice. Noteworthy are his more elaborate system of controls and the increase in numbers of subjects tested. Among his conclusions are the following:

The most rapid increase in accuracy of swallowing grains occurs during the three initial practice days, whether these three days immediately succeed the time of hatching or come after a period of artificial delay. A part of the increase is attributed to general physiological development, which occurs during the first few days of postnatal life, irrespective of practice in pecking. Delayed practice is followed by accuracy of swallowing which at the initial test is no greater than that observed in one-day-old animals. (p. 90)

Another investigation on the accuracy of pecking in chicks was reported by Moseley (30). She verified the data of Breed on the relatively complete development of the pecking response at the time of hatching, but, unlike Breed, found a decrease in the rate of improvement of this response in chicks fed artificially for various periods of time after hatching. Moseley believes that learning, in the accepted sense, accounts primarily for increased accuracy in seizing objects, whereas striking and swallowing are more nearly unlearned responses.

Noting certain shortcomings in the earlier experiments on maturation and learning in chicks, Cruze (14) repeated and extended them under highly controlled conditions. The experimental conditions imposed on 8 groups of chicks from the time they were taken from the dark brooder are shown in Table 3. The hunger motivation was kept as nearly constant as possible by force-feeding of chicks that were not allowed to peck or allowed only a limited number of pecks per day. Data on the hits and misses at grains and also on the number of hits accompanied by swallowing reactions were collected. Figure 6 illustrates the number of swallowing responses for

TABLE 3

EXPERIMENTAL CONDITIONS FOR EIGHT GROUPS OF CHICKS (p. 380)

Group	Number in Each Group	Age in Hours When Taken from Dark Room	Number of Test Pecks Allowed Each Day	Method of Subsequent Feeding
A	26	24	25	Natural
B	25	48	25	Natural
C	25	72	25	Natural
D	25	96	25	Natural
E	25	120	25	Natural
F	25	24	12	In dark for 20 days
G	25	24	25	In dark for 20 days
H	26	24	12 for 10 days 25 for next 10	In dark for 20 days

groups *A* to *E*, which were tested, respectively, on the first to fifth days after hatching. The records are based on a 25-peck sample. For all groups there is a low initial accuracy followed by a rapid gain. The rapidity of gain is greater for those that began pecking at more

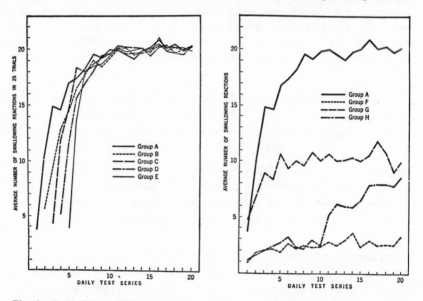

Fig. 6. (*Left*) The swallowing reactions of five groups of chicks taking their initial tests at one, two, three, four, and five days, respectively, after hatching. (*Right*) The average number of swallowing reactions of chicks allowed different amounts of daily practice. [After Cruze (14).]

advanced ages, hence they quickly reach the same level of attainment as the others, in spite of the fact that those which began pecking early had, *in toto,* more practice than those beginning late (see Table 3). To evaluate the influence of different amounts of practice upon the chick's pecking efficiency during the first 20 days after hatching, a further experiment was performed. Beginning at 24 hours after hatching, group F was allowed 12 pecks daily; group G, 25 pecks daily; and group H, 12 pecks for the first 10 days and 25 for the remaining 10 days. All were given supplementary food by force-feeding each day, in order to keep them growing normally and to maintain approximately the same degree of hunger in all groups. The results of this experiment are graphically represented in Fig. 6b. It is apparent that 12 pecks were insufficient to promote rapid and steady gain. Even 25 pecks were far inferior to unrestricted pecking, although it promoted gain in proficiency at a rate that greatly exceeds 12 pecks. This carefully conducted investigation brings out many other interesting relationships between the contributions of the factor of maturation and learning during the post-hatching development of feeding responses. In summary, Cruze concludes that:

The pecking reaction in chicks is an integration of both learned and unlearned activities. Maturation during the first five days of the life of a chick seems to be sufficient explanation for the reduction and near elimination of missing errors, although under all normal conditions practice effects aid in this elimination. Accuracy in the total response including the consummatory response of swallowing seems to be very definitely the result of learning. More mature chicks develop accuracy in this reaction more rapidly than chicks which are less mature. The degree of accuracy attained with such chicks seems to be determined, to a large extent, by the amount of practice allowed. (p. 208)

3. **Modifiability as related to age in different species.** Since action systems mature with characteristic tempo and sequence in different species, it would seem that the rate of learning should reflect differences in maturational rates with respect to the action systems involved. Supporting this tentative hypothesis is the fact that domestic animals appear to achieve intellectual and emotional maturity at a much earlier point in their total life-spans than man. Laboratory experiments prove conclusively that this is true in the case of albino rats, for which an abundance of relevant data is available. Bearing on this same point are the comparative studies of the ape and the child by the Kelloggs (23). A seven-and-a-half-months-old female chimpanzee was brought into the home of the investigators and reared for one year with a boy that was two months older. As far as possible, these scientists treated the two infants alike for a period of one year. At the outset the chimpanzee learned diverse actions and inhibitions, such as obedience to spoken commands, manifesta-

tions of affection, opening of doors, skipping, manipulation of eating utensils, and bathroom habits, at a rate much faster than the child. Toward the end of the experiment, however, the child's adaptiveness was rapidly outdoing that of the ape in those respects in which it was inferior at the outset. Moreover, the child continued to enlarge the breech between them in those activities in which it had surpassed the ape at the outset, in spite of its relative immaturity in sensori-motor equipment.

Among the points clearly established by this study are the facts that learning rate under appropriate conditions for experience re-flects the level of maturation reached by ape and child, and that characteristic differences in maturational rate persist despite the similarity of training to which both were subjected. These points have a practical bearing on certain topics frequently discussed in genetic psychology. When, for example, should specific training be given? And what will be the beneficial or deleterious effects of this training on the maturative processes in the same and in other action systems?

That some optimal amount of practice or use of an immature action system *per se* accelerates the maturational rate is quite gen-erally believed by trainers of animals and teachers of children. But so far as the author knows, crucial data to support this suppo-sition have never been brought forward, although it is one of the most revered and widely-voiced hypotheses of genetic psychology. What seems equally plausible and more in line with scattered evi-dences is the hypothesis that:

(a) Maturational development is always primary and development by learning secondary in point of time. At all times maturational develop-ment sets the upper limits for types and levels of habit formation, and habits merely reflect or conceal, as the case may be, the maturational level reached.

(b) Habits do not accelerate or retard maturational development ex-cept as they affect fundamental nutritional processes underlying somatic growth or maintenance. To illustrate, if young rats of weaning age are given a balanced diet in which cracked corn, oat flakes, or cracked wheat are constituents, soon it will be obvious that some litters leave untouched the cracked corn, some the oat flakes, and some the cracked wheat, whereas others eat the mixture as a whole. Only the latter grow at the optimal rate, and only the latter manifest their puberal sexual responses at the normal age. Eating habits of the discriminators have failed to supply them with all the nutrient demanded for normal somatic and functional development. Those animals that form the most superior foraging and eating habits have, in general, the most accelerated postnatal development.

Instinctive Behavior

Unlearned patterns of behavior, occurring alike in all members of a species and serviceably complete on the occasion of their first appearance, are usually called innate or instinctive reactions. Examples of the earliest manifestations of such reactions in the yucca moth and in the fetus or newborn vertebrate have already been presented. Now we shall turn our attention to typical examples of instinctive or "species-constant" reactions that make their appearance at physiological epochs or in cyclic fashion in adolescent or adult life.

1. **Hoarding.** The collection of nest or food materials in great quantities is characteristic of many species of animals. When these collections appear to be excessive, particularly in the case of food, the term *hoarding* is applied. In the valleys of California one species of woodpecker drills small holes in the bark of trees or in the sides of buildings for the storage of acorns that they secure in vast quantities from the native oaks. Everyone is aware of the exploits of the common grey squirrel, which in season caches an overabundance of nuts in the ground or under a bed of forest leaves. The European hamster hoards grain in such excesses that in time of famine the less provident human beings of that region, in dire need of sustenance, have been known to raid its stores. The pack rat is notorious for the size of its mound and the variety of objects that it drags together. Since analogous collecting "habits" have characterized the peoples of every culture in historic times, special experiments on animal hoarders were required to assure us that these patterns of behavior deserve to be called instinctive rather than learned.

Experimental studies with the common laboratory rat show that no conditioning process or tuition is required to elicit the hoarding of food. Nevertheless, there are many factors and circumstances that will either inhibit or facilitate the occurrence of this response. Usually a period of emotional adaptation to new surroundings assists, whereas unfamiliar, strange housing hinders elicitation of hoarding. Under conditions of low temperature and of food privation hoarding is more easily instigated than when temperature and food satiation are relatively high. Hoarding is likely to be increased somewhat by past experience of food privation and certain types of psychological frustration. Possibly also variations in illumination or of the *social milieu* are important variables with which the time and vigor of hoarding are correlated. Even specific position habits or other details about the home environment may play a role in the manifestation of hoarding; nonetheless the primary mechanism underlying this response in rats, as in many other species, appears to be acquired by a process akin to maturation rather than to learning; hence one continues to designate this species-constant behavior by the term *instinctive* (29).

Much remains to be learned about possible kinships between hoarding of food, gathering of bedding or nesting materials, retrieving of young by parturient females, and still other unlearned patterns of behavior in which transportation of objects appears as an occasional, highly-motivated, species-constant pattern of behavior, serving as it does some essential need of the individual or of the species.

2. Hibernation. No single theory can be invoked as yet to explain hibernation, but experimental studies have uncovered many interesting facts concerning hibernating animals. Researches have been addressed to the task of explaining: (*a*) the tendency of certain warm-blooded animals to assume the temperature of the surrounding medium; (*b*) absence of shivering and spontaneous movements; (*c*) loss of consciousness; (*d*) profound reduction in the rate of metabolism; (*e*) prolonged state of hypoglycemia without convulsions; (*f*) subsequent awakening; and (*g*) instigation of breeding activities that may take place in some species of animals almost immediately after hibernation, even though they are in a state of chronic inanition, when reproductive functions in most animals are at a low ebb.

Some years ago lethargic effects due to pituitary deficiency were considered as causal factors in inducing hibernation. Inquiring into the evidence supporting this theory, Rasmussen (32) made a microscopic study of the hypophysis of the woodchucks that he sacrificed in every month of the year. His painstaking correlations show, in effect, that the hypophysis does not have an instigating or causal relation to hibernation in the woodchuck. Also, inquiries on possible roles played by different concentrations of CO_2 in the blood and by the so-called "hibernating gland" (multilocular adipose tissue commonly found in rodents, but not confined to hibernators) were to no avail in explaining the onset or maintenance of this torpid state.

Perhaps the most that should be said of our present knowledge on hibernation, as a species-constant type of behavior, is that competent physiologists no longer regard it as a "miracle of nature," but merely as one among many other baffling biological sequences that, like the intricacies of reproductive behavior, they hope ultimately to understand.

3. **Migration.** An important Bertillon-like innovation in the study of animal migrations was introduced during the present century. This consists of systematic trapping and marking of migratory animals (or, as in the case of salmon, labeling and release of specimens reared in captivity), followed by registration of pertinent facts concerning the classification of each specimen, probable age, physical condition, place of capture, state of the weather, association with others of its kind, date of release, and so on. These pertinent facts are kept in a central file against the time when this same animal may be captured again and another comprehensive report returned to the central bureau (26).

Since the United States Department of Agriculture began taking an active part in systematizing studies of bird migrations by sponsoring the work of "banding stations" located in various parts of the western hemisphere, literally thousands of individual reports on migratory birds have been processed. Collation and interpretation of these reports have provided an abundance of species-constant information concerning: seasonal movements; migratory routes or fly-ways used; spring and autumn destinations; rate of movement; stopovers; rare but informative differences in time of departure and of fly-ways used by young and old; orienting cues over land and sea; hazards overcome; relation of migration to pituitary and gonadal functions; seasonal instigation of endocrine changes by radiant energy; origin of migration in the species; and possible affinities in the migration of mammals, birds, reptiles, amphibians, and fishes.

Differing chiefly in detail from the mass of knowledge now being accumulated on birds is that on the migration of eels, salmon, flounders, seals, and many other acquatic animals of great economic value. So great is the detail on all of them that for an accurate account the reader must turn to recent special reviews of the literature.

4. **Problems common to all studies of instinctive behavior.** Long ago, the comparative anatomists systematized their task by agreeing to base comparisons on approximately ten structural subdivisions, such as: skin or integument, supporting or connective tissue, and

the eight major systems—muscular, digestive, respiratory, nervous, circulatory, urinary, reproductive, and endocrine. As yet, however, comparative psychologists have not reached an equivalent agreement for systematic work on innate action systems. One finds that they construct short, medium, and long lists of instinctive responses pertaining to (a) alimentation and elimination; (b) thermoregulatory acts involving nest building, burrowing, huddling, brooding, and hibernation; (c) postures and movements related to defense or aggression; (d) reproductive behavior, involving display, courtship, and other foreplays that anticipate the insemination reflexes; (e) social processes pertaining to the rearing of young; (f) acts or postural attitudes that reflect the social status of individuals within a group; (g) aggregating tendencies that characterize entire populations of a geographical area; and so on.

Disregarding the problem of classification of innate behavior, however, and directing one's attention to a specific instinctive response, or aggregate of responses clinging together as in the instance of the "sexual instincts," one finds that most of them offer tangible problems for the beginning of research that, although differing in detail, are somewhat analogous to those presented by the maternal behavior of pigeons, domestic fowl, rabbits, guinea pigs, mice, or rats.

In the case of maternal behavior in the rat, which has been more extensively investigated than any other of the above named, the most obvious problem was that of discovering the constant components of the maternal cluster. They are nest building, nest maintenance, parturition, nursing, defense, and retrieving. Then followed, as in job analysis or in time and motion studies in industry, many types of research that had as their aim: (a) description of the specific patterns of response involved in each type of maternal activity; (b) determination of the role of specific external stimuli by which maternal behavior could be aroused; (c) determination of endogenous factors that activate, prolong, and terminate the components of maternal behavior; (d) investigation of the roles of the special senses and of localized areas of the cerebral cortex in maternal behavior; (e) determination of the conditions under which the components of maternal drive are manifested in varying degrees of intensity; and (f) discovery of which conditions cause and which correct pathological manifestations of maternal behavior. Many of the detailed reports on this subject can be found in the monographs of Wiesner and Sheard (49) and of Beach (5).

5. **Origin.** As yet there is no satisfactory conception of the origin or disappearance of instinctive responses in the racial history of a species. The theories most vigorously championed by Lamarck, Charles Darwin, and the neo-Darwinians, who rely chiefly on the mutation theory of de Vries, have grave limitations that have been duly considered many times during the past century (31, 41, 42). Probably most evolutionists today would favor some combination of the theory of mutation and the Darwinian conceptions of continuous variation, isolation, and natural selection.

Bibliography

1. Allen, E., Danforth, C. A., and Doisey, E. A.: *Sex and Internal Secretions.* Baltimore: Williams and Wilkins, 1939.
2. Angulo y González, A. W.: The Prenatal Development of Behavior in the Albino Rat, *J. Compar. Neurol.,* 1932, **55,** 395-442.
3. Avery, G. T.: Responses of Foetal Guinea Pigs Prematurely Delivered, *Genet. Psychol. Monogr.,* 1928, **3,** 247-331.
4. Ball, Josephine: The Effect of Testosterone on the Sex Behavior of Female Rats, *J. Compar. Psychol.,* 1940, **29,** 151-168.
5. Beach F. A.: *Hormones and Behavior.* New York: Paul B. Haeber, Inc., 1948.
6. Bird, C.: The Effect of Maturation upon the Pecking Instinct of Chicks, *Pedag. Sem. and J. Genet. Psychol.,* 1926, **33,** 212-233.
7. Brooks, C. M.: The Role of the Cerebral Cortex and of Various Sense Organs in the Excitation and Execution of Mating Activity in the Rabbit. *Amer. J. Physiol.,* 1937, **120,** 544-553.
8. Carmichael, L.: The Development of Behavior in Vertebrates Experimentally Removed from the Influence of External Stimulation, *Psychol. Rev.,* 1926, **33,** 51-58. Idem. 1927, **34,** 34-47.
9. ——— The Growth of the Sensory Control of Behavior Before Birth. *Psychol. Rev.,* 1947, **54,** 316-324.
10. ——— An Experimental Study in the Prenatal Guinea-Pig of the Origin and Development of Reflexes and Patterns of Behavior in Relation to the Stimulation of Specific Receptor Areas During the Period of Active Fetal Life. *Genet. Psychol. Monogr.,* 1934, **16,** 337-491.
11. Coghill, G. E.: Correlated Anatomical and Physiological Studies of the Growth of the Nervous System in Amphibia: VI. The Mechanism of Integration in Amblystoma Punctatum. *J. Compar. Neurol.,* 1926, **41,** 95-152.
12. ——— *Anatomy and the Problem of Behavior.* Cambridge: Cambridge University Press, 1929.
13. Crew, F. A. E.: Studies in Intersexuality. *Proc. Royal Soc. of London,* 1923, **95B,** 256-278.

14. Cruze, W. W.: Maturation and Learning in Chicks. *J. Compar. Psychol.*, 1935, **19**, 371-409.

15. Detwiler, S. R.: Experimental Studies on Morphogenesis in the Nervous System. *Quart. Rev. Biol.*, 1926, **1**, 61-86.

16. Domm, L. V. and Van Dyke, H. B.: Precocious Development of Sexual Characters in the Fowl by Daily Injections of Hebin: II The Male. *Proc. Soc. Exper. Biol. and Med.*, 1932, **30**, 349-350.

17. Hall, C. S.: Emotional Behavior in the Rat: I. Defecations and Urination as Measures of Individual Differences in Emotionality. *J. Compar. Psychol.*, 1934, **18**, 385-403.

18. Hamilton, J. B.: Precocious Masculine Behavior Following Administration of Synthetic Male Hormone Substance. *Endocrinology*, 1938, **23**, 53-57.

19. ———— Induction of Penile Erection by Male Hormone Substance. *Endocrinology*, 1937, **21**, 744-749.

20. Jackson, C. M.: *The Effects of Inanition and Malnutrition upon Growth and Structure.* Philadelphia: P. Blakiston's Sons, 1925.

21. Jennings, H. S.: *The Biological Basis of Human Nature.* New York: W. W. Norton and Company, 1930.

22. Kao, Han: Notes on the Congenital Behavior of Rabbits, M.A. thesis deposited in the Stanford University Library, 1927.

23. Kellogg, W. N., and Kellogg, L. A.: *The Ape and the Child.* New York: McGraw-Hill, 1933.

24. Kun, H.: Psychische Feminierung und Hermaphrodisierung von Männchen durch weibliches Sexualhormon. *Endokrinologie*, 1933, **13**, 311-323.

25. Langworthy, O. R.: The Behavior of Pouch-Young Opossums Correlated with the Myelinization of Tracts in the Nervous System, *J. Compar. Neurol.*, 1928, **46**, 201-248.

26. Lincoln, F. C.: *The Migration of American Birds.* New York: Doubleday, Doran, 1939.

27. Marquis, D. G.: The Criterion of Innate Behavior. *Psychol. Rev.*, 1930, **37**, 334-349.

28. Morgan, C. L.: *Habit and Instinct.* London: Edward Arnold, 1896.

29. Morgan, Clifford T.: The Hoarding Instinct. *Psychol. Rev.*, 1947, **54**, 335-341.

30. Moseley, D.: The Accuracy of the Pecking Response in Chicks, *J. Compar. Psychol.*, 1925, **5**, 75-98.

31. Munn, N. L.: *Psychological Development.* Boston: Houghton Mifflin Co., 1938.

32. Rasmussen, A. T.: Theories of Hibernation. *Amer. Natur.*, 1916, **50**, 609-625.

33. Rogers, Fred T.: Studies of the Brain Stem: VI. An Experimental Study of the Corpus Striatum of the Pigeon as Related to Various Instinctive Types of Behavior. *J. Compar. Neurol.*, 1922, **35**, 21-59.

34. Rowan, W.: *The Riddle of Migration.* Baltimore: Williams and Wilkins, 1931.

35. Shepard, J. F. and Breed, F. S.: Maturation and Use in the Development of an Instinct. *J. Animal Behavior,* 1913, **3**, 274-285.
36. Shirley, M.: *The First Two Years,* Vol. 1: *Postural and Locomotor Development.* Minneapolis: University of Minnesota Press, 1931.
37. Small, W. S.: Notes on the Psychic Development of the Young White Rat. *Amer. J. Psychol.,* 1899, **11**, 80-100.
38. Stockard, C. R.: *The Physical Basis of Personality.* New York: Norton & Co., 1931.
39. Stoltenberg, C.: Unpublished manuscript from the Department of Anatomy, Stanford University. Abstract published in the *Proceedings of the Ninth International Congress on Psychology,* 1929, p. 414.
40. Stone, C. P.: Recent Contributions to the Experimental Literature on Native or Congenital Behavior. *Psychol. Bull.,* 1927, **24**, 36-61.
41. ———— Multiply, Vary, Let the Strongest Live and the Weakest Die— Charles Darwin. *Psychol. Bull.,* 1943, **40**, 1-24.
42. ———— Methodological Resources for the Experimental Study of Innate Behavior as Related to Environmental Factors. *Psychol. Rev.,* 1947, **54**, 342-347.
43. ———— The Age Factor in Animal Learning: II. Rats on a Multiple Light Discrimination Box and a Difficult Maze. *Genet. Psychol. Monogr.,* 1929, **6**, 125-202.
44. ———— Effects of Cortical Destruction on Reproductive Behavior and Maze Learning in Albino Rats. *J. Compar. Psychol.,* 1938, **26**, 217-236.
45. ———— Precocious Copulatory Activity Induced in Male Rats by Subcutaneous Injections of Testosterone Propionate. *Endocrinology,* 1940, **26**, 511-515.
46. Tolman, E. C.: The Nature of Instinct. *Psychol. Bull.,* 1923, **20**, 200-218.
47. ———— The Nature of the Fundamental Drives. *J. Abnor. and Soc. Psychol.,* 1926, **20**, 349-358.
48. Tracy, H. C.: The Development of Motility and Behavior Reactions in the Toadfish (Opsanus tau), *J. Compar. Neurol.,* 1926, **40**, 253-370.
49. Wiesner, B. P., and Sheard, N. M.: *Maternal Behavior in the Rat.* Edinburgh: Oliver and Boyd, 1933.

CHAPTER 4

Motivation of Animal Behavior

PAUL THOMAS YOUNG
University of Illinois

B roadly conceived, motivation is the process of arousing and sustaining behavior or of changing the pattern of an activity in progress. Some psychologists would limit the definition of motivation to the determination of purposive behavior alone, but, in the broad meaning of the word, all behavior, whether purposive or not, is motivated, i.e., causally determined through release and transformation of energy.

The history of psychology is strewn with theories of instinct, propensity, wish, desire, need, and mental force. Critics have pointed out that the use of such terms gives only a pseudoexplanation of behavior. To say that a man works because he has an instinct of workmanship or that a dog fights because of a fighting propensity is to offer no real explanation of behavior. Scientific explanation always adds something to the facts to be explained, either by relating them to additional facts (in the present or in the past) or by making a hypothesis that can be tested.

The problem of explanation within psychology is broader than the problem of motivation. Psychologists recognize that behavior is determined by many factors. No single explanation can be fully adequate. As a matter of fact when a psychologist seeks to explain the facts of behavior he turns in one of several directions:

1. He attempts to explain in terms of the genes and the mechanisms of heredity.
2. He explains chemically in terms of hormones and other chemical factors that act directly upon tissues and organs.
3. He explains in terms of stimulus and response, distinguishing between external patterns of stimulation and internal excitations.
4. He explains in terms of gross and microscopic structure of the body. The structural organization of the nervous system is especially important in an explanation of the facts of behavior.
5. The structure of the sociocultural environment is regarded as an

important determinant of man's activity. The child is a biological organism growing up in a social and cultural environment. As he becomes socialized he acquires the behavioral patterns characteristic of his group.

6. The psychologist also seeks explanation within the conscious experiences of individuals. Especially important to the student of human motivation are affective experiences (distress, relief, enjoyment, satiation), perceptual experiences that are based upon past experiences, pictures in memory and imagination, conscious purposes and expectancies. In everyday life as well as in ethics, religion, and law, a motive is regarded as a conscious determinant of action.

There are thus a number of ways in which the psychologist seeks to explain the facts of human and animal behavior. The kind of explanation that a student of motivation is especially interested in may be characterized as *dynamic*. Motivation is a contemporary dynamic process occurring always within an organism. Motivation is conceived in terms of the energetics of activity in relation to the regulation and patterning of behavior.

The Level of Activity

Behavior is made of a variety of specific patterns of activity. The rat, for example, may be observed to eat, drink, urinate, defecate, sleep, breathe, copulate, run, fight, preen, dig, burrow, gnaw, climb, vocalize, etc. Each activity has its own characteristic pattern by which it can be recognized and defined.

Under laboratory conditions certain activities are cyclic, occurring with a regular periodicity. Two illustrations of activity cycles are described below: (a) the running cycle in the female rat, and (b) the diurnal drinking cycle.

The rate of running activity can be determined by means of a rotating drum similar to the running wheels that are used in a zoo for exercising of squirrels and other small animals. In the laboratory a counter is attached to the central axis of the drum so that the number of revolutions per hour or per day can be measured. Rats sometimes run in the activity wheel for hours at a time with relatively few pauses. The number of revolutions per hour or per day, however, varies with conditions.

The mature female rat, when not pregnant or lactating, exhibits regular periodic variations in the level of running activity. Figure 1 illustrates the results from an experiment in which the rotating-drum technique was utilized. The vertical axis of the figure shows the number of revolutions made per day by the rat. The horizontal axis gives the age of the animal during successive days of the experi-

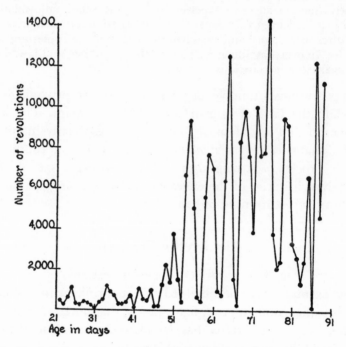

Fig. 1. **Onset of the Activity Cycle of a Female Rat at Puberty.** [After Wang (25).]

ment. The female is relatively active for a few hours during estrus (rut) and relatively less active between successive periods of estrus. The peaks of high activity for the average adult female rat occur with a periodicity of about 4.7 days.

This estrous rhythm is absent with the immature female. The onset of the activity cycle at puberty is shown in Fig. 2. The cycle persists from puberty throughout the reproductive period of the rat; it is suspended during pregnancy and lactation. It can be eliminated by ovariectomy and restored by transplantation of ovarian tissue or by the administration of ovarian hormones. The periods of heightened activity coincide with the periodic liberation of quantities of follicular hormone into the blood of the animal.

The second illustration of an activity rhythm is the diurnal drinking cycle of the rat. A continuous record of drinking activity can readily be obtained by means of an apparatus diagrammed in Fig. 3. This apparatus, used in the writer's laboratory, operates on the

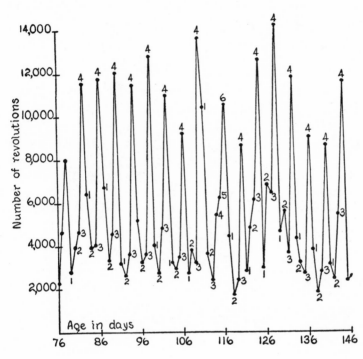

Fig. 2. **Typical Activity Cycle of a Female Rat.** [After Richter (16).]

principle of the inverted-bottle devices for watering. When an animal drinks out of the cup at the base of the apparatus, bubbles of air rise into the vertical container, thus reducing the partial vacuum above the water and permitting the water to fall into the cup. The level of water in the drinking cup is at all times approximately constant, but the water in the tube falls at a rate determined by the rate of drinking. A cork float on the surface of the water is attached to a non-absorbent filament and this filament, in turn, is attached to a recording pen that drops vertically across a moving paper. The falling pen gives a graphic record of the drinking and non-drinking activity of the rat and it shows continuously the rate of drinking and the periods of non-drinking (32).

Figure 4 presents a two-day continuous record of the drinking activity of four rats. The animals were housed in individual cages and each had an unlimited supply of laboratory chow and unre-

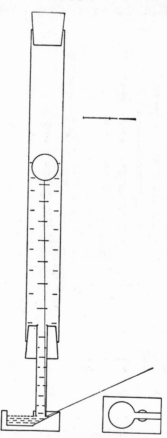

Fig. 3. Drinking Cup and Part of Apparatus for Continuous Recording of the Rate of Drinking (32). The essential part of this apparatus is a lucite block drilled out to make a one-inch circular drinking cup which is located inside the animal's cage. A nonabsorbent filament (keeping the same length in water and in air) connects a cork float with a recording pen (not shown in the drawing), which drops vertically in front of a moving paper. The graphic record indicates periods of drinking and nondrinking and changes in the rate of acceptance.

stricted access to a drinking cup containing distilled water. The parallel vertical lines mark off time in units of six hours. These curves are typical of the records obtained. Inspection shows that during the morning hours and the early afternoon the rats do relatively little drinking. They drink mostly in the late afternoon and at night. There is a well-marked diurnal rhythm of drinking and non-drinking. It is assumed that this rhythm is a learned adaptation to the diurnal alternations of light and dark.

It is well known that the rat is a nocturnal animal. He is relatively more active during night than day. This statement applies not only

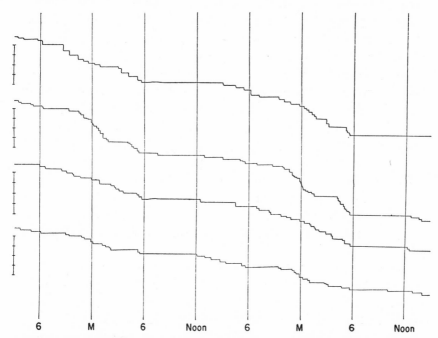

6   M   6   Noon   6   M   6   Noon

Fig. 4. Diurnal Drinking Curves of the Rat (32). The graph shows periods of drinking and nondrinking of distilled water. The records were obtained from four rats recording simultaneously. The step-wise drops are due to the fact that the recording pen moves only when bubbles of air rise in the container (see Fig. 3). Vertical cross-lines have been added to mark time in six-hour units. The scales at the left indicate the quantity of water consumed; the unit for each scale is 10 grams.

to drinking but also to feeding, running, and probably to most of the specific activities that together determine the general level of activity.

Various other forms of apparatus have been devised for recording the level of activity. In the triangular activity cage, for example, every movement made by the subject leaves a mark on the record regardless of its nature. The triangular activity cage is supported at the corners by tambours so that every movement made by the subject changes the pressure in a pneumatic system. Quantitative differences in the gross amount of activity can also be recorded unanalytically with a stabilimeter—a cage supported by springs.

Quantitative records of the level of activity are important in studies of the endocrine glands. Surgical removal of certain glands—pituitary, adrenals, thyroid, parathyroids, gonads—results in a marked lowering of the level of activity. The removal of glands sometimes reveals new and unexplained rhythms of activity.

Measurements of the level of activity have also shown important relations between activity and age, temperature, illumination, sex, periodicity of feeding, and other conditions. The general level of activity falls during fatigue, sleep, and sickness. It rises with painful stimulation, and with situations that threaten the security of the organism calling forth the emergency reactions (29).

Homeostatic Drives

The cells of the organism are surrounded by lymph and blood. From these fluids they withdraw the substances necessary for growth and survival. This physicochemical environment of the cells remains relatively constant, as Claude Bernard and later Cannon (7) pointed out.

The water content of the cellular environment remains relatively constant. There is also a relative constancy of blood sugar, protein, fat, sodium, and calcium. The oxygen supply within the blood is maintained at a relatively stable level. The acidity of the blood is kept at a point close to neutrality. There is a remarkable stability of internal temperature; if the temperature departs but a few degrees from the normal level, the physician suspects some inner disturbance. The external temperature, of course, varies widely from the tropics to the poles but despite this the temperature of the *milieu interne* is held approximately constant by temperature-regulating mechanisms of the body.

To designate a relatively constant internal state Cannon coined the word *homeostasis* (plural *homeostases*). The word does not imply a stability that is absolutely constant but rather a condition that varies, within limits, about a mean. To maintain homeostasis the fluid matrix of the body must be safeguarded. The organism must somehow find water, carbohydrate, fat, sodium, calcium, and so forth, in its physical environment. It must obtain oxygen. It must remain within a certain range of temperatures. In order to maintain homeostasis the organism requires certain substances and energy conditions. The physical needs of the body can be defined objectively in terms of the substances and energy conditions required to maintain homeostasis. Metabolic needs can be defined as the requirements of an organism for growth, normal activity, health, or survival itself.

Richter (17, 18), extending the doctrine of Bernard and Cannon, has argued that behavior is a manifestation of self-regulatory mechanisms for the maintenance of homeostasis. The basic motivations of behavior, he believes, are the deep biological urges to maintain constant internal states. Freeman (10) has extended the concept of homeostasis by placing an emphasis upon the neuromuscular processes of self-regulatory behavior. When an activity in progress is blocked, he points out, the organism tends to mobilize additional energy. The energy reinforcement serves to carry the activity in progress to completion, thereby restoring equilibrium. Other writers have attempted to extend the concept of equilibrium into the area of social behavior and personality adjustment.

In any event, certain basic motivations are related intimately to the maintaining of internal conditions which are essential for survival and growth. These motivations will be designated as the *homeostatic drives*.

Thirst

According to Cannon's well-known theory, thirst is of local origin. Thirst, he believes, is normally the consequence of a drying of the mucous membranes of the mouth and pharynx when the salivary glands fail to keep this region moist. The dehydrated membranes stimulate cutaneous nerves, which, in turn, excite the organism and mediate the experience of thirst.

Although the experience of thirst is usually localized in the region of the mouth and pharynx, the bodily basis of thirst is more general. This was demonstrated by Bellows (6) who operated upon dogs, placing a fistula so that water would pass through the mouth and pharynx and thence outside of the body. Moistening of the mouth and pharynx brought only temporary relief; but when water (equal in amount to the water deficit of the body) was introduced directly into the alimentary tract the act of drinking was permanently inhibited. It required ten to fifteen minutes, however, after the water had been introduced below the pharynx for a permanent satisfaction of thirst to develop. Thus watering the animal directly without letting water enter the mouth brought permanent satisfacion of thirst whereas passing water through the mouth and out through the fistula brought only temporary relief. Bellows concluded that there are two processes in the satisfaction of thirst which normally supplement and follow each other: (a) a buccal and pharyngeal process, and (b) a subpharyngeal process.

Another investigator, Adolph (1), also using the sham-drinking technique, distinguished between the drinking response and the drive to drink. He observed that when water taken by a dog left the body through a fistula, the rate of drinking remained nearly constant for considerable periods of time. The rate of response, however, varied with the water deficit of the body and was roughly proportional to the water deficit. Dogs that were severely desiccated spent about 20 per cent of their time in drinking. In one extreme instance, 71 liters of water (4.7 times the body weight) passed through the mouth in a 24-hour period. When water was introduced directly into the alimentary tract the urge to drink was satiated before there was time for the water to enter the blood stream and offset the water deficit. Some mechanism, therefore, appeared to check the drive to drink before the bodily need for water could be fully met.

In behavioral studies upon thirst the degree of physiological drive is usually controlled by depriving the animal of water for some specified number of hours. Thus one reads of a 24-hour thirst drive or a 48-hour drive. It is, of course, reasonable to assume that the need for water increases directly with the duration of water deprivation. Studies by Warner (26), however, relying upon the obstruction method (see pages 83-84), have shown that the frequency with which a rat crosses a charged grill to reach water is maximal after about 24 hours of water deprivation. When the period of deprivation is increased from one to six days the strength of the behavioral drive decreases.

A logical conclusion from studies with the obstruction method is that the behavioral drive, measured by this method, is not a dependable index of bodily need. The need for water increases directly with the duration of water deprivation but the behavioral drive does not. *Need* for water is one thing; *behavioral thirst drive* is something else.

Another difficulty with the duration of deprivation as a measure of the strength of drive is suggested by the well-marked diurnal drinking rhythm pictured above in Fig. 4. If the duration of deprivation is less than a day (for example, six or ten hours), the time of day during which the privation is imposed is a matter of considerable importance. A water deprivation from six A.M. till noon would have little effect since the animal rarely drinks during these hours. This deprivation would not be comparable in the strength of thirst created to one from midnight to six A.M.

In an attempt to obviate the difficulty of controlling the strength of thirst drive through deprivation Heyer (12) developed a technique of injecting salt solutions subcutaneously. The dosage was at the rate of three grams per kilogram of body weight for a 15 per cent solution of sodium chloride. The site of the injection was under the relatively loose skin along the rat's back and nape of the neck.

An injection of NaCl produces dehydration of the cells of the body. By varying the concentration of solution and the size of the dosage the degree of dehydration can be controlled. The sodium does not penetrate the cells directly but raises the osmotic pressure of the extracellular fluid. This withdraws water from the cells, which thus share in the general dehydration. A few minutes after a salt injection the animals commence to drink; they continue drinking, presumably, until the effects of dehydration are neutralized.

Heyer's method of producing dehydration has an obvious advantage over deprivation in experiments utilizing thirst motivation: The method permits the building up of a thirst drive of controllable magnitude at any time the experimenter wants it. Experiments upon motivation and learning can be designed without the necessity of fixed periods of deprivation to produce a degree of thirst. There is, however, one disadvantage: The injection arouses a painful disturbance in the animals. Some rats accept the hypodermic needle more or less complacently; others become emotional and develop attitudes of hostility toward the experimenter.

Hunger and appetite, palatability, feeding habit

The ingestion of food is regulated by three main groups of determinants, which are considered below: (a) the organic state (hunger and appetite, degree of approach to satiation); (b) the physical and chemical properties of the foodstuffs (relative palatability); and (c) the existing food habits or attitudes.

(a) The hunger pang—as Cannon and Washburn, Carlson, and other physiologists have shown—depends upon the contractions of an empty stomach. When the smooth muscle of an empty stomach contracts the hungry subject experiences "a dull ache or gnawing sensation referred to the lower mid-chest region and the epigastrium.

It is the organism's first strong demand for nutriment, and, not satisfied, is likely to grow into a highly uncomfortable pang, less definitely localized as it becomes more intense."

Although there can be no reasonable doubt concerning the physiological facts of hunger, this local-action theory of hunger is generally regarded by psychologists as incomplete and inadequate as an explanation of food-seeking behavior. For one thing the local-action theory does not account for specific hungers or appetites.

Richter (17, 18) has shown that when the components of an adequate diet are presented in separate containers, the laboratory rat is able to select and balance a diet that maintains normal growth and activity. Wild Norway rats, however, with garbage-pail habits and living under conditions of stress, are less able to adapt to self-selection or cafeteria conditions of maintenance.

Self-selection feeding experiments demonstrate the existence of independently varying appetites or specific hungers. There are appetites for protein, fat, carbohydrate, water, sodium, phosphorus, calcium, thiamine, riboflavin, pyridoxine, and doubtless for other substances. In addition to the appetites revealed by laboratory animals there are various acquired cravings of man—for alcoholic beverages, for morphine, cocaine, heroine, and other drugs. Also there are "perverted" appetites that appear in man and animal during malnutrition, sickness, pregnancy and lactation, and that follow surgical removal of some ductless gland. Examples of parorexia are: coprophagia (eating of feces), infantophagia (eating of the young), osteophagia (bone eating), and the grass eating of dogs and cats when sick. In diabetes, the patient may develop an intense craving for sugar and other sweets. In hookworm disease the patient may indiscriminately eat earth, paper, chalk, starch, hair, and clay. Human pregnancy is often accompanied by unusual food cravings that vary from person to person.

Thus there is ample evidence to support the view that there are independently varying appetites for different kinds of substance. *Independent variability,* however, is not of itself an adequate criterion for the demonstration of separate appetites. Independent variability might well depend upon the characteristics of the foodstuff apart from any organic hunger or craving.

The writer suggests that the criteria for a demonstration of separate appetites or specific hungers should be two: independent variability in food acceptance, and a demonstration that such independent variability depends upon some internal organic condition rather than upon the properties of the foodstuff or upon a well-formed habit. If the relative acceptance of a foodstuff can be shown to depend upon the presence or absence of a gland, for example, when the properties of the foodstuff itself are held constant, that fact demonstrates the existence of an organic appetite or specific hunger.

(b) That food selections of men and other animals depend upon characteristics of the foodstuff is fairly obvious. It is commonly recognized that the taste, smell, temperature, texture, appearance, and other sensory characteristics of a food are the basis for accepting, preferring, or rejecting. Foods differ in the degree of their "sense appeal." The problems of analyzing palatability are clearly bound up with problems of affectivity.

Human subjects report that some foods are more enjoyable to eat than others. Some foods are *liked* and others *disliked*. Non-humans may equally experience degrees of enjoyment associated with the eating of various kinds of food, but with animals we are limited to an objective analysis of behavior. We can, however, analyze food preferences, the rates at which animals consume different kinds of food, and the many complex conditions that regulate food acceptance and rejection. An objective account of affectivity can be given in terms of the reactions to different kinds of foodstuff.

Three of the most useful methods for investigating the relative acceptability of foodstuffs will now be described. The first of these is the writer's method of choice or preference that depends upon brief exposures of the test foods.

Figure 5 shows a preference tester with cover removed to reveal the parts. Test foods are located in two glass cups or vials shown by the arrow at *F*. Liquid or solid foods can be presented, a pair at a time. The foods can be raised or lowered from the floor by means of a lever indicated by *L*. When a test of preference is given, the rat is placed in the box, *B*, and the door is lowered. After the rat has remained for one minute in the box the experimenter raises the door and the animal is free to come out to the foods. When he accepts one food, both are lowered out of reach. The exposure is brief so that the animal is forced to choose. The procedure is such that the rat is trained to return to the starting-box before getting another nibble of food. When the rat is inside the box the door is lowered and immediately raised for another run. With this procedure the

Fig. 5. Food Preference Tester. *B* shows the location of the starting-box in which the rat is placed before a test and to which he returns between choices. *F* indicates the location of the foods presented during a test. *R* is a rod used by the experimenter for interchanging the relative positions of the test foods. *L* is a lever for raising or lowering the foods.

animal learns to shuttle back and forth between box and foods and on each round trip he makes a single choice. When the foods are lowered the experimenter interchanges their relative positions by turning the rod, *R*, and raises the foods to the plate for the next choice.

Some typical results, obtained with an earlier model of the preference tester, are given on page 75 (28).

Ten rats from the same litter, four males and six females, were used as subjects. They were maintained upon an adequate prepared diet, and, commencing at the age of 101 days, they were given individual tests of preference between all pairs of the following test foods:

Fresh milk standardized at 4 per cent butterfat (M).
Pure butterfat, free from salt, prepared for the experiment (B).
Cane sugar, granulated, extra fine (S).
White flour made from wheat (F).
Whole wheat flour, from selected wheat, ground for the experiment (W).
Dehydrated milk, a commercial powder (known as Klim, which is milk spelled backwards) (D).

The test foods, presented in pairs to each rat, become arranged into transitive series from the most to the least acceptable. The results for the ten rats are shown in the table. The test foods are

Rat Number			Preferential Sequence			
40	S	M	W	D	B	F
41	M	S	W	D	B	F
42	M	S	D	W	F	B
43	M	S	D	W	F	B
44	M	S	W	D	B	F
45	M	S	W	D	F	—
46	M	S	W	D	F	B
47	M	S	W	D	B	F
48	M	S	W	D	F	B
49	M	S	W	D	F	B
Total group	M	S	W	D	F	B

arranged in order, for the individual animal and for the group as a whole, so that any food is preferred to all of the foods shown to the right of it in the table. For example, for the group as a whole, milk is preferred to sugar. Both of these foods are preferred to whole wheat powder, and so on.

The writer has found in repeated experiments that when the diet is held constant, a group of test foods becomes arranged in a transitive series extending from the most to the least palatable. The series is relatively stable for a given set of experimental conditions but it can be changed by changing the diet.

The uniformity and stability of food preferences, with laboratory rats, is surprising. We have all heard the adage *De gustibus non est disputandum*. This is hardly correct for the rat! The tabulation of food preferences reveals marked uniformity, stability, and consistency.

The results can be taken to indicate that the food selections of the rat are dependent upon the kind or quality of food presented. In other experiments it has been proved that the rate of running

Fig. 6. Individual Cages for Preference Tests with a Self-selection Technique.
(Photograph through the courtesy of Dr. C. P. Richter.)

on the apparatus is dependent upon the quality of the foodstuff. Rats run faster to a highly palatable food than to one of lower palatability.

A second method for studying relative food acceptance is the self-selection or cafeteria method employed extensively by Richter and others. The animal is housed in a cage that presents in separate containers from one to twenty kinds of food (the number varying with the purpose of the experiment). The quantity of food presented is measured before and after a 24-hour exposure. The difference between initial and final measurements is the daily intake (recorded in grams or cubic centimeters).

Figure 6 pictures several cages of the type used in an experiment to be described below. In the middle row of cages each rat is offered a choice between two test fluids presented in the graduated inverted bottles. The bottles are clamped to the cage so that the openings are inside and readily accessible to the subject. At the top and bottom of the photograph are shown portions of cages provided with three containers for fluids, and a tin box containing a solid food. The animal is given a free choice among the dietary components that are presented continuously.

In one experiment rats were given a choice between distilled water and sugar solutions of varying concentration. The general procedure was to start the experiment with both bottles filled with distilled water. After a few days a sub-threshold concentration of sugar solution was substituted for water in one of the containers. From day to day the concentration of this solution was gradually increased until a preferential threshold was reached. Then the concentration was steadily raised above the threshold from day to day and the daily intake recorded.

Figures 7a and 7b show two types of curve obtained by Richter and Campbell (19). In the first type of curve (7a), illustrated by intake of glucose, there is a preferential threshold and a well-defined optimal concentration (about 10 per cent). As the concentration is raised above the optimal value the preference reverses. Where the curves for glucose and water cross, there is, theoretically, an indifference point at which no preference exists. In the second type of curve (7b), illustrated by lactose, distilled water is preferred to the sugar solution. As the concentration, from day to day, is steadily increased above the preferential threshold the preference becomes increasingly pronounced.

The present writer has tested a variety of fluids and to date there have been found only these two types of curve. If distilled water is preferred to the test fluid, the graph resembles that for lactose. If the test fluid is preferred to water, the graph resembles that for glucose (although in some curves the optimum and indifference point are not reached).

A third method for studying relative food acceptance is one that bridges the gap between the first two through recording continuously the rate of acceptance of the test foods. One form of the method was

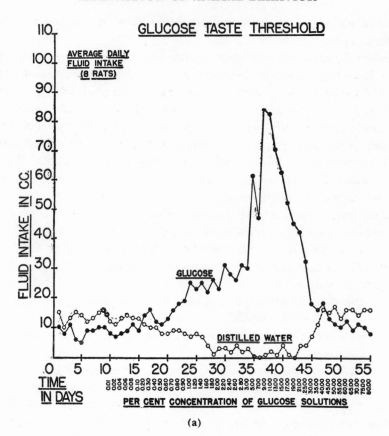

(a)

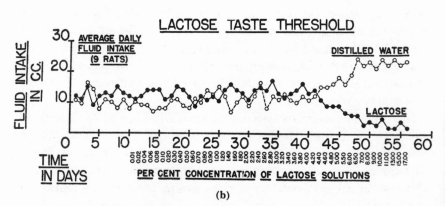

(b)

Fig. 7 (a and b). Curves Showing Result of Preference Tests with Distilled Water and Solutions of Glucose (above) and Lactose (below). [After Richter and Campbell (19).]

described previously and illustrated in Figs. 3 and 4. Periods of drinking and non-drinking are clearly recorded, and the rate of drinking is shown by the graphic records. When several fluids are presented simultaneously, the record indicates the preferences among them as well as changes in preference.

Other instrumental techniques are available for recording the rate of behavior. Examples are Skinner's bar-pressing apparatus, Warden's obstruction apparatus, Hull's straightaway for measuring the speed of locomotion toward food, and the numerous mazes, discrimination boxes, and other forms of apparatus employed in laboratories of animal behavior. With almost every one of these instruments it can readily be shown that the rate of behavior depends upon the factors mentioned above—the organic state (hunger and appetite) and the characteristics of the foodstuff (relative palatability). The recording instruments reveal clearly a third factor (habit) that is often the main concern of psychologists.

(c) When recruits for the U. S. Army came together from various regions of the country they brought with them the food habits and attitudes characteristic of their home localities. The Quartermaster Department was concerned over the fact that the men reacted differently to the Army chow.

A clear-cut illustration of the importance of food habits in the regulation of food acceptance is found in an experiment by Young and Chaplin (31). Rats maintained upon a self-selection, or cafeteria, diet were given a choice between two of the dietary components— sugar and casein. On the preference tester they consistently preferred sugar to casein. Then the casein was permanently removed from the regular diet thus creating a protein deficiency. Protein starvation increasingly developed. When placed upon the preference tester, however, the rats continued to prefer sugar to casein (the needed food). At this point in the experiment a different kind of preference tester (with the foods in fixed positions and widely separated as in a Y-maze) was employed. When tested with the new apparatus the reverse preference (of casein to sugar) at once developed in all animals. Two kinds of preference were present simultaneously! When placed upon the apparatus with which they had been trained before protein starvation they continued to select sugar regardless of its position. When tested with the new technique the animals consistently showed a preference for casein. One preference agreed with bodily need; the other did not. The final conclusion reached, after several control experiments, was that: *Preferential food habits tend to form in agreement with metabolic needs, but an established habit may persist as a factor regulating the selection of food regardless of need.* Thus an animal may automatically, mechanically, select a food to which he has been habituated regardless of need.

The psychologist would like to know how food habits come into existence, upon what they rest, how they operate in regulating the process of feeding. These are basic questions.

One view concerning the origin of food habits is that the animal learns to accept a food that meets a bodily need and that aids in restoring homeostasis. This view, however, meets with certain difficulties: marked food preferences develop in the absence of metabolic need; animals accept with avidity a sweet-tasting substance (saccharin) that meets no need; animals sometimes take more than they need of a substance and thereby develop symptoms of excess; in experiments they sometimes fail to select foods in agreement with known needs; they occasionally accept toxic substances with fatal result; and they are dominated by habits and attitudes regardless of bodily needs (30). Obviously *need* is one thing; *food acceptance* is something else.

A better hypothesis is that sensory contact with a food arouses an affective reaction in the subject—an immediate liking or disliking that depends upon the characteristics of the foodstuff as well as upon the prevailing organic state and existing food habits. Instead of starting from the concepts of homeostasis and bodily need, this interpretation starts with the observed facts of food acceptance: the uniformity, consistency, and stability of food preferences; the transitive series or hierarchies of food preference that have been repeatedly found; the dependence of food acceptance upon the characteristics of the food object as well as upon the chemical state of the organism; the positive correlation between the strength of the food-seeking drive and the measured level of palatability; the fact that adequate motivation can be obtained with a food incentive in the absence of need; and so forth (30).

Food-seeking drives, we believe, are organized on the basis of a hedonic principle. When an animal is deprived of some needed food a pattern of deficiency symptoms develops. There are different kinds of deficiency syndrome corresponding to different kinds of dietary deficiency. A partial starvation (insofar as it has a psychological effect) produces a specific form of distress. Painful stimulations from the environment and frustrations also produce distress.

The diagram in Fig. 8 illustrates the fact that affectivity may move from indifference to distress. There are mild, moderate, and intense

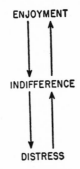

ENJOYMENT

INDIFFERENCE

DISTRESS

Fig. 8. Diagram to Show Relationships among Affective Processes.

degrees of distress, but affectivity may depart from indifference in another direction. When an animal is free from every known metabolic need, when he is healthy, active, and in the presence of plenty, he still accepts foods that are supplementary to the diet. He accepts some foods with apparent enjoyment. Different degrees of enjoyment are shown objectively in the rate of acceptance and in relative food preference. The enjoyment of food is usually reduced by the approach of satiation, by frustration, or by distraction in one form or another.

The hedonic theory of drive assumes that animals *organize* patterns of behavior that relieve distress or that continue enjoyment. They do not organize patterns that increase distress nor those that reduce enjoyment.

Determinants of maternal behavior

Some authors have referred to a maternal drive or instinct as if there were a single underlying cause of maternal activity. Actually there are several interlocking determinants.

Maternal behavior in the rat is complex, being composed of separate activities such as parturition, removal of the fetal membranes, cleansing the newborn, retrieving the young and gathering the scattered young together, nest building and repairing of a damaged nest, hovering over the young, nursing, licking the young and licking one's self, defense of the young upon occasion, and so on. Primiparous females display activities similar to those of multiparous animals—activities directed toward the care of the young (22). To look for a single underlying cause of these diverse phenomena is to over-simplify the picture.

According to one theory, maternal behavior is said to depend upon activity of the mammary glands and the suckling of the young. This hypothesis has been tested by surgically removing the mammary glands prior to pregnancy or immediately after pregnancy (27). In the absence of mammary glands rats showed the same patterns of maternal behavior as those exhibited by intact females. Most of the operated animals retrieved the young. They sat on the nest crouching over the young in a nursing posture. They shifted the young under them as frequently as normal mothers. In the absence of stimulation from the mammary glands, and with suckling of the young rendered impossible, these mothers still showed quite normal maternal behavior. We are forced to conclude, therefore, that the continuation of maternal behavior is not dependent upon the secretion of milk nor upon suckling the young. Incidentally, the experiment showed also that assuming of the nursing posture is a primary response and not merely a secondary adaptation to the act of nursing.

Removal of the mammary glands did not interfere with return of the estrous cycle after delivery of a litter. Nor was nest building reduced by the operation. In some animals nest building was even increased despite the fact that suckling was rendered impossible.

With intact animals nest building is closely associated with birth and care of the young. The parturient rat exhibits a strong tendency to build a nest and also to retrieve the young if they move away from the nest. The tendency to retrieve is of maximal intensity soon after parturition and from maximum it diminishes at a variable rate. How long retrieving persists at a lower level of intensity depends upon the organic condition of the mother as well as upon the presence or absence of small young. If the young are beyond a certain age, the mother rat does not retrieve them at all. Retrieving normally ceases shortly after the fifteenth day of lactation, but, at this time, if small young from another litter are introduced, the mother again retrieves them, although at the same time she fails to retrieve her own larger young. Apparently the presence of a satisfactory maternal object (small young) combines with the organic state of the mother to induce retrieving. The stimulus-pattern for retrieving is not very specific, for the mother rat retrieves young mice, kittens, chicks, as well as the young of some litter other than her own.

Maternal behavior is dependent upon internal secretions synchronized with, but not induced by, parturition. In the gland transplantation experiments of Steinach it was shown that feminized male guinea pigs exhibit maternal behavior. Actual "lactation" was reported by several observers of such animals. It is believed, therefore, that the ovarian secretions incite maternal behavior and that there is a hormonal basis for continuance of the maternal patterns. But these patterns also depend upon the presence of suitable maternal objects. As Stone has put it, there are interlocking relations between the organic and environmental conditions of behavior.

Determinants of sexual behavior

The much discussed Kinsey (13) report is a mine of information concerning human sexual activity; it provides a basis for comparing the sexual behavior of man with that of other animals. Kinsey's bibliography is useful to anyone who wishes to study a particular aspect of sexual activity. A review of the literature upon sexual drive, by Stone (20), constitutes a good introduction to experimental studies with animals.

One method that has been extensively used in the analysis of sexual drive is the obstruction method of Warden (26) and collaborators. The method has a wide applicability, having also been used for the study of hunger, thirst, exploratory behavior, and the maternal drive. The obstruction method requires the animal to cross a charged grill to reach the goal object and make the consummatory reaction. The general plan of the Columbia University obstruction box is shown in Fig. 9.

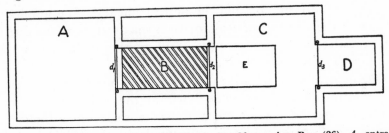

Fig. 9. Floor Plan of the Columbia University Obstruction Box (26). *A*, entrance compartment; *B*, obstruction compartment with charged grill on the floor; *C* and *D*, a divided incentive compartment; *E*, release plate which automatically opens a door, d_3, releasing the incentive animal from compartment *D*. Manually operated doors for closing off entrance and incentive compartments are located at d_1 and d_2.

In experiments upon sexual drive, the mate is placed in compartment D. When the subject crosses the charged grill, B, and depresses the floor plate, E, the mate is automatically released from D into compartment C. An animal to be tested is placed in compartment A. When doors, d_1 and d_2, are raised the subject is free to cross the charged grill to the mate. Complete sexual union is not ordinarily permitted but the subject is lifted back from C into A. The frequency of crossing the grill during a standard period of 20 minutes constitutes a measure of the strength of drive. Approaches to the grill and contacts with it are also recorded.

Typical results are those obtained by Warner, reported by Warden (26). The upper curve in Fig. 10 shows the average number of crossings of the grill (solid line), contacts with it (dot-dash line), and approaches to it (dash line), for groups of female rats. The sexual receptivity of the female is periodic (see Figs. 1 and 2) with a periodicity, on the average, of about 4.7 days. The base line of Fig. 10 marks off successive changes in the histological character of the vaginal secretions during one complete estrous cycle of the rat. These successive changes are designated as: recuperative, early inactive, inactive, late inactive, early cornified, cornified, late cornified, post ovulative, recuperative. The strength of the female sexual drive, as indicated by graphs based upon all three criteria, is seen to vary regularly with the stage of the estrous cycle.

The lower curve in Fig. 10 gives the average number of crossings (solid line), contacts (dot-dash line), and approaches (dash line) for groups of male rats. The strength of the male drive does not show a cyclic variability. Instead the strength of the male drive varies with the period of deprivation following sexual satiation. The base line of the lower curve, therefore, records the interval of time elapsed between sexual satiation and the obstruction test. The graph indicates that the strength of male drive is maximal at about one day after copulation to satiation (when grill crossing is the criterion), or (with other criteria) in less than a day.

One general difficulty with the obstruction method is that a complex motivating state is aroused within the subject. Whether in testing the sexual urge, hunger, thirst, or some other biologically basic motivation, the subject is confronted with the necessity of crossing a charged grill to reach the goal-object. A conflict is thus set up between pain avoidance and the primary motivating state that is under investigation. There are unknown complications of this conflict. Nevertheless, the validity and reliability of the method have

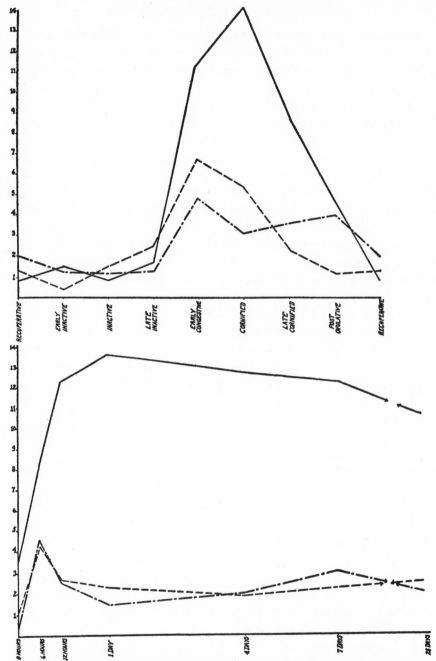

Fig. 10. Variations in the Strength of the Female and Male Sexual Drives as Determined by the Obstruction Apparatus. [After Warner (26).] Upper curve, female sexual drive; lower curve, male. Solid lines show frequency of crossing the charged grid. Dot-dash lines show frequency of contacts with the grid. Dash lines show frequency of approaches to the grid.

been determined (21) and the method has been quite extensively used. What is needed is an unambiguous, operational definition of the sexual drive—a definition based upon actual mating performance rather than a less direct type of behavior such as the tendency of a male to cross an electrically charged grid to reach the receptive female.

A more direct approach to the determinants of sexual behavior has been made by Beach and Holz-Tucker (4). During a test the male is placed in a circular observation cage, 34 inches in diameter and 30 inches high. After a three-minute period of adaptation, a receptive female is deposited quietly in the center of the cage. Each test lasts ten minutes from the time of the first complete or incomplete copulation by the experimental male. Various measurements of sexual behavior are made. Latency is defined as the number of seconds elapsing between the time that the receptive female is placed in the observation cage and the time the male executes his first sexual mount. Another measure is simply the presence or absence of mating behavior. A castrated male, for example, is given a negative score if he fails to copulate. When the test is positive the frequency of copulation per test constitutes another measure.

Using this direct method Beach and others have studied the effects of castration upon sexual behavior and the effects of injecting androgen (male sexual hormone) upon castrated animals.

When male rats are castrated their latency is markedly increased and the frequency of copulation per test is markedly decreased. In other words, their sexual potency is decreased by an operation that removes from the blood the testicular hormones. It was found that injections of androgen (testosterone propionate) restored sexual potency. There was, moreover, a direct relation between the measures of sexual potency, on the one hand, and the number of micrograms of androgen injected per day (1 microgram = .001 mg.), on the other.

Beach found that the amount of hormone necessary to maintain sexual performance at or near the preoperative level was dependent upon the behavioral criterion selected as a measure. In the main, however, 50 to 75 micrograms per day is a dose that will maintain the sexual drive of the rat at its preoperative level. When castrated males are given a daily injection of 100 to 500 micrograms of androgen they exhibit sexual behavior equal or superior to that shown prior to the operation.

This work is significant in that it indicates clearly a quantitative relation between the strength of sexual drive exhibited in behavior and the number of micrograms of androgen injected into the animal. In a further study, Beach and Levinson (5) observed structural changes in sensory mechanisms correlated with the presence or absence of androgen.

Figure 11 shows the histological changes in the sexual receptor mechanisms of the male rat following castration and the partial return to normal when androgen is administered. The first view shows the genital papillae of the normal rat. It is the mechanical stimulation of these structures, during coition, that produces the response of ejaculation. Such stimulation excites tactile corpuscles and sensory nerves that are located beneath them. The result of castration is shown in the second view (with higher magnification). The papillae have almost disappeared and the surface of the skin is smooth. Beach and Levinson suggest that the weakened sexual drive of the castrated male is, in part, due to lowered sensitivity in the copulatory organ. There are, presumably, other changes due to castration, for androgen acts directly upon the complex neural mechanisms. The third view shows regeneration of the genital papillae after four weeks of treatment with androgen. This regeneration is associated with a return of sexual drive toward its normal strength. The fourth view, with a high magnification, shows the genital papillae and underlying tactile corpuscles of a normal rat.

These observations are of theoretical interest in that they demonstrate the close interrelations among the chemical action of hormones, structural changes in the organism, and behavior. If we are attempting to explain sexual behavior, we must take account not only of the chemical determinants but also of the histological and gross structural changes that they produce. We must remember, also, that structure and function are everywhere interdependent.

Other homeostatic drives

In addition to thirst, hunger and appetite, and the determinants of maternal and sexual behavior, there are other primary motivations that might well be considered in a study of homeostatic drives.

To survive, the organism must obtain oxygen. If a man is submerged, there ensues an immediate *air hunger* with a struggle to reach the air. Failing in the attempt a man will drown in a few minutes, for oxygenation of the blood is one of the basic conditions of survival. Again, overexertion produces a biochemical condition of *fatigue* that requires rest to remove from the blood an excessive

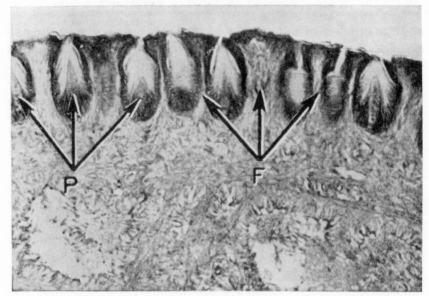

(1)

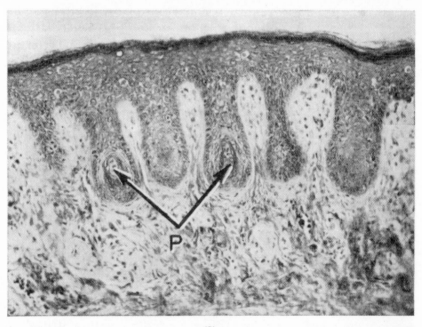

(2)

Fig. 11. **Structural Changes in the Genital Papillae of Castrated Male Rats before and after the Administration of Androgen.** [After Beach and Levinson (5).] (1) A section of the integument of the glans penis of a normal male. *F* indicates cross sections through epithelial folds and *P* sections through genital papillae. (2) This view is a similar section four weeks after castration, with no administration of androgen. *P*

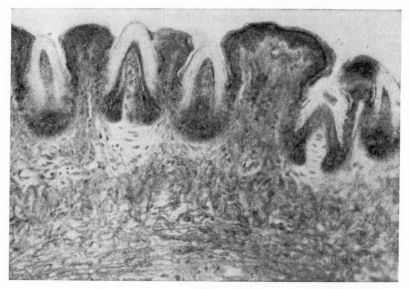

(3)

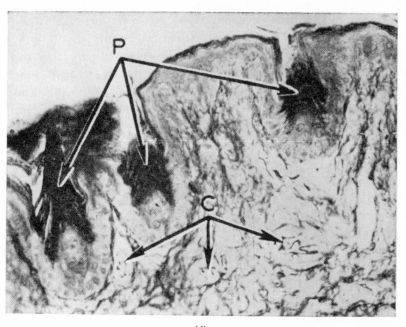

(4)

indicates remnants of former genital papillae; the surface is smooth. (3) A similar cross section of a rat castrated for four weeks and then treated with androgen. This rat was given 75 micrograms of testosterone propionate daily for 28 days before the section was made. The magnification of the first view is less than that of the other two. (4) This view, with high magnification, shows the normal genital papillae at *P* and the underlying tactile corpuscles at *C*.

89

quantity of CO_2 and sarcolactic acid. There is a chemical basis for the demand of a fatigued organism to rest and relax. Further, the *urge to sleep* is not to be confused with fatigue. A man may be sleepy without being fatigued or he may be fatigued without being sleepy. Often, of course, he is both sleepy and fatigued. Sleep, whatever its organic nature, is necessary for survival and the loss of sleep, as we all know, brings a lowering of efficiency and comfort in work. Still other basic drives are the *urges to urinate and to defecate.* The eliminative drives depend upon mechanical pressure of urine against the wall of the bladder or of fecal matter against the wall of the colon and rectum. If elimination is impossible, these pressures become increasingly painful. Elimination is just as essential for maintaining homeostasis and for survival as the ingestion of food. Also there are powerful urges in the interest of *temperature regulation.* The organism seeks to avoid extremes of cold and heat. As noted above, the cells of the body can survive only if maintained within a fairly narrow thermal range. The physiological mechanisms of temperature regulation need not be considered here but brief mention should be made of the fact that behavior cooperates in the process. Finally, *painful stimulation,* whether from the environment or from the internal tissues, produces a powerful urge to avoid it. The *pain-avoiding drive* is basic. All of these primary motivations drive the organism to act in a manner that brings relief, restores homeostasis, and permits survival.

Environmental Controls of Behavior

The homeostatic drives are primary in the sense that a physiological mechanism underlying purposive behavior has been demonstrated for each one of them. These primary drives, therefore, can be differentiated in terms of their organic bases. Moreover, the homeostatic drives are primary in the further sense that they relate to basic needs for survival of the individual and the race. The homeostatic drives are dependable in the sense that people in all societies, regardless of time and place, are driven by biological necessity to eat, drink, eliminate, breathe, be active, rest, sleep, mate, care for the young, and avoid painful stimulations and the extremes of temperature. Although patterns of behavior vary widely from culture to culture, the biological needs and bodily mechanisms that underlie these primary patterns are uniform throughout.

To designate a drive as secondary, however, does not mean that it is unimportant. There are fundamental trends in behavior that cannot be related to any primary motivation, but that nevertheless are of great importance in human and animal life. Psychologists have found it convenient to work in the laboratory with the homeostatic drives, and they have neglected or belittled the potentialities of the secondary motivations.

Play

The scientific analysis of playful behavior has lagged behind the analysis of other forms of fundamental activity because play does not fit into the general pattern of the homeostatic drives. There is no play gland or play muscle, no neural integration known to be common to all forms of play. Moreover, there is no identifiable pattern of behavior that is common to the different forms of play. The playful cat pounces upon a moving leaf, utilizing a familiar reflexive pattern; the playful dog romps around the yard; the playful colt kicks up his heels in the field; the playful child engages in innumerable activities—running, jumping, dancing, dressing a doll, and so forth. What do all forms of playful behavior have in common? It is difficult to find any single answer in terms of traditional physiological psychology.

Current beliefs concerning the concept of play have been summarized by Beach (2) as follows. (a) It is commonly assumed that playful behavior, in animals as well as in man, is a pleasant, enjoyable activity. (b) Play is usually regarded as characteristic of the immature animal rather than the adult. The child plays more frequently than the grown up (although adults, of course, do play). (c) It is often supposed that playful behavior lacks biological utility. Play, in other words, has no immediately useful result. (d) Play, as noted above, assumes diverse forms. Dogs, horses, apes, children, and other creatures, play in different ways. (e) In the higher forms of organism play is more frequent and more variable than in the lower forms. Moreover, in the higher forms playful behavior occupies a relatively longer period of the life span than it does in lower forms.

There has been much speculation about the nature, causation, and significance of play, but relatively little objective research upon playful behavior. Analysis of playful behavior, however, can be made through controlled observations and experiments as the study of maternal behavior, courtship and mating, food selection, territory defense, social dominance, learning, and similar phenomena have already yielded to the objective methods. To the present writer the fundamental characteristic of playful behavior is the enjoyment associated with the activity in its early (unhabituated) stages. Play and other interesting activities raise a question concerning an hedonic basis of behavior.

Manipulation and exploration

It is commonly recognized that when an animal is placed in a novel environment he engages in exploratory activity. When a rat, for example, is first placed in a maze he runs about, looking, sniffing, touching objects. If the animal is hungry, he explores before eating; if sexually stimulated, he explores before mating. Rats will even cross a charged grid of the obstruction apparatus (Fig. 9), enduring discomfort, to continue exploration of a Dashiell checkerboard maze. When, through repeated exploration, the animal has become thoroughly habituated to the environment, exploratory patterns disappear.

It may be said that exploration is a response to an environmental factor—novelty—and that such exploration has the advantage of acquainting the organism with potential threats and sources of danger in the environment. Exploratory behavior is *environmentally* determined. In this respect it differs from the primary physiological drives.

In some experiments upon the solving of mechanical puzzles by monkeys, Harlow (11) has utilized a non-homeostatic drive—the drive to manipulate. He has shown that monkeys persist in the manipulation of gadgets that resemble human puzzles. The puzzle presents no extrinsic reward such as food, nor does the activity reduce any known organic need.

A sample of the apparatus employed in Harlow's studies is pictured in Fig. 12. It consists of a metal-edged unpainted wooden base to which is attached, flush, a hasp restrained by a hook. The hook, in turn, is restrained by a metal peg attached to a chain. (Four of these units are shown in the illustration.) By removing the peg the monkey can lift the hook and then open the hasp. Nothing is obtained by these manipulations. Solution of the puzzle does not lead to food, water, sexual gratification, nor to relief from pain or from high or low temperatures. The persistent manipulative behavior of the monkey clearly does not fit into the pattern of the homeostatic drives. All that can be said is that the device is a puzzle that in some way invites the manipulations of the monkey.

Harlow proposes the view that an externally-elicited drive may operate to channel behavior, and that the manipulations in some way provide intrinsic reward. The curiosity motive, frequently at-

Fig. 12. Monkey Solving Mechanical Puzzles Without Food Incentives or Other Extrinsic Reward. [Photograph through the courtesy of Dr. H. F. Harlow (11).] The picture shows very clearly that there can be no food beneath the mechanical devices that the animal manipulates.

tributed to human infants and children, can be characterized in much the same way.

Emergency reactions

When a cat is pursued by a barking dog the first reaction is flight and escape, but if the cat is cornered, the pattern changes to one of attack. So far as we know, the difference between flight and attack does not lie in the internal bodily changes associated with the two reactions, but rather in the dynamic relationship between the organism and its external situation. Flight is an avoidance, a negative reaction to a threatening or dangerous situation. Attack is a positive reaction to the same type of threatening situation. If the cat is lucky enough to escape into a tree, she may persist for half an hour or more in a state of emotional excitement. If she is injured, pain complicates the organic state.

Cannon has referred to the bodily changes that occur in a biological crisis as *emergency* emotions. Considered as a group they are seen to involve a common pattern of internal bodily changes that prepare the organism for a vigorous struggle or a race for life. The increased secreting of the adrenal glands, the more rapid liberation of sugar from the liver, the acceleration of the heart beat and of respiration, and other bodily changes, all prepare and organize the animal for a vital struggle that involves energy expenditure at a high level.

The internal bodily changes of the emergency reaction can be differentiated clearly from those of hunger, thirst, fatigue, and other homeostatic drives. But the pattern of internal changes during the emergency reaction is the same for fear, rage, pain, and great excitement. These emotional patterns can be distinguished, however, on the level of behavior. Fear is associated with flight; rage with hostile attack; pain with bodily injury; excitement with the absence of a persistent incentive orientation.

Emotional behavior is different from the homeostatic drives in that it is aroused initially by an environmental situation, such as the encounter with a barking dog, whereas the homeostatic drives evoke behavior through internal bodily arousals.

The distinction between organic and environmental conditions of behavior, however, is in the last analysis arbitrary and one that is made only for convenience. Behavior is always a dynamic interrelation between organism and environment. The physical environment is the source of food, air, water, mates, thermal energy, and other requirements of life; it is also a source of enemies, injury, poison, pain, and death. A fundamental analysis of motivation can never lose sight of the environmental controls of behavior.

Specific Incentives

A distinction is commonly drawn between motives and incentives. *Motives* are internal determinants of behavior, such as organic states of hunger, thirst, fatigue, and specific determinations to carry out some course of action. *Incentives,* by contrast, are external determinants. The goal-objects toward which purposive behavior is directed are sometimes called incentive-objects. It is not so much the object itself (food, mate, young), however, that is the goal of activity, as the consummatory reaction (eating, copulating, mothering) for which the object is required. Incentives, also, are conditions that facilitate purposive behavior. The spur and the whip applied to the horse speed up the running; these painful stimulations act as incentives. The word of praise to a pupil, the gold star placed after his name, the prize to be won, constitute incentives to the school child. These are environmental conditions that facilitate purposive activity.

The terms *reward* and *punishment* are commonly employed in experimental literature dealing with specific incentives. These terms, as others have pointed out, often imply moral evaluations. A reward is bestowed for good or right conduct. A punishment is inflicted for error and, presumably, to correct error. A reward brings enjoyment or relief from distress. A punishment brings pain or some other distress that impels the animal to gain relief. When we use these terms we will keep in mind the psychological facts rather than the ethical implications. We will review an experiment upon pain avoidance and then a group of experiments dealing with various aspects of so-called rewards.

Acquisition of a Pain-Avoiding Drive

In an experiment upon fear Miller (14) employed the apparatus shown in Fig. 13. The left compartment was painted white and the right black to give a clear sensory difference. The floor of the white compartment consisted of a grid through which an electric shock could be delivered to the feet of the rat. Between these two compartments was a door painted visibly with white and black stripes. The door could be opened in one of three ways: (a) The experimenter could open it by pressing a button; (b) The rat could open it by turning a roller-like wheel located immediately above the door; (c) The rat could open it by pressing a bar in the wall of the white compartment.

In preliminary trials a rat was placed in the apparatus and given opportunity to explore. Miller reports that the animals showed no preference for either compartment (although rats normally do prefer dark places to light). When the animals received a shock, however, they escaped through the open door into the black compartment. Following a number of shocks, the rats would run out of the white compartment into the black even when the grid was not charged. In other words, painful shock associated with the white compartment produced pain-avoiding behavior. The animals quickly learned to avoid the white room.

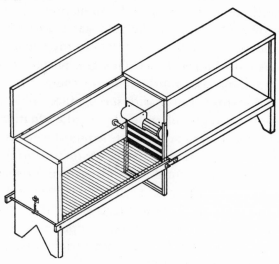

Fig. 13. Apparatus for the Study of Pain-avoiding Patterns of Behavior.
[After Dr. N. Miller (14).]

After preliminary training, during which the animal was shocked, a rat was placed in the white compartment without a shock. The door, which had previously been open, was closed. The only way the rat could open the door was by rotating the wheel above the door. In another series the only way the animal could open the door was by pressing the lever projecting from the wall.

Rats learned to operate the gadgets and to escape from white to black compartments. Control tests showed that the learning of these instrumental habits was dependent upon the fact that the rats had previously received moderately strong electric shocks during the early stages of training.

Miller writes that when rats were dropped into the white compartment on non-shock trials, following their training in the same compartment with shock, they exhibited fear. They urinated and defecated, showing tenseness, and they acted as if frightened. He believes that fear motivated the activities through which the animals learned to escape into the black compartment. The adaptive patterns were learned as a means of escaping the painful stimulating situation. Fear, he believes, is an acquired drive.

We would interpret the facts of this neat experiment with a slightly different emphasis. The painful shock clearly produced an affective disturbance that may be called painful excitement. After a few painful shocks in the white compartment, the animal, through learning, was affectively disturbed when placed in the white compartment without a shock. In a state of emotional excitement (perhaps with expectation of pain) the rats made efforts to escape the pain-threatening environment. In these efforts they learned to turn the wheel or to press the bar. In other words, they acquired techniques for avoiding painful stimulation or a situation that threatened painful stimulation. What they learned was a pain-avoiding drive. There was probably a transition from emotional upset to a well-organized purposive activity of escape.

Pain, we know, has different psychological effects, depending upon its intensity. In weak degree a painful stimulation serves as a signal for some impending event with little affective arousal; a weak pain is *instructive* to the subject. In moderate degree pain becomes an *incentive;* the subject acts more or less vigorously to avoid the painful distress. In high degree pain is *disruptive.* In agony the emotional disorganization is simply endured when little can be done about it.

Experiments Upon Reward

Rewards have been varied in many ways. Some of the experiments dealing with variations in reward are considered in the following paragraphs.

Appropriateness of reward

An appropriate reward is one which satisfies a need and brings a drive to quiescence. Water, for example, is an appropriate reward when the animal is thirsty; food, when he is hungry. If a thirsty animal when satiated upon food is offered further food as a reward, the offering is inappropriate and irrelevant to the need.

It has been shown by M. H. Elliott (29) that if the physiological drive be shifted from hunger to thirst during the course of maze learning, and the reward simultaneously changed from food to water, the performance curve continues throughout to show improvement with practice. There is little disturbance produced by a shift of drive, provided the incentive-object is also shifted so that the drive-incentive relation remains an appropriate one. This agrees, of course, with the common finding that Johnnie continues to learn his arithmetic when a new plan of motivation is introduced after a former plan is found to be ineffective.

When the appropriateness of the reward is changed during the course of learning there is a marked change in the curves of performance. An inappropriate reward is clearly less effective than an appropriate reward as a determinant of the level of performance.

Substitution of one reward for another

In one form of the delayed reaction experiment, a monkey is seated on a chair about eight feet away from two tin cups, both of which are on the floor. The experimenter raises one of the cups and obviously puts a piece of banana under it. Then he places a screen in front so that both cups are out of sight. After a delay the subject is commanded to "come get the food." He jumps from the chair and runs round the screen at the end near to the container. He picks up the can, seizes, and eats the food.

Monkeys are able to delay their response. Presumably there is a representative factor through which the animal can anticipate finding the food under the cup that covered it up. There is an expectancy that a particular kind of food will be found under a particular cup.

In this experiment Tinklepaugh (24) tried substituting one kind of food for another. If, when the cup is out of view, a piece of lettuce is substituted for banana, the monkey shows what, in human terms, would be called "disappointment." After the delay the monkey is told to "come get the food." According to one account, the animal jumps down from the chair, rushes to the proper container, and picks it up, extending the hand as if to seize the food. Then the hand drops to the floor without touching the lettuce. The animal looks around the cup and behind the screen; stands up and looks under and around her. She picks up the cup and examines it inside and out. She has occasionally turned toward the human observers and shrieked at them in apparent anger. After several seconds of searching she glances toward the other cup (which she has been taught not to look into) and walks away leaving the lettuce untouched on the floor. Although the lettuce is rejected when a piece of banana is expected, the lettuce is accepted under other circumstances. Banana, however, is more palatable than lettuce.

If the subjects had been trained to expect lettuce and banana was substituted, the behavior differed. In most trials they made their choices and seized the food without noticeable signs of emotion and without hesitation. There probably was a factor of "surprise," but this was not shown in behavior, whereas the "disappointment" pattern in the reverse setting was clearly apparent.

The experiment was repeated with twin boys, aged four years and nine months, jelly beans (preferred) and chocolate buds being used as rewards. The results were similar. In this experiment the child was seated on a chair. The candy was clearly displayed and placed under one of the bowls. After a delay of one minute the child was asked to "come get the candy." When one kind of reward was substituted for another the behavior of the boys was similar to that of the monkeys but in addition the boys exclaimed: "Why that kind of candy!" or, "You changed it!"

The experiment shows that the monkey and the small boy may build up an expectancy for a particular kind of reward, that relative to this expectancy there may be an affective disturbance commonly described either as disappointment or as surprise.

Quantity of reward

In experiments in which the quantity of reward was systematically varied, Crespi (9) presented rats with 1, 4, 16, 64, or 256 pellets of a standard food. The subject was required to run down a 20-foot runway from a starting box to a square food box at the far end. Time was automatically recorded at each quarter-length of the runway. Time spent in retracing was added to time for the sector from which retracing commenced.

With practice, the animals ran more and more directly and quickly to the food. To keep the strength of hunger drive at a constant level there was a single run per day. Obviously there could be no more than one run per day because with varying quantities of food consumed the strength of hunger would be reduced by varying degrees. Following reward and feeding there was a food deprivation of 22 hours before the next trial.

Crespi found consistent differences in the speed of locomotion dependent upon the quantity of food reward. With practice these differences became increasingly clear. He found, as Hull had previously observed, speed-of-locomotion gradients that differed with the stage of habit growth.

Differences in the speed of locomotion dependent upon the quantity of reward were observed in all four sections of the runway. Figure 14 shows the average time in seconds required to run the

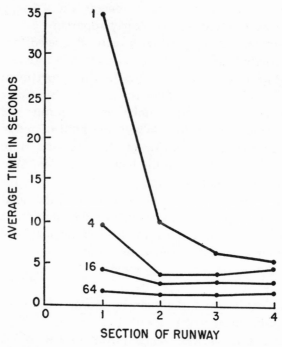

Fig. 14. Speed-of-locomotion Gradients for Rats with Different Quantities of Reward. [After Dr. L. P. Crespi (9).] The curves show average speed-of-locomotion gradients, after 20 daily trials, for rats running to rewards of 1, 4, 16, or 64 pellets of Purina chow, each pellet weighing 1/50 of a gram.

four successive sections of the runway when 1, 4, 16, or 64 pellets were presented as a reward. The data plotted in the curves are for days 21 to 25, following 20 days of practice. During these five days, following practice, the speed-of-locomotion gradients vary progressively all the way from a gradient with marked negative acceleration to one with complete flatness, as the quantity of incentive is increased successively from 1 to 64 pellets.

In another experiment rats were first trained to run for a given quantity of reward. Then, during a test period, the quantity was either increased or decreased. The results demonstrate that rats develop an expectancy for a certain quantity of incentive just as Tinklepaugh's work with monkeys (described above) demonstrated that animals learn to expect a certain kind of food. Crespi suggests that the *value* of a reward is proportional to the discrepancy between the level of expectation and the level of attainment. When an animal is rewarded by incentive quantities that are below the level of expectation there are signs of frustration that are proportional to the degree of negative deviation. The attainment of amounts of reward above the level of expectation produces elation in proportion to the degree of positive deviation.

Quality of reward

A number of experiments have been carried out upon the kind or quality of reward (29). The writer's experiments upon food preference (see pages 73-76) demonstrate that relative palatability and choice are dependent upon the kind of food presented. Moreover, the rate of running or of bar pressing is positively correlated with the level of acceptability of the food reward.

From the point of view of hedonic theory, quality and quantity are intimately related. The continuum of palatability is an affective dimension (Fig. 8); test foods become arranged along this continuum according to the degree of their acceptability. If a food is eaten continuously, there is a more or less regular approach to satiation. But, within limits, the duration of enjoyment of a food is related to the duration of the animal's contact with it.

When Crespi varied the quantity of food reward he actually varied the duration of affective arousal with one and the same kind of food reward. We would argue that both the intensity of affective process and its duration are important variables in any study of the quality and quantity of reward.

Removal and introduction of reward (latent learning)

In his classical experiments Pavlov reported that a conditioned reflex gradually diminishes or becomes extinguished if it is not occasionally reinforced by the natural stimulus. Thus, if the salivary reflex of a dog has been conditioned upon the ringing of a bell, the repeated ringing of the bell in the absence of food leads to a reduction in the number of drops of saliva per minute. With repeated soundings of the bell the saliva does not flow at all—the conditioned reflex becomes extinguished. Pavlov found that an extinguished response tended to reappear spontaneously if there was an interval between tests, but the response tended to become permanently extinguished if it was never reinforced with meat powder. To preserve a conditioned reflex there must be occasional reinforcement. Pavlov believed that experimental extinction was a form of inhibition.

Pavlov's well known result can be interpreted in terms of the removal and presentation of a reward. So long as the sounding bell is a dependable signal of food the CR remains. When the bell is no longer a dependable signal the CR tends to disappear but it may later be reestablished. The result is similar to findings in trial-and-error learning of a maze.

When a rat has learned to run a maze for a food reward in the goal box he continues to run as long as the food is there. If the food is suddenly and permanently removed and the well-practiced rat is given non-rewarded runs, the curve of performance runs backward. For a few runs the animal goes promptly to the goal box. Then he begins to take more time in approaching the empty goal box. He goes into blind alleys, makes errors, becomes increasingly variable from trial to trial, until finally the level of his performance is similar to that of a naïve rat. Has he *unlearned* the maze? Seemingly so, but if food is again placed in the box, he will quickly relearn it. The phenomenon is not so much one of learning and unlearning as it is a demonstration of the fact that behavior is goal-directed and dependent upon motive satisfaction.

Experiments upon removal and introduction of reward and change of reward have given rise to the concept of latent learning. In 1918 Szymanski (23), in a study of factors that can serve as incentives to learning, formulated a general principle: If an animal fails to learn the maze because of inadequate motivation, but nevertheless goes through it, exploring actively, this facilitates subsequent learning when adequate motivation is provided.

To assume that exploratory behavior is unmotivated, and that the novelty of an environment that arouses exploratory behavior is inadequate motivation, is gratuitous. Exploratory activity is a dependable pattern. It can be induced in the rat by putting the animal in a new environment or by changing some factor in his accustomed environment. The goal of exploratory behavior might be described as familiarity or acquaintance with the environment, for when a rat has become habituated to an environment his exploratory behavior typically ceases.

Through exploration an animal learns. He learns to find his way about and he loses the affective disturbance initially aroused by a strange environment. The habit-organization learned through exploration may be utilized in subsequent activity when a reward is introduced. What the animal learns through exploration has been described as latent learning. (See page 152.)

Symbolic reward

If a chimpanzee can exchange a poker chip for a bit of food, the animal will work to obtain the chip. Again, if a dog can exchange a small rubber ball for food, he will work to obtain the ball. In other words, an object that is instrumental in producing food may itself be adequate as an incentive. The object is a symbol of food.

In an experiment upon symbolic reward Cowles (8) showed that chimpanzees will work for discs that can be exchanged for food. Further, if 10 to 30 discs are required before the exchange can be made, the animals will work steadily to accumulate the discs. Once the chimp has learned to work for the token it can be used as an incentive in the solution of a wide variety of laboratory problems. It is as if the animal were being paid for his services. In the laboratory, chimpanzees have learned to form simple right- or left-position habits, to form five-choice position habits, to make visual discriminations of size, to make visual color-pattern discriminations, and to delay their responses, when the reward is a token of food.

When a token of one color is exchangeable for food and a token of a different color is not exchangeable the chimpanzees learn to discriminate between the "good and the bad money." They show a preference for the tokens that can be exchanged for food. Moreover, in terms of the work accomplished, the incentive value of food tokens is greater than that of the non-food tokens. In other words, the fact that a token can be exchanged for food makes it adequate as an incentive in experiments upon learning.

Food tokens that can be exchanged for food immediately prove to be more effective as incentives than those that can be exchanged only when a group of them has been collected during successive trials. Hence, animals as well as men, will work for a symbol.

Delay of reward

In experiments upon the delay of reward the subject can make a critical discrimination, but, instead of being rewarded immediately, he is forced to wait. There is nothing he can do but wait—for a few seconds or a few minutes. As the interval of delay increases, the effectiveness of the reward (as an incentive to performance) rapidly diminishes. The general conclusion from this work is that to be maximally effective an incentive must be immediate (29).

Principles of Motivation

The above discussion has presented representative studies upon animal motivation. It is now time to consider principles of motivation and some fundamental concepts.

Set and tension

In his experiments upon the delayed reaction (see page 163) Hunter found that some of his subjects could delay their responses by maintaining a bodily orientation toward the place where a light signal had flashed. Other subjects, including children, were able to delay their responses without an overt posture. Some internal mechanism represented for them the internal pattern of response.

Hunter's work justifies a distinction between *neuromuscular* and *neural* set. A neuromuscular set is outwardly manifest in bodily posture and preparation for a specific pattern of response. A neural set is not revealed overtly. It is latent but still remains as a readiness to react according to a specific pattern.

A neuromuscular set, with its pattern of tonic changes in skeletal muscles, implies a persistent stimulation of the proprioceptors. This persistent stimulation is a definite source of motivation. As long as the organism is tensely set for a specific action there is motivating tension. The tension may relax during sleep or other activity but *set* then persists as a neural readiness. If a man resolves to take a trip one week from date, this determination persists. At times the environmental situation redintegrates the set along with proprioceptive tension, but for many hours the set exists simply as a neural readiness.

Innumerable neural predispositions—such as those for hostile attack, fear-avoidance, love-approach, and the specific determinations to act—are latent most of the time. It requires an appropriate environmental situation to redintegrate these predispositions, to build up the tension that makes them dynamically active determinants of behavior.

The hedonic factor

If an individual is placed in a situation that produces distress, he acts immediately to relieve that distress. If placed in a situation that produces enjoyment, he acts to continue the enjoyment. When placed repeatedly in a situation that arouses an affective process his behavior in that situation is much the same from time to time. Through repetition of the situation and exercise he learns to react so that he will relieve distress and continue enjoyment. At any time, there is an hedonic principle in the *organization* and *regulation* of behavior.

The strength of a determination is directly related to affective intensity and duration. The more intense the enjoyment or relief, the stronger the drive as shown by rate of running, latency in response, and so on. The longer its duration, the stronger the drive.

Appetite and aversion

If appetites and aversions are analyzed fundamentally, both are found to be processes that relieve distress. Appetites relieve an internal, organic distress through positive, adient behavior. Aversions remove an external source of distress by negative, abient behavior. Appetites and aversions, therefore, have one common feature: both are behavioral patterns that reduce or remove distress.

Some appetitive behavior, however, has been organized to continue enjoyment rather than to relieve distress. Psychologists have paid too little attention to the distinction between enjoyment and relief. The playful behavior of a healthy, well-rested animal does not appear to be directed toward the relief of any distress; it is generally interpreted as pleasant activity. Again, a rat learns to run to a food when there is no indication of distress or need. Moreover, he learns to run faster to a preferred food than to a non-preferred (practice being constant) when there is no sign of distress arising from contact with the food. The obvious interpretation is that there are different intensities of enjoyment and that the strength of appetitive behavior reflects these affective differences.

In summary, a food appetite is an acquired drive (motive) to find and ingest a particular kind of food. An aversion is an acquired drive (motive) to get away from some stimulus-object that produces distress (painful stimulation, bright light, and so forth). The aversion is based upon relief from distress. The appetite, upon relief or upon a more positive enjoyment.

Mechanisms of homeostatic drives

The homeostatic drives have certain common characteristics, namely: (a) a persistent condition in the tissues; which gives rise to (b) a sustained stimulation of afferent nerves; from the latter (c) a release of energy in nerves, muscles, and other tissues, which changes the activity level; and (d) in developed organisms, goal-directed behavior; with (e) a goal-object or a consummatory reaction that is capable of removing the persistent tissue condition mentioned in (a), thus restoring homeostasis.

Some physiological drives are dependent upon a mechanical pressure on receptors located in the walls of hollow viscera, or in ducts. With others, the chemical state of the tissues is an important factor. Beach (3) has considered in detail the relation between hormonal secretions and behavior. (See Chapter 5.)

Need and drive

A need is a lack *of* something *for* something, for example, a lack of oxygen for survival. The metabolic needs of organisms can be described objectively in terms of specified criteria such as survival, growth, reproduction, activity, and so on. Social needs, conceivably, can be described in terms of social criteria, such as maintaining status, conforming to the group standards, and so forth. If a need is a *lack,* the lack of itself does not explain behavior. A need, in fact, may have no apparent relation to behavior.

It is important to be clear about the concept of *need* because psychologists are using the term in a dynamic sense as a substitute for *drive* or *motive.* It is common to read about some alleged need as if it were a tension that motivates behavior. So employed, the term carries a dynamic meaning. A need may be: (a) a lack, or deficit, or (b) a tension that motivates or drives behavior.

The central motivating state

It is misleading to isolate separate drives and to treat them as if they were independent units. The plain fact is that when one motivating factor is changed the total motivating state varies. The factors that determine behavior are complex, interdependent, and closely interlocking.

Thirst and hunger, for example, are interrelated. If an animal is deprived of water, his food intake drops. The sexual drive and hunger are interrelated; food deprivation weakens the sexual urge in both animals and men. Again, exploratory behavior, in the rat, is interrelated with other patterns. If an animal is hungry or thirsty or sexually aroused, he will explore a novel environment before eating or drinking or copulating. Again, the degree of nest-building activity varies with the reproductive state of the female, with age, with external temperature, and other conditions. Further, the appetites for fat and for carbohydrate are opposed so that when one increases the other decreases and vice versa. Also, the level of general activity varies with the endocrine balance, with age, sex, hunger and thirst, external temperature, noise, and other conditions. Finally, the specific patterns of behavior that appear at any time are dependent upon the organic sets, attitudes, and habit organizations existing at the moment. Thus the determinants of behavior are complexly interrelated, interlocking.

To avoid atomistic analysis Morgan (15) has postulated a *central motivating state* (C. M. S.), which, he writes, has certain general properties:

(*a*) The C. M. S. is partly self-perpetuating. Neural activity, once it has been initiated, tends to continue and it may initiate peripheral bodily changes that themselves are sources of motivating stimulation.

(*b*) The C. M. S. has behavioral properties: (1) It may affect the level of general activity; (2) it may produce local bodily changes that are specific, for example, rhythmic contractions of the empty stomach; (3) it may create a readiness of the organism to perceive or to react.

(*c*) The C. M. S. evokes specific forms of behavior. For example, the condition of estrus in the female creates a readiness for specific patterns of sexual behavior.

(*d*) The C. M. S. may prime the organism for appropriate stimulations from the environment. When the environmental conditions are present, the pattern is called forth. The mother rat, for example, is primed to retrieve small young and does so when they are present in her surroundings. The male is primed to mount when a receptive female is present.

The inciting motivation may be from the environment but the C. M. S. predisposes the organism toward specific patterns of appropriate activity.

Conclusion

We have considered some of the facts and principles relating to the analysis of motivation. The principles seem diverse, but actually they are interrelated and not exclusive. A general theory of motivation is possible today, for the diverse facts and principles fit into a single pattern.

Bibliography

1. Adolph, E. F., Measurements of Water Drinking in Dogs, *Amer. J. Physiol.*, 1939, **125**, 75-86.
2. Beach, F. A., Current Concepts of Play in Animals, *Amer. Natur.*, 1945, **79**, 523-541.
3. ——— *Hormones and Behavior*. New York: Hoeber, Inc., 1948.
4. ——— and Holz-Tucker, A. M., Effects of Different Concentrations of Androgen Upon Sexual Behavior in Castrated Male Rats, *J. Compar. and Physiol. Psychol.*, 1949, **42**, 433-453.
5. ——— and Levinson, G., Effects of Androgen on the Glans Penis and Mating Behavior of Castrated Male Rats, *J. Exper. Zoöl.*, 1950, **114**, 159-171.
6. Bellows, R. T., Time Factors in Water Drinking in Dogs, *Amer. J. Physiol.*, 1938, **125**, 87-97.
7. Cannon, W. B., *The Wisdom of the Body*, Rev. Ed. New York: W. W. Norton & Company, Inc., 1939.
8. Cowles, J. T., Food-tokens as Incentives for Learning by Chimpanzees, *Compar. Psychol. Monogr.*, 1937, **14**, No. 71, p. 96.
9. Crespi, L. P., Quantitative Variation of Incentive and Performance in the White Rat, *Amer J. Psychol.*, 1942, **55**, 467-517.
10. Freeman, G. L., *The Energetics of Human Behavior*. Ithaca, N. Y.: Cornell Univ. Press, 1948.
11. Harlow, H. F., Harlow, M. K., and Meyer, D. R., Learning Motivated by a Manipulative Drive, *J. Exper. Psychol.*, 1950, **40**, 228-234.
12. Heyer, A. W., Jr., Studies in Motivation and Retention. III. A Methodological Approach to the Independent Manipulation of Tissue Dehydration and Time of Water Deprivation, *Compar. Psychol. Monogr.*, 1951, **20**, No. 106.
13. Kinsey, A. C., Pomeroy, W. B., and Martin, C. E., *Sexual Behavior in the Human Male*. Philadelphia: W. B. Saunders Company, 1948.
14. Miller, N. E., Studies of Fear as an Acquirable Drive: I. Fear as Motivation and Fear-reduction as Reinforcement in the Learning of New Responses, *J. Exper. Psychol.*, 1948, **38**, 89-101.
15. Morgan, C. T., *Physiological Psychology*. New York: McGraw-Hill Book Company, 1943.
16. Richter, C. P., Animal Behavior and Internal Drives, *Quart. Rev. Biol.*, 1927, **2**, 307-343.

17. ——— Total Self Regulatory Functions in Animals and Human Beings, *Harvey Lecture Series,* 1942-43, **38,** 63-103.

18. ——— Biology of Drives, *J. Compar. and Physiol. Psychol.,* 1947, **40,** 129-134.

19. ——— and Campbell, K. H., Taste Thresholds and Taste Preferences of Rats for Five Common Sugars, *J. Nutr.,* 1940, **20,** 31-46.

20. Stone, C. P., *Sex and Internal Secretions,* 2nd Ed. (E. Allen, Ed.). Baltimore: Williams and Wilkins, 1939, pp. 1213-1262.

21. ——— *Comparative Psychology,* Rev. Ed. (F. A. Moss, Ed.). New York: Prentice-Hall, Inc., 1942, Chapter 4, pp. 65-97.

22. Sturman-Hulbe, M., and Stone, C. P., Maternal Behavior in the Albino Rat, *J. Compar. Psychol.,* 1929, **9,** 203-237.

23. Szymanski, J. S., Versuche über die Wirkung der Faktoren, die als Antrieb zum Erlernen einer Handlung dienen können, *Pflüger's Archiv für die gesamte Physiologie,* 1918, **171,** 374-385.

24. Tinklepaugh, O. L., An Experimental Study of Representative Factors in Monkeys, *J. Compar. Psychol.,* 1928, **8,** 197-236.

25. Wang, G. H., Relation Between "Spontaneous" Activity and Oestrus Cycle in the White Rat, *Compar. Psychol. Monogr.,* 1923, **2,** No. 6, p. 27.

26. Warden, C. J., *Animal Motivation, Experimental Studies on the Albino Rat.* New York: Columbia University Press, 1931.

27. Wiesner, B. P., and Sheard, N. M., *Maternal Behaviour in the Rat.* Edinburgh: Oliver and Boyd, 1933.

28. Young, P. T., Relative Food Preferences of the White Rat (II), *J. Compar. Psychol.,* 1933, **15,** 149-165.

29. ——— *Motivation of Behavior, the Fundamental Determinants of Human and Animal Activity.* New York: Wiley and Sons, Inc., 1936.

30. ——— Food-seeking Drive, Affective Process, and Learning, *Psychol. Rev.,* 1949, **56,** 98-121.

31. ——— and Chaplin, C. P., Studies of Food Preference, Appetite and Dietary Habit; III. Palatability and Appetite in Relation to Bodily Need, *Compar. Psychol. Monogr.,* 1945, **18,** No. 95, p. 45.

32. ——— and Richey, H. W., Diurnal Drinking Patterns in the Rat, *J. Compar. and Physiol. Psychol.,* 1952, **45,** 80-89.

CHAPTER 5

Internal Secretions and Behavior

WILLIAM C. YOUNG

The University of Kansas

The Endocrinological Background

The internally-secreted substances or *hormones* are variously defined, but no definition departs widely from that given by the English physiologist, Starling, in 1914. He defined a hormone as "any substance normally produced in the cells of some part of the body and carried by the blood stream to distant parts which it affects for the good of the body as a whole." In general, the hormones are regulatory of growth, metabolism, and reproduction, and since these properties are characteristic of all protoplasm, the widespread occurrence of hormones should not be surprising. Actually, however, the extent to which such substances occur has only recently been appreciated. Much of the growth and differentiation of the higher plants is influenced by substances whose actions are reminiscent of those of the hormones of animals (47). Organs of internal secretion are found in many invertebrates and are known particularly in the Arthropoda (12, 40). Finally, the endocrine organs of man, except for the placenta, and possibly the parathyroid, which has not been identified with certainty in the fishes, are found throughout the vertebrate series. Their structure and functions, as far as they are known, are adequately described in elementary textbooks (22, 48), but for the benefit of those to whom the subject is relatively new, a thumbnail sketch has been prepared.

The generally recognized organs and tissues of internal secretion in man are the hypophysis or pituitary body, the thyroid gland, the parathyroid glands, the adrenal or suprarenal glands, the islands of Langerhans in the pancreas, the mucosa or inner layer of the gastrointestinal tract, the testes in the male, the ovaries in the female, and the fetal portion of the placenta. Although their status is equivocal, it is believed by many that the kidney and liver produce substances that justify the inclusion of these organs among the glands of internal secretion, but inasmuch as no hormones

110

they produce are known to have any direct effect on behavior, the kidney and liver will not be mentioned again in this chapter.

The hypophysis is located near the center of the head and ventral to the brain to which its *pars nervosa* is attached. It is a compound gland composed of an adenohypophysis which develops from a dorsally-directed evagination from the oral cavity or embryonic mouth, and a *pars nervosa* or neurohypophysis which develops from a ventrally-directed evagination from the embryonic diencephalon, a part of the brain. The adenohypophysis is composed of *pars distalis* and *pars tuberalis* which constitute the anterior lobe, and the *pars intermedia*. The latter is closely associated with the *pars nervosa* and with it constitutes the posterior lobe. These relationships can easily be visualized from the diagram given below:

$$\text{Adenohypophysis} \begin{cases} \textit{Pars tuberalis} \\ \textit{Pars distalis} \\ \textit{Pars intermedia} \end{cases} \begin{array}{l} \\ \end{array} \text{Anterior lobe}$$

Neurohypophysis or *Pars nervosa* } Posterior lobe

Pars tuberalis and *pars intermedia* are not known to have any functional activity in man and other mammals, although *intermedin,* the hormone of the *pars intermedia,* disperses the pigment granules within the cytoplasm of the melanophores in many fishes, amphibians, and reptiles. It is an agent therefore in the darkening of the skin that occurs when the animals are in a cool, dark habitat.

Pars distalis is more nearly entitled to the appellation "master gland" than any other gland in the body. It elaborates a *thyrotrophic principle,* which is necessary for the functional integrity of the thyroid gland, a *corticotrophic principle (ACTH,* about which so much is being written because of its relation to rheumatoid arthritis), which stimulates all or at least a part of the adrenal cortex, a *somatotrophic* or *growth principle,* which is believed by many to be a discrete substance without which normal growth is impossible, and three *gonadotrophic principles.* The first of these is the *follicle-stimulating hormone (FSH),* which is responsible for much of the growth of the graafian follicle of the ovary until shortly before its rupture. The *luteinizing hormone (LH)* is the second of the gonadotrophic principles. It is thought to be secreted during the later stages of follicular development and it stimulates the preovulatory swelling or final growth of the follicle, ovulation, and the formation of the corpus luteum. The luteinizing hormone also exerts a trophic action on the internal secretory elements of the testis. Because of this action, it is also known as the *interstitial cell-stimulating hormone (ICSH).* About the time the luteinizing hormone begins to function in the cycle of the female it seems probable that a third gonadotrophic principle is produced. This is the *luteotrophic hormone (LTH),* which is necessary for the functioning of the corpus luteum. It appears to be identical with the *lactogenic principle* that is associated with the secretion of milk and possibly with the appearance of parental behavior.

All the hormones of the *pars distalis* are proteins and most exert their action on other organs of internal secretion rather than on the tissues responsible for the final response in the organism. An illustration will clarify this statement. The pituitary gonadotrophin, follicle-stimulating hormone, has been said to act on the growing graafian follicle in the ovary. This structure then secretes hormones that act on the female genital tract and on the tissues mediating reproductive behavior. It is the changes in these tissues that are responsible for the final response in this particular sequence of events.

There are exceptions to the statement that the hormones of the *pars distalis* act on other organs of internal secretion rather than on tissues associated with the final response. Thyrotrophic hormone is thought to act directly on the tissues of the eye socket as well as on the thyroid. Growth hormone acts on the skeleton and many of the soft tissues, including those of the viscera. Lactogenic hormone acts on the mammary glands and possibly on the tissues mediating parental behavior, as well as on the corpus luteum. It is also thought to induce the return of the salamander, *Triturus viridescens,* at the termination of the land phase, to the water habitat (35). Anterior pituitary hormones, in addition to their action on the interstitial cells of the testis, induce male feathering in the African weaver finch (51) and antler growth in the Virginia deer (50).

Pars nervosa, that part of the pituitary which is derived from the diencephalon and remains connected with the hypothalamus, is commonly thought to elaborate two principles, a *vasopressor* and *antidiuretic hormone,* and an *oxytocic hormone* whose site of action is the musculature of the uterus. Nerve fibers are contained in this part of the gland. It is possible, therefore, that impulses from the many stimuli that affect the functioning of the anterior pituitary traverse pathways in the *pars nervosa.* Stimuli that are known to affect this part of the pituitary are cold, warmth, seasonal changes in the length of day, the approach of darkness in many nocturnal animals, copulation in certain species such as the rabbit and cat, and psychic and physical trauma.

The thyroid gland is derived from the embryonic pharynx or throat, and in the adult lies on the ventral side of the trachea near its junction with the larynx. It is composed of ovoid to spherical follicles whose walls are a single cell-layer in thickness. The lumen is filled with colloid that contains *thyroid hormone.* Synthesis of this hormone is stimulated by thyrotrophin from the anterior pituitary, but the conditions under which it is released to the blood are not understood. Storage of the hormone by the thyroid is unique; in other glands precursors of the hormones or the hormones themselves are found in granules or droplets in the cells that produce them, but they are not stored extracellularly, as in the thyroid. The thyroid hormone does not appear to have a specific target organ; rather it increases the rate of oxidation in cells throughout the body. Such an action might account for the widespread effects of hypo- and hyperthyroidism in man; in these states abnormalities of growth, metabolism, and behavior are pronounced. Similar effects are not encountered in all species and under all conditions. Certain laboratory mammals such as the guinea pig and even the Rhesus monkey are tolerant of very wide fluctuations in thyroid activity, including thyroidectomy (25). Young animals seem more dependent on adequate supplies of the hormone than do older animals (17).

The parathyroid glands are the smallest of the endocrine glands. Their location in the adult is variable, but in most species they are embedded in the substance of the thyroid or are on its posterior surface in the capsule. Like the thyroid, they are derived from the wall of the embryonic pharynx, but their course of differentiation and structure in the adult are entirely different, and they function independently of stimulation by the hypophysis. They are composed of densely-packed groups or cords of cells separated by a network of tiny blood vessels called *sinusoids*. The action of the parathyroids is closely identified with the metabolism of calcium and phosphorus, but there is still no agreement with respect to the sites of action. Some investigators are of the opinion that their hormone, *parathormone*, acts on the bone-destroying cells of the bone marrow, others believe that it acts on the uriniferous tubules of the kidney. In either case blood calcium is high in hyperparathyroidism and low in hypoparathyroidism, blood phosphates are low in hyperparathyroidism and high in hypoparathyroidism.

Important endocrine tissues are closely associated with the alimentary tract. The first of these is the *islet tissue of the pancreas*. The second is presumed to lie within the mucosa or inner layer of the upper parts of the small intestine and is known as an endocrine tissue only by its physiological activity. The islet tissue or *islands of Langerhans* are distributed throughout the substance of the pancreas. Each island is composed of cells that stain more lightly than the other cells of the pancreas when the most commonly used tissue stains are used. Certain of these cells, the B cells, secrete *insulin*, which is the anti-diabetogenic hormone and which acts to facilitate the storage and utilization of carbohydrate. The second gastrointestinal principle is *secretin*. Its production has not yet been identified with any cell-type, nor is its chemical nature known, but its action was demonstrated in 1902 when Baylis and Starling (2) discovered its role in stimulating the flow of pancreatic juice.

The three endocrine organs whose description follows, suprarenal gland, testis, and ovary, comprise the most interesting group from the standpoint of behavior because certain of the hormones they secrete are related more directly to discrete patterns of behavior than any mentioned heretofore. Except for the suprarenal medulla, which is thought to originate in association with the autonomic nervous system (motor nerves to the blood vessels, visceral organs, iris, salivary glands, muscles of the hair and sweat glands), all arise from the epithelium of the coelom or body cavity. They produce hormones known as *steroid hormones* that are very similar chemically.

The suprarenal gland is composed of an outer cortical portion and central medulla; their separate origins are indicated above. The cortex contains columns of cells that extend radially between the capsule of the gland and the medulla. The outer ends of the columns are rounded and this region is called the *zona glomerulosa*. Some investigators believe that this portion of the gland functions independently of pituitary stimulation by corticotrophin and secretes *desoxycorticosterone* (21). The hormone is thought to be associated with sodium and potassium metabolism. The columns internal to the glomerulosa are more or less parallel and constitute the *zona fasciculata*, which passes over into a *zona reticularis*. The latter may not be functional. The *zona fasciculata*, on the other hand, secretes substances that are of the utmost importance for the functioning of the body and abundant proof exists that it is subject to pituitary control. The hormones it elaborates, *corticosterone, cortisone*, and others that are less well known, are thought to be involved in carbohydrate metabolism, in the functioning of the defense mechanisms, in the maintenance of the structural integrity of the mesenchymal tissues composing and surrounding the smaller blood vessels, in the control of basal heat production, and probably in other activities as well. Cells are seen within the medulla that have an affinity for the salts of chromic acid and therefore are known as *chromaffin cells*. Between them, nerve cells and rather poorly defined connective tissue cells are found. The chromaffin cells secrete *epinephrin* or *adrenalin*. Both cortex and medulla are very sensitive to environmental change and respond quickly to situations in which the elements of hunger, fright, pain, anger, and excitement in general are involved.

The testes are composed of large numbers of coiled tubules known as *seminiferous tubules* in which spermatozoa are produced. The internal secretory elements are the *interstitial cells*, which lie between the seminiferous tubules. The dependence of the interstitial cells on the luteinizing hormone of the pituitary has already been mentioned. *Testosterone*, which is the hormone secreted by the interstitial cells, is responsible for the maintenance of the male genital tract and for the morphological and behavioral characters that impart maleness to an animal.

The functioning of the ovary, like that of the testis, is dependent on pituitary gonadotrophins whose actions were described in the section dealing with the pars distalis of the pituitary. From the brief description it will be apparent that two ovarian structures having endocrine activity are recognized; the *graafian follicle* in which the ovum develops, and the *corpus luteum*, which develops from the tissues of the graafian follicle after its rupture or *ovulation*, as it is called. *Estradiol* is believed to be the hormone of primary importance that is produced by the graafian follicle, although *estrone*, which also has physiological activity, may also be secreted by the same tissue. *Progesterone* is produced in small quantities during the later stages of follicular development, but it is best known as the hormone of the corpus luteum. This structure secretes estradiol as well.

Singly or together, in what is known as a *synergistic response*, the *estrogens* (estradiol and estrone) and progesterone act on the female genital tract to condition it for implantation of the fertilized ova. The estrogens must act first, and no amount of estrogen is sufficient to sensitize the *endometrium* or inner lining of the uterus for implantation. Sensitization does not occur until progesterone has exerted its influence, but the latter hormone is ineffective unless an estrogen has previously been present and has primed or conditioned the tissues for the action of progesterone. The estrogens, and in some rodents estrogens and progesterone in another type of synergistic relationship, act on the tissues mediating mating behavior. These hormones are also responsible for other characteristics that distinguish a female from a male.

The fetal placenta is included among the organs and tissues having internal secretory activity because of its demonstrated activity in producing a variety of hormones important for reproduction. One of these, *chorionic gonadotrophin*, which is especially abundant in the human female, bears many resemblances to the pituitary gonadotrophins, luteinizing hormone and luteotrophic hormone. It is the substance contained in urine which, when injected into the estrous rabbit, stimulates luteinization of the larger graafian follicles, thus giving the positive *Friedman Test* for pregnancy. Chorionic gonadotrophin is thought to function by prolonging the life of the corpus luteum during the early weeks of pregnancy (24). In this way the continued production of progesterone and estrogens is assured and the endometrium on which these hormones act is thereby maintained in a condition suitable for the development of the newly implanted embryo. Cells of the fetal placenta are also thought to produce estrogens and progesterone. It is this activity in mammals, including man, that permits the removal of the ovaries from the pregnant female during the latter part of pregnancy without necessarily precipitating abortion. The secretion of estrogens and progesterone by the placenta probably explains, too, the heightened sex drive of spayed female rats following their treatment with placental extracts (33), for as we will point out elsewhere, these are the hormones, regardless of their origin, that induce the display of sexual behavior in female rats.

The Hormones and Behavior

Most of the hormones enumerated above are related to behavior in one way or another, but the relationship is not always direct in the sense that specific qualitative and quantitative changes in behavior follow the administration of preparations of glandular origin or the removal of tissues or organs elaborating such substances. The action of hormones secreted by the gonads on the tissues mediating reproductive behavior fulfills these requirements more nearly than that of any other endocrine substance.

Not to be confused with glands such as the testis and ovary, whose effects on behavior are direct, is a group of endocrine organs whose action is tentatively regarded as indirect. The abnormal functioning of these glands is reflected in increased irritability, mental retardation, indifference, and even preference for certain foods. Their actions in creating these abnormal behavioral states probably are the results of abnormalities of metabolism rather than the direct consequences of an action of a hormone on the central nervous tissue associated with such behavior. With certain minor exceptions, the pituitary, thyroid, adrenal cortex, and parathyroid belong in this category.

There is a third relationship between the hormones and behavior that touches all of us as we adjust ourselves to new situations and to environmental stimuli. This is the effect of different behavioral states on hormonal action. It is well known that impulses arising from fright, anger, and psychic trauma are conveyed to certain endocrine organs where they are excitatory or inhibitory. Possibly the adrenal medulla is preeminent in this respect, but effects of different behavioral states on the adrenal cortex and the pituitary are also known and will be described.

Direct effects on behavior

1. **The male.** The connection between the testis and male behavior is a matter of long historical record. Experimental studies were reported as early as 1849 when Berthold demonstrated by means of testes transplanted from their normal site to locations elsewhere in the body that the maleness of the cock is conferred by substances carried in the blood and originating in testes from which all nerve connections had been severed. Many vertebrates, at all phylogenetic levels from fish to man, have since been studied. The evidence is clear from this work, which is reviewed by Beach (7), that courtship and mating activity are under the control of this gland. The development of the testis, whether it is a part of the general process of growth and maturation or seasonal, is correlated with sexual activity. Removal of the testes is followed by a decrease in the strength of sexual behavior, if not with its disappearance. Finally, substances extracted from the testis and administered to castrated males restore the pattern of behavior that characterized the individual prior to removal of the gonads.

Among mammals the relationship between the testis and behavior is best known for the albino rat, guinea pig, rabbit, cat, and dog, and for the Rhesus monkey, chimpanzee, and man among the primates. In all, pursuit of the female leading to copulation with ejaculation is the ultimate in sexual behavior, but in the lower mammals there are many elements, such as sniffing and licking of the ano-genital zone, mounting and intromission without ejaculation, which constitute lower degrees of sexual behavior. Stone (42, 43) showed as a part of the first comprehensive study of male behavior that these elements appear in sequence as the males mature and, except for the elements of lowest degree, that they disappear in the reverse order following castration. Their reappearance in the order of appearance during adolescence can be brought about by suitable treatment of the castrate with the male hormone, testosterone (5, 8, 44). The waxing and waning of this behavior under controlled conditions provides additional proof for the role of testosterone in the development and maintenance of sexual behavior in the male.

Many investigators have tried to determine the site of action of the male hormone, but a completely satisfactory answer cannot yet be given. Beach (4) in a consideration of the problem based on his studies and those of others expresses doubt that the effects are confined to a restricted region of the brain or to the activation of any one type of sensory receptor. He postulates the existence in the forebrain of a *central excitatory mechanism,* connected *afferently* with the *peripheral receptors,* such as those for sight, smell, touch, and hearing, and *efferently* with *motor centers* that mediate the specific mating responses. It is further postulated that the central excitatory mechanism and the motor centers are stimulated by the male hormone. The latter increases the excitability of the central excitatory mechanism and lowers the threshold of the motor centers. *In such a system maximum arousal would occur following strong multisensory stimulation of the cortical and motor centers that had been brought to a peak of excitability by the male hormone.* Responses would be less intense under the conditions (a) of a deficiency in any one or more types of the peripheral receptors such as eyes, nose, ears, or (b) of a low level of excitation within the central excitatory mechanism or the motor centers.

This theory would explain why the ease of arousal of the male rat or rabbit is lessened following destruction of any one of the receptors mediating vision, smell, hearing, or cutaneous sensitivity in the region of the snout and genitalia, or following ablation of a part of the cerebral cortex. It would explain too why animals subjected to this latter operation can be reactivated by the adminis-

tration of testosterone, provided of course that the amount of destruction has not been too great (5).

An unexplained peculiarity of the relationship between the testis
and male behavior is that the changes that occur following castration
are not as abrupt as they are in the genital tract and other tissues
that are influenced by testosterone action. Not only in man, but also
in many lower vertebrates, relatively long intervals elapse following
removal of the testes before the basic level of castrate behavior is
reached (43). It is difficult to account for the gradual decrease in
sexual excitability in the castrated adult male. There is no evidence
for any storage of testosterone. There may perhaps be a conditioning
of the tissues that mediate male behavior, with the result that they
are capable of responding to stimulation after the testes have been
removed. On the other hand, no evidence for such a conditioning
is seen in the females of lower mammals in which overt sexual
behavior disappears immediately following removal of the ovaries.
Finally, the adrenal cortex not only produces hormones that are very
similar chemically to those secreted by the testis, but also is thought
to be the source of male hormones as well. Many investigators have
suggested therefore that, in the absence of the testes, this gland
may be an extra-testicular source of male hormone. If, however, the
adrenal cortex is an important source of this substance, it is difficult
to understand why castrational changes in the genital tract, in contrast to those in behavior, should be so abrupt. Whatever explanation
is finally accepted, the fact that castration of the adult is not followed
immediately by a change to the condition seen in the long-term
castrate may account for the lack of agreement among investigators
concerning the effect of castration on male sexual behavior.

It must not be assumed from what has been said with respect to
the testis hormone and behavior that this substance acts alone and
independently of other factors. *Even when the structure of the testis
is normal and fertile spermatozoa are produced, or when equal
amounts of hormone are present as in injected castrated males, the
response is not always the same.* Individuals are found that do not
achieve intromission or ejaculation. Other animals achieve copulation with ejaculation, but the interval between the beginning of the
test and ejaculation is unusually long. Often these patterns are
repeated from test to test and the individual is clearly set apart from
others by some peculiarity in his pattern of behavior (46).

Age is one of the most prominent of the factors that are known to be involved in these differences in behavior, although the changes that take place as the male matures, passes through the period of greatest reproductive activity, and then becomes senile have not been studied systematically. In a general way it seems clear that the amount of testosterone that will induce copulation in prepuberal males and in senile males is greater than that required for the restoration of copulatory activity in castrated young adults. There are also indications that the changes associated with sexual maturation occur relatively rapidly, whereas those associated with the decrease in sexual activity take place more slowly.

The interval between copulations is important (45). In general, copulation with ejaculation is followed by a period during which the male is incapable of sexual arousal equal to that preceding the ejaculation, despite the circumstance that there probably is no loss of hormone during copulation comparable with the loss of fuel during combustion.

Different females elicit different responses. Among laboratory mammals receptive females are more excitatory than non-receptive females. Among the primates below man strong preferences are shown that cannot be correlated with estimations of the quantity of secreted hormone (16). These preferences are assumed to have a psychological basis, for there is abundant evidence that, as mammals have evolved, psychic and cultural factors have become more important, while the importance of purely hormonal factors has decreased. It must not be concluded, however, as some authors have done (15), that gonadal secretions in the adult human male have become completely subordinate to psychic centers. To be sure, numerous clinical reports contain references to the survival of libido following castration, but in others a gradual loss of sexual desire is stated to have occurred. In still others the administration of testosterone to castrates is claimed to have been followed by an arousal of libido. If this result follows, it seems unlikely that a deficiency of hormone would be without effect. The stumbling block to an accurate determination of the relationship between the level of testis hormone and the strength of sexual drive in the human male is the circumstance that the objective tests adapted to laboratory mammals are not suitable for man. If such were devised, the possibility would have to be anticipated that the vigor of sexual behavior subsequent to castration would be found to be less than that prior to the operation.

The level of activity of the thyroid is thought by many to be importantly related to the vigor of sexual behavior in the male. Kinsey, Pomeroy, and Martin (28) go so far as to state that the thyroid hormone produces, if anything, more marked results on the sexual activity of the human male than does the testis hormone. The report by Petersen, Spielman, Pomeroy, and Boyd (34) that a thyroidectomized bull would not mate except when given thyroid hormone or testosterone has been widely cited. We may not assume, however, that all species react to reduced levels of thyroid function in this manner. The administration of drugs that inactivate the thyroid does not prevent male rats from mating (26). In the author's laboratory, thyroidectomy has not affected the intensity of the sexual reactions displayed by male guinea pigs nor has the administration of thyroxine done this unless the resulting loss of weight exceeded approximately 15 per cent.

An important, if not the most important, factor contributing to differences in the sexual behavior of individuals is variation in the responsiveness of the tissues to hormonal stimulation. The importance of tissue reactivity has not always been emphasized, but it can be and often is as vital for the response that is shown as is the secretion of the hormone. If, in an animal, the tissues that normally mediate sexual behavior are unresponsive to quantities of hormone that are adequate for the stimulation of other reactions in the body, that animal might as well be without testes as far as his behavior is concerned. His sexual excitability is no greater than that of the castrate and he is infertile because he will not mate. The point that has been made for the female in which the corresponding condition has been found to exist (55), is applicable with equal force to the male. *The testis (or any gland of internal secretion) possesses a potentiality of action that is limited by the responsiveness of the tissues on which its secretions act.*

This conclusion is supported by the work of Heller (23), who showed that the amount of spontaneous running activity displayed by intact male rats given testis hormone was not proportional to the amount he injected. Additional evidence is coming from experiments being conducted by Mr. Jerome Grunt in the author's laboratory. Male guinea pigs, homogeneous with respect to age, diet, manner of caging, and past sexual experience, were found to differ greatly in the strength of their sexual drive. It could be presumed from the circumstance that if their testes were normal the differences in the quantities of secreted hormone were not sufficient to account for the range of sexual behavior. Proof that the amount of hormone was not involved came after castration when replacement therapy with testosterone was given. Every animal received the same amount daily; nevertheless, the degree of sexual excitability returned to the level peculiar to the individual prior to castration.

This result provides further evidence that the sensitivity of the tissues is of the utmost importance for the response to a hormone. Such being the case, we ask: To what can these variations in sensitivity or responsiveness be attributed? With differences in age, diet, past sexual experience, the manner of caging, and the condition of the female excluded, the role of what is variously referred to as the *somatic, constitutional,* or *genetic factor* suggests itself. The existence of such a factor receives tacit recognition in the numerous references to strain differences, but there is little reason to doubt that it is operative at the level of the individual as well.

2. **The female.** Much of what was said concerning the hormonal control of mating behavior in the male is as applicable to the female. In both sexes, changes in behavior that lead to copulation and therefore to bringing together the male and female germ cells are a prerequisite for reproduction. As in the male, age is important. Developing young females become responsive to smaller and smaller quantities of hormones until a point is reached beyond which there is little change, at least until old age. The relationship of responsiveness to hormonal action during this latter period has not been investigated. The sensitivity of the tissues mediating mating behavior varies in adult females of the same age as it does in males, and is an important factor in shaping the character of the response that is shown.

Striking differences between the male and female are encountered when we come to the specific processes of reproduction and to the hormones that are involved. The abrupt termination of overt sexual behavior after spaying in the female has already been contrasted with the gradual waning of sexual excitability following castration in the male. Within the reproductive season the production of spermatozoa is continuous, that of ova is cyclic. Except for periods of recovery following ejaculation, the rut of the male is continuous, the heat periods of the female are cyclic. In many species the role of the male in reproduction terminates with copulation, but not so in the female. Depending on the species, she must construct a nest or be prepared for an incubation period. If she is a mammal, the requirements of gestation will involve few if any changes in the behavior pattern that normally provides for sustenance and safety, but there is much to be anticipated in the form of young to be fed and cared for until they can lead an independent existence. In the female this entire sequence of events has a hormonal basis, but unlike the male, in which one hormone is thought to act, two estrogens, progesterone and the lactogenic principle of the pituitary may be involved.

The relationship between the ovarian hormones, estradiol, estrone, and progesterone, and mating behavior as it exists in the rat and guinea pig can very properly serve as a starting point in a discussion of the subject. Mating behavior in the rat is composed of at least three elements or components and in the guinea pig of at least two. The first, which is shown by both species, is the assumption of the copulatory stance or posture on tactile stimulation of the back. When the reaction is strong it is indicative of the willingness of the female to accept the male. Beginning with the time when this response can first be obtained, there is a striking change in behavioral mien. From an animal that will vigorously reject any tactile stimulation of the ano-genital region, she becomes passive and will submit to any manipulation or attention by the male. During this time the female is said to be in *heat* or *estrus*.

The second component of the pattern is also displayed by females of the two species. It is a male-like mounting activity directed at other animals in the cage regardless of sex. It is shown for the most part about the beginning of the heat period. This behavior is not of constant occurrence in either species, and is seen more commonly in the guinea pig than in the rat.

Students of vertebrate embryology learn that the young fetus contains the beginnings of the genital tracts of both sexes, but that as development proceeds the female genital tract undergoes involution in the male and is represented in the adult by only a few vestigial structures. There is a comparable involution of the male genital tract in the developing female. The situation with respect to the nervous tissues mediating reproductive behavior may not be unlike that described for the tissues of the genital tracts. There may be a differential development of such a nature that the tissues mediating female behavior become dominant in the female, and those mediating male behavior become dominant in the male, *but in either sex the tissues homologous with those of the opposite sex may still be represented.* In the case of the female the tissues mediating male behavior can be stimulated by ovarian hormones present at the time of heat. In the case of the male, the tissues mediating female behavior, although subordinate, can be stimulated by the hormone secreted by the testis. Such an explanation would explain the tendency of some females to display male-like behavior at the time of heat and the tendency of some males to display elements of the female pattern under the conditions of strong stimulation described by Beach (3).

The third element composing mating behavior is a spontaneous running that is measured most accurately in the revolving drum and that may amount to as much as 15 or 20 miles during the estrous period of the albino rat. It was the first of the three components of the sexual behavior pattern to receive attention and has been studied as a discrete element only in the rat (see chapter 4).

The willingness to copulate and the display of male-like mounting activity can be induced experimentally in spayed females by the injection of estradiol or estrone followed 24 to 48 hours later by the injection of a small quantity of progesterone (9, 14). The reaction to the two hormones administered in the order described above is an example of the synergistic response between estrogen and progesterone that is encountered elsewhere in the female, particularly in the uterus.

Once estrous behavior has been displayed and run its course, it will not be shown again until the animals have been reinjected with the two hormones. Progesterone alone is ineffective. Estradiol or estrone given alone usually does not induce heat unless very large quantities are administered. Even then the course of heat tends to be interrupted and it does not follow the pattern of sudden appearance and gradual decline that is seen following the injection of estrogen and progesterone (53).

Certain reactions, such as the display of parental behavior, can be stimulated by the presence of other animals, apparently in the absence of any glandular tissue that is thought to induce parental behavior in intact females (29). Estrous behavior on the other hand, is not shown by ovariectomized animals, even when they are with animals that are in heat. The possibility was tested in a very simple experiment. When some of the spayed females in a cage were injected with estrogen and progesterone, the uninjected animals did not display any of the elements of the sexual behavior pattern, despite the circumstance that the animals in heat nuzzled and pursued them and mounted them actively. Not even conditioning injections of estrogen raised the animals so treated to a point of excitability where estrous behavior displayed by other animals was contagious. Heat responses by the animals injected only with estrogen were not shown until they had received a small quantity of progesterone (58).

Results from experiments involving the injection of estrogen and progesterone suggest what happens in intact females of these species. The animals are first conditioned for heat and mounting activity by estrogens produced by the developing graafian follicle; later they are brought into heat by the first small quantities of progesterone that are secreted prior to ovulation.

There is at least one difference in the relationship of these hormones to the copulatory response on the one hand, and to the display of male-like mounting behavior on the other. The length of heat is not proportional to the number of developing graafian follicles in intact females or to the amount of injected estrogens when spayed females are tested. The amount of mounting behavior is proportional to the number of developing follicles and to the quantity of injected estrogen, at least within the limits of the amounts that have been used experimentally. The meaning of this observation is not clear, unless mounting behavior, as a homologue of the pattern characteristic of the male, is controlled by a mechanism different from that which mediates the copulatory response.

The hormonal control of spontaneous running activity is still different (56). Production of this component of the sexual behavior pattern is obtained only *when the hormone estrone is given continuously*. Single injections are not effective. Estradiol induces only a small increase in the amount of running, and supplementary progesterone is without any apparent effect.

From what has been said about the hormonal control of mating behavior in the female rat and guinea pig, it can be concluded that the three elements of the pattern are induced by ovarian follicular hormones. They are displayed simultaneously because in a given cycle all the follicles develop simultaneously, but they are not shown in the same relative proportion because the elements of the behavior pattern are believed to be mediated by different nervous mechanisms each of which has its own sensitivity to the hormone or combination of hormones to which it responds.

As far as we know, the dual nature of the hormonal control of the copulatory response is not encountered in other species, save the mouse (39) and hamster (19). In many species, the cow, horse, goat, cat, dog, ferret, rabbit, sheep, Rhesus monkey, and chimpanzee, there is no evidence that progesterone is necessary. In the sheep and goat, on the contrary, Fraps, Scott, Simmons and Phillips (20) have shown that progesterone acts to terminate estrus. Also the estrogen-induced sexual activity of the Rhesus monkey is reduced by the subsequent administration of progesterone (1). These observations are not inconsistent with the demonstrated action of progesterone in the rat and guinea pig. In these species the small amounts initially produced may pull the trigger that releases the estrous mechanism, while the larger amounts thought to be produced as ovulation is approached may have an inhibitory effect.

It will be recalled that the sexual behavior characteristic of the male is thought to have become modified as the higher mammals have evolved. The equally clear evidence for evolutionary changes in the behavior of the female has been reviewed by Young (53). Briefly it has been found that, in mammals below the primates, heat is confined to the last hours or days of the follicular phase, which is approximately the first half of the cycle. In primates below man the period during which the female is sexually receptive extends throughout much if not all of the follicular phase, although willingness to accept the male may be shown during the luteal phase or second half of the cycle as well. Most observers are agreed, however, that sexual excitability is less then, particularly if proper allowance is made for the social relations at the time of the observations (52, 57, 60). In the human female the period of receptivity has become further extended and sexual relations occur during the luteal phase as well as during the follicular phase. Whether it can be concluded from this circumstance that sexual reactions in the human female have become emancipated from hormonal control is a moot point. As in the male, psychic and cultural factors have become ascendent, but evidence is still not conclusive that these factors do not operate against a background of hormonal action.

The sites of action of the hormones that induce the display of mating behavior in the female are uncertain. Beach (4) suggests that the ovarian hormones exert their effects on the female very much as the testis hormones do on the male; that is, by increasing the excitability of the central excitatory mechanism, which is cortical, and by lowering the threshold of the motor circuits mediating the pattern of behavior. Other investigators, on the other hand, seem more inclined to think in terms of hormone action on a center in the anterior hypothalamus. Brookhart, Dey, and Ranson (11) demonstrated that female guinea pigs with lesions one millimeter above the ventral surface of the hypothalamus did not display mating reactions following the injection of estrogen and progesterone, even though they injected 4 to 6 times the amount of estrogen necessary to condition a spayed animal with intact neural centers. They concluded that the lesions damaged a central mechanism that is indispensable to estrous reactions. Kent and Liberman (27) have shown that a minute quantity of progesterone placed in direct contact with the hypothalamus of hamsters previously injected with estrone is effective in inducing heat sooner than a larger quantity injected subcutaneously.

Admittedly, these observations cast an attractive light on the hypothesis that mating behavior in the female is mediated by a center in the anterior hypothalamus, but it is difficult to believe that cortical centers are not involved, even in lower animals. To be sure, partial, and even complete decortication of rats and cats does not always abolish mating responses, but it is clear from the data reviewed by Beach (7) that many partially decorticate animals are affected and the responsiveness to estrogens is often lowered. It may be that the female can tolerate a more severe cortical injury than the male without loss of the capacity for displaying sexual behavior. If so, the cortical contribution to sexual behavior probably is less in females than in males, but for the present this suggestion should have no more than tentative acceptance.

As in the male, differences between individuals homogeneous with respect to age, diet, and previous sexual experience are the rule rather than the exception (54). Furthermore, guinea pigs when spayed and injected with estrogen and progesterone give responses that tend to be similar to those shown prior to ovariectomy (10). It has been concluded, therefore, that in the females of lower mammals the character of the pattern of sexual behavior is largely determined by factors inherent in the tissues.

The lack of relationship between the character of the pattern of sexual behavior and gonadal activity has been demonstrated by the reactions of female guinea pigs and rats that were ovariectomized within 24 hours after birth and given a single treatment of estrogen and progesterone at an interval after the operation (49). The response of the animals spayed at birth and injected 30 days later was not different from that of animals ovariectomized on the thirtieth day and injected two days later. It was concluded from this experiment that the change in responsiveness to estrogenic stimulation that occurs during the first 30 days of life in the guinea pig and rat is not dependent on the presence of the gonads. In another experiment females received the first injection of estrogen and progesterone 24 months after ovariectomy performed at the time of birth. Again, the response did not differ from that shown by the control animals. It is apparent therefore that the maintenance of normal responsiveness to estrogenic stimulation is not dependent on the presence of the gonads.

A confirmation of these results was given by Beach (6) who had the good fortune to come across a 90- to 100-day old female rat in which there was a congenital absence of ovarian tissue. Following treatment with estrogen and progesterone she displayed all the elements of the mating pattern shown by normal females in heat. In this case, as in the animals from which the ovaries were removed within a day after birth, the differentiation of the neural structures that mediate sexual behavior did not depend on the presence of ovarian tissue.

The role of the hormones in the production of parental behavior is difficult to evaluate. Riddle (37) indicated soon after the first experiments in this field had been described that the view that parental behavior is induced by lactogenic hormone from the anterior pituitary could not be accepted without reservation. He and his associates had found that hypophysectomy of virgin female rats leads to display of parental instinct. Leblond (29) later reported that mice and rats whose pituitary glands had been rendered inactive before puberty developed parental behavior when placed with newborn young. Finally it was stated that maternal drive is exhibited by female and male rats during injections with each of a variety of hormones: prolactin, progesterone, desoxycorticosterone, intermedin, luteinizing hormone, and thyroxine; also with phenol (carbolic acid), a non-hormonal substance (38). It is obvious from these data and from other experiments reviewed by Beach (7) that more is involved than merely the action of a specific pituitary hormone. Up to the present, the problem has not been resolved beyond this point.

Indirect effects on behavior

When thought is given to the relationship between the gonads and behavior that has just been described, it will be realized that maintenance of certain behavioral states is one of the primary functions of the substances produced by these glands. Their hormones probably induce the behavior associated with reproductive performance by initiating chemical changes in the specific tissues that mediate such behavior. Quite a different relationship exists between other endocrine organs (such as the thyroid, adrenal, parathyroid, pituitary and islands of Langerhans) and behavior. Their primary action is on carbohydrate metabolism, mineral metabolism, oxidative processes, and so on, but inasmuch as normal behavior depends on the normality of these processes, it also depends on the glands regulating their vital activities. It is suggested that when these glands are functioning normally, little relationship is seen between their activity and behavior, but when they function abnormally or not at all, deviations in behavior are encountered.

This generalization is illustrated by the relationship of the thyroid to behavior. Thyroid hormone is regulatory of oxidations throughout the body. An excess increases and a deficiency decreases the rate of oxidations. In many mammals including man the gland is also necessary for normal differentiation and growth. When it is absent from birth therefore and the condition is not treated, growth and development of the brain as well as of other organs and tissues are incomplete. The victim of this misfortune is a cretin and as such is usually an idiot or an imbecile. When deficiencies of thyroid function manifest themselves during the juvenile years or later myxedema develops. In such individuals, according to Means (32), memory is slow but usually accurate, and there is a lowering of emotional drive and a decreased rate of cerebration. The condition is associated with a decrease in irritability and reaction time by the nervous tissues that are involved.

Overactivity of the thyroid gland, as in thyrotoxicosis, decreases the reaction time and heightens the irritability of the nervous tissues. Patients suffering from this disease are nervous and restless. Frequently there is emotional instability and in a few individuals actual psychoses develop. Means comments, however, that it is only the occasional thyrotoxic patient who does not retain comparatively normal mental function. His suggestion that it is the potential psychotic who has his mental disease made manifest by the strain of thyroid overactivity is reminiscent of what was said earlier about the importance of the somatic factor for endocrine reactions.

Interesting relationships between the endocrines and behavior are described by Richter (36). There is an increase in nest-building activity by rats following thyroidectomy. It will be recalled that the thyroid hormone, because of its calorigenic action, is important for the maintenance of a constant body temperature. When the hormone is deficient or absent, the heat-regulating mechanisms are seriously disturbed. Removal of the anterior pituitary has the same effect; this is explained in part by the dependence of the thyroid on thyrotrophin secreted by the pituitary. Changes in behavior help to compensate for the removal of these glands. Thyroidectomized or hypophysectomized rats build much larger nests than intact animals, presumably in an effort to cover themselves and conserve heat. Similarly, hypothyroid men and women dress more warmly and use more blankets.

Comparable changes in behavior are reflected in the choice of diets following adrenalectomy, pancreatectomy, and parathyroidectomy. Compensation for the loss of sodium that follows adrenalectomy is made by the inclusion of much larger than normal quantities of sodium salt in the diet when such animals are given access to a variety of mineral solutions. The selective consumption of calcium solution was increased and of phosphorus solutions decreased following parathyroidectomy of rats. In this way a change in behavior helped compensate for the low blood calcium and high blood phosphates that follow parathyroidectomy. Pancreatectomized rats, when offered a carbohydrate, a fat, and a protein in separate containers, rejected the carbohydrate and ate larger than normal amounts of fat and protein. Corresponding changes in behavior are recorded for man. Addisonian patients, that is, those whose adrenal cortex has been destroyed or is non-functional, crave very large amounts of table salt and foods having a high salt content. Children with parathyroid deficiency crave food or substances with a high content of calcium.

Richter explains these changes in behavior as an effort by the individual to compensate for the failure of the physiological or chemical regulation that normally contributes to homeostasis, which is the maintenance of a constant internal environment. Under conditions of normal endocrine activity, fluctuations in the rate of oxidations or in the nutritive state that would be reflected in nest-building, clothing, or dietary adjustments would be so slight as to remain unnoticed. On the other hand, when deviations from normal levels are brought on by endocrine malfunction, there is an unconscious effort to adjust by means of changes in behavior.

The behavioral state and endocrine activity

The first endocrine gland we think of as an example of one whose activity is strongly influenced by the behavioral state of the organism is the adrenal medulla. The late Doctor Walter B. Cannon's (13) description of the action of this gland under conditions of stress is one of the classics of American physiology. In a series of experiments representative of the scientific method at its best, Cannon and his associates demonstrated that when cats, dogs, and rabbits are subjected to conditions under which there is an arousal of emotional excitement as in rage, fear, and the sensation of pain, there is a detectable increase in the amount of adrenalin in the blood. The hormone serves to stimulate reactions in the body, such as acceleration of the heart rate, increase in the number of circulating red-blood cells, and prolongation of the capacity for muscular exertion, all of which are adaptive in the physical struggle for existence. It is as though the recognition of danger were sufficient to release an endocrine mechanism that serves to mobilize the resources of the body for emergency action. This is precisely the sequence of events that Cannon postulated. These reactions do not occur when adrenalectomized animals or animals from which the nerve supply to the gland has been destroyed are exposed to stimuli that arouse a degree of emotional excitement that is provocative of adrenalin secretion in intact individuals. In an animal of the first type adrenalin is not produced, and in one of the second type the stimulus originating during stress cannot reach the gland.

Secretion of adrenalin under conditions of emotional excitement is not limited to laboratory mammals. In man, for whom it is convenient to use the presence of sugar in the urine as an indicator of adrenalin secretion, glycosuria was found in students after difficult examinations, in players after participation in a football game, and in a spectator after watching an exciting game. One is tempted to suspect that the excitement of pleasure may also be productive of a heightened adrenalin secretion and glycosuria.

The opinion is general that psychic trauma affects the secretory activity of other endocrine glands as well as the adrenal medulla, but the possibility has not been subjected to the careful scrutiny and to the critical test of experiment that characterized Cannon's studies of the adrenal medulla. As a result, a formulation of the relationship between the behavioral state and the action of other endocrine glands, comparable with that given us for the relationship between the behavioral state and the adrenal medulla, does not exist. Nevertheless, the information that has been brought together is too impressive to be ignored.

As the literature is reviewed, it is obvious that the term psychic trauma is used to include the reaction to sharp or prolonged pain, shock, fright, fear, worry, sorrow, strife, indeed to any emotional disturbance to which adaptive responses are required. We find mentioned in this category apprehension over a change of occupation, the shock following aerial bombardment during the two World Wars, the shock following an automobile accident, the fear of pregnancy. The glands mentioned as being involved are the thyroid, the adrenal cortex, and the gonads in males and females. In the case of these four glands, hypophyseal control over their functioning exists and there is abundant evidence that the impulses, whether they are excitatory or inhibitory to pituitary action, reach the *pars distalis* by way of the hypothalamus in the brain.

In situations in which the thyroid is involved, as in the development of thyrotoxicosis following psychic stress (32), it is presumed that the trauma is in some way followed by an increased production of thyrotrophin, which, in turn, activates the thyroid to secrete excessive quantities of thyroid hormone.

The most elaborate theories concern the relationship between psychic and physical trauma and the activity of the adrenal cortex. The sequence of events is described by Selye (41) in a review of what he has called the *general adaptation syndrome*. Shortly after a preliminary *"shock phase,"* defined as "a condition of suddenly developing, intense, systemic (general) damage," there is a *"counter-shock phase"* characterized by an enlargement of the adrenal cortex and other morphological as well as physiological evidence of hyperactivity. He postulates that the damaging agent present during the "shock phase," through a hypothetical toxic metabolite produced under its influence, stimulates the anterior lobe of the pituitary to discharge corticotrophic hormone (ACTH). Secretion of the latter is followed by an enlargement of the adrenal cortex and an increased production of cortical hormones. These substances, by counteracting the effects of the initial damage, raise the resistance to stress.

The entire sequence of events bears some resemblance to the reactions associated with the adrenal medulla under conditions of fear, rage, and pain. Both are defensive endocrine responses stimulated by an abrupt change in the behavioral state of the organism. It would seem, however, from the numerous discussions of the subject that there are important differences. The adrenal medulla has come to be regarded as protective in emergencies of short duration. The adrenal cortex is thought to be protective in situations in which the stress is prolonged and in which the derangements of metabolism are more profound. The response of the adrenal medulla to emotional stress is direct; that is, it is not mediated by another endocrine organ. The reaction of the adrenal cortex is always by way of the anterior pituitary, although the route of stimulation that leads to corticotrophin production by this gland may not always be the same. Following stress it is postulated that an increased tissue utilization of cortical hormone lowers the level in the blood and thereby stimulates the pituitary to increased production of corticotrophin, presumably during the "shock phase." Long (31) suggests that a second route of anterior hypophysis-adrenal cortex activation is by way of the adrenal medulla. The sequence of events in this case would be as follows: stress → epinephrine production, presumably during the "shock phase," → stimulation of the anterior pituitary → increased corticotrophin secretion.

Not all effects of the behavioral state on endocrine activity are excitatory as are those described for the thyroid, the adrenal medulla, and the adrenal cortex. Evidence exists for the view that severe emotional stress is inhibitory to pituitary gonadotrophic function. The consequences are a cessation of cyclic ovarian and uterine activity and the development of *amenorrhea*, which is the abeyance of the menses (18). Uncertainty exists with respect to the site of action within the pituitary. Observations on the chimpanzee, in which prefollicular, follicular, and luteal phases and menstruation are readily distinguishable externally, suggest that the amenorrhea frequently seen during adolescence or that which often follows pregnancy and lactation is associated with a failure of follicular development, and therefore with a failure of the follicle-stimulating hormone to function (59). Data obtained during a study of four clinical cases (30) suggest, however, that the arrest can also occur during the luteal phase and therefore be the consequence of an inhibition of luteinizing or luteotrophic hormone action. If this is true, the pituitary gland as it produces gonadotrophins is vulnerable to emotional disturbance at all stages of the process, but acceptance of such a conclusion from limited data would be hazardous. Not only must more data be collected, but they must be controlled with respect to the emotional stability of the individual, the nutritional state, age, and the time of the cycle during which the stress occurred.

Bibliography

1. Ball, J., Effect of Progesterone Upon Sexual Excitability in the Female Monkey, *Psychol. Bull.*, 1941, **38**, 533.
2. Bayliss, W. M. and Starling, E. H., The Mechanism of Pancreatic Secretion, *J. of Physiol.*, 1902, **28**, 325-353.
3. Beach, F. A., Female Mating Behavior Shown by Male Rats after Administration of Testosterone Propionate, *Endocrinology*, 1941, **29**, 409-412.
4. ————— Analysis of Factors Involved in the Arousal, Maintenance and Manifestation of Sexual Excitement in Male Animals, *Psychosom. Med.*, 1942, **4**, 173-198.
5. ————— Relative Effects of Androgen upon Mating Behavior in Male Rats Subjected to Castration or Forebrain Injury, *J. Exper. Zool.*, 1944, **97**, 249-285.
6. ————— Hormonal Induction of Mating Responses in a Rat with Congenital Absence of Gonadal Tissue, *Anatom. Rec.*, 1945, **92**, 289-292.
7. ————— *Hormones and Behavior.* New York: Paul B. Hoeber, Inc., 1948
8. ————— and Holz-Tucker, A. M., Effects of Different Concentrations of Androgen upon Sexual Behavior in Castrated Male Rats, *J. Compar. and Physiol. Psychol.*, 1949, **42**, 433-453.
9. Boling, J. L., and Blandau, R. J., The Estrogen-Progesterone Induction of Mating Responses in the Spayed Female Rat, *Endocrinology*, 1939, **25**, 359-364.
10. ————— Young, W. C., and Dempsey, E. W., Miscellaneous Experiments on the Estrogen-Progesterone Induction of Heat in the Spayed Guinea Pig, *Endocrinology*, 1938, **23**, 182-187.
11. Brookhart, J. M., Dey, F. L., and Ranson, S. W., The Abolition of Mating Behavior by Hypothalamic Lesions in Guinea Pigs, *Endocrinology*, 1941, **28**, 561-565.
12. Brown, F. A., Jr., *The Hormones* (G. Pincus and K. V. Thimann, Eds.). New York: Academic Press, Inc., 1948, Chapter 5, pp. 159-199.
13. Cannon, W. B., *Bodily Changes in Pain, Hunger, Fear and Rage.* New York: D. Appleton and Company, 1929.

14. Dempsey, E. W., Hertz, R., and Young, W. C., The Experimental Induction of Oestrus (Sexual Receptivity) in the Normal and Ovariectomized Guinea Pig, *Amer. J. Physiol.*, 1936, **116**, 201-209.

15. Feiner, L., and Rothman, T., Study of a Male Castrate, *J. Amer. Med. Ass.*, 1939, **113**, 2144-2146.

16. Fish, W. R., Young, W. C., and Dorfman, R. I., Excretion of Estrogenic and Androgenic Substances by Female and Male Chimpanzees with Known Mating Behavior Records, *Endocrinology*, 1941, **28**, 585-592.

17. Fleischmann, W., Comparative Physiology of the Thyroid Hormone, *Quart. Rev. Biol.*, 1947, **22**, 119-140.

18. Fluhmann, C. F., *Menstrual Disorders: Pathology, Diagnosis and Treatment*. Philadelphia: W. B. Saunders Company, 1939.

19. Frank, A. H. and Fraps, R. M., Induction of Estrus in the Ovariectomized Golden Hamster, *Endocrinology*, 1945, **37**, 357-361.

20. Fraps, R. M., Schott, R. G., Simmons, V. L., and Phillips, R. W., The Suppression of Estrogen-Induced Heat in Ovariectomized Sheep and Goats by Progesterone, *Anat. Rec.*, 1946, **96**, 570.

21. Greep, R. O., and Deane, H. W., The Cytology and Cytochemistry of the Adrenal Cortex, *Annals N. Y. Acad. Sci.*, 1949, **50**, 596-615.

22. Grollman, A., *Essentials of Endocrinology*. Philadephia: J. B. Lippincott Company, 1941.

23. Heller, R. E., Spontaneous Activity in Male Rats in Relation to Testis Hormone, *Endocrinology*, 1932, **16**, 626-632.

24. Hisaw, F. L., The Placental Gonadotrophin and Luteal Function in Monkeys (*Macaca mulatta*), *Yale J. Biol. and Med.*, 1944, **17**, 119-137.

25. Jailer, J. W., Sperry, W. M., Engle, E. T., and Smelser, G., Experimental Hypothyroidism in the Monkey, *Endocrinology*, 1944, **35**, 27-37.

26. Jones, G. E. Seegar, Delfs, E., and Foote, E. C., The Effect of Thiouracil Hypothyroidism on Reproduction in the Rat, *Endocrinology*, 1946, **38**, 337-344.

27. Kent, G. C., Jr., and Liberman, M. J., Induction of Psychic Estrus in the Hamster with Progesterone Administered via the Lateral Brain Ventricle, *Endocrinology*, 1949, **45**, 29-32.

28. Kinsey, A. C., Pomeroy, W. B., and Martin, C. E., *Sexual Behavior in the Human Male*. Philadelphia: W. B. Saunders Company, 1948.

29. Leblond, C. P., Extra-Hormonal Factors in Maternal Behavior, *Proc. Soc. Exper. Biol. and Med.*, 1938, **38**, 66-70.

30. Loeser, A. A., Effect of Emotional Shock on Hormone Release and Endometrial Development, *Lancet*, 1943, **244**, 518-519.

31. Long, C. N. H., The Mechanism of Secretion of the Adrenal Cortical Hormones, *Science*, 1950, **111**, 458-459.

32. Means, J. H., *The Thyroid and its Diseases*. Philadelphia: J. B. Lippincott Company, 1948.

33. Nissen, H. W., The Effects of Gonadectomy, Vasotomy and Injections

of Placental and Orchic Extracts on the Sex Behavior of the White Rat, *Genet. Psychol. Monogr.*, 1929, **5**, 451-547.

34. Petersen, W. E., Spielman, A., Pomeroy, B. S., and Boyd, W. L., Effect of Thyroidectomy upon Sexual Behavior of the Male Bovine, *Proc. Soc. Exper. Biol. and Med.*, 1941, **46**, 16-17.

35. Reinke, E. E., and Chadwick, C. S., The Origin of the Water Drive in *Triturus viridescens*. I. Induction of the Water Drive in Thyroidectomized and Gonadectomized Land Phases by Pituitary Implantations, *J. Exper. Zool.*, 1940, **83**, 223-233.

36. Richter, C. P., Total Self Regulatory Functions in Animals and Human Beings, *Harvey Lectures*, 1942-1943, Series 38, pp. 63-103.

37. Riddle, O., Physiological Responses to Prolactin, *Cold Spring Harbor Symposia on Quantitative Biology*, 1937, **5**, 218-228.

38. Riddle, O., Hollander, W. F., Miller, R. A., Lahr, E. L., Smith, G. C., and Marvin, H. N., Endocrine Studies, *Carnegie Institution of Washington Yearbook,* 1941-42, **41**, 203-211.

39. Ring, J. R., The Estrogen-Progesterone Induction of Sexual Receptivity in the Spayed Female Mouse, *Endocrinology,* 1944, **34**, 269-275.

40. Scharrer, B., *The Hormones* (G. Pincus and K. V. Thimann, Eds.). New York: Academic Press, Inc., 1948, Chapter 4, pp. 121-158.

41. Selye, H., The General Adaptation Syndrome and the Diseases of Adaptation, *J. Clin. Endocrin.,* 1946, **6**, 117-230.

42. Stone, C. P., The Awakening of Copulatory Ability in the Male Albino Rat, *Amer. J. Physiol.,* 1924, **68**, 407-424.

43. —— The Retention of Copulatory Ability in Male Rats Following Castration, *J. of Compar. Psychol.,* 1927, **7**, 369-387.

44. —— Copulatory Activity in Adult Male Rats Following Castration and Injections of Testosterone Propionate. *Endocrinology,* 1939, **24**, 165-174.

45. —— and Ferguson, L. W., Temporal Relationships in the Copulatory Acts of Adult Male Rats, *J. Compar. Psychol.,* 1940, **30**, 419-433.

46. —— Ferguson, L. W., and Wright, C., Consistency in Lengths of Post-ejaculatory Quiescent Periods in Adult Male Rats, *Proc. Soc. Exper. Biol. and Med.,* 1940, **45**, 120-121.

47. Thimann, K. V., *The Hormones* (G. Pincus and K. V. Thimann, Eds.). New York: Academic Press, Inc., 1948, Chapters 2 and 3, pp. 5-119.

48. Turner, C. D., *General Endocrinology*. Philadelphia: W. B. Saunders Company, 1948.

49. Wilson, J. G., and Young, W. C., Sensitivity to Estrogen Studied by Means of Experimentally Induced Mating Responses in the Female Guinea Pig and Rat, *Endocrinology,* 1941, **29**, 779-783.

50. Wislocki, G. B., Aub, J. C., and Waldo, C. M., The Effects of Gonadectomy and the Administration of Testosterone Propionate

on the Growth of Antlers in Male and Female Deer, *Endocrinology*, 1947, **40**, 202-224.

51. Witschi, E., Effect of Gonadotropic and Oestrogenic Hormones on Regenerating Feathers of Weaver Finches (*Pyromelana franciscana*), *Proc. Soc. Exper. Biol. and Med.*, 1936, **35**, 484-489.

52. Yerkes, R. M., *Chimpanzees*. New Haven: Yale University Press, 1943.

53. Young, W. C., Observations and Experiments on Mating Behavior in Female Guinea Pigs, *Quart. Rev. Biol.*, 1941, **16**, 135-156, 311-335.

54. ———— Dempsey, E. W., Hagquist, C. W., and Boling, J. L., Sexual Behavior and Sexual Receptivity in the Female Guinea Pig, *J. Compar. Psychol.*, 1939, **27**, 49-68.

55. ———— Dempsey, E. W., Myers, H. I., and Hagquist, C. W., The Ovarian Condition and Sexual Behavior in the Female Guinea Pig, *Amer. J. Anat.*, 1938, **63**, 457-487.

56. ———— and Fish, W. R., The Ovarian Hormones and Spontaneous Running Activity in the Female Rat, *Endocrinology*, 1945, **36**, 181-189.

57. ———— and Orbison, W. D.: Changes in Selected Features of Behavior in Pairs of Oppositely Sexed Chimpanzees during the Sexual Cycle and after Ovariectomy, *J. Compar. Psychol.*, 1944, **37**, 107-143.

58. ———— and Rundlett, B., The Hormonal Induction of Homosexual Behavior in the Spayed Female Guinea Pig, *Psychosom. Med.*, 1939, **1**, 449-460.

59. ———— and Yerkes, R. M., Factors Influencing the Reproductive Cycle in the Chimpanzee; the Period of Adolescent Sterility and Related Problems, *Endocrinology*, 1943, **33**, 121-154.

60. Zuckerman, S., *The Social Life of Monkeys and Apes*. London: Kegan Paul, Trench, Trübner, 1932.

CHAPTER 6

Learning: General Introduction

W. T. HERON

University of Minnesota

Introduction

Learning is a phenomenon that occurs throughout the entire animal scale. In all adult vertebrates there is no behavior, with the possible exception of the simple reflexes, that is free from at least a modicum of learning. It is likewise true that learning is based upon native mechanisms. Because of the interdependence of learning and native behavior, it is difficult to set off the one from the other. This difficulty is increased by virtue of the fact that the formulation of a definition of learning is an extremely perplexing problem. One cannot hope to give a solution upon which there will be universal agreement, but any definition certainly would involve the concept of change of behavior to what is, at least superficially, a constant environment. One might therefore say that to learn is to change reactions through interaction with the environment.

What are the ways in which reactions may change? They are: (*a*) a reaction may cease to occur, or perhaps, more strictly speaking, the probability of the occurrence of the reaction decreases; (*b*) a reaction may change its form—for example, running instead of walking; (*c*) the probability of the reaction occurring is increased.

It is specified by many authorities that the change in reaction should result in an adaptation of the organism to its environment if it is to be designated learning. That would eliminate as learning all changes that do not contribute to the preservation of the organism.

It is specified by other authorities that the change in reactions should be in the direction of decreasing the amount of energy that the organism uses to get to his goal.

Broadly considered, these specifications are unnecessary. Learning designates any change in reactions arising from interaction with the environment, not attributable to maturation, regardless of the result to the organism.

There is a second way in which the term learning may be used. One may refer to a change within the organism that does not at the moment make itself apparent in its reactions. In this case one is referring to acquisition rather than performance. When latent learning is discussed later in the chapter, it will be evident that learning is used in the sense of acquisition. It will also be obvious, however, that the only indication of acquisition is in terms of performance.

Distribution of Learning Ability in the Phylogenetic Scale

The ability to learn is preëminently a characteristic of the normal human being. However, this capacity is also present, in varying degrees, in animals below man in the phylogenetic scale. In fact, there is evidence that indicates that all species (from the unicellular animals upward) are capable of learning. Only some species have been investigated in this connection, but the sampling is sufficient to justify the statement.[1]

To be sure, the extent to which modification of reactions takes place varies widely in different species. One would not expect a paramecium, for example, to learn a problem in calculus; but then a paramecium does not meet calculus problems in its environment. However, if by some decree of an experimenter it were required to do so or die, it would be forced to the latter fate. In other words, the relatively simple organization of the paramecium does not permit it to solve these complex problems. Generally speaking, there is a low positive correlation between the position of each species in the phylogenetic scale and the complexity of the tasks that it is able to learn.

There are many factors that prevent this correlation from approaching perfection. One of the outstanding of these is the extent to which instinctive behavior is predominant in some animals, particularly the insects. In many of these organisms, the instinctive equipment is so closely, so rigidly adjusted to the normal environment of the species that it is only with great difficulty that their behavior can be modified through experience.

It is interesting to compare the relative advantages and disadvantages of the two modes of getting on in the world. This comparison

---

[1] A summary of the knowledge concerning the learning ability of different species is given by M. F. Washburn, *The Animal Mind*. New York: The Macmillan Company, 1936.

is most vivid when made between the human species, which emphasizes learning as the chief mode of adaptation, and the social insects, which use primarily the instinctive approach.

For practically all of human learned behavior we can find a prototype in instinctive behavior. A few examples are: the cultivation of plants for food; the care of other animals for food; and the carrying on of organized warfare. It is apparent that the behaviors are very similar whether learned or instinctive. A comparison of the two leads to the following conclusions:

1. Adaptation to rapidly changing environmental conditions can usually be made more efficiently through learned rather than through instinctive behavior.
2. New modes of adaptation can be handed down quickly to offspring in the form of social inheritance by animals that use learning as the chief mode of adaptation.
3. Previous learning can be incorporated into present learning, thus making a cumulative process within the individual. This, although possible, is less characteristic of instinctive behavior.
4. Adaptation by learning, however, usually requires a long tutorial period for each individual. This is not a very efficient procedure.
5. Learned behavior is subject to forgetting so that behavior once learned may not later be available to the organism and the learning process must be repeated. Forgetting does not occur in instinctive behavior.
6. Learning frequently leads to conflicts in the life of the individual and thus may produce neurotic conditions. These phenomena usually lead to much inefficiency, at least from the point of view of the social group. Animals that adapt primarily by instinct do not suffer conflicts and neuroses.
7. Organisms exhibiting little else than instinctive behavior are more homogeneous. In organisms that rely upon learning there is great heterogeneity of capacity and attainments. This tends to produce a disruption of the social group.
8. In those organisms that rely upon learning there is always the possibility that the individual will form habits that are undesirable from the point of view of either his own or group welfare. The danger of undesirable behavior is minimized in the instinctive organisms.
9. Other comparisons may be made, but the above are enough to indicate the nature of the problem.

Nature, speaking metaphorically, is performing an experiment to determine the relative effectiveness of these two modes of adaptation. On the one hand she has endowed the social insects with practically complete instinctive equipment and placed them at the apex of the development of the invertebrate animals. Standing at the apex of the vertebrate series is man with his highly developed learning equipment.

To a large extent man and the insects are enemies and competitors. Only time can tell if the issue between instinct and learning will be joined to the point of decision.

Although, as we have indicated, learning ability is found throughout the phylogenetic scale, in this chapter we shall confine ourselves to learning phenomena in the mammalian series. Some limitations must be fixed, and it is the mammals that have received the most experimental attention in recent years.

Typical Methods of Studying Animal Learning

Scientists of America, Germany, and Russia have contributed their respective methods for the study of learning in animals.

Conditioning

The Russian scientist, Pavlov, has developed the *conditioned* response (CR) method of conditioning. Pavlov and his students studied conditioning for more than a quarter of a century. In addition, there are thousands of conditioning experiments described by researchers in other parts of the world. Consequently there has grown around the method a terminology peculiar to it. Also the various phenomena of conditioning have formed a basis for the formulation of theories of learning. The conditioned response is looked upon by some theorists as the fundamental paradigm of all learning. They believe that even the most complex of human activity can be reduced to the principles of conditioning. Because of this great emphasis it is desirable that at least a few of the terms and principles of conditioning become a part of the student's psychological equipment.

To start with, the experimenter has within his control a stimulus that will elicit the reaction in which he is interested. In the case of Pavlov, this *unconditioned stimulus* (US) was usually the stimulation of food in the mouth of a hungry dog. The reaction was salivation. The secretion of saliva as the result of oral food stimulation in a hungry dog may be considered a matter of hereditary constitution. However, any stimulus that will elicit the desired response at the start of the experiment is the US, even though its production of the response is the result of previous learning.

In conditioning, the learning consists of causing a previously ineffective stimulus to produce the behavior that is elicited by the US. This is done by producing the presently ineffective stimulus slightly before the US. Eventually this new stimulus will elicit the response, and it is called the *conditioned stimulus* (CS).

However, after the CS has been caused to elicit the response, it is found that any other stimuli in the same sensory modality as the CS will also produce the response, although usually to a lesser extent. Pavlov used the term *generalization* to indicate this phenomenon. There has been some discussion in recent years concerning the reality of generalization. Lashley and Wade (30) categorically deny that training from one stimulus, the CS, "irradiate to produce association with similar stimuli, with a strength of association proportional to the degree of similarity." Hull (16), who uses what he terms primary stimulus generalization as an integral part of his theory, is not convinced by Lashley and Wade's arguments.

Another important phenomenon associated with conditioning is that of *experimental extinction*. It happens that in Pavlov's experiments the US also played the role of an incentive. At least this is true when he was using food as the US. In order to establish a conditioned response, the dog must be hungry (the drive) and, of course, the food is the proper source of satisfaction for this hunger.

In the conditioned response, as in all learned behavior, when the incentive is consistently withheld or rendered ineffective by a previous satiation of the drive, the learned activity deteriorates. In the case of conditioning this means that the conditioned response gradually reduces in magnitude upon successive repetition of the CS without the US. This reduction of the CR is termed *experimental extinction*.

A rather unusual phenomenon associated with experimental extinction is known as *spontaneous recovery*. If, as a result of successive applications of the CS without the incentive, the CR is reduced markedly and the animal is then allowed to rest, the CR will be found to have recovered to a slight degree. Spontaneous recovery is soon eliminated if the CS is again given a few times without the incentive.

Most authors designate Pavlov's work on conditioning as *classical conditioning*, and designate those cases of conditioning in which the US is not simultaneously the incentive as *instrumental conditioning*. In many of the latter situations the US is not identifiable by the experimenter. Some writers speak of its nonidentifiability as simply a result of lack of sufficient acuity of observation, and thereby imply that the US must be there. Other authorities (47) insist that there is no use in assuming that which cannot be identified, and speak of such apparently uninstigated behavior as *operant*. An example of this behavior that has been extensively studied is bar-pressing by the rat.

The apparatus is arranged so that when the hungry animal presses the bar a bit of food drops down within his reach. The stimulus, if any, that initiates the bar-pressing is not apparent. However, a CS may be quickly connected to this behavior and the bar-pressing in the absence of food may be extinguished to the CS. Experimental evidence with reference to instrumental conditioning has been widely used in the development of some of the theories of learning.

The student should remember that in both classical and instrumental conditioning the experimenter is limiting his observations to only a small portion of the animal's behavior. Likewise, his attention is fixed upon a limited portion of the stimulus complex in which the animal operates. Because of such necessarily restricted observations we are sometimes led to erroneous ideas. For example, diagrams are often drawn that imply that the response to the CS is identical with that to the US. Such is never the case if the complete responses made to the respective stimuli are examined.

Likewise, the animal is living in a flux of stimuli. An identical stimulus complex is never possible from one time to another, no matter how conscientious the experimenter is in the control of the situation. In this connection it is probably safe to say that Pavlov and his students exercised a much greater control over the stimulus complex of their experimental animals than any other researchers. Certainly their control was much closer than that found in the work of those who use problem boxes, mazes, and so on, or even that found in the work on instrumental conditioning.

If one examines conditioning in a historical perspective it becomes apparent that the Aristotelian law of contiguity covers the process. It is obvious that, in conditioning, the experimenter manipulates the situation so that the CS is brought into a contiguous relationship with the response. Thus it may be said that a connection or association is formed between them. The exception to this arrangement is found in the *trace* conditioned response. In this case the CS is given and terminated before the US with its accompanying response is presented to the animal. Perhaps Pavlov, being a physiologist rather than a psychologist, knew nothing of the "law of contiguity," but nevertheless he assumed that, in order to get a connection, a contiguity must exist. He hypothecated that the CS leaves a trace in the nervous system that remains to bridge the gap between the CS and the US. Because only a short interval of time can be used between the CS and US, he assumed that this trace must be of short duration and unstable. The concept of the trace is, of course, in the nature of a hypothetical construct designed to account for the observed facts.

There are a number of other terms and concepts used in the field of conditioning, but these are left for discussion in reference to the formation of discriminations and the development of learning theory.

Trial and error

Of the American methods, the two that are most often used are: (a) the problem box method, which was first employed under controlled experimental conditions by Thorndike (50), and (b) the maze method, contributed by Small (48).

The maze is, essentially, a tortuous pathway, usually with some blind alleys or *culs-de-sac*. It is particularly adapted to the rat, although it has been used with other species, including the human being. The rat, because it is easily maintained in good health, multiplies rapidly, is active and alert, and is economical to feed, is used a great deal by experimenters in the field of animal psychology. Many experiments on learning have the rat as the subject and the maze as the problem. Figure 1 shows the ground plan and detail of a maze that has been used by several investigators. It will be noted that the maze is composed of T-shaped units, a unit that has become the standard in maze construction.[2]

The problem box is a box or cage with a door fitted in it. This door is held shut by a latch or hook. In some experiments, the animal is placed inside the box, his task being to learn how to open the door in order to get out and to secure his food—the usual incentive. In others, the problem is to get into the box. The problem box has never been as widely used as the maze, probably because an error is not as easily defined and recorded as in the latter. It is, however, a very useful technique for some species, such as monkeys and apes, that are not particularly adapted to the maze situation.

The maze and problem-box techniques are most frequently used in

---

[2] A comparison of many different patterns of mazes will be found in L. H. Warner and C. J. Warden, "The Development of a Standard Animal Maze," *Archives of Psychology*, 1927, No. 93, pp. 1-35.

experimentation on trial-and-error learning. This is the "type" of learning that has been emphasized by American investigators, probably because of the influence of Thorndike (50), who conducted one of the primary investigations in the field of animal psychology. He used cats in a simple latch-type problem box, with hunger as the drive. He noted that on its first introduction to the box, the cat

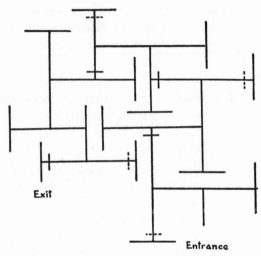

Exit

Entrance

Fig. 1. The Floor Plan of the Stone Multiple-T-Maze. This particular pattern was devised by Stone and used in a number of investigations. The short solid lines indicate doors that are let down behind the rat to prevent retracing. The dashed lines represent dummy doors, causing the blind alley and the true path to have the same appearance to the animal from the choice point.

would make a number of reactions, such as clawing, scratching, pushing, mewing, biting, striking, and so forth. These movements were performed more or less at random throughout the entire area of the box. Eventually, provided the cat persisted in its behavior, it would by chance hit the latch and the door would fly open. The cat could then walk out of the box and eat its food. The following day the cat was again put into the box and the whole procedure repeated. As days went by, the behavior of the cat tended to be more and more concentrated in the region of the latch. This fact would cause the hitting of the latch more quickly. The end result was that the cat eliminated practically all movements within the box except those required to trip the latch, and was then able to escape from the box immediately. Thus we have the completion of a process of trial-and-error learning.

Because the maze and problem-box techniques do emphasize trial-and-error learning to the exclusion of other possibly more intelligent types of behavior, Köhler, the German psychologist, has criticized them. In this connection, Köhler (28) writes:

American animal psychology makes animals (or people) seek the way out of the mazes, over the whole of which there is no general survey from any point inside; the first time they get out is, therefore, necessarily a matter of chance, and so, for these scientists, the chief question is how the experience gained in such circumstances can be applied in further tests. In intelligence tests of the nature of our roundabout-way experiments, everything depends upon the situation being surveyable by the subject from the outset.

Köhler likewise objects to Thorndike's use of problem boxes. He writes a criticism in the following strain:

It is somewhat astonishing to find that (in Thorndike's experiments) cats and dogs were frequently placed in cages containing the extreme end only of one or the other mechanism, or allowing a view of ropes or other parts of the mechanism, but from which a survey over the *whole* arrangement was not possible.

Insight

To overcome the difficulties that he believes to be inherent in the traditional American experimentation, Köhler makes use of the "roundabout" method. Experiments of this type are designed in such a manner that the animal can survey the situation and has the opportunity to understand, if he can, the relationships involved.

The term *insight* has been emphasized by the German *Gestalt* school of psychology, of which Köhler is one of the leading proponents. However, its point of emphasis—that some of the lower animals may react to a relationship if given the opportunity—has been shown, although not emphasized, in earlier experiments. For example, Kinamann (27) showed that monkeys will react to a relationship between two greys rather than to either of two specific greys.

However, without attempting a specific definition of insight, we may observe the results of an experiment that indicates this ability. Professor Köhler's chimpanzee, Sultan, which had previously learned to rake in food with a bamboo pole, was one day presented with two poles that could be fitted together to form a longer stick. The food, a banana, was placed on the ground outside the cage. It was just far enough away so that Sultan could not reach it with either pole no matter how hard he tried. When this proved futile he pulled a box toward the side of the cage outside of which lay the banana. This is an example of what Köhler called a "bad error." Soon, however, he performed a "good error." He pushed one stick out as far as it would go and with the other stick in his hand gradually pushed the loose stick towards the objective. By this means he actually touched the banana. This procedure meant, however, that the stick on the ground had to be handed back to him by the experimenter.

The experiment continued for over an hour and it looked as if Sultan was going to fail the test. Köhler, therefore, returned to the house leaving the keeper to watch Sultan who had retained his sticks. Sultan had apparently also abandoned the problem and squatted in the cage playing with the sticks, as is the habit of chimpanzees. As he played, apparently indifferent to the lure, he found himself accidentally holding one stick in each hand in such a way that the two sticks lay in a straight line. He pushed the smaller a little way into the larger stick and while so doing started running towards the side of the cage where the banana was located. He extended the double stick between the bars and began to draw in the banana.

However, the sticks came apart. This was a minor misfortune for Sultan, but a fortunate circumstance from the experimenter's point of view, because Sultan now took the two sticks and firmly pushed them together, then proceeded to go after the fruit again. This indicated to the experimenter that the animal had really grasped the relationship between the length of the double pole and securing the banana.

This grasping of relationship, especially in the sudden fashion as indicated by Sultan putting the sticks together on the run, is an example of insight. Another is an experiment performed by Tolman and Honzik (53) with rats. The apparatus is a form of the elevated-pathway type of maze, that is, the alleys are formed by strips of wood without sidewalls. These strips are raised a sufficient distance from the floor to prevent the rats' jumping off. The diagram of the maze is shown in Fig. 2. The gate is arranged so that the weight of the rat upon it will cause it to lower and allow the animal to go through. As soon as he is through, however, it closes again so that he cannot go back.

The animals are given preliminary training in the apparatus in order to accustom them to the experimental situation and also to set up in them preferential tendencies with reference to the three pathways to the food. Rats as a rule will learn rather quickly to take the shortest pathway to food when several of various lengths are presented to them. Consequently, in this experiment, the animals will soon learn to prefer Path *1*, of the three possibilities. To persuade them to take one of the other pathways, it is necessary to put block *A*

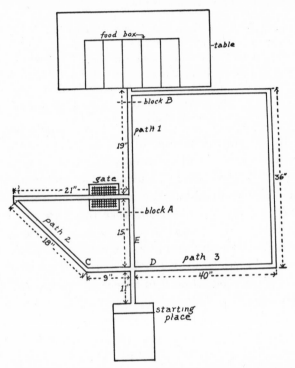

Fig. 2. Ground Plan of Elevated Maze Used by Tolman and Honzik. (See text.)

in Path *1*. This forces them to return to the bifurcation of the paths and to choose either Path *2* or Path *3*. Of these, the rats will prefer Path *2*. This is shown by the fact that of a total of 1,357 runs made by the 15 rats with block *A* in place, 1,229 (90.57 per cent) were on Path *2*, and the remainder on Path *3*.

At this point, then, the situation is as follows: If the rats are put in the maze without blocks of any kind, they will, in the vast majority of cases, take Path *1*; if, however, Path *1* is blocked at *A*, they will, in the majority of cases, take Path *2*. The crucial test trial to determine whether the animals show insight is initiated by removing block *A* and putting in block *B*. The animals will run to block *B* over Path *1*, but they will, of course, have to return to the bifurcation of the paths. The tendency, as indicated before, is now to take Path *2*. However, if the animals show insight into the situation, they will take Path *3*, because under these circumstances, with the block at *B*, Path *2* is also blocked so far as getting to the food is concerned. The results show that 14 of the 15 rats took Path *3*. The following quotation is taken from the authors' report:

> If the taking of Path 2 or Path *3* after return from block *B* were a matter of pure chance, similar to the tossing of a coin, the probability of 14 out of 15 rats taking Path *3* and one rat taking Path 2 would be .00046. The actual result of 14 rats taking Path *3* and one rat taking Path 2 on the first test run indicates, therefore, a very decided "loading" in favor of Path *3*, in spite of the fact that the "loading" during the training period was just the reverse, viz., in favor of Path 2.

This "loading" consists presumably in the ability of the animal to grasp the relationship of the position of block *B* to the commoness of Paths *1* and *2* at this point. That is, the animal shows "insight." It should be emphasized that this experimental setup allows the animal to survey the total situation, since there are no sidewalls on the maze. Tolman and Honzik (53) also used a maze of a similar pattern with sidewalls and a similar experimental procedure, with negative results. These results give support to Köhler's contention that the animal must be allowed to survey the total situation if it is to grasp relationships.

In view of the interest in the problem of insight it is unfortunate that no precise definition of that term is available. It should be emphasized that a reaction to a relationship is not sufficient to impute to the animal any extraordinary ability. If a positively phototropic animal is placed between two lights of different intensities, the path that the animal travels will be determined by the relative intensities of the two lights. The animal here is reacting to a relationship, but its reaction is not a proof of insight. Of course, a tropism is a native and relatively invariable type of behavior.

Is one to believe, then, that there is evidence of insight when the animal, in a situation for which it does not have a native response, proceeds to react to a relationship? What are the distinguishing characteristics of insight? Pechstein and Brown (43) have searched the literature on this subject and listed what they call the "criteria of insight learning." In a somewhat abbreviated form these are: (*a*) immediate solution of the problem; or (*b*), if the problem is complex,

almost immediate solution preceded by some trial-and-error behavior; (*c*) reaction to the situation as a whole; (*d*) responses to
meaningful relationships in a situation; and (*e*) in this response,
evidence of mental activity, that is, survey of the problematical
situation and maintenance of an attitude of concentrated attention.
Even to the most casual reader it should be obvious that some of these
criteria raise more questions than they answer—for example, what is
a meaningful relationship, to whom is it meaningful, and from what
point of reference?

The Learning Curve

In the study of learning, it is convenient to represent the learner's
progress by graphical means. American methods usually represent
the speed of behavioral modification by the rate at which time or
errors are eliminated. The tendency in recent years has been to
place greater reliance upon error records, especially in the maze
problem.

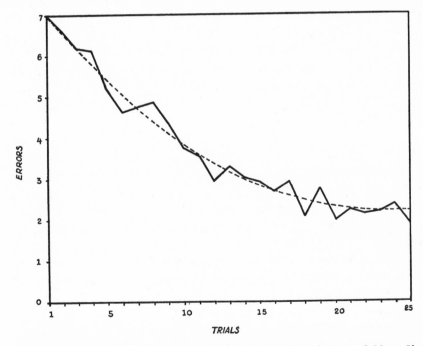

Fig. 3. Learning Curve of a Group of Rats on a Multiple-T Type of Maze. If a
sufficient number of trials were given, the curve would continue its downward course
until it reached the base line. The solid line is from the data. The dashed line is inserted to illustrate the general form of the curve.

The rate of elimination of errors is most conveniently shown by plotting a learning curve. Figure 3 shows a learning curve based upon the mean error record per trial of a group of 103 rats that were given one trial per day in running a maze for 25 days. The dashed line has been inserted to bring out more clearly the general form of the curve. It is seen that there is a relatively rapid descent (ascent if correct responses are used instead of errors) of the curve in the first few trials, and that the rate of descent gradually decreases with progressive trials. This type of curve is for this reason called a *negatively accelerated curve,* and is the usual form of the curve based upon trial-and-error learning. It is characteristic of much human as well as animal learning.

If, however, some factor that affects the course of learning is varied, there will be a change in the rate of descent of this curve as compared with the curve obtained under the standard control conditions. The learning curves are, therefore, useful in showing graphically the effect of changing experimental conditions. The curves may also have a further value if subjected to an adequate mathematical analysis (60). This question, however, is beyond the scope of this book.

While it is possible to picture the progress of both conditioning and insight learning in graphical form, the fact is that such graphs do not add greatly to the understanding of the experiments in those fields.

The Relation of Learning to Certain Variable Factors

A determination of the factors that affect the course of learning is of great theoretical and practical importance. Theoretically it helps us to understand better the fundamental nature of learning; and from the standpoint of practicality, every teacher, parent, and industrialist is interested in finding the factors that will increase the speed and efficiency of learning. Many factors suspected of influencing the course of learning have been investigated. Within the compass of this book it is impossible to discuss them all. Only a few will be chosen to indicate to the reader some of the possibilities.

Motives and incentives

To be able to learn, any organism must be active. This activity need not be in the skeletal muscles nor even in the other effectors of the body, although it is likely that in all cases the effectors are active to some degree. Possibly the activity may be confined to the nervous system, but regardless of locus it must be taking place somewhere in the organism. That state of activity that is related to a specific learning process is known as the *motive,* or, in the lower animals, *drive.* The *incentive* is that condition or situation that, when it is attained by the organism, tends temporarily to reduce the drive.

In the case of the human subject, motivation is recognized as a very potent factor in behavior even by the most casual observer. Nevertheless, human motivation is so complex as to be almost beyond our present comprehension. In the human being there are not only the native biological drives—for example, hunger, thirst, sex— but also a great superstructure of learned motives through which the underlying native foundation is seen only obscurely.

The lower animals, however, have stuck closer to the biological "springs of action." The animal grows hungry and eats; it becomes thirsty and drinks; its sex glands periodically become active and it engages in normal sex behavior. When these and a few other needs are taken care of, the animal is quiescent. Thus it presents a much simpler situation for the study of drives than does the human subject.

Even in the case of the animal, however, the relation of drives and incentives to learning is not entirely clear. So while it is no more than common sense to say that *speedy* learning cannot occur without the influence of drive, there is the question of whether the drive and its corresponding incentive actually affect the process of acquisition or only the performance of the act.

Blodgett (2) was the original investigator of this matter, using rats as subjects. His general procedure was to allow hungry rats (hunger was the drive) to explore a maze, but without finding food (the incentive) at the exit of the maze. He used three groups of animals. Group 1 (the control group containing 36 rats) ran the maze individually once a day for seven days, and were "allowed to eat for *three minutes in the food box at the end of each run."* Group 2 (containing 36 rats, litter mates of Group 1), was treated like Group 1 except that it found no food in the food box *for the first six days.* Each rat was kept in the food box for two minutes, and one hour later was fed in another cage. On the seventh, eighth, and ninth days, they were treated exactly as Group 1 had been. Group 3 (containing 25 rats) was treated like Group 2 except that food was introduced on the third day instead of the seventh.

Figure 4 shows the error curves for these three groups. It is quite obvious that little or no learning occurs, to judge by performance, as long as the incentive is not given at the completion of the run. However, some acquisition is taking place, as is shown by the very great drop in the curves for Groups 2 and 3 on the day following that on which they first found food in the food box. This acquisition has been termed by Blodgett *latent learning*.

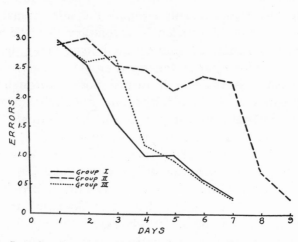

Fig. 4. Learning Curves of Blodgett's Three Groups of Rats. (See text.)

Since Blodgett's original experiment, the research on latent learning has been pushed vigorously because of the significance of the results for learning theory. Rival theorists are seemingly willing to rest their case on the answer to this question of the reality of latent learning. The theoretical implication will have to wait for a subsequent chapter (Chapter 8). Now it is possible only to present some of the conflicting evidence in a way that points out the main lines of attack.

Recent investigators have for the most part used a simple T-maze as their apparatus. This simplification arises out of their desire to reduce the situation to its fundamentals and to eliminate, as far as possible, complicating factors. The issue of latent learning has reduced itself to this question: Can the animal learn the location of an incentive although he does not partake of the incentive either because the appropriate drive is satiated or because the incentive is behind barriers that permit it to stimulate only his distance receptors? Or to put the matter in the terminology of rival theorists: Can the animal learn a "cognition" of the location of an incentive during a period in which he is stimulated by the incentive but is not "reinforced" by it?

The general plan of the experiments is to place water in the goal box at the end of one arm of the T-maze and food in the goal box at the other end. The animals are then treated in one of the following ways:

1. One drive (either hunger or thirst) is raised to a high level by deprivation of the proper incentive and the other is satiated. The animals are then run in the T-maze and, of course, find an appropriate incentive in one arm. They are, however, forced to go to the other goal box an equal number of times where they are presumably stimulated by the inappropriate incentive but do not partake of it because of their satiated condition for the corresponding drive. After some specified number of trials the experimenter reverses the drive condition so that the formerly inappropriate incentive becomes the appropriate one. Latent learning in this experiment would be indicated if the animals immediately were to reverse their preferred turn at the bifurcation of the T and go the side of the previously inappropriate incentive. Kendler (25) did an experiment of this kind and found in the test trial that the animals continued to go into the arm that had led to the appropriate incentive during the training. Thus the animals did not show latent learning in his experiment.

2. The two drives (hunger and thirst) are satiated and the animals are allowed to run for a specified number of trials through a T-maze in which water is in one arm and food in the other. Since the animals are satiated they will partake of neither of these. The animals are caused to go to each arm an equal number of trials. The test is to raise one drive while leaving the other satiated and to determine if the animals will now go to the arm that contains the appropriate incentive to a significantly greater extent than chance expectation. Meehl and Mac-Corquodale (41) performed an experiment of this type. Their results indicate that latent learning did occur, or, in other words, some rats did form cognitions of the locations of the respective incentives. They question, however, that these cognitions are formed in the absence of reinforcement and, therefore, speak of them as "phenomenological cognitions." Their discussion of this point becomes too theoretical to be treated here.

3. A third variation is to use one unsatiated and one satiated drive. The appropriate incentive for the unsatiated drive is put in both goal boxes while the incentive for the satiated drive is put in only one. The animal is forced by experimental manipulation to go an equal number of trials to each end of the T-maze where he can partake of the incentive appropriate to his unsatiated drive. In the test trial the drives are reversed in reference to the state of satiation. The question is: Will the animals now go, beyond chance expectation, to the end where they

had previously experienced the inappropriate incentive since it has now become an appropriate one? Kendler and Mencher (26) did an experiment of this type and found that the rats had not formed a cognition of the location of the inappropriate incentive during the training trials.

4. Still a fourth variation that might be tried, although no one seems as yet to have performed the experiment, would be to use two unsatiated drives (hunger and thirst) and put the incentives in the goal boxes as in method 1. However, the incentives could be covered in such a way that they would stimulate the distance sense organs of the animal but the animal could not partake of them. The animals would be forced to go an equal number of times to each side for the purpose of equating their turning tendencies. The test would consist in satiating one drive and predicting that the animals would go to the side of the incentive appropriate to their remaining unsatiated drive if latent learning had taken place. This technique would have at least one advantage over method 2 in that the animals would be much more active and thus the time spent by the experimenter would be greatly decreased.

It has been indicated that the experimenters have concentrated on the T-maze in investigating the latent learning problem in order to simplify the situation. It is obvious, however, that many factors are still involved that may be influential to a degree unknown. For example, what do forced trials do to the learning of the animal or what do they do to prevent an animal from attaining an appropriate incentive by the use of barriers? Is there a phenomenon of frustration to contend with? What is the influence of secondary reinforcers in these experimental situations? Many other questions of a like nature remain unanswered.

Regardless of how the question of acquisition without reinforcement may be settled, there are many problems concerning the relationship of drives and incentives to learning that are less ambiguous in their solution. For example, can the drive determine which of two or more potential habits will function at the moment? Leeper (31) and Hull (14) have evidence that the rat will behave in accordance with the prevailing drive of the moment. On some days the animals were thirsty when put in the problem situation; on others they were hungry. The apparatus was arranged so that a rat could find water by turning right or food by turning left at a certain point. Both routes were equally available at all times. Will the rat on thirsty days turn right and on hungry days turn left? The rats could and did learn to do this.

Whether it is correct to say that the animals were reacting on the

basis of hunger or thirst is rendered doubtful by the results of a
somewhat similar experiment by Heron (11). After having trained
the animals, this experimenter ran a control in which the animals
were deprived of both food and water. These animals reacted as if
they were hungry, but when water was pumped into their stomachs
they acted as if they were thirsty. Also, if they were given both food
and water before running, they acted as if they were thirsty, although
running slowly. It would appear that these animals were reacting
as if thirsty when their stomachs were full, and as if hungry when
their stomachs were empty regardless of how the stomach got empty
or full. It is obvious that we need much more experimental evidence
before the so-called "drive stimuli" are understood.

Another problem of great interest is the probable effect of delaying
access to the incentive after the animal has completed the performance. Likewise, when punishment is used for incorrect responses,
what will be the effect of delaying the punishment after the error
has been made? The answer to the question of delayed access to food
is to be found in the work of Wolfe (61). He used a single T-maze
in which the problem was to learn which way to turn for food.
There was a detention chamber in both the correct and incorrect
pathway immediately beyond the bifurcation of the central pathway.
If the rat turned correctly he was detained according to the schedule
given in the first column of Table 1 and then released and allowed
to go to the food. If the animal turned incorrectly it was detained
according to the same schedule and then returned to the entrance for
another trial.

TABLE 1

(*Since there are only two alternatives in the simple T-Maze, the mean expected chance
success is 50 per cent. The D/σ ratios are calculated on the basis of the obtained mean
percentage of success in relation to the mean chance expectancy.*)

Delays	Mean % of Success	D/σ
0 seconds	78.5	13.6
5 "	75.0	11.4
30 "	63.3	5.5
1 minute	60.5	4.4
1½ "	61.8	4.9
5 "	61.3	4.9
10 "	58.5	3.4
20 "	54.8	1.9

The data of Table 1 indicate that all except the 20-minute group
scored successes significantly above chance; in other words, learning
had occurred. However, beginning with the 30-second delay there

is a marked decrease in the number of successes.' Therefore, the conclusion is that incentive should be given as quickly as possible after
the act that it is intended to reward.

A similar situation obtains with reference to punishment. Warden
and Diamond (57) have carried out experiments relative to this question, using a very simple problem with rats. The punishment used
was electric shock. In this case a delay of four seconds produced a
marked increase in errors over a zero-second delay.

The above conclusions regarding the effect of delayed reward and
punishment have been called into doubt by Perin's (44) experiment
on delayed reward in which an effort was made to eliminate the
effects of secondary reinforcers. This concept of secondary rewards
has been emphasized by Hull (15). He believes that any stimulus
that is present at the time an organism is receiving a primary reward
(that is, a reward that satisfies a biological drive) becomes rewarding
also. According to this notion the stimuli from the sides of a food
box acquire reward value to the animal.

Therefore, to get the pure effect of delaying a reward these secondary rewards would have to be rendered ineffective or delayed
also. When Perin did this he found that no learning will occur if
the incentive is delayed for about 35 seconds, based upon an extra-
polation of his curve from the 20-second group. However, it is fairly
certain that Perin did not have complete control of the secondary
rewards, and Spence (49) believes that if such control were complete
there would be no learning beyond a zero delay.

The whole question of the effect and value of punishment has
been reopened by the experimental results of a number of investigators, notably, Thorndike (51), Muenzinger (42), and Tolman (54).
Although these results are most significant in relation to theories in
learning, which is not the province of this chapter, we may give them
some attention at this point.

Figure 5 is a reproduction of a diagram from a report by Muenzinger. This experimenter used rats in a light-dark discrimination experiment. As the figure indicates, he used three groups: no-shock;
shock for correct response; and shock for wrong response. All groups
received food for correct responses and in each trial were left in the
apparatus until they made the correct response. Although conditions
were somewhat different, the results of this experiment are in general
accordance with the Warden and Aylesworth experiment, but it is
surprising that there is no statistically significant difference between

the shock-right and shock-wrong groups. It would have been heresy a few years ago even to have considered giving punishment for correct responses; yet in this experiment it seems to make little difference for which kind of response the punishment is given. The results

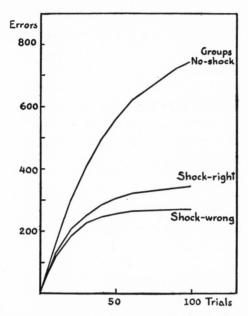

Fig. 5. Cumulative Error Curves of Three Groups of Rats Treated as Indicated on the Graphs. (From Muenzinger.)

of the other investigators mentioned, while differing in many respects from those of Muenzinger, all agree in questioning the traditional concept of the effect of punishment in learning.

Other factors in relation to learning

Extended space has been given to motivational factors in relation to learning because of their great systematic and theoretical importance. Even there, however, the discussion has not been complete because of space limitations. The same limitations make it impossible to discuss the many other factors that have been investigated in relation to learning. A partial list of these factors is: (a) distribution of practice; (b) whole versus part learning; (c) length of material to be learned; (d) emotional disturbances; (e) sex; (f) drugs; (g) ligation of arteries supplying the brain; (h) temperature; (i) oestrous cycle; (j) endocrine glands; (k) surgical interference with the nervous system; (*l*) positive and negative transfer; (*m*) retroactive inhibition; (*n*) wakefulness; (*o*) brain lipids; (*p*) age; (*q*) diet; (*r*) tuitional controls; and (*s*) electroshock.

Cues Used in Learning

"If amount of experimentation is indicative, then the rat has the human being thoroughly puzzled as to how it finds its way through and finally learns the maze." This sentence, taken from the first revision of this book, was written almost ten years ago. The puzzlement continues, if, in fact, it has not grown worse.

In experiments on sensory discrimination (see Chapter 10) there is no problem, since the animal is forced to use a certain sense organ if the experiment is well controlled. In maze learning, however, the solution is not nearly so easy.

An analysis of the situation produces the following statements: (*a*) Certain factors in the environment may act upon the organism to force it to go in certain directions without the intervention of the sense organs, for example, gravity, friction, and so forth; (*b*) Intramaze cues—olfactory, visual, tactual, and other stimuli—may be associated by the animal with certain turns in the maze and may help it to learn the correct path, such cues serving as signposts; (*c*) The cues mentioned in category (*b*) may lie in the extramaze environment; (*d*) The rat may conceivably use only intraorganic cues—for example, kinesthesis; (*e*) It is inconceivable that the factors in category (*a*) could account for learning by themselves, but it is possible that these factors could act together with those in any other category or in any combination of these categories; it is also possible that the organism can shift from cues in category (*b*), (*c*) or (*d*) to cues in any other category or combination of categories; (*f*) It is possible that the organism can integrate sensory processes from various sources with which to form a sort of map of the maze, and from then on be relatively free from the necessity of relying upon cues, although it would seem that the organism would occasionally have to check its position on the map through the use of sensory information. An analysis of this sort is admittedly made from the if-I-were-the-rat position and only partially on the basis of experimentation, but, nevertheless, it should serve to indicate to the reader the complexity of the problem.

Watson (58) was one of the early workers on this problem and he thought he had solved it. By a process of eliminating sensory fields, he came to the conclusion that the rat must learn the maze by the use of the muscle sense (kinesthesis). He found that the animal could run the maze when one after another of its sense organs had been eliminated, although each elimination was performed, for the most part, in a different group of animals. Watson, however, knew of no method of eliminating the muscle sense, consequently he could give no positive proof of his contention by elimination. However, by means of a special maze in which the alleys could be shortened or lengthened, he believed that he had found positive proof. If, after the rat has learned the maze, the alleys are shortened, it will, according to Watson, run into the walls; or, if the alleys are lengthened, it will try to turn before the end of the alley. These and other data caused him to make the statement, "We seem forced to conclude that in the rat kinaesthetic arcs are the only ones necessary at any stage of the formation of this habit." He therefore resolved the "maze habit process into the functioning of a serially chained kinaesthetic arc system."

This doctrine has received widespread attention and has been applied to many human habits of everyday life. It has also initiated much research, the result of which has been, however, to question Watson's conclusion that the maze habit is simply a concatenation of kinesthetic arcs. Watson himself realized that the situation might not be as simple as he had described it. For example, he states that the animals are confused by a 180-degree rotation of the maze. This, of course, should not occur if kinesthetic arcs alone are concerned, since the units in the maze still bear the same relation to each other.

Hunter (18), in order to test what the animal can accomplish with kinesthesis, designed the temporal maze diagrammed in Fig. 6. In this maze, when the rat is forced to go twice to the right and then twice to the left (that is, RRLL), it fails to learn the problem. In this situation there are no differential cues for the second right turn and the second left turn unless the animal can derive such cues from his kinesthetic impulses. Apparently the rat is not able to do this. More will be said of this problem later.

More recently Hunter (20) has published an experiment that indicates that rats can learn a maze using kinesthetic impulses alone. Blinded animals were used, the maze was systematically rotated around its vertical axis, and the units of the maze were systematically interchanged from trial to trial. These conditions would seem to make impossible the use of either extra- or intramaze stimuli as differential cues. So far as sensory information goes, therefore, only kinesthetic cues remain.

Another attack upon this general problem was made by Macfarlane (35), who taught rats a maze in the usual fashion, and then filled the

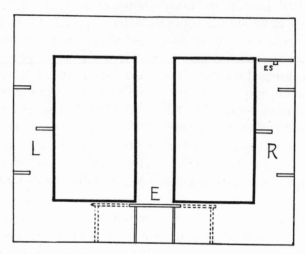

Fig. 6. The Temporal Maze. A stop, *ES*, may be inserted into either alley, *R* or *L*, to prevent the animal from completing a tour on the wrong side. The animal is inserted into the apparatus at *E*. The stop just below *E* may be shifted into the positions indicated by the dotted lines in order to force the animal into the central alley again after the completion of each tour. (After Hunter.)

maze with water in such a way that the animals had to swim. He found that this change caused very little disturbance in error score. The same procedure in the reverse order was also used, with the same result. He maintains that the change from running to swimming, or vice versa, must have been a change in the kinesthetic pattern, and that, therefore, if kinesthesis was effective in guiding the animal, there should have been a disturbance.

Lashley and Ball (29) attempted to eliminate, by double hemi-sections of the cord in the cervical region, most of the proprioceptive impulses in rats that had learned a maze. They then retested these animals in the maze and found almost perfect retention. They believe that they eliminated or controlled all exteroceptive cues. They con-clude that the best explanation of their results is that the maze habit is controlled by some sort of central mechanism that will function independently of sensory cues. Ingebritsen (22) later performed a similar operation on rats before they had learned, and found that they could learn the maze as well as retain it, as Lashley and Ball had shown.

These various experiments indicate that the maze habit is far from being as simple as it was formerly conceived to be. To complicate the problem still further, there is evidence that the rat learns in some way the general location of the food box with reference to the starting box. This is shown by the fact that when physical obstacles are removed, it will go to the food over a path that it has never taken before, and that is, as near as possible, a straight path from the entrance to the food box. Dashiell (4), who has studied this phenomenon extensively, believes that it must have some sort of intraorganic basis.

Tolman is particularly partial to the sixth possibility listed above. In a long series of experiments he has contrasted "place-learning"

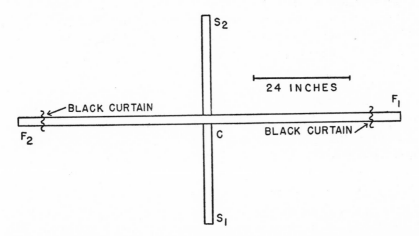

Fig. 7. **Elevated Maze Used in Place Versus Response Learning.** (Modified from Tolman, Ritchie, and Kalish.) S_1 and S_2: starting points; F_1 and F_2: food boxes; C: center point.

with "response-learning." In one of the simpler of these studies (55) he used an elevated maze of the design shown in Fig. 7. Sometimes the animal was started at S_1, and sometimes at S_2. The "response-learning" group is required to make a right-hand turn at C. Consequently if they started at S_1, they would receive food at F_1; if they started at S_2, food would be received at F_2. The "place-learning" group, on the other hand, always received food at F_1 regardless of whether they started at S_1 or S_2.

In this experiment the latter group learned quickly, but the "response-learning" group had great difficulty. Tolman believes that if there are marked extramaze cues, place-learning is simpler than response-learning. In the further development of this idea with a number of experimental techniques, he comes to the conclusion that animals may form "cognitive maps" and that they use these maps in getting from place to place. A further development of this point would verge into a discussion of theoretical points of view (see Chapter 8).

The problem is further complicated by what, for want of a better name, is called *preferential tendencies*. Thus, Yoshioka (63) and others have found that rats will group themselves into those that tend to go right, and those that tend to go left, at points where the path bifurcates.

There is also evidence that the making of one turn will tend to inhibit an immediate turn to the same side (5) (59). In other words, the occurrence of an act seems to inhibit its immediate repetition. Thus, a sequence of right or left turns would be harder to learn than an alternating sequence, other factors being equal.

MacCorquodale and Meehl (34) have shown that rats learn to stay out of blind alleys even when the reward factor does not enter into the situation. They believe that the blocking of the animal's forward progress and having to twist its body around in order to escape from the blind alley acts as a negative incentive. This may be related to some naturalistic tendency of the animal to stay out of situations in which it might be trapped by an enemy coming upon it from behind.

Experimental evidence is thus making it more and more apparent that maze learning is an extremely complex process. This fact is reflected in the increasing complexity of the theories designed to account for maze as well as other learning, which are discussed in another chapter.

Complex Learning Processes

The human being credits himself with what have traditionally been called "higher mental processes." Examples of these are: reasoning, imagery, thought, and judgment. Learning is a large factor in all of these processes and in them it presumably manifests itself in a complex manner. Therefore, learning will be considered from this point of view as found experimentally in animals.

Delayed reaction

The delayed-reaction experiment was suggested by Carr. It was Hunter (17), however, who put the suggestion into effect and who wrote the now classical monograph on the subject. The essential principle of this experiment is to present the animal with a stimulus to which it habitually or instinctively reacts, then to withdraw the stimulus and allow the animal to make the reaction in its absence. The idea is that since the stimulus is absent at the moment of reaction, the animal must be reacting to some substitute for that stimulus; hence the term "representative factor."

There are two general methods for testing delayed reactions, both of which were used by Hunter. They are the *indirect method* and the *direct method.* In the *indirect method,* the experimenter has to

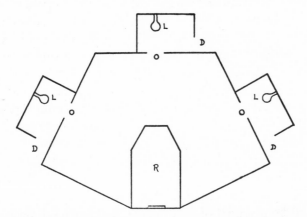

Fig. 8. Simplified Ground-plan Drawing of Delayed-reaction Apparatus Used by Hunter. A light *L* may be made to shine through any of the openings *O*. When the animal goes through the lighted opening, he will find food at position *D*. The animal is inserted in box *R*, which has glass sides so that he can see which opening is lighted. If the animal attempts to go through an opening that is not lighted, he will find his path obstructed by movable blocks (not shown here).

set up in the animal an association between the stimulus and the reaction before he can start on the delayed-reaction experiment. Figure 8 shows the ground plan of the three-choice apparatus that Hunter used with his animals. In this particular experiment, light was used as the stimulus. The animal was taught to go to the lighted opening to get his food. Thus the lighted opening became the signal for food. When the animal had learned this association, a light at one of the openings was turned on and then off while the animal was still confined in the release cage. After a given interval of time had elapsed, the animal was released to determine whether it would go immediately to the door that it had last seen lit. The doors are illuminated in a random order so the animal cannot react correctly by learning to go always to a certain position.

In the case of the *direct method,* the animal, by virtue of its hereditary constitution or past experience, already has a reaction to the stimulus. Therefore, the experimenter need not spend time in preliminary training to form this association. Hunter used this method with some of the children whom he studied. He set three boxes before a child and let the child see him drop a favorite plaything into one of the boxes. The child's attention was then otherwise engaged until the specified time had elapsed. It was then allowed to approach the boxes, the test being whether the child would reach into the box into which it had seen the plaything dropped. It was, of course, not allowed to see into the boxes. This direct method can be successfully used with the higher animals such as monkeys, apes, and man, but is not very practicable with animals lower in the scale.

In a delayed-reaction experiment there are two important questions to be considered. First, what is the maximum interval that may separate the presentation of the stimulus and the reaction without seriously decreasing the correctness of the reaction? Second, how is the animal able to bridge the interval; that is, what "representative factors" does it use?

The question of the length of delay is the less interesting of the two and will be disposed of first. There is no general answer to this query because the maximal delay under one set of conditions may be quite different from the maximal delay under another set. In other words, the length of delay is partially a function of the experimental conditions.

In his experiment described above, Hunter found that the maximal delay for the rat was ten seconds. In an experiment by Honzik (12), the rat was shown to be able to delay for at least 45 seconds. Honzik's apparatus is shown in Fig. 9. In this apparatus, a white curtain indicates the correct door, and a black the incorrect. In a comparison of the two experiments, this is probably a difference of minor importance.

A second difference of much greater significance is the fact that the animals were allowed to run toward the white curtain in their delay trials. They could not, however, in these trials, push aside the curtain, because it was backed by a wooden block. As soon as an animal had made the reaction to the curtain, the screen was lowered and a black curtain substituted for the white one. At the end of the

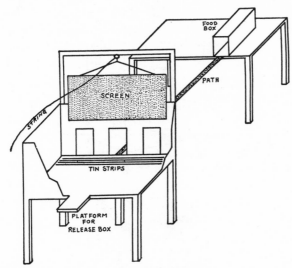

Fig. 9. Delayed-reaction Apparatus as Used by Honzik. The path to the food box shown leading from the middle door can, of course, be moved to any of the three openings. The tin strips were used to give the rats an electric shock if they made an incorrect response.

delay period the screen was raised. If the animal could in some way remember where he had last seen the white curtain, he would be able to make the correct reaction. Honzik believes that this running toward the stimulus in the delay trials gave the animals the following advantages: (*a*) it could be made certain that the rat had actually received the stimulus, and (*b*) the running toward the stimulus would probably also reinforce the stimulus and hence enhance the animal's ability, after the delay, to react correctly to the place where it had been.

McCord (40) has devised conditions that show a still longer delay by the rat. He used the apparatus diagrammed in Fig. 10. In this experiment the experimenter indicates the correct door to the animal by extending his arm through the doorway with the food cup in his hand. The animal was confined in a cage on the jumping stand during the delay period. With this arrangement delays of four minutes with 78 per cent accuracy were obtained and even longer delays gave results somewhat above the 25 per cent correct accounted for by chance.

The author believes that the longer delays were owing to "better structured psychological fields for the responding animals." This

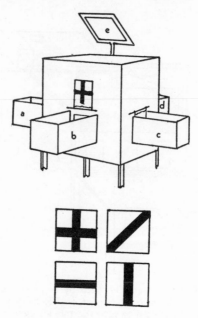

Fig. 10. A Diagram of the Apparatus Used by McCord (modified from McCord). The rat jumps from a round stand (not shown) in the middle of the apparatus to one of the food boxes *a, b, c, d,* from which he has last seen the experimenter's hand holding the food cup protruding through the door. During the delay period the rat is prevented from jumping by a circular restraining cage resting on top of the jumping platform. One door is shown open and the diagrams on the doors are shown below. There is a mirror at *e* through which the experimenter observes the animal.

terminology is of Gestalt origin. Presumably the better structure prevailed in three aspects of the animal's psychological field: (*a*) in the behavioral or motorial dimension, because the animals were required to jump rather than run, and because there was required a 90 per cent turn of the animal for each choice; (*b*) in the motivational dimension, because the animals were never fed during the training period except in the apparatus and were never allowed to feed except after a correct response, and also because the animal in this experiment is on a small platform from which it endeavors to escape; and (*c*) in the cognitive dimension, which would be influenced by the patterns on the doors. These patterns presumably serve to enrich the environment and give the animal more to hold on to.

Maier (36) taught rats to run up inclined paths from a floor to a table top for food. There were three of these paths, one of which he would allow the animal to traverse three times in succession. The rat was then removed to an adjoining room. At some later time, it was returned to the table top and allowed to run to the floor by a fourth path. The object was to see whether the animal would go around to the path that it had used in the last three trials and go up it to get food. Maier found that the rats were able to accomplish this after the elapse of several hours.

He called this delayed reaction. If it is accepted as such, the length of delays that he used successfully are the longest ever recorded for the rat. However, Tolman (52) has pointed out that this cannot be called a delayed reaction in the usual sense of the term, since the rat experiences the total situation preceding the delay, rather than a sign (for example, light) that merely signifies the total situation.

Loucks (32) has performed an experiment on "delayed alternation." He used an apparatus similar to the Hunter temporal maze (Fig. 6). In this apparatus, he required that the animal learn the single alternation; that is, $R L R L$ or $L R L R,$ depending upon which way the animal turned on the first trial of each day. Now it is obvious, of course, that the animal can be delayed between the trials, and since there are no differential cues in the external environment, it must remember which way it turned on the last trial to be able to turn correctly in the present one. The cue received by the animal from the preceding trial differs, of course, from the cues used by Hunter and Honzik in that it is something within the animal, and not imposed upon it from an outside source, for example, light. Loucks was able to use delay periods as long as five minutes. This method has also been used successfully with raccoons (6).

Cowles (3) secured maximum delays by allowing the animal to traverse the path to the goal once as the pre-delay presentation but without receiving food at the goal. This method gave maximum delays of about ten minutes, although Cowles did not aim at determining the outside limits of delay. If the animals were allowed to traverse only a part of the path to the goal at the pre-delay presentation, the delays were less but still greater than if the rats were confined in the delay chamber after the fashion of the Hunter experiment. It would seem then that the extent to which the animal is allowed to practice the response in the pre-delay presentation determines to an important degree his ability to make that response in the post-delay test.

With animals higher than the rat in the phylogenetic scale, longer delay periods can, as a rule, be used successfully. In Hunter's experiments, the dog was found capable of maximal delays of five minutes, and the raccoon responded correctly with a delay of 25 seconds. Older children were capable of delays of at least 25 minutes. It is quite probable that all these animals would be capable of longer delays under other conditions.

Methods of bridging the interval

The above brief summary of results with reference to the length of delay indicates that there is a rough correlation between the position of the animal in the phylogenetic scale, and the length of the interval that may elapse between stimulus and reaction without seriously affecting the accuracy of the latter. This fact is of great interest, but the question of how the various species bridge the gap is perhaps of greater significance, although the answer is much more difficult to discover.

However, there are some experimental data that are relevant to this inquiry. In Hunter's experiments, the rats and the dogs kept a gross bodily orientation. When the light was flashed, they would orient either their whole bodies or their heads in the direction of the light, and during the delay period they maintained their orientation. When they were released, they followed their noses, so to speak, and were able to go to the correct box. If this orientation was disturbed, the animals were unable to react correctly. The raccoons and the children, on the other hand, did not need to maintain the orientation in order to react correctly. This fact led Hunter to venture the theory that raccoons were capable of "sensory thought," or what is more commonly called "imageless thought." He indicates that this is a lower type of ability than thought with images, though the latter, of course, he will concede to children.

It has been shown, however, since Hunter's experiment, that even a rat is able to make a successful delay without gross bodily orientation. These results were obtained by Honzik (12), McAllister (39), and McCord (40), among others. Walton (56) has shown also that the dog need not maintain his orientation in order to delay successfully. Likewise, apes and monkeys rarely, if ever, maintain orientation during the period of delay.

However, there is another kind of bodily orientation, not an apparent one, that might occur in the animal. This orientation would consist in the maintenance of a muscular tension, the muscle in which the tension would be maintained varying with the position of the stimulus. The device would have to be such that it would not be disturbed by a shift in the gross bodily orientation, since at the moment of response the animal must necessarily be oriented, in the Hunter and similar types of apparatus, as he was when he received the stimulus.

It is hardly conceivable that a device of this sort could be used successfully to bridge the long delays with correct response that are found in the primates. However, with the rat, the longest delay with correct response has been a few minutes at the most (Maier's work excepted). Under these conditions it might work very well. A case in which it would not work is that of McCord's experiments (see Fig. 10). Since here the rat may be oriented toward any point on the circumference of a circle and can respond without reorienting to the position which obtained when the stimulus was given, it would be impossible to use a tension as a guide to correct responses.

In order to test the muscular-tension hypothesis in a situation where tension could conceivably be used, Loucks (32) gave his rats a general anaesthetic during the period of delay. If there was a muscular tension involved, it certainly would be destroyed by the relaxation of the muscles caused by the anaesthesia, and the animal would be unable to make correct responses. It was found, however, that the rats could respond correctly after the anaesthesia.

McAllister (39) likewise caused the animals to dig through sand during the period of delay, on the supposition that this activity would make it difficult to maintain a muscular tension. He found that the animals could react correctly under these conditions. It is apparent, therefore, that the evidence is very much against the maintenance of a differential muscular tension as a device used by the rat to bridge the delay in delayed reaction experiments.

It has been suggested that the bridging could be done by the use of symbolic representation of the pre-delay stimulus. An analysis of the delayed reaction experiment indicates that the ability to use symbolism by itself is not sufficient to solve the problem. Suppose that two boxes, one black, one white, are being used, and that the subject is able to think in words, "black" and "white." Suppose the food is put in the white box. The subject says to himself, "white."

Now he must either continue to make this response during the period of delay or he must reinstate the response when it is time to choose a box. If the delay is a long one it is hardly likely that the response will be continued during the delay period. There must be, therefore, some way of reinstating the response, "white" at the end of the delay. Responses are not reinstated spontaneously, that is, without causal antecedents. What could the causes be? What produced the response in the first place? Of course, it was the visual stimuli resulting from the experimenter's dropping food into the white box. These stimuli, however, are only a part, the most effective part to be sure, of a large complex of stimuli. The response, "white," is instigated in the first place not only by the whiteness of the box but also by stimuli coming from the experimenter's hand, the food, the relative position of the two boxes, and so forth, including intra-organic stimuli. The symbol, white, stands not only for the whiteness of the box but for a complex of which whiteness is only a part. After the delay period has passed and it is time to open a box this complex that originally excited the response "white" has been subtracted from and added to. The visual stimuli from food and hand are gone and if the boxes have been shifted, the stimuli depending upon the relative positions of the boxes are also gone. In addition there are stimuli arising from the opening of the restraining device, the change in position of boxes, and so on. The symbolism, whiteness, can only be useful to the animal if it can be effectively reinstated by this changed complex of stimuli. The ease of performing the delayed reaction experiment, therefore, will depend not only upon the use of symbolism or other representative factors, but also upon the facility of the animal in reinstating the symbol in response to a changed stimulus nexus, assuming that the symbolic response is not constantly maintained during the delay period. From this point of view, other factors being equal, enrichment in the similarity of stimuli before and after the delay period should increase the ease with which the problem is solved.

Perhaps it is premature to speak of symbolic processes in animals. Even for human beings this subject has not received satisfactory treatment. Seward (46), after giving his definition of symbolism, considers a number of experiments done with animals. He tries to determine if the animal would have to use symbolism as defined in order to solve the problem. He considers that only under special conditions of running the delayed reaction experiment would there be the slightest need to assume that the animal is using symbolism.

These conditions would seem to have been met in MacCorquodale's (33) modification of McCord's experiment. The latter believed that the diagrams on the doors helped the animal to make a long delay but MacCorquodale showed that the animals did not follow the diagrams when they were interchanged during the delay period. That is to say, if a diagram, for example the plus sign, in a certain doorway was designated as the correct symbol in the pre-delay presentation, but during the delay the symbol was moved to another doorway, the animals continued to jump to the pre-delay position rather than to the pre-delay diagram. If the rats had responded correctly to the diagram it would seem that symbolism would have been indicated according to Seward's analysis of the problem.

MacCorquodale's experiment stimulated Handlon (10) to do a further modification of McCord's work. His results were similar to those obtained by MacCorquodale except that he insists that the animals can be made to react to the diagrams on the doors if the problem is made difficult enough through increasing the length of delay or removing the animal from the apparatus during the delay period.

It will be noted, however, that he presented the animals with the diagrams during the pre-delay period and simply replaced them with blank doors for the post-delay trial. Under the long delays the accuracy for the animals decreased as compared to what it was when the diagrams were not replaced. This is not sufficient evidence that the diagrams were used as *discriminative* cues. Rather, it may be simply an indication that a change in the stimulus complex will disturb the behavior of the animals. If the general illumination of the room had been changed or if a loud noise had been introduced, the experimenter might have gotten similar results, yet neither of these stimuli could be considered *discriminative* cues. It is not unreasonable to suppose that an increase in difficulty of a problem would be accompanied by a greater disturbance from a change in the stimulus complex. For example, unusual noises might not disturb a person doing light reading but if he were reading and trying to comprehend some very obtuse material, such noises could have a very upsetting effect.

If Handlon wished to investigate the effectiveness of the door diagrams as *discriminative* cues it is surprising that he did not use the ordinary method of determining if the behavior of the animals could be guided by the cues. The way to do this is, of course, to change the position of the diagrams during the delay period.

Since Handlon has not proved that the animals were using the diagrams on the doors as discriminative cues his results do not satisfy Seward's requirements for the presence of symbolic behavior. However, in the next chapter results will be given for primates that make it practically obligatory that symbolic behavior be attributed to these animals.

Neither MacCorquodale nor Handlon designed their experiments in an optimum manner for the investigation of the effectiveness of nonpositional cues in the delayed-reaction experiment. A more satisfactory procedure would be to shift the diagrams during the delay period when the minimal delays were being used. In other words, every effort should be taken to minimize the positional factor and to force the animals to rely on nonpositional cues. Once having learned to react on the basis of the positional factor, it is not surprising that the animal should have difficulty in making a change.

Although the delayed-reaction experiment was originally designed to test for imagery or some other "higher mental process" in the animal, there is now a tendency to regard it as simply a discrimination problem to be learned in one presentation. The argument is based primarily on the results of experiments in which the pre-delay presentation is made progressively more similar to the post-delay test. As this similarity increases, the maximum delay increases. Presumably, as the pre-delay presentation is made more similar to the post-delay trial the influence of secondary reinforcers is increased and this factor accounts for the successful increase of length of delay.

Only Maier (36) has given primary reinforcement, that is, food, at the pre-delay presentation, and he got extremely long delays for the rat. As already indicated, Tolman does not think that Maier's experiment should be called delayed reaction, but a thorough analysis will perhaps show no fundamental difference between it and the typical delayed-reaction experiment.

The double-alternation problem

We have had occasion to mention several times the single-alternation problem in the temporal maze (on p. 160 is shown a ground-plan diagram of the apparatus). It will be remembered that in the single-alternation problem the animal is required to make in succeeding trials the following sequence of turns: $R L R L$, and so forth. Hunter

(19) also has used the double alternation, in which the endeavor is made to teach the animal the $R R L L R R L L$ sequence of turns.

A little consideration will show that there is a significant difference between the single- and double-alternation problems. In the former, a turn to the right presents a cue to the animal that in some way determines his turn to the left in the succeeding trial. Likewise, his turn to the left presents cues that determine his turn to the right in the next trial. In the latter, the turn to the right must at one time present cues to the turn to the right, and at another time (the second, for example) cues to turn to the left. This is, of course, impossible, as it is inconceivable that identical causes should produce two different effects. The same situation obtains for the turns to the left.

Under such conditions, therefore, if the animal is to learn the double alternation problem he must supplement the cues received on his tours by some other factor, or factors, that may act in a differential manner. Hunter suggests the following possibilities: There may be (a) a cumulative piling up in the nervous system of the retained effects of the responses already made; or (b), a symbolic process, as, for example, "the human subject would have no difficulty with double alternation, if he supplemented his responses with the verbal behavior, 'It is two, two, I first go two right, then two left, etc.'"

Hunter is inclined toward the latter hypothesis. In his original work with the rat (18), he found that this animal could not learn the double-alternation problem even with the smallest possible number of trials in the series, namely, $R R L L$. He had already found that the rat could not do the delayed-reaction experiment unless it kept the gross bodily orientation. In a later experiment (19), he found that raccoons could do the double alternation to the extent of $R R L L$, but could not extend the series to $R R L L R R L L$. He is inclined, therefore, to believe that the raccoon, but not the rat, can use a symbolic process. The cat (23) and dog (24) can also respond $R R L L$ but not beyond.

Recent work (21) using a double-alternation pattern in a spatial maze, but so arranged that there would be no constant orientational cues, has indicated that some rats can, with great difficulty, learn the double-alternation sequence. Hunter and Hill (21) feel that this can only mean that the animals are using a symbolic process, however rudimentary.

It has also been shown that the rat can learn to press two levers in a double alternation pattern (45). Seward, in the article previously mentioned, does not feel that it is necessary to assume symbolic processes in order to account for double alternation.

The multiple-choice problem

The essential feature of the multiple-choice apparatus is a series of similar compartments. These compartment are not all used at any one trial, but they are used in groups of a given number, let us say, for example, groups of three. At one trial, the three compartments on the right end of the series of ten are open; at another trial, those on the left end; at another, those in the middle, and so on. Of the group of three open compartments, only one contains food. This one, however, in any particular experiment, always bears the same spatial relationship to the open compartments. For example, the food-bearing compartment may always be the left one in the group of three. In this case, therefore, the problem for the animal is to learn always to go to the left compartment of the group of three open compartments, no matter where that group may be located in the total series. This method was first used in principle by Hamilton (9) and later developed by Yerkes (62).

It is obvious that the behavior of the animal in this problem must necessarily be of the trial-and-error sort, at least in the beginning, because there is no "insightful" way in which it can determine the compartment containing the food. Later, of course, it may suddenly grasp the system that the experimenter is using and after that make few, if any, errors. This phenomenon would be indicated by a sudden drop in the learning curve.

Abstractions and generalizations

The question to be considered here is whether an infra-human animal is able to abstract from a number of somewhat similar situations an element or several elements to which it will learn to make a reaction in such a way that if it is presented with a new situation containing these elements, it will react as it did in the training situations. If it is capable of doing so, there is justification for declaring that the animal has formed a concept.

The essential nature of concept formation in the human being will give us the cues concerning the direction that experiments with concept formation in animals must take. Fields (7) paraphrased a quotation from Hull (13) that clearly states this process in the human child:

A young child finds himself in a certain situation (white equilateral triangle, apex up; area, 28 square centimeters), reacts to it by approach, and hears it called "triangle." In a somewhat different situation (white equilateral triangle, apex down; area, 28 square centimeters), he hears that called "triangle." Later, in a still different situation (black equilateral triangle, rotated 30 degrees; area, 55 square centimeters), he hears that called "triangle" also. There is no obvious label as to the essential nature of the situation, which precipitates at each new appearance a more or less acute problem as to the proper reaction. And so the process goes on with right-angle, isosceles, and scalene triangles, until the day finally comes on which the child makes the specific language response, "triangle," whenever any of the foregoing classes of figures are presented. This child now has a meaning for the shape "triangle." Upon examination, this meaning is found to be actually a characteristic more or less common to all triangles, and not common to squares, circles, etc. But to the child, the process of arriving at this meaning, or concept, has been largely unconscious. The formation of the concept has never been an end deliberately sought for itself. It has always been the means to an end—the supremely absorbing task of physical and social reaction and adjustment.

If this is the way in which the child learns a concept, what must be the procedure in investigating conceptual learning in animals? Obviously, the language response in the case of the animal is not available; but is this necessary? Not at all! Another type of response may easily be substituted, for example, an approaching response. Assume that the animal is to be taught the concept of triangularity. It will be necessary to present the animal with a triangle and some other shape, a circle, for example, to be discriminated from it. When the animal learns this discrimination the triangle is rotated slightly and again the discrimination is established. Then the triangle is rotated a few more degrees and the discrimination again established, and so on with many changes in the triangle in many respects, such as size, brightness, color—if the animal has color vision—shape, and so forth. When the animal has learned to react positively to all these triangles, figures are presented to him that he has never experienced before but that include the characteristics of triangularity, for example, three small circles as arranged in the form of a triangle, one circle at each corner. If the animal continues to react positively to these figures without further training, it is a fair assumption that a concept of triangularity has been formed.

The above procedure is essentially that which Fields (7) used with the rat as a subject, and he comes to the conclusion, "When white rats are given a training period specifically designed to provide a large number of different 'triangle experiences,' the rats are able to perfect a type of behavior which is fully described by the implications inherent, in our case, in the term 'concept.' "

It should be noted that other experiments also might be used to indicate that animals are capable of abstractions; for example, the experiments showing that animals will react to "larger than" or "brighter than" relationships. The animal may be said to have abstracted such a relationship from the situation in the training series in such a way that the reaction to this relationship will occur again with stimuli of a different absolute size, or brightness, and so forth.

The use of tools

The use of tools has generally been considered one of the outstanding achievements of the human being. Whether animals can use tools is a question for the animal psychologist to answer. But first, what is a tool? For the purposes of this discussion, a tool is defined as any manipulable object used by the animal as an intermediary link between itself and its objective. By this definition, it is apparent that tool-using is widespread among animals. Some examples are: the use of wood shavings to secure water by the rat (8); the use of a lever by cats to secure food placed upon one end of the lever by the experimenter (1); and the use of boxes or other objects by apes to secure food otherwise out of reach (28).

Reasoning

This term has come into the literature of experimental animal psychology chiefly through the work of Maier (37). He states, "The term *reasoning* implies that something new has been brought about, and that in some way, past experiences have been manipulated. It, therefore, seems that behavior patterns made up of two isolated experiences characterize what is meant by behavior which is the product of reasoning" (38).

With this statement in mind, two of Maier's many experiments may be examined. The first experiment uses three tables that differ from each other in several respects. These tables are connected by elevated pathways, as shown in Fig. 11. The rat is allowed an opportunity to explore this situation and to run from one table to another over the pathways, thus becoming familiar with the experimental situation. This period of exploration is called "Experience 1."

The animal is now removed to one of the tables (for example, X, Fig. 11) and fed a small amount of food on that table. This is "Experience 2." It is now removed to one of the other tables, perhaps Y. Now if the rat combined "Experience 1," that is, knowledge of

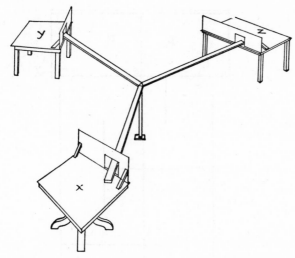

Fig. 11. Diagram Showing Arrangement of Tables in Maier's Experiment on "Reasoning."

the pathways, with "Experience 2," it will go directly from Table Y to Table X, where it has just been fed and where it will receive more food. The problem can be varied from trial to trial by giving the preliminary food on different tables and also by starting the animal from different tables.

An experiment of a more complex nature was also used. The layout of the experimental situation in this case is shown in Fig. 12. A and B represent the two halves of a large table. These halves are separated by a cardboard partition (o-p) over which the rats, with difficulty, may scramble. A maze of the elevated-pathway type starts in the small box at point X and ends in the wire cage at point Y. Before this maze and the box and cage are connected to the table, however, the rats are allowed to explore the table top thoroughly and to learn to scale the partition. When this is accomplished, they are taught the maze by being put in the box at X, from which point they are allowed to run to the food in the cage at Y.

After learning this, the rat is placed on the table at point *M*, with the food, of course, inside the cage. This begins the test trial. As is to be expected, the animal will spend a good deal of time trying to get into the cage, which is impossible. Eventually, the animal will scale the wall, and now comes the critical point. Will the animal run directly over to the box at *X* and enter it in order to get on the

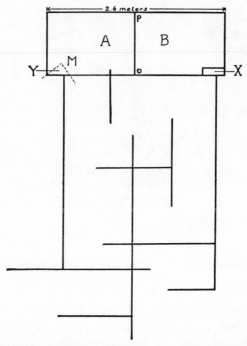

Fig. 12. The Combination of Table and Maze Used by Maier in Experiments on Rats.
The table is divided into halves *A* and *B* by the partition *o-p*.

maze so that it may run around to the food at *Y*? Maier found that his rats did go almost directly to the box, after scaling the wall. They scrambled into the box, although they had never entered it before on their own initiative, and ran around the maze to the food.

The discerning reader will realize that the device of describing these experiments in terms of Experiences 1 and 2 can equally well be applied to the Tolman and Honzik experiment. In that case, Experience 1 is the acquaintanceship of the rat with the various pathways to the goal. Experience 2 is the finding of the block at point *B* in a common part of Paths *1* and *2*. The rat relates these two experiences and takes Path *3*. The ease with which the same description may be applied to both the "insight" and the "reasoning" experiments raises the question of whether both terms are needed. As a matter of fact, a little further analysis makes some of these experiments seem remarkably like the delayed-reaction experiment with a minimal delay.

Conclusion

It has been impossible to attempt an exhaustive account of learning in the infra-primates in the space of one chapter. A selection of topics has been made, but for each of these topics much more could be written. Some of the topics were selected to give the reader the vocabulary and mechanics for further study of learning. Others were selected because of their fundamental importance to an understanding of learning.

Since the previous revision of this book, there has been a marked change in the type of experimental problem done by the students of learning. Previously the vast majority of the researches were on the factors that may affect the efficiency of learning. During the past ten years the great bulk of the research material is related to the problem of the theory of learning and behavior. This revolution has been based on the movement to develop a systematic theory of behavior led by Tolman (52), Skinner (47), and especially Hull (15).

It is the feeling of these men and many others that the days when the student in psychology starts out his research with the "I-wonder-what-would-happen-if" attitude should be numbered. If psychology is to make any significant advance in the future, researches must be planned and integrated in the light of some comprehensive system of approach.

In psychology, as in other sciences, there will always be room for those who wish to shoot in the dark on the chance of making a lucky hit, but the majority of research men will wish to trade their shotguns for rifles and have their target at least dimly in sight.

Bibliography

1. Adams, D. K., Experimental Studies of Adaptive Behavior in Cats, *Compar. Psychol. Monogr.*, 1929, 6, No. 27, pp. 1-166.
2. Blodgett, H. C., The Effect of the Introduction of Reward upon the Maze Performance of Rats, *Univ. Calif. Publications in Psychol.*, 1929, 4, 113-134.

3. Cowles, J. T., "Delayed Response" as Tested by Three Methods and Its Relation to Other Learning Situations, *J. Psychol.*, 1940, **9**, 103-130.

4. Dashiell, J. F., Direction Orientation in Maze Running by the White Rat, *Compar. Psychol. Monogr.*, 1930, **7**.

5. Dennis, W., Spontaneous Alternation in Rats as an Indicator of the Persistence of Stimulus Effects, *J. Compar. Psychol.*, 1939, **28**, 305-312.

6. Elder, J. H., and Nissen, H. W., Delayed Alternation in Raccoons, *J. Compar. Psychol.*, 1933, **16**, 117-135.

7. Fields, P. E., Studies in Concept Formation, *Compar. Psychol. Monogr.*, 1932, **9**, No. 2, pp. 1-70.

8. Fritz, M. F., A Note on the Use of Tools by the White Rat, *J. Genet. Psychol.*, 1930, **27**, 330-331.

9. Hamilton, G. V., A Study of Trial-and-Error Reactions in Mammals, *J. Animal Behav.*, 1911, **1**, 33-66.

10. Handlon, Joseph H. Jr., Perceptual Factors in Delayed Response, *Univ. Calif. Pub. Psychol.*, 1950, **5**, 289-320.

11. Heron, W. T., Internal Stimuli and Learning, *J. Compar. and Physiol. Psychol.*, 1949, **42**, 486-492.

12. Honzik, C. H., Delayed Reaction in Rats, *Univ. Calif. Pub. Psychol.*, 1931, **4**, 307-318.

13. Hull, C. L., Quantitative Aspects of the Evolution of Concepts, *Psychol. Monogr.*, 1920, **28**, No. 1, pp. 1-85.

14. ——— Differential Habituation to Internal Stimuli in the Albino Rat, *J. Compar. Psychol.*, 1934, **16**, 255-273.

15. ——— *Principles of Behavior.* New York: Appleton-Century Co., 1943.

16. ——— The Problem of Primary Stimulus Generalization, *Psychol. Rev.*, 1947, **54**, 120-134.

17. Hunter, W. S., The Delayed Reaction in Animals and Children, *Behav. Monogr.*, 1912, **2**, No. 1, pp. 1-85.

18. ——— The Temporal Maze and Kinaesthetic Sensory Processes in the White Rat, *Psychobiology*, 1920, **2**, 1-17.

19. ——— The Behavior of Raccoons in a Double Alternation Temporal Maze, *J. Genet. Psychol.*, 1928, **35**, 374-388.

20. ——— A Kinesthetically Controlled Maze Habit in the Rat, *Science*, 1940, **91**, 267-269.

21. Hunter, W. S. and Hall, B. E., Double Alternation Behavior of the White Rat in a Spatial Maze, *J. Compar. Psychol.*, 1941, **32**, 253-266.

22. Ingebritsen, O. C., Maze Learning After Lesion in the Cervical Cord, *J. Compar. Psychol.*, 1932, **14**, 279-294.

23. Karn, H. W., The Behavior of Cats on the Double Alternation Problem in the Temporal Maze, *J. Compar. Psychol.*, 1939, **27**, 201-208.

24. Karn, H. W. and Malamud, H. R., The Behavior of Dogs on the

Double Alternation Problem in the Temporal Maze, *J. Compar. Psychol.*, 1939, **27**, 461-466.

25. Kendler, Howard H., An Investigation of Latent Learning in a T-Maze, *J. Compar. and Physiol. Psychol.*, 1947, **40**, 265-270.

26. Kendler, Howard H. and Mencher, Helen Chamberlain, The Ability of Rats to Learn the Location of Food When Motivated by Thirst—An Experimental Reply to Leeper, *J. Exper. Psychol.*, 1948, **38**, 82-88.

27. Kinamann, A. J., Mental Life of Two Macacus Rhesus Monkeys in Captivity, *Amer. J. Psychol.*, 1902, **13**, 98-148 and 171-218.

28. Köhler, W., *The Mentality of Apes*. New York: Harcourt Brace & Company, Inc., 1925.

29. Lashley, K. S. and Ball, J., Spinal Conduction and Kinaesthetic Sensitivity in the Maze Habit, *J. Compar. Psychol.*, 1929, **9**, 71-105.

30. Lashley, K. S., and Wade, M., The Pavlovian Theory of Generalization, *Psychol. Rev.*, 1946, **53**, 72-87.

31. Leeper, R., The Role of Motivation in Learning: A Study of the Phenomenon of Differential Motivational Control of the Utilization of Habits, *J. Genet. Psychol.*, 1935, **46**, 3-40.

32. Loucks, R. B., Efficacy of the Rat's Motor Cortex in Delayed Alternation, *J. Compar. Neurol.*, 1931, **53**, 511-567.

33. MacCorquodale, K., An Analysis of Certain Cues in the Delayed Response, *J. Compar. and Physiol. Psychol.*, 1947, **40**, 239-253.

34. ———— and Meehl, P. E., On the Elimination of Cul Entries without Obvious Reinforcement, *J. Compar. and Physiol. Psychol.* (In press).

35. Macfarlane, D. A., The Role of Kinaesthesia in Maze Learning, *Univ. Calif. Pub. Psychol.*, 1930, **4**, 277-305.

36. Maier, N. R. F., Delayed Reactions and Memory in Rats, *J. Genet. Psychol.*, 1929, **36**, 538-550.

37. ———— Reasoning in White Rats, *Compar. Psychol. Monogr.*, 1929, **6**, No. 3, pp. 1-93.

38. ———— Reasoning and Learning, *Psychol. Rev.*, 1931, **38**, 332-346.

39. McAllister, W. G., A Further Study of the Delayed Reaction in the Albino Rat, *Compar. Psychol. Monogr.*, 1932, **8**, No. 37, pp. 1-103.

40. McCord F., The Delayed Reaction and Memory in Rats. I. Length of Delay, *J. Compar. Psychol.*, 1939, **27**, 1-37.

41. Meehl, Paul E., and MacCorquodale, Kenneth, A Further Study of Latent Learning in the T-Maze, *J. Compar. and Physiol. Psychol.*, 1948, **41**, 372-396.

42. Muenzinger, K. F., Motivation in Learning. II. The Function of Electric Shock for Right and Wrong Responses in Human Subjects, *J. Exper. Psychol.*, 1934, **17**, 267-277 and 439-448.

43. Pechstein, L. A., and Brown, F. D., An Experimental Analysis of the Alleged Criteria of Insight Learning, *J. Educat. Psychol.*, 1939, **30**, 38-52.

44. Perin, C. T., A Quantitative Investigation of the Delay-of-Reinforcement Gradient, *J. Exper. Psychol.*, 1943, **32**, 37-51.

45. Schlosberg, H., and Katz, A., Double Alternation Lever-Pressing in the White Rat, *Amer. J. Psychol.*, 1943, **56**, 274-282.

46. Seward, John P., The Sign of a Symbol: A Reply to Professor Allport, *Psychol. Rev.*, 1948, **55**, 277-296.

47. Skinner, B. F., *The Behavior of Organisms: An Experimental Analysis*. New York: D. Appleton-Century Co., 1938.

48. Small, W. S., An Experimental Study of the Mental Processes of the Rat, *Amer. J. Psychol.*, 1899, **11**, 133-165.

49. Spence, K. W., The Role of Secondary Reinforcement in Delayed Reward Learning, *Psychol. Rev.*, 1947, **54**, 1-8.

50. Thorndike, E. L., Animal Intelligence, An Experimental Study of the Associative Processes in Animals, *Psychol. Rev. Monogr.*, Supplement ii, 1898, No. 4, pp. 1-109.

51. ——— *The Fundamentals of Learning*. New York: Columbia University Press, 1932.

52. Tolman, E. C., *Purposive Behavior in Animals and Men*. New York: The Century Co., 1932.

53. ——— and Honzik, C. H., "Insight" in Rats, *Univ. Calif. Pub. Psychol.*, 1930, **4**, 215-232.

54. Tolman, E. C., Hall, C. S., and Bretnall, E. P., A Disproof of the Law of Effect and a Substitution of the Laws of Emphasis, Motivation and Disruption, *J. Exper. Psychol.*, 1932, **15**, 601-614.

55. Tolman, E. C., Ritchie, B. F., and Kalish, D., Studies in Spatial Learning. II. Place Learning versus Response Learning, *J. Exper. Psychol.*, 1946, **36**, 221-229.

56. Walton, A. C., The Influence of Diverting Stimuli During Delayed Reaction, *J. Animal Behav.*, 1915, **5**, 259-291.

57. Warden, C. J., and Diamond, S., A Preliminary Study of the Effect of Delayed Punishment on Learning in the White Rat, *J. Genet. Psychol.*, 1931, **39**, 455-462.

58. Watson, J. B., *Behavior: An Introduction to Comparative Psychology*. New York: Henry Holt & Company, Inc., 1914.

59. Weitz, J., and Wakeman, M. L., "Spontaneous" Alternation and the Conditioned Response, *J. Compar. Psychol.*, 1941, **32**, 551-562.

60. Wiley, L. E., and Wiley, A. M., Studies in the Learning Function, *Psychometrika*, 1937, **2**, 1-19 and 107-120.

61. Wolfe, John B., The Effect of Delayed Reward upon Learning in the White Rat, *J. Compar. Psychol.*, 1934, **17**, 1-21.

62. Yerkes, R. M., and Coburn, C. A., A Study of the Behavior of the Pig Sus Scrofa by the Multiple-Choice Method, *J. Animal Behav.*, 1915, **5**, 185-225.

63. Yoshioka, J. G., Frequency Factor in Habit Formation, *J. Compar. Psychol.*, 1930, **11**, 37-49.

CHAPTER 7

Primate Learning

HARRY F. HARLOW
University of Wisconsin

The ultimate goal of the psychology of learning is the discovery of the laws governing acquisition and retention in the human organism. If all the desirable experimental controls could be imposed upon man, he would make the most satisfactory subject for the investigation of learning. Unfortunately, human beings cannot be maintained in laboratories for all or even substantial portions of their lives. Outside the laboratory, their manner of living and their learning experiences can in no way be rigidly limited. Nor can they be induced to accept more than modest alterations in their internal environment and anatomical integrity.

For these reasons theoretical psychologists have sought primary recourse to other animals in the hope that study of their behavior might supply data yielding generalizations applicable to man. Serious dangers, of course, are attendant upon such an approach, since the laws governing the behavior of a particular species may not only be inapplicable, but even inimical to comprehending the behavior of another species. Maximal advantage and minimal risk are involved if closely related species possessing similar sensory, motor, and homeostatic mechanisms are chosen. The animals whose behavior is most likely to aid us in understanding human learning are those belonging to man's own order, the primates, particularly the anthropoid apes and monkeys. Indeed, after we have thoroughly explored and analyzed the learning of our closest phyletic relatives, we may be able to make intelligent guesses as to the applicability of learning data obtained from dogs, cats, rats, and cockroaches, to the learning behavior of monkeys, anthropoid apes, and human beings.

The emphasis on the conditioned response paradigm in the recent literature of comparative psychology has directed psychological research toward problems that suggest greater concern of the learning theorists with rat learning per se than with the implications of such learning for a broad theory applicable to higher organisms, including man. The Skinner Box and the single-unit T-maze are admirable apparatus for the study of certain simple kinds of learning problems—but the kinds are extremely limited. Neo-Behaviorists have promised that thorough analysis of the conditioned response would reveal that more complicated problems fall within the schema. But 40 years of intensive work on the conditioned response and simple discrimination problems have thus far cast little illumination on the nature of the more complex learning tasks that challenge man. Actually, simple problems usually permit only simple analysis. Far more precise and effective analysis can probably be carried out on tasks of greater complexity than the conditioned response and spatial discrimination. It is the belief of the writer that there is far greater hope of understanding the simple learning phenomena from study of the moderately complex than there is of understanding the complex from study of the simple.

The purpose of the following section is to present a survey of some of the problems that can be solved by subhuman primates and may, perhaps, be solved by various subprimate organisms, and to present these in a classificatory system that will indicate certain of the relationships among the problems as complexity increases. Such a survey is designed to put conditioned response learning and spatial discrimination learning in proper perspective with relation to a wide variety of other problems.

Representative Learning Problems

Conditioned response learning

Conditioning has been little studied in the subhuman primates, although several investigations indicate that conditioned responses may be rapidly formed and well retained by these animals. There is no reason to believe, however, that monkeys and apes condition more efficiently than many subprimate species. The particular value of primates as subjects lies not so much in the rapidity with which they acquire habits as in the complexity and range of learning problems they can master.

In an investigation that demonstrated ready reversal of conditioned stimulus–unconditioned stimulus relationships in monkeys, Harlow (10) conditioned his subjects with fear- or avoidance-producing unconditioned stimuli in five trials or less. Almost equally efficient conditioning of monkeys was reported by Harris (19), who found that fewer than 10 to 12 paired presentations of a tone and a weak electric shock produced unmistakable conditioned responses measured by recording or observing movement of a stabilimeter (see Fig. 1). The main purpose of this experiment was the determination of absolute thresholds for a wide range of frequencies, rather than the discovery of the speed with which such conditioned responses could be established.

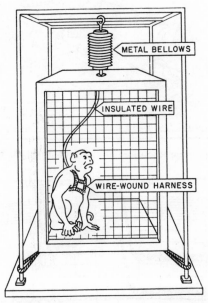

Fig. 1. **Stabilimeter Used in Testing Auditory Conditioned Responses by Monkeys.**

Such data are not meant to imply that all conditioned responses are formed readily in monkeys. In a study reported by Hilgard and Marquis (20), conditioning of the corneal reflex, originally elicited by a puff of air, to the substitute stimulus, light, was continuous and orderly, but slow. After 300 paired-stimulus presentations, the four monkeys had still not attained an average of 80 per cent frequency of response. Slowness of acquisition in this instance may have resulted from the nature of this particular reflex or from the physical restraint imposed by the apparatus. Figure 2 schematizes the apparatus and presents a sample photochronographic record of a conditioned eyelid response.

The attempts to condition avoidance responses in infant chimpanzees have produced results comparable to those found in human infant conditioning studies. Riesen (36) subjected one chimpanzee at two days of age to mild shock upon contact with a large yellow and black striped disc attached to a rod and presented by the experimenter. After a month of daily training, the infant still showed no evidence of learned avoidance. Normal seven-month-old chim-

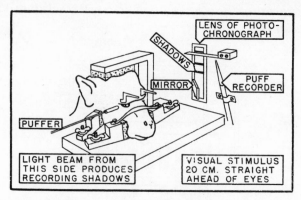

Fig. 2a. Photochronographic Recording of Conditioned Eyelid Responses by Monkeys.

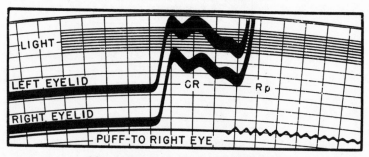

CR-CONDITIONED RESPONSE
Rp-UNCONDITIONED RESPONSE TO PUFF

Fig. 2b. Photochronographic Record of Conditioned Eyelid Response.

panzees, on the other hand, showed avoidance after one or two shocks from the disc. Two more seven-month-old animals—one raised in complete darkness and another in an environment permitting only homogeneous, unpatterned light—were shocked twice a day for six and nine days, respectively, before showing conditioned whimpering responses, and 15 and 13 days before showing consistent avoidance responses. These findings on visually deprived animals suggest the importance of experience in determining ease of acquisition in this simple learning situation and are consistent with results on initial learning experiences of monkeys with the more complex problems discussed in the next sections.

It is apparent from these various investigations that primates condition rapidly under some conditions and with great difficulty under others. There is no evidence at the present time to indicate that any measure of efficiency of conditioned response acquisition will separate primates from subprimates. More effective differentiating criteria are the variety and complexity of learning situations that the organism is able to master.

Spatial discrimination learning

Spatial discriminations are taught by rewarding only the responses made to a particular positional cue among alternate available positional cues. In the simplest spatial discrimination problems, rats are trained to choose either the right or left alley in a one-unit

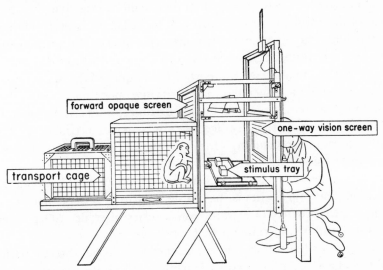

Fig. 3. Wisconsin General Test Apparatus. Correct response to right-position habit is illustrated.

T-maze, and primates are trained to select the right or left object of two identical objects covering foodwells. Figure 3 illustrates correct response by a monkey trained on a position discrimination. The Wisconsin General Test Apparatus is depicted in this drawing. Failure of the test-wise monkey to solve such problems in a single trial is the exception, not the rule. Efficient performance on spatial discrimination problems has been reported for subprimate animals.

Nonspatial discrimination learning

The problems thus far described are simple, in that learning may be accomplished with little or no interference of stimulus cues. Simple conditioned response learning theoretically involves no trained stimulus interference inasmuch as only one stimulus (the conditioned stimulus) elicits a response that is reinforced. Other persistent stimuli in the situation are present before, during, and after reinforcement. Discriminative conditioning involves interference only because of responses elicited by a range of stimuli following reinforcement of a particular stimulus. Essential interference is limited to the similarity in physical properties of the stimuli within the generalization range. The same phenomenon holds for spatial discrimination in which interference may result from generalization of spatial locus of reward. A host of spatial discrimination (and closely related spatial delayed response) studies demonstrate that the closer the positions of the choice stimuli, the less efficient is performance.

Additional factors operate in nonspatial discrimination learning, such as black-white discrimination by the rat and object discrimination by the chimpanzee or monkey. These nonspatial discrimination problems present associated, but varying, positional cues along with the consistently rewarded color or object cues. As Spence (44) has pointed out, correct choice on any particular trial results in "ambiguous reinforcement," for both a particular positional cue (right or left side) and a particular nonpositional cue (black or white color) are rewarded. In such situations interference between the positional and object cues is inevitable. Learning is dependent upon differential frequency of reward over a series of trials—100 per cent for object and 50 per cent for each position.

Monkeys without previous experience on object discrimination problems have been reported by Harlow (14) to solve these problems readily after preliminary adaptation that probably involved some incidental learning. Four animals given their initial laboratory problem of discriminating objects differing in form and color, averaged only 4.2 errors before attaining a criterion of 20 correct responses in 25 trials. Since very rapid nonspatial discrimination learning has been reported for rats trained to choose between all-black and all-white alleys of a maze, there is no reason to believe that the rapid learning of the monkeys differentiates them from all subprimates. Experienced monkeys, however, may solve series of such problems *practically without error* after the initial blind trial, and comparable performances by any subprimate have yet to be demonstrated. Perhaps monkeys and men can be differentiated from subprimates in terms of their ability to attain immediate or almost immediate solution of a *series* of nonspatial or object discrimination problems.

Rapid discrimination learning has been demonstrated in chimpanzees by Nissen, Riesen, and Nowlis (34). The discrimination data were obtained during the investigation of other and complex learning processes. Variations in method in the monkey and chimpanzee studies make it impossible to compare directly the performance of these species on series of discrimination problems, but the indications are that both species respond efficiently.

Multiple-sign learning

The nonspatial or object discrimination problem presents a task in which reward of the positional cues and object cues is ambiguous on any particular trial. There is one necessary differential factor— the differential attributes of the stimuli—to which the organism must respond to solve the problem. Simultaneously, the animal must ignore the other variable stimulus factor—the position of the reward.

Fig. 4. Correct Responses by a Monkey Tested on the Oddity Problem.

More complex problems can be devised in which there is ambiguous reward of *more than two cues* on individual trials. Solution of these problems demands consistent response to only one cue over the series of trials. Such problems are described by Harlow (11) as multiple-sign problems, by Lashley (23) as generalizations of a second (or higher) order, and by Nissen (29) as ambivalent cue problems.

One situation of this class is the oddity problem, illustrated in Fig. 4. Two different pairs of identical stimuli are used, but only three stimuli are presented together. The odd stimulus, the stimulus singly represented, is rewarded, and trial sequences are so arranged that a member from each pair of stimuli is odd on half the test trials. On any given trial there is reward of the position, the object, and single representation, but over the series of trials only single representation is rewarded 100 per cent of the time. The other stimulus and situational variables—the position of the reward and the particular object rewarded—must be disregarded by the animal if he is to master the problem.

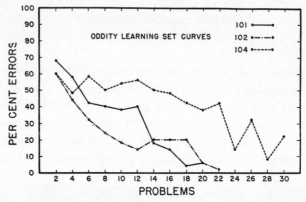

Fig. 5. Oddity Learning by Three Representative Monkeys. The animals whose data are presented in the above figure were trained on a series of oddity problems, a new problem being tested for 24 trials each day.

Oddity-problem solution by monkeys was first demonstrated by Robinson (38) at California and has since been investigated by workers at the Wisconsin Laboratory (43, 6, 27). It has been found that monkeys take from 400 to 1500 trials to reach a criterion of 90 per cent correct responses. During acquisition, perseverative positional and perseverative object errors decrease rapidly, but there is no discontinuity in the elimination of these error-producing factors, and both are present to some extent even after the learning criterion has been attained. Three individual oddity learning curves representing superior, average, and poor performance within a group of eight monkeys are shown in Fig. 5.

Nissen and McCulloch (33) have reported efficient performance by chimpanzees on oddity problems. After a long series of preliminary training procedures, these investigators presented a single odd stimulus with 11 identical stimuli. Both of their chimpanzee subjects showed rapid mastery and effective generalization of this oddity problem, but again the differences in method and apparatus between the chimpanzee and monkey studies make any direct comparisons unwarranted.

The matching problem is a multiple-sign situation very similar to the oddity problem. Matching was first studied by Kohts (22), who trained a young chimpanzee to select from many objects on a tray the particular object identical with the one she held in her hand. Though Kohts used the technique primarily for testing visual capacities, she also made some tests of memory and abstraction.

Kohts' technique was standardized for monkeys, and her fundamental procedures were subjected to rigid laboratory controls by Weinstein (48). Variations of his basic apparatus are illustrated in Figs. 7, 17, 18, and 19. In the simplest form the test tray is divided into a sample compartment having a single foodwell and a choice compartment having two or more foodwells. All wells are covered by objects. The subject is trained to displace the sample object, which is rewarded, first, and then to select the identical or most nearly similar choice object.

The matching and oddity problems are obvious complements. In the first instance, the subject is required to choose from three or more objects, the identical (nonodd) ones, and in the second, the one odd (nonidentical) object in a group of three or more objects. As might be expected, monkeys require about the same number of trials to master either of these problems.

Successful matching by seven chimpanzees was obtained in from 177 to 547 trials by Nissen, Blum, and Blum (31) using a somewhat different technique. The sample object was placed in the middle compartment of a three-compartment tray, with the result that the two matching objects were always adjacent. The Wisconsin oddity and matching studies have shown that the arrangements of stimuli that separate the identical objects by the nonidentical object produce the most frequent and most persistent errors. This difference in stimulus arrangement and other procedural differences make it impossible to equate the performance of monkeys and chimpanzees on matching problems, but the proficiency of the chimpanzee in both learning and generalizing the matching cannot be questioned.

The facility with which monkeys and chimpanzees learn and generalize second-order sign problems is in contrast with the difficulty that these problems occasion for subprimate animals. An attempt was made by Lashley (23) to train rats on the oddity problem, using the jumping box apparatus that had proved so successful in discrimination learning. The animals were trained initially to choose a cross presented along with two circles, and next, to choose a circle presented with two crosses. Alternate testing was then begun in the hope that the rats might eventually come to choose whichever figure was odd. Instead, after the third to fifth reversal, the animals either refused to jump or jumped persistently to one figure in spite of repeated falls.

Rose (39) trained rats to select a black curtain after a right maze turn and a white curtain after a left maze turn, in each case regardless of the relative position of a black-white pair of curtains. After prolonged practice this matching of movements with particular color stimuli was apparently attained. The performance was easily disturbed by extraneous cues, however, and no evidence is presented for generalization of the matching to other stimuli. The study does indicate that rodents may be able to solve second-order sign problems.

Limited success in the solution of matching problems by pigeons has been reported by Skinner (42). The birds were trained to peck at a red- or green-illuminated key, thus switching on a red light behind one and a green light behind the other of two keys located on either side of the originally lighted key. Pecking at the side key of the same color as the center key was rewarded with food. Both the color of the center light and the position of the matching light were randomly changed from trial to trial. This matching technique is comparable to that used with the chimpanzees, in that the sample is always the center one of three objects; the sample and the correct choice object are always adjacent, unlike the arrangements in the studies with the monkeys. No data are reported for the pigeons' matching performance, but Skinner states that the birds showed increased rate of response to the matching stimulus so long as the sample was given prior to simultaneous presentation of the three stimuli. No report is made of the relative rates of response to the matching and nonmatching keys. Several statements, however, imply relative lack of adaptation to changing situations. After matching behavior has been well established, for example, "the behavior of matching survives unchanged when all reinforcement is withheld" [(42), p. 214]. Furthermore, a record is presented of a bird that had learned matching under regular reinforcement conditions but that had reverted to a color preference when switched to periodic reinforcement. Subjected at that stage to reinforcement of opposites rather than matches, the bird showed increased rate of response to opposites, decreased to matches. Again switched to matching, the subject increased its rate of matching responses and decreased its rate of opposite responses. The changes in rates, however, do not suggest high-level efficiency in spite of the many thousands of responses made during the course of the study.

There is, then, evidence that at least some second-order sign problems can be solved by subprimates; there is overlapping in the requisite abilities of different genera, orders, and classes. It appears, however, that primates are far more facile than any other animals in learning multiple-sign problems. As we shall see, primates are capable of solving much more complex problems of this type.

Monkeys can solve combined matching-nonmatching or oddity-nonoddity problems, these being third-order multiple-sign problems. In half the trials of the combined matching-nonmatching test the subject displaces the sample stimulus and receives a food reward, a sign for selecting the like member of the two choice stimuli. On the other trials, response to the sample stimulus is unrewarded, a sign for selecting the choice object that is unlike the sample. Four monkeys mastered this problem after training by stepwise procedures. First they learned matching to a criterion of 45 correct responses in 50 trials, and then nonmatching to the same criterion. Finally, the problem was complicated by presenting matching and nonmatching trials in an irregular order. The subjects took from about 1200 to 2900 trials altogether, with a mean of approximately 1900 trials, to reach the criterion.

Three other rhesus monkeys were trained at the Wisconsin Laboratory on the combined oddity-nonoddity problem. Yellow and black test trays served, respectively, as signs for response to oddity and to nonoddity, the latter being defined as choice of both like objects. The training procedure was stepwise, patterned after that already described for the matching-nonmatching problem, and the results were similar. The mean number of total trials to attain the criterion of 45 correct responses in 50 was about 2100.

Both the combined matching-nonmatching and the oddity-nonoddity problems are third-order multiple-sign problems, for their solution requires response to one more factor than is required for solution of the component parts. In matching-nonmatching this additional factor is a food sign—the presence or absence of food under the sample; and in oddity-nonoddity, it is a board sign—the yellow or black color of the test tray. In these problems the reward of position, object, and even numerical representation of the objects is ambiguous on any particular trial.

The classification of problems in terms of the numerical order of the multiple signs necessary for their solution does not imply a hierarchical order of difficulty or even a separation into distinct problem types. Different second- and third-order sign problems may vary greatly in their ease of solution, and this variation is probably not constant among individuals within a species or even among species. Furthermore, it is probable that many second-order sign problems are generally more difficult than many third-order sign problems, and that similar relationships hold among multiple-sign problems of numerically higher orders.

Third-order multiple-sign problems that have proved troublesome for both monkeys and chimpanzees are Weigl-principle matching and oddity problems introduced by Harlow (11, 12), who adapted the problems from some of the principles of the well-known Weigl Test of Abstraction used clinically with human beings. In these two problems the animal must choose among three nonidentical stimuli, two of which are alike or similar in color, and two alike or similar in form. At Wisconsin four monkeys were trained on Weigl matching and three on Weigl oddity. In the matching tests a color response was required when the sample was rewarded and a form response when the sample was not rewarded. Differential board signs were used in the oddity testing. When the objects were presented on an orange tray, the color-odd object was correct, and presented on a cream-colored tray, the form-odd object was rewarded, as illustrated in Fig. 6.

Seven chimpanzees were tested at the Yerkes Laboratory on modified Weigl matching (31). The problem utilized differential colors of the boards as cues for color or form response, and only the two end stimuli served as choice objects. Since this situation does not give the animal his color-form cue from the sample, it would be better described as a simplified Weigl oddity problem.

All three investigations utilized a stepwise procedure, but the exact nature of the steps varies in the different studies. In all cases the final step involved randomly interspersed color-correct and form-correct trials. The Wisconsin studies further complicated the task by: (a) adding one or two stimuli to the choice objects, (b) substituting new sets of color-form objects, and (c) testing with sets of stimuli in which colors and forms were similar but not identical.

All the monkeys trained on Weigl oddity solved the original problem in less than 4000 trials, and the two animals tested further, effectively generalized the three complicating modifications. Three of the four monkeys trained on Weigl matching attained solution of all the training steps and generalization tests at a statistically significant level in 2400, 4650, and 5600 trials, respectively. One of the three monkeys failed to generalize the Weigl matching problem to a four-choice-object situation.

Fig. 6. **Weigl-Principle Oddity Test.** *Left.* Object odd in respect to form chosen on cream-colored tray. *Right.* Object odd in respect to color chosen on orange tray.

Only one of seven chimpanzees solved the simplified Weigl problem, and she took 6725 trials. Another gave a "promising" performance on the last step of the test. Descriptions of the behavior of the subjects show that both monkeys and chimpanzees had grave difficulty with this test; but the striking finding is the superiority of the rhesus monkey over the chimpanzee, a superiority that cannot be explained in terms of the difficulty of the test situation. This does not, of course, imply intellectual pre-eminence in the rhesus monkey. Differential personality characteristics in the species could account for differences in performance.

A fundamentally different type of multiple-sign problem is the complex ambivalent-cue situation devised by Nissen (29). Four stimuli—a small white square, a small black square, a large white square, a large black square—were arranged to form four discrimination-problem pairs, as illustrated by the following schema:

$$w \; (+) \; vs. \quad b \; (-)$$
$$B \; (+) \; vs. \; W \; (-)$$
$$W \; (+) \; vs. \; w \; (-)$$
$$b \; (+) \; vs. \; B \; (-)$$

A very flexible stepwise procedure was used in presenting the various stimulus combinations to the five chimpanzees. The final step involved mixed presentation of the four discriminations. A fixed schedule of stepwise training and more rigid criteria for step mastery were used in a repetition of this experiment with monkeys at the Wisconsin Primate Laboratory (35).

Four of the five chimpanzees mastered the problem in from about 1000 to 1500 trials. The one failure was attributed by Nissen to motivational-emotional factors. Four of the six monkeys solved the problem in approximately 1800 to 2300 trials. One monkey failed the last step, and the other was discontinued because of emotional difficulties. Trials-to-learn is not, however, a valid index of the difficulty value of the problem for the two species because the procedures used are not strictly comparable. Inspection of the data suggests that the chimpanzees and the monkeys did about equally well in the early steps of the problem, but that the chimpanzees were clearly superior on the last step.

In an attempt to discover the complexity of multiple-sign problems solvable by the rhesus monkey, Harlow (11) conducted a series of tests, illustrated in Fig. 7, on four rhesus monkeys. The animals were first taught the combined matching-nonmatching problem, to which was later added certain sign-differentiated antagonistic position problems. The first pair of position problems was elicited in a situation providing identical choice objects that were unlike the sample. When food was under the sample, the monkey was trained to select the distant choice object; when there was no food under the sample, the monkey was required to select the near choice object. After these habits were mastered, randomly intermixed matching, nonmatching, and sign-differentiated position trials were presented. A new test was then introduced in which choice and sample objects were identical. When food was under the sample object, the monkey was rewarded for choice of the closer object, and when no food was beneath the sample object, the more distant choice object was the one rewarded. The final stage of the problem consisted of randomly presented trials for matching, nonmatching, and both types of antagonistic position habits.

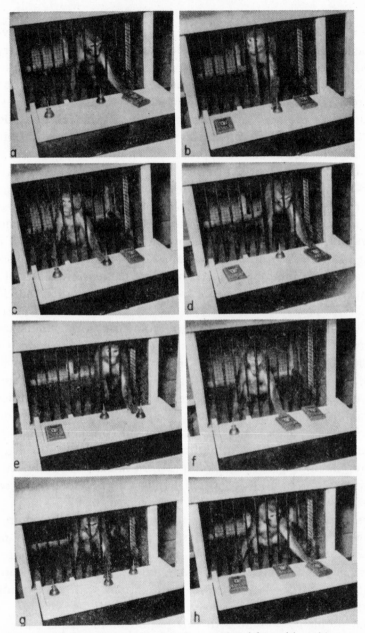

Fig. 7. Matching Problem. a. Food under sample; right-position object correct. **b.** Food under sample; left-position object correct. **Nonmatching Problem. c.** No food under sample; right-position object correct. **d.** No food under sample; left-position object correct. **Antagonistic position habits. e.** Food under sample; right-position object correct. **f.** No food under sample; left-position object correct. **g.** Food under sample; left-position object correct. **h.** No food under sample; right-position object correct.

This complex multiple-sign problem was solved by the four animals in from 2550 to 3770 trials, and all showed a high level of proficiency both on the total problem and on its four basic arrangements, each of which involved four stimulus configurations. One monkey made only a single error in the last 100 test trials. The sign-differentiated antagonistic position habits occasioned little interference with the matching-nonmatching problems. This, no doubt, resulted from the basic differences in the stimulus configurations.

In an effort to attain or approach the limit of complex reactions in chimpanzees, Nissen (30) tested one animal in 401 sessions over a period of three years. Stimuli were 16 pairs of plaques. Members of a pair differed only in size, but each pair differed from every other pair in one of four other characteristics: color, form, presence or absence of margin, and presence or absence of a green peg in front of the plaque. The number of variables determining correct response increased as training progressed and more habits were added. Habit I required only response to size; concurrent mastery of I and II demanded responsiveness to size and color; addition of the next two habits required responsiveness to size, color, and form; the next four habits added to the previous cues the essential cue of margin; and the last eight habits demanded simultaneous responsiveness to all five cues. Choice on every trial was between the larger and smaller of two plaques, but the size correct for the trial was determined by any combination of the other four variables.

The subject made steady progress on this problem, although, as might be expected, new stimulus pairs tended to be learned and differentiated progressively less rapidly. In the last 15 sessions, which required differentiation of all 16 habits, the percentage of correct responses ranged from 76 to 100 with a mean of 83.

Nissen points out that when members of a group of discrimination problems differ in many respects, the pattern difference is not a necessary cue. For this reason the chimpanzee's behavior is not fifth-order sign learning—the situation does not offer five-cue ambivalence. What one probably has is 16 discriminations with the stimuli so designed as to maximize habit interference.

The problems presented in this section of the paper have been selected because they represent the range of abilities thus far effectively tested in subhuman animals. These problems appear to belong to a single large class having considerable community in the factors that produce intraproblem interference and, hence, difficulty of solution. Although detailed analysis of the role of the variables abetting and hindering learning has been made only for the simpler of these problems, there is every reason to believe that the same analytical techniques may be applied with profit to the more complex tasks. When experimental, not deductive, analysis is made of the actual variables operating in such problems, we may expect to gain breadth of insight into the nature of learning problems of importance to human beings.

The principles operating in multiple-sign learning are apparent in everyday human behavior. The meanings of signs and symbols are repeatedly restricted, amplified, or reversed by the meanings of associated signs; in the simplest possible terms, this is the role of context in meaning. In oddity and matching, the meaning of a specific object *as a sign* changes from trial to trial. This is analogous to the problem the child faces in learning to use the words "I" and "you." The meanings of these words change according to the speaker. When the child is talking, "I" refers to himself, "you" to the person addressed. When the child is addressed, he is no longer "I" but "you." If your opponent leads the ace of spades and you are blank in the suit, you are expected to trump; if your partner leads the ace of spades and you trump it, you may be criticized. There is a vast difference between a girl who is "awful pretty" and one who is "pretty awful." The auditory physical stimuli "hole" and "whole" refer to nothing or everything and are differentiated strictly in terms of related signs. Multiple-sign responsiveness so pervades human behavior that it is accepted as a natural and automatic way of behaving. Recognizing the infinite number of human multiple signs and their vast complexities gives some appreciation of the degree of separation of the human being from the subhuman primate, and at the same time stresses the importance of analyzing such behavior in the animal laboratory if we are to comprehend learning of significance for man.

The Concept of Learning Set

There appears to be little correlation between position on the phyletic scale and speed of solution of any single, simple problem. We have already seen that rate of conditioning and facility of formation of spatial discriminations does not differentiate rodent from primate. It is questionable whether a single object discrimination problem can differentiate animals within the mammalian class. Such a test has not succeeded thus far in clearly separating sheep, cows, horses, chimpanzees, and human aments (9). The extremely complicated problems described in the preceding section do appear to separate animals of different phyletic levels. The explanation may in part reside in the fact that the acquisition of these more complicated problems entails solution of a series of simpler tasks. The acquisition of the oddity problem, for example, may be considered as involving a long sequence of discrimination reversals because the subject is repeatedly required to shift his object choice from trial to trial.

The partial analysis of complex problems in terms of the learning of sequences of simpler problems suggests the value of studying directly the cumulative effect of multiple learning problems—that is, *interproblem learning*. The promise of such an approach is further strengthened by the observation that multiple-, not single-, problem learning is characteristic of the adjustments that animals generally and man especially make outside the laboratory.

Formation of learning sets

The nature of this interproblem learning was investigated by Harlow (15), who trained eight rhesus monkeys on a series of 344 object discrimination problems utilizing a different stimulus pair for every discrimination. Each of the first 32 problems was 50 trials long; the next 200 problems, 6 trials; and the last 112 problems, an average of 9 trials. Learning curves showing the percentages of correct responses on the first six trials of these discriminations are presented in Fig. 8. These data demonstrate that the animals' ability to solve discrimination problems progressively improved. The monkeys gradually *learned how to learn* individual problems with a minimum of errors, a process designated by the term *learning set*. The animals attained such mastery that if they chose the correct object on the first trial, they rarely made an error on subsequent trials. If they chose the incorrect object on the first trial, they immediately shifted to the correct object and subsequently responded almost perfectly.

Efficient as the six-trial discriminations are for producing rapid learning, it appears that still shorter problems may lead to one-trial learning in even fewer total trials. Braun, at Western Psychiatric Institute in Pittsburgh, presented 451 discrimination problems to eight rhesus monkeys. The first 8 problems were run for 50 trials,

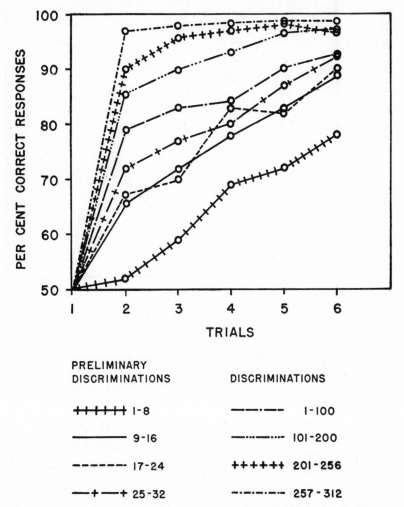

DISCRIMINATION LEARNING CURVES

Fig. 8. Discrimination Learning Curves on Successive Blocks of Problems.
(Harlow's data.)

the next 24 for 10 trials, the next 35 for 6 trials, and the final 384 for 3 trials. The results are presented in Fig. 9.

The data of Figs. 8 and 9 show a transition in the form of the learning curves for successive blocks of problems. The initial curves are S-shaped—the type described in the literature as typical "trial-and-error" curves. The final curves are discontinuous at Trial 2—the type frequently referred to as "insight" curves.

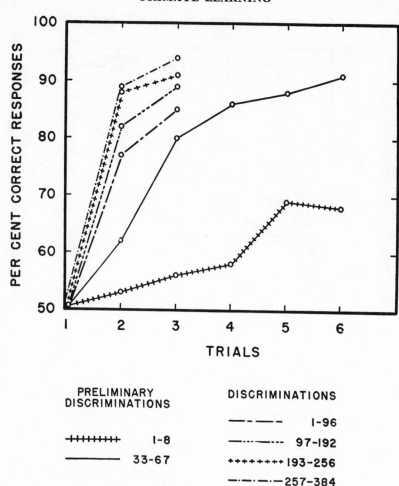

Fig. 9. Discrimination Learning Curves of Successive Blocks of Problems.
(Braun's data.)

Interproblem learning studies have also been conducted on various other kinds of learning problems at the Wisconsin Laboratory. The eight subjects of the discrimination learning series were also given 112 discrimination reversal problems (15). Each problem consisted of a discrimination phase of 7, 9, or 11 trials, followed by a reversal phase of 8 trials in which the reward value of the stimuli was reversed. Thus, the stimulus correct in the first phase became suddenly, and without warning, incorrect in the second phase. On initial reversal problems the monkeys made many errors, but before they had completed the 112 problems, they were reversing their responses in a single trial. The efficiency of reversal performance is indicated by the 97 per cent correct Reversal Trial 2 responses on the final 42 problems of the series (see Fig. 10).

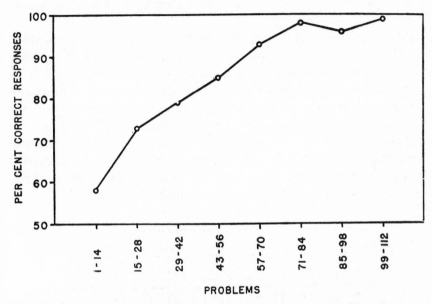

Fig. 10.   Discrimination-Reversal Learning-Set Curve Based on Trial-Two Responses of the Reversal Phase.

A more complex situation, the oddity problem, has also been subjected to the learning-set approach (17). Four normal monkeys and eight with extensive brain damage were trained on a series of 60 oddity problems, each of which utilized a different double pair of objects. Twenty-four trials were given per problem. All the animals showed progressive interproblem improvement, and the normal monkeys reached the point at which they were making 90 per cent correct responses on the *first trial* of new oddity problems.

None of the work with chimpanzees parallels the multiple-problem studies with the monkeys, but an investigation by Nissen, Riesen, and Nowlis (34) is sufficiently comparable to consider along with the learning-set studies. These investigators presented two chimpanzees with sequences of discrimination reversals utilizing a single pair of stimuli. The reversals were in ten-trial units for the first 900 trials and six-trial units for the next 900 trials. The initial two trials of each unit were delayed responses, the remaining trials discrimination responses. One animal was continued for 1800 additional trials. The subject that received a total of only 1800 trials made rapid progress and eventually attained a high level of proficiency. The other subject showed only slight progress, if any, over the course of her 3600 trials. The performance of the successful chimpanzee was described, appropriately, as "learning to learn."

Although there has been no systematic research on multiple-problem solution in subprimate animals, there is enough evidence in the literature to suggest that these lower organisms may form learning sets. Pavlov reported that dogs learn successive conditioned responses with progressively greater rapidity, and this finding has been confirmed by others. Similarly, Krechevsky found that rats learn discriminations in fewer and fewer trials when tested on a series of such problems. Unfortunately, the studies have never been carried to a point that permits plotting precise learning-set curves or determining the independence of multiple learning sets.

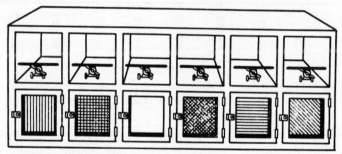

Fig. 11. Apparatus Used in Testing Matching in Children. (Door colors indicated by patent-office standards.)

Although man must form hundreds or even thousands of learning sets in the course of a lifetime and manipulate them with a skill far beyond that of any other animal, there are few human researches demonstrating the phenomenon, especially beyond the child level. At the University of Wisconsin a few studies (15) have been conducted that indicate that young children easily form discrimination and discrimination-reversal learning sets in situations paralleling those presented to the monkeys. A more complex organized response pattern, however, has been reported by Roberts (37) in an experiment conducted at the University of Iowa with 40 children ranging from three to seven years of age.

Nine learning situations comprising three color-, three form-, and three size-matching problems were presented in balanced order to three groups. The apparatus, illustrated in Fig. 11, was a two-story multiple-choice box with compartments for presenting the stimulus objects and matching stimulus cards. Stimuli were so arranged that only one pair matched on any trial. The general plan for the three groups of problems is illustrated by the color-matching situation. Problem 1 presented six like-colored airplanes in the upper compartments and differently-colored cards, one of which matched the airplanes, in the lower compartments. For Problem 2, the airplanes varied in color and the cards were uniformly colored. In Problem 3, both airplanes and cards varied in color. Parallel arrangements were provided for size-matching and form-matching.

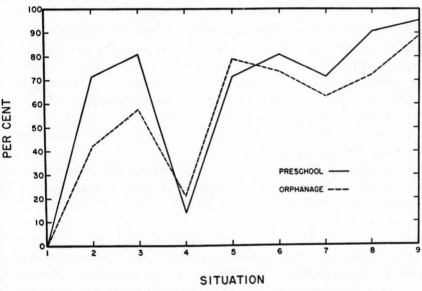

SITUATION

Fig. 12. Percentage of Zero Learning Trials in Each of Nine Situations for 21 Preschool and 19 Orphanage Children.

The experimental design thus permits study of transfer of habit under conditions of both slight and substantial changes of situation. The results in terms of errorless transfer for combined subject groups are shown in Fig. 12. It is apparent that transfer is marked within groups of problems but consistently decreases on the first situation in new problem groups. Over the series of the three problem groups, however, there is a cumulative transfer effect comparable to that found within problem groups.

Operation of learning sets

If we compare the oddity learning-set data with the data previously presented on the learning of a single oddity problem, we find that oddity is mastered as rapidly when a small number of training trials is presented for each of a large number of problems, as when all the trials are presented on a single problem. At the same time the training under multiple-problem conditions provides for much greater generalization of performance than does one-problem training. Habits are restrictive and have limited adaptive value; learning sets are generalized and have far greater adaptive breadth. Furthermore, it has been found that learning sets, once formed, are well retained and can be relearned months or even years later in a small fraction of the time taken for their original formation.

A number of antagonistic learning sets may be acquired by an animal and remain elicitable by appropriate stimuli and with amazingly little interference. Learning sets may operate, then, as if they were relatively isolated and discrete units. Evidence for the integrity and relative functional isolation of learning sets is illustrated by an experiment on six monkeys with object discrimination learning experience but without previous training on positional discriminations. These animals were given seven blocks of 14 problems each, starting with a block of 25-trial object discriminations and followed by a block of 25-trial positional discriminations that alternated left- and right-position problems. The remaining five blocks of problems continued the alternate presentation of 14 object discrimination problems and 14 right-left positional discriminations. Figure 13 presents curves showing the percentages of correct responses on total trials for these alternate blocks of antagonistic discriminations. The complex positional-discrimination learning-set curve shows progressive improvement throughout the series, whereas the object discrimination curve begins at a high level of accuracy, shows decrement on the second block, and subsequently recovers. By the end of the experiment the two basically antagonistic learning sets operated in succession with a minimum of interference. Between each two blocks of object discriminations there were 350 trials in which no object was differentially rewarded, and between each two blocks of positional discriminations there were 350 trials in which no position was differentially rewarded. Despite this, the monkeys learned to shift from one problem to the other with amazing ease and efficiency.

This relative functional isolation of learning sets is undoubtedly a basic mechanism in facilitating solution of complex problems. It enables an animal—particularly at the primate level—to respond in terms of an organized habit pattern and to shift readily to another habit pattern if consistently successful responses are not attained. Man possesses this ability to try out alternate problem solutions to a far greater degree than other animals, but the mechanism is also apparent in monkeys, as illustrated in a study by Zable and Harlow

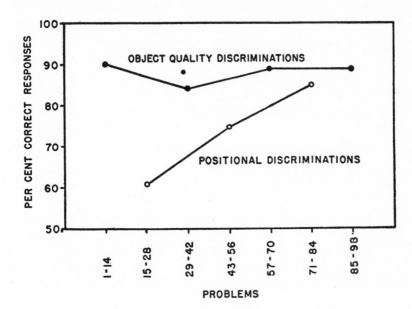

Fig. 13. Learning Set Curves for Problems with Alternating Object and Positional Discriminations, Based on Total-Trial Responses.

(52). Three subjects were given 60 trials a day on a single pair of objects: a funnel and a saltcellar. For 15 trials the funnel was correct, for 15 trials the saltcellar was correct, for 15 trials the right position was correct, and for 15 trials the left position was correct. The only cue for problem shifts was the failure of reward of a previously correct response. The order in which the four different parts of the problem were presented changed from day to day in an irregular, predetermined manner for the 30 days of the experiment. Two of the three monkeys solved 70 per cent of the shifts with 2 errors or less and over 90 per cent of the shifts in 4 errors or less. The poorest of the three subjects solved about 80 per cent of the shifts in 4 or fewer errors. The efficiency of the performance is evident when it is recognized that an average of 1.5 errors is essential before the animal can be informed of the nature of the shift.

One of the obvious characteristics of learning sets is that of changing problems that were originally solved slowly and with difficulty into problems that are solved quickly and easily. The process of reduction of problem difficulty through the formation of learning sets may carry on continuously to problems of ever increasing complexity. Solution time required for new and more complicated problems may be reduced through the simultaneous maintenance of a number of these relatively discrete organized response patterns that furnish the animal with multiple alternate approaches. The rigidity of fixed and relatively unchangeable habits so characteristic of some of the lower animals gives way to the plasticity of behavior and the ability to shift set that are typical of the primates.

Variables Influencing Learning in Primates

It is obvious that a large number of variables operate to influence the efficiency of learning in animals. The goal of a psychology of learning is to determine the functions of these variables in specific situations and to discover the degree of generality of these functions over broad kinds and classes of learning situations. Before any such goal can be attained, a vast number of precisely scaled functions must be determined for many tasks with many species of animals. Failure to obtain such data has led learning theorists to overestimate the importance of certain classes of variables and to ignore or underestimate the importance of others.

Interfering factors

We have already seen that various animals trained on long series of problems of a particular kind eventually may solve new problems of that kind with extreme rapidity, often on first presentation if the experimental situation affords immediate solution. Such data suggest the possibility that all problems can be solved in a single trial if the animal has already eliminated interfering influences. Obviously, there is a vast multiplicity of factors that can interfere with problem solution; moreover, the importance of any particular factor varies during the course of learning an individual problem or series of problems. It is possible to demonstrate the presence of important interfering factors and even to estimate the role they play in the learning of many problems.

One factor that operates in most, if not all, learning situations is that of *stimulus preference*. It is relatively easy to train an animal to do something that comes "naturally" but far harder to train him to respond in opposition to innate or acquired tendencies. If we present to a naive monkey a large black bottle and a small jar lid on a two-foodwell tray, the animal will choose the jar lid. Should the jar lid be rewarded, the problem presents no difficulty. If the black bottle is rewarded, however, learning is very slow indeed. In the previously cited study (16), in which monkeys were trained on over 300 discrimination problems, stimulus-preference errors were quite frequent early in the series, but were the first type of error to be suppressed effectively.

Response preference may also serve as an important and even persistent interfering factor. Monkeys and chimpanzees rapidly learn to solve problem boxes that open if a plunger is pulled out, but have difficulty in solving problem boxes if the plunger must be pushed in. The role of response preference is also illustrated by the rake problem, which monkeys, gibbons, chimpanzees, and children solve readily if the food is placed near the angle of the handle and blade. All subjects encounter greater difficulty if the bait lies to the side of the blade and greatest difficulty if it lies beyond the rake. Pulling-in is the preferred response, sidewise motion next most preferred, and moving the object away from the body least preferred. Response preferences are undoubtedly of great importance in all manipulatory and motor-skills learning.

Both sensory and motor preferences may be partly or completely determined by training; they are not merely a function of innate potentialities. In discrimination reversal problems, for example, the difficulty on the early trials of the reversal phase is occasioned by the experimentally induced or, at least, enhanced preference for the stimulus rewarded previously. Similarly, a subhuman primate trained to solve a problem box by turning a crank to the right, encounters difficulty if the operation of the crank is reversed so as to demand a left turn.

Another interfering factor—or category of factors—is related to the tendency of animals to shift spontaneously to an alternate response pattern or patterns *even though the initial response pattern has been consistently rewarded.* There are many basic mechanisms that might be operating here. It is possible that the effort or work entailed in making a response progressively raises the threshold for the elicitation of that response. An hypothesis more in keeping with the data on primates, however, suggests a tendency to explore the available components of a given situation. If a monkey chances to select the correct stimulus on the first trial of a discrimination, he will show an increasingly strong tendency to "try out" the other stimulus as trials progress. If, on the other hand, the first trial is incorrect and on the second trial he shifts to the correct stimulus, the likelihood of again choosing the incorrect stimulus will be significantly less. This factor, named *response shift* by the author, is an extremely persistent mechanism in monkeys and probably in all primates. Its operation may be more limited in lower animals, such as the rat, which fall readily into stereotyped habits of little adaptability or plasticity.

There is, nevertheless, evidence that the mechanism of response shift does operate in rats. Dennis reported a strong tendency for these animals on successive early trials to alternate position choices at the first three choice points of a multiple-unit maze. For example, if on Trial 1 they turned right at the first choice point, they showed a strong tendency to turn left at this point on Trial 2, even though the initial right-going response was correct. Krechevsky's "hypotheses" in rats also are suggestive of a response shift mechanism. Furthermore, the well-known tendencies of rats—and other animals—to fall into simple alternation habits would be in keeping with the operation of a response shift factor.

In many learning situations the relationship between the stimuli and the reward can become apparent only over a series of trials. On any one discrimination trial, for example, object and position are either both rewarded or both unrewarded. This ambiguity can be eliminated only by trials in which the position of the stimuli is reversed. *Ambiguity of reward* is an intrinsic interfering factor in many problems. In discrimination learning by monkeys it accounts for a large percentage of errors in the early stages of learning. Harlow (16) found its persistence to be intermediate between stimulus preference and response shift.

Drive and incentive variables

Most investigators working with subprimates have found that learning is facilitated when the drive state appropriate to the experimental incentive is high as defined by length of deprivation. Rats trained on a maze to a water incentive commonly learn more rapidly if water-deprived than if water-sated; rats working on a Skinner Box emit more responses one day after feeding than one hour after feeding. Many theoreticians have been so impressed by the drive variable that they have made it a key principle to their learning theories.

Support for the importance of deprivation as a condition influencing the *rate* of elicitation of a learned response by monkeys was obtained in a study using a Skinner-type device. Pressing a lever of a vending machine delivered a peanut, and the number of responses

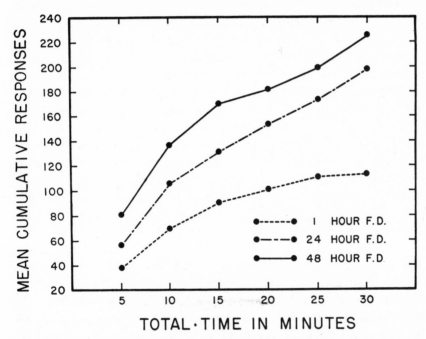

Fig. 14. Mean Cumulative Responses at Successive Five-Minute Intervals under Three Deprivation Conditions.

made in six successive five-minute periods was the measure of elicitation of the learned response. Each of nine subjects was tested for three days under each of three food deprivation periods: 1, 23, and 47 hours. The results, presented in Fig. 14, show a high positive relationship between degree of food deprivation and frequency of elicitation of the learned response.

There is, of course, no a priori reason for believing that the relationship between deprivation and rate of response will hold for other learning measures. Two studies by Meyer (25) indicate that there may be no significant relationship between the period of food deprivation and the *efficiency* of performance of monkeys on dis-crimination problems. In the initial experiment 12 naive rhesus monkeys were given a series of 168 discrimination problems, 56 after each of the food deprivation periods of 1 hour, 6 hours, and 23 hours. *No significant differences were found in performance under the three conditions.*

Subsequently, the same animals were tested on 108 discrimination reversal problems, divided equally among the deprivation periods of 1 hour, 23 hours, and 47 hours. Records were taken of the prereversal and reversal errors, and forward and total cage activity measured by the number of times the subject crossed the lines dividing the cage floor into quadrants. *No significant differences were found between periods of deprivation and any of these response measures* even though the experiment was of such power that error differences of a few per cent would have been significant. The uniform failure of differences to appear suggests that, over the deprivation range studied, *food deprivation is an unimportant variable in discrimina-tion-type learning by monkeys.* It should be pointed out that in these experiments the deprivation was for the standard maintenance diet of dog biscuits, carrots, and oranges, and the incentive foods were peanuts and raisins.

The effect of food deprivation on problem solving in the chim-panzee was studied by Birch (4), who tested 6 young chimpanzees after 2, 6, 12, 24, 36, and 48 hours of food deprivation on 6 patterned string problems, 10 stick problems, and 1 hooked-rope problem. *No significant differences were obtained for string-test performance under the various conditions.* Of the 15 differences between per-formance and hours of deprivation obtained for the other 11 prob-lems, only two were significant. All 15 of these measures were for *time*, not proficiency, whereas the string-test measures were for proficiency. Observational evidence, which was in accord with trends from the more objective data, led Birch to conclude that intermediate conditions of motivation were most desirable for problem-solving activities. Intense motivation led the chimpanzees to concentrate on the goal to the relative exclusion of the other essential factors; under conditions of low motivation, the animals were easily diverted from the problem. As has been pointed out by Nissen, great distractibility is a fundamental characteristic of chimpanzee behavior, particularly in young animals.

Certain very interesting observations of primate learning behavior have been reported. Test-wise, stable, and friendly chimpanzees have been observed to continue working on a problem and to show improvement in performance for a considerable period after showing no interest in the reward. Both chimpanzees and monkeys have been reported to solve problems without receiving rewards directly. One chimpanzee learned discrimination problems by observing the performances of a chimpanzee friend. A monkey trained to solve discriminations of a modified delayed response type in a single trial was given a series of these learning problems so arranged that reward appeared every second problem, then every third, and finally every fourth. In spite of the fact that most problems were *never rewarded* the animal continued to perform at a highly efficient level; indeed, there was little evidence of experimental decrement until the subject simply refused to respond in the test situation.

Efficiency of performance by both chimpanzees and monkeys has been shown to be influenced by the amount and kind of incentives used. Nissen and Elder (32) tested chimpanzees on delayed response tests with different amounts of banana incentive. They reported that the delay limit for these animals was a direct function of the amount of reward. The effect of low-, intermediate-, and high-preference incentives on delayed response performance by monkeys was measured by Maslow and Groshong (24). Efficiency of performance was positively related to the preference value of the incentive, but the experimenters stressed the relatively small behavioral differences occasioned by the relatively great variation in food preferences.

The behavioral significance of a given amount of reward can be understood only in terms of the monkey's experiences with the rewards available for the performance of a given task. Eight monkeys previously trained to a high level of proficiency on discrimination reversal problems that provided a single piece of food reward per trial, were subsequently trained by Meyer (26) on a series of multiple discrimination-reversal problems that for any particular reversal offered one or three pieces of food per trial. On consecutive reversals within a problem the amount of reward might increase, decrease, or remain constant. At the beginning of the experiment, performance efficiency was high and about equal for all conditions of reward. Subsequently, the effectiveness of the previously acceptable single piece of food progressively declined, and the effectiveness of the triple reward progressively increased; the over-all level of performance for all conditions combined, however, remained the same. Performance was most efficient when the transition was from small to large and least efficient when transition was from large to small. These data show very clearly that amount of reward has little meaning in terms of its physical characteristics alone. The reinforcing characteristics of a given amount of reward cannot be a simple function of the capacity of that reward to reduce a homeostatic drive, but must, at least, be related to the maximum and minimum amounts of reward previously obtained in the particular situation.

Work or effort variables

The effects of varying conditions of effort on monkeys' learning performance was studied by Davis at the Wisconsin Laboratory. Nine animals were trained, to a criterion of 23 correct responses in 25 trials, to choose the larger of two gray squares having side lengths of approximately 1.625 and 1.0 inches, respectively. The subjects then received 648 trials in which the 1-inch square was paired with

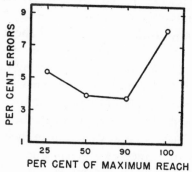

Fig. 15. Performance of Monkeys as a Function of Reach Effort on Discrimination Generalization Tests.

any one of three squares having linear dimensions of 1.125 inches, 1.25 inches, or 1.375 inches. The larger square was rewarded in each instance. These generalization pairs were presented under four different conditions of effort measured by the distance the monkey was forced to reach for the stimuli. Maximum reach, the farthest distance the animal reached for a piece of food on 95 per cent or more food presentations, had been determined for each subject by the method of limits and confirmed by the method of constant stimuli. Maximum reach and reach points at 90, 50, and 25 per cent of the maximum reaching distance were employed. High-level performance was obtained at all four reach points, but efficiency was best at the middle distances and poorest at the maximal distance, as shown in Fig. 15. These data suggest a tendency for extreme effort to interfere with performance, but it is notable that the 90 per cent reach point, which entailed a high degree of effort, gave maximally proficient performance. Such data strongly indicate that there is no simple linear relationship between work and learning performance.

Stimulus variables

Although careful and detailed psychophysical tests indicate that monkeys, chimpanzees, and human beings are nearly identical in their visual acuity and in their ability to discriminate hue and brightness, there is every reason to believe that they differ enormously in their perceptual responses, particularly where detail vision is concerned. Human beings differentiate immediately small patches of color, small figures, and figures of different size centered in homogeneous surrounds. Chimpanzees and monkeys (14), on the other hand, have difficulty in discriminating such detail. They appear most nearly to resemble man in differentiating color detail, next in form detail, and least in size detail. Failure to recognize these limitations of perceptual performance and their significance for learning has resulted in unnecessary confusion in the literature.

Both monkeys and chimpanzees can learn to discriminate multi-dimensional objects very rapidly, as already indicated. Objects differing only in over-all color or external form are also discriminated with ease. It has been claimed that monkeys and chimpanzees can differentiate stereometric, three-dimensional objects much more facilely than they can differentiate essentially planometric, two-dimensional objects, and the common naive behavioristic explanation given is that stereometric stimuli afford additional real or implicit proprioceptive cues conditioned on previous manipulatory responses. Harlow (13) found no significant differences in monkeys in discrimination performance on otherwise equated stereometric and planometric stimuli. Since no differences have yet been demonstrated between stereometric and planometric discriminations tested under comparable conditions, it would appear that explanations to account for the nonexistent differences are premature.

Although our knowledge of the exact role of the perceptual variables influencing learning in chimpanzees and monkeys is incomplete, it is almost profound in comparison with our scanty knowledge of the perceptual characteristics of subprimate animals. An attack on visual perception in the rat was made by Lashley (23) in some preliminary experiments. The number of subjects and number of trials per test were often limited, and, although suggestive data were obtained, the work cannot be regarded as definitive. Lashley has stressed "the tendency of the rat to base his reactions upon such relations as distance, or direction, where a human subject identifies a total geometrical figure" [(23), p. 182]. He goes on to say, "Observations of the rat in the maze and free-field have suggested that the chief function of vision in the animal's adaptive reactions is for general orientation, with little or no visual identification of specific objects" [(23), pp. 182-183].

Instrumentation

The data on learning set show that once an animal has had experience on a variety of problems of a single type, it may come to solve at once new problems belonging to this class. Immediate solution is one of the criteria used by many in defining "insightful behavior." There are reasons to believe that no insightful behavior can take place without antecedent practice. Riesen's (36) data on the slow learning of single problems by visually naive monkeys and chimpanzees strongly support this position. Most tests that have been supposed to measure static and innate capacities have been subsequently shown under appropriate circumstances to measure functions that are sometimes overwhelmingly improved by practice. Patterned string tests of monkeys (18) and chimpanzees (7), multiple-choice tests of chimpanzees (45, 50), and delayed response tests of monkeys (28) and chimpanzees are noteworthy examples. Acceptance of the concept of innate capacities for insight has so dominated the thinking of investigators that increments in performance have frequently been interpreted as adaptation to the problem rather than obvious transfer of learning.

The construct of insight learning gained acceptance from Köhler's (21) demonstrations of instrumental problem solution in chimpanzees. Köhler was impressed by the suddenness with which some problems were solved, by the frequent unity and coherence of the action sequence preceding solution, and by the change in the chimpanzee's facial expression, which often accompanied success.

Köhler's observational data are, however, far from satisfactory for the formulation of scientific theory. The early learning histories of his animals were unknown; the subjects were apparently allowed experience with instruments without continuous observation by scientifically trained individuals; the sequences of problems were not designed so as to control transfer effects from simple to complex problems.

When factors such as these are kept under reasonable control, it becomes clear that experience and training play a very large role in the solution of even simple instrumentation problems, and that no complex instrumentation problem has ever been reported to be solved by any animal, including man, in the absence of previous opportunity for practice on related problems.

More than 20 years ago a comprehensive study of box stacking was conducted by Bingham (3) under rigid, scientific conditions. Four immature chimpanzee subjects were tested on eight problems ranging in difficulty from placement and use of one cuboidal box to placement, stacking, and use of four cuboidal boxes, and placing, upending, and use of an oblong box atop a large basal cube. It was Bingham's conclusion that solution of the box problems demanded little if any behavior that was strictly new, and that novelty and originality appeared solely in the regrouping of former experiences. This, of course, does not imply that a solution or partial solution cannot appear suddenly. Once past experience with *any kind of problem,* discriminative or manipulative, has become organized, response patterns are available for elicitation by appropriate stimulation. The organized patterns generalize widely and can be easily combined and recombined.

The box-stacking data provide no exception to the rule that *insightful behavior on instrumentation problems apparently occurs only in animals that have had previous opportunity for experience in related situations.* Six four- to five-year-old chimpanzees, born and reared in the laboratory, were tested by Birch (5) on the hoe problem with the food lying near the junction of the handle and blade. Only two of the six subjects solved this extremely simple problem within a 30-minute period. One of these solutions was clearly accidental, and the other was made by a chimpanzee that had been observed to use sticks regularly in spontaneous play. Even after being given opportunity for stick play in their cages for three days, five of the subjects failed the single-stick problem. The one that succeeded was again the one that had used sticks adaptively in his cage before the experiment began!

Schiller (40) conducted a more extensive series of instrumental problems on 25 chimpanzees of from one to 15 years of age. A series of 12 stick problems of graduated difficulty was employed. Gradual learning by "specific experience" characterized all subjects, including the oldest. The youngest required hundreds of trials to master the simplest single-stick problems. The three- to four-year-olds solved a series of single-stick problems in about a hundred trials each, but failed on multiple-stick problems in which sticks were placed on different platforms. Even the oldest animals failed to solve their initial problem—a single straight stick with food beyond it—on the first trial. They learned much more rapidly than the younger animals, they generalized solutions more broadly, and they were able finally to solve problems of greater complexity than the younger subjects. But even the oldest animals made frequent gross, stupid errors in situations in which they had had previous experience.

All the true anthropoid apes—gorilla, orangutan, and chimpanzee—have been reported to stack boxes, but only one monkey, a cebus, has been observed to do so. Bierens de Haan reported that this monkey gradually learned to stack four boxes, often overturning them during stacking but appearing to show less difficulty with this "static understanding" than did Köhler's chimpanzees. No primate other than man has been known to stack more than four boxes.

The solution of rake problems and of single- and multiple-stick problems has been reported for gorillas, orangutans, and monkeys as well as for chimpanzees. Sticks have been used by these various primates as objects to pull in a reward, knock down a reward, climb up to obtain a reward, and to push a reward out of a pipe.

Reports by Romanes and by Klüver, and unpublished observations by the present author, give every indication that some cebus monkeys may solve instrumentation problems as complex as any ever reported solved by the apes. Figure 16 shows typical tool-problem solutions by a cebus monkey at the Wisconsin Laboratory. A complete motion picture record was obtained of the initial pole-climbing success. Like all "insight" solutions, this first solution was impressively sudden. But, if the law of gravity were not to be repealed, how could such a problem be solved other than suddenly? Study of the photographic records reveals that a very considerable amount of tentative pole arranging and climbing preceded correct solution. Furthermore, much behavior following the initial success is short of perfection. The cebus sometimes placed the pole too far from the food and sometimes at an acute rather than a right angle before starting to climb. With practice he became highly proficient at pole climbing

Fig. 16a. Solution of Instrumentation Problems by a Cebus Monkey. (Multiple-stick problem.)

Fig. 16b. Solution of Instrumentation Problems by a Cebus Monkey. (Pull-in by friction problem.)

and even combined the pole climbing with the single-box problem. Even after success in combining these problems, he frequently made such errors as placing the pole adjacent to the box rather than on the box. Similar evidence of limited insight and gradual acquisition of

Fig. 16c.   Fig. 16d.

Fig. 16c and d.   Solution of Instrumentation Problems by a Cebus Monkey. c. Stick as a
knocking-down instrument. d. Stick as a climbing instrument.

instrumentation problems are reported for apes tested under controlled observational conditions.

The cebus monkeys have consistently proved to be superior to
the rhesus monkeys in the solution of instrumentation problems.
Warden, Koch, and Fjeld (47) tested five rhesus and three cebus
monkeys on both single- and multiple-rake problems and found
the cebus to be clearly superior both in terms of the mean performance of the groups and in terms of the maximum attainments

of the most successful animal. But we know very little of the significance of these differences. The data on other kinds of learning problems suggest that the cebus is no more efficient and is possibly less efficient than the rhesus monkey. It is possible that the differences

Fig. 16e. Solution of Instrumentation Problems by a Cebus Monkey.
(Combination of box and stick problems.)

in instrumentation abilities relate more to innate propensities toward manipulation than to intellectual factors.

Data on human children lend support to the position that instrumentation problems are solved by primates only after practice. Five box-stacking problems and four stick problems were presented by Alpert (1) to 40 nursery school subjects of from 19 to 49 months of age. Successful children took two to three learning sessions to solve the simplest box problem. Only one solution was immediate, and 17 subjects failed completely in the allotted five experimental sessions. Comparable difficulty was encountered by the children in the stick problems. The ineptitude of the children in these tool situations is particularly striking in view of the commonness with which young children use boxes, blocks, chairs, and sticks in their play and even in practical problems of obtaining forbidden incentives.

Fig. 16f. Solution of Instrumentation Problems by a Cebus Monkey.
(Stick and pipe problem.)

In spite of the large number of observational studies, our knowledge of instrumentation behavior in the primates is very limited. It is tedious to control early experience on instrumentation tasks; it is hard if not impossible to devise series of problems of equal or near equal difficulty. There have been no systematic attempts to measure generalization precisely from one problem to another. Nor has anyone tried to determine exactly the various kinds of response patterns required for solution of tool problems and to determine the degree to which these variable action patterns may be combined, recombined, and coordinated. Experimental analysis of instrumentation behavior is a task for the future, and one that may never be solved satisfactorily. Possibly what is most needed to give new life to this old problem is a relatively novel approach by an investigator who is not thoroughly steeped in the knowledge of bygone failures.

Delayed Response

The delayed response problem was first devised to test the ability of animals to respond to a stimulus not physically present. Attention of investigators was next directed to the essential mechanism of delay, for if animals can solve these problems without maintaining orientation to the stimulus during the delay, some central representative factor must be present. This factor may well operate with different levels of efficiency in various animals, and its efficiency is doubtless influenced by many circumstances.

Variables that influence delayed response

The ability of primates, from lemur to man, to solve delayed responses has been demonstrated in numerous researches, and this ability is roughly related to the position of the species within the primate order. Under comparable conditions monkeys and apes have been able to delay longer than lower animals, whose performances on simple spatial delayed responses have already been discussed (Ch. 6). One experiment at Wisconsin was designed to assess for monkeys the relative importance of other variables. The effects of learning (1536 trials), length of delay (5-, 10-, 15-, and 20-second periods), and amount of reward (1, 2, 3, and 4 pieces of food) were simultaneously studied. Identical objects were used in half the tests and dissimilar objects in the remainder. The stimuli were further classified into familiar and unfamiliar, the latter being defined as objects employed for only a single trial. For half of the eight animals a screen was lowered in front of the objects during the delay interval; for the others the test tray was simply kept out of reach.

Progressive reduction in errors continued for over a thousand trials and provided conclusive evidence for learning. Differences in performance attributable to length of delay were statistically significant, although the maximum difference, that between the 5- and 20-second delays, was only 3 per cent. Error scores decreased with increase in the amount of reward, but, as the experiment progressed, the differential effectiveness of the three larger incentives declined. The interpolation of the opaque screen during the delay interval increased the number of errors by 50 per cent. No significant differences were found in the use of familiar and unfamiliar objects, but errors were 25 per cent less frequent for dissimilar as compared with identical

objects. The monkeys thus were aided by nonspatial cues in a problem solvable by spatial cues—a finding noteworthy because of the
difficulty encountered by monkeys and apes in the solution of nonspatial delayed responses.

Complex delayed response

Although superior to lower animals in the length of delays they
can effect under comparable conditions on simple delayed response,
primates demonstrate their greater abilities more strikingly in performance on modified delayed response problems, such as multiple
delayed response and nonspatial delayed response. No subprimate
has been reported to date to have solved either of these types of
delay problem.

Tinklepaugh (46) introduced multiple delayed response in a series
of studies employing two rhesus monkeys, two immature chimpanzees, four human children, and five human adults. One test was
confined to monkeys and chimpanzees. The subjects were taken to a
number of different rooms and in each were allowed to watch the
experimenter place a piece of food under one of two identical containers. The animals were then returned to the rooms in which the
containers had been baited and were permitted to make a single
choice in each room.

The chimpanzees were clearly superior to the monkey subjects in
terms of the percentage of correct choices with number of rooms
constant, and in terms of the maximal number of pairs of containers
solved in any series The mean score of the monkeys tested on five
pairs of containers was 79 per cent correct in contrast to the 90 per
cent average made by the two chimpanzee subjects on a series twice
as long.

Tinklepaugh's second test method consisted of arranging from
three to 16 pairs of containers in a 20-foot circle within a large room.
The subject sat on a stool in the center during the baiting process and
afterward was permitted to respond to the various pairs in turn.
The data of Table 1 show the clear superiority of the chimpanzees
over the monkeys and the apparent superiority over the children. It
should be emphasized, however, that delayed reaction training and
experience were not equal for human and subhuman subjects. Although Tinklepaugh did not find consistent improvement with practice, his experiment was not adequately designed to test practice
effects.

TABLE 1

MEAN PER CENT CORRECT RESPONSES ON MULTIPLE DELAYED-REACTION TEST

Subjects	Number of Pairs of Test Objects		
	4	8	16
Monkeys	74	61	
Chimpanzees		88	78
Children			63
Adults			75

An interesting test indicating that monkeys and chimpanzees can remember the nature as well as the location of food is Tinklepaugh's substitution test. In this situation, he baited the correct container with banana, and during the delay interval substituted a less preferred food, lettuce for the monkeys, and carrot or orange for the chimpanzees. Surprise, disappointment, and resentment were indicated by facial expression, bodily attitude, and vocalizations. The monkeys commonly refused to accept the nonpreferred lettuce, but the chimpanzees, after hesitation and delay, would carry the orange or carrot away and eat it at their leisure.

Another modification of the delayed response problem is that devised by Harlow, who baited the correct one of two containers, and, while the monkey watched, altered the position of the objects. Two kinds of shift trials were employed, one that restored the containers to their original position, and one that left the objects in the reverse position. Four of ten monkeys attained a criterion of 75 per cent correct responses on the last 20 trials of both problems. As might be expected the shift that reversed position offered by far the greatest difficulty.

Many studies have investigated the ability of monkeys and chimpanzees to make nonspatial delayed responses, that is, to respond, after a delay interval, to the baited object regardless of its position. This type of delayed response was demonstrated first in the chimpanzee by Yerkes and Yerkes (51). These investigators placed in the corners of a room four boxes and baited one of them while the subject watched. The chimpanzee was then taken away, and the positions of the boxes were shifted before he was brought back to make a choice. Nonspatial delays as long as 30 minutes were attained after prolonged training. Subsequently a series of nonspatial delayed response studies was carried out at the Yerkes Laboratory by Nissen and co-workers. Their basic technique, illustrated in Fig. 17, was to bait one of two differently colored, vertically placed doors, and to rotate these doors into a horizontal position during the delay interval.

The three chimpanzees tested were given long preliminary training and subjected to a wide variety of special procedures during the course of the experiment. Positive evidence for nonspatial delayed response was demonstrated for all subjects, and delays as long as 40 seconds were obtained.

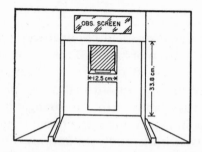 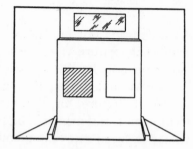

Fig. 17.   **Apparatus for Nonspatial Delayed Response Testing.** *Left.* Discrimination box as it appears at time of baiting for delayed response trials. *Right.* Discrimination box in position for responses after delay, and for all regular discrimination learning procedure.

An extremely efficient technique for testing nonspatial delayed response is Weinstein's adaptation of his matching-from-sample method. The delayed reactions are run by first presenting the sample stimulus alone, and after the animal has responded to it, interposing a screen, removing the sample stimulus and placing the choice stimuli, and then removing the screen. If the animal is to select correctly, he must remember the sample object, not merely its position. Using two monkeys that had already learned to match from sample, Weinstein trained the animals in approximately 2000 trials to respond to 15-second delays with 75 per cent accuracy. After additional training, one subject was successful on *30- and 60-second delays even when as many as five choice objects were presented.*

A more complicated nonspatial delayed response involving memory for differential objects was then tested on this single subject. Two stimuli were placed in the sample compartment over foodwells made of brass cups designed to form a collar that would hold immobile a socket attached to the base of an object. The incorrect sample stimulus was rendered immobile in this way; the correct stimulus had no attached socket and could be easily pushed aside. After the monkey responded to the sample objects, the opaque screen was lowered, the samples were removed, and five choice objects were placed over foodwells. One of these choice objects was identical with the correct sample, and one was identical with the incorrect sample (see Fig. 18). In less than a thousand total training trials, the monkey succeeded in making 60-second delayed responses with 60 per cent accuracy on the last 50 trials, a frequency three times as great as would be expected by chance. Improvement with training was progressive, and with trials held constant, efficiency of performance was negatively correlated with length of delay. Since at the end of the experiment the monkey was still improving, there is every reason to believe that he could have attained even greater proficiency with more prolonged training.

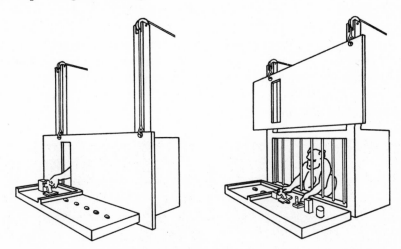

Fig. 18. **Nonspatial Delayed Response to Differential Sample Objects.**

Chimpanzees have also been found to perform effectively on nonspatial delayed responses employing a matching technique. Finch (8) presented two subjects with a three-compartment apparatus having the sample object section in the middle rather than on one end. Two animals previously experienced on nonspatial delays were trained to match from sample and then were given more than 400 delayed matching trials. The procedure for delayed matching was to raise the shutter to the center compartment, allow the subject to make a response, close the center shutter, and then, after the appropriate delay interval, to raise the shutters to the adjacent choice compartments. On the last 400 trials, the chimpanzees averaged 91, 81, 69, and 61 per cent correct responses for delay intervals of 2, 10, 20, and 40 seconds, respectively.

A study by Simpson and Harlow (41) shows that monkeys can make nonspatial delayed responses to the color or form attribute of objects as well as to objects as units. Two rhesus monkeys already skilled in differential color-form matching (Weigl-principle matching) were subjected to an adapted form of the delayed matching-from-sample technique. A single sample object was presented alone. If it was rewarded, the monkey was required to effect a delayed color-matching response; if it was not rewarded, a delayed form-matching response was required. One choice object matched the sample in color, and the other matched in form. Approximately 3500 trials were given during the course of a seven-step training procedure using the maximum delay interval of 12 seconds on the last step. Both subjects attained the criterion of 80 per cent correct responses in the last 25 trials, and both made significantly better than chance scores on color and form trials analyzed separately in the last step of the experiment.

A variation of this test using four instead of two choice objects is shown in Fig. 19. Somewhat less efficient performance occurred in the pictured situation.

Fig. 19. Successful Response to a Weigl-Principle Delayed Reaction by a Rhesus Monkey. *Left.* Response to the sample object with no food in the foodwell. (Color matching would be required if a food reward were beneath the sample.) *Right.* Selection of the choice object matching the form of the sample object. (The darker circle matches the color of the sample object.)

Significance of delayed response

Delayed response studies are of historical interest because they represent the attempts by comparative psychologists to attack the "higher mental processes." Early, as well as present-day, investigators have assumed that delayed response involves the use of some representative factor that requires a higher order of ability than discrimination learning. Furthermore, the additional assumption has appeared in the literature that nonspatial delays are set apart from spatial delays by some process of symbolism. Why there should be any intrinsic difference between memory for position and memory for objects has never been clarified.

Successful delayed response performance is possible only if an animal learns discrimination *reversal* problems in a *single* trial to an implicit (secondarily reinforced) reward and retains this learning for the period defined by the delay. One-trial reversal learning is itself a difficult kind of problem and is mastered only after considerable practice. The implicit reward of the learning is no doubt an additional complicating factor. In a spatial delayed response problem the position of the object previously rewarded by food must frequently be abandoned on the next trial for the opposite position previously rewarded only implicitly. In a nonspatial delayed response problem, the object previously rewarded by food must frequently be forsaken on the next trial for the secondarily rewarded object. Delay is only quantitatively different in delayed response problems from that in discrimination problems, since some delay is involved in all discrimination learning, whether between response to the stimulus and the obtaining of food or between successive trials.

It is to be expected that animals learn somewhat more rapidly to do single-trial spatial discrimination reversal problems than spatial delayed response problems, which involve all the factors of difficulty of the former plus the limitations imposed by implicit reward. Any assumption, however, that delayed response is intrinsically more difficult than discrimination learning is unwarranted. Monkeys learn in a few hundred trials to perform almost without error on 10-second spatial delayed reactions but after 10 times this number of trials they still fail to solve in a single trial many simple detail discriminations involving no unessential delay. Delayed response performance is *more* or *less* difficult than discrimination-learning performance, depending on the specific nature of the problems being compared.

Monkeys with large bilateral lesions in the frontal lobe solve object discriminations with facility but have great difficulty in solving delayed response problems. These data have been taken to support the position that the delayed response was a higher type function than discrimination learning. Confounding this finding is the fact that monkeys with large posterior lesions solve delayed response problems as efficiently as do normal monkeys, but show very marked impairment on discrimination problems. Thus neither the operative nor normal behavioral data support the position that delayed response performance occupies a hierarchical position different from that of discrimination learning.

Still another unestablished assumption found throughout the literature of comparative psychology is that space learning is more natural and easier for animals than is object learning. It is possible that this is so. It may be, however, that this is true for the nocturnal rodent but not for the diurnal primate. It is also possible that the entire concept is meaningless or even fallacious. Rats learn a right-left discrimination more rapidly than they learn a triangle-circle discrimination, but the position discrimination is arranged so that there is no ambiguity of reinforcement whereas the object discrimination involves this additional error-producing factor. Comparison of problem difficulty cannot be made as long as the essential operations involved in testing are grossly different. Furthermore, triangles and circles may be difficult object discriminations for rats; certainly these lowly rodents learn to discriminate all-black alleys from all-white alleys much more readily.

To test the prepotency of object as opposed to positional choice in rhesus monkeys, a small experiment was carried out at Wisconsin on four animals. Eight ambiguous discriminations were run each day for 10 days. In these discriminations the positions of the A and B stimuli of a pair were held constant for 2, 4, 8, or 16 trials, after which a single test trial was presented in which the position of the objects was reversed. The previously correct position was rewarded on half the discriminations, and the previously correct object was rewarded on the other problems. In 95 per cent of the critical trials the monkeys chose on the basis of *object, not position,* previously rewarded. Furthermore, the greater the number of ambiguous pretest trials, the greater was the tendency to choose object. Over the course of the experiment the proportion of object choices increased.

Of course, these animals had had much previous experience on object choice, but if position were prepotent, some trend to position choice should have appeared in this experiment. The data show at the least that, if there is a natural preference for position, it can be completely obscured by training. And, one might ask, has differential space and object training ever been controlled in any experiment with rats or monkeys? To control such training would demand immobilizing the animal from birth, if not before. Until such procedures are effected, natural preferences are a philosophical, not a psychological, concept.

Since monkeys and, presumably, chimpanzees can become proficient object-oriented animals, there would appear to be every reason to believe that they should solve nonspatial delayed responses with skill. Observation of monkeys performing on matching problems reveals that the monkey often spends many seconds in "vicarious trial-and-error" behavior (VTE) between the choice objects without looking back at the sample before choosing. This and other observations convinced the Wisconsin workers that nonspatial delayed response could be readily demonstrated in monkeys by appropriate techniques.

The difficulty that animals show on nonspatial delay is more likely a function of the complex procedures that must be taken to insure that the possibility of spatial delayed response has been ruled out, than a function of intrinsic difficulty in object memory. The assumption that nonspatial delay involves some special symbolic function in an animal as object-aware as the primate cannot be justified.

Generalization, Transposition, and Concept Formation

Generalization and transposition

If either chimpanzees or monkeys are trained to a *single* stimulus and subsequently tested on the training stimulus in combination with a second stimulus differing from it in a single dimension, they most often choose the training stimulus. The farther on the continuum the new stimulus is from the training stimulus, the greater is the frequency of choice of the training stimulus; the nearer on the continuum the new stimulus is to the training stimulus, the less is the frequency of choice of the training stimulus. Selection of the new stimulus under these conditions of training has frequently been described as an example of the phenomenon of *stimulus generalization.*

If trained to select one of two stimuli on the continuum rather than the positive stimulus presented alone, monkeys and chimpanzees, when subsequently presented the positive training stimulus with one proportionately farther out on the continuum in the positive direction, choose the new stimulus most often. This phenomenon has been described as *transposition,* and its fundamental nature has been the basis of theoretical controversy. The actual data obtained on both chimpanzees and monkeys are somewhat inconsistent from one situation to another, suggesting the operation of many variables at present incompletely understood.

Generalization of learned responses to the physical characteristics of stimuli is by no means limited to discrimination learning situations. Generalization of oddity responses was studied in detail by Bromer (6), who found very considerable transfer to new pairs of colors when the form of the training stimuli was held constant, but less generalization when the color remained constant and the form changed. Other data on both chimpanzees and monkeys consistently indicate that generalization of oddity response to color is superior to that of form. Studies on both oddity and Weigl-oddity demonstrate numerical generalization—an animal trained to oddity on a three-foodwell board generalizes the learned oddity response to four- and five-foodwell situations.

Concept formation

Sixteen monkeys were trained by Andrew and Harlow (2) to differentiate a triangle from a circle to the criterion of 45 correct responses in 50 consecutive trials. Subsequently, they were tested for generalization in 50 new situations including, among others, tests of rotation of the positive stimulus, tests with new triangles and new negative figures, and tests with incomplete figures. Generalization was slight, the more triangular figure being chosen only 55 per cent of the time. After the monkeys had been trained on 50 triangularity situations, however, and subsequently tested on 50 different triangularity situations, they chose the more triangular stimulus over 75 per cent of the time. Training on a single discrimination produced little generalization, whereas additional training on a multitude of situations produced considerable generalization. Similar results have been reported for rats, cats, dogs, and chimpanzees. Unfortunately, no study thus far has held amount of practice constant for the single situation as opposed to the multiple situation.

As indicated, there are many investigations in which animals have been trained to differentiate a large variety of triangles from many other forms. Studies of this type, in which generalization is to a particular characteristic of stimuli varying in multiple additional ways, are commonly described as *concept formation*. The data indicate that monkeys and chimpanzees are generally superior to cats and dogs on such generalization tests, and that cats and dogs are superior to rats, whether success is measured by initial responses to changed situations or by rapidity of learning in new situations. Two-

year-old children have proved, however, to be superior to all subhuman animals.

By far the most dramatic study of subhuman concept formation
is the color categorization research by Weinstein (49), who trained
two monkeys to make generalized color-matching responses. The most
striking data were obtained on a single monkey originally trained
to match on the basis of identity and later trained to sort on the basis
of similarity. The correct response to presentation of a red triangular
sample object was selection of all the red objects from a mixed group
of red and blue objects; correct response to a blue elliptical sample

Fig. 20. Color Categorization by a Rhesus Monkey.

object was sorting out all the blue objects. After prolonged training
the subject attained high proficiency in these differential color
matches even when size, form, brightness, and saturation of the
stimuli were varied from trial to trial and the number of correct
objects ranged from zero to eight. When no choice object was correct,
the monkey was rewarded for inhibiting response for 30 seconds.
Finally, the monkey was trained to respond to all red objects when
handed an unpainted triangle, and to select all blue objects in
response to an unpainted ellipse. Figure 20 illustrates these categorization responses.

Weinstein's monkey demonstrated in the final stage of training a truly amazing ability to conceptualize or categorize red and blue to stimuli having no physical characteristic in common with any of the choice objects. Furthermore, many of the choice objects had relatively small areas of the appropriate color and much larger areas of different colors. In all previous concept studies the animals were trained to respond positively to one of the test stimuli, but in the Weinstein study, *not responding* to stimuli that lay outside the category was as important an aspect of the problem as was responding to stimuli within the category. This is a much more precise and rigid criterion of concept than ever before applied to the behavior of any subhuman animal. Human concepts, it should be noted, are *ex*clusive as well as *in*clusive, and the former aspect may be much more intellectually demanding than the latter.

Summary

The data presented in this chapter indicate the range of learned behaviors available to the subhuman primate. In both variety and complexity, the problems that fall within the repertory of the primate contrast sharply with those testable on rodent or carnivore. Under appropriate taming and testing conditions, the monkey becomes a stable test animal, willing, eager, and able. Even a modest laboratory can maintain a primate colony, and modern techniques of experimental design and statistical analysis are such that the behaviors of even small groups can be effectively and quantitatively assessed. Compensating for the size and maintenance cost of the monkey is the fact that large amounts of work can be obtained each day from these animals. The industry of the monkey is such that the major laboratory problem is more often that of obtaining experimenters than obtaining monkeys.

The barest beginning has been made so far in the psychological study of the subhuman primates. Only one anthropoid ape, the chimpanzee, has been subjected to detailed investigation, and only one monkey, the rhesus monkey, has been used in other than scattered investigations. Exhaustive investigation of the behavioral capabilities of the gorilla, orangutan, and gibbon will take place as adequate populations of these anthropoids become available. Many of the hundreds of species of monkeys must possess special abilities and propensities whose experimental analysis and exploitation would reveal further knowledge of primate behavior, including man's. The obsessive curiosity of the instrumentally oriented cebus monkey remains unprobed and unquantified; the absence of competition in the howler monkey has been observed in the wild but is still unanalyzed in the laboratory; the unfissured brain of the marmoset is ideally designed for countless studies in physiological psychology. Other species, too, offer inviting research possibilities. The emotional stability of the young baboon should make him an ideal laboratory primate. Only his growth rate and well-developed canine teeth kept us from choosing him as our first monkey species for detailed study. The pig-tailed macaque consistently out-performed the rhesus monkey in our early studies and may well bear intensive investigation. One great subfamily of primates, those with sacculated stomachs, has yet to point to any representative in psychological research.

The available testing techniques will certainly be vastly improved, expanded, and redesigned to permit more detailed analyses. The relative efficiency of existing techniques is as much a tribute to the ability of the animals as to the ability of the scientists, for the exploitation of almost any technique will provide new and valuable data. Two primate laboratories, even though staffed by men of good will, cannot exhaust the research possibilities on primates in the next quarter-century, nor can they design and standardize *all* the needed apparatus, techniques, and methodology.

There can be little doubt that the comparative psychology of the future will place heavy emphasis on primate research. The use of primates in other scientific fields has rapidly expanded: biological and physiological primate laboratories are common, and facilities for maintaining subjects are becoming standardized. Adequate financial support is to be expected. There is no reason to believe that psychological rodentology will wane, but there is reason to hope that a better balance between rodentology and primatology will obtain in the future.

Bibliography

1. Alpert, A., The Solving of Problem Situations by Preschool Children, *Teach. Coll. Contr. Educ.*, 1928, **323**, 69.
2. Andrew, G., and Harlow H. F., Performance of Macaque Monkeys on a Test of the Concept of Generalized Triangularity, *Comp. Psychol. Monogr.*, 1948, **19**, 1-20.
3. Bingham, H. C., Chimpanzee Translocation by Means of Boxes, *Comp. Psychol. Monogr.*, 1929, **5**, 91.

4. Birch, H. G., The Role of Motivational Factors in Insightful Problem-Solving, *J. Comp. Psychol.*, 1948, **38**, 295-317.

5. ——— The Relation of Previous Experience to Insightful Problem-Solving, *J. Comp. Psychol.*, 1945, **38**, 367-383.

6. Bromer, J. A., A Genetic and Physiological Investigation of Concept Behavior in Primates, Unpublished Ph.D. thesis, Univ. Wis., 1940.

7. Finch, G., The Solution of Patterned String Problems by Chimpanzees, *J. Comp. Psychol.*, 1941, **32**, 83-90.

8. ——— Delayed Matching-from-Sample and Non-spatial Delayed Response in Chimpanzees, *J. Comp. Psychol.*, 1942, **34**, 315-319.

9. Gardner, L. P., and Nissen, H. W., Simple Discrimination Behavior of Young Chimpanzees: Comparisons with Human Aments and Domestic Animals, *J. Genet. Psychol.*, 1948, **72**, 145-164.

10. Harlow, H. F., Experimental Analysis of the Role of the Original Stimulus in Conditioned Responses in Monkeys, *Psychol. Rec.*, 1937, **1**, 62-68.

11. ——— Responses by Rhesus Monkeys to Stimuli Having Multiple-Sign Values, *Studies in Personality* (Q. McNemar and M. A. Merrill, Eds.). New York: McGraw-Hill Book Company, 1942, 105-123.

12. ——— Solution by Rhesus Monkeys of a Problem Involving the Weigl Principle Using the Matching-from-Sample Method, *J. Comp. Psychol.*, 1943, **36**, 217-227.

13. ——— Studies in Discrimination Learning by Monkeys: III. Factors Influencing the Facility of Solution of Discrimination Problems by Rhesus Monkeys, *J. Gen. Psychol.*, 1945, **32**, 213-277.

14. ——— Studies in Discrimination Learning in Monkeys: V. Initial Performance by Experimentally Naive Monkeys on Stimulus-Object and Pattern Discriminations, *J. Gen. Psychol.*, 1945, **33**, 3-10.

15. ——— The Formation of Learning Sets, *Psychol. Rev.*, 1949, **56**, 51-65.

16. ——— Analysis of Discrimination Learning, *J. Exp. Psychol.*, 1950, **40**, 26-39.

17. ——— Meyer, D. R., and Settlage, P. H., Effect of Large Cortical Lesions on the Solution of Oddity Problems by Monkeys, *J. Comp. and Physiol. Psychol.*, 1951, **44**.

18. Harlow, H. F., and Settlage, P. H., Comparative Behavior of Primates: Capacity of Monkeys to Solve Patterned String Tests, *J. Comp. Psychol.*, 1934, **18**, 423-435.

19. Harris, J. D., The Auditory Acuity of Pre-adolescent Monkeys, *J. Comp. Psychol.*, 1943, **35**, 255-265.

20. Hilgard, E. R., and Marquis, D. G., Conditioned Eyelid Responses in Monkeys, with a Comparison of Dog, Monkey, and Man. *Psychol. Monogr.*, 1936, **47**, 186-198.

21. Köhler, W., *The Mentality of Apes*. New York: Harcourt, Brace and Co., 1925.

22. Kohts, N., Recherches sur l'Intelligence du Chimpanzé par la

Méthode de «Choix d'après Modèle». *J. Psychol. Norm. Path.,* 1928, **25**, 255-275.

23. Lashley, K. S., The Mechanism of Vision: XV. Preliminary Studies of the Rat's Capacity for Detail Vision, *J. Gen. Psychol.,* 1938, **18**, 123-193.

24. Maslow, A. H., and Groshung, E. P., Influence of Differential Motivation on Delayed Reactions in Monkeys, *J. Comp. Psychol.,* 1934, **18**, 75-83.

25. Meyer, D. R., Food Deprivation and Discrimination Reversal Learning by Monkeys, *J. Exp. Psychol.,* 1951, **41**. (In press)

26. —————— The Effects of Differential Rewards on Discrimination Reversal Learning by Monkeys, *J. Exp. Psychol.,* 1951. (In press)

27. —————— and Harlow, H. F., The Development of Transfer of Response to Patterning by Monkeys, *J. Comp. and Physiol. Psychol.,* 1949, **42**, 454-462.

28. —————— The Effects of Multiple Variables on Delayed Response Performance by Monkeys, *J. Genet. Psychol.,* 1951. (In press)

29. Nissen, H. W., Ambivalent Cues in Discriminative Behavior of Chimpanzees. *J. Psychol.,* 1942, **14**, 3-33.

30. —————— Analysis of a Conditional Reaction in Chimpanzee, *J. Comp. and Physiol. Psychol.,* 1951, **44**, 9-16.

31. —————— Blum, J. S., and Blum, R. A., Analysis of Matching Behavior in Chimpanzee, *J. Comp. and Physiol. Psychol.,* 1948, **41**, 62-74.

32. Nissen, H. W., and Elder, J. H., The Influence of Amount of Incentive on Delayed Response Performance of Chimpanzees. *J. Genet. Psychol.,* 1935, **47**, 49-72.

33. Nissen, H. W., and McCulloch, P., Equated and Non-equated Stimulus Situations in Discrimination Learning by Chimpanzees: III. Prepotency of Response to Oddity through Training, *J. Comp. Psychol.,* 1937, **23**, 377-381.

34. Nissen, H. W., Riesen, A. H., and Nowlis, V., Delayed Response and Discrimination Learning by Chimpanzees, *J. Comp. Psychol.,* 1938, **26**, 361-386.

35. Noer, M. C., and Harlow, H. F., Discrimination of Ambivalent Cue Stimuli by Macaque Monkeys, *J. Gen. Psychol.,* 1946, **34**, 165-177.

36. Riesen, A. H., Arrested Vision: In Which Chimpanzees Raised in the Dark Shed Light on the Relationship Between Visual Experience and Visual Development. *Sc. Amer.,* 1950, **183**, 16-19.

37. Roberts, K. E., Learning in Preschool and Orphanage Children: An Experimental Study of Ability to Solve Different Situations According to the Same Plan, *Univ. Ia. Stud. Child Welf.,* 1933, **7**, 88.

38. Robinson, E. W., A Preliminary Experiment on Abstraction in a Monkey, *J. Comp. Psychol.,* 1933, **16**, 231-236.

39. Rose, E. L., Spatial and Temporal Bases for the Establishment by Rats of Contrary Discrimination Habits, *Univ. Calif. Publ. Psychol.,* 1939, **6**, 189-218.

40. Schiller, P. H., Innate Constitutents of Complex Responses in Primates, Personal Communication.
41. Simpson, M. M., and Harlow, H. F., Solution by Rhesus Monkeys of a Non-spatial Delayed Response to the Color or Form Attribute of a Single Stimulus (Weigl Principle Delayed Reaction), *J. Comp. Psychol.*, 1944, **37**, 211-220.
42. Skinner, B. F., Are Theories of Learning Necessary? *Psychol. Rev.*, 1950, **57**, 193-216.
43. Spaet, T., and Harlow, H. F., Solution by Rhesus Monkeys of Multiple Sign Problems Utilizing the Oddity Technique, *J. Comp. Psychol.*, 1943, **35**, 119-132.
44. Spence, K. W., The Nature of Discrimination Learning in Animals, *J. Genet. Psychol.*, 1936, **48**, 362-370.
45. ——— The Solution of Multiple Choice Problems by Chimpanzees, *Comp. Psychol. Monogr.*, 1939, **15**, 54.
46. Tinklepaugh, O. L., Multiple Delayed Reaction with Chimpanzees and Monkeys, *J. Comp. Psychol.*, 1932, **13**, 197-236.
47. Warden, C. J., Koch, A. M., and Fjeld, N. A., Instrumentation in Cebus and Rhesus Monkeys, *J. Genet. Psychol.*, 1940, **56**, 297-310.
48. Weinstein, B., Matching-from-Sample by Rhesus Monkeys and by Children, *J. Comp. Psychol.*, 1941, **31**, 195-213.
49. ——— The Evolution of Intelligent Behavior in Rhesus Monkeys, *Genet. Psychol. Monogr.*, 1945, **31**, 3-48.
50. Yerkes, R. M., Modes of Behavorial Adaptation in Chimpanzee to Multiple-Choice Problems, *Comp. Psychol. Monogr.*, 1934, **10**, 108.
51. ——— and Yerkes, D. N., Concerning Memory in the Chimpanzee, *J. Comp. Psychol.*, 1928, **8**, 237-271.
52. Zable, M., and Harlow, H. F., The Performance of Rhesus Monkeys on Series of Object-Quality and Positional Discriminations and Discrimination Reversals, *J. Comp. Psychol.*, 1946, **39**, 13-23.

CHAPTER 8

Theoretical Interpretations of Learning

K. W. SPENCE

State University of Iowa

Introduction

Nature and function of theories in science

Before considering the various theories of learning phenomena, we shall find it helpful to recall the function that theories serve in science. Their role is best understood in terms of the description of the task that the scientist sets for himself. What is it that the scientist is attempting to do?

Briefly, it may be said that the primary aim of the scientist is to develop an understanding or knowledge of a particular realm of events or data. Such scientific understanding consists in formulated relationships between concepts that have reference to the particular events under observation. Thus, beginning with the sense data or events provided by observation, the scientist abstracts out of them certain ones on which he concentrates. To particular descriptive events and patterns of events he assigns, arbitrarily, language symbols (concepts), and then formulates the relationships observed to hold between these events (or concepts) in the form of laws. These observed regularities or laws provide at least partial explanation of the particular events under consideration, for explanation in science basically consists in nothing more than a statement of the relations of a particular event to one or more other events. In the more highly developed sciences, such as physics, these empirical concepts are typically *measurable* concepts, or variables, and the relationships or laws are frequently expressed in terms of mathematical functions.

While such empirical laws relating experimental variables (that is, relatively directly observable magnitudes) provide for explanation of particular events, scientists usually have attempted to develop still more generalized formulations, theories as they are termed, that will serve as a basis for deriving and predicting these lower-order empirical laws. Physicists, in particular, have been highly successful in formulating sets of assumptions (postulate systems) involving high-order theoretical constructs that have served to integrate laws (the interrelations of which were quite unknown prior to the theory) into a single system of knowledge. A good example of the integrating power of such theories is the deduction of the various laws of optics, such as reflection, refraction, interference, polarization, dispersion, and so forth, from the Maxwell electro-magnetic wave theory of radiation.

Theories, in the sense described above, are to be found only in the older, more highly developed sciences, in which many lower-order laws have already been established. In the earlier stages of development of physics, that is, prior to the discovery of the empirical laws by experimentation, and in the less highly developed social and biological sciences of today, the term theory usually has had a quite different meaning. In present-day psychology theorizing consists primarily in guessing at the nature of the lower-order empirical laws. This involves hypotheses as to what other variables besides those we already know determine a particular behavior event, plus further guesses as to the nature of the functional relations holding between these relevant variables and the response. Because of the greater complexity and interrelatedness of psychological phenomena, the behavior scientist has had great difficulty in experimentally isolating elementary situations in which the number of variables is limited, or has not been able to find a satisfactory means of measuring all the relevant variables in the system under observation. In this circumstance he has been forced to offer what have come to be called intervening variables as a device to aid in the formulation of the empirical laws. These are hypothetical constructs that are assumed to intervene between the environmental events on the one hand and the measurable behavior properties on the other (77, 91).

The postulation of intervening variables has been particularly fruitful in the area of learning, and the two leading present-day theorists in this field, Hull (27) and Tolman (91), have explicitly acknowledged their theorizing as being of this form. Hull's constructs of habit ($_sH_R$), inhibitory potential (I_R), reaction potential ($_sE_R$), and so on, and Tolman's sign-Gestalt-expectation, demand, and so forth, are well-known examples of this type of theoretical construct.

The task of the theoretical psychologist

The task of the theoretical psychologist may be described, in terms of the above conception of scientific theory, as consisting in the discovery and statement of the functional relations (laws) holding between certain classes of events. Specifically he is interested in discovering the laws holding between three classes of variables: (*a*) response or behavior variables, (*b*) environmental (physical and social) variables, and (*c*) organic (neurophysiological) variables. The response variables are usually referred to as the dependent variables and the others (environmental happenings and organic condition of organism) as the independent, manipulable variables.

Referring more specifically to the problem of learning, the psychological theorist is interested in ascertaining the interrelations holding between certain kinds of behavior changes and such manipulable experimental variables as, for example, numbers of practice trials, temporal relations between various stimulus aspects, nature and amount of the reward, and certain organic conditions such as neurological lesions.

Classification of theories of learning

In learning, the behavior of the organism in the same situation changes with successive practice occasions. This fact has led the learning psychologist to infer that certain changes also occur inside the organism. Unable to record or measure these events, he has been forced to speculate or theorize as to their nature. The manner in which psychologists have conceived or defined these hypothetical learning changes provides the basis for designating the main theoretical issues and the different positions taken with respect to them (76, 79, 88).

Cognition versus association issue. A major division of opinion among learning theorists is the one concerned with the conception of the nature of the hypothetical learning changes. Thus one group of theorists, the associationists [Thorndike (84), Hull (27), Guthrie (16)] has employed the notion of a functional connection or some kind of linkage becoming gradually established or strengthened with successive practice occasions. Within this point of view one may find different preferences with respect to whether physiological concepts (for example, receptor-effector connections in the nervous systems) or nonphysiological ones (for example, associations, bonds, habits) are employed. The theorist preferring the physiological notion is usually interested primarily in the intrinsic properties of his hypothetical constructs, whereas the theorist employing nonphysiological constructs is more likely to specify (define) their properties in terms of antecedent environmental events. As an example of the latter, we shall see that Hull (27) has defined his hypothetical learning construct, habit, as a mathematical function of certain antecedent environmental variables.

Opposed to the above conception of learning in terms of the incremental growth of a functional linkage or association may be grouped a number of psychologists [Köhler (36), Koffka (35), Lewin (44), Tolman (87), Adams (1), and Zener (99)] who favor what has been designated the *cognition* theory of learning. According to the views of this group, learning is but a part of the more inclusive problem of the *organization* of the cognitive structure of the individual. As such, learning is to be conceived in terms of the organization into some kind of whole of the perceptual systems of the subject, or, more briefly, learning consists in perceptual *organization* and *reorganization*. Thus, in any learning experiment, such as classical conditioning, a pattern of stimulus events occurs, and as a consequence of the organism experiencing it, a cognitive structure or pattern representative of the stimulus relationships is assumed to develop. The subsequent behavior of the organism to the initial conditioned stimulus is, in part, determined by this cognitive structure. In contrast to the associationist's conception of a gradual and incremental strengthening of the hypothetical learning change (bond, connection, habit) with successive practice occasions, the cognitive theorists tend to think of a cognitive pattern becoming clearer and/or changing in structure with practice. The notion of a continuous growth-like process is often vigorously rejected. Instead, they argue that the structure may change suddenly in as yet unpredictable ways. The cognitive theorist has been somewhat vague about the dimensions of change that these cognitive patterns undergo during learning.

As in the case of the association theorists, one finds within the cognition group differences with respect to which the intrinsic properties of the hypothetical construct are emphasized. Thus such psychologists as the Gestalt group (Köhler, Koffka) tend to concern themselves extensively with the physiological nature of the hypothetical learning change (electric brain fields, and so on), whereas Tolman and Lewin almost completely ignore such properties. Tolman, like

Hull, usually proposes that his hypothetical learning construct be defined in terms of the antecedent environmental variables.[1]

S-R versus S-S issue in learning

A second issue that divides learning theorists is very closely related to the first. This disagreement is whether the change, conceived either as an associative link or an organized cognition, involves relating sensory and motor processes (S-R) or sets of sensory (perceptual) processes (S-S). While the association theorists tend to hold to the S-R view, it should be pointed out that there is no necessary reason for them to take sides on this issue, which is concerned entirely with the intrinsic, physiological properties of the hypothetical change. Indeed, Hull's mathematically defined construct of habit involves no implication of an S-R or S-S association. Only when Hull identifies this construct with the physiological notion of a receptor-effector connection does he become an S-R theorist. All of his mathematical theorizing (and this is the only portion of the theory that is employed in accounting for the experimental findings) would apply equally well to either S-R or S-S associations.

The cognition theorists, on the other hand, appear to be much more thoroughly committed to the view that learning involves establishing relations (organizations) between sensory or perceptual processes. Certainly all of them have taken a definite and explicit stand on the matter. Thus the Gestaltists, and such other psychologists in this group as Lashley, Adams, Zener, Lewin, and Tolman, conceive of learning in terms of the formation of cognitive patterns in which are organized the successive perceptual processes occurring in a behavior sequence.

Reinforcement versus nonreinforcement (contiguity) issue. A third and one of the most important areas of disagreement among learning psychologists has to do with a set of conditions that one group believes to be essential if the hypothetical learning changes, whatever their intrinsic nature, are to occur. More specifically, the controversy is over the role of motivation and reward in learning. One group has taken the position that learning requires the presence of some kind of motivating or drive state and the occurrence of a reinforcing (goal)

---

[1] The difficulties encountered in attempting to classify learning theorists is probably best shown by the fact that among the cognition theorists listed above, Tolman has explicitly stated that his theory is associationistic (90). Nevertheless, Tolman subscribes in entirety to the fundamental notions of the cognition group as outlined.

situation. While theorists holding to this view acknowledge that responses contiguous with a stimulus situation may become functionally related (associated) with it, they make the further assumption that a necessary condition for establishing these functional connections is the presence of some form of reinforcement. The outstanding exponent of this theoretical position today is Hull (27).

On the other hand, another group of psychologists has taken an opposite view. They deny the necessity for introducing the concepts of motivation and reinforcement in explaining learning. Reinforcement of the response is not a necessary condition for its strengthening. Provided satisfactory perceptual conditions are present, the occurrence of the stimulus events in some close temporal relationship or the response in contiguity with the situation are sufficient conditions for the learning to occur. Association by contiguity, or sequence in experience, is the primary principle governing learning according to this view. Representatives of both the association (S-R) and cognition (S-S) viewpoints are to be found supporting this nonreinforcement position. Thus, Guthrie (16, 17) and Rexroad (63), both S-R theorists, have formulated association-by-contiguity theories of learning while almost every cognitive theorist seems to have shown a preference for the contiguity principle. Tolman (88, 90) and Leeper (43) have been the most explicit exponents among this latter group.

A third position, representing somewhat of a compromise in this issue of contiguity versus reinforcement, has existed for some time and has lately been gaining many new adherents. Psychologists adopting this view believe that there are two basically different learning processes. In one of these, classical emotional conditioning in which the effectors involved (smooth muscles or glands) are under the control of the autonomic nervous system, the learning is assumed to be governed by the principle of contiguity. In the case of the second type, the principle of reinforcement is said to operate. The latter class is much the more extensive, including classical defense conditioning involving striated muscles, instrumental conditioning, and trial-and-error learning; in fact, all complex forms of problem-solving in which the responses involve striated muscles. The current proponents of this two-factor theory are Skinner (70, 71), Schlosberg (68), Thorndike (9), Maier and Schneirla (48), and its latest convert, Mowrer (54).

Discussions of the reinforcement-nonreinforcement issue are likely to appear confusing to the beginning student for the reason that the protagonists have not always clearly distinguished between three very different kinds of notions: (a) the law of effect as an empirical statement, (b) a general statement of the theory of reinforcement, and (c) special hypotheses that attempt to specify further the properties of reinforcing events. Thus, contiguity theorists such as Tolman and Guthrie would heartily concur with the following statement of the empirical law of effect: "Responses that lead to certain types of environmental events (called rewards) subsequently become stronger and are retained, whereas responses that lead to certain other types of after-effects (called non-rewards) become weaker and eventually disappear" (79).

However, learning theorists opposed to a reinforcement theory would deny that "rewards" are responsible for bringing about the increment or change in the hypothetical learning factor (association, cognition, and so on). To quote Tolman on this point: "... the 'Law of Effect' may hold descriptively for 'performance,' it does not hold for learning *per se* ... Food and lack of food, shock and lack of shock, open path and blind end, the word *right* and the word *wrong*—these do not stamp in or stamp out; they result" [(88), p. 386].

Reinforcement theorists, on the other hand, do assume that the environmental events consequent to a response are responsible for the change in the hypothetical learning factor. In the case of those events (that is, rewards) that are known to result in an increased likelihood of occurrence of the response, the theorist holding to a general reinforcement theory assumes that "rewards" operate in some *unspecified* manner to strengthen the functional connection of the response to its eliciting stimulus. So long as the properties of this class of events (rewards) are not specified, other than that they lead to increased response strength, a theorist may be said to be supporting a general reinforcement interpretation. Many problems in learning do not require the theorist to go beyond such a general statement of a reinforcement theory.

Specific hypotheses as to the nature of reinforcers and their mode of operation have been offered by a number of psychologists. The earliest conception stemmed from the doctrine of hedonism. This hypothesis assumed that pleasant consequences strengthened response tendencies they followed, whereas unpleasant experiences weakened responses. Thorndike's original theory of learning was of this type, although he later abandoned it. The hedonistic theory of learning was developed to its highest degree by Troland (94), who offered both a psychological and a parallel physiological account in terms of retroflex action of the thalamus. For the most part the hedonistic theories have been merely speculative in nature and have not provided for satisfactory experimental test.

A second type of special hypothesis as to the nature of reinforcement that has been suggested is that reinforcement involves relief or reduction of a need or drive. Early formulations of this type were given by Kuo (39) and Perrin and Klein (62). Hull (27) has hypothesized that a primary reinforcing state of affairs involves either a reduction in what he calls the drive level of the organism or reduction in the intensity of a drive stimulus resulting from a basic need or motivating condition. The reduction of drive level or drive stimulation is assumed to set going the reinforcing process, which is left unspecified. As yet very little in the way of experimental testing of these hypotheses has been offered. They have served primarily to specify, in terms of more definite experimental operations, variations in the time of occurrence and amount of reinforcement.

From this discussion of the main theoretical issues dividing learning psychologists and the different positions taken with regard to them, it is readily apparent that the number of possible different kinds of theories would be rather large. Actually, as we have seen, there has been a marked tendency for those who take the same position on the first issue (associationism vs. cognition theory) to side together on the second issue (S-R vs. S-S). Furthermore, a large majority of the S-R association theorists have tended to accept the principle of reinforcement for most learning, while the S-S cognition theorists almost without exception have opposed the reinforcement position.[2] As a consequence we find that the majority of learning psychologists today fall into one of two theoretical camps, either the S-R Association-Reinforcement group or the S-S Cognition-Contiguity group.

---

[2] There are two major exceptions to this tendency. Woodworth (97) has offered a theory of learning that emphasizes both its perceptual character and the principle of reinforcement. Guthrie (16) on the other hand, employs the concepts of stimulus, response, and association, but rejects the principle of reinforcement. These two positions are not treated in the present discussion primarily because of lack of space. The S-S type of reinforcement theory exemplified by Woodworth's formulation has never been worked out in any detail. Guthrie's S-R contiguity theory was outlined in the 1942 edition of *Comparative Psychology* (pp. 298-310). Few, if any, changes or additions have been made in it since. A promising attempt to cast the Guthrie type of theory into a mathematical form similar to that of Hull has recently been offered by Estes (10).

In our subsequent discussion of the detailed theoretical viewpoints, these two positions will be taken as the point of departure. First, their main constructs and assumptions will be presented. Following this, the manner in which each deals with the detailed experimental data provided by different simple learning situations will be treated. Emphasis will be placed on those data that are most critical with respect to the opposing theoretical interpretations.

The *S-R* Association-Reinforcement Theory

Introduction

Contemporary *S-R* theories of learning begin with observed correlations between stimulation and response.[3] Changes in the response made to the same situation with successive practice occasions are first studied and described. On the basis of these observed changes under a variety of conditions, attempts are made to formulate the laws relating the response measures to the manipulated experimental variables.

In his *Principles of Behavior,* Hull begins with the behavior phenomena observed in two types of learning situations, classical and instrumental conditioning. The simplicity of these experimental setups makes them, he believed, particularly strategic starting points for the discovery of some of the basic concepts and laws describing learning and performance. Once available, these concepts and laws would, he assumed, aid us in our attempt to understand and explain more complex learning phenomena. Hull did not mean to imply here, as has sometimes been mistakenly interpreted (21), that the concepts and laws discovered in connection with these two simple types of learning experiments would be sufficient to account for *all*

---

[3] Both the stimulus and response are described at a molar, common-sense level, rather than in molecular, physiological units. Thus a response is described either in terms of the effects it produces in the environment, such as depressing the lever of a Skinner Box, or in terms of the changed spatial relations of the organism in its environment, for example, entering a blind alley, approaching the positive stimulus, and so on. No note is taken of differences in the detailed movements or motor pattern of the activity. Thus, all movements of the organism that result in the same environmental change are regarded as a single-response class.

On the stimulus side the same level of description is employed. Moreover, the stimulus situation is regarded as a complex affair with many different aspects or components that may vary from one trial to another (43, Chap. 13). Quite contrary to the criticisms of some of its opponents, *S-R* theory does not regard the stimulus in even the simplest learning situation as consisting in rigid and unchanging elementary units.

learning behavior. It is obvious that the more complex learning situations must involve new variables and hence additional laws. Hull merely assumed that these situations would involve, at least in part, the same factors (and hence laws) that operate in simpler learning situations. He believed that a precise knowledge of the latter would make it easier to understand how the new and old variables might combine to produce the more complex behavior phenomena. The discovery of the new laws would thus be greatly facilitated.

But even the simple conditioning experiments present such a wealth of data involving so many experimental variables that the formulation of the laws interrelating them is not a simple matter. Thus the data of the typical classical conditioning experiment present a picture showing how the response variable, known as the conditioned reaction, varies or changes with the manipulation of certain experimental variables. Several measurable aspects of response are studied as functions of these manipulable experimental variables and the data so obtained may be plotted in the form of several curves. Thus, in Pavlov's experiment with dogs (57), the increasing magnitude of the C.R. in terms of amount of saliva secreted, or the latency of the C.R., is plotted against the number of reinforcements or combined presentations of the conditioned and unconditioned stimuli. But it has been shown that the response measures are also a function of such other variables as the intensity and duration of the conditioned stimulus (C.S.), the intensity and nature of the primary, unconditioned stimulus (U.S.), the time interval between the onset of the C.S. and the U.S., the time of deprivation of food, and so forth.

Faced with the task of formulating the empirical laws holding within this set of variables, Hull, as we have already indicated, followed the same procedure as Tolman did, namely, that of introducing intervening variables between the environmental variables on the one hand, and the response variables on the other. Briefly, this technique consists in defining a series of hypothetical constructs in step-wise fashion and by means of specific mathematical functions. The construction starts from the independently manipulable environmental variables, for example the conditioned stimulus, number of practice trials, and so on, and ends with assumptions relating the various measures of behavior to the final members in the chain of intervening hypothetical constructs.

Theoretical constructs and principles

1. The construct of stimulus trace (s). The first of Hull's constructs that need concern us has to do with stimulus reception. The stimulation of an end organ, for example, by the C.S. is assumed to initiate an afferent impulse or stimulus trace (s) that consists of two segments, (a) an input segment that varies in magnitude in some characteristic fashion for each receptor with the intensity and duration of the stimulation, (b) a perseverative segment that decreases in magnitude according to a decreasing, negatively accelerated function of the time after termination of the stimulus. The functional connection or relation established in learning is assumed by Hull to occur between the response (effector activity) and the phase of the stimulus trace that coincides temporally with it.

2. The principle of reinforcement. With this concept of stimulus trace before us, we may now state in its most general form the *principle of reinforcement*. According to this principle, whenever an activity (R) of an organism occurs coincidently with a stimulus afferent impulse or trace (s) and the conjunction is accompanied by a "reinforcing state of affairs," there will result an increment in the strength of the habit tendency $(\triangle_s H_R)$ for the stimulus producing s to evoke that response.

3. Need, drive, and drive stimulus. To clarify Hull's expression, *a reinforcing state of affairs,* we must first consider the concepts of need, drive (D), and drive stimulus (S_D). The term *need* refers to hypothetical states of the organism that result from two kinds of antecedent circumstances in the environment that are under the control of the experimenter: (*a*) lack of various environmental objects, such as food, water, and so on, for varying periods of time, and (*b*) intense forms of stimulation, such as electric shock, and so forth. The concept of drive (D) is conceived by Hull as a nonspecific state or general condition of the nervous system to which all the specific needs contribute. D represents, then, the total effective drive strength operating in the organism at a given moment. In a particular experimental situation, the value of D is assumed to be determined not only by the relevant need (that is, the need for which the goal object in the experiment is appropriate) but also by all other needs, primary or secondary, present at the time. Drive stimulus (S_D) refers to the hypothetical, internal afferent impulses aroused by a particular need. Each need, presumably, arouses its own peculiar interoceptive stimulation, so that there are as many kinds of drive stimulation as there are different need states.

For the psychologist interested primarily in learning phenomena, none of these hypothetical states or events need ever be observed directly. They are intervening variables, defined in terms of specific antecedent conditions that are under his control. In each instance with manipulation of one of these conditions, the hypothetical needs, drive level, and drive stimuli can be assumed to be present. By means of more refined quantitative assumptions, varying amounts of these states can be postulated. This is precisely what Hull has done.

4. Primary and secondary reinforcement. Hull has tentatively proposed that a primary reinforcing state of affairs is to be identified with either a reduction in level of drive (D) or with a decrease in the intensity of the associated drive stimulus (S_D). In the case of each need, some act of the organism initiates a sequence of events that culminates in a decrement in the drive, and it is this reduction in drive level that activates the reinforcing mechanism. The clearest instance of the occurrence of such a primary reinforcing state of affairs is the cessation of a noxious stimulus that would occur with escape from electric shock. Presumably the attainment of the various types of goal objects in the environment, such as food and water, represents the onset of external stimulation rather than the reduction of drive or internal drive stimulation, and is an instance of what Hull calls *secondary reinforcement* rather than *primary reinforcement*. Such stimulus events have come to possess reinforcing properties, Hull postulates, because in the past experience of the organism they have occurred repeatedly and consistently with a primary reinforcing event. Thus, a feeding or goal box becomes a secondary reinforcing agent according to this assumption because it has in the past repeatedly accompanied hunger reduction.

5. Secondary motivation. In similar fashion, Hull has assumed that there are secondary motivations or needs that contribute to the total drive strength (D) of the moment and provide for drive stimulation. One such secondary state of motivation is known as *fear* or *anxiety*. When the internal emotional response is aroused by some C.S. that in the past has repeatedly been accompanied by noxious stimulation, we speak of the motivational state aroused by the C.S. as an acquired or secondary one.

6. Habit strength ($_sH_R$). The principle of reinforcement specifies the necessary motivational and reinforcement conditions that must hold on the occurrence of a trial if an increment in the strength of a habit tendency is to occur. In his *Principles of Behavior*, Hull introduced four subprinciples in connection with this principle that, in effect, qualified further the manner in which habit $(_sH_R)$ was assumed to develop. These four postulates hypothesized that habit strength $(_sH_R)$ is a function of four experimental variables: (a) number of reinforced trials (N); (b) magnitude of the reinforcing agent (W); (c) time of delay of reinforcement (T_G); and (d) time between the onset of the C.S. and the occurrence of the U.S. (T_S).

More recently Hull (28) has made a rather radical change in his formulation, and he now considers that only one of these variables, the number of reinforcements, determines the amount of habit strength. The other three variables are now assumed, as we shall see later, to enter into the determination of another intervening variable, excitatory potential $(_sE_R)$, but not habit.

The postulate relating the growth of habit strength to number of reinforced trials assumes that the function $_sH_R = f(N)$ is exponential. In this type of "growth" function, as it is termed, the increment of growth $(\triangle_sH_R)$ on any trial is always a constant fraction (F) of the potential growth as yet unrealized. Thus, if we conceive the amount of habit growth possible as 100 units, the constant fraction of growth resulting from a single reinforcement as 1/10, and the habit as beginning at zero strength, the increment of habit strength for the first trial would be 10; for the second trial, $9 = 1/10$ of $(100 - 10)$; for the third, $8.1 = 1/10$ of $(100 - 19)$, and so forth. Summation of such a set of values would give a negatively accelerated curve of habit growth.[4]

7. **Nonassociative factors determining response strength.** The construct of habit $(_sH_R)$, represents the hypothetical learning or associative factor in Hull's formulation. The measurable characteristics of the learned response at any moment will depend, however, upon a number of other nonassociative factors. For each of these Hull has introduced an intervening variable defined in terms of the environmental conditions that he assumes determine it.[5]

---

[4] For the mathematically trained reader this postulate may be stated as follows:
$$_sH_R = A\,[1 - (1 - F)\,^n]$$
Where A equals the limit to which the habit will grow and F is a constant determining the rate of approach of the function to its maximum. A and F are presumably parameters characteristic of individual learners.

[5] The following presentation of Hull's reformulation of his theory is not strictly in accord with the version presented by Hull in a recent article (28), but represents a somewhat simplified treatment that the present writer favors.

(a) *Stimulus dynamism* (V). Properties of the stimulus situation eliciting the response determine its strength. Thus, in the classical conditioning situation the intensity of the C.S. (S), the length of time it has been acting (T_s), and, if it has ceased to be present, the length of time since its cessation (T'_s) all have been shown to determine the response strength (12, 13, 34, 65). These experimental vari-ables are each assumed to determine the magnitude or intensity of the stimulus trace (s) and to this intervening variable the symbol V is assigned.

$$V = f(S, T_s, T'_s)$$

(b) *Incentive motivation* (K). The properties of the reinforcing stimulus also appear to determine the strength of the response being learned. In the case of classical conditioning involving food as the U.S., and in instrumental learning problems involving positive goal objects such as food, water, and so on, the magnitude of the reward has been shown to affect the response measure, for example, to lower or increase response latency, increase or decrease running speed, and so forth (8, 98). Delay of the incentive has also been shown to deter-mine the level of performance attained in any simple learning situa-tion (18, 59, 61). With these facts in mind, Hull has postulated an in-centive motivational factor (K) that is assumed to be a function of the magnitude (G) and time of delay (T_G) of the reward following the occurrence of the response to be learned.

$$K = f(W_G, T_G)$$

(c) *Primary motivation or drive* (D). This hypothetical factor has already been discussed in connection with the problem of reinforce-ment. The evidence of a number of studies points clearly to the fact that response strength varies with such experimental variables as time of deprivation of goal objects, and, in the classical defense type of conditioning situation, with intensity of the unconditioned stimu-lus (S_u) (56, 58). The intervening variable, drive, may be assumed to be a function of these two types of experimental variables.

$$D = f(T_d, S_u)$$

The three hypothetical factors, V, K, and D, may be lumped together and thought of as the nonassociative factor (M) determining response strength. Hull has assumed that they interact in a multi-plicative manner with each other and with the associative factor,

habit, to define another hypothetical construct, excitatory potential $_sE_R$.

$$M = f(V \times K \times D)$$
$$_sE_R = f(M \times _sH_R)$$

In changing his formulation of these factors from that in the
Principles of Behavior to the above form, Hull has revealed an admirable readiness to be influenced by the experimental findings.
However, the evidence with respect to the role of some of these variables is not as yet clear cut. The studies of Grant and Schneider (12,
13) would seem unequivocally to indicate that habit strength $(_sH_R)$
is not a function of the properties of the C.S. (S, T_S, T'_S). Similarly,
the experimental findings of Crespi (8) and Zeaman (98) suggest that
Hull is on firm ground in his interpretation that habit strength is
not a function of magnitude of the goal object (W_G). The experimental evidence with respect to such variables as the time of delay
of reward (T_G) in instrumental learning or the intensity of the U.S.
in classical conditioning is not so clear cut. Further evidence is required before we can be certain that these various experimental
variables affect response strength through a nonassociative factor or
the associative factor $(_sH_R)$. The problem is important in Hull's
system because of the property of relative permanence assigned to
$_sH_R$ by Hull [(27), p. 109]. Thus, if it should turn out that time of
delay of reward does determine habit strength, then learning under
short delay will establish a high level of habit strength that would
not be reduced if the delay period were subsequently increased. On
the other hand, if time of delay of reward affects a nonassociative
factor (K), increase of reward delay would lead to prompt decrease
of K and an immediate reduction of response strength.

8. **Inhibitory factors determining response strength.** In addition
to the factors determining the *excitatory* potential of a stimulus to
evoke a response, Hull has postulated a further set of intervening
variables that refer to negative or *inhibitory* factors in behavior. The
two most important of these constructs are inhibitory potential (I_R)
and oscillation $(_sO_R)$. Inhibitory potential is conceived as being
composed of two components, reactive inhibition (I_R) and conditioned inhibition $(_sI_R)$. Reactive inhibition is a hypothetical state
that is assumed to develop with each occurrence of the response and
to dissipate in the interval between occurrences. The amount of I_R
that will accumulate over a series of trials is hypothesized to be a
function of the amount of work involved in the act (W), the number

of occurrences of the act (n), and the duration of the time interval between response occurrences (F).

$$I_R = f(W, n, F)$$

Reactive inhibition is further assumed to produce a primary motivational state (need for rest) that is comparable to such other motivational states as pain or tissue injury. The goal response, that is, the response leading to alleviation of this need state, consists in ceasing to make the act or "not responding." As this latter response becomes conditioned to the stimulus complex, it tends to inhibit the making of the original response. This conditioned inhibitory tendency is designated by Hull as $_sI_R$.

The two components of inhibitory potential (I_R), reactive inhibition (I_R) and conditioned inhibition ($_sI_R$) are assumed by Hull to summate and jointly oppose excitatory potential. The net effective excitatory potential is designated as $_s\bar{E}_R$. These relations may be represented mathematically as follows:

$$\dot{I}_R = (I_R + {_sI_R})$$
$$_s\bar{E}_R = {_sE_R} - \dot{I}_R$$

Hull has postulated the intervening variable, behavioral oscillation ($_sO_R$), on the assumption that measures of behavior of living organisms, in addition to showing such systematic changes as occur in learning experiments, also exhibit a random variability. Behavioral oscillation is assumed to fluctuate in amount from trial to trial according to the normal probability function. This factor is also conceived to be inhibitory, acting against effective reaction potential ($_s\bar{E}_R$) to determine a further intervening variable, the momentary effective reaction potential ($_s\dot{\bar{E}}_R$).

$$_s\dot{\bar{E}}_R = {_s\bar{E}_R} - {_sO_R}$$

Finally, Hull assumes a threshold value ($_sL_R$) of excitatory potential that must obtain before an observable response will occur. That is, the momentary effective excitatory potential must be greater than this threshold value before a stimulus will evoke a response. It will be noted that neither of these latter constructs, $_sO_R$ or $_sL_R$, is defined in terms of antecedent environmental conditions; rather each is to be looked upon as a hypothetical variable characteristic of the individual or species. Hull has also made a number of other specific assumptions about them on the basis of relevant experimental data (Hull, Felsinger, and others).

9. Relation of response measures to intervening variables. Completion of this theoretical structure is achieved by relating various measures from learning experiments to one or the other, or some combination of these intervening variables. Thus, the four measures employed most frequently in classical and instrumental conditioning are related to the intervening variables as follows:

(*a*) *Reaction latency* ($_{s}t_{R}$). Reaction latency is a negatively accelerated, decreasing function of the momentary effective reaction potential ($_{s}\dot{\bar{E}}_{R}$).

$$t = a\dot{\bar{E}}^{-b} + c$$

(*b*) *Reaction amplitude* (*A*). The amplitude of responses, mediated by the autonomic nervous system, for example, the galvanic skin response, is an increasing linear function of the momentary effective reaction potential ($_{s}\dot{\bar{E}}_{R}$).

$$A = d\dot{\bar{E}} - f$$

(*c*) *Number of trials to extinction* (*n*). The number of trials required to extinguish a response to some criterion is a linear function of the effective reaction potential ($_{s}E_{R}$).

$$n = hE - j$$

(*d*) *Reaction probability* (*p*). The probability (*p*) of a response occurring to the conditioned stimulus is a normal integral (s-shaped) function of the amount that $_{s}E_{R}$ exceeds the threshold ($_{s}L_{R}$). This is an implication that follows from the definitions already given the oscillatory inhibitory potential ($_{s}O_{R}$), the reaction threshold ($_{s}L_{R}$) and effective reaction potential ($_{s}\bar{E}_{R}$).

By means of these last assumptions and the earlier ones relating $_{s}E_{R}$ to *N*, Hull is able to describe the form that curves of conditioning using these response measures should take. There should be nothing particularly surprising about the fact that such theoretically derived curves fit the data of these conditioning studies. The theoretical constructs and their interrelations were literally chosen so as to make them do so. The purpose underlying their formulation, it will be recalled, was to be able to formulate the laws describing the relations between the changing behavior in a learning situation and the various experimental variables that determine the nature, rate. and limit of this change.

A number of other constructs and principles employed by Hull in his treatment of simple learning phenomena will only be mentioned here; the principles of primary and secondary generalization, interaction between stimulus traces, summation of excitatory potentials, competition between incompatible reaction potentials, and so on. All play important roles in Hull's theory of behavior. Some of these, along with a number of further constructs not required in dealing with conditioning, will be treated later in connection with simple trial-and-error learning and discrimination learning.

S-S Cognition-Contiguity Theory
Introduction

Approaching the task of psychology as being concerned with the ascertainment of the variables determining behavior and the nature of their interrelations, Tolman (91), like Hull, conceives of learning as providing one class of these variables. Experience with any set of environmental events, Tolman assumes, leads to the acquisition or development on the part of the organism of certain kinds of hypothetical sets or *cognitive structures*. These cognitions are introduced as intervening variables that refer to organizations or connections that become established among the perceptual systems of the subject. Learning is thus conceived as involving the formation and modification of these cognitive patterns representative of the relations within the environment and of the organism's own relations to the environment, rather than the strengthening or weakening of stimulus-response tendencies.

Theoretical constructs and principles (laws)

In his most recent theoretical treatment of learning, Tolman (92) suggests that there are six different classes or types of relations that are learned.[6] These different kinds of learning may be thought of

---

[6] Unfortunately for the student just beginning the study of learning, Tolman's writings on the subject involve the introduction of a great many new and rather bizarre terms (for example, sign-Gestalt readiness, means-end-capacity). The difficulty is further aggravated by his penchant for suggesting new and different terms for what is essentially the same concept. Thus, one type of cognitive structure acquired in a number of learning situations has been variously termed means-ends-expectation, sign-Gestalt-expectation, hypothesis, cognition-as-to-what-is-related-to-what, and, most recently, field-expectancy.

Still further confusion is provided by Tolman's ever changing conception of the

as involving the modification (acquisition, deacquisition, and forgetting) of different classes of cognitive structures, each of which is specified in terms of distinguishable environmental-organismic or intra-environmental relations or sequences. The six classes of cognitions or relations listed by Tolman are: cathexes, equivalence beliefs, field expectancies, field cognition modes, drive discriminations, and motor patterns. Since he believes there is little or nothing known at present of the laws governing the acquisition of the last three, these will not be discussed further.

1. Cathexes. These refer to cognitions concerning relations or connections between various kinds of goal objects and drive satisfactions, for example, the knowledge that a particular food satisfies the hunger drive. On the basis of such cathexes and the existence of a particular drive, organisms respond appropriately to goal objects presented by the immediate environment.

2. Equivalence beliefs. These are cognitions with respect to the relation that some environmental object or event has to primary goal objects. As a consequence of such established cognitions, these secondary objects come to serve as subgoals; they provide some kind of drive reduction and are striven for just as primary goal objects themselves.

3. Field expectancies. These refer to cognitions (knowledge) about relations and sequences among events in the environment. As the result of moving about in its environment, the organism "tends to acquire an apprehension not only of each group of immediate stimuli as it impinges upon him but he also tends to acquire a 'set' such that, upon the apprehension of the first group of stimuli in the field, he becomes prepared for the further 'to come' groups of stimuli and also for some of the interconnections or field relationships between such groups of stimuli" [(92), p. 145]. The student familiar with the earlier writings of Tolman will recognize this intervening variable as that which was formerly termed *sign-Gestalt-expectation,* although sometimes Tolman has also used this latter

---

number of different types or kinds of learning that may be distinguished. In the chapter on learning theories in the first edition of *Comparative Psychology* (88), Tolman specified four different classes of learning. Three years later he distinguished seven classes based on the different types of environmental sequences involved in the various kinds of laboratory learning situations (90). In his most recent treatment Tolman (92) offers still a different kind of analysis of the types of connections or relations that organisms have to learn about themselves and the world in which they live. For the most part we shall follow this most recent treatment of Tolman, identifying when necessary the new and old concepts.

concept to refer to the more general notion of cognition as employed here.

These hypothetical cognitive structures become acquired, modified, and extinguished under a variety of conditions. The postulated relations of the environmental variables to these intervening variables constitute the definitions of them and provide us, as we have indicated previously, with guesses as to the laws governing learning. It is characteristic of Tolman's theorizing, however, that it never gets much beyond the programmatic stage, with the result that instead of providing specifically defined constructs, as does Hull, he merely discusses in a general way three classes of experimental variables and laws that play, he believes, an important role in learning.

(a) *Laws or principles relating to stimulus organization.* Like the Gestalt psychologists, Tolman stresses the active, selective, organizing processes that the organism performs on the environmental stimulation it receives. Experimental variables that influence perceptual organization also play an important role in learning. As yet, however, very little is known experimentally concerning these factors in learning. Tolman suggests two such laws, *belongingness* and *fusibility* (87). The former refers to certain conditions that make the components of the cognition "belong together" or stand out as a unit or figure from the background of surrounding experience. The law of *fusibility* asserts that same signs and significates (stimuli) will fuse into cognitive structures more readily than will others. Thus, according to this principle, odors would become more readily conditioned to the salivary reflex, and noises to avoidance responses, than would other forms of stimulation.

(b) *Laws relating to sequence of events in experience.* The law of *association by contiguity*—that learning "arises as a result of some specific sequential pattern (spatial and temporal) of environmental stimulus-objects presented to the animal on one or more occasions" [(90), p. 202]—states a necessary condition for the learning of cognitive patterns (sign-behavior means-significate relations). Other factors that may be subsumed as sub-principles under this fundamental principle of contiguity in experience are those of *frequency* (exercise) and *recency*. Thus the more frequently and recently the components of a cognitive structure have occurred in past experience, the clearer and more highly differentiated is the cognition. Other variables that would be included in this group are such temporal factors as the delay of the goal object following a response, and, in classical conditioning, the time interval between the onset of the conditioned and unconditioned stimuli.

(c) *Laws or principles relative to motivational and reward conditions.* Tolman has shown even more hesitancy about the role of motivational-reward factors in learning. On the basis of the early latent-learning studies from his own laboratory (30, 93), he was led to reject the principle of reinforcement or effect as a law of learning. Although recognizing that the need-satisfying value of a significate (stimulus object) may affect performance, Tolman nevertheless rejected the notion that it in any way affects the formation of cognitions (sign-Gestalt-expectations). The law of effect, he held, was a law of performance rather than of learning.[7]

More recently Tolman (92) has modified his views of the role of motivation and reinforcement in learning. On the basis of the findings of a series of studies involving the learning of a simple, single-choice maze situation under various motivational-reward conditions (14, 30, 33, 80, 81, 82), he has suggested that possibly the learning of some of the types of cognitions, specifically cathexes and equivalence beliefs, does involve *reinforcement.* As he writes: "... the consummatory reactions to these new objects do reduce the corresponding drives. Hence here I believe, with Hull, in the efficacy of reinforcement or need-reduction [(92), p. 146]." In the case of field-expectancies, however, he still rejects the notion that a principle of reinforcement is necessary. Adequate perception and ability to remember and associate the contiguous experiences is a sufficient condition for the acquisition of such perceptual organizations. The experimental findings have also required him to postulate a *law of motivation* (not reinforcement) to the effect that adequacy of perception is a function of the motivational state of the organism. Thus one of these simple T-maze studies (11, 32, 82) has shown that rats were unable to learn which of two alternative paths led to water when hungry or which path led to food when thirsty. Tolman's explanation of this failure was that the rats did not "perceive" the water and food under such motivational conditions.

Tolman has also suggested a *law of emphasis.* Cognitions are acquired more or less readily as the result of certain types of strong, inciting conditions accompanying the stimulus events. This law is

---

[7] The manner in which Tolman conceives that goal objects affect performance will be treated more in detail in the later discussion of specific learning situations.

based on the observation that either pleasant or painful experiences, for example, pleasant odors, electric shock, seem to speed up learning. He believes this is due to the emphasizing or compelling nature of these conditions rather than their satisfying or annoying characteristics.

The concepts of primary and secondary demands

In addition to these hypothetical learning constructs (cognitions), Tolman has introduced a number of other intervening variables that he defines in terms of the manipulable environmental variables and subject variables. The most important of these from the point of view of our present interest are the constructs of primary and secondary demands (89). Primary demands or demands for drive reduction are defined in terms of some controlling maintenance schedule such as feeding schedule, drinking schedule, oestrus cycle schedule, and so on.

$$\triangle_{DR} = f(T_D),$$

where $\triangle_{DR}$ represents a primary demand for drive reduction and T_D represents time of deprivation of some goal object.

Secondary demands are defined in terms of primary demands (or other secondary demands ultimately defined in terms of primary demands) and cognitions (cathexes, equivalence beliefs, field expectancies) concerning the relations that various environmental objects have to the intervening secondary-demand objects and the final primary demand. These relationships may be made clear by means of the following simple instrumental learning situation. Suppose we have a runway with a starting box at one end and a goal box containing food at the other. If a hungry animal placed at the starting box is permitted to run to the goal box and obtain a piece of food, it will be found that its starting time (time elapsing between raising the door in the starting box and leaving the box) and time on the runway to the goal will show a steady decrease on successive trials until a limiting, or asymptotic, value is attained. The increased speed of response reflects an increase in what Tolman refers to as the behavior readiness (B_P) to run down the maze path. Behavior readiness is thus an intervening variable somewhat analogous to Hull's excitatory potential ($_sE_R$):

$$R_t = f(B_P)$$

The behavior readiness with respect to the pathway is said to be a function of the secondary demand for this pathway ($\triangle_P$) which, in turn, is defined as being a function of the cognition (field expectancy) that the pathway leads to food ($C_P \rightarrow F$) and the secondary demand for food ($\triangle_F$).

$$B_P = f(\triangle_P)$$
$$\triangle_P = f[C_P \rightarrow F, \triangle_F]$$

The secondary demand for food is, in turn, a function of the cognition (cathexis) that the particular food leads to hunger reduction plus the primary demand for hunger reduction ($\triangle_{HR}$).

$$\triangle_F = f[C_F \rightarrow HR, \triangle_{HR}]$$

Each of the cognitions, of course, is a function of the previous training experiences that the subject has had with the particular stimulus objects, that is,

$$C_P \rightarrow F = f \text{ (Training experiences)}$$
$$C_F \rightarrow HR = f \text{ (Past experiences with food)}$$

Tolman does not offer any specific guesses or suggestions as to the nature of the functions defining any of these intervening variables, stating that he prefers to proceed to ascertain them empirically by a set of "standard" experiments in which all but one of the independent experimental variables is held constant. The obtained functional relation holding between any one independent variable and some quantifiable aspect of observable behavior defines objectively one of the intervening variables. Each intervening variable is to be defined by such a standard experiment. Unfortunately, the matter, even in simple learning situations, is not so simple. There would be no scientific economy in having a single intervening variable for each independent experimental variable. Furthermore, such experiments do not provide directly the nature of the functional relations holding between the more highly derived intervening variables that are defined, in part, by other intervening variables, nor the relations between the final set of intervening variables and the empirical response measures. On the basis of the available data one has to make guesses as to these relations, as Hull has done. So far Tolman has not offered such hypotheses, and for this reason his theorizing is as yet only in the blueprint stage.

Classical Conditioning

Theoretical interpretations of classical conditioning

Early interpretations of the classical conditioned-response experiment by psychologists (Watson, Guthrie) stressed the temporal factors in this type of learning situation. In classical conditioning the onset of the conditioned stimulus (C.S.) is always in some constant temporal relation to the onset of the unconditioned stimulus (U.S.) and hence to the unconditioned response (U.R.). This controlled arrangement gave emphasis to the necessity for contiguity or close temporal sequence of these events if the learning was to occur. While there was some recognition of the role of motivation in determining the C.R., this factor was stressed relatively little.[8] Moreover, not even the most ardent of the early reinforcement theorists (Thorndike) thought to offer a reinforcement interpretation of this type of learning. Indeed, Thorndike (85) regarded classical conditioning as a special form of learning that appeared to have different laws from those of trial-and-error learning.

With respect to the integration of classical conditioning with other forms of learning, two points of view have dominated the thinking of psychologists until recently. One was that conditioning revealed the basic principle of learning to be that of association by contiguity. The problem for the theorists (for example, Watson, Guthrie) holding this view, was to show how this principle could also account for trial-and-error learning in which, because of the influence of the work and writings of Thorndike, the law of effect held sway. The second point of view was that held by Thorndike, mentioned above; namely, that there are two kinds of learning, (*a*) classical conditioning, which is governed by the principle of association by contiguity, and (*b*) other, more complex forms of learning in which the principle of reinforcement is operative. In 1937 Hull (26) suggested the possibility of a third position. This was that conditioned-response learning and trial-and-error learning are special cases of the operation of a single set of principles, a central one of which is the principle of reinforcement.

---

[8] The fact that Pavlov employed the expression "reinforcement by the U.S." would appear to contradict this statement. The meaning of the term "reinforcement" for Pavlov, however, was that of "facilitation of action," not the notion of an after effect strengthening an S-R tendency.

S-R reinforcement interpretation of classical conditioning

The reinforcement interpretation of the C.R. experiment may be made clear with the help of Fig. 1, which has been taken from Hull [(27), p. 77]. According to this conception, the U.S., electric shock, serves not only the function of evoking the leg flexion, but is also assumed by Hull to set up, at its onset, a drive state (D) and a drive stimulus trace or drive receptor impulse (s_D). The cessation of the shock is assumed to lead to a decrease in the strength of the drive state and cessation of the drive stimulus trace, that is, to a reinforcing state of affairs. The occurrence of the reinforcing state of affairs in conjunction with the coincidence of the stimulus trace of the C.S. and the response of leg flexion leads to the establishment of habit strength (sH_R) between the stimulus trace and the response. It will be recalled that this process of habit growth is assumed to be a cumulative process, the increments of habit strength on successive trials becoming smaller and smaller with the result that the curve of growth approaches a limiting value.

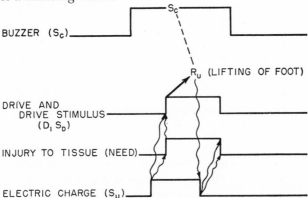

Fig. 1. The S-R Reinforcement Interpretation of Classical Conditioning. The R_u terminates the shock (S_u), which in turn terminates the drive (D) and drive stimulus (S_D). The latter presumably provides for the reinforcing state of affairs that sets up the habit $(S_C H_R)$.

Such defense types of response to noxious stimulation provide the simplest instance of classical conditioning involving primary reinforcement. The Pavlovian type of conditioned-response experiment represents a somewhat more complex situation in which the U.S. (food), in addition to eliciting the U.R., provides for secondary reinforcement rather than primary reinforcement. The drive state (D) in this instance is provided by the hunger resulting from food deprivation.

S-S contiguity interpretation of classical conditioning

In sharp contrast to the S-R reinforcement interpretation of classical conditioning, the S-S contiguity theorists assert that such learning involves the integration into some kind of cognitive structure of the sensory processes aroused by the C.S. and the U.S. As a result of the conditioning procedure, the first stimulus (C.S.) acquires the functional properties of the second (U.S.), namely that of eliciting the response. While these theorists have not been specific about the course of development of this cognitive organization as have the S-R theorists, they have hypothesized that contiguity of occurrence of the inner events resulting from the stimulation is a requisite condition for its establishment. There is no need to assume, they claim, a motivational state and a reinforcing event.

Experimental evidence relative to the rival interpretations of classical conditioning

The issues between these opposed interpretations have been responsible for a number of experimental studies that have been directed toward their settlement. While some of the findings have been relevant to the issue, and hence critical of it, certain others have not. A consideration of both types of studies will provide us not only with a picture of the status of the present evidence on the problem, but also with some of the difficulties that arise, particularly when superficial and uncritical thinking occurs in such matters.

1. **Relative effectiveness of avoidance and nonavoidance procedures in conditioning.** One experimental finding that has been cited by opponents of the reinforcement theory (2, 48) as failing to support this type of interpretation is the superior conditioning obtained by Brogden, Lippman, and Culler (7) under what is known as *avoidance conditioning* as compared with *nonavoidance conditioning*. In the former procedure the occurrence of a C.R. (that is, a response prior to the onset of the U.S.) prevents the noxious U.S. from occurring, whereas in nonavoidant conditioning the subject receives the U.S. regardless of the occurrence or nonoccurrence of the C.R. In the experiment cited, an attempt was made to condition guinea pigs to run in a rotating cage to the sound of a 1000-cycle tone that preceded the U.S. (shock) by two seconds. In terms of per cent of occurrence of C.R.'s, the curve for the avoidance group rose steadily to a level of 100 per cent in an average of 200 trials.

The nonavoidance group started out as well for the first hundred trials, but then fell behind, and, after reaching a maximum of about 50 per cent C.R.'s at 325 trials, finally fell below 20 per cent at 500 trials.

According to reinforcement theory, some of its critics have claimed, the nonavoidance group should have shown the superior conditioning, for it always received a shock and hence reinforcement (pain reduction) occurred on every trial (2). Indeed, the question might be raised as to why the avoidance group attained such a high level of conditioning at all under this procedure, for as conditioning develops there occurs an increasing proportion of nonreinforcements.

However, these critics failed to take into consideration one very important factor that was apparent even in the report of the original study, but that was brought out more clearly in a subsequent study (69) in which the experimenter designed his apparatus to record more precisely how the subjects behaved on each trial. The latter experiment showed that once a conditioned running response occurred to the tone, the onset of the shock in the nonavoidance group tended to elicit, not a more vigorous running response, but an incompatible, nonrunning response (crouching, sprawling, and so on). Analysis of the data revealed that if the response made to shock on a particular trial was continued running, the frequency of conditioned running on the ensuing trial increased from 40 per cent to 50 per cent. But the frequency of C.R.'s on the next trial dropped from 40 per cent to 20 per cent when the response to shock on the previous trial had been some type of nonrunning. It is apparent from this analysis that counterconditioning of an incompatible (nonrunning) response was responsible for the poor performance of the nonavoidance group and that this finding is not, as claimed, inconsistent with a reinforcement theory.

It has probably occurred to the reader that if one had a situation in which the response made to the U.S., once the C.R. begins to occur, is the same as the C.R., except that it is possibly more vigorous, this complication of counterconditioning would not be a factor and conditioning would be expected to occur more readily with the nonavoidance technique. Some evidence that the nonavoidance procedure was slightly better than the avoidance procedure when the response conditioned was leg flexion in the white rat has been reported by Schlosberg (67), but his evidence was extremely meager and inconclusive. A recent experiment by Logan (45) compared the effectiveness of the two procedures in eyelid conditioning in human subjects. In this study, in which the U.S., electric shock, continued to elicit the same response as the conditioned anticipatory response (eyelid closure), it was found that the nonavoidance group showed significantly superior conditioning to the avoidance group.

The explanation offered by the reinforcement theorist of the fact that conditioning does occur in avoidance conditioning despite the increasing failure of primary reinforcement to occur with increase in conditioning is that the C.S. becomes conditioned to an emotional (fear) response. With the onset of the C.S. this emotional response occurs, resulting in an increase in the drive level; the termination of the C.S. produces a cessation of the emotional response and hence a reduction in the drive. Such reinforcement is present whether or not primary reinforcement, dependent on the occurrence and cessation of the U.S., is present. This hypothesis, which was suggested by Mowrer (53), has received experimental support in the finding that avoidance conditioning occurs more effectively if the C.S. terminates the instant the C.R. occurs, instead of a few seconds before or a few seconds afterward (55).

In summary, it will be seen that the superiority of the avoidance over the nonavoidance technique of conditioning found by Brogden, Lippman, and Culler is not unfavorable to the reinforcement theory, as claimed by its critics. Not only is this result quite satisfactorily explained in terms of counterconditioning but results of the opposite nature were found to occur when such counterconditioning did not occur. While this latter result (superiority of nonavoidance over avoidance) is in agreement with reinforcement theory, it cannot be interpreted as refuting the S-S contiguity theory. The fact that the sequence of events, C.S.-U.S., does not occur consistently in avoidance conditioning, but is increasingly replaced by the sequence, C.S.-no-U.S., should, theoretically, lead to interference (confusion, ambiguity) in the development of the cognitive structure and hence to poorer performance. Unfortunately, neither Tolman nor any other proponents of this type of theory have ever got around to considering in detail the effects on cognition development of such a variable as variation of the proportion of occurrences of the U.S. following the C.S. Until the theory is more developed these experimental facts have no significance one way or the other for it.

2. **Experiments in which U.R. is elicited without exciting a pain receptor.** An interesting conditioning experiment that has sometimes

been cited as providing evidence in favor of the sensory integration (S-S) interpretation and as opposed to the S-R association conception is the finding reported by Loucks (46). He was unable to obtain conditioning of leg flexion in a dog to a buzzer when the response was elicited by direct faradic stimulation of the appropriate area of the motor cortex. The fact that there was no activation of the second afferent process (that corresponding to the U.S.) led Maier and Schneirla (48) to interpret the result as evidence that such learning consists in some kind of integration of the two sensory processes. The lack of one of the sensory processes, they reasoned, precluded the development of the organization and hence the appearance of the conditioned response. Moreover, they argued that the hypothesis that the association involved a linking of the afferent event corresponding to the C.S. and the efferent process leading to the U.R. was also refuted, as these two processes were left intact and yet no conditioning occurred.

But the S-R reinforcement theorist would inquire as to the source of the reinforcement in the experiment. The direct stimulation of the cortex by faradic shock does not arouse any pain receptors and hence noes not provide for the cessation of drive receptor impulses (that is, reinforcement) with the cessation of the shock. With no reinforcement present, conditioning should not be expected. This interpretation receives support from a second part of the experiment in which Loucks did provide for reinforcement in the form of the presentation of a piece of food following the occurrence of leg flexion. Under this arrangement the conditioning did occur just as the S-R reinforcement theory would predict.

Loucks and Gantt (47) have reported still another study that strongly supports the interpretation that reinforcement in the form of pain (drive) reduction plays a critical role in classical conditioning involving skeletal responses. These investigators found that leg flexion of the dog could not be conditioned to a buzzer when elicited by faradic stimulation in the region of the spinal cord containing kinesthetic fibres. However, conditioning did occur when the shock was applied to the posterior root ganglion. In the latter case pain fibres were involved and with this stimulation and its cessation the conditions were set for drive reduction and thus a reinforcing state of affairs. Both of these experiments are thus seen to offer strong support of the S-R reinforcement theory of learning and not to favor the contiguity interpretation that rejects reinforcement.

3. Studies employing the pupillary response to light stimulation. A number of careful studies (22, 83, 96) have recently reported failure to obtain conditioning of the pupillary response with a light as the U.S. The conditions of these experiments have provided the necessary contiguity of the sensory events (or S-R events) and yet conditioning has consistently failed to occur. Most significantly, conditioning of the pupillary response has been obtained when electric shock instead of visual stimulation served as the U.S. (19, 20). The implication of these studies, like those of Loucks, is clear. They point to the conclusion that classical conditioning does not occur with mere contiguity of the stimulus-aroused events. Some form of reinforcement, primary or secondary, is required. The studies with the pupillary response are also of significance for the two-factor theory of conditioning (cf. p. 244). The pupillary response is under the control of the autonomic nervous system and thus, according to the two-factor theory, falls into the group of responses that do not require reinforcement. Obviously, the evidence of these studies does not support this theory.

4. Sensory preconditioning studies. In concluding this discussion of the experimental evidence from classical conditioning bearing on these rival theoretical interpretations, mention should be made of the studies of what is known as sensory preconditioning (5, 6, 29). In this type of experiment two stimuli (for example, a tone and a light) are presented together prior to conditioning. After one of them has been made a C.S. to some response, the other is tested to see if it will evoke the same response. Positive results have been interpreted as evidence that sensory integration occurred during the original combined presentation of the two stimuli without any reinforcement.

The findings from these studies have been somewhat equivocal. From the point of view of reinforcement theory, moreover, the experimental design has been very inadequate. In the presentation of the two stimuli in the preconditioning series the onsets of the two stimuli have been simultaneous, a condition that has been shown experimentally to be very unfavorable in the regular conditioning situation. Provided it were arranged to have the onset of one of the stimuli in the preconditioning series occur a half-second before the other and provided the second stimulus is relatively intense so as to produce a mild drive state and hence, with its cessation, a reinforcing state of affairs, the reinforcement theorist would expect to obtain more positive results in this type of experiment than have been obtained thus far. If either of the stimuli employed in the preconditioning is very weak, or even if the stimulus occurring second is weak and the first is strong, very much less or no sensory preconditioning would be expected on the basis of reinforcement theory. Sensory preconditioning studies designed along these lines would provide important evidence with respect to the reinforcement issue. The studies that have been conducted so far have no significance in this regard.

Simple Trial-and-Error Learning

Analysis of simple trial-and-error learning

In classical conditioning, the second, or reinforcing, stimulus is entirely independent of the behavior of the subject and occurs according to a fixed temporal arrangement determined by the experimenter. In all other experimental arrangements that have been employed in the study of animal learning, the occurrence or nonoccurrence of

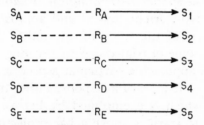

Fig. 2. Diagram Representing Simple Trial-and-error Learning. $S_A - - - - S_E$ represent different aspects of the environment to which the subject responds $(R_A - - - - R_E)$. $S_1 - - - - S_5$ signify the environmental events subsequent to each response.

the reinforcing stimulus (the demanded significate in Tolman's terms) is determined by the response of the subject. Typically, these more complicated learning situations involve a number of different response alternatives that lead, usually, to different subsequent stimulus events. One of the responses (the successful or correct one) leads to an environmental object or place for which, by virtue of an antecedent maintenance schedule or the presence of a noxious stimulus, the subject has a need. The other responses (unsuccessful or erroneous responses) do not lead to the needed goal-object or, as in some instances, they lead to it but only after greater amounts of time and/or effort.

Figure 2 presents in diagrammatic form such trial-and-error learning. $S_A \ldots S_E$ represent different aspects of the environment to which the subject may respond. $R_A \ldots R_E$ signify the different instrumental responses that can be made in the situation, and $S_1 \ldots S_5$ refer to the environmental events subsequent to each response. While the responses have been designated by a single R, it should be understood that each R refers to a series or sequence of acts. Each instrumental sequence begins with orientating and approaching (locomotion) responses to the part of the environment containing one of the stimulus aspects and ends either with locomotion or some distinctive manipulative act (depressing a lever, lifting a latch, pulling a loop, and so forth). The final act in the correct instrumental sequence either brings the subject to the needed goal-object or brings the goal-object to it. In the case of incorrect acts, other stimulus-objects may be attained but not the one for which the subject is at the moment motivated.

A variety of such trial-and-error situations has been used. The most typical (for example, the problem box and simple T-maze) may be described as *spatial-discrimination situations* in which the subject has to learn to orient toward and approach one particular aspect (spatial locus) of the environment rather than others. In a somewhat different type of trial-and-error learning problem the subject has to learn to approach a particular aspect of the situation and then learn to make one kind of a response rather than another to it. Such a situation, which is exemplified by Perin's experiment (60) in which rats had to learn to move a bar projecting into a box to the left rather than to the right, might be described as involving response differentiation in addition to discrimination of spatial cues. Still another type of learning situation is the *nonspatial-discrimination problem* in which the aspects of the environment that are to be approached or avoided do not keep their spatial relations constant. Examples of this are learning to discriminate differences of brightness, form, and so forth. This latter type of learning problem is referred to as discrimination learning.

At the beginning of simple trial-and-error learning, the correct (goal-attaining) response is not the strongest among the alternatives, with the result that at first erroneous responses occur. Finally the correct response takes place and the first trial is completed. Successive trials typically show a lesser number of occurrences of the erroneous responses until finally the correct response occurs promptly at the beginning of each trial. This process is a fairly complex one involving the weakening and disappearance of erroneous responses, and, simultaneously, the strengthening and more and more prompt occurence of the correct response sequence.

A limiting case of such trial-and-error learning is the type of problem known as instrumental conditioning. In this type of learning the response to be learned is, as in trial-and-error learning, instrumental in bringing about the goal stimulus. It differs from trial-and-error learning in that the experimenter attempts to arrange conditions in such a way as to make the correct, goal-attaining response the one most likely to occur from the beginning. Thus the course of such learning primarily represents the strengthening of the tendency to make this response; it is not complicated by the simultaneous weakening of the incorrect responses. In actual practice this condition is probably seldom attained. Thus most instrumental learning situations (for example, Skinner Box) are only limiting cases of trial-and-error learning in which the occurrence of erroneous responses, and hence the necessity for extinguishing them, is minimized.

In our treatment of the theoretical interpretations of these various kinds of trial-and-error learning, we shall limit ourselves primarily to two situations: simple selective learning, involving spatial discrimination such as the single-choice-point maze, and nonspatial-discrimination learning. These two learning problems have provided some of the most interesting and relevant experimental data with respect to the rival theories.

S-R association interpretation of simple selective learning

According to the *S-R* theory, all forms of trial-and-error learning involve the relative strengthening of the correct (goal-attaining) stimulus-response tendency as compared with the competing, incorrect *S-R*'s As shown below, in the single-choice-point T-maze we have two competing *S-R*'s, one of which leads to the needed goal object (S_G) and one to an empty goal box (S_O) or some other nongoal object.

$$\begin{array}{c} S_{l.} \\ S_R \end{array} \quad \begin{array}{ll} \xrightarrow{\quad \bar{E} \quad} & R_A \longrightarrow S_G\,(-) \\ \xrightarrow{\quad E \quad} & R_A \longrightarrow S_O\,(+) \end{array}$$

Depending upon the initial strengths of the two competing effective excitatory potentials ($_{S_L}\bar{E}_{R_A}$, $_{S_R}E_{R_A}$), which, in turn, will be primarily a function of transfer from past experience, the subject will at first respond in a chance manner to the two alleys or show an initial preference for one or the other. With successive reinforcement of the correct response and nonreinforcement of response to the incorrect alley, $s_L E_{R_A}$ will increase in strength because of the increase in habit strength $(s_L H_R)$, while $s_R \bar{E}_{R_A}$ will decrease in strength because of the accumulation of inhibition resulting from nonreinforcement (I_R).[9] As the difference between the two competing response potentials increases in favor of $s_L \bar{E}_{R_A}$, the likelihood of occurrence of the stronger (correct) response will increase until it finally reaches 100 per cent.[10]

The essential notion underlying this theory of selective learning is that one of the competing excitatory potentials acquires greater strength than the other, that is, $s_L E_{R_A} > s_R E_{R_A}$. While an important factor underlying the increased strength of the correct excitatory potential $(s_L \bar{E}_{R_A})$ is the increase in habit strength that results from each reinforcement, there is also another *nonhabit* (that is, nonassociative) factor that must be considered. Reference is being made here to the role played in this type of learning by the so-called fractional anticipatory goal reaction (r_G) and its interoceptively produced cue (s_G). In his earlier theoretical articles on maze learning (23, 24) and problem solving (25), Hull made considerable use of this mechanism. Its function in the present kind of learning has been discussed briefly by Spence (79).

Figure 3 shows the relations that this mechanism $(r_G \rightarrow s_G)$ has to the correct response in the present type of situation. The cues at the entrance to the left alley, or rather the traces of these cues, (see p. 249, after a number of trials, become conditioned (classical) to the goal response (R_G). Stimulation by the cues at the entrance of the left alley will evoke, through generalization, such components of this goal response (r_G) as can occur without the actual presence of the goal object (for example, in the case of food salivation, chewing movements, and so on). The interoceptive stimulus cue (s_G) produced

---

[9] There is some disagreement among S-R theorists concerning the detailed assumptions about the weakening of a response tendency with nonreinforcement. Space does not permit discussion of these alternative conceptions here; the discussion will primarily be concerned with the increasing strength of excitatory potential with reinforcement.

[10] This relationship between probability of response occurrence (R_p) and the magnitude of the difference between the effective excitatory strengths of the competing responses is derivable from the assumptions made concerning the oscillation $(s O_R)$ of the two competing excitatory potentials. The matter is not treated here, since it is not relevant to the theoretical issues to be discussed.

by this classical conditioned response will itself became conditioned to the instrumental locomotor response and thus becomes a determiner of its excitatory strength. Presumably it does this in two ways: (a) the s_G acquires habit strength ($s_G H_R$) to the instrumental locomotor response, and (b) through the intensity of its trace, which presumably increases with the increased strength of r_G as the latter becomes more strongly conditioned, s_G determines the nonassociative factor, K. Recalling that

$$_sE_R = f\,(K \times {_sH_R}),$$

it will be seen that this mechanism determines the excitatory strength of the instrumental response in two ways. That is, it contributes a component to $_sH_R$ and it determines the value of K.

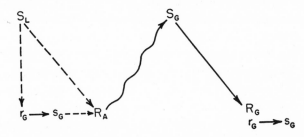

Fig. 3. **As the Result of Classical Conditioning the Fractional Anticipatory Goal Response r_G Moves Forward and Occurs at S_L.** The s_G resulting from r_G becomes conditioned to R_A.

Reference to the earlier discussion of this factor, K, in Hull's theory (p. 252) will show that two experimental variables were assumed to determine its magnitude: (a) the magnitude of the reward, and (b) the period of its delay. A large reward would be expected to lead more quickly to a preference for the correct path of the T-maze than a small reward (64), while a long delay of the reward would be expected to lead to slower adoption of the correct response than no delay or a short delay of reward (56). The fractional anticipatory goal response and its interoceptive cue are here suggested as providing the mechanism underlying this incentive motivational factor, K. We shall return to a further consideration of this mechanism in connection with certain experimental studies of simple selective learning that will be treated later. We turn now to a brief treatment of the S-S contiguity theory of this type of learning.

S-S cognition interpretation of simple selective learning

Tolman's theory of simple selective learning represents an extension of that given for instrumental learning on page 260. Instead
of the single secondary demand for the maze pathway based on the
cognition (field expectancy) that the pathway led to food plus the
secondary demand for food, we have in this choice type of maze
situation two competing secondary demands, one for the left path
and one for the right path. According to this theory, response to the
left path will eventually occur more frequently than the response
to the right path (assuming as before that food is on the left side)
because there develops a stronger secondary demand for the left
path $(\triangle_L)$ than for the right path $(\triangle_R)$. These secondary demands
for the two paths are, in turn, functions of: (a) the cognitions (field
expectancies) that the left alley leads to food $(C_L \rightarrow F)$ and the right
alley to an empty box $(C_R \rightarrow B)$, and (b) the secondary demands for
food $(\triangle_F)$ and the empty box $(\triangle_B)$. These latter demands, in turn,
are functions of the cognitions (cathexes) as to the relation of these
objects to the primary demands for consummation that they satisfy.
Thus the strength of the demand for food is based on the cognition
that food satisfies the hunger drive plus the primary demand for
hunger reduction, that is:

$$\triangle_F = f (C_F \rightarrow HR, \triangle_{HR}).$$

Similarly the demand for the empty box would presumably be based
on some such primary demand as that for exploration $(\triangle_{ER})$ and
the cognition that the box would provide for some kind of reduction
of this primary demand, that is:

$$\triangle_B = f (C_B \rightarrow ER, \triangle_{ER}).$$

In this type of experimental situation the demand for the left
alley will be stronger than that for the right alley because the demand
for food is greater than the demand for the empty end box and not
because there is a difference in the strength or clarity of the cognitive
items. These relationships may be represented as follows:

$$B_L > B_R \text{ if } \triangle_L > \triangle_R$$
$$\triangle_L = f(C_L \rightarrow F, \triangle_F) > \triangle_R = f(C_R \rightarrow B, \triangle_B) \text{ if } \triangle_F > \triangle_B$$
$$\triangle_F = f(C_F - HR, \triangle_{HR}) > \triangle_B = f(C_B \rightarrow ER, \triangle_{ER}) \text{ if } \triangle_{HR} > \triangle_{ER}$$

As yet, however, Tolman has never specified the nature of any of these functions, nor has he specified how cognitions (cathexes, field expectancies, and so forth) change with successive experiences (trials). He has suggested that the cognitions become clear and differentiated, rather than stronger. Presumably the differential demands for the two alleys will not develop until the cognitions have become clear, but whether and how degrees of clearness of the cognitions lead to degrees of demand differentiation is not made explicit.

Experimental tests of theories of simple selective learning

Since both the S-S and S-R types of learning theories are able to predict that a subject will come to choose the alley leading to the goal object for which it is motivated, learning data from this standard type of simple-choice situation do not provide critical evidence with respect to them.[11] A number of modifications of this simple learning situation, however, have been employed by the present writer and his students in an attempt to test the cognition theory. The first of these investigations (81, 82) employed a single-choice maze in which one of the paths led to an end box containing food and the other to one containing water. The subjects, white rats motivated for water and satiated for food, were given 60 training trials in which they had experience with both pathways and the contents of their end boxes. Since the subjects were satiated for the food they did not eat it but presumably only "perceived" it as a visual, odorous object. A test was then given in which the motivation of the subjects was shifted from thirst to hunger. According to Tolman's theory, as formulated at the time of the experiment, the subjects should have acquired not only the cognition that one of the paths led to water but also that one led to food, since the perception of this alley entrance was followed in experience by the perception (seeing, smelling, and so on) of the food. Motivated as the subjects were in the test trial for food and satiated for water there should have been a greater demand for the path leading to food than for the path leading to water and consequently the path leading to food should have been taken.

$$[\triangle_L = f\,(C_L \rightarrow F, \triangle_F) > \triangle_R = f\,(C_R \rightarrow W, \triangle_W)]$$

But the experimental findings were quite the opposite. All 20 subjects continued to go down the path leading to water. This finding,

---

[11] The programmatic nature of Tolman's theorizing precludes, of course, the use of any refined quantitative findings in testing these two theories.

which is predictable on the basis of S-R theory, was subsequently confirmed by Kendler (32) and Gleitmann (11).

A difficulty with this first experiment from the viewpoint of the cognition theory was the asymmetry of the two paths at the completion of the training period, so far as their need-satisfying properties were concerned. It could be argued that the subjects might be responding on the basis of the cognition that the left path led to need-satisfaction, whereas the right path did not. In order to eliminate this possibility two further types of experiment were conducted.

In one of these, the subjects were motivated for water that was to be found at the end of each of the alleys. One of the goal boxes also contained food. The experimental question was whether or not the animals, while motivated by thirst, would also acquire the cognition that one of the alternative paths led to food, and whether or not they would be able to use this knowledge to respond appropriately when motivated for food on a subsequent test. According to Tolman's cognition theory the expectation was that the animals should respond appropriately on the test trials, as they should have acquired the field expectancy that one of the alleys led to food. The results of three studies of this type have been somewhat equivocal. Two (30, 33) have been negative, the subjects responding in purely chance fashion on the test trial. A third study (95), however, has given positive results (5 per cent level of significance) in two parts of the experiment and negative results in a third part.

In a third variation of this simple-choice type of experimental situation, one of the end boxes contained food and the other water. However, the subjects were satiated for both of these goal objects and a different incentive was employed to motivate the subjects to perform in the maze during the training period. In the first study of this type conducted (80, 81) the motivational-reward condition employed was that of wanting to get to a social cage containing cage mates of the same sex after being isolated in small confining cages for a period of time prior to each trial. A number of other studies have used this experimental design either with this same source of motivation (49) or some other, such as need to escape prodding (31), need to get back to the home cage (52), or need to escape anxiety-eliciting cues (86).

The results of these studies have also been conflicting although they have, on the whole, been much more negative than positive to the cognition theory. That is, when motivated for one or the other of the goal objects, food or water, the subjects have not responded by choosing the appropriate path. Three of the studies (31, 52, 80) did give positive results on the first test but negative results on a second test in which the subjects were motivated for the goal object (food or water) for which they had not been motivated on the first test. Two studies (49, 86) gave uniformly negative results on all tests.

As a result of these experimental findings Tolman (92) has been led to modify his earlier views as to the conditions necessary for the acquisition of the cognitions (field expectancies) involved in this type of experiment. He now suggests that the motivational conditions of the moment play a much more important role than had previously been realized in determining if there is adequate perception of the goal-object (significate). Unfortunately, he has not been able to offer any generalization with respect to this variable that would permit one to account for all of the conflicting experimental results. To assume, as he has, on the basis of one kind of result [14, (33)], that thirsty animals apparently do not "perceive" the presence of food, merely gets him into trouble when confronted with another study (95) in which the subjects apparently were able to perceive the food while thirsty. Another question that might be asked is why, in one study (80), did subjects successfully perceive and therefore learn about the location of food and water while motivated to get to a social cage, and, in another, fail to learn when the social reward was brought nearer to the point at which the significates (food and water) were located (49). Obviously cognition theory needs considerable elaboration and reformulation before it can adequately account for these seemingly conflicting data.

One further point to be emphasized about the implication of these studies is that, quite contrary to common belief (21), they have no bearing on the question of whether or not reinforcement is necessary for the hypothetical learning change to occur. All these experiments involved some form of motivation and a reinforcing state of affairs of some kind. Indeed, it was impossible to conduct such an experiment in the absence of these conditions (80). Thus the question whether or not cognitive structures can be established through contiguity or sequence in experience of sign, behavior, and significate *without a reinforcing state of affairs of any kind* cannot be answered by this experimental design. In terms of Tolman's theoretical constructs this type of experiment can tell us only whether expectancies concerning significates (goal objects) for which there is not at the

moment any need, can be established on the basis of some other motivational state and accompanying or closely following significate
that does have reward value. Or, in other words, these experiments
provide tests of the adequacy of only the S-S cognition portion of
Tolman's theory that learning is a matter of forming relations (organizations) between perceptual processes.

Turning now to the S-R interpretation of these experimental findings, a number of writers (30, 49, 52, 75, 81) have attempted to show
how they may be accounted for in terms of the *fractional anticipatory
response mechanism* discussed above. First, an experiment by Kendler (30), in which the objects in both goal boxes were relevant to
the existing motivations of the subject during the training period,
will show the decisive role that this mechanism can play in such a
situation. Using a single T-maze, one path of which led to food and
the other to water, Kendler had his subjects (rats) *both* hungry and
thirsty during learning. In the subsequent test trials only one of the
needs, hunger or thirst, was present. It was found that the subjects
were able to respond appropriately a highly significant number of
times. As the responses to both pathways were reinforced equally
it is reasonable to assume that their habit strengths $(_sH_R)$ were
strengthened to the same degree during training. How then is the
differential response on the test trials to be explained?

A suggestion made by Spence (30, 75) was that the cues at the
entrance to the path leading to water through conditioning in
the training series come to elicit the fractional anticipatory drinking
act (r_w) and, in turn, the proprioceptive cue (s_w) from this act becomes
conditioned to response of approaching and locomoting in this alley.
Similarly, the fractional anticipatory eating response (r_f) becomes
conditioned to the other alley entrance, and the proprioceptive cue
(s_f) from it becomes conditioned to the behavior of entering this
alley. During the test series, when only one need is operative, the
anticipatory act related to the goal object for which the subject is
motivated, will, because of the greater strength of the particular drive
stimulus (see the principle of stimulus dynamism) be stronger than
the other, and hence will produce the stronger proprioceptive cue.
For example, if the subject is thirsty, s_w will be stronger (more intense) than s_f. The intensity of these conditioned proprioceptive cues
(s_w, s_f) determines, it will be recalled, the nonassociative factor, K,
and hence the excitatory strengths of the responses of entering and
continuing down the paths to which they are conditioned. The

greater intensity or strength of s_w when thirsty and not hungry leads to the implication that the excitatory potential of the response to the alley leading to water will be stronger than that of the response of entering the food alley. In other words, in the test series the relative excitatory strengths of the competing responses will be a function of the relative strengths of the two fractional anticipatory goal responses and their proprioceptive cues (factor K). These latter will, in turn, be dependent upon which need is present and which is absent.

The application of this principle to the experiments in which the subjects were motivated for some incentive (for example, social goal) other than food and water in the training series is similar. The sight of the food (or water) is assumed to evoke, as the result of past experience, conditioned fractional eating (drinking) responses. As described above, these responses would become conditioned to the cues of their respective alley entrances, the reinforcement being provided by the social goal, or possibly the sight of the food or water itself (secondary reinforcement).

Now these fractional anticipatory goal responses would be much weaker in this type of experiment than Kendler's (30) as the subjects do not actually eat or drink during the training period but are merely stimulated visually, tactually, and so on. This would imply that weaker r_g's would be conditioned to the alley cues and consequently the interoceptive cues (s_g) would also be weaker. The poorer test results obtained under these conditions as compared with the test data of Kendler's study in which the subjects ate or drank instead of just seeing the food and water might possibly be related to the fact that the absolute differences in the strengths of the proprioceptive cues is less in the test series of this experiment than in Kendler's.

Still another and even more promising possible explanation of the relatively poorer results in the studies in which the food is seen and not eaten is the possibility that the weaker fractional anticipatory goal responses elicited under these conditions are interfered with by the competing goal response made to the incentive for which the subject is motivated. This hypothesis would seem particularly apropos to the predominantly negative findings obtained in the experiments in which the subjects, motivated for water, found water in both end boxes and saw food in one of them (14, 34). The suggested explanation is that under thirst motivation the presence of the water dispenser in the end box, with its tendency to evoke strong anticipatory drinking responses, interfered with the occurrence of the weaker conditioned fractional eating response (r_f) evoked by the sight of the food. Thus the latter was prevented from becoming conditioned to the traces of the cues from the alley entrance. When made hungry in the test trial, the cues at the alley entrance leading to food would thus not evoke any anticipatory eating response with the result that the differential s_f would not be present to give an advantage to the excitatory potential of responding to this alley over that of the other. Hence the animals would be expected to respond in chance fashion.

In this connection it is interesting to note that in the Kendler (34) and Grice (14) experiments, in which the test results were negative, food and water were in the same goal box. In the Walker experiment (95), on the other hand, in which positive test results (significant choice of the food alley) were obtained, there were two separate goal boxes at the end of each alley, with food in the first one and water in the second. The separation of these two goal boxes would be expected to result in less interference of the conditioned fractional eating response to the sight of food by the anticipatory drinking response. Presumably this would provide for greater likelihood of the r_f becoming conditioned to the maze cues. One prediction that may be made on the basis of this hypothesis is that the greater the separation (in time and/or space) of the food and water, the more likely will the test results be positive. The logic behind this derivation is that the greater the separation the less will be the interference with the r_f to food by the r_w and hence the greater the likelihood that the r_f would become conditioned to the cues at the entrance to the alley leading to food.

Probably the most important conclusion to be drawn from this discussion of these experimental findings on simple selective learning and their implication for the rival theoretical interpretations is that no theory is at present sufficiently complete to account for all the detailed findings. The cognition type theory, as formulated at the present time, has been shown to be inadequate to account for the facts. The S-R theory, especially with the elaboration of Hull's earlier concept of the fractional anticipatory goal response, has been able to suggest a number of experimental variables, for example, the degree of separation of the goal objects, the incompatibility of the responses made to the goal objects, and so on. These are important determiners of learning in this type of situation. In contrast to the state of our knowledge about classical and instrumental conditioning, in which we have already managed to isolate the major variables determining the strength of the conditioned response and have even been able to ascertain in fairly precise form the nature of the relations (laws) holding among the variables, our knowledge of such simple selective learning is much less complete and much less developed. Our theorizing in this area is still in the stage of ascertaining what variables are important for this type of behavior.

Discrimination Learning

Analysis of discrimination learning

Discrimination learning, as exemplified in the choice type of situation in which the animal must learn to approach and enter a lighted alley and not a darkened alley, or to jump toward a card containing a triangular form and not to a card containing a circle, and so forth, is, as was described earlier, a type of simple trial-and-error learning. It differs from such situations as the problem-box and single-choice-point maze in that the cue aspects of the environment do not keep their spatial relations constant. Instead, the positive cue is presented in random order on the left and on the right side with the negative cue necessarily being on the opposite side each trial. The subject must learn to approach always the positive cue on whichever side it may be, and not to approach the negative cue.

As a consequence of this shifting of the position of the positive and negative cues in this type of learning situation, it will be seen that responses to the spatial cues, for example, the left and right alleys, or left and right boxes, and so on, are reinforced part of the time and not reinforced part of the time. Thus, in the initial stages of learning, approaching responses to these spatial cues are reinforced approximately only 50 per cent of the time. As the discrimination is learned this proportion increases until at the point of mastery it is 100 per cent. In other types of simple trial-and-error learning (single-choice-point maze, problem box, and so forth), responses to the various stimulus aspects are either always reinforced or consistently followed by nonreinforcement.

Analysis of the pre-solution period of such discrimination learning in animals has shown that it is marked by the occurrence of systematic response tendencies, or, as they have been termed by Krechevsky, hypotheses (37). These hypotheses, which may be precisely defined in statistical terms as responses that occur within a block of trials with a frequency beyond the limits of chance expectancy, have consisted predominantly of spatial responses, particularly left- or right-position habits. While for the most part they tend to be present from the beginning of learning, they also have been observed to develop during the course of learning.

Theoretical interpretations of discrimination-learning phenomena, including the presence of these hypotheses during the pre-solution period, follow fairly closely the main division of learning theories we have been considering. One, referred to as the noncontinuity theory, falls within the class of theories that we have designated as the S-S cognition type. Among its chief proponents is Lashley (41, 42) who was listed among the psychologists favoring this type of theory, and another, Krechevsky (Krech), carried out his first studies on hypotheses in Tolman's laboratory (37). The opposing continuity interpretation (50, 51, 71, 72, 73) is developed within the framework of the S-R association theory.

Noncontinuity (cognition) interpretation of discrimination learning

Based on a suggestion originally made by Lashley, the noncontinuity theory (38, 42) assumes that the systematic response tendencies or hypotheses exhibited in the presolution period represent attempted solutions of the problem that are based on the cognitive belief that the particular cues selected signify or lead to the demanded significate. It assumes further that while an animal is responding on the basis of one of these initial, incorrect hypotheses or cognitions, no learning occurs with respect to the relevant cue. Thus, if the subject is responding on the basis of a position (for example, left) hypothesis it learns nothing, develops no cognition, with respect to the relevant stimulus cue. Eventually it gives up the position hypothesis, tries some other hypothesis until, finally, it hits upon the correct hypothesis. Only from then on does it learn anything (form cognitions) about the relation of the correct stimulus cue to the significate or goal object.

Continuity (association) interpretation of discrimination learning

In contrast, the continuity theory emphasizes the continuous nature of the learning process. Discrimination learning is conceived to be a cumulative process of building up with each reinforcement the excitatory strength (habit, associative strength) of the positive cue to evoke the approaching response, as compared with the excitatory tendency of the negative stimulus cue to evoke the response of approaching it (71, 73). This process is assumed to continue until the excitatory strength of the positive cue is sufficiently greater than that of the negative cue to offset any other differences in excitatory strength that may exist between the stimulus complexes, of which these cues are members. Thus the difference in excitatory strengths of the cue stimuli must be greater than the difference between the excitatory strengths of the position cues, for example, the left and right alleys, before learning will be complete.

As long as the animal is receiving discriminably different stimulation from the positive and negative discriminanda from the start of training, differential associative tendencies will be developed with respect to them from the beginning. Such would be the case for example in learning a brightness-discrimination problem involving a lighted versus a darkened alley. However, this requirement would not necessarily hold true in a pattern- or form-discrimination problem. In such situations the animal would first have to learn to make receptor-orienting acts that would provide discriminably different stimulation from the two stimulus patterns before differential excitatory (associative) tendencies with respect to these stimulus cues would develop. This latter point is particularly important for the main point at issue between the two rival theories—whether the animal, while responding on the basis of an irrelevant hypothesis, for example, a position habit, learns anything with respect to the relevant cues. While positive evidence of such learning would provide a disproof of the noncontinuity theory and support for the continuity interpretation, it should be noted that negative evidence would not disprove the continuity theory. The continuity theorist would accept negative evidence as opposing his theory only in the case of the simple brightness-discrimination situation in which the receipt of discriminably different stimulation is assured. Negative findings in a pattern discrimination situation might, on the other hand, be a consequence of failure of the initial receptor-orienting adjustment of the subject to provide discriminably different stimulation from the two stimulus figures. As we shall see, the evidence on this issue is importantly related to the type of discrimination problem involved and to the precautions taken by the experimenter to insure discriminably different stimulation during the period the subject is responding with the irrelevant hypothesis.

Experimental tests of theories of discrimination learning

In order to test the opposed implications of the continuity and noncontinuity theories with respect to the question of whether the animal learns anything with respect to the relevant stimulus cues while responding systematically on the basis of some other irrelevant cues, Spence (77) employed the following experimental design. Two groups of albino rats, 20 in each group, learned a white-black discrimination problem. Prior to the learning both groups were trained until they had acquired a strong position habit to their preferred side with the black and white cues absent. The experimental group was then given 20 trials in which response to the stimulus that would be negative in the subsequent learning situation was rewarded. The control group was reinforced 50 per cent of the time on both white and black stimuli during this prelearning period of 20 trials. Following elimination of the position preference the regular learning problem was presented. The implications of the two theories are clear. According to the noncontinuity interpretation, no learning would take place with respect to the black and white cues during the 20-trial prelearning period in which the subjects were responding with the position habit, hence there should have been no difference in the subsequent learning of the white-black problem by the two groups. On the contrary, the continuity theory would predict a difference between the groups. The experimental group should have been relatively retarded in their learning, for the consistent reinforcement of responses to the stimulus that was subseqeuntly to be negative should have built up the excitatory strength of this cue to a value greater than that which was to be positive. The subsequent learning would require that the direction of this difference be reversed. Indeed, this theory would predict that, following the elimination of the position preference, the experimental subjects should start the learning problem at a point below 50 per cent.

The experimental results were in complete agreement with the continuity theory and contrary to the implication of the noncontinuity theory. The experimental group was significantly retarded as compared with the control group. Furthermore, as predicted by the continuity theory, the experimental group began its learning well below the 50 per cent point, taking approximately 50 trials before it reached this level of performance.

Two further investigations (9, 65) have since employed essentially this same experimental design but have differed in that they involved pattern discrimination instead of brightness differences. One of these studies (65) required the subjects, pigmented rats, to discriminate between patterns of horizontal and vertical black and white stripes. The results again agreed entirely with the continuity theory and were contrary to the implications of the noncontinuity theory.

The third study, that of Ehrenfreund (9), involved learning to discriminate between upright and inverted white triangles on black cards. This experiment is interesting because it was run under two different conditions of stimulus reception. In one condition the stimulus figures were so presented that the receptor-orienting acts that the subjects had acquired in the preliminary training were unlikely to provide discriminably different retinal stimulation from the figures during the period in which the groups were responding with position habits. In the preliminary training with this jumping type of apparatus, in which the subject is trained to jump to the open window, it learns to fixate and jump towards the lower part of the window. When the stimulus cards bearing the figures are placed in the window, the subjects fixate the bottom part of the card and jump against it. Presumably this fixation precludes the reception of discriminable patterns of stimulation from the figures, with the result that differential associations with respect to these cues do not develop in the initial training trials. Successful learning of such a discrimination requires that the subject modify its receptor-exposure adjustment so as to receive differential stimulation from the cue figures before jumping towards them. Only after such differential stimulation is provided can differential excitatory tendencies develop.

By placing the forms on the upper portion of the stimulus cards in the first condition of his experiment, Ehrenfreund further assured the lack of differential stimulation during the prelearning period. Under this condition no difference was found in the subsequent learning of the experimental and control groups. In the second condition of his experiment Ehrenfreund arranged the apparatus in a manner calculated to assure the reception of discriminably different stimulation from the cue figures from the first trial of their presentation. This was accomplished by raising the level of the jumping platform of the apparatus so that the subjects jumped to the cards at the level of the stimulus figures. Under this condition a difference between the experimental and control groups was obtained, the experimental group being significantly retarded in all measures of learning. This result, like those of the other two studies, was contrary to the noncontinuity theory and in agreement with the theoretical analysis offered by the continuity viewpoint.

The findings of these three experiments clearly establish the fact, contrary to the implication of the noncontinuity theory, that differential learning with respect to the relevant cues does occur while the subject is responding systematically on the basis of other irrelevant cues. Ehrenfreund's study, moreover, provides a possible explanation of the failure of Krechevsky to find similar results in an earlier study with pattern vision (41). Other recent studies that have provided evidence in support of the continuity conception of discrimination learning and contrary to the noncontinuity interpretation are those of Grice (15) and Bitterman and Coate (3).

Summary

Theoretical interpretations of such simple learning phenomena as classical and instrumental conditioning, simple selective learning, and discrimination learning differ with respect to a number of issues: (a) whether the hypothetical learning change is to be conceived in terms of the incremental growth of associative (habit) processes or in terms of the organization of the cognitive structure of the organism; (b) whether the changes involve the association or functional linking of afferent with efferent processes (S-R) or the organization of afferent (perceptual) systems (S-S); (c) whether or not the learning changes require for their occurrence the presence of some kind of motivational state and reinforcing state of affairs. Two main theoretical positions, designated as the S-R association-reinforcement interpretation and the S-S cognition-contiguity theory, are outlined and their implications examined in relation to the relevant experimental data from the four types of simple learning listed above.

Bibliography

1. Adams, D. K., A Restatement of The Problem of Learning, *Brit. J. Psychol.*, 1931, **22**, 150-178.
2. Birch, H. G., and Bitterman, M. E., Reinforcement and Learning: The Process of Sensory Integration, *Psychol. Rev.*, 1949, **56**, 292-308.
3. Bitterman, M. E., and Coate, W. B., Some New Experiments on The Nature of Discrimination Learning in The Rat, *J. Compar. and Physiol. Psychol.*, 1950, **45**, 198-210.

4. Blodgett, H. C., The Effect of The Introduction of Reward Upon The Maze Performance of Rats, *Univ. Calif. Publ. Psychol.*, 1928, **4**, 114-134.

5. Brogden, W. J., Sensory Preconditioning, *J. Exper. Psychol.*, 1939, **25**, 323-332.

6. ⸺⸺ Test of Sensory Pre-Conditioning With Human Subjects, *J. Exper. Psychol.*, 1942, **31**, 505-517.

7. ⸺⸺ Lipman, E. A., and Culler, E. The Role of Incentive In Conditioning and Extinction, *Amer. J. Psychol.*, 1938, **51**, 109-117.

8. Crespi, L. P., Amount of Reinforcement and Level of Performance, *Psychol. Rev.*, 1944, **51**, 341-357.

9. Ehrenfreund, D., An Experimental Test of The Continuity Theory of Discrimination Learning with Pattern Vision, *J. Compar. and Physiol. Psychol.*, 1948, **41**, 408-422.

10. Estes, W. K., Toward A Statistical Theory of Learning, *Psychol. Rev.*, 1950, **57**, 94-107.

11. Gleitman, H., Studies in Motivation and Learning: II. Thirsty Rats Trained in a Maze With Food But No Water; Then Run Hungry, *J. Exper. Psychol.*, 1950, **40**, 169-174.

12. Grant, D. A., and Schneider, D. E., Intensity of The Conditioned Stimulus and Strength of Conditioning. I. The Conditioned Eyelid Response to Light, *J. Exper. Psychol.*, 1948, **38**, 609-696.

13. ⸺⸺ Intensity of The Conditioned Stimulus and Strength of Conditioning. II. The Conditioned Galvanic Skin Response to an Auditory Stimulus, *J. Exper. Psychol.*, 1949, **39**, 35-40.

14. Grice, G. R., An experimental Test of The Expectation Theory of Learning, *J. Compar. and Physiol. Psychol.*, 1948, **41**, 137-143.

15. ⸺⸺ The Acquisition of A Visual Discrimination Habit Following Response to a Single Stimulus, *J. Exper. Psychol.*, 1948, **38**, 633-642.

16. Guthrie, E. R., *The Psychology of Learning*. New York: Harper and Brothers, 1935.

17. ⸺⸺ Conditioning: A Theory of Learning in Terms of Stimulus Response, and Association, *41st Yearbook Nat. Soc. Study Educ.* Bloomington: Public School Publishing Company, 1942.

18. Harker, G. S., An Experimental Investigation of The Effect of Changes in The Delay of Reinforcement Upon Level of Performance of An Instrumental Response. Unpublished Ph.D. Thesis, University of Iowa, February, 1950.

19. Harlow, H. F., The Effect of Incomplete Curare Paralysis Upon The Formation of Conditioned Responses in Cats., *J. Genet. Psychol.*, 1940, **56**, 273-282.

20. ⸺⸺ and Stagner, R., Effect of Complete Striate Muscle Paralysis Upon The Learning Process, *J. Exper. Psychol.*, 1933, **16**, 283-294.

21. Hilgard, E. R., *Theories of Learning*. New York: Appleton-Century-Crofts, Inc., 1948.

22. ⸺⸺ Dutton, C. E., and Helmick, J. S., Attempted Pupillary Con-

ditioning at Four Stimulus Intervals, *J. Exper. Psychol.*, 1949, **39**, 683-689.

23. Hull, C. L., Goal Attraction and Directing Ideas Conceived As Habit Phenomena, *Psychol. Rev.*, 1931, **38**, 487-506.

24. ———— The Concept of The Habit-Family Hierarchy and Maze Learning, *Psychol. Rev.*, 1934, **41**, 33-52; 134-152.

25. ———— The Mechanism of The Assembly of Behavior Segments in Novel Combinations Suitable for Problem Solution, *Psychol. Rev.*, 1935, **42**, 219-245.

26. ———— Mind, Mechanism and Adaptive Behavior, *Psychol.*, Rev., 1937, **44**, 1-32.

27. ———— *Principles of Behavior*. New York: D. Appleton Century, 1943.

28. ———— Behavior Postulates and Corollaries—1949, *Psychol. Rev.*, 1950, **57**, 173-180.

29. Karn, H. W., Sensory Pre-conditioning and Incidental Learning in Human Subjects, *J. Exper. Psychol.*, 1947, **37**, 540-544.

30. Kendler, H. H., The Influence of Simultaneous Hunger and Thirst Drives Upon the Learning of Two Opposed Spatial Responses of The White Rat, *J. Exper. Psychol.*, 1946, **36**, 212-220.

31. ———— A Comparison of Learning Under Motivated and Satiated Conditions in The White Rat, *J. Exper. Psychol.*, 1947, **37**, 545-549.

32. ———— An Investigation of Latent Learning in a T-Maze, *J. Comp. and Physiol. Psychol.*, 1947, **40**, 265-270.

33. ———— and Mencher, H. C., The Ability of Rats to Learn The Location of Food When Motivated by Thirst—An Experimental Reply to Leeper, *J. Exper. Psychol.*, 1948, **38**, 82-88.

34. Kimble, G., Conditioning as a Function of the Time between Conditioned and Unconditioned Stimuli, *J. Exper. Psychol.*, 1947, **37**, 1-15.

35. Koffka, K., *The Principles of Gestalt Psychology*. New York: Harcourt, Brace & Company, Inc., 1935, p. 720.

36. Köhler, W., *Gestalt Psychology*. New York: Horace Liveright, 1929.

37. Krechevsky, I., Hypotheses in Rats. *Psychol. Rev.*, 1932, **39**, 516-532.

38. ———— A Study of the Continuity of the Problem-Solving Process, *Psychol. Rev.*, 1938, **45**, 107-133.

39. Kuo, Z. Y., Giving Up Instincts in Psychology, *J. Philosophy*, 1921, **18**, 645-664.

40. Lashley, K. S., *Brain Mechanisms and Intelligence*. Chicago: University of Chicago Press, 1929.

41. ———— An Examination of the Continuity Theory as Applied to Discriminative Learning, *J. Gen. Psychol.*, 1942, **26**, 241-265.

42. ———— and Wade, M., The Pavlovian Theory of Generalization, *Psychol. Rev.*, 1946, **53**, 72-87.

43. Leeper, R., The Role of Motivation in Learning; A Study of the Phenomenon of Differential Motivational Control of the Utilization of Habits, *J. Genet. Psychol.*, 1935, **46**, 3-40.

44. Lewin, K., Field Theory and Learning, *41st Yearbook Nat. Soc. Study Educ.* Bloomington: Public School Publishing Company, 1942.

45. Logan, F. A., A Comparison of Avoidance and Nonavoidance Eyelid Conditioning. M.A. Thesis, University of Iowa, February, 1950.

46. Loucks, R. B., The Experimental Delimitation of Structures Essential for Learning: The Attempt to Condition Striped Muscle Responses with Faradization of the Sigmoid Gyrus, *J. Psychol.*, 1935, **1**, 5-44.

47. ———— and Gantt, W. H., The Conditioning of Striped Muscle Responses Based Upon Faradic Stimulation of Dorsal Roots and Dorsal Columns of the Spinal Cord, *J. Compar. Psychol.*, 1938, **25**, 415-426.

48. Maier, N. R. F., and Schneirla, T. C., Mechanisms in Conditioning, *Psychol. Rev.*, 1942, **49**, 117-133.

49. Maltzman, I. M., An Interpretation of Learning under an Irrelevant Need, *Psychol. Rev.*, 1950, **57**, 181-187.

50. McCulloch, T. L., Comment on The Formation of Discrimination Habits, *Psychol. Rev.*, 1939, **46**, 75-85.

51. ———— and Pratt, J. G., A Study of The Pre-solution Period in Weight Discrimination by White Rats, *J. Compar. Psychol.*, 1934, **18**, 271-290.

52. Meehl, P. E., and MacCorquodale, K. A., Further Study of Latent Learning in The T-Maze, *J. Compar. and Physiol. Psychol.*, 1948, **41**, 372-396.

53. Mowrer, O. H., Anxiety Reduction and Learning, *J. Exper. Psychol.*, 1940, **27**, 497-516.

54. ———— On the Dual Nature of Learning—A Reinterpretation of "Conditioning" and "Problem-solving," *Harv. Educ. Rev.*, 1947, **17**, 102-148.

55. ———— and Lamoreaux, R. R., Avoidance Conditioning and Signal Duration—A Study of Secondary Motivation and Reward, *Psychol. Monog.*, 1942, **54**, No. 5.

56. Passey, G. E., The Influence of the Intensity of Unconditioned Stimulus Upon Acquisition of a Conditioned Response, *J. Exper. Psychol.*, 1948, **38**, 420-428.

57. Pavlov, I. P., *Conditioned Reflexes* (Trans. by G. V. Anrep). Oxford Univ. Press, 1927.

58. Perin, C. T., Behavior Potentiality as a Joint Function of the Amount of Training and the Degree of Hunger at the Time of Extinction, *J. Exper. Psychol.*, 1942, **30**, 93-113.

59. ———— A Quantitative Investigation of the Delay of Reinforcement Gradient, *J. Exper. Psychol.*, 1943, **32**, 37-52.

60. ———— The Effect of Delayed Reinforcement upon the Differentiation of Bar Responses in White Rats, *J. Exper. Psychol.*, 1943, **32**, 95-109.

61. Perkins, C., The Relation of Secondary Rewards to Gradients of Reinforcement, *J. Exper. Psychol.*, 1947, **37**, 377-392.

62. Perrin, F. A. C., and Klein, D. B., *Psychology*. New York: Henry Holt and Co., 1926.

63. Rexroad, C. N., An Examination of Conditioned Reflex Theory, *Psychol. Rev.*, 1933, **40**, 457-466.

64. Reynolds, B., Acquisition of A Simple Spatial Discrimination as a Function of the Amount of Reinforcement, *J. Exper. Psychol.*, 1950, **40**, 152-160.

65. —— The Acquisition of a Trace Conditioned Response as a Function of the Magnitude of the Stimulus Trace, *J. Exper. Psychol.*, 1945, **35**, 15-31.

66. Ritchie, B. F., Ebeling, E., and Roth, W., Evidence for Continuity in the Discrimination of Vertical and Horizontal Patterns, *J. Compar. and Physiol. Psychol.*, 1950, **45**, 168-180.

67. Schlosberg, H., Conditioned Responses in the White Rat: II. Conditioned Responses Based on Shock to the Foreleg, *J. Genet. Psychol.*, 1936, **49**, 107-138.

68. —— The Relationship between Success and the Laws of Conditioning, *Psychol. Rev.*, 1937, **44**, 379-394.

69. Sheffield, F. D., Avoidance Training and the Contiguity Principle. *J. Compar. and Physiol. Psychol.*, 1948, **41**, 165-177.

70. Skinner, B. F., Two Types of Conditioned Reflex and a Pseudo-Type. *J. Gen. Psychol.*, 1935, **12**, 66-77.

71. —— *The Behavior of Organisms.* New York: Appleton-Century, 1938.

72. Spence, K. W., The Nature of Discrimination Learning in Animals, *Psychol. Rev.*, 1936, **43**, 427-449.

73. —— The Differential Response in Animals to Stimuli Varying within a Single Dimension, *Psychol. Rev.*, 1937, **44**, 430-444.

74. —— Continuous versus Non-Continuous Interpretations of Discrimination Learning, *Psychol. Rev.*, 1940, **47**, 271-288.

75. —— Symposium: Learning as Related to Need and The Subsequent Motivation of Such Learned Behavior, *Psychol. Bull.*, 1941, **38**, 721.

76. —— Theories of Learning, Chap. XII in Moss, F. A. (Ed.), *Comparative Psychology* (rev. ed.). New York: Prentice-Hall, Inc., 1942.

77. —— The Nature of Theory Construction in Contemporary Psychology. *Psychol. Rev.*, 1944, **51**, 47-68.

78. —— An Experimental Test of the Continuity and Non-Continuity Theories of Discrimination Learning. *J. Exper. Psychol.*, 1945, **35**, 253-266.

79. —— Theoretical Interpretations of Learning, Chap. in *Handbook of Experimental Psychology*, Stevens, S. (Ed.). New York: John Wiley and Sons, 1951.

80. —— Bergmann, G., and Lippitt, R., A Study of Simple Learning under Irrelevant Motivational Reward Conditions, *J. Exper. Psychol.*, 1950, **40**, 539-551.

81. Spence, K. W., and Lippitt, R., "Latent" Learning of a Simple Maze Problem with Relevant Needs Satiated, *Psychol. Bull.*, 1940, **37**, 429.

82. ———— An Experimental Test of the Sign-Gestalt Theory of Trial-and-Error Learning, *J. Exper. Psychol.*, 1946, **36**, 491-502.

83. Steckle, L. C., and Renshaw, S., An Investigation of the Conditioned Iridic Reflex, *J. Gen. Psychol.*, 1934, **11**, 3-23.

84. Thorndike, E. L., *The Psychology of Wants, Interests, and Attitudes*. New York: Appleton-Century, 1935.

85. Thorndike, E. L. et al., *The Fundamentals of Learning*. New York: Teachers College, Columbia University, 1932.

86. Thune, L., Dusek, R., and Spence, K. W., Learning under Relevant and Irrelevant Needs, *Amer. Psychologist*, 1949, **4**, 352.

87. Tolman, E. C., *Purposive Behavior in Animals and Men*. New York: Century, 1932.

88. ———— Theories of Learning (Chap. XII), *Comparative Psychology*, ed. by F. A. Moss. New York: Prentice-Hall, Inc., 1934.

89. ———— Demands and Conflicts, *Psychol. Rev.*, 1937, **44**, 158-169.

90. ———— The Acquisition of String-Pulling by Rats—Conditioned Response or Sign-Gestalt? *Psychol. Rev.*, 1937, **44**, 195-211.

91. ———— The Determiners of Behavior at a Choice Point, *Psychol. Rev.*, 1938, **45**, 1-41.

92. ———— There is More Than One Kind of Learning, *Psychol. Rev.*, 1949, **56**, 144-155.

93. ———— and Honzik, C. H., Introduction and Removal of Reward and Maze Performance in Rats, *Univ. Calif. Publ. Psychol.*, 1928, **4**, 241-256.

94. Troland, L. T., *The Fundamentals of Human Motivation*. New York: Van Nostrand, 1928.

95. Walker, E. L., Knotter, M. C., and DeValois, R. L., Drive Specificity and Learning: The Acquisition of a Spatial Response to Food under Conditions of Water Deprivation and Food Satiation, *J. Exper. Psychol.*, 1950, **40**, 161-168.

96. Wedell, C. H., Taylor, F. V., and Skolnick, A., An Attempt to Condition the Pupillary Response, *J. Exper. Psychol.*, 1940, **27**, 517-531.

97. Woodworth, R. S., Reinforcement of Perception, *Amer. J. Psychol.*, 1947, **60**, 119-124.

98. Zeaman, D., Response Latency as a Function of the Amount of Reinforcement, *J. Exper. Psychol.*, 1949, **39**, 466-484.

99. Zener, K., The Significance of Behavior Accompanying Conditioned Salivary Secretion for Theories of the Conditioned Response, *Amer. J. Psychol.*, 1937, **50**, 384-403.

CHAPTER 9

The Neurology of Learning

DONALD G. MARQUIS

University of Michigan

The ability of an animal to learn—the ability to modify its behavior on the basis of previous experience and to adapt successfully to new situations—depends upon the structure and organization of its central nervous system. The difference between an untrained dog and a dog that has been taught to "beg" when food is held out, is a difference in the brain. The dog's reaction, of course, involves the functioning of receptors, sensory nerves, motor nerves, and muscles, but the modification produced by the training is a modification of brain function. The neural connections from the receptors to the brain and from the brain to the muscles are fixed and unchangeable. When a man learns through long practice to aim and shoot a gun accurately, he has not trained the eye or the finger—he has altered the brain processes in such a way that his movements are more precisely related to the visual stimulation.

The synaptic connections between sensory neurons and motor neurons are all located in the central nervous system, and are organized in functional systems of their own. Some of these systems are quite direct, involving only one or two synapses. Reactions that are mediated by such direct systems are usually rapid, inevitable, and stereotyped. Examples are the knee jerk, the flexion of a limb to pain stimulation, and the blink following touching of the cornea. These reactions are called reflexes; they are unlearned and they are practically unmodifiable by any kind of training.

In addition to the direct neural systems that underlie reflex behavior, there are indirect systems also connecting the sensory and motor neurons. Branches from the sensory neurons make synaptic connections with other neurons running to the brain. Neurons descending from the brain make synaptic connection with the motor neurons that go to the muscles. Within the brain are many systems that may be involved in the reaction to a stimulus. For example, the response of an individual to a sudden loud pistol shot may be analyzed into several components that ordinarily merge imperceptibly into a total reaction called "startle." About one tenth of a second following the shot there is a reflex response consisting of a bodily start, blink, and so forth. This is mediated by the direct neural systems below the level of the brain. Shortly thereafter a readjustment of the bodily posture occurs, which is mediated by systems of the midbrain and cerebellum. Visceral reactions, such as increased heart rate, involve still other systems (in the hypothalamus and medulla). About three tenths of a second after the shot, the individual may voluntarily turn his head and eyes in the direction from which the shot was heard. This reaction involves the cortical systems of the cerebral hemispheres.

The neural systems that mediate the several components of the total reaction to any situation constitute a hierarchy. The higher systems exercise a certain control over the functioning of the lower systems, and when the brain is removed by surgical operation the lower systems are sometimes observed to be hyperactive.

Evolution of the Brain

The fundamental plan of the nervous system of higher animals is seen in its most simple form in the worm. Each segment of the animal contains a ganglion—a collection of synapses—that connects the sensory neurons with the motor neurons. Each ganglion is connected with the others by a longitudinal bundle of neurons running the length of the body. At the head end of the animal is a cephalic ganglion that may be considered the forerunner of the brain in vertebrates. It receives many neurons carrying impulses from the sensitive anterior part of the body, and by means of its neural connections with the segmental ganglia it functions to integrate the activity of the various muscles and to control the direction of locomotion of the animal in response to stimulation of the head.

The brain of the vertebrate animal is much more complex, and many structurally differentiated portions can be distinguished. The size of the brain relative to the spinal cord increases progressively in the vertebrate series from fish to man. At the same time there is a greater increase in the development of the cerebrum than in any of the other portions of the brain. These evolutionary developments are related primarily to three important factors: (a) In the higher animals there is a marked development of the sense organs located in the head, and a corresponding increase in the sensory cerebral systems, particularly those of vision and hearing; (*b*) the elaboration of the response mechanisms of posture, locomotion, and manipulation in the higher animals is accompanied by an enlargement of the cerebral systems controlling muscular movement; (*c*) the increased learning ability and intelligence of the higher animals is associated with a pronounced development of the cortex of the cerebrum. The increased size of the sensory and motor systems of the cortex does not account for the total increase, and in the higher mammals a progressively greater portion of the cerebrum consists of association systems that are concerned with the complex sensory-motor integrations of intelligent, adaptive behavior.

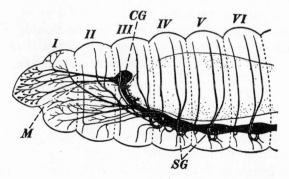

Fig. 1. **Brain and Anterior Portion of the Earthworm's Nervous System.** *CG,* cephalic ganglion; *M,* mouth; *SG,* segmental ganglia. [After Rogers (23).]

It is now well established that learning ability does not depend exclusively upon cerebral functioning. Some degree of modifiability seems to be a property of all neural tissue. The possibility of learning has been clearly demonstrated in lower invertebrate animals whose brains are rudimentary and contain no true cortical tissue. Furthermore, in a mammal such as the dog, certain simple types of learning are possible after lesions of the cerebrum, including all the cortical tissue. With expert care a decorticate dog may be maintained in good health for years. After recovery from the immediate effects of the operation, the dog is able to stand and walk about. It will eat when food is placed in its mouth, but it is unable to locate food placed in the room. Although reflex responses to light, sound, touch, and pain are present, the animal seems unable to utilize such stimuli in its adaptive behavior. It bumps into walls and other obstacles, and when it happens to head into a corner, it continues to push forward rather than turn around. However, several investigators have found that simple conditioned responses, such as leg withdrawal, can be established by prolonged training with intense stimuli (4, 1). The conditioned response is not as precise or adaptive as it is in normal dogs. A discrimination between two different stimuli is even more difficult to establish, and probably represents the limits of learning ability in the decorticate dog.

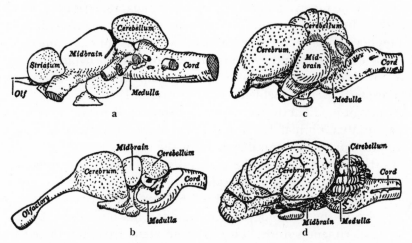

Fig 2. **Successive Stages in the Evolution of the Vertebrate Brain. a.** Codfish brain; **b.** Alligator brain (*Crosby*); **c.** Dove brain; **d.** Dog brain.
[From Newman (20).]

The effects of removal of cerebral hemispheres are much more severe in the higher vertebrates than in the lower. As the brain systems develop in size and complexity in the phylogenetic series from fish to man, many functions that originally had their anatomical basis in lower systems are taken over by the cerebrum. This progressive shifting of dominance to the higher systems is termed *encephalization,* and is a fundamental principle of the evolution of the central nervous system.

Encephalization has been found in every type of function that has been studied: motor, sensory, and learning. In the absence of the cerebrum, the fish and the bird show no detectable disturbance of motility; the rat, cat, and dog demonstrate impaired posture but are able to stand and walk; the monkey can sit with help but is unable to walk. In the sphere of visual functions, the fish shows no impairment after removal of the cerebrum; the bird has some disturbance of detail vision; the rat cannot discriminate visual patterns but can distinguish the brightness, position, and distance of objects; the cat, dog, and monkey can react only to brightness differences; and man is completely blind (17).

A similarly-graded series of effects is observed in the learning abilities of vertebrates after decortication. No impairment has been observed in the fish; some slight disturbances of retention have been found in the pigeon; while learning is restricted to simple conditioning in the rat, cat, and dog. The most comparable data for human beings is furnished by the observations of anencephalic children— babies born without any cerebral hemispheres because of some defect in their embryological development. Although such babies may survive for several years they show none of the evidences of learning that are seen even in feebleminded children (21).

Although modifiability is a general property of neural tissue, it is apparent that normal learning in the higher mammals is largely dependent upon the neural systems of the cortex.

Do the various parts of the cerebral cortex contribute equally to learning ability, or is there a localization of particular kinds of learning in specific regions of the brain? This question is one of the most important in the neurology of learning and has been the subject of much experimental study. Two extreme views have dominated the discussion during the past 50 years. The first view considers that each habit depends on a neural modification that is localized in a particular part of the brain. The other view regards learning as a function of the entire brain; the neural process underlying a particular habit may occur in one region of the brain as well as in any other. Recent experimental evidence favors a position intermediate between these two extremes.

Methods of Studying Cerebral Functions

There are several different experimental techniques that contribute to the identification of the neural systems involved in particular habits. In certain cases, anatomical methods are able to demonstrate the course of nerve pathways. Although single neurons are too small to be followed individually, neurons of similar function are often grouped in bundles that can be traced by microscopic study. In this way the course of the neurons running from the sense organs to the brain has been followed in detail, and their termination in particular regions of the cortex has been identified. These regions are known as the *primary sensory areas* (see Fig. 3). In the same way, some of the motor pathways carrying nerve impulses from the brain to the muscles have been anatomically determined. The cortical region from which such neurons originate is called the *motor area.*

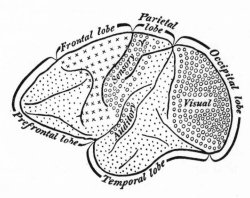

Fig. 3. Functional Regions of the Cortex of the Monkey (lateral view of the left cerebral hemisphere). *o o*—primary sensory areas; *x x*—primary motor areas; . . . —association areas. [After Walker (27).]

Another method of tracing functional neural pathways makes use of artificial stimulation with chemicals or electricity to set up nerve impulses at various points along the pathway. For example, if an electrical current is applied to a point in the motor area of the cortex it will produce a particular muscular movement. Within the motor area the excitable points are arranged in a definite order. From the top of the area toe movements are elicited; just below that, foot movements; then knee, hip, trunk, hand, arm, neck, and face. Electrical stimulation of the primary sensory areas has been carried out with human patients who are undergoing a surgical operation on the brain. In such operations local anesthesia is sometimes used and the patient is normally conscious. Stimulation of the sensory areas does not produce any movements. Stimulation of the visual area may cause the patient to see flashes of light, sometimes brilliantly colored. Stimulation of the somatic sensory area (cutaneous and proprioceptive) results in a tingling in some part of the body. The various parts of the body are represented in the somatic sensory area in the same order as in the motor area.

Recent improvements in amplifying and recording apparatus have made possible the development of electrical techniques for the localization of neural systems. A minute electrical disturbance accompanies the passage of an impulse along a neuron. The electrical effect is measured as a difference in potential between the active part and the inactive part of the neuron. By placing the recording electrodes at various points in the central nervous system, it is possible to localize the pathway of impulses resulting from sensory stimulation such as a flash of light or a pressure on the skin. The electrical method has provided refinement of the anatomical methods in locating the primary sensory areas of the cortex and promises to yield valuable data concerning the connections of the cortical association areas.

Perhaps the most widely used method of investigating cerebral localization is the destruction method. A region of the brain is removed by surgical operation, and the animal is carefully studied to determine what functions and performances have been impaired. The ability of operated animals to learn particular habits can be compared with that of normal animals. Retention of a habit can be studied by training the animals before they are operated and testing them afterwards to discover if the learning has been retained or if it can be re-acquired. Comparable data can be secured from human beings by the study of patients who have suffered destruction of particular areas of the brain as a result of disease or accident. The results of all such studies by the destruction method present certain serious difficulties in interpretation. The investigator is never able to study the normal functioning of a cortical area by destroying that area; he can only study the symptoms of abnormal functioning that result. Furthermore, if a certain operation produces no observable effect upon learning ability, it is not justifiable to conclude that the destroyed region does not normally function in the learning process. After removal of one eye an individual will still be able to see; this fact does not prove that the eye had no visual function.

The experimental study of cerebral localization has benefited greatly from the development and improvement of techniques of training animals, and from more accurate methods of measuring learning ability. In the following pages the evidence will be examined for the localization of simple habits, complex serial learning, and reasoning. Only the findings on mammals will be included and, whenever data are available, special emphasis will be placed on the study of primates.

Simple Habits

A simple habit is one that involves the learning of a particular response to some definite stimulus change. Conditioning, trial-and-error learning, and easy discrimination learning are the commonly studied examples. We have said (p. 294) that conditioned responses can be established in dogs after complete removal of the cerebral cortex, but the limits of learning ability in the decorticate animal have not been fully studied. Dogs have been trained by shocking the paw to withdraw the leg to conditioned stimuli of sound, touch, heat, and light. With adequate methodological precautions, these conditioned responses are not significantly different from those in normal animals. Moreover it is possible to train a dog in a simple discrimination—to raise its paw to a light stimulus and not to respond to a bell stimulus (1).

More extensive knowledge of the differences between cortical learning and subcortical learning is obtained from studies of the effect of removal of parts of the cerebral cortex.

Motor cortex

Since any habit involves some motor response we can study the effect of removal of the motor areas of the cortex. In general, no impairment of simple conditioned responses is found. Conditioned salivation, eyeblinking, and foot withdrawal have been successfully established in dogs after removal of the motor cortex.

If the habit involves more complex coordination, as in skilled performance, the results are different. The most extensive study of the effect of lesions of the motor cortex on manipulative habits is one by Lashley (10). Rats were trained in a series of five different latch-box problems. Four of these problems required some kind of manipulative skill—pulling a string, tearing a paper strip, and so forth. The other required the animal to step on each of two platforms before getting food. Operations on the motor cortex did not affect the performance on the double-platform problem, but the ability to learn the skill problems was considerably impaired. A most interesting result of the experiment was the finding that the degree of impairment was roughly proportional to the amount of cortical tissue destroyed, the correlations ranging for the different problems from .48 to .72. Similar impairment of manipulative skill learning has been observed in chimpanzees after operation on the motor areas of the cerebrum.

Visual cortex

Anatomical and electrical study has shown that the nerve fibers from the eyes make connections with two systems in the brain. One system is complete at a subcortical level (midbrain); the other involves the primary visual areas in the occipital lobes of the cortex. Each of these systems can function independently of the other in certain visual performances.

If the cortical visual system is destroyed by surgical removal of the occipital lobes in the rat, cat, dog, or monkey, the animal will seem to be completely blind. It fails to locate its food dish by sight, bumps into obstacles, and does not blink when a threatening gesture is made toward the eyes. Careful study shows, however, that not all visual function has been lost. Many unlearned responses to optic stimulation are unimpaired. The reflex pupillary constriction and the eyeblink to a bright light are unaffected, and the optic nystagmus evoked by continuous movement of a striped visual field is normal. It is significant to note that optic nystagmus can be elicited in the operated animals with stripes that are just as fine in detail as the threshold values for normal animals (26). The resolving power, or acuity, of the subcortical system is no less than that of the cortical system. The reaction to a single moving stripe, however, shows a clear impairment. There is normally no reflex response to such a stimulus, and while normal animals will sometimes follow a moving stripe with their eyes, the operated animals fail to make any response.

In addition to the unlearned responses that are mediated by the subcortical visual system, it is possible to establish certain habits by training after removal of the occipital cortex. In all mammals that have been studied, with the exception of man, a discrimination between two different intensities of light can be learned after such an operation (16). Moreover, the rate at which the habit is learned is not significantly different from normal, and the threshold of discrimination is not seriously impaired. In transposition tests the animals continue to choose on the basis of relative rather than absolute brightness. Attempts to establish discrimination habits based on the shape, size, or color of visual stimuli have yielded negative results, although there is some evidence in cats of an imperfect discrimination between moving and stationary stimuli.

Although the subcortical visual system is capable of mediating light discrimination, its destruction does not abolish the ability. The cortical and subcortical systems evidently provide alternative mechanisms for this habit.

The analysis of the light-discrimination ability remaining after removal of the cortical visual system has yielded some interesting results. Smith (25) has shown that discrimination is possible only if the tests are carried out in a room that is dark or very dimly illuminated. If the general illumination is high, the operated cats fail the test, although normal animals can react correctly under any conditions of illumination. Klüver (7) has demonstrated that the monkey, after removal of the occipital lobes, cannot respond to differences in stimulus brightness but only to differences in the total amount of light entering the eyes. A monkey that has been trained to react to the brighter of two stimulus patches will respond to a large dim patch rather than a small bright patch if the total light from the former is greater.

Although the ability to learn a habit of light discrimination is not destroyed by removal of the cortical visual system, the retention of a habit learned prior to operation is completely abolished. The animals are able to relearn the habit in about the same number of trials that were necessary for the original learning. This finding suggests that the cortical system, if intact, is involved in the habit, but that after its removal the habit can be mediated by the subcortical system. In contrast with the discrimination habit, a simple conditioned-eyelid response to a flash of light is normally a subcortical function. Removal of the occipital lobes in the dog does not result in any amnesia for the training carried out prior to operation (18, 28).

Discrimination of size and visual form or shape depends entirely on the cortical system. Destruction of the subcortical visual centers does not prevent such learning, while destruction of the cortical visual area abolishes permanently the ability to learn even the simplest distinctions of form. Partial destruction of the visual cortex, however, does not seriously disturb form discrimination. From careful studies of human patients with accidental destruction of only part of the visual cortex we know that they will have a "blind spot" in the corresponding part of the visual field, but that they can move their eyes so that the image of an object will fall on a part of the retina which is connected to the intact portion of the cortex. In such cases, therefore, we would not find any loss of ability in form discrimination.

Experiment shows also that memory for habits of pattern discrimination is not localized in any particular part of the area. If rats are trained to discriminate an erect from an inverted triangle, the habit will be abolished by a complete destruction of the visual cortex, but any part of the visual cortex can be destroyed without disturbing the habit (12). Within this area there is an equipotentiality of function for such learning.

Auditory cortex

The experimental studies of learning based on other sense modalities are less complete than those in the field of vision. The rate of learning a simple differential response to noise is not significantly inferior to normal in rats after destruction of the auditory sensory areas of the cortex, although an amnesia for learning before operation may result (22). Man is rendered completely deaf by comparable destruction, and monkeys have not yet been adequately studied in this respect. Habits requiring the localization of the sound source are affected in much the same way as sound intensity discriminations. Experiments with rats, cats, and dogs agree that the localization habit is lost after removal of the auditory cortex but that it can be relearned (19).

Neural mechanism of learning

The evidence summarized so far shows that the learning of a simple habit involves a change in the nervous system that can be localized approximately in one of the areas of the cortex or subcortex of the brain. The precise nature of the neural modification is a subject for speculation. Neurophysiological research has been concerned primarily with the functioning of peripheral neurons and with the brief changes involved in excitation and propagation of the neural impulse. This work has led to the conclusion that the neuron is an independent anatomical unit; that impulses are propagated in an all-or-none manner throughout its length; and that one neuron excites another primarily through the region of contact between the two at a synapse. If cortical neurons function in the same way, it must follow that the modifications due to learning are alterations at the synapses that cause impulses to traverse a path different from that before the learning.

There is at present no satisfactory theory of the nature of the relatively permanent synaptic changes that would account for learning. The nature of the excitation process itself is a matter of controversy, and extensions of electrical, chemical, or growth theories to the phenomenon of learning are without any basis in fact.

It is entirely possible that neural functioning in the cortex will be found to be qualitatively different from that in the lower systems. Some investigators have suggested that cortical integration may depend upon electrical fields set up by patterns of neural activity, and independent of the particular anatomical locus. The advance in techniques for the study of the electrical effects of cortical activity may be expected eventually to offer a solution to this problem.

Serial Maze Learning

An extensive series of experiments has been carried out by Lashley (9, 13) to determine the effect of cerebral lesions on maze-learning ability in rats. He found that impairment of this ability does not depend upon the location of the region destroyed, but upon the amount of destruction. Correlations between the number of errors during learning and the surface extent of the cortex destroyed in different animals are 0.65 and 0.86 for two types of mazes.

The maze habit does not depend upon any single sensory or motor function. Rats can still learn to run the correct pathway after the elimination of any one sense function, although their performance is seriously impaired if several senses are destroyed. It is possible that the deterioration in the maze performance following cerebral lesions may be due primarily to sensory defects. Lesions in any area would affect one or another sense function, and larger lesions would result in a greater deterioration because of the effect on several senses. This interpretation is unquestionably a factor in the explanation of the equipotentiality of cerebral areas for maze learning, but more recent evidence indicates that it cannot be the complete explanation.

Each sensory area participates in two different kinds of function. In addition to its specific sensory function, the area contributes to some more general function concerned with integrations above a simple sensory-motor level. If the functions of the visual cerebral area are purely sensory, then removal of the eyes and removal of the cerebral area should result in equally severe deterioration. But this is not the case. Cerebral destruction results in significantly greater deterioration than removal of the eyes. Furthermore, the cerebral visual area contributes to maze-learning ability even in blind animals. A group of rats were blinded in infancy and later trained in maze performance. The removal of the cerebral visual areas produced a marked retardation in the rats' ability.

Reasoning and Complex Abilities

Certain types of adaptive behavior that involve the integration of isolated experiences to achieve a new solution, or the use of implicit symbolic processes, may be differentiated from rote-learning tasks. Reasoning ability clearly involves something more than simple sensory or motor function, and it might be expected that tasks involving reasoning could be impaired by cerebral lesions that do not affect sensory discrimination or motor performance. It is also important to determine whether reasoning ability is localized in specific regions of the cortex, or whether the various regions function equally in such tasks.

Maier (14) has compared a rote-learning task in rats with a task whose solution requires that the animal combine two habits on which it has had previous training. The latter task was more susceptible to cortical injury than the former. No particular region of the cortex was found to be essential, and the impairment of reasoning was roughly proportional to the amount of cortical tissue destroyed. Other defects in complex abilities have been investigated by Krechevsky with similar results. In one situation, rats were confronted by a maze that allowed several different but equally adequate solutions. Rats with destruction of a portion of the cerebrum were inferior in arriving at a simple generalized solution, and they investigated fewer possible solutions than the normal animals. Another test required an *umweg* type of solution. The rat could reach food by a short path that necessitated losing sight of the food for a short time, or he could reach it by a long path on which the food remained visible. In contrast with normal animals, the operated rats continued to run on the long path (8). In both of these test situations, the degree of behavior impairment showed no relation to the location of the cerebral lesion, and in the first it was proportional to the amount of the destruction. In general, operated animals show less variability (more stereotyped reaction) in problem-solving situations.

The delayed response is another example of a complex ability that depends upon symbolic function for successful performance. Tests are made in monkeys by first permitting the animal to observe a piece of food being concealed under one of two inverted cups. After a specified interval of delay, the animal chooses one of the cups, and if it is the one under which food was hidden, it secures the reward. Normal monkeys can perform correctly with delays of 30 seconds after very little practice. Jacobsen (6) found that this ability is completely abolished by removal of the prefrontal areas of the cortex, although lesions of comparable extent in any other cortical region, except the visual associative area (11), result in no impairment.

Removal of the prefrontal areas in monkeys does not produce any detectable sensory or motor deficit. Discrimination learning and simple motor habits are performed as well by them as by normal animals. The precise nature of the ability that is abolished with the prefrontal areas has been the subject of further interesting investigation. Jacobsen and his collaborators found that after operation chimpanzees will continue to use sticks as tools to reach pieces of food, but will have difficulty in solving the problem if the necessary sticks and food are not simultaneously present in the visual field. On the basis of such tests it might be supposed that the operation results in a specific disability to react to symbolic memories, that is, to objects that are not present to the senses at the time of response. Finan, however, has found that monkeys can perform delayed response tests after prefrontal operation when the testing conditions are somewhat altered (3). If, on the first portion of the test, the monkey does not merely look at the food on the right or left, but actually approaches or eats it, it is able, after an enforced delay, to choose the correct side. These observations suggest that the operated monkeys fail to learn the correct side with a single unrewarded presentation of the stimuli. Another line of analysis is that of Malmo (15), who found that monkeys without prefrontal cortex could perform the usual delayed-response test if there was darkness during the delay interval. The memory of the preliminary stimulus presentation is evidently interfered with by the activities during the interval (retroactive inhibition), and darkness reduces such interfering activities to a minimum. By this hypothesis, the defect following removal of the prefrontal areas would be a greater susceptibility to interference from activities interpolated in the retention interval. This interpretation is further supported by experiments in which monkeys without prefrontal cortex were able to perform delayed-reaction tests when they were under light sedatives (nembutal or dial).

Interest in the nature of the functions of the prefrontal cortex is heightened by the current use of prefrontal operation in the treatment of mental disorder. In hundreds of cases there has been some improvement of symptoms without significant impairment of intellectual and problem-solving abilities. Recent careful analysis of mental performance on a variety of tasks indicates, however, that there is a demonstrable deficiency in attention comparable to that in the monkeys. Patients are unable to perform well in the face of distractions resulting from extraneous stimuli or on tasks involving two simultaneous requirements such as canceling and counting different letters in a printed page (24). The impairment was reduced when the patients were given small doses of nembutal.

Memory Functions

In some cases injury to the brain results in amnesia or forgetting of previous learning, even though the organism still has the ability to learn the task again. There is no single region of the brain responsible for memory function. This makes psychological sense, because memory is involved in every kind of learned response. We have noted earlier that after removal of the visual cortex, animals are unable to perform a learned brightness discrimination but can relearn the habit with ordinary training. Similarly a sound discrimination is abolished by removal of the auditory cortex but can be relearned. In both cases the new habit involves other parts of the brain, presumably subcortical.

Human patients with damage to the temporal lobe sometimes have serious difficulty in remembering the names of objects. For example, if such a patient is shown a pencil he may recognize and know what to do with it but be unable to recall its name. Once he has heard the word "pencil" he recognizes it as correct and can repeat it. This symptom is called amnesic aphasia and is related to the language disturbances described in the following section.

Temporary damage to the brain caused by a severe blow on the head or by drugs such as alcohol may produce amnesia for events in a particular period of time only. A head injury ordinarily causes forgetting for a period preceding the trauma; the more severe the injury, the longer the period. In recovery from the effects of the trauma the memories return not in order of their importance but in order of time. The long-past memories are the first to return and the most recent ones will be recovered last or not at all.

Recently this problem has been attacked experimentally. Intense brief electric shocks to the head—strong enough to produce a convulsion—have been found valuable in the treatment of patients with mental disorder. The same kind of sudden shock can be used with animals to study the effect on learning and memory. Rats learn a maze much less well if the daily practice periods are followed by such electroshocks. The impairment is probably due to the fact that the shocks disrupt memory and prevent the animals from carrying over what they learn from one day to the next. Duncan (2) has shown that the impairment is greatest when the shock follows the training trial immediately, and is progressively less if the interval between training and shock is increased up to one hour.

The disrupting effect of electroshock is more apparent on complex skills than on simple habits. The impairment is not due to the punishing effect, as shown by the fact that the same shock administered to the hind legs has little effect. The resulting convulsion, however, is important. If animals are anesthetized before receiving the shock there is no convulsion and the disturbance of memory is significantly less.

Language Functions

In man, the most striking disturbances of higher integrative functions are those concerned with the language mechanism. It is in the use of written and spoken language that man is most clearly differentiated from other animals, and the cerebral organization for language functions reflects this difference. All the simpler sensory and motor functions are represented in both hemispheres of the cerebrum; in general, the right side of the body is represented in the left hemisphere, and vice versa. Language functions, however, do not have this bilateral representation; they are mediated in one hemisphere only. In right-handed individuals this is the left hemisphere, and the entire right hemisphere can be removed without resulting in aphasia, that is, disturbance of the language functions. Within the left hemisphere there are several regions in the frontal, parietal, and temporal lobes that function together for the understanding and speaking of language. Since the limits of cerebral destruction due to disease and accident are not as precise as can be obtained experimentally in animals, the localization of specific language performances in man is not a matter of complete agreement. In general, cortical destruction in the frontal region of the language areas results in a loss or impairment of the motor skills of speaking or writing. In certain cases, there seems to be little disturbance in the understanding of printed or spoken words. The patient knows what he wants to say, but cannot get it out, although there is no paralysis of the vocal apparatus, and all the sounds in speech can be made separately. Cortical destruction in the language areas of the parietal region produces an aphasia that most affects reading; destruction in the temporal region results in impaired understanding of oral speech. Other lesions may produce more or less isolated impairment of writing, ability of music appreciation, of arithmetical abilities, or of understanding of word-meanings. The most common type of aphasia seen in a hospital clinic exhibits some degree of impairment in all such functions, since the commonest type of cerebral destruction is seldom restricted to a single functional region of the brain.

Intelligence

It should be clear from the preceding discussion that intelligence is not a function that can be localized in any particular region of the brain. Recent statistical analysis of intelligence tests has clearly shown that there is no single unitary ability involved in those performances usually called intelligent. A more refined analysis of human abilities must be made before there is any hope of studying the cerebral mechanisms involved. And there is no evidence to support the belief that the current analysis of intelligence into verbal ability, memory, number ability, space perception, and so forth, will have any meaning in terms of the underlying cerebral functions. The most carefully studied effects of cortical destruction—aphasia, prefrontal lobe defect, and temporal lobe defect—do not correspond to any current psychological categories such as attention, abstraction, synthesis, or memory. It will be surprising if memory, for example, is found to be a single ability. Indeed, one of the most striking characteristics of one type of aphasia is the retention of recognition memory coupled with the almost complete loss of recall memory.

The Nature of Cerebral Localization

We may now return to the question raised at the beginning of this chapter and examine the evidence for and against theories of localization of function in the cerebral cortex. Anatomical and physiological study has clearly demonstrated the existence of localized primary sensory and motor areas, and destruction of these regions leads to specific deficiencies whose nature depends upon the locus of the cortical lesion. Lashley has stated the conception of nonlocalization most specifically. This theory is based primarily upon the two concepts of equipotentiality and of mass action.

The theory of equipotentiality states that within the entire cortex for certain functions, and within specialized areas for others, the subordinate parts are all equally capable of performing the functions of the whole. This has been found to be the case in many of the experiments described above. The cortical system and the subcortical system are equipotential for the ability of brightness discrimination, and the various regions within the cortical visual area are equipotential for pattern discrimination. The different parts of the whole cortex are equipotential for latch habits, for maze learning, and for reasoning tests in rats. In many of the other experiments, however, abilities were found to be dependent upon specific regions of the cerebrum. Most of the examples of equipotentiality, it will be noted, were observed in studies of rats, and there are other reasons to believe that the specificity of localization increases in the higher animals. This cannot be the entire explanation of the difference, however. It is more likely that those functions for which there is equipotentiality of receptor and effector function will be the ones for which equipotentiality of cerebral function is found. For example, an individual's reaction to an apple will survive the destruction of any particular region of the retina as long as the apple can be seen at all. Correspondingly, the reaction will survive the destruction of any particular region of the visual area of the cortex. If the individual, moreover, is permitted to identify the apple by smell, taste, or touch, as well as vision, the reaction will survive the destruction of any single region of the total cortex, but will be abolished by destruction of the entire cortex.

The theory of mass action states that the degree of impairment of a function is proportional to the extent of the cortex destroyed. This has been found true of the latch habit, the maze habit, and some of the reasoning tests in rats. In other performances no relation between deterioration and size of lesion has been found. This theory is not merely a restatement of the theory of equipotentiality; for it has been shown that, although the parts of the visual area are equipotential for pattern discrimination, there is no relation between impairment of learning and extent of lesion. The mass action relationship is observed in the case of functions which involve widespread cortical regions as a result of multiple sensory control or multiple types of integration. The relationship may be due to the increasing involvement of additional systems, or it may be due to some dynamic nonlocalized facilitating function of the cortical mechanism.

Recovery of Function After Cerebral Lesions

Further evidence concerning the plasticity or specificity of the neural mechanisms involved in learning is available in studies of recovery of function. After injury to a portion of the brain, many of the habits and abilities that were temporarily impaired will subsequently show improvement. Not all the performances recover at the same rate, however, and there are several factors influencing the degree of recovery. These facts may be illustrated by description of the effects of removal of the visual areas of the cerebrum in dogs.

The following description is a composite one based on the study of several animals (16, 18). A dog was trained before operation in two habits; first, a conditioned eyelid blink to a light signal, and second, a discrimination between a bright and a dim light to secure food reward. On the second day following the operation, the dog was normally healthy and active but it behaved as if it were totally blind. Brief experimental tests demonstrated that neither the conditioned response to light nor the discrimination habit could be performed. By the fifth postoperative day, however, the conditioned eyelid response had returned at about its normal strength, although no training had been given. The temporary loss of the conditioned response for the first few days was not due simply to the anesthesia and the general effects of the operative procedure, for other dogs showed retention of the response at the end of the first day following an equally severe operation on a different, nonvisual region of the brain.

The discrimination habit, on the contrary, never showed any spontaneous recovery. When retraining was undertaken, the habit was relearned by the dog in about as many trials as had been required for the original preoperative learning. This was true whether the retraining was begun one week after operation or six months later. Once relearned, the habit was performed about as well as in the normal animal.

Some of the performances of the dog never showed any recovery, either with or without retraining. The dog was never able to locate food or avoid obstacles by sight, and there was permanent loss of all pattern or form vision. In the course of weeks and months, however, there was a noticeable improvement in the dog's ability to get around. In its living cage and in other familiar surroundings the dog seldom bumped into walls or objects. When the experimenter entered its room the dog would run to the front of the cage, and, when released, it would follow the experimenter down the hallways. Careful observation showed that this recovery did not depend at all on visual ability but was based rather on the substitution of effective use of auditory and cutaneous cues.

From the example described above, and from many corresponding studies, it is apparent that there are several mechanisms for the recovery of function after cerebral injury. Spontaneous recovery, not dependent upon retraining, apparently results from the restitution of normal function in nerve cells that have been temporarily incapacitated. An injury invariably produces, in addition to total destruction of some nerve cells, a partial impairment of surrounding and functionally related regions of the brain. There is no actual regeneration or new growth of cells in the central nervous system, but "sick" cells regain their vigor, and habits dependent on them show spontaneous recovery. This may be clearly observed, for example, in the first few days following an incomplete destruction of the cerebral motor area in the monkey. On recovery from the anesthetic, the limbs affected by the operation are completely paralyzed; by the following day, gross movements may be observed; after a week, relatively fine movements of the hand and fingers will be achieved.

After the spontaneous recovery is complete and the degree of impairment of function has become stable, it is still possible to reestablish certain habits by the processes of learning. In habits such as locomotion, the necessary practice occurs naturally in the course of ordinary daily activities. In other cases, specific training procedures must be carried out to guarantee the relearning. It has been demonstrated that systematic exercise will produce a measurable degree of improvement in patients whose paralysis has been constant for years. Patients with aphasia of long standing can learn to use new words after persistent training.

The fundamental problem of recovery through re-education is that of the specific neural structures involved in the new learning. Is the organization of cortical functions sufficiently plastic to permit the remaining brain regions to take over the functions lost by destruction of one region? Before we try to answer this question, we must distinguish between two kinds of re-education. The first kind involves the substitution of new habits that accomplish much the same ends as the habits lost. For example, if an individual suffers a paralysis of the right hand, he may subsequently learn to write by using his left hand and to sweep by holding the broom with his left hand and right elbow. The dog described above that had lost the ability to distinguish objects visually learned to avoid obstacles on the basis of tactile and sound stimulation. Substitute habits of this type are mediated by the regions of the brain normally involved in such learning, and the problem of plasticity of neural organization does not arise. It is apparent that the limits of this kind of recovery are set by the number and the effectiveness of possible substitute habits. A widespread cortical destruction will consequently permit less substitutive recovery than will a small restricted injury.

The second kind of re-education involves the re-acquisition of habits that are apparently identical with those lost through brain injury. We have seen that a dog, whose discrimination between bright and dim lights was abolished by removal of the visual cortex, could subsequently be retrained to perform this habit correctly. Many studies have demonstrated the relearning of motor habits by animals after destruction of the cortical motor area. In such cases it is apparent that some part of the nervous system is functioning vicariously for the destroyed part. Some investigators have believed that the organization of brain functions was so plastic that almost any part of the cortex might take over the functions of other parts. More recent evidence, however, has shown that vicarious function is limited to certain neural systems that are normally concerned with the function in question.

The limits of vicarious function have been most clearly determined for the motor and visual systems. When an animal has recovered certain motor abilities following destruction of the motor area in one cerebral hemisphere, no impairment of the recovered functions results from destruction of the corresponding area in the other hemisphere, or from cutting the corpus callosum that connects the two hemispheres. Reappearance of the paralysis will be caused, however, by more extensive injury to the motor system of the same hemisphere (for example, the premotor cortex or the subcortical systems of the corpus striatum). Similarly, when an animal has relearned the brightness discrimination habit following destruction of the visual cortex, no impairment of this performance results from destruction of any region of the remaining cortex. The habit is permanently abolished, however, by the additional destruction of the subcortical visual systems in the midbrain. The midbrain is not simply a duplicate neural system for the visual cortex; it normally functions in reflex reactions to optic stimulation and its destruction alone does not impair brightness discrimination. It is a part of the total visual system, and in the absence of the visual cortex is able, with training, to take over a limited part of the cortical functions.

Several factors are important in determining the rate and amount of recovery under training. As in any learning situation, the nature of the training procedures and the motivation of the subject will influence the achievement. It has been noted that, in general, the larger the brain lesion the less the recovery. A large lesion not only produces a greater deficiency, but also, through its widespread destruction of neural tissue, seriously limits the possibilities for re-education.

Another factor determining the degree of recovery is the age of the individual. Clinical and experimental results indicate clearly that the possibilities of restitution of function are better for young than for old individuals. Some remarkable instances of recovery have been demonstrated following brain lesions in early infancy. If the cortical motor area is removed in a baby monkey there is eventually almost complete recovery, whereas the removal of the same region in an adult animal produces a permanent and rather severe deficiency in movement. An extensive lesion of the rat's brain, involving 40 per cent of the cortex, practically incapacitates the adult animal for maze learning, but if a comparable destruction is made in infant rats the impairment is barely detectable. Similar studies have been made with respect to visual pattern discrimination and maternal behavior in rats. The explanation of such results is not clear. There is no evidence for the regeneration of destroyed brain tissue, but it may be that the remaining portions of the brain are better able to

acquire new functions during the stages of growth and differentiation than during the adult period. At the same time it must be
pointed out that some types of brain damage will have a greater
effect in young than old persons. Hebb (5) has shown that lesions
of comparable severity have more effect on verbal intelligence if
they occur at an early age. The early lesion prevents the formation
of the many concepts that constitute the basis for intellectual development, while the later lesion occurs after the essential concepts have
been learned.

Bibliography

1. Bromiley, R. B., Conditioned Responses in a Dog after Removal of
   Neocortex, *J. Compar. and Physiol. Psychol.*, 1948, 41, 102-110.
2. Duncan, C. P., The Retroactive Effect of Electroshock on Learning,
   J. Compar. and Physiol. Psychol., 1949, 42, 32-44.
3. Finan, J. L., Delayed Response with Pre-Delay Reenforcement in
   Monkeys after the Removal of the Frontal Lobes, *Amer. J. Psychol.*,
   1942, 55, 202-214.
4. Girden, E., Mettler, F. A., Finch, G., and Culler, E., Conditioned
   Responses in a Decorticate Dog to Acoustic, Thermal, and Tactile
   Stimulation, *J. Compar. Psychol.*, 1936, 21, 367-385.
5. Hebb, D. O., *Organization of Behavior: A Neuropsychological
   Theory*. New York: John Wiley and Sons, Inc., 1949.
6. Jacobsen, C. F., Studies of Cerebral Function in Primates, *Compar.
   Psychol. Monogr.*, 1936, 13, No. 63, 3-60.
7. Klüver, H., Visual Functions after Removal of the Occipital Lobes,
   J. Psychol., 1941, 11, 23-45.
8. Krechevsky, I., Brain Mechanisms and Umweg Behavior, *J. Compar.
   Psychol.*, 1938, 25, 147-173.
9. Lashley, K. S., *Brain Mechanisms and Intelligence: A Quantitative
   Study of Injuries to the Brain*. Chicago: University of Chicago
   Press, 1929.
10. ――― Studies of Cerebral Function in Learning. XI. The Behavior
    of the Rat in Latch Box Situations, *Compar. Psychol. Monogr.*,
    1935, 11, No. 52, 5-42.
11. ――― The Mechanism of Vision. XVIII. Effects of Destroying the
    Visual "Associative Areas" of the Monkey, *Genet. Psychol. Monogr.*,
    1948, 37, 107-166.
12. Lashley, K. S., and Frank, M., The Mechanism of Vision. X. Post-
    operative Disturbances of Habits Based on Detail Vision in the Rat
    after Lesions in the Cerebral Visual Areas, *J. Compar. Psychol.*,
    1934, 17, 355-391.
13. Lashley, K. S., and Wiley, L. E., Studies of Cerebral Function in
    Learning. IX. Mass Action in Relation to the Number of Elements
    in the Problem to be Learned, *J. Compar. Neurol.*, 1933, 57, 3-55.

14. Maier, N. R. F., The Effect of Cerebral Destruction on Reasoning and Learning in Rats, *J. Compar. Neurol.*, 1932, 54, 45-75.

15. Malmo, R. B., Interference Factors in Delayed Response in Monkeys after Removal of the Frontal Lobes, *J. Neurophysiology*, 1942, 5, 295-308.

16. Marquis, D. G., Effects of Removal of the Visual Cortex in Mammals, with Observations on the Retention of Light Discrimination in Dogs, *Research Publications of the Association for Research in Nervous and Mental Disease*, 1934, 13, 558-592.

17. ——— Phylogenetic Interpretation of the Functions of the Visual Cortex, *Archiv. Neurol. and Psychiatry*, Chicago, 1935, 33, 807-815.

18. Marquis, D. G., and Hilgard, E. R., Conditioned Lid Responses to Light in Dogs after Removal of the Visual Cortex, *J. Compar. Psychol.*, 1936, 22, 157-178.

19. Neff, W. C., and Yela, M., Function of the Auditory Cortex: the Localization of Sound in Space, *Amer. Psychol.*, 1948, 3, 243.

20. Newman, H. H. (Ed.), *The Nature of the World and of Man.* Chicago: University of Chicago Press, 1926.

21. Nielson, J. M., and Sedgwick, R. P., Instincts and Emotions in an Anencephalic Monster, *J. Nervous and Mental Diseases*, 1949, 110, 387-394.

22. Raab, D. H., and Ades, H. W., Cortical and Midbrain Mediation of a Conditioned Discrimination of Acoustic Intensities, *Amer. J. Psychol.*, 1946, 59, 59-83.

23. Rogers, C. G., *Textbook of Comparative Physiology.* New York: McGraw-Hill Book Company, 1927.

24. Sheer, D., The Effect of Frontal Lobe Operations on the Attentive Process. Unpublished Dissertation, University of Michigan Library, 1951.

25. Smith, K. U., Visual Discrimination in the Cat. V. The Postoperative Effects of Removal of the Striate Cortex upon Intensity Discrimination, *J. Genet. Psychol.*, 1937, 51, 329-369.

26. Smith, K. U., and Warkentin, J., The Central Neural Organization of Optic Function Related to Minimum Visible Acuity, *J. Genet. Psychol.*, 1939, 55, 177-195.

27. Walker, A. E., *The Primate Thalamus.* Chicago: University of Chicago Press, 1938.

28. Wing, K. G., The Role of the Optic Cortex of the Dog in the Retention of Learned Responses to Light: Conditioning with Light and Food, *Amer. J. Psychol.*, 1947, 60, 30-67.

CHAPTER 10

Discriminative Behavior in Animals

K. U. Smith

University of Wisconsin

The Nature of Discriminative Behavior

By the term discrimination we mean differential or selective response of animals to differences in stimulation in the receptor environment. In the most obvious instances of discrimination, the animal distinguishes one stimulus pattern from another, and reacts in some way in relation to this difference. The patterns of stimuli that are involved in such reactions are quite diverse. Visual and auditory stimuli are the most typical and well known physical agents for discrimination response, but the animal's life depends at all times on reactions cued or guided by tactual, static, gustatory, and olfactory stimulation. Discrimination of environmental stimuli represents the major differential basis of all behavior.

The marks of the discriminative response are usually quite clear. As noted above, differences in environmental stimulation are always involved. This environmental situation produces or alters sustained patterns of physiological activity in the receptors, the nervous system, and the effector mechanisms of the animal. The patterns of internal bodily activity, thus defined in part through the external stimulation, have as one result the production of an overt response that bears some direct relation to the environmental field of stimulation acting on the animal. The responses displayed as a resultant of the integration of the environmental and the physiological events may be quite diverse under different circumstances. The discrimination reaction may be nothing more than a local limb reaction, or it may be a very generalized pattern of behavior such as an emotional startle response. In using the term discrimination, we do not refer to a particular type of response, for all types of reactions of the organism may involve the processes of discrimination or differentiation between environmental patterns of stimulation. As a matter of fact, there are few forms of overt response that do not involve as one aspect some relatively specific form of discrimination.

Given any particular pattern of discriminative reaction, as for example, body orientation, head turning, limb lifting, or emotional response, the relation between the environmental stimulation and the response itself may be significant for understanding the discrimination. In some cases, there is only a time correlation between the occurrence of the response and the environmental stimulation. The response, say lifting of a limb, occurs consistently when a given stimulus is presented. In other cases, there is a temporal and spatial correlation between the environmental stimuli and the response. The animal localizes or orients toward the discriminated stimulus pattern. Finally, an on-going response, which is occurring spontaneously or with reference to other stimulus patterns, may be altered in some respect by a discriminated stimulus. Breathing rate may be interrupted, and a recurring limb response may be changed in rate of occurrence. Thus the reactive marks of discriminative behavior are specific to the situation in which the animal is responding.

From the above we arrive at the general definition that discriminative behavior consists of temporally discrete patterns of reaction or transient changes in an observed reaction that occur in relation to or may be correlated with patterns of receptor stimulation. Both simultaneous and successive differentiation of stimuli are typical of the discriminative behavior of animals.

The forms of discrimination

Before going further with definitions, let us take a look at examples of different forms of behavior ordinarily considered to be of a discriminative nature. We can, more or less arbitrarily, distinguish between three different forms of such behavior: stimulus detection, stimulus comparison, and stimulus classification.

In stimulus detection, the animal responds to an isolated pattern of environmental stimulation. Figure 1 shows how different aspects of behavior may be displayed in this process, as the animal may give a specific or general reaction when the stimulus occurs, show a change in a recurring pattern of behavior, or orient toward or away from the stimulus. In observing vertebrates as well as the simplest forms of invertebrate animals, one can demonstrate the different types of behavior indicated. Careful consideration of the process of stimulus detection shows that it involves both successive and simultaneous differentiation of an environmental stimulus from a general pattern of receptor stimuli.

Stimulus comparison represents a common form of discrimination in animals. In such behavior the animal responds comparatively to two or more stimuli that occur either simultaneously or successively in the receptor field. Typical examples are simultaneous comparison between two patterns of light, or successive comparison between two or more odoriferous sources. In either of these cases the comparative behavior consists of a differential patterning of response with respect to the alternative stimuli.

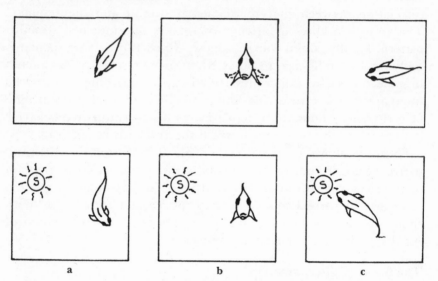

Fig. 1. **Types of Detection Behavior. a.** The discriminated stimulus is related to change in position of the body. **b.** The discriminated stimulus is related to cessation of fin movements. **c.** The animal orients toward the discriminated stimulus.

The differential response that occurs in comparative discrimination may be (a) an absolute differentiation of reaction in which the response occurs to one of the alternative stimuli but not to the others, (b) orientation toward or localization of one of the stimuli, (c) a differential change in some reactive characteristic of the response, its magnitude, latency, rate, or duration with respect to the different alternative stimuli. Figure 2 diagrammatically illustrates these three types of discriminative comparison.

Figure 3 illustrates a typical type of learned discriminative response of the common cat. In this setup, the cat has learned to discriminate comparatively between two light panels of different brightness. This discrimination is made at the end of a runway table, on which the animal is released. In the experiment shown, the cat must react to the brighter light panel. If it proceeds down the runway leading to the dark panel, an electric shock is delivered to the paws through

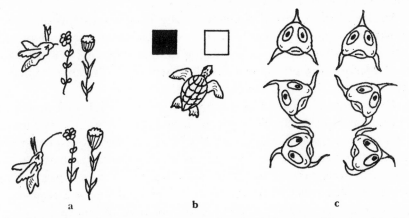

Fig. 2. **Types of Comparative Discrimination in Animals. a.** The hummingbird moth extends its tongue to only certain types of flowers among those approached. **b.** The turtle orients to the brighter of two stimuli. **c.** The fish shows discriminative eye and fin movements of different magnitude in relation to different degrees of rotation of the head.

Fig. 3. **A Typical Type of Discrimination Apparatus for Study of Learned Response to Differences in Light Intensity.**

grills located at the end of the table and on the runway. Response to the lighter panel enables the cat to obtain food inside the box, the door of which opens when the pedal is pressed. The black and white cards are reversed in position in random fashion in order to eliminate the possibility of response based on position.

In stimulus classification behavior, the animal responds selectively in turn to several alternative stimuli, or matches one or more of such stimuli with simultaneously existing sample patterns. We shall call the ordering type of response discriminative ordering and the matching response, discriminative matching.

Discriminative matching is a natural phenomenon of behavior in animals at different levels in the phyletic scale. Bees and other insects will respond to particular artificially baited patterns of color, among a variety of such patterns, in terms of the similarity between the specific patterns and the color of the flowers they are working. Among a variety of artifactual forms, some fish will match and respond to those forms most closely matching the form of the mate.

Discriminative ordering is based upon relative effectiveness of different magnitudes of stimulus patterns to bring about selective response. Thus, insects, fish, turtles, and other animals will display a graded frequency of response to simultaneously presented, varying patterns of color, or patterns of light intensity. It is thus possible to scale behaviorally the relative effectiveness of different magnitudes or arrangements of stimuli in a given physical dimension. The reader will recognize that this is the process that is followed in setting up psychological or behavior scales for the human subject also.

Figure 4 illustrates two examples of complex discrimination of the nature of discriminative ordering and discriminative matching. In Fig. 4a we observe a diagrammatic simplification of a common aspect of behavior in insects. Light patterns of equally graded steps in physical intensity, from low to high, produce a curvilinear trend in frequency with which a swarm of insects will respond to these stimuli. The brightest panel attracts the largest number of insects. On the next brightest panel, 8, there are two thirds as many as on the brightest, and on panel 7, only one half as many as on panel 8. Thus the insects scale or order the light intensities in a quantitative way different from the equally graded steps in brightness.

Figure 4b shows how primates (25), for example, may be trained to match one of several diverse stimuli to a sample stimulus pattern. The animal is first trained to respond to the various boxes underneath the presented patterns. After such learning, it is then taught that only one stimulus pattern will be associated with the food. This is the pattern that is most like the sample. As already noted, the elementary aspects of stimulus-matching behavior are observed in the response of insects, fish, and birds to artifactual arrangements of nests, mates, and other objects of biological significance to them. The common response of birds pecking at reflections of themselves in mirrored surfaces is an example of matching behavior.

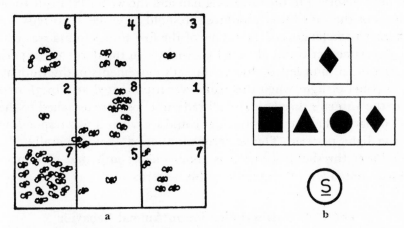

Fig. 4. Types of Stimulus Classification Behavior. a. Insects distribute themselves at different frequencies on light panels of graded brightness levels. b. Monkeys match one of four stimulus patterns with respect to a given sample.

The Level of Discriminative Abilities in Animals

It is a common assumption that the higher animals, especially human individuals, are far advanced above the lower forms in making highly refined discriminations. Actually there is no evidence for such a view. Capacity for discrimination should be viewed in terms of the special adaptations that the living organism, either primitive or advanced, has evolved in relation to its environment. For example, day insects are especially sensitive to differences in wave lengths of light, and are capable of response to short wave lengths of light in the ultra-violet range that the human eye never sees. The mammals among the ungulate and carnivorous groups far excel the human being in detection of faint odors, particularly animal odors, and utilize these capacities in the hunt for prey and food as well as in the avoidance of enemies. The common mouse, rat, and bat display auditory acuity for high frequency vibrations that are supersonic with respect to the human ear. Whereas human subjects perceive sound frequencies up to 20,000 cycles per second, the rat and bat have been judged to hear vibrations as high as 50,000 cycles per second. Spiders have exceedingly sensitive receptors for perception of mechanical vibrations of the body, which are used to detect the presence of intruders or prey on the web.

A good example of the high level of development of animal vision has been observed in the cat. Bridgman and the writer (2) made some studies of the cat's lower absolute threshold of visual sensitivity for different wave lengths of light. One of the first things found was that the experimenter could not use his own eyes in the darkened experimental room in order to observe the cat's movements in discriminating a panel of light when this panel was illuminated at a brightness near the animal's threshold. Small radium clips were attached to the cat's collar so that the experimenter could see when it was responding to the light pattern. The experiment showed that, generally, the cat's lower threshold of vision is about one-seventh that of human subjects tested with the same stimulus patterns.

The Role of Discrimination in Animal Behavior

The mechanisms of stimulus discrimination define the main avenues of reaction used by animals to orient to their environmental surroundings, secure food, avoid enemies, and, in fact, keep the physiology of the living system in proper adjustment to the environment. Examples will be given here to illustrate some of the more striking roles of discrimination in the lives of animals.

All animals are equipped at birth with discrimination reactions in terms of which initial behavior toward the parent and toward the general environment is guided and controlled. The young mammal in seeking food is guided to the mother's nipple by sensory discrimination. It retains its orientation to gravity in terms of similar differential sensitivity to stimuli set up through motion of its own body. It seeks warmth and cover through cutaneous temperature discrimination.

Making an adequate visual discrimination is a matter of life or death to the newly hatched loggerhead turtle. On a tropical or subtropical sand beach, the female loggerhead, one of the great sea turtles, prepares a nest, lays her eggs, covers them, and returns to the ocean, never to revisit the nest site. The nest is a hole in the sand about 2½ feet deep and 1 foot in diameter, located from 25 to 100 feet from the ocean's edge. When the eggs hatch, about 50 days later, the young turtles mill around in the cavern under the sand. As the sand covering them sifts down among the egg shells they are gradually raised to the level of the beach. When the young turtles are able to emerge from the nest, they move directly and rapidly to the ocean. Without parental or social guidance, either by day or by night, the newly hatched turtle finds its way from the nest site to the ocean and thereafter to the open reaches of the Gulf Stream.

This migration of the young loggerhead turtle has been a mystery until recently. Some people thought that the turtle discriminated the color of ocean water from the green foliage of the terrain back of the beach. Others thought that the animal was geotropic, that is, was guided by the sloping contour of the beach as it dropped toward the ocean's edge. Daniel and the writer (3) showed that the migration of young turtles depends entirely on their ability to discriminate faint differences in light intensity between the white surf of the ocean and other areas in their environment. At all times, except on moonless nights when the ocean is almost completely quiet, the surf of the ocean is more brilliant than any other area of the turtle's immediate environment. On moonless summer nights the brightness of the surf is due in part to the phosphorescence of the water. If the ocean is very quiet on a moonless night, some of the baby turtles get lost. It was also shown in this study that olfaction, hearing, and geotropic orientation are not critical for the migration. An interesting fact about the visual discrimination of the young turtles is that their forced orientation toward the brighter of several light patterns is lost as soon as they begin to eat, some seven to ten days after they have hatched.

Animals depend continually upon discriminative reactions in order to control movements of the body in the environment. The story of auditory discriminations in bats represents one of the most interesting discoveries about animal discrimination in recent years. The studies of Griffin and Galambos (4, 7) disclosed that these small animals maintain their remarkable ability to avoid obstacles in night flight by emitting supersonic waves of about 50,000 vibrations per second. These vibrations have the property of greater directional specificity than sounds of lower frequency audible to the human ear.

They are thus directionally reflected from obstacles and this echo is discriminated by the bat. Figure 5 illustrates the principles involved in this self-generated sound and echo relation.

Griffin and Galambos (4) first confirmed earlier work that if the bat's hearing is impaired, it is unable to avoid objects in flying at night, but that if it is merely blindfolded, there is no disturbance of its ability to avoid obstacles. Next, they observed that if the mouth and nose of the animal are covered, the animal shows defects in its flying. These two facts suggested that self-emission of sounds and

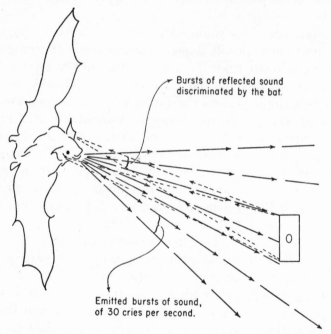

Bursts of reflected sound discriminated by the bat.

Emitted bursts of sound, of 30 cries per second.

Fig. 5. The Principle of Object Localization and Discrimination by the Bat.

auditory discrimination were both involved in the bat's location of objects. More refined experimental techniques were thereafter used to investigate the cries of bats (7). A supersonic analyzer was employed to convert the high frequency vibrations emitted by the animal to record form. It was found that the sounds emitted and discriminated by the animal vary but are usually above 50,000 vibrations per second, which is at least 30,000 vibrations above the maximum frequency perceived by the human ear. They also found that the rate of the cries emitted is between 30 and 50 per second.

The significant aspect of this study is not that bats hear supersonic vibrations, since dogs, rats, mice, and other mammals are also known to hear such frequencies, but that the bat is the only known animal to make use of the echo principle of radar and sonar in discriminating the position of objects in its environment. As if that were not enough, Griffin and Galambos found that the essential feature of the echo detector, namely the suppression of the emitted signal so that the echo can be detected, is also found in bats. They found that when the bat's squeak is being produced, a muscle in the ear contracts and closes the ear to the emitted squeak. As soon as the squeak is over the ear opens up so that the echo can be heard.

Animals depend upon ultrasensitive chemical discriminative mechanisms to guard them from danger and to aid in the search for food. It has been known for some time that animals, including man, possess chemical analyzers far more accurate than the best chemical techniques in the detection of certain substances. Hasler and Wisby (10) have demonstrated clearly the remarkable nature of the chemical discriminative reactions of certain fish. The purpose of their study was the use of fish for the olfactory assay of pollutants, especially phenol pollutants, in lake and stream water. They attempted to set up a discrimination between phenol and p-chloro-phenol in the blunt-nose minnow. The minnows were trained, in a specially devised aquarium (Fig. 6), to associate the odor of one substance with food and the other with electrical punishment. In such an aquarium, it was possible to inject continuous streams of water from either end of the tank, to introduce the olfactory substance into either stream and then clear the water rapidly through charcoal filters, to punish the fish at either end of the tank by means of electrodes, and to give food in a feed trough at either end of the tank. The two odoriferous substances were released into the tank, one in conjunction with food and the other in conjunction with electric shock, under conditions of control of all extraneous factors that might affect the response of the minnows.

The biological assay of phenolic compounds by methods like this is of the nature of recognition and not quantitative analysis. In the experiment described, the trained minnows were observed to discriminate dilutions of phenolic compound about 20 times more accurately than does man. Further studies showed that minnows can learn to make discriminations between water from two different streams, and that they retain this discrimination after a forgetting period. Work is being extended to discover the nature of this type of discrimination and its retention in salmon as an approach to understanding salmon migration. Hasler and Wisby also employ their methods for appraising the selective discrimination of fish in

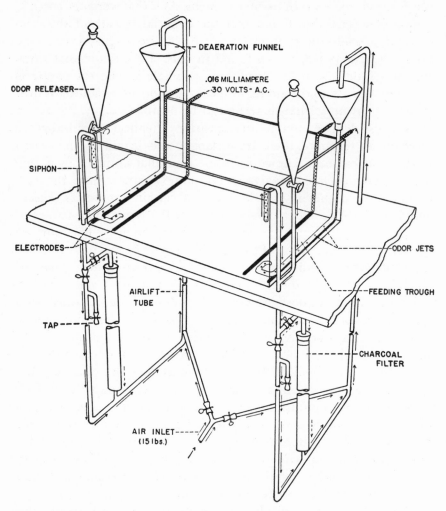

Fig. 6. The Aquarium Setup Used by Hasler and Wisby (10) to Train and Test Fish in the Comparative Discrimination of Odors.

recognition of water plants and the detection of prey by lampreys.

The discriminative reactions of animals provide not only the mechanisms for detection and orientation, but also are closely interrelated with the physiological processes of drive. The effectiveness of certain stimuli in producing discriminative reaction may be shown to change with deprivation or with alteration of physiological states associated with motivation. Thus, discriminative reaction acts as a part of the regulatory system of the animal body that maintains the proper adjustment of physiological state of the organism.

In animal behavior, discriminative mechanisms are evolved that adjust in a highly refined manner the quantitative characteristics of response with the degree and extent of stimulation in complex situations. The rate of head and eye movements in the detection and discrimination of moving stimuli is a good example of such mechanisms. Cats, dogs, monkeys, guinea pigs, and most other mammals display such automatically adjusted behavior not only in the presence of real movement of visual stimuli but also in relation to conditions of apparent visual movement, such as seen in the phi phenomenon or in the motion picture (18).

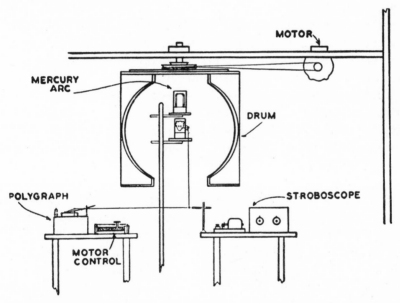

Fig. 7.   The Arrangement of Apparatus Used to Induce and Record Responses to Visual Apparent-movement in the Guinea Pig (18).

We can demonstrate stimulus-correlated discriminative response to conditions of apparent movement in animals by means of the rather complicated setup shown in Fig. 7. The apparatus consists of a moving drum, arranged with striated ribs that are painted white on their inside surface. When the striations of the drum are illuminated by the flashing light of the stroboscope, the inside of the drum is seen as a sharply contrasting field of black and white stripes. The animal, in this case a guinea pig, is placed in a box holder inside the drum. A string is attached to the nose of the guinea pig and connected to a recording lever in order to register the head movements on a polygraph paper record.

In making observations, the drum, located in a darkened room, is rotated at a given speed. The stroboscope is then turned on and the flash frequency is adjusted to be: (a) greater than frequency of movement of stripes passing a given point, in order to produce apparent movement of the stripes in the same direction as the real movement; (b) less than the stripe frequency, to produce apparent movement opposite in direction from that of the real movement of the drum; (c) equal to the stripe frequency, in order to make the stripes look as if they were standing still. In this setup it can be shown that the rate of head movements in the animal varies as a function of the direction and rate of the stroboscopic or apparent movement. Thus, what is ordinarily thought to be a very complex perceptual discrimination occurs in many animals and may be described in quantitative behavioral terms.

The examples given in this section indicate one of the main characteristics of discriminative behavior—its role in the maintenance of adaptive conduct of the animal. It is through understanding of discrimination that the mechanisms of such conduct can be clarified. On the other hand, consideration of the biological significance of the particular discriminative response, as shown here, leads naturally to detailed examination of significant features of such responses that may be overlooked and misunderstood unless the adaptive aspect of the behavior is kept clearly in mind. This functional approach to the problems of discrimination, by giving a broad meaningful framework to detailed experimental analysis, can be depended upon to guide investigation along systematic lines and to avoid the dangers of purely logical orientation to problems of this field.

Definition of the Problems of Discrimination

In studying the processes of discrimination one may approach the problem in a number of ways. There are at least five major problematic areas to be considered: the description of the behavior itself, and its psychophysical, psychophysiological, dynamic, and motivational characteristics. Extensive study is needed to determine how different quantitative properties correlate with one another, and to what extent these properties define the level and stability of the discriminative behavior.

The problems of describing discriminative reactions

When we desire to specify exactly the type of response or the aspect of response that is being observed and studied, we refer to the reactive characteristics of the response, which identify the pattern of the response and the quantitative features that it displays. The pattern of the response may be specific or general and may involve different muscular or effector mechanisms. The quantitative features of the response may vary from one pattern of behavior to another, but such properties as magnitude, frequency, duration, rate, and latent period of reaction will be common to most types of discrimination. In order to measure discriminative behavior, we measure one or more of these reactive properties of a given type of response. All evidence about behavior indicates that its causation can be defined only in terms of the conditions affecting particular patterns or trends in response that can be subjected to experimentation and analysis. Accordingly, the scientific problem of discriminative behavior is the determination of those characteristics or conditions of occurrence of known patterns of differential behavior that are described in terms of their observable reactive properties.

The psychophysical problems of discrimination

In this area we are concerned mainly with describing the qualitative and quantitative relations or functions between the physical properties of stimulation and specified patterns of response. Generally speaking we want to know, given a certain form of response, how different properties of this response will vary under different conditions of stimulation.

The psychophysiological problems of discrimination

Once we know how a given discriminative response takes place or varies with certain kinds of stimulation, in short when we can identify some of the reactive and psychophysical characteristics of a reaction, we may inquire into the relations between this behavior and the anatomical and physiological processes of the body. We may attempt to investigate how different structures and processes in the receptors, nervous system, effector system, and other parts of the body are qualitatively and quantitatively related to the discriminative response and its psychophysical functions.

The dynamic problems of discrimination

Like all other forms of behavior, discriminative reactions are not always stable entities. They develop and change in time in relation to a variety of causes. These change characteristics of the discriminative response represent an area of most active experimental interest today. Growth changes, learning phenomena, extinction and forgetting changes, generalizations and transfer, inhibitive changes, fatigue phenomena, and variations related to adaptation are some of the main dynamic features of discriminative behavior. In the analysis of the time changes in discriminative behavior, we deal with alteration of the known reactive features, psychophysical features, or psychophysiological characteristics of a given discriminative response on a measurable time scale.

The motivational problems of discrimination

There is another feature of change in discriminative reactions that may be related to emotional and need states of the animal. Various animals have their perceptions of the environment modified when they are in sexual heat, hungry, thirsty, or are otherwise affected by deprivation of specific bodily requirements. Emotional patterns of behavior, set up by environmental stimuli, give rise in the same way to variations in accompanying discriminative responses. Although it is possible to deal with these questions of motivation in discrimination in terms of the psychophysical, dynamic, and physiological characteristics of behavior, we arbitrarily distinguish these problems because of the complex factors of physical stimulation, deprivation, and the periodicity of physiological states involved.

Analysis of the Problems of Discrimination

The reactive aspects of discrimination

As noted before, discriminative behavior is a relatively consistent pattern of response, which may be observed and measured in different ways. Study of the following reactive aspects of a given segment of behavior yields information about animal discrimination:

a. Presence or absence of the response to a given pattern of stimulation.

b. Relative frequency of occurrence (relative number of correct or incorrect reactions) in conjunction with repeated presentation of the stimulus to be discriminated.

c. Relative duration of the response.

d. Relative response time or latent period.

e. Relative velocity of a movement made in response to different stimuli.

f. Relative magnitude of response made to different stimuli.

g. Relative rate of repetition of a response made to different stimuli.

Scientific investigation of discrimination always involves as a first step specification of: (a) the pattern of response to be studied, whether a general movement, a leg response, pupillary response, orientation, and so on; (b) the reactive property or properties of behavior, for example, magnitude, response frequency, rate, which are to be measured; and (c) the form of discrimination involved.

The apparatus, recording, and stimulus presentation problems of analyzing animal discrimination depend on the special reactive features of response that are to be studied. Generalizations about these technical problems are difficult to make without being misleading. However, the following points may be made:

1. **Apparatus.** Simple apparatus arrangements for control and restraint are possible when orientation patterns of behavior are used. When duration, magnitude, rate of response, or any type of relative change in response is investigated, more complicated devices for control of the animal are usually necessary. Some of the common forms of apparatus for training, control, and restraint of the subject animal, as used in learned-discrimination experiments, are shown in Fig. 8.

2. **Recording.** Special recording devices are necessary when features of reaction such as response time, change in rate, response magnitude, and similar reactive properties are measured or observed as critical variables in the discrimination experiment. The experiment on apparent movement, already cited, gives an example of the type of device that may be used to investigate relative magnitude and rate of eye movement. Recording devices used in discrimination experiments consist of numerical counters, time clocks, kymographic recording devices, and oscillographic devices.

3. **Stimulus presentation.** The problems of stimulus presentation can become quite difficult in some studies of discrimination. Hasler and Wisby's (10) studies give an indication of the problems of presenting controlled olfactory stimuli to fish. Obviously, the first

problems of stimulus presentation depend on the sensory channel or channels under investigation. But once the nature of the stimulus variables involved in the discrimination are known and controlled, there still remains the question of how the olfactory, visual, tactual, or auditory stimuli will be presented. The so-called psychophysical methods of presentation to be used in the animal experiment will

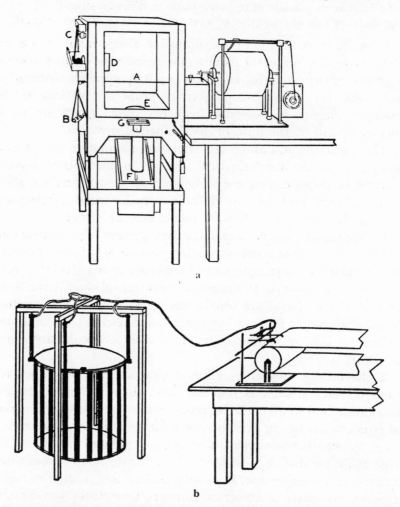

Fig. 8. Methods for Analyzing Learned Discriminative Response in Animals. a. Apparatus for training and observing the cat's detection and response to objects (20). In this apparatus, the animal, by depressing the string (*A*), can deliver small rubber balls into the box from the magazine (*C*). When these are placed in the chute (*E*), the apparatus automatically gives the animal access to food. **b.** Stabilimeter device (19) for pneumatically recording unlearned and conditioned detection and comparison responses in medium-sized laboratory animals. **c.** Conditioning apparatus for

be defined by the form of the discriminative response. The psycho-physical *method of limits* is used especially for the investigation of detection behavior. *Methods of constant stimuli* are especially adapted to studies of visual and auditory comparison behavior. The *methods of adjustment,* as used in human experiments on discrimination, have little application in animal studies because of the limited

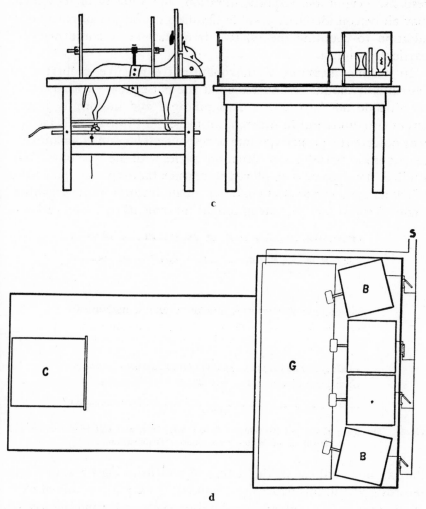

c

d

studying detection and comparison of stimuli by dogs. In this apparatus, flexion of the hind leg is conditioned and recorded. **d.** Multiple discrimination setup for analyzing discrimination in cats. Visual patterns are presented in the front panels of the boxes (*B*). The animal depresses the lever on the box presenting the positive stimuli, and thus gains access to food inside the box. Electrical shock may be given through the levers and the grill (*G*).

abilities of the subjects. Stimulus classification behavior has been investigated by methods comparable to that of constant stimuli.

4. Quantitative indication of the discriminative response. The precision of investigation of discrimination in animals can often be improved by development of methods for measuring some quantitative reactive aspect of the response. Latent period, rate of response, response magnitude, response duration, and velocity of movement may all be considered as possible significant measures of reaction in addition to counting the relative frequency of response made to particular stimuli.

In making measures of the quantitative reactive properties of response, it should be understood at the outset that such aspects of reaction do not have universal significance and uniformity in different situations and in different animals. To illustrate this fact we may observe the property of rate of response. The rate of an animal's reactions in discrimination situations varies with the type of reaction studied, the apparatus employed to register the response, the nature of the animal, and a variety of other innate features in the organism. Figure 9 shows how the rate of tongue movements naturally varies in

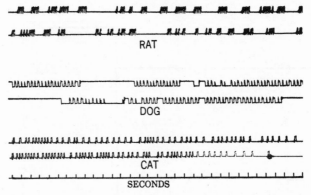

RAT

DOG

CAT

SECONDS

Fig. 9. The Rate of Tongue Movements in the Rat, Dog, and Cat in Detection and Drinking of Water after 24-hour Deprivation.

the rat, dog, and cat in the detection and drinking of water. The records given in this figure are obtained by having the animal close an electronic circuit of sub-threshold strength each time the tongue comes into contact with the water.[1] The pairs of records shown were obtained after a 24-hour water deprivation. The top curve of each

[1] The type of apparatus used for obtaining these records was originally designed by William E. Kappauf.

pair represents the start of the drinking after deprivation. The bottom curve of each pair shows the lapping rate near the time of satiation. The rate of response for the rat is quite different from that of dog and cat. The rat's lapping rate occurs in bursts of five or six responses separated by one- or two-second intervals. The dog drinks in irregular periods but laps regularly in these periods. The cat's rate of response waxes and wanes without interruption.

Species differences in properties of the same discriminative response, in this case rate of response in detection of fluid, will define the degree of control essential for obtaining comparable measures of discrimination in different animals. In the same way, specification of known modes of variation in such response with level of motivation, diurnal variation, and other variables may be demanded for detailed analysis of various conditions affecting discrimination.

The psychophysical aspects of discrimination

Most of the literature on animal discrimination deals with psychophysical problems. Some of the phenomena involved may be described briefly.

1. General limits of sensitivity. It is always of popular and scientific interest to know the answers to such questions as whether spiders hear, to what extent fish see color, how well dogs can smell, and so on. Such problems have been investigated in almost all phyla of animals. Here are some of the more popularly discussed questions and their answers.

Even the lowest of animals detect and comparatively discriminate most types of stimuli to which the human animal responds. In effect they smell, taste, see, and feel, when these terms are meant to imply that differential behavior occurs under conditions of varied stimulation.

Evidence indicates that all animals discriminate in some way gravitational and acceleratory forces acting upon the body, although different sensory channels are used in different animals. In some animals such behavior depends on special cyst organs, in others on cutaneous receptors, and in higher mammals on visual receptors, muscle receptors, skin receptors, and the receptors located in the vestibular labyrinth.

Cutaneous and muscle sensitivity, covering sensitivity to pressure, temperature, and vibratory stimuli, are highly developed in all animals. Insects have exceptionally developed discriminative reactions for control of flying as well as detection of mechanical changes in the environment. Detection of temperature changes is a very critical part of animal behavior. Such detection may be observed most clearly in cold-blooded animals, in which rate of responding of the heart, respiratory system, and other repetitive reactions change with variations in temperature.

Taste sensitivity for solutions detected by the human tongue as sour, salt, sweet, and bitter seem to be much the same in different animals.

Olfactory discrimination, as already mentioned, is found in marine animals as well as in land animals. Fish are especially sensitive to some substances. Extreme olfactory sensitivity, as found in some mammals, like the dog and deer, is the result apparently of the great elaboration of the nasal chambers in these animals and is not due to any special development of the olfactory receptor cells. There is apparently considerable uniformity in types of odors discriminated in all animals.

Only a relatively few animals of the earth hear sounds in a true sense, that is, are sensitive to air borne or water borne vibrations of the audible range near that of the human ear. Stridulating insects hear, as do fish and other marine vertebrates. These animals, as well as frogs and reptiles, respond to sound frequencies of a very limited range. The range of frequency discrimination in hearing is most extensive in small mammals like the rat and bat.

One of the most widely discussed of all problems of discrimination is that of animal color vision. Here again only a few of the hundreds of thousands of different animals respond selectively to equated differences in wave lengths of light. This term *equated differences* in wave lengths is a very critical problem in determining whether animals "discriminate color." If an animal is presented with light patterns of different wave lengths, which are adjusted in intensity to make them of equal brightness for the animal's own eyes, one may appraise accurately the subject's ability to discriminate these wave lengths (or "color"). On this basis, some few infrahuman animals have been shown to discriminate color. Up to the present, more than 400 specific studies dealing with this problem, mostly giving negative or nonconclusive results, have appeared in the psychological literature. Some of the positive results have been found for bees, the fruit fly, day birds, monkeys, and apes. It is fairly certain that most infraprimate mammals are color blind. The evidence for color vision in reptiles is good but not conclusive. Amphibia and fish probably do not discriminate color. At best the evidence for such discrimination is controversial.

2. Relative sensitivity in discrimination. The problem of the efficiency with which different forms of stimulus energy can produce discrimination is a basic psychophysical aspect of animal discrimination. We define this problem as the relative amount of stimulus energy for a given receptor system or for different receptor systems that is necessary to bring about an equivalent level of response to stimulus variables. The nature of such a scientific experiment can be illustrated by reference to work upon vision in the cat. Bridgman (1) set up an experiment to measure the minimum amount of light

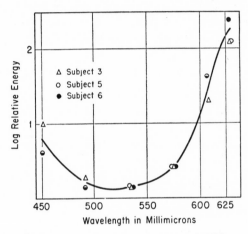

Fig. 10. The Curve Sensitivity in Detection of Lights of Different Wave Lengths at Absolute Threshold Level in the Cat. (From the data of Bridgman.)

energy necessary for the cat to detect different wave lengths of light. The cat responded by pressing a lever on a single-discrimination box. The threshold of detection was defined as that minimal level of light energy at each wave length that would cause the animal to press the lever 75 per cent of the time when the spectral light was presented in the panel of the discrimination box. Following this procedure, the absolute threshold was determined for narrow wavelength bands with maxima approximately at 450, 490, 540, 580, 615, and 630 millimicrons. Bridgman's results are shown in Fig. 10. In this graph, the relative level of radiant energy, expressed in logarithmic units, necessary to produce equivalent response (absolute threshold response) is plotted against the wave length. The results show that, at very low illuminations, the cat discriminates the presence of different wave lengths of light in much the same way as the human eye. The animal is most sensitive to wave lengths in the yellow and green areas of the spectrum and less sensitive to the red and blue regions.

Following experiments generally like those just described, relative sensitivity in discrimination of various properties of visual stimuli in addition to wave length can be specified for different animals. In addition, relative sensitivity functions have been worked out for auditory stimuli, taste sensitivity, and to some extent olfactory sensitivity, in a wide variety of different infrahuman animals.

3. Psychophysical variation in discriminative behavior. In addition to problems of relative sensitivity, the psychophysics of animal discrimination deals with the question of variation in the capacity to

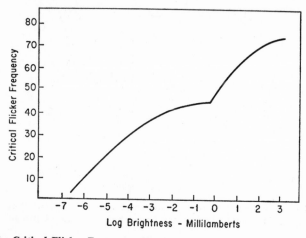

Fig. 11. The Critical Flicker Frequency for the Cat in Flashes per Second at Different Brightness Levels. [Modified from the data of Kappauf (11).]

differentiate stimuli in relation to alteration of the stimulus conditions themselves. We may take as an example the variation in comparison thresholds of discrimination of flickering lights for the cat. The data plotted in Fig. 11 are those obtained by Kappauf (11). The curve given in this figure shows that, as the level of brightness of a flickering light is increased, the rate of flicker must be increased before the cat responds to this light as a fused constant pattern. This fusion level, expressed in flashes per second, is called the critical flicker frequency, or *CFF*. Critical flicker frequency may be determined for the cat and other animals by setting up a learned discrimination between a constant and flickering light of equal total illumination. After the discriminative response is learned, the rate of flicker of the one light may be increased until the discrimination breaks down, or until the critical fusion frequency is reached. Observations must also be made by having the animal respond when the rate of flicker is set above fusion level and then reduced until the discriminative response appears to be consistent. In the experiment described, precautions were taken to prevent position cues and other secondary factors from influencing the animal's behavior. In order to obtain the results shown in Fig. 11, the critical fusion frequency was determined for different illumination levels of the two light sources discriminated. The data plotted here represent the smoothed curves for two cats. In these animals, the curve shows two segments, the "rod" and "cone" functions, comparable to the curves of human subjects. Cats show individual differences in this discrimination. Other cats studied by Kappauf failed to show the higher or "cone" segment of the curve.

Scientific studies such as these, as well as those described for relative sensitivity, provide a permanent record of certain aspects of animal behavior of importance in understanding biological phenomena of response. In addition, such studies serve as a foundation for further experimental and theoretical work on the psychophysiology of animal and human behavior.

It is impossible to describe here the scope of experimentation on the analysis of the psychophysical variations in animal discrimination. Extensive experimentation, involving different sensory mechanisms, has provided knowledge especially of the following areas: (a) the nature of the pitch and loudness discrimination in hearing; (b) visual acuity, size, form, brightness, movement, and distance discrimination in animal vision; (c) olfactory discrimination and its stimulus basis; (d) the nature and functions of taste discrimination. As noted before, much of what is known today about the environmental control of adjustive behavior and its physiological basis has been provided by analyses of animal behavior.

4. **The psychophysical organization of discriminative behavior.** Besides the questions of stimulus limits of response, and the variation in these limits as a function of different conditions and parameters of stimulation, many important problems of discrimination center around the phenomena of behavioral organization in relation to the stimulus pattern. One of the most active fields of research in animal

behavior currently is concerned with this area of "perceptual" organization. Under this general topic we deal with such subjects as space discrimination, discrimination of apparent movement, sensory contrast and mixture phenomena, sensory integration, object discrimination, and the "perceptual constancy" phenomena. Space permits a discussion of only a limited number of these controversial problems.

One of the most critical problems of sensory integration is concerned with the interplay of vision, touch, kinesthetic, and vestibular mechanisms in the control of posture, and discrimination orientation based on these sensory systems. The equivalence and integration of action of vision and the vestibular system in defining differential eye, head, and body responses to movement of the environment and of the animal body in space has been established experimentally. In many animals, including man, optic nystagmus, when elicited under appropriate conditions, shows the same general characteristics found for vestibular nystagmus. The former is produced by movement of the visual environment, the latter by acceleration of movement of the blinded animal in space. Through these two discriminative systems the animal is provided with a speed recorder (the optic system) and an acceleration recorder (the vestibular system), which, working together, provide an essential control of differential behavior for all velocities and changes in velocity of movement of the animal body in space.

The study of perceptual discrimination in animals sometimes brings into proper focus the nature of certain responses that mistakenly have been thought to represent highly evolved and complicated forms of perception. Discrimination based on conditions of apparent movement stimulation is a case in point. In Gestalt psychology and in earlier types of mentalistic theories of psychology, apparent movement vision has been thought of as a high order of perception requiring the most advanced stages of cortical evolution. Such discrimination, however, can be observed to occur in the common guinea pig, as well as in birds and reptiles. In fact, animals deprived of the cerebral cortex, the surface layers of the brain, make equally good discriminative responses based on apparent movement stimulation. Methods of study utilizing the principle of the stroboscope have been described earlier. These methods and results have illustrated that apparent-movement vision has a primitive behavioral status, as a differential type of reaction, and that its related discrimination functions are of the same order as for real movement stimulation.

Color perception in infrahuman animals represents an almost untouched field of investigation. Color contrast phenomena have been observed in insects, and probably occur in all animals possessing color vision. Color mixture and similar integrative sensory processes have been described in monkeys and chimpanzees by Grether (5) in studies based on observations of animals trained to open food compartments located in relation to the stimulus panels to be discriminated. Grether has shown that the mixture proportions for color discrimination in monkeys and chimpanzees approximate those for color mixture in human vision. An exception noted in these studies, which were conducted by determining the equivalence of certain color mixtures with predetermined white and yellow samples, is that both the monkey and the chimpanzee require more of the red component in a red-green mixture than is required by the human eye to produce a mixture equivalence with a white light.

Object identification in animals has been investigated in a number of interesting studies. A current application of knowledge in this field is the use of radio-produced sounds simulating those made by female mosquitoes to attract males to a lethal trap. Extensive studies on the use of interrelated sensory cues to provide adequate object identification in insects and fish have shown a complexity of perceptual discrimination in these species comparable to that shown by mammals.

In the higher animals, the experimental analysis of object discrimination has uncovered important aspects of animal perception. Harlow's (9) studies on the rhesus monkey are of special significance, inasmuch as they show that the monkey learns to identify common objects and make consistent discriminations between them on the basis of a single previous presentation of these objects to the animal. In these experiments, the monkey is rewarded with food for choosing the one of two objects that arbitrarily has been designated as the correct choice. In successive trials new pairs of different objects are introduced, and response to one of each of these pairs is reinforced as just described. Eventually, it is found that a single presentation of a new pair is sufficient for the animal to make consistent discrimination thereafter between the two objects of the new pair. In addition, it has been shown that equally rapid identification is learned when the animal is to recognize an odd object among several others or to recognize that a reversal has been made in the object of a pair that has been designated as correct.

These studies are of significance in showing that the infrahuman primate learns to integrate compound sensory cues into sustained patterns of behavior in a way reminiscent of the rapidity and flexibility of the human mode of reaction. Harlow's work also has a bearing on the interpretation of perceptual generalization which will be presented below.

The description of the psychophysical organization of discriminative response is a problem of considerable significance in theoretical psychology. Relative to this topic we wish to know to what extent animals possess the ability to discriminate in terms of perceived similarities, and on what basis response in terms of similarity is developed.

The most noteworthy fact about this subject, contrary to many current writings in the field, is that, in most animals, discriminative responses are organized in very specific ways prior to and independently of specific learning. In invertebrates, and in most vertebrates, situations may be set up in which a variety of stimuli is responded to, without training, as equivalent or identical. The constancy of response of newly hatched or newly born animals to certain patterns of visual, auditory, tactual, olfactory and gustatory stimuli indicates that unlearned discriminative organization exists. As an example, take the equivalence of response of newly hatched turtles to a variety of light patterns. The natural discriminative responses in detection, comparison, and classification of stimuli are obviously not based upon the specific, absolute, quantitative values of stimulation. Relative difference in intensity in light stimulation is the critical factor for elicitation of the natural light-controlled responses of most animals, as for example, the turtle, the young rat, and the newborn monkey. The same is true for pattern and movement discriminations and for other varieties of responses that may be produced without training in almost all animals. In other words, the relational aspect of discriminative behavior is not necessarily due to learning, but may be said to be a basic psychophysical and psychophysiological property of response.

Identification of patterns of stimuli that are made to vary in some physical respect occurs also in animals without apparent training. Very complex mechanisms of identification of mates, of food sources, and of nest sites may be demonstrated in insects, in fish, and in most migrating birds. Mammals possess these primary perceptual organizations as well (8). The nursing female dog or cat, in caring for offspring for the first time, rarely confuses the newborn young with inanimate objects substituted for the kittens or puppies. Here again absolute aspects of stimulation are unimportant. The young of another female may be introduced, or the number of kittens or pups may be changed, without disturbing the maternal discriminations of the nursing female. In a word, the absolute values of physical stimulation change, but the discriminative responses of the female persist as if nothing has happened. Certain relative conditions of stimulation, within limits, define the identification and acceptance of the young.

In a succeeding section, the question of discriminative similarity and generalization, as based on learning experiments, will be discussed. At that point, it will be advantageous to remember that, before an animal learns to detect, compare, or classify patterns of stimuli in a specific situation, it already makes organized discriminative reactions to all of these stimuli. New organizations of discriminative response that appear as a result of learning are simply modifications of well established modes of discrimination.

The dynamic aspects of discriminative behavior

Discriminative responses, like other aspects of behavior, display features of change in time. The change properties may be referred to, for want of a better name, as the dynamic aspects of the discriminative response. Phenomena that have been investigated include those concerned with maturation, learning, retention, adaptation, extinction, inhibition, and generalization of discrimination. A limited number of these aspects of discrimination will be discussed.

1. **Maturational phenomena.** Maturational aspects of discrimination are investigated by relating changes in reaction to age of development and excluding as far as possible specific practice and learning in the functions to be studied. The development of visual acuity in kittens (24) has been studied by subjecting the young kittens to discrimination tests beginning shortly after birth. Observations were made of placing reactions to surfaces and eye and head responses to moving striations of different widths. The method of testing discriminative responses to moving lines is shown in Fig. 12. The kitten is held in a small box holder and its differential head and eye movements to movement of the striated drum are observed. The result of these experiments (Fig. 13) show that there is a

gradual development of visual acuity in the young kitten beginning shortly after the eyes open. Response to wide striations (5 cm.) begins on the average at 14 days, response to 2.5 cm. lines at around 16 days, and acuity nears its maximum at 24 to 26 days. Tactual placing of the forelimbs for standing matures before effective vision. These same placing responses may be elicited by visual stimulation only when the visual acuity of the kittens has reached its maximum development.

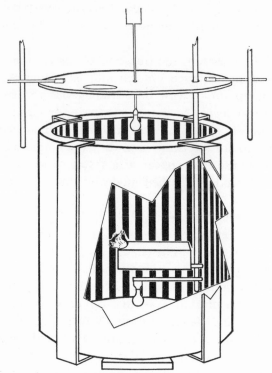

Fig. 12. The Method of Observing Unlearned Discriminative Movements of the Head and Eyes in Young Kittens (24). These responses are made to movement of the striated inner surface of the drum.

Methods of studying embryonic behavior have been developed for mammals and for inframammalian species. Observation of differential detection and comparison behavior is possible in some forms. In animals hatched from eggs, such as the turtle, it is sometimes possible to find highly complex forms of discriminative behavior existing prior to the time of hatching. For example, young loggerhead turtles that are released prematurely from the egg display light-discrimination reactions identical to those which take place after hatching.

The study of maturation of discriminative response offers a fertile and as yet relatively untouched field of investigation in animal psychology. Such investigation not only discloses the order and time of integration of response, but also provides meaningful data for understanding the scope and character of adult modes of discrimination.

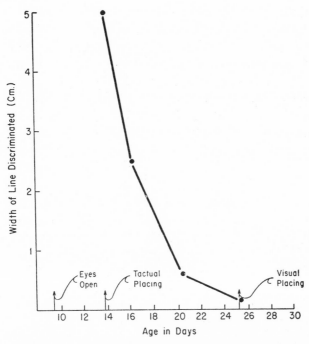

Fig. 13. The Development of Visual Acuity in the Young Kitten in Relation to the Time of Eye Opening, and the Appearance in Development of Tactual and Visual Placing Reactions of the Front Limbs. Visual acuity is expressed in terms of the width in centimeters of the lines discriminated.

2. Discrimination learning. The learning of discriminations has been investigated in many different ways in animal psychology. Typically, detection behavior is learned more easily than comparison behavior, and these two are learned apparently with greater facility than matching behavior. This difference between detection and comparison learning may be said to be true irrespective of the so-called type of learning or response involved. It appears that the

matching type of response is learned only with difficulty by monkeys and by young children.

The rate of development of learned discriminations based on different stimulus characteristics, using similar methods of procedure, has been determined for some animals. In the rat, discriminations based on distance and position are acquired much faster than those based on visual pattern (13). Responses to number differences are not learned at all. The common dog and cat learn to respond to sound differences with greater rapidity than to visual differences. Work with monkeys seems to show that discriminations of stimulus objects varying in several dimensions are learned more rapidly than similar responses made to stimuli differing in a single dimension.

Table 1 summarizes some basic facts about the nature and extent of learning of comparative discriminations in the cat. Brightness discrimination is learned with considerable rapidity. Form discrimination is more difficult for the animal to acquire. When four or five stimulus patterns are used, the learning, in terms of trials, is more rapid than when only two patterns, one positive and one negative,

TABLE 1

THE NUMBER OF TRIALS REQUIRED BY THE CAT TO LEARN DIFFERENT COMPARATIVE DISCRIMINATIONS

Type of Discrimination	Number of Animals	Number of Trials Required to Learn	Range
Brightness discrimination	11	120	100-160
Form discrimination			
a) two patterns	3	413	320-520
b) three patterns	3	387	200-480
c) four patterns	3	307	240-400
Object relations			
Relative position of two objects with respect to one another	4	120	100-200
Relative connection between objects (strings and food containers)	10	Does not learn simple relative connections between objects	

are presented to the animal. Discrimination based on relative position is learned with about the same ease as brightness discrimination. When the animal is required to discriminate between objects in terms of their continuity or connection with a third object, no learning occurs if the factor of positional cue is eliminated in the training.

Some of the most noteworthy studies of learning and discrimination in recent literature have been reported by Harlow (9), whose investigations were partly described earlier. In these experiments, monkeys are trained to make comparative discriminations between objects varying in more than one stimulus dimension. Learning curves for response in different and successive discrimination-problem situations have been obtained. Some of the results are presented in Fig. 14. A group of monkeys is given a first problem of discriminating between two objects. After 50 trials in this situation, the animals are then presented with new pairs of objects in the succeeding blocks of trials. In the first series of eight problem discriminations of this nature, the level of correct response for the second trial on each

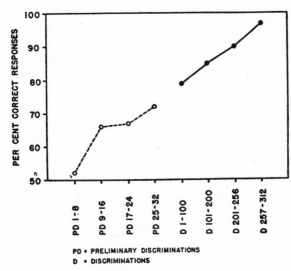

Fig. 14. A Learning Curve Based on Performance in the Second Trial of Each of a Series of Successive Blocks of Trials in which Monkeys Are Presented with Different Pairs of Objects to Be Discriminated (9). The lower curve is based on training on successive blocks of problems of eight problems to each block, the higher curve on successive blocks of problems of 100 problems to each block.

problem is less than 3 per cent above chance response. In the preliminary series of 32 problems, the curve of correct response for the second trial rises gradually. In the final discrimination series, the curve for the second trial response continues to rise to near 100 per cent correct response. These results show that in successive discrimination problems the animal becomes more and more efficient until, at the final stages of learning, a single presentation of the stimulus is sufficient to enable the monkey to differentiate between the new stimulus objects. In other words, monkeys, like man, learn to handle new discrimination problems with great efficiency within a constant environmental and behavioral matrix, when opportunity is afforded for such learning. The results prove, in addition, that the ability to learn and to generalize to new discrimination situations is apparently more dependent on this situational learning factor than any other variable that has yet been studied. Situational learning is the means whereby the animal really achieves efficiency in organizing diverse combinations of stimuli into a consistent mode of behavior, independently of the physical or psychophysical identity of the stimulus patterns presented.

There have been attempts to formulate theoretically the problem of learned discriminative response. Such theories deal mainly with the learning of comparative discriminations.

Spence (21, 23) proposes that in comparative discrimination there is a gradual cumulative strengthening of the connections between the positive stimulus and its response. At the same time there is a gradual and continuous weakening or extinction of the connections between the negative stimulus and its response. When this dual strengthening and weakening of the positive response and the negative response proceeds to a critical point, the discriminative comparison takes place. This theory is an application of the principles of conditioning and cumulative reinforcement through effect to the understanding of discrimination.

According to Lashley (14), the innate factors of neural organization are critical in determining in part the learning and the phenomena of generalization in discrimination. He denies the rigid relationship between stimulation, "reinforcement," and response strength assumed in conditioning theory, as outlined above, and points up facts of individual differences in animals, the psychophysical complexity of discriminative response, and the occurrence of discrimination with only limited reinforcement as support for his view.

Köhler's (12) theory of discriminative learning ascribes the acquisition or development of comparative discrimination to perceptual organization of the situation by the animal. Such organization, given the name of closure, is based on relational factors between the stimuli to be discriminated and their associated receptor and neural processes. The occurrence of closure brings about intelligent understanding or insight that is characterized by rapid solution of the discrimination problem by the animal. Such an explanation of discrimination learning has been called a "non-continuity theory" in contradistinction to a "continuity theory" such as that of Spence, which embodies the principles of conditioning in an explanation of discriminative learning.

3. Discriminative generalization. By generalization of a discriminative response we mean that an already established response, made in relation to specific stimuli, is extended or recurs without further training when the animal is confronted with a different environmental pattern of stimulation.

The phenomenon of generalization or transfer of response has been described in psychological literature under a variety of names. Among others, the terms induction, transfer of training, abstraction, irradiation, transposition, concept formation, stimulus equivalence, and perceptual constancy have been used to signify this feature of discrimination. The preferred term depends on the theoretical orientation of the experimenter.

The study of discriminative generalization is of primary theoretical importance because the observations concerned with this dynamic aspect of response have been taken to signify the basic nature of the psychophysical and psychophysiological organization of behavior. The current controversies in the psychology of perception concerning fundamental definition of stimulus and response stem from the fact that the discriminative reactions of animals are never delimited by specific environmental patterns of energy but are organized psychophysically with reference to diverse patterns of such energy.

The critical experimental control in the generalization experiment is that of eliminating training or learning when the animal is tested for extension of the established response to the new or changed stimulus situation. Without going into this matter in detail, it should be noted that this control is very difficult, if not almost impossible, to achieve in experimental study of animals, and that the results of most generalization studies are quite arbitrary because of this limitation in experimental method.

A typical experiment (17) dealing with comparative discrimination of visual form in the cat will illustrate the method of studying generalization. In Fig. 15 a series of visual patterns used in the experiment is shown. The cat was presented with the combination of four forms, a triangle and three circles, shown at the top of the figure, and was trained to respond positively to the triangle and negatively to the circles. When the animal had learned this discrimination, the various combinations of figures, numbers 2 to 12, were presented to the animal in successive periods of three trials each. In the training, the animal received food for response to the triangle, and an electric shock for response to the circles. In the generalization tests, the animal received no food, nor was it punished for response to any of the changed figures. The column of forms marked (+) shows the forms generally responded to positively by twelve cats used in an extended study. The columns of figures marked (−) represent figures generally avoided by the animal in the generalization test.

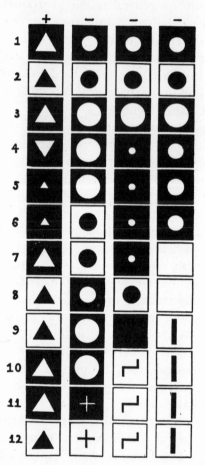

Fig. 15. The Patterns of Stimuli Effective in the Generalization of a Comparative-Discriminative Response in the Cat.

It may be concluded that the cat displays an undisputed ability to extend the learned discrimination of triangles and circles to new combinations of figures in which the relative brightness of figure and ground, the size of the figures, and the nature of the patterns themselves have been changed with respect to the forms used in training. Another important result of this experiment is that either through "latent" or indirect effects, the animal learns to respond to some of the changed figures in a definite way, even though no "reinforcement" of food or punishment is given. For example, some animals start reacting to the vertical bar as first given in combination 9, and it is found that the frequency of this response increases as the tests containing this figure are continued. The fact of persistence of a learning effect in this and similar generalization studies makes it essential to keep present hypotheses about generalization, equivalence, transposition, and response constancy on a very tentative or trial basis. It is obvious that the range and extent of generalization has not been adequately determined because of the difficulty inherent in controlling the persistence of learning during generalization test sequences.

This discussion of generalization in discrimination would not be complete without reference to fact and theory about the factors defining generalization. The nature and extent of generalization vary for different types of discrimination response. Detection reactions generally appear to be more subject to generalization than reactions involving discriminative comparison and classification.

The type of response itself defines its range of generalization. Specific movements, for example limb reactions or eye movements, have a more limited natural stimulus organization than general body movements and emotional patterns of response.

Level of motivation and need deprivation define level of generalization, as already noted. In the case of unlearned detection behavior, Schlosberg, Duncan, and Daitch (16) have given a fine description of change in the generalization in sex recognition patterns of fish after protracted isolation of the male from the female.

Learning defines the extent and range of generalization. First of all, through learning itself, new patterns of stimulation become effective in defining a given response. In addition, as Harlow (9) has shown through his studies, specific training in response to successively different combinations of stimuli causes the monkey to improve greatly in extending an already learned pattern of response to changing stimuli. A major factor defining generalization in learned reactions is the general environmental and reactive matrix in which the response has been learned. The dog or cat, conditioned to sound, does not generalize the learned response to similar tones outside the experimental situation. The principles underlying the specificity or lack of generalization of the learned discriminative response to the particular situation in which it is evolved are not clearly understood. This feature of generalization in animals corresponds in some ways to the specificity found for learned reactions in human situations.

"Physical similarity" of stimuli within a given dimension defines indirectly the range of generalization, as the study in form perception has indicated. We use the word indirectly here to signify the fact that the animal generalizes to different stimulus magnitudes of the same stimulus dimension on the basis of its intrinsic psychophysical and psychophysiological organization. Similarity, then, does not exist for the animal in a physical sense, but is a question of the organization of behavior in the animal.

In comparison behavior, in which the animal is discriminating on the basis of differences, there has been considerable controversy as to whether relative differences in the discriminated stimuli or absolute difference values are more important in defining generalization of the response. From many different studies, it would appear that if the learned stimulus pairs are changed but little in absolute magnitude, relative differences are important in maintaining the response. It is observed, however, that marked change in absolute magnitude of each of a stimulus pair, keeping relative difference constant, is sufficient to bring about failure of generalization in some situations.

Generalization of a discriminative response may occur across modalities of stimulation. Both detection and comparison responses may be generalized in this way, but, as a rule, with greater facility in one direction. For example, learned visual responses are generalized with ease to situations involving auditory stimuli. Learned responses based on auditory stimuli are not typically generalized to discrimination situations involving visual stimuli.

The psychophysical limits of sensitivity and comparison define the range of generalization, if other factors are not operative in defining this range. Generalization of a detection type of response to a comparative discriminative response may occur (6).

To obtain a curve of generalization with respect to the effectiveness of stimuli of the same dimension as the training stimulus presents grave difficulties of experimentation, as already noted. One attempt (6) to secure such a curve with monkeys has indicated, more than anything else, that the stimuli of a given dimension, to which monkeys generalize after being trained on a particular stimulus value, show no marked differences in effectiveness in producing the generalized response.

Current controversial theories about generalization of discriminative responses follow the pattern of learning theory, and are concerned primarily with comparative discrimination. One theory (21, 22) explains generalization of comparative discriminations in terms of generalization of detection reactions that are made with respect to the separate positive and negative stimuli. The generalization of these detection responses is taken for granted as a basic characteristic of behavior. Lashley (14) assumes that generalization is typically based on relational values of the compared stimuli, which are associated with or set up neural gradients in the brain. He holds that these gradients underlie the existence of abstract concepts of size and form, which he attributes to the animal. Field theorists also have attributed such abstractions to the animal, but account for their existence more explicitly in terms of configural relations in the physical environment and between the animal and its environment.

The psychophysiological aspects of discrimination

This area of scientific study, as previously noted, deals with the question of the relations existing between the known reactive, psychophysical, and dynamic properties of discriminative response and the anatomical and functional processes within the animal body. Several distinct types of relation between discrimination and bodily mechanisms may be specified, although because of present limited knowledge, exact specification of such relations may be made only in terms of the particular methods used in controlled observation of the physiological system. Experimental studies have been made especially of the correlations between behavior properties of discriminative response and (a) anatomical organization, (b) effects of injury, (c) electrical phenomena, and (d) chemical states in the physiological system. Similar observation of the effects of deprivation and of biophysical events in the body, as related to discrimination, are possible but have not been investigated widely in animals.

The psychophysiological relations just noted may be analyzed with respect to various parts of the physiological system, the receptors, the nervous, muscle systems, and glandular mechanisms. Studies thus far conducted deal mainly with the correlations between observed discrimination and features of the receptors. Considerable work has been reported on the effects of cortical injury on discrimination.

An example will serve to point up fact and method in this field of research. For some time a question has existed whether there is any physiological difference between various types of learned discriminative response, especially between detection and comparison behavior. Wing (26) has performed the basic experiment, which grew out of a series of earlier studies. He has shown that the visual areas of the cortex in the dog are necessary for maintaining a differential conditioned response based on reaction to a particular direction of change in light intensity. The same cortical areas may be destroyed, however, without disturbing seriously a response based on detection of the presence or absence of the light stimulus. These results were obtained with the apparatus shown in Fig. 8C, which was modified to use a food incentive on conditioning the animal. Two groups of animals were trained, one group in the detection type of response and the other in the comparison type of reaction. Surgical operations were then performed in which the striate or visual areas of the cortex were removed. After operation the animals were retested. As noted above, those animals trained in comparative discrimination lost this response after the surgical operations, whereas the other group of dogs, those trained to detect the presence or absence of the stimulus light, retained the reaction subsequent to the operation.

Experiments such as these show, as do the extensive important studies of receptor functions in animal discrimination, that it is possible to investigate any critical aspect of discriminative reaction—reactive, psychophysical, dynamic, or motivational—in relation to particular aspects of physiological function. It may be emphasized again that such psychophysiological study today represents the basic foundations of many aspects of medical science, as well as giving the factual framework to sound description of behavior generally.

Numerous examples could be given of experiments concerned with the functions of the brain and their correlation with different properties of discriminative response. Lashley's (13) studies on the rat are the earliest attempts to define neural correlates of visual discriminative behavior. Extensive research has been done by others on the cat, dog, and monkey, in hearing as well as vision. Some of the results of this work may be summarized briefly.

Injury to the auditory areas of the cortex has little or no effect on the learning or psychophysical limits of auditory discrimination responses, especially those based on sound intensity.

In vision, a very interesting situation occurs in regard to division of labor at different levels of the nervous system in defining various aspects of discriminative response. Discriminative detection is not an exclusive function of the cortex. Visual discriminative comparison behavior, however, may be disturbed, or in some cases abolished, by removal of the visual areas of the cortex. In the case of brightness and flicker discrimination, removal of the visual cortex abolishes the learned response, but the animal can relearn these discriminations. Studies have shown that the recovery of such discriminative ability may take months or years before preoperative ability is regained.

Learned discriminations of visual form and of movement of visual patterns are completely or very nearly abolished by destruction of the cortical centers of vision. Such operated animals can still orient, in terms of unlearned head and eye movements, to complex moving patterns, displaying just as good visual acuity as that of the normal animal. Operated animals can also give these unlearned optokinetic responses to apparent movement in much the same way as normal animals. In other words, the neural system of vision is highly differentiated both at the cortical level and at the subcortical level for resolution of visual pattern necessary to produce selective unlearned discriminations of moving complex stimuli. Only the cortex, however, is organized for maintaining learned and unlearned responses to isolated patterns in the visual field, either stationary or moving.

It should be emphasized that the present data concerning the functions of the brain in vision indicate two main conclusions. The major injury effect of destruction of the cortical visual centers is found not in the basic psychophysical capacities of intensity, form and flicker discrimination, but in the disorganization of the comparison type of learned discriminative response. Certain specialized reactions involved in visual fixation and in placing and hopping responses of the limbs are also disturbed. The second conclusion to be drawn from this work is that the problem of neural organization in discrimination is far more complex than has sometimes been indicated. Specifically, the simplified theory that the visual cortex is required for pattern and space discrimination but not for discriminations based on light intensity does not find justification in fact.

Another aspect of discrimination should be noted with respect to its psychophysiological correlates. Modern theory of perception and learning often implies that transfer of learning and generalization in discrimination is a high order of abstraction or configural organization that requires the functioning of the cortical centers. Wing and the writer (27) have shown that generalization of conditioned detection reactions to light occurs when the cortical centers of vision are destroyed. If an animal is trained, then subjected to an operation involving ablation of the visual cortex before generalization tests are given, and thereafter tested for generalization of the light controlled response to sound stimulation, it is found that transfer to the sound stimuli takes place much as if the animal were normal. Thus, systematic proof for cortical mechanisms as the basis of generalization and equivalence have not been provided, notwithstanding the assumption of a high order of neural integration for these discriminative phenomena. Harlow (9) has been able to show, however, that the monkey's ability to learn in successive but different discrimination problems, as described earlier, is retarded by extensive ablation of cortical tissue.

Speculations about the neural mechanisms of discriminative response have been based on results of experiments of the sort just described as well as on inferences from behavior itself. One long standing theory of comparative discrimination, based on traditional anatomical ideas about the functions of the neurone and its synapse, postulates specific alternative neural connections between stimulus and response with selection dependent on the relative strength of such connections. "Neural gradients" and differences in electrical fields within the brain have also been proposed as differential neural factors in discrimination. The various divisions of labor in the nervous system in defining visual discrimination, as described earlier in this section, as well as the previously noted compound behavioral properties of the discriminative response, force us to discount very radically any physiological theory that relies upon a single causative framework to describe the neural phenomena of discrimination as now known. The known electrophysiological, chemical, anatomical, and injury-induced phenomena in discrimination cannot be correlated now by any restricted theory of neural causation. The systematic statement made earlier in this section about the physiological properties of discrimination may be repeated with profit as a foundation for experimentally guided theory: Exact specifications of such relations may be made only in terms of the particular methods used in controlled observation of the physiological system.

The relation of receptor processes to the psychophysiological problems of discrimination represents a broad area of study in psychology, dealing especially with the determination of receptor mechanisms involved in certain forms of discriminative response. The reader must be referred to other sources for discussion of special problems of animal behavior in this field.

The motivational aspects of discrimination

The study of the relation between motivational aspects of behavior and discriminative phenomena is a very difficult field of research. Motivation, as usually discussed in psychology, represents a complex interrelation between environmental stimulation, deprivation of materials and sources of energy required for maintenance of bodily functions, and periodically recurring physiological states. Several aspects of animal discrimination have been related to different conditions of motivation. It has been shown that the rat can learn to make differential discriminative reactions in a maze specifically in relation to an imposed state of deprivation. The rat learns to turn one way if hungry and another way if thirsty. This is not a surprising demonstration, for it is evident that many of the differential organizations of behavior in animals, including discriminative behavior, are established with reference to periodically recurring states of need. A more subtle aspect of discriminative behavior may be noted in connection with periodically recurring motivational states in animals. The common female cat shows marked variation in tactual sensitivity on the hind quarters during different stages of the oestrus cycle. Female animals with young typically show changes, which are not observable at other times, in discriminative response to other animals. The protective behavior of the barnyard hen with chicks is an example. Changes in discrimination are sometimes related to specific chemical states within the animal body. Working with rats, Richter (15) has made very important observations on the effect of removal of the adrenal cortex, which is one of the main organic mechanisms for the control of salt metabolism. After its removal, the rat's sensitivity in discrimination of salt solutions is increased greatly, so that solutions of salt concentration normally not detectable by the animal will be effective in producing selective drinking.

General reactive states, such as extreme emotion, hibernation, sleep, tonic immobility, and physiological disorder and sickness constitute periods of motivational change in which discriminative response is altered greatly. Sensitivity to visual and auditory stimuli is greatly affected, and the typical organization of the animal's discrimination is changed during these periods. Broadly speaking, perception in these states can be interpreted only in terms of the present need and physiological status of the animal. One of the main unsolved problems of animal behavior is represented by the way in which such motivational conditions, or the derivatives of such states that are developed through learning, define and organize animal perception.

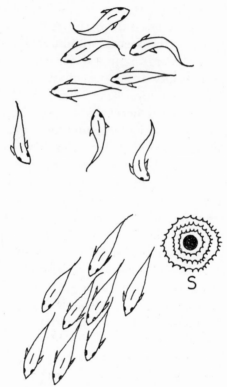

Fig. 16. Induction of a Social Pattern of Motivated Behavior by a Discriminated Stimulus.

There is another relationship between discrimination and motivational behavior that should be noted. Motivation, as a state of the organism defined by both external and internal conditions, represents a matrix of behavior in which certain forms of response and given levels of activity persist over a period of time. The animal seeks food when hungry, sexual mates in states of heat, fluids when thirsty.

A similar matrix of activity may often be established by a discriminated stimulus. For example, in the female rabbit, oestrus and accompanying sexual activities are induced by copulation with the male and the tactual discriminations involved in this act. Similarly, in certain types of social behavior the motivational matrix, as just described, is established through the action of the discriminated stimulus. The herding of animals, the flocking of birds, and the schooling of fish are understandable in part through mechanisms of this nature. Figure 16 illustrates how a type of innately organized social behavior may occur through the action of a discriminated stimulus. Under normal circumstances, fish do not school systematically in feeding, but an environmental stimulus, which is detected or compared, may bring about the schooling response. Investigation will show that the motivated pattern of behavior also depends on detection by individual fish of members of the same species and their movements. Many other common forms of social behavior in animals also display critical reactive, psychophysical, psychophysiological, and dynamic properties of discriminative behavior.

Theory of discrimination

A general theory of discrimination is of significance only as a means of giving a systematic picture of such behavior. A general theory is not of significance in predicting discriminative behavior inasmuch as the reactive aspects and conditions of differential responses are too diverse to be brought under any single causative scheme of explanation and description. This chapter has presented a general descriptive, mechanistic theory of discrimination that indicates the nature and conditions of discriminative response. This descriptive scheme can be reviewed by way of summary of the chapter.

Discriminative behavior consists of reactions made in relation to physical differences in stimulation. Several forms of discrimination may be observed, stimulus detection, stimulus comparison, and stimulus classification, and different types of responses may occur in connection with these forms of discrimination. In addition, the discriminative response may be described in terms of the receptors or sensory channels concerned.

Discriminative behavior is never a reaction pattern "forced" or "caused by" the physical environment alone. Physical stimulation occurs in conjunction with a matrix of physiological activity and sustained patterns of behavior within the animal body, and this integrated pattern of effective circumstances is the foundation of the behavior. In addition, most phenomena of discriminative behavior are generally understandable only within the framework of the adaptive mechanisms of response that serve to maintain the life of the individual animal.

In order to describe the discriminative response itself we may observe and measure the reactive properties of the behavior. The terms of this description are the particular pattern of the response and those quantitative features that the response displays. Relative frequency, velocity, change in velocity, rate, change in rate, magnitude, change in magnitude, latent time, and duration are reactive properties that may be observed and specified for certain patterns of discriminative behavior. The interrelations of these properties for most forms of discrimination are not known.

Prediction and causation of a particular form and type of discriminative behavior may be specified in terms of known relations between given aspects of the response and the various conditions under which the behavior occurs. We may distinguish four different relational aspects of discrimination: (a) psychophysical properties, (b) psychophysiological properties, (c) dynamic properties, and (d) motivational properties. These aspects of discrimination should be kept clearly in mind. Theoretical attempts to explain one aspect in terms of another lead to nothing but confusion.

The known psychophysical aspects of discrimination enable us to describe and predict the limits of sensitivity, the variations in sensitivity, and the nature of psychophysical organization of a given type of response with respect to different conditions of stimulation.

The psychophysiological properties of discriminative behavior are best described in terms of the particular methods used to define the relations between response and bodily structure and physiological processes. We can specify today significant correlations between certain receptor and neural processes and discriminative reaction in terms of the chemical, electrophysiological, injury, and narcotic aspects of bodily function.

The dynamic properties of discrimination define ways in which such behavior may evolve and change in time. Such changes may be plotted in terms of the reactive properties of response and in terms of its psychophysical features. Generally, these dynamic properties of discrimination can be defined with respect to modes or types of change in behavior that can be distinguished. Maturation changes, including change with advanced age, and changes related to learning and to different conditions of learning are significant in understanding the organization of discriminative response. Special studies have been made of phenomena of inhibition, extinction, adaptation, fatigue, forgetting, and generalization in discrimination which provide further insight into prediction of differential behavior.

We distinguish as separate the so-called motivational properties of discriminative behavior, although it is recognized that motivation itself may be described in terms of certain physiological states, environmental conditions, and learned habits that define it. These integrated states of behavior may be shown to be related to discrimination in definite ways. It has been proved that change in motivation may serve as the basis for discrimination, may define the level of psychophysical sensitivity, may determine the nature of generalization and organization for certain forms of discriminative response, and may in turn be defined by the action of discriminating stimuli.

The exact formulation of knowledge and theory of the nature of discriminative response through experiment represents a most important area of scientific psychology of general theoretical significance. The extension of knowledge in this field is also of special importance in applied psychology, as well as in related fields of medicine, agriculture, conservation, and industry.

Bibliography

1. Bridgman, C. S., The Visibility Curve of the Cat at Absolute Threshold, *Psychol. Bull.*, 1937, **34**, 792.
2. ———— and Smith, K. U., The Absolute Threshold of Vision in Cat and Man with Observations on Its Relation to the Optic Cortex, *Amer. J. Physiol.*, 1942, **136**, 463-466.
3. Daniel, R. S., and Smith, K. U., The Migration of Newly Hatched Loggerhead Turtles Toward the Sea, *Science*, 1947, **106**, 398-399.
4. Galambos, R., and Griffin, D. R., Obstacle Avoidance by Flying Bats: The Cries of Bats, *J. Exp. Zool.*, 1942, **89**, 475-490.
5. Grether, W. F., Chimpanzee Color Vision, *J. Compar. Psychol.*, 1940, **29**, 167-192.
6. Grandine, L., and Harlow, H. F., Generalization of the Characteristics of a Single Learned Stimulus by Monkeys, *J. Comp. and Physiol. Psychol.*, 1948, **41**, 327-338.
7. Griffin, D. R., and Galambos, R., The Sensory Basis of Obstacle Avoidance by Flying Bats, *J. Exp. Zool.*, 1941, **86**, 481-506.

8. Harlow, H. F., Studies in Discrimination Learning by Monkeys: II. Discrimination Learning Without Primary Reinforcement, *J. Gen. Psychol.,* 1944, **30**, 13-21.

9. —— The Formation of Learning Sets, *Psychol. Rev.,* 1949, **56**, 51-65.

10. Hasler, A. D., and Wisby, W. J., Use of Fish for the Olfactory Assay of Pollutants (Phenols) in Water, *Trans. Amer. Fish Soc.,* 1950, (in press).

11. Kappauf, W. E., Flicker Discrimination in the Cat, *Psychol. Bull.,* 1936, **33**, 597-598.

12. Köhler, W., *Gestalt Psychology.* New York: Liveright, 1929, p. 403.

13. Lashley, K. S., The Mechanism of Vision. XV. Preliminary Studies of the Rat's Capacity for Detail Vision, *J. Gen. Psychol.,* 1938, **18**, 123-193.

14. —— An Examination of the "Continuity Theory" as Applied to Discriminative Learning, *J. Gen. Psychol.,* 1942, **26**, 241-265.

15. Richter, C. P., Salt Taste Thresholds for Normal and Adrenalectomized Rats, *Endocrinology,* 1939, **24**, 367-371.

16. Schlosberg, H., Duncan, M. C., and Daitch, B. H., Mating Behavior of Two Live-bearing Fish, *Xiphophorus hellerii* and *Platypoecilus maculatus, Physiol. Zool.,* 1949, **22**, 148-161.

17. Smith, K. U., Visual Discrimination in the Cat. III. The Relative Effect of Paired and Unpaired Stimuli in the Discriminative Behavior of the Cat. *J. Genet. Psychol.,* 1936, **48**, 29-57.

18. —— The Neural Centers Concerned in the Mediation of Apparent Movement Vision, *J. Exp. Psychol.,* 1940, **26**, 443-466.

19. —— An Improved Stabilimeter Method for Recording Activity in Laboratory Mammals, *J. Exp. Psychol.,* 1940, **27**, 89-93.

20. Smith, M. F., The Establishment and Extinction of the Token-Reward Habit in the Cat, *J. Gen. Psychol.,* 1939, **20**, 475-486.

21. Spence, K. W., The Nature of Discrimination Learning in Animals, *Psychol. Rev.,* 1936, **43**, 427-449.

22. —— The Differential Response in Animals to Stimuli Varying Within a Single Dimension, *Psychol. Rev.,* 1937, **44**, 430-444.

23. —— Continuous Versus Non-continuous Interpretations of Discriminative Learning, *Psychol. Rev.,* 1940, **47**, 271-288.

24. Warkentin, J., and Smith, K. U., The Development of Visual Acuity in the Cat, *J. Genet. Psychol.,* 1937, **50**, 371-399.

25. Weinstein, B., Matching-from-sample by Rhesus Monkeys and by Children, *J. Compar. Psychol.,* 1941, **31**, 195-213.

26. Wing, K. G., The Role of the Optic Cortex of the Dog in the Retention of Learned Responses to Light: Conditioning with Light and Food, *Amer. J. Psychol.,* 1947, **60**, 30-67.

27. —— and Smith, K. U., The Role of the Optic Cortex in the Dog in the Determination of the Functional Properties of Conditioned Reactions to Light, *J. Exp. Psychol.,* 1942, **31**, 478-496.

CHAPTER 11

Individual Differences

CALVIN S. HALL

Western Reserve University

Introduction

That members of a species differ among themselves is as apparent as the fact that species differ one from another. Just as each species has developed special modes of behavior that enable it to cope more or less successfully with its environment, so each individual member of the species displays its own unique modes of adjustment within the limits set by the species. Cougars, for example, "earn" their living by stalking deer, but not all cougars are equally successful in this vocation. Variation within a species is an absolute necessity if the evolutionary process is to operate along the lines of Darwin's formulation, since "survival of the fittest" through natural selection assumes that some members of a species are better qualified to adjust to the contingencies of existence than are other members. The study of individual differences as a research area in comparative psychology has its origins, therefore, in the evolutionary doctrine. The final goals towards which all such studies are directed are (*a*) accurate and comprehensive descriptions of individual organisms, and (*b*) explanations as to how the individual organism acquires its unique organization.

The study of individual differences has practical implications as well as theoretical ones. For example, it has been found that not all dogs make good guides for blind people. Some breeds are better than others for this type of work, and even within a talented breed there are wide differences among individual animals. Since the training of a "seeing eye" dog is lengthy and expensive, it is important to identify the talented dogs at an early age before training has begun. The assessment of dogs for "seeing eye" training is a problem of measuring individual differences, with which the present chapter is concerned.

363

The Measurement of Individual Differences

The test situation

The first step in measuring individual differences is to decide just what aspects of behavior one is going to observe and under what conditions he is going to observe them. Suppose, for example, the comparative psychologist wishes to study individual differences in sexuality among adult male chimpanzees and decides to use frequency of copulation as the measure of sexuality. Having made this decision, he must then think about the conditions under which the observations are to be made. He may choose to observe copulatory activity among chimpanzees living in a state of nature. If he does he will find that naturalistic studies have many drawbacks. Not only does the investigator have to go to chimpanzee country, but he also has to make sure that he will be able to identify and observe the same animals over a period of time when he gets there. Moreover, he must take into account that copulatory activity is influenced by numerous circumstances over which he will have no control, and that unless he can obtain some measure of these influences and correct for them, his data will be contaminated by irrelevant factors. Field studies, whatever their merits may be in other respects, are not well suited for studies of individual differences.

Most studies of individual differences have been made on laboratory animals, and since the laboratory rat is inexpensive to maintain, is easily bred, and has a fairly wide repertoire of behavior, it is the favorite mammal for all types of psychological investigations including those of individual differences. Cats, dogs, monkeys, and chimpanzees are also used, but to a lesser degree than rats. Accordingly, instead of studying individual variation in sexuality among chimpanzees in the tropical forests of Africa, the comparative psychologist will find it more convenient to investigate copulatory frequency among rats residing in a laboratory colony.

In order to obtain pure measures of copulatory frequency he will need to exclude any condition that might adulterate the results. For example, if the physical setting under which the observations are made do not remain constant with respect to noise, temperature, light, and so on for all animals, then the copulatory frequency of one rat may differ from that of another because the setting in which the copulations occur is not the same for the two rats. Moreover, since copulation involves a female partner, it is necessary to make certain that variation among the consorts is not producing differences among the males. In short, if one wants to secure pure measures of a given behavior it is necessary to standardize the conditions under which the observations are to be made, so that conditions are uniform for all animals. This is called a standard test situation, or simply a *test*.

Reliability

What are the requirements of a good test? The first requirement is, as we have already said, that the test be the same for all animals. Sometimes this requirement is a difficult one to meet. In the case of copulatory frequency, the most difficult condition to standardize is that of the female partners. It is not easy to provide similar partners for all male rats; consequently, the differences in copulatory activity between animals may be due to variation among the consorts.

Fortunately, there is a way of determining whether variation among a group of animals is due to factors within the animals themselves or whether the variation is being produced by extraneous circumstances. Suppose we observe copulatory frequency in a group of rats one day, and the next day the same animals are retested. If the frequencies change in such a manner that one rat that copulates a great deal the first day relative to the group as a whole copulates only moderately or slightly the second day, and another rat copulates only moderately the first day and a lot or a little the next, and that similar fluctuations occur in other members of the group, then the test situation is said to be an unreliable one. An unreliable test is one that does not give consistent results on successive observations. An unreliable test is a worthless test since it does not measure an individual in a stable way. How is a rat to be classified on a scale of sexuality if it has many copulations one day, few the next, and a moderate number the third day?

It has probably occurred to the reader that inconsistent behavior may not be due to the test but to the animal. This is quite possible and that is why it is important not only to standardize the test situation itself so as to rule out external sources of variation, but also to standardize the way in which the animals are handled, cared for, fed, and otherwise treated between tests. If everything is as completely standardized as possible both within and without the test situation, and the behavior of the individual animals still varies in an unpredictable manner from test to test, then it is useless to continue with the investigation.

However, most forms of behavior that have claimed the attention of comparative psychologists do yield consistent results when conditions are standardized. For example, the early mazes used to measure learning ability in the rat were not very reliable. But as they were improved both in design and in length, as more care was taken in giving the animals preliminary experience with various features of the maze, for example, alleys, turns, doors, and as the handling and care of the animals were regimented, they became more reliable. Individual differences in maze-learning ability can now be measured with great consistency. However, in order to obtain stable individual differences, it is essential that the maze be a long one, preferably more than ten units, and that the animals be tested in the maze at least ten times. Tryon (30) found that if animals are "run" once a day through a maze having 20 choice-points, the scores in terms of the total number of errors made during 18 trials are virtually without any inconsistency whatsoever. This means that the maze-learning ability of the individual rat can be as precisely measured as physical characteristics like height and weight. Another way of saying the same thing is that the score earned by a rat represents only his capacity for learning the maze; it is not influenced by irrelevant factors.[1]

Over how long a period of time is it necessary for variation among animals in a given behavior to remain stable? Suppose that rats are tested in a maze in January and are retested the following January. A year is a long time in the life span of a rat, the equivalent of forty years in the lifetime of a human being, and it might be expected that maze-learning ability would undergo changes during the year. If these changes differed from rat to rat, so that a bright young rat turned out to be a dull or mediocre old rat, then consistency throughout the life-span could not be claimed for maze learning. This is a separate problem and should not be confused with the consistency of individual differences at a given point in the life of a group of animals. Maze-learning ability should be reliably measured when the rats are young as well as when they are old, but it is not necessary for the animals to remain consistent over a long period of time in

---

[1] For an authoritative discussion of the reliability of mazes and a list of references on this subject up to 1942, see Tyron (34).

order that the test be reliable. The question is, can this behavior be reliably measured in this test situation at this time?

The investigator should also be on the alert for conditions that may spuriously increase the reliability of a test. In order to illustrate a spurious factor, imagine that three rats, *A, B,* and *C* are placed respectively in three activity wheels, *X, Y,* and *Z,* in order to obtain measures of what is called "voluntary activity." The three activity wheels, it is assumed, differ mechanically in one important respect, namely, *X* is very hard to turn, *Y* is moderately hard to turn, and *Z* is easy to turn. At the end of the first five days in the wheels, Rat *A* has turned only a few revolutions, Rat *C* has turned many, and Rat *B's* activity lies between the other two. At the end of the next five days, the same relative order is found, and it is concluded that individual differences in "voluntary activity" remain stable over a ten-day period. But this stability is due to the fact that the wheels differ markedly with respect to ease of turning. Rat *A* has had to work much harder to turn the wheel than either Rat *B* or *C.* Each rat differs consistently from the other two because the test situations are consistently different for the three rats. If Rat *A* and been put in *Z,* it would have turned many, rather than few, times because *Z* is so much easier to turn than *X.* This spurious factor can be eliminated by making certain that the test situations are identical for all animals. If they cannot be made identical, then the animals should be shifted around from one test situation to another so that the final score for each animal is the sum of the scores obtained in a number of different test situations. We learn from this discussion that the presence of uncontrolled factors may increase reliability spuriously as well as lower it.

There is another source of unreliability, namely, the unreliability of the observer. Ordinarily, the animal's behavior in a test situation is observed and recorded by the experimenter. Let us suppose that behavior in a maze is under observation, and that the experimenter records the elapsed time between the rat's entry in the maze and his emergence into the food box at the end of maze, and further that he notes whether the rat goes into a blind alley or takes the correct path at each choice point. These are fairly simple records that do not tax the efforts of an experienced investigator, yet it is surprising how fallible even a trained observer can be in making simple observations. As the observations increase in complexity, accurate observing becomes more difficult. For example, the writer and S. J.

Klein, in their study of aggressive behavior in rats (19), were required to make judgments regarding the degree of aggression manifest by each rat. Six types of aggressive behavior, ranging from frequent, vigorous nosing to fierce wrestling and biting, were delineated. Two rats were placed together in a cage for five minutes and if any aggression was observed during that time, a judgment was made as to the intensity of the aggression displayed. In order to check the reliability of the observer, two observers made independent ratings of the same rats. One observer rated the rats when tested in the afternoon; the other observer rated them at night. There was substantial agreement between the two raters with respect to the *number* of aggressive encounters engaged in by each rat, but less agreement for *severity* of aggression. It will be noted that two factors might have accounted for the inconsistencies found; one is the fallibility of the observers' judgments of the behavior and the other is the inconsistency of individual rats in expressing aggression during the two test periods on the same day.

When conditions are carefully standardized and raters are trained to observe well defined aspects of behavior, the consistency of ratings can be made very exact. Tryon (35), for example, had three trained raters observe and rate hiding, avoidance, escape, and vocalization behavior in a group of rats on two successive days. The raters agreed almost perfectly in their judgments of these fairly complex activities.

Let us summarize what we have learned from this discussion of the reliability of measurement. A test situation is said to be reliable if the animals maintain the same relative position to one another when they are retested, and an observer is said to be reliable when his observations agree with those of a second observer. A test may be made more reliable by standardizing procedures and by using a set of well-defined and explicit categories of behavior. If a test of behavior cannot be devised that yields stable differences among a group of animals, then it is impossible to investigate individual differences in that behavior. However, it has been possible to devise reliable tests for those aspects of behavior that the comparative psychologist has chosen to study. Reliable measures of learning, activity, emotionality, drives, and aggressiveness are now available for the psychologist who wishes to study individual differences in these traits (15).

One final word concerning reliability. Statistical procedures are used to arrive at an index of consistency. This index is called a reliability coefficient, and it is a number whose maximum value is 1.00.

A reliability coefficient of 1.00 means that the test measures individual differences with perfect consistency. In practice, perfect reliability is rarely found. A test is said to have sufficient reliability if it yields a coefficient of at least .90. The student will usually find in published reports of investigations of individual differences, the simple statement, "This test has a reliability coefficient of .93," or whatever the value may be. This is a shorthand way of saying that the test is a reliable one.

There are several ways of computing the reliability of a test but it would take too much space to discuss these methods. The student will find an adequate discussion of this topic, as well as an account of what statistical operations should be followed in order to obtain a reliability coefficient, in any textbook of psychological statistics.[2]

Validity

Let us assume that the test that has been devised to measure variation among animals in a given trait is a reliable one. There is still one other criterion that a good test must meet—it must also be a *valid* test. A valid test is one that measures what the investigator says it measures. For example, if a comparative psychologist invents a test to measure persistence, he should be able to demonstrate that the test actually measures the trait of persistence and not some other type of behavior. Many tests used with animals are said to have "face validity," which means that investigators agree that the test measures what it is said to measure. An activity wheel is a valid test of voluntary activity because it permits the animal to run whenever the animal feels the urge, and that is precisely what is meant by voluntary activity. A maze is a valid test of maze-learning ability for the obvious reason that in this test the animal is given an opportunity to demonstrate his ability to learn a maze. Fighting is a valid measure of aggressiveness because fighting is a direct expression of aggressiveness. For the same reason copulatory frequency is a valid measure of the sex drive.

Some tests do not have "face validity," and in these cases their validity must be established. The writer, for example, wanted to measure individual differences in emotionality or fearfulness (12). He devised a simple test that consisted of placing a rat in a brightly lighted circular enclosure, seven feet in diameter. The floor of the field was covered with linoleum so that it could be easily washed

---

[2] A good discussion of the concept of reliability will be found in R. L. Thorndike (28).

after each animal had been removed from the field. The animal was left in the field for two minutes and if during that. time it defecated or urinated a notation of the occurrence was made. The next day the rat was retested in the same manner, and thereafter each day for a total of 12 trials in all. The score consisted of the number of trials in the field during which defecation or urination occurred. Since each rat had 12 possibilities of excreting in the field the maximum score was 12, and the minimum score was zero. Stable individual differences were found showing that the test is a reliable one. Do the scores, number of trials during which excretion occurred, really measure fearfulness? Can it be said that an animal with a score of 12 is more fearful than one with a score of less than 12? Although it is well known that defecation and/or urination do occur during great fear in lower animals as well as in man, how do we know that the rat in the field is undergoing fear? May it not excrete just because it has to and not because it is afraid? These questions had to be answered by demonstrating the test's validity. In order to do this, another test of emotionality had to be found with which the results of the first test could be compared. Accordingly, the writer formulated the proposition that a hungry rat that was afraid in the field would not eat even though appetizing food was there in the field for it to eat. Not eating in the field became the second test of fearfulness, and was conducted in the following manner. A hungry rat was placed in a field that contained food, and records were kept for a two-minute period whether the rat defecated and urinated and whether it ate any food. Tests were made daily for 12 days, and from the test two sets of scores were derived. One set consisted of days during which excretion occurred (zero through 12) and the other set consisted of days during which the animal did not eat (zero through 12). It was found that a rat that obtained a high excretion score also had a high not-eating score, and a rat that obtained a low excretion score had a low not-eating score. In fact, a rat rarely began to eat in the field until a trial or two after defecation or urination had stopped. Since there is reasonable justification for assuming that each test by itself is a measure of fearfulness, the fact that a group of animals are ranked in approximately the same order on both tests clinches the matter and establishes the validity of both tests as measures of emotionality. Since the excretion measure is the more convenient one to use, it has been adopted as a standard test of fearfulness. Other studies using a similar rationale, but different tests against which to compare the field-excretion test, support the conclusion that it is a valid measure of fearfulness (3, 8, 35).

We may summarize this discussion of validity by saying that unless a test possesses "face validity," by which is meant agreement among qualified judges that the test measures what it purports to measure, then it is necessary to *validate* the test by showing that it ranks a group of animals in the same order as another test, which is assumed to measure the same trait, ranks them.

Situational generality

Individual differences in a particular mode of behavior may be reliably and validly measured, so it may be said that one animal learns a particular maze better than another animal or that one animal is more fearful than another animal in the field situation. Yet these statements may have only limited descriptive value if learning ability and fearfulness are not general characteristics of the animal. That is, if the rank orders of a group of animals tested on two different mazes do not agree, then any statements about the comparative learning ability of the animals can only be made with respect to their performance on a particular maze and not on mazes in general. A trait is said to have situational generality, if a sample of animals maintains approximately the same rank order in a number of reliable and valid test situations. This state of affairs is portrayed in the following hypothetical illustration, in which the numbers represent the relative ranks of the animals, 1 being the highest rank, 2 the next highest and so on.

MAZE-LEARNING ABILITY

	Maze 1	Maze 2	Maze 3	Maze 4	Maze 5
Rat A	1	1	1	1	1
Rat B	2	2	2	2	2
Rat C	3	3	3	3	3
Rat D	4	4	4	4	4
Rat E	5	5	5	5	5

In actual practice, exact agreement in scores is never found; the investigation is usually satisfied if there is approximate agreement. Let us now examine the experimental findings on this question to see whether the traits that have been studied are general or specific.

Learning ability. Rats tend to maintain the same rank order when run on different mazes, so that we are justified in concluding that maze-learning ability is a general characteristic of the rat (29). A rat that learns one maze quickly will tend to learn other mazes quickly. This implies that there are stable factors within each rat that determine its unique level of performance in a variety of maze situations.

Moreover, Tryon has shown that when the maze situation is altered after the animals have reached a high level of learning, namely, by turning off the lights so that the rats are now running in the dark, or by taking several units out of the maze, thus breaking up any possible serially chained responses, or by throwing a blanket over the maze to muffle sounds, individual differences before and after such alterations remain very consistent. The rat that runs the maze well in the light continues to turn out a superior performance in the dark. An inferior maze learner remains inferior when the pattern of the maze is shortened. Tryon feels that these results indicate that differences between rats are not controlled by sensory or kinesthetic stimuli, but by "higher generalized distance-direction behavior sets" (31).

However, when rats learn a maze and then learn to get out of a problem box, they display no consistency in the two sets of scores obtained (10). A good maze learner is not necessarily a good problem-box learner. The same disparity is found when a group of rats learns a maze and then learns to discriminate between two sensory signs (10). Likewise, there is no relationship between the ease with which a rat learns to solve a problem box, and its performance in a discrimination task (10). These findings negate the hypothesis that learning ability is a general characteristic and support the hypothesis that there are numerous fairly specific learning abilities.

Fearfulness. Parker (23) has done the most extensive investigation of the generality of fearfulness. He obtained excretion scores in six different situations. In one test situation, a rat was placed in a suspended bucket which was dropped suddenly, and in another the rat was slowly squeezed into a smaller and smaller space. In neither case, was the rat physically harmed. Four other equally dissimilar situations were used. The results indicate clearly that the degree of fearfulness as measured by excretion is a fairly generalized characteristic of a given rat, since a rat that defecated a great deal in one test situation was also likely to defecate a great deal in each of the other five situations.

Anderson's studies (3) provide further evidence that fearfulness is a generalized trait. He used the field-excretion test and a test that does not employ defecation or urination as a sign of emotionality. In the second test, the animal is put in a U-shaped stovepipe and the measure of fearfulness is the amount of time it takes to emerge from the stovepipe. It is assumed that a fearful rat will remain in the stovepipe longer than a fearless rat will. Although the results of these two tests do not agree closely, there is a distinctly significant relationship between them. The rat that emerges slowly from the stovepipe is also likely to defecate in the field. Since these are quite different test situations, it appears that fearfulness is a comparatively stable component of an animal's make-up.

Aggressiveness. Similar results have been found for aggressiveness. For instance, the writer and S. J. Klein (19) rated the same rats for aggressiveness under four different conditions. During one test, the rats were thirsty but no water was available in the test cage; during the second test the animals were thirsty, and a water bottle from which only one animal could drink at a time was in the test cage; during the third test the animals, all of whom were males, had been deprived of the company of females several days before the third test was begun; and during the fourth test, conditions were normal. Each animal behaved very consistently throughout the four tests. Fighters remained fighters and pacifists remained pacifists despite altered test circumstances.

Activity. Although different tests of individual differences in activity have been employed, namely, the activity wheel that the rat turns by running, the activity cage that rests on tambours that respond to changes of the animal's position in the cage, and ambulatory activity in a large enclosure that permits freedom of movement, there have been no studies of the generality of activity in these various situations.

Sex drive. Anderson (2) measured individual differences in the strength of the sex drive in the following five ways: (*a*) copulation frequency; (*b*) amount of time a male rat spent near a wire screen that separated him from a female in heat; (*c*) time required by a male to dig through sand to a receptive female; (*d*) speed with which a male rat ran down a 27-foot-long runway to a female at the other end; and (*e*) the number of times in 12 minutes a male rat would cross an electrified grid to a female. There is a fairly marked tendency, but by no means perfect, for these five tests to rank the rats in the same order. A rat with a high copulatory frequency, which is the most direct measure of sexuality, tends also to spend a lot of time near the screened-off female, to run or dig rapidly, and to take more shocks to get to a female.

Exploratory drive. Anderson (2) also tested a group of rats in seven different tests of the exploratory drive, and found about the same results as he did for the sex tests. An animal that explored a great deal in one situation tended to explore a great deal in other situations.

Hunger drive. In contrast with sex and exploratory drives, individual differences in the hunger drive seem to be devoid of generality. One test ranks the same animals in a completely different fashion than another test does. Thus, an animal with intense hunger motivation cannot be identified by a single test, since if another test is used that same animal might display weak hunger motivation. The strength of an animal's hunger drive apears to be specific to the type of test situation employed (2).

Thirst drive. Anderson (2) came to the same conclusion for thirst as he did for hunger. There is no such thing as a consistent and stable level of drive for water in individual rats as there is for the sex and exploratory drives.

Some traits like maze-learning ability (but not learning ability in general), fearfulness, aggressiveness, sexuality, and exploratory drive may be characterized as possessing situational generality; other characteristics like the hunger and thirst drives are specific to the test situation used. Why some traits should be general and others specific is not clearly understood.

Developmental generality

As we have seen in the last section, situational generality prevails for many of the characteristics that have been investigated. In these studies, the research design usually consists of testing a group of animals of a given age in a variety of situations.

In this section, we shall discuss another type of generality, namely, the stability of individual differences in a particular trait when animals are tested at different stages of their development. Will a rat that is superior in maze learning when it is young maintain its superiority throughout its life? The student should not confuse this question with one concerning age differences. It may be that a young rat will learn faster than an old rat, but that is not our present concern. It is a question of *relative* status or rank in the group. Even though a rat may not learn as readily when it is old as it did when young, does it nevertheless rank high among a group of rats in maze-learning ability at both ages?

Maze learning. Tryon's study concerning this question is definitive as are so many of his carefully designed investigations of individual differences in maze-learning ability (30). He showed that individual differences remained very stable over a period of eight months, which is more than a third of the average rat's life span.

Fearfulness. Although there has been no systematic study of developmental generality for this trait, a fairly high relationship was found between emotional defecation at the age of 25 days when rats' ears were clipped (clipping is done for the purpose of identifying individual rats) and defecation in the field when the same rats were 105 days old (6).

Aggressiveness. The writer and S. J. Klein (19) found very stable differences in aggressiveness in rats over a period of three months. A pugnacious eight-months-old rat is still pungacious at 11 months.

Activity. Individual differences in activity as measured by the revolving wheel remain very constant between the sixth and ninth month of a rat's life (26).

Sex drive. Over a four-months period the copulatory frequency of a male rat will remain fairly consistent. If the rat is a sexual extremist as a young adult, he will remain a sexual extremist relative to other rats as a middle-aged adult (2).

Although there is a paucity of evidence for developmental generality, what there is suggests that the animal's rank in a group remains quite constant over a period of several months. It would be interesting to investigate the constancy of an animal's relative position in a group throughout its lifetime.

Organismic generality

The question to be discussed in this section may be stated as follows: Will animals maintain their same relative position with respect to a given measurable trait when the animals themselves are altered in some systematic manner? The type of study we have in mind is illustrated by one made by Anderson (1). He tested a group of rats in activity wheels under the following conditions: (a) unmotivated, (b) hungry, (c) thirsty, and (d) sexually aroused, and found high consistencies between the four activity measures, even though the average activity of the whole group changed markedly under changed motivation. Thus the average hungry animal makes about three times as many revolutions as the average non-hungry animal does, yet the relative position of each rat in the group under the two conditions remains about the same. A hyperactive rat when hungry is also relatively hyperactive when well fed.

More studies of this type, in which animals themselves are changed in some planned way to see if their rank order varies or remains constant, are needed.

The Organization of Traits

In the preceding pages, evidence has been presented that shows that individual differences in a variety of characteristics can be reliably and validly measured, and that such traits as maze learning, activity, aggressiveness, sexuality, and fearfulness possess both situational and developmental generality. In this section, we shall consider the question of how these various characteristics are interrelated. We shall be concerned with such questions as the following ones: Is a very active animal a superior maze learner? Does an animal that has a strong hunger drive also have a strong thirst drive? Is a fearful rat a pacifistic rat? Do marked aggressiveness, hyperactivity, and a strong sex drive go together? These are questions that have to do with the way in which the traits are organized within an animal. If we could describe completely the configuration of traits in an animal, which we cannot do at our present state of knowledge, we would then have a complete understanding of the psychological nature of that animal. Let it be understood that questions of causality are not involved in the present discussion. If it is found that an active rat is a good maze learner, that does not permit us to say that a high activity level is the reason why a rat learns readily or that good maze-learning ability causes the rat to be more active. We are concerned at this time only with trait organization; questions of causality will be taken up in the next section.

Trait relationships

Most of the studies in this area present evidence for the interrelationship or lack of it between relatively few traits, often only two. Although it is possible to make some inferences about the organization of a number of traits that have been studied two at a time, ideally generalizations should be based upon results obtained from a sample of animals that have been assessed for a large number of characteristics. There are a few studies of the latter type. Let us first, however, confine our attention to the more prevalent type of study where a group of animals is measured with respect to a few traits. The literature is so extensive that we can discuss but a few of the many studies.

Fearfulness and activity. Billingslea (7, 8) found a moderate positive relationship between emotional defecation in the field and voluntary activity in the wheel after the rats had become used to the activity-wheel situations. This means that a timid rat is likely to be more active than a bold rat.

Fearfulness and maze-learning ability. Fearful rats make more errors and take more time in running a maze than fearless rats do (2). They tend to explore, and are overcautious.

Fearfulness and aggressiveness. Fearful rats, as might be expected, are less aggressive than fearless rats (8, 19).

Fearfulness and sexuality. Individual differences in timidity are negatively correlated with individual differences in sexuality, which means that the timid rat indulges in less copulatory activity than a bold rat does (1, 2, 3, 4).

Fearfulness and persistence. There is no relationship between persevering at a task and fearfulness. The test of perseverence or persistence required the animal to tear its way through a number of thicknesses of paper to get to food (7, 18, 37).

Fearfulness and stereotyping of response. Stereotypy is measured in an apparatus consisting of five pathways of equal length, all of which lead to food. A stereotyped performance means that a rat takes the same path on successive trials. The opposite of stereotypy is variability, which signifies that a rat varies its path on successive trials. In this situation, a fearful rat tends to vary its response more than a fearless rat does (13).

Fearfulness and audiogenic seizures. An audiogenic seizure is like an epileptic attack. It is produced by exposing a rat or mouse to a sound of high frequency. Fearful animals have fewer audiogenic seizures than fearless animals (22).

In the foregoing investigations, the relationship of fearfulness to each of seven other characteristics has been determined. These findings may be integrated in such a manner that the psychological make-up of the fearful or fearless rat with respect to the seven traits can be described. The following list of traits characterize the fearful animal as compared with the fearless animal.

The fearful animal is:

1. more active
2. a poorer maze learner
3. less aggressive
4. less sexual
5. more variable
6. less susceptible to audiogenic seizures
7. neither more nor less persevering.

If individual differences in sexuality as measured by copulatory frequency are taken as the trait against which to compare other characteristics, the following contrasting profiles emerge. One profile is that of a highly-sexed rat, the other is that of a sexually sluggish rat. These profiles are based upon the extensive investigations of E. E. Anderson (1, 2, 3, 4).

The over-sexed rat is:

1. a better maze learner
2. a heavy eater
3. a light drinker
4. less fearful
5. more active.

The under-sexed rat is:

1. a poorer maze learner
2. a light eater
3. a heavy drinker
4. more fearful
5. less active.

By comparing these profiles with those for a fearful and a fearless rat, one inconsistency will be observed. We learn from the first profiles that a fearful rat is *less* sexual and *more* active, and from the second profiles that a highly-sexed rat is *less* fearful and *more* active. These findings do not hang together, since greater activity is associated in the former case with less sexuality and in the latter case with more sexuality. One can only wonder why this inconsistency exists and attempt to resolve it through further work. It may interest the student to speculate as to why the sexual "athlete" is a heavy eater but a light drinker, and why the situation is reversed for the sexual "sluggard." Would we find the same results with humans, and if so, what would they mean?

Factor analysis

A complex method for discovering the basic pattern of traits in an animal is *factor analysis*. Although limitations of space prevent an adequate discussion of this method, the essential features of factor analysis may be described rather simply. Scores are obtained for a group of animals in a variety of test situations, and the relationships between these scores are determined by computing coefficients of correlation. A coefficient of correlation tells the degree to which the rank order of the animals on one test or variable agrees with the rank order of the same animals on another test. If the animals tend to maintain about the same ranks on the two tests, that is, if Animal *A* is the best on both tests, Animal *B* is next best, and so on, the two sets of scores are said to be positively correlated. If one has obtained ten sets of scores from ten different tests, and correlates each set with every other set, there will be 45 coefficients of correlations. One then asks, "How many factors (basic traits) will account for these interrelations?" The answer to this question is found by performing certain mathematical operations, called factor analysis, on a table of correlation coefficients.

Vaughn's study of factors in rat learning may be used to illustrate the method and to show what information may be obtained about the nature of the determiners of individual differences (37). Vaughn tested a group of 80 rats in ten different test situations, and obtained therefrom 34 distributions of scores. By correlating the other 33 with each distribution, 561 coefficients were obtained. At this point, factor analysis was initiated, with the consequence that four factors were identified, namely, speed, timidity, insight learning, and transfer, and four others were extracted which could not be identified. What is the psychological significance of the identified factors? The speed factor refers to the capacity of a rat for moving rapidly through space. Hence, if a rat has a large amount of this factor, it will perform well in any situation where speed is required. Similarly, if an animal is timid, his performance in strange situations will be adversely affected. The same argument can be made for the factors of insight learning, and transfer. Factors are assumed to be basic determiners of behavior. A basic determiner is a property of the animal which influences its conduct in a variety of situations. The goal of factor analysis is to identify all the basic factors so that a pure test of each factor may be devised. With a battery of such tests it would be possible to describe in fairly complete fashion the psychological organization of an animal. In a sense, this is the main goal of psychology, to understand fully the basic components of the individual organism and the way in which these components are and become organized.

Another example of an attempt to determine the organization of abilities in the rat, with special consideration given to learning abilities, is an investigation made by R. L. Thorndike (27). He tested a group of animals on two alley-type mazes, two elevated mazes, two problem boxes, a conditioned-response situation, and the Columbia obstruction apparatus. All but the obstruction apparatus, which measures drive strength, are learning tests. From these tests, 32 scores were obtained for each rat. Each distribution of scores was correlated with every other distribution, and the resulting interrelationships were subjected to factor analysis. Thorndike concluded that three factors could be identified: (a) a general maze learning ability, (b) a transfer factor, and (c) a conditioned-response factor. Van Steenberg (36) was not satisfied with Thorndike's method of analysis, and re-analyzed Thorndike's table of intercorrelations into the following ten factors: (a) visual perception, (b) wildness, (c) motility or speed, (d) drive, (e) problem-solving ability, (f) alternating tendency, (g) visual insight, and three others that were not identified.

One other example of factor analysis will be described. Geier, Levin, and Tolman (11) tested 57 male albino rats in two test situations, an open field and a simple-discrimination apparatus. From these two situations, 29 scores on as many variables were obtained. The intercorrelations between the 29 distributions of scores were analyzed by a factor method devised by Tryon (32), and resulted in the identification of four factors: (a) open-field timidity, (b) cognitive reactivity, (c) unsystematic variability, and (d) lack of motivation.

A promising new method of studying the organization of traits within the individual animal consists of correlating animals rather than traits. What does it mean to correlate animals? Let us consider a study by Searle that illustrates this new method (25). Searle wanted to know if the animals of a strain that had been selectively bred for superior maze-learning ability were like one another in the organization of their traits, and if, at the same time, they were dissimilar to rats that had been selectively bred for inferior maze-learning ability. He measured a group of rats from each strain on 30 variables which resulted in 30 scores for each rat. He then took each bright rat and correlated its 30 scores with the 30 scores earned by every other bright rat, and found fairly sizeable relationships. This means that the bright rats as a group are similarly constituted. He followed the same procedure with a group of dull rats, and obtained similar results for them. One dull rat is pretty much like another dull rat in its organization. He then correlated each bright rat with each dull rat and obtained no significant relationships, which enabled him to conclude that a bright rat is not organized in the same way as a dull rat is. How is each organized? Searle says that the bright rat is characteristically a hunger-motivated rat, that it takes short paths rather than long ones, that it is not highly motivated to escape from water, and that it is timid in open spaces. The dull rat is relatively disinterested in food, average or better in water motivation, and fearful of the mechanical features of the test apparatus. This method is particularly valuable when one is looking for "types," since animals that can be shown to resemble one another belong together as a "type." It is conceivable that there are a few basic kinds of organizations in any given species. If so, such a method as the one described should provide the necessary proof.

Although it has been impossible to include in this chapter a discussion of all the studies that bear upon the question of an animal's psychological organization, it may be said fairly that the comparative psychologist has hardly scratched the surface of this highly important region of psychology. It is still pretty much virgin territory, despite the pioneering efforts of a few investigators.

The Causes of Individual Differences

There is general agreement among all observers that members of a species differ among themselves with respect to their psychological make-up. There is far less agreement as to the reasons for these differences. Some psychologists are of the opinion that heredity factors, the genes, are the primary determinants of individual differences. Other psychologists prefer to look for the causes of variation in the differential experiences of animals. This controversy is the age-old one of nature versus nurture or heredity versus environment.

There is no longer any reason to doubt the efficacy of both nature and nurture as determinants of individual differences, since the evidence clearly indicates that either genes or experiences or both can and do operate to make organisms dissimilar.

The influence of heredity

It is well known that the genes are the important agents of hereditary transmission and that the genes of one organism differ from those of another organism, except in the case of identical twins. It is possible by the method of selective inbreeding to obtain animals that are alike genetically, except for the inevitable sex difference. This method consists of testing a group of animals for some trait and selecting for breeding those that resemble one another in the trait and that also have a close family relationship, preferably brother and sister. The offspring of these selected matings are tested for the same characteristics as their parents were, and closely related, similar behaving animals are again bred together. Selective inbreeding is continued for a number of generations, and after 20 or 30 generations the animals of a given line will all be alike or nearly alike genetically; that is, they will be practical equivalents of identical twins.

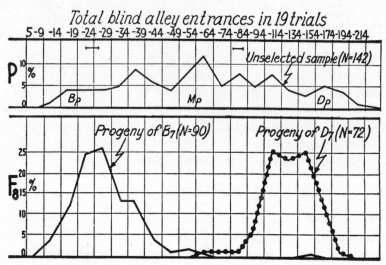

Fig. 1. Comparison of the Distribution of Scores on a 17-unit T-maze Made by the Parental Generation *(P)* and the Eighth Filial Generation *(F_8).* [After Tyron (34), pp. 344-345]. *Above.* This distribution represents the scores obtained by an unselected sample of 142 laboratory rats. For selective inbreeding of superior maze learners, animals with low scores (those at the left end of the scale) were selected for breeding. For selective inbreeding of inferior maze learners, animals with high scores (those at the right end of the scale) were selected for breeding. *Below.* The distribution on the left represents the scores obtained by the bright strain after eight generations of selective inbreeding. The distribution on the right represents the scores obtained by the dull strain after eight generations of selective inbreeding. It will be observed that there is still variation in maze-learning ability within each strain. We are told that this variation still exists after 22 generations of selective inbreeding.

The method of selective inbreeding and the significance of the results obtained therefrom may be illustrated by Tryon's study of the genetics of maze-learning ability (33). Tryon took a large sample of laboratory rats and ran them through a complicated 17-unit maze. There was wide variation in the performance of the rats on the maze as measured by the number of entrances into blind alleys during 19 trials. Some rats made fewer than ten errors and others made more than 200 errors. The distribution of scores made by the parental

stock is shown in the upper part of Fig. 1. These individual differences, it may be assumed, are due to both genetic and experimental
factors.

The brightest rats were bred together and the dullest rats were
bred together, and the offspring of each "type" were tested in the
same maze. The brightest of the bright "type" and the dullest of
the dull "type" were then mated and their offspring were tested for
maze-learning ability. This was kept up for a number of generations, until two strains, one consisting of superior maze learners, the
other consisting of inferior maze learners, were established. The two
strains bred true; that is, the offspring of the bright strain could be
depended upon to learn the maze rapidly and the offspring of the
dull strain could be depended upon to learn the maze slowly. The
distribution of scores for the bright and dull strain in the eighth
generation appears in the lower part of Fig. 1. This result proves
conclusively that individual differences in maze-learning ability are
produced, in part, by genetic constitution. Similar findings for voluntary activity (9, 24), emotionality (14), audiogenic seizures (16, 22,
38), aggressiveness (19), "hypotheses" (21), temperature preferences
(20), and other psychological characteristics have been obtained.[3]

The influence of experience

Under the rubric "experience," a diversity of factors has been
included, for example, prenatal influences, infantile experiences,
illness, diet, specific types of training, physiological functioning,
routine handling, drive states, and so on. Innumerable experiments,
many of which have been discussed in other chapters of this book,
testify to the importance of experience in producing changes in the
psychological organization of an animal. We need not discuss these
experiments or their implications here.

However, in order to point up the importance of nongenetic determinants of variation within a species, we may refer again to
Tryon's selective inbreeding experiment. It will be recalled that he
found wide variability among rats of the parental stock. Through
selective inbreeding two strains were obtained, and although the
variation within each strain was noticeably less than the variation
within the original parental stock, there was still considerable variation even though the members of a strain supposedly had identical
genetic constitutions (see Fig. 1). That is, if genetic constitution

[3] For a recent digest of the literature on the genetics of behavior see (17).

alone were responsible for individual differences, then there should be no differences when genetic constitution is made alike for animals. The fact that intra-strain variability still exists shows that experiential factors are a contributing cause of individual differences. Other selective inbreeding studies yield results that are consonant with those found by Tryon.

Conclusion

Within recent years, the study of individual differences has been neglected by comparative psychologists. Since the decade of the 1930's, when Anderson, Tryon, the present writer, and others were actively engaged in investigations of individual differences, there has been little work done in this important field. Comparative psychologists have been interested more in general psychological functions, for example, learning and motivation, than in the organization of the individual animal. With the advent of clinical psychology as a major field of psychological endeavor, it may be expected that there will be a revival of interest in studying individual differences among various species of animals, especially mammals. Clinical psychology is concerned with the psychological organization of the individual and with the developmental history of that organization. The student of individual differences has precisely the same interests. Since experiments using lower animals are often more feasible and more informative than experiments using human beings, it would seem that comparative psychology might be of considerable service to clinical psychology in testing some of the working hypotheses of the latter field. For example, one of the major propositions of the clinician is that the infantile experiences of the person play a large role in determining his psychological organization. Obviously, experiments that aim to test this proposition encounter many obstacles when one attempts to use human subjects. On the other hand, they are quite easily performed on lower animals (19a).

We have seen in this chapter that the groundwork for studying the psychological organization of the individual has been laid. Numerous reliable and valid tests of significant psychological traits have been made available. Testing procedures and apparatus have been standardized, and a solid core of information regarding the nature and causation of individual differences has been accumulated. It would appear that this research area promises numerous, easily obtained rewards to the investigator.

Bibliography

1. Anderson, E. E., Interrelationship of Drives in the Male Albino Rat. I. Intercorrelations of Measures of Drives, *J. Compar. Psychol.* 1937, 24, 73-118.

2. ———— The Interrelationships of Drives in the Male Albino Rat. II. Intercorrelations between 47 Measures of Drives and Learning, *Compar. Psychol. Monogr.*, 1938, 14, No. 72, pp. 1-119.

3. ———— The Interrelationship of Drives in the Male Albino Rat. III. Interrelations among Measures of Emotional, Sexual and Exploratory Behavior, *Ped. Sem. and J. Genet. Psychol.*, 1938, 53, 335-352.

4. ———— The Sex Hormones and Emotional Behavior. I. The Effect of Sexual Receptivity upon Timidity in the Female Rat, *Ped. Sem. and J. Genet. Psychol.*, 1940, 56, 149-158.

5. ———— and Anderson, S. F., The Sex Hormones and Emotional Behavior. II. The Influence of the Female Sex Hormone upon Timidity in Female Rats, *Ped. Sem. and J. Genet. Psychol.*, 1940, 56, 159-168.

6. Biel, W. C., and O'Kelly, L. I., The Effect of Cortical Lesions on Emotional and Regressive Behavior in the Rat. I. Emotional Behavior, *J. Compar. Psychol.*, 1940, 30, 221-240.

7. Billingslea, F. Y., The Relationship between Emotionality, Activity, Curiosity, Persistence and Weight in the Male Rat, *J. Compar. Psychol.*, 1940, 29, 315-325.

8. ———— The Relationship between Emotionality and Various other Salients of Behavior in the Rat, *J. Compar. Psychol.*, 1941, 31, 69-77.

9. Brody, E. G., Genetic Basis of Spontaneous Activity in the Albino Rat, *Compar. Psychol. Monogr.*, 1942, 17, No. 5, 1-24.

10. Commins, W. D., McNemar, Q., and Stone, C. P., Interrelations of Measures of Ability in the Rat, *J. Compar. Psychol.*, 1932, 14, 225-235.

11. Geier, F. M., Levin, M., and Tolman, E. C., Individual Differences in Emotionality, Hypothesis Formation, Vicarious Trial and Error, and Visual Discrimination Learning in Rats, *Compar. Psychol. Monogr.*, 1941, 17, No. 3, 1-20.

12. Hall, C. S., Emotional Behavior in the Rat. I. Defecation and Urination as Measures of Individual Differences in Emotionality, *J. Compar. Psychol.*, 1934, 18, 385-403.

13. ———— Emotional Behavior in the Rat. IV. The Relationship Between Emotionality and Stereotyping of Behavior, *J. Compar. Psychol.*, 1937, 24, 369-375.

14. ———— The Inheritance of Emotionality, *Sigma Xi Quarterly*, 1938, 26, 17-27.

15. ———— Temperament: A Survey of Animal Studies, *Psychol. Bull.*, 1941, 38, 909-943.

16. Hall, C. S., Genetic Differences in Fatal Audigenic Seizures between Two Inbred Strains of House Mice, *J. Heredity,* 1947, **38**, 2-6.

17. —— The Genetics of Behavior, *Handbook of Experimental Psychology* (S. S. Smith, Editor). New York: John Wiley and Sons, Inc., 1951.

18. —— and Klein, L. L., Emotional Behavior in the Rat. VI. The Relationship between Persistence and Emotionality, *J. Compar. Psychol.,* 1941, **32**, 503-506.

19. —— and Klein, S. J., Individual Differences in Aggressiveness in Rats, *J. Compar. Psychol.,* 1942, **33**, 371-383.

19a. —— and Whiteman, P. H., The Effects of Infantile Stimulation upon Later Emotional Stability in the Mouse, *J. Compar. and Physiol. Psychol.,* 1951, **44**, 61-66.

20. Herter, K., Das Thermotaktische Optimum bei Nagetieren, ein mendelndes Art- und Rassenmerkmal, *Zeitschrift für Vergleichende Physiologie,* 1936, **23**, 605-650.

21. Krechevsky, I., Hereditary Nature of "Hypotheses," *J. Compar. Psychol.,* 1933, **16**, 99-116.

22. Martin, R. F. and Hall, C. S., Emotional Behavior in the Rat. V. The Incidence of Behavior Derangements Resulting from Air-blast Stimulation in Emotional and Non-emotional Strains of Rats, *J. Compar. Psychol.,* 1941, **32**, 191-204.

23. Parker, M. M., Experimental Studies in the Psychobiology of Temperament in the Adult Albino Rat, *Ph.D. Dissertation,* Ohio State University, 1939.

24. Rundquist, E. A., The Inheritance of Spontaneous Activity in Rats, *J. Compar. Psychol.* 1933, **16**, 415-438.

25. Searle, L. V., The Organization of Hereditary Maze-Brightness and Maze-Dullness, *Genet. Psychol. Monogr,* 1949, **39**, 279-325.

26. Shirley, Mary, Studies on Activity. II. Activity Rhythms; Age and Activity; Activity after Rest, *J. Compar. Psychol.,* 1928, **8**, 159-186.

27. Thorndike, R. L., Organization of Behavior in the Albino Rat, *Genet. Psychol. Monogr.,* 1935, **17**, No. 1, pp. 1-70.

28. —— *Personnel Selection.* New York: John Wiley and Sons, Inc., 1949, Chapter 4.

29. Tryon, R. C., Studies in Individual Differences in Maze Ability. III. The Community of Function Between Two Maze Abilities, *J. Compar. Psychol.,* 1931, **12**, 95-116.

30. —— Studies in Individual Differences in Maze Ability. IV. The Constancy of Individual Differences: Correlation between Learning and Relearning, *J. Compar. Psychol.,* 1931, **12**, 303-345.

31. —— Studies in Individual Differences in Maze Learning. VI. Disproof of Sensory Components: Experimental Effects of Stimulus Variation, *J. Compar. Psychol.,* 1939, **28**, 361-415.

32. —— *Cluster Analysis.* Ann Arbor: Edwards Brothers, 1939.

33. ———— Genetic Differences in Maze Learning in Rats. (In National Society for the Study of Education, *The Thirty Ninth Yearbook.*) Bloomington, Illinois: Public School Publishing Co., 1940.

34. ———— *Comparative Psychology,* Rev. Ed. (F. A. Moss, Ed.). New York: Prentice-Hall, Inc., 1942, Chapter 12, pp. 330-365.

35. ———— Tryon, C. M., and Kuznets, G., Studies in Individual Differences in Maze Ability. IX. Ratings of Hiding, Avoidance, Escape and Vocalization Responses, *J. Compar. Psychol.,* 1941, **32,** 407-435.

36. Van Steenberg, N. J. F., Factors in the Learning Behavior of the Albino Rat, *Psychometrika,* 1939, **4,** 179-200.

37. Vaughn, C. L., Factors in Rat Learning, *Compar. Psychol. Monogr.,* 1937, **14,** No. 3, pp. 1-41.

38. Witt, G., and Hall, C. S., The Genetics of Audiogenic Seizures in the House Mouse, *J. Compar. and Physiol. Psychol.,* 1949, **42,** 58-63.

CHAPTER 12

Problems and Principles of Animal Sociology

NICHOLAS E. COLLIAS
University of Wisconsin

The present discussion will be restricted primarily to intraspecific phenomena in order to avoid extensive overlap with community ecology. In practice the loose and vague term *social* is frequently used as a convenient designation for all relations of individuals of the same species to each other. Sometimes it is restricted to mutually beneficial relations, but since such relations often are problems for investigation the broader usage seems more practical, convenient, and accurate in most cases, and is adopted here.

The extent of the aggregating tendency in nature has not been fully appreciated, and some degree of aggregation is the rule rather than the exception (1, 3). Only the main types of groups will be considered here; there is no end of minor variations on certain central themes. Darwin considered factors influencing the life of the individual and success in leaving progeny as two aspects of the struggle for existence. The problems of survival and of reproduction are both individual and group problems in the sense that natural selection operates both on individuals and on groups. Vertebrate animals to a large extent can be classified according to the relative degree to which the individual or the group bears the brunt of the struggle for existence (17). Allee (1) has presented a general classification of animal groups based on the degree of social integration. Some use of this will be made in the present chapter.

In the following pages social phenomena will first be considered from the standpoint of the individual, and then from the viewpoint of the group, including both relatively close and coherent social groups and the relationship of these to population density. This will be followed by a brief discussion of the physiological aspects of social life, and finally, of the evolutionary aspects of social adjustments.

Social Problems of Individuals

When a shortage of food or potential mates exists only a limited number of individuals can be accommodated in a given locality and this results in competition. The competition is often indirect and formalized, that is, the animals may compete for social status in a dominance hierarchy or for territory, and if successful in these endeavors, attain some degree of precedence to food or mates. There is also some evidence for sexual selection of prospective mates.

Dominance hierarchies

Consideration of dominance hierarchies as based on aggressive-submissive interactions can be divided into three problems from the viewpoint of individuals, (a) evidence for the existence and nature of dominance hierarchies, (b) effects on individuals of a given rank in a hierarchy, and (c) the basis for the establishment and maintenance of the hierarchy.

The nature of a social hierarchy may be illustrated by the classical case of the pecking order in a flock of hens, where each hen, except the one lowest in the hierarchy, pecks certain subordinates without being pecked in return. Table 1 illustrates an actual case, based on about 40 days observation, of a flock at the morning and afternoon feeding periods.

TABLE 1

DOMINANCE HIERARCHY IN A FLOCK OF FIVE WHITE LEGHORN HENS, SHOWING NUMBER OF TIMES EACH HEN IN THE COLUMN TO THE LEFT PECKED OR THREATENED EACH HEN IN THE ROW ABOVE.

	A	B	C	D	E
A		216	101	156	32
B			32	78	25
C		1		104	50
D					39
E	1				

Hen A was the despot of the flock and frequently drove all other hens away from the food hopper in the morning. Hen E was at the bottom of the social order and tended to avoid the other hens and was therefore not pecked so often by each of its dominants as were other hens. Very rarely a subordinate pecks back at a dominant bird; E once pecked A, and C once pecked B. In such cases if the despot happens to take notice and is not engrossed in feeding it immediately assumes the typical fighting pose, leaps upon the unruly subordinate and often pecks and chases it about during the rest of the period of observation. Not infrequently, flocks contain triangular pecking relations, that is *A* will dominate *B*, *B* will dominate *C*, which in turn dominates *A*. Changes in the social hierarchy are very rare in small flocks of hens and a given dominance order may persist for months or even years.

While there is evidence for the existence in nature of dominance hierarchies for many birds and mammals, as well as for a few lizards and fishes (17, 19), detailed numerical data are still scarce and desirable. Such hierarchies are particularly in evidence during critical periods of food shortage. Recently, we managed to gather sufficient data indicating the existence of a dominance hierarchy among ring-necked pheasants wintering in a tall-grass marsh near Madison, Wisconsin. Dominance was decided mainly on the basis of aggressive displacement of one bird from a food supply by another bird. Table 2 gives an example of a dominance hierarchy among wild passerine birds. It will be noticed that in a few cases subordinate birds displaced their presumed dominants from the food supply. These apparent exceptions depended on the territorial relations of the birds and will be discussed later in this connection.

TABLE 2

Dominance Hierarchy at a Winter Feeding Station in a Flock of Male Great Tits (Parus major) in Scotland, Showing the Number of Times Each Bird in the Column to the Left Dominated Each Subordinate in the Row Above [After Brian, (14)].

	A	B	C	D	E	F	G
A		20	19	17	7	22	21
B	8		24	4	1	17	26
C				1	4	10	6
D			7			3	8
E			1	2			9
F							4
G							

The second problem in our discussion of social hierarchies concerns the effects of a given social status on an individual. For one thing, it is obvious that the top-ranking individual receives far less punishment, if any, compared to other members of the group. This relative freedom from fear is associated with considerably more freedom and independence of movement.

Precedence to food as a result of high social status has been known to lead to increased growth rate, as in the case of immature green sunfish (4), and Norway rats kept in a large enclosure. Calhoun (cf. Collias, 18) observed that class differences in rats tended to perpetuate themselves, since rats born to dominant parents established near a central food source grew much larger than rats born in less favorable situations, and their larger size in turn helped them to win higher dominance status and therefore precedence to the food.

Aggressive competition for mates has been observed in many vertebrates as well as in certain insects, spiders, and cuttlefish. Quantitative data have been presented for precedence to mates according to rank in the dominance hierarchy for roosters, and for free-ranging rhesus monkeys. Among domestic roosters confined to the same pen, some of the birds of low social status may be so strongly subordinated that they fear to approach the hens even in the absence of the dominant cock, resulting in what has been termed "psychological castration." On the other hand, the most dominant hens in a flock frequently mate less often than do their subordinates.

The more dominant roosters sire more progeny, as was shown by Guhl and Warren using males of different genetic constitution for plumage factors so that the color of each chick evidenced its father. Hens and wasps (*Polistes gallicus*) at or near the bottom of their dominance hierarchy lay fewer eggs than do more dominant individuals. Among highly social insects all eggs of the colony are frequently layed by one queen. Queen bees may fight with and kill young rival queens.

At times high rank in the dominance hierarchy may favor residence in a given area. A great many birds establish territories during the breeding season, areas which they defend from intruders, usually with success; but in many instances it is now known that birds may occasionally be driven from their territories by very dominant individuals of the same species. In seven aquaria each containing four sunfish, which were observed before territories were established, Greenberg (36) found that territories were taken up strictly in accordance with rank in the preceding dominance hierarchy.

Social acceptance in a group is known to be related to dominance status in flocks of some birds. Alien valley quail released near a covey are not permitted to join the flock for some time and are relegated to the bottom of the dominance hierarchy. In small flocks of hens, aggressive newcomers that attained first, second, or third place in the dominance hierachy apparently became assimilated within three days of their introduction, whereas newcomers at or near the bottom of the hierarchy required from three to six weeks before they were permitted to mingle and feed with the other hens without being continually chased away (25).

Dominant animals have greater freedom of movement, and this may give them more learning opportunities as compared with subordinate individuals. The most dominant sunfish learn to swim an aquarium maze to a food reward significantly faster than do more subordinate fish when the fish are run as a group (36). Diebschlag (24) states that he could reduce the speed of learning of a pigeon very considerably by putting into the same room a more dominant pigeon, even though the latter might be confined in a closed cage. According to Mowrer (45) the problem-solving capacities of subordinated rats are likely to be considerably impaired, and they become fearful of eating in the experimental situation even though no other animals are present. Socially subordinate rats are more likely to freeze and remain at one spot in a maze or puzzle box than are rats more dominant in the home cage (53). Gordon (32) has pioneered the application of learning tests to wild animals in their native setting. Using a variety of mazes, problem boxes, and string-pulling tests he observed considerable individual differences in the learning performance of wild chipmunks and ground squirrels. In all of these experiments the best performers were usually at or near the top of the dominance order as determined by noting chasing sequences in relation to food competition. Few of the animals in the lower half of the dominance scale would even participate in the learning tests, and those that did were likely to be interfered with by more dominant animals.

Another general problem concerns the manner in which the social hierarchy is established and maintained. As a rule, social rank in the dominance hierarchy is established by fighting, bluffing, or passive submission at the initial encounter between individuals or during an early series of such encounters (16, 17). Success in initial encounters depends on a variable complex of factors and is generally favored by maturity, maleness, familiarity with the locale, help from other individuals, high social status in the home group, isolation from dominating individuals, experience in winning, signs of fear or unaggressiveness in the opponent, body weight, endurance, skill, endocrine balance, good health, and various unknown factors. Some of these differences are genetic [cf. Potter, (52)], others are not.

It is obvious that in such a complex the precise contribution of each factor to success will vary from one situation to the next. Many of the variables involved can be evaluated only by statistical means, for example by multiple regression, as was done in one study with white leghorn hens (17). Two hundred initial encounters were staged in a neutral pen using in each encounter two moderately-inbred white leghorn hens from different flocks. Factors of major importance in deciding the outcome of the staged encounters were male hormone output by these hens as indicated by comb size, and slightness of molt. Social rank in the home flock had much less influence, and weight differences were of only slight importance. Previous experiments had shown that treatment of subordinate hens with male hormone increased aggressiveness, while treatment of very dominant hens with doses of thyroxin sufficient to cause severe molting decreased aggressiveness during initial encounters.

Once established the social order is maintained by the habit of subordination reinforced by more or less frequent threats or attacks from dominant individuals. Occasionally a hen that has become ill and very weak will maintain her dominance status up to or until a few days before her death.

Dominance rank may vary in different groups. Individual hens rotated daily from one flock to another may become assimilated members of as many as five different flocks, and simultaneously maintain a different status in the hierarchy of each flock (25).

Changes in an established dominance hierarchy as a rule are uncommon and seem to come about through active revolt by subordinates which, by fighting, cause a reversal of position. Instabilities of relative position in the dominance order are most likely to occur in recently established groups, among closely ranked individuals, and particularly in cases where a very aggressive individual has, through one circumstance or another, been forced into a subordinate position, or in cases where the aggressiveness of subordinate individuals for physiological reasons undergoes a decided increase. In six out of eight cases, when green sunfish that were at the top of the dominance order in their respective tanks were placed into a strange group, they went first to the bottom of the dominance hierarchy as is usual for newcomers, but within an hour fought their way to the top of the new order (36).

Territoriality

Territorialism, or defense of a given area, is best known among freshwater fish, lizards, and birds. The territorial phenomenon grades into dominance hierarchies. Precise laboratory studies on chameleons (35) and green sunfish (36) have shown that one individual may, on a given area, dominate two or more other individuals which may in turn defend small portions of this same area against each other. The same phenomenon has been noted for western fence lizards in the field. Considerable territorial overlap occurs among wild chipmunks and ground squirrels, and they exhibit a definite chasing order on this more or less neutral ground (32).

Territorialism has certain important functions for the individual. One of these is protection from despotism. Among chipmunks and ground squirrels in the field (32), as in wintering flocks of titmice (14), the closer an individual is to its home range the more likely it is to dominate other individuals at any given locality. Thus the dominance order for great tits given in Table 2 parallels the distance of each individual's territory from the food station. By moving the food station back and forth into the territory of A or B, reversal of dominance relations could be secured at will. Among song sparrows a territorial male is virtually undefeatable while on his territory (46). Gamecocks, each with a harem of hens, have been observed to respect one another's territory in a farm yard; for over 12 months in one case they were never seen to start fights with each other and seldom trespassed (27).

Possession of a territory facilitates securing of a mate and successful reproduction. In species of birds in which males establish territories before arrival of the females, the latter go to those males that have established territories. Dominant roosters are especially likely to interfere with attempted matings with the hens by subordinate cocks, and occasionally a subordinate cock may even interfere with copulation by a dominant rooster. Fish, lizards, and birds often direct most of their territorial defenses against members of their own sex. Once a pair of jewel fish is well settled they drive off other jewel fish from their territory regardless of sex (47).

Another problem concerns the factors leading to successful establishment and maintenance of territories. The most important factor in establishment seems to be prior residence. Even among wandering species not territorial in the strict sense, prior residence in a general locality increases the chances of securing dominance during initial encounters with strangers, as in the case of the viviparous fish, *Platypoecilus maculatus,* in aquaria (10).

Territories are advertised and maintained by use of special signals. Among song birds establishment and maintenance of territory is accompanied by vigorous singing contests as well as by special threat postures and aggressive attacks. Special displays are also used by fish and lizards to supplement active fighting in defense of their territories, and, as in the case of birds, the intruder drops its display when it retreats. Mammals frequently mark the area in which they live with odors from special glands, urine, and feces (37). The penis of the male pigmy hippopotamus is hooked backwards, and its tail, covered with bristles, is capable of a rapid vibratory motion that functions to scatter widely the feces and urine. A dog has been observed to urinate 132 times in 2½ hours. Dogs are said to be able to learn to distinguish the trail of one dog from that of another (54).

Tradition may play an important role in the maintenance of territory. The individual male song sparrow returns to or remains on the same territory from year to year and is generally successful in evicting other males that may have entered during his absence. Young song sparrows tend to settle near their birthplace (46).

Sexual selection between individuals

Darwin presented the theory of sexual selection many years ago to help explain the differences between male and female in coloration or special ornaments, but experimental verification has been slow in coming. Noble and Curtis (47) found that in 36 tests a female jewel fish would invariably lay her eggs opposite an artificially reddened male in preference to a paler male, both males being in adjacent aquaria. Half of the males were reddened by injecting them with yohimbine, the other half were made paler by injecting them with adrenaline. The authors stated that if any difference in movement between two males could be detected, these males were not used in the experiment. Eight gravid females were similarly exposed to two pale males in nonbreeding condition, one male being stained with neutral red. Each female spent over twice as much time before the reddened male as before the unstained control.

American chameleons display to the female by erecting a red throat fan. The conspicuous red flash of this fan among the green leaves serves to attract the female. Normal males were approached in a discrimination apparatus by females in breeding condition 28 times in contrast to only 8 approaches of such females to males that had the fan fastened down with collodion (35).

Cooperative Aspects of Group Life

The ecological role of aggregations

The grouping habit has an important function in the facilitation of survival, growth, and reproduction of individuals (1, 2, 3).

Aggregation clearly enables many animals to achieve a higher degree of environmental control. Mice, like bobwhite quail, have an increased tendency to huddle together when cold, and this helps them to maintain their body heat. When the temperature falls below 13° C. honeybees form a cluster within which the temperature is raised by the fanning of their wings by the central bees; a bee isolated from the group may die of the cold. Termite colonies build nests that regulate humidity and enable some species to live in deserts despite their susceptibility to death from evaporation. The mound nest of certain ants and termites helps them to maintain themselves in periodically flooded grasslands. Beaver colonies construct dams that help maintain the water level suitable for their various activities.

Aggregation enables many aquatic organisms to survive better under critical environmental conditions. Water isopods resist fatal drying better if they are aggregated. A small group of goldfish moves about less and consumes less oxygen per fish than do solitary goldfish; the group is also less easily poisoned by low concentrations of toxic chemicals in the environment. If a group of the small marine flatworm, *Procerodes,* is placed in fresh water, some of the individuals survive decidedly longer than do isolated worms. The main reason for this is that the first worms to die give off calcium into the medium, and calcium is known to have a protective action for marine animals placed in freshwater.

Animals often meet their food problems as a group. Location of the food is facilitated by increasing the number of searchers. The sight of one animal feeding or moving toward food quickly attracts others of the same species. This is probably the way in which vultures locate carrion. Wolves often hunt in packs when food gets scarce. A type of automatic food sharing is shown by grouped goldfish that regurgitate food particles into the water which are then taken up by other fishes of the group. Such grouped fishes show increased growth compared to solitary fishes; part of this effect may be due to some specific growth-promoting factor since a dilute extract from the skin of goldfish has growth-promoting powers. Food sharing is one of the integrating forces in colonies of social insects. Food storage is seen in colonies of beavers, ants, and bees. Many ants keep plant lice from which they derive certain secretions; some ants even build sheds for their domestic animals. The fungus-growing ants and termites have solved their food problem by adopting agriculture. The lower termites feed on wood and depend on protozoa in the gut to digest the wood. These protozoa are shed at each molt so that a freshly molted termite is dependent on other individuals for reinfection. In other words, colony life is essential among lower termites to enable them to be able to digest their food.

Animals frequently meet the enemy problem as a group. This involves detection of the enemy, warning signals, hiding, fleeing, deflection of the attack, or active defense. Some animals like pronghorn antelope and geese have sentinels that do not feed with the others, but keep a watch for danger. Colonies of certain ants, bees, and termites have individuals that guard the entrance to the nest and do not permit strangers or enemies to enter. The California ground squirrel gives different kinds of warning chirps to indicate the presence of a snake, raptorial bird, or mammalian predator. From the appropriate chirps the course of a hawk could be traced along a canyon wall or over rolling hills, while the snake chirp was found to be the most convenient way for human observers to locate rattlesnakes on the area of study (29). An excellent example of a visual warning signal is the white rump patch of the American antelope, which is very conspicuous when the hairs of the rump are raised. The alarm is flashed from one animal to another across the plains, and the animals then run together into a small, compact group (56). An injured European minnow (*Phoxinus laevis*) gives off a substance from its skin that stimulates other minnows to concentrate and to quickly seek cover. Skin extracts diluted some hundreds of times were effective in inducing this alarm response (30).

Decrease in numbers of animals in a group to a very low level can have deleterious effects on reproduction. Harmful or lethal genes are usually recessive, and are more likely to become homozygous when the population is very small. Sex ratios are likely to be disturbed in very small populations and the chances of a male and female meeting one another is decreased. Granary beetles of the genus *Tribolium* lay eggs at a greater rate if more than one pair of beetles is present in the flour medium. Various kinds of protozoa divide more slowly in a very sparse than in a medium population density. The flagellate protozoan, *Chilomonas,* releases a specific chemical substance that accelerates the rate of reproduction of associated individuals.

The care of the young by their parents provides numerous and striking examples of cooperative behavior and social service. Creation of a favorable environment for the young is well illustrated by the nests of birds and of termites and ants. The ability of very young birds to regulate their body temperature is poor, and they are generally brooded by the parents both in the nest and, in many cases, after they have left the nest. Many kinds of young birds and mammals have special distress calls that function to inform their parents when they are lost or in some difficulty, and the parents in turn have special calls that serve to attract their young ones to them.

Feeding of the young is characteristic of higher animals, such as birds, mammals, termites, ants, and bees. Many young domestic animals, such as chickens and lambs, learn to feed on the same foods and at the same time as does the mother. Young kittens will kill mice or rats after seeing their mother do so, and tend to attack the same kind of rat or mouse as does the mother.

Defense of the young by parent birds or mammals is a well known phenomenon. Special warning notes, to which the young respond promptly by hiding or fleeing, are often given by the parents when they perceive danger. "Injury-feigning" as a means of deflecting the attack of a predator from the young is known among many birds.

Young animals are often highly sensitive to disease. Cichlid fish and the female scarab beetle, *Copris hispanis* (26), probably help protect the eggs and young from infection by mold. The first milk secreted after parturition by cows, ewes, goats, sows, and mares is known as colostrum and contains many times the number of antibodies against certain diseases as is found in the milk later secreted (44).

General mechanisms of group integration

The general mechanisms of group integration include selection of a given habitat and specific locality, the balance of specific tolerances and specific attractions with disrupting influences, repetition of social ceremonies or experiences, socialization of the young, contagious behavior, and leadership (17, 18).

The location of the winter crow roosts in New York State has not changed appreciably for 50 years or more, and their pattern of distribution coincides with that of the original or natural vegetation rather than with changes subsequently wrought by man. Bass Rock, a tiny island in the Firth of Forth in Scotland, is a famous breeding site for gannets, and these birds are known to have been breeding on this particular island for at least 500 years. Austin (5) observed that 75 per cent of 2,400 banded and subsequently recaptured individuals of the common tern returned to their natal colony for their first nesting. This attachment increases with age, and many individuals nest from year to year within a few feet of formerly occupied nest sites. A progressive amalgamation of certain small, scattered groups into a few large colonies indicates that site tenacity is modified by group adherence.

The dependence of group formation on the balance between social attraction and such disrupting forces as individual aggressiveness is well illustrated by a flock of song sparrows in late winter or early spring. The winter flock may break up on a warm day into individual or pair territories; with a succeeding cold spell the flock may reform, the territories be released, and the sex pairs be disunited. Ants, bees, and termites have a specific colony odor. Individuals from strange colonies placed in the nest are attacked; but if they are protected for a length of time sufficient to allow them to acquire the colony odor they are accepted.

The existence of very large crowds of aggressive species of animals, including instances among schools of fish, flocks of birds, and herds of mammals, makes it evident that their aggressive impulses must be inhibited, perhaps by crowding, to enable them to form such large groups. It has been observed in the cichlid fish *Aequidens latifrons*, crowded into small water holes as a result of the dry season, that fighting increases with crowding up to a certain point and then decreases (12).

Specific attractions that lead to the formation and integrated behavior of various social groups depend on signal-response patterns, the principles of operation of which have been reviewed by Tinbergen (59) with emphasis on the more innate aspects. The term "social signal" is here used to refer to social cues regardless of the relative importance of innate or conditioned contributions. Social signals and responses will be considered separately.

Signals that function to bring animals of the same species together use various sensory modalities, such as olfactory, auditory, visual, tactile, and thermal. The European minnow has been trained to distinguish over 15 different species of fish by odor (33). Blinded European minnows are attracted by water from which other minnows have been' removed more than by water that had contained no minnows (30). The female dog urinates frequently when she is in heat, and lays down a series of odor trails that converge upon her most frequent residence. Male dogs show a greater tendency to examine oestrous than nonoestrous female urine (8). The schooling of fish depends particularly on visual stimuli, and such schools tend to break up in the dark. Any small object moving alongside the aquarium attracts zebra fishes, but a large moving object repels them (13). The songs of the males of birds, frogs, and certain insects attract females of the species. Social responses to warmth are exemplified by the way in which baby chicks gather next to the artificial heat units of electric brooders. Usually, various sensory modalities cooperate to produce a specific social group, for example, schooling of young catfishes (*Ameiurus melas*) normally depends on visual and tactile stimuli as well as on water vibrations set up by the tail (9). The stimuli may be reacted to simultaneously or successively.

Social signals of animals are not necessarily within the range of human sensory organs. Insect songs are often too high in pitch to be heard by the human ear (51). A variety of insects is known to see ultraviolet, and among some butterflies the females, but not the males, reflect ultraviolet (40).

Social signals have various properties. They are specific, and present evidence indicates that animals recognize not only species and sex, but in some instances individuals as well, by means of distinctive odors, voices, or facial characteristics. In the European minnow, according to Göz (33), blinded individuals could be trained to distinguish individual minnows independently of age or sex. The innate specificity of social signals is not absolute, but varies about an optimum. Clucking, as by a broody hen or a phonograph record of her voice, attracts recently hatched chicks. There is an optimum intensity, rate, and quality for clucking, all of which can be varied within wide limits and still be effective (21). The optimum stimulus is not necessarily the normal one. Oyster catchers show incubation responses to artificial eggs, and prefer an egg several times normal size to a normal egg (60). Social signals are complex, that is, they can be broken down into combinations of simpler stimulus properties. The red spot near the tip of the beak of the parent herring gull stimulates the young to peck at it and facilitates feeding. Experiments with models prove that not only the presence and color of the spot, but the degree of its contrast with the rest of the bill coloration modify the frequency with which the young peck at the beak of the parent. The red spot also helps direct the feeding responses, since models with the spot placed on the forehead instead of on the beak not only receive much fewer pecks, but many of these are directed at the spot on the forehead (61). Different aspects of social signals may summate to enhance the response. The male grayling butterfly follows each passing female; the optimal stimulus situation is a dark female fluttering in the typical way of a butterfly, as near to the male as possible. A white, sailing model of a "female" evokes relatively few responses by the male, and this model could be improved just as well by painting it dark as by presenting it in a fluttering motion (59). Social signals are frequently repetitive and rhythmic. A lost chick regularly repeats its distress call hundreds of times until its mother responds; the clucking of a broody fowl is likewise repeated and rhythmic and serves to quiet and attract the chick.

The frequency of giving signals may vary with factors of the physical environment. For example, the frequency of singing by crickets increases with temperature in a precise way that can be mathematically expressed (51).

The nature of the response to social signals varies with the type of response and with the general external and internal situation.

In general, it is probably true that animals respond to relations in social objects, although the matter has not been much investigated. Models of male sticklebacks with a red back stimulate much fewer fighting responses by a male three-spined stickleback than do models with the red in the normal position on the belly.

A response may serve as the signal for the next response in a reaction chain, as has been shown for the interaction of male and female sticklebacks in the various steps leading to the laying and fertilization of the eggs in the nest built and guarded by the male. Secondary adjustments may facilitate reaction chains; among pigeons and chickens it is known that one sex may compensate by increased provocative behavior for relatively low sexual motivation in the opposite sex.

A response may be in the nature of an increase or a decrease in a given behavior pattern; for example, the clucking of a hen not only inhibits the distress calls of her chicks, but frequently causes them to emit notes of very different character, which we have termed "pleasure notes." Many stimulus situations may result in the distress call, for example cold, hunger, restraint, unfamiliar places, and visual or auditory absence of companions; but whatever situations favor distress calls also inhibit the characteristic pleasure notes. The converse is equally true (21). This suggests the existence of neural systems that are balanced against each other.

On the motor side, Darwin (22) long ago observed that hostile dogs display exactly the opposite motor patterns from friendly or submissive dogs. He described these differences in considerable detail and used this and other cases as illustrations of his "principle of antithesis," which he suggested was one of the general principles of emotional expression in both man and other animals. The aggressive and submissive behavior patterns of many vertebrates are now known to be similarly antithetical. Here again the existence of two neural systems balanced against one another is suggested.

When an animal is placed in a social situation that is apparently conducive to the development of both fear and aggressiveness, apparently extraneous activities may result that may function in a tension-reducing capacity.

Tinbergen (59) has pointed out that an innate social signal is not merely a device evoking one special motor response, but rather serves to lower the threshold of one group of functionally related motor patterns. For example, the sight of a territorial intruder lowers the threshold for all fighting behavior, including biting, threatening, chasing, and so on. The various motor patterns can be classified under various drives or subdrives resulting in a hierarchial organization. In turn, each motor pattern can be broken down into a hierarchy of physiological levels.

Changing of the threshold of a social response may be due to exposure to the appropriate social signal, or simply to physiological changes with lapse of time, as in the reduction of sexual drive in old age with isolation from mates. Rats highly motivated in a sexual sense show wide stimulus generalization, and attempt to mate with a variety of unsuitable objects such as other males (7). With very high motivation, a specific social-behavior pattern may take place in the absence of anything remotely resembling a social signal. For example, it has long been known that broody hens that have never had nor seen chicks will cluck. Raising of the threshold of response may be due to specific fatigue, as in the case of sexual satiation in roosters.

Repetition of social ceremonies in the sense of repeated exchange of positive social contacts and experiences is an important basis for social integration among animals (18, 55). The members of a social group become conditioned to one another and social experiences that apparently provide mutual satisfactions, including sexual and parent-young relations, may function strongly to maintain the group. For example, a nesting pair of black-crowned night herons practices a greeting ceremony in which the long nuptial plumes of the crown are erected. Removal of these plumes tends to dissociate the pair and the birds stand apart and may seek new mates. Mutual preening among birds, and licking or grooming among mammals is of rather general occurrence, particularly within the sex pair or family. Courtship feeding is very common among birds. Mutual exchange of food and chemical or tactile stimuli is widespread among the more social insects such as termites, wasps, ants, and bees.

Socialization of the young is a highly important basis for group integration. Doves and pigeons reared by another species may, after they reach sexual maturity, associate with the species that reared them in preference to their own. Both innate and learned factors are probably involved in species recognition. Noble and Curtis (47) have observed that certain species of cichlid fish that develop red breeding colors are attracted most by red early in life, whereas those that develop black breeding colors are attracted more by black early in life. Association with the parents strengthens an inherited tendency to swim toward moving discs of the same general color as the parents, since young reared in isolation are slow to respond.

Many young vertebrates are more closely aggregated as juveniles than as adults, and such early aggregation may strengthen the social tendency. Isolation of young catfishes, zebra fishes, and young chicks greatly weakens their aggregating tendency. Certain species of locusts have a gregarious phase and a more solitary phase. The gregarious phase can be induced from the solitary phase by rearing the young under crowded conditions. The reverse is also true.

Play is a widely known phenomenon among animals and birds, although it is difficult to define. The play-fighting of young cockerels, the wrestling of young bear cubs, the slides of otters, the races of lambs, and the general exploratory activities of young birds and mammals serve as illustrations. Play probably helps condition the young to cooperative, group-positive behavior, as C. R. Carpenter has suggested for monkeys. The various concepts of play have been reviewed by Beach (6).

Leadership of one individual initiates or stimulates similar activities by other individuals and often considerably enhances group cooperation (3, 18). The leader of group movements often acts as sentinel for the group, as in blue geese and red deer. Goldfish learn to run a simple maze to a food reward more quickly in the company of experienced individuals, and rats soon learn that the direction taken by an experienced leader means a food reward. The matter of leadership to food has been analyzed to a considerable extent in honeybees by Karl von Frisch (3). Bees go out from the hive and look for flowers with nectar and pollen from which they make their honey stores. When a bee finds a good food source, it releases an odor from a special scent gland that attracts other bees in the vicinity. When it returns to the hive it informs other bees of food sources near the hive by a special round dance, while a waggle-tail dance means a greater distance to a food source. On a vertical comb if the waggle dance proceeds upwards, the food source lies in the direction of the sun, if the dancer proceeds to the right the food source is to be found to the right of the sun at the same angle by which the direction of the dancer deviates from the vertical, etc.

The factors that make for leadership have not yet been much studied. Leadership may shift from one individual to another as in white pekin ducks, or it may reside more consistently with one individual as with female red deer. The role of experience has been indicated. The group leader may also be chief despot of the group, as among stallions and rhesus monkeys. Often a female leads, as in the case of sheep, where generally the oldest ewe is the leader. American antelope in the Yellowstone Park area migrate south in the fall in bands that are usually led by does; about once in 20 cases a buck leads the way (56). Leadership may grow out of family relations. Among many birds and mammals the young follow the parents about and develop a strong attachment to the parent, which is based on the food, warmth, and other types of security secured from the parent as well as on innate factors. Another source of leadership is the widespread tendency of animals to do the same thing at the same time, a phenomenon sometimes designated as contagious behavior. Examples of behavior that has been shown to be contagious in birds or mammals include running, swimming, bathing, feeding, preening, resting, homing, fear, predation, certain vocalizations, and pair formation [cf. Collias (18)].

Social Behavior and Population Density

Population problems include establishment, growth, maintenance, spread, and limitation of numbers of individuals in relation to the capacity of the habitat. Social behavior plays an important part in each of these aspects of population regulation. Conversely, changes in population density may exert important influences on social integration (3, 17, 18).

Establishment and maintenance of a species in new localities is often facilitated by social habits. The geometric rate of increase of populations in itself facilitates establishment once a local population has attained some numbers. Some of the harmful effects of very small numbers, including distorted sex ratios, deleterious inbreeding, and inadequate control of the biotic and physical environment, were described in the preceding section. From 1875 to 1939 the number of breeding colonies of the fulmar petrel in the British Isles increased from 2 to 208. Small colonies of fulmars were frequently present during the breeding season in various localities from one to five years before breeding, and after breeding began there was some evidence that fewer eggs or young were produced per breeding pair in very small colonies than in the larger ones (28).

Social mechanisms may help to regulate age and sex ratios. As a population grows, the proportion of young in the population tends to decrease. Among flour beetles (*Tribolium*) the rate of cannibalism of the eggs by larvae and adults increases with population density (3). Among termites the presence of mature males, females, or soldiers, respectively, inhibits the development of the same caste from undifferentiated nymphs, which then remain as workers. Apparently, special inhibitory substances in the exudates of each caste are eaten by the nymphs. This provides a mechanism whereby the proportion of castes could be automatically controlled, and there is some evidence that the ratio of soldiers to workers tends to a constant figure, regardless of the proportions at the start [cf. Emerson (3)].

Many regulatory factors help limit a population. These have been summarized by Thomas Park (3). When the various external factors are made favorable, it has been demonstrated that limitation of population density to a fluctuating equilibrium may still occur because of intrinsic social factors. These operate by causing mortality directly, by restriction of reproduction, and by forcing emigration. Normally, however, social factors operate in conjunction with environmental factors, such as food shortage, predation, or disease.

Cannibalism of eggs and young by older individuals is very widespread in the animal kingdom, and has been demonstrated to limit population growth in flour beetles (3), guppies in large aquaria (13), and black bass in rearing ponds. Laboratory populations of the vole, *Microtus agrestis,* show an excessive mortality component between conception and weaning, in good part due to resorption of fetuses or killing of the young. Habitual litter eating is a phenomenon well known to stock breeders. Among the termites cannibalism increases if nitrogenous food is deficient and presumably helps to restrict colony size in relation to the food supply.

The most remarkable case known of social control of population density is probably drone elimination by honeybees. This elimination usually occurs in the fall when the food source diminishes. Workers herd the drones into corners of the hive and cut them off from the food supply; ultimately the weakened drones are dragged away and left to die outside the hive entrance.

Social behavior may limit high population density by restricting reproduction. In very crowded flour beetle populations fecundity is reduced, mainly through conditioning effects of the beetles on their flour medium.

Increased emigration at high population densities may be caused by social factors. Larvae of the granary beetle, *Rhizopertha dominica,* burrow into grains of wheat in which they feed and pupate. A larva that enters an occupied hole is repulsed by an attack that may be fatal unless one larva emigrates to another wheat grain. This is reminiscent of the territorial relations of many vertebrates, which force many individuals into suboptimal habitats at times of high population density. The compressibility of territories varies greatly with food supply, abundance of nest sites, and with different species, but in many cases territorialism probably helps to stabilize population density. In crowded colonies of the common tern, desertion of nests, fighting, and mortality from fighting is said to increase with diminishing size of territories (48). A typical beaver colony consists of an individual family. Yearlings are tolerated, but two-year olds are attacked and driven from the colony in the spring just before the young are born (11). The swarming of honeybees is an example of a highly specialized mechanism for preventing local overcrowding by division of the old colony, and leads to the spread of the species into new territory. As the nurse bees increase in number, they secrete a superabundance of brood food and construct queen cells from which new queens emerge. When a queen emerges from the hive with the swarm she emits a special odor that causes the swarm to cluster about her. Scouts are said to leave the swarm and look for a new place for the colony to settle. Swarming can be delayed or prevented by reducing the number of the bees, or by removing the queen cells.

Population density exerts a reciprocal influence on social organization. Increase in population density of wild turkeys is paralleled by increase in the average size of flocks. In low-density populations of valley quail social barriers are more rigid and newcomers are not readily admitted. Possibly this helps facilitate survival in the species as a whole by permitting a closer organization within covies. In flocks of domestic fowl with a continually shifting membership, there is more strife, and the average individual gets less to eat and does not maintain body weight very well, as compared with individuals in a flock with a more stable membership.

Physiological Aspects of Social Adjustments

The physiological basis of social adjustment is best known for vertebrate animals, and particularly for reproductive mechanisms. Endocrine and neural mechanisms of reproductive behavior have been reviewed in detail elsewhere [Chapter 5; also, 7, 20]. The following brief summary is designed only to illustrate certain major principles of physiological control of social mechanisms. Such principles serve to integrate a great many facts in studies of social behavior. For example, knowledge of the action of sex hormones systematizes much that is known about reproductive behavior.

Hormones and reproductive behavior

Seasonal adjustment of the breeding season depends on both ecological and physiological factors. In general, the breeding season for each animal is so adjusted that the young are produced at the time of year most favorable for their growth and survival. For many

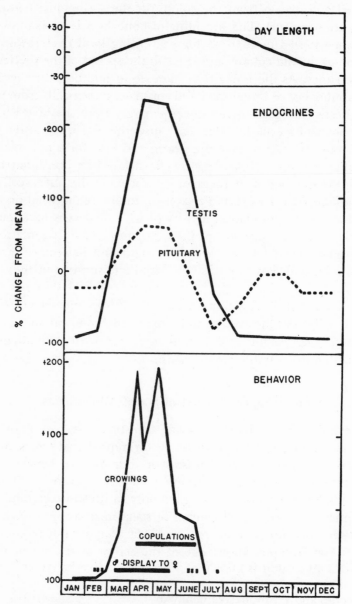

Fig. 1.   Chart Illustrating Control of Seasonal Breeding Behavior in Ring-necked Pheasants (see text). After Greeley (34), Collias (20), and Taber (58).

birds and mammals of the northern hemisphere that breed in the spring and summer it has been demonstrated that increase in day-length is the important factor stimulating gonad development, and variations in other factors exert only a modifying or inhibiting influence. For example, ring-necked pheasants subjected to artificially increased day-length have bred in midwinter. Eventually, the birds cease to respond despite continued exposure to increased day-length.

The relationship of the breeding cycle in ring-necked pheasants exposed to the natural increase in day-length is illustrated by Fig. 1. Increase in day-length acts at least in part through the pituitary gland. For the curves of testis weight and pituitary potency, F. Greeley (34) each month examined 12 game-farm cocks reared in large outdoor pens. The gonad-stimulating powers of the anterior pituitary were assayed by noting the growth-promoting effect on the testis when an extract was injected into chicks of the domestic fowl. Crowing signalizes the establishment of territories. The number of crowings by unconfined pheasants was counted from one spot in a marsh during the breeding season and are graphed in Fig. 1, using only data from days with favorable weather conditions for crowing. The temporary drop in the center of the curve is probably due to the dispersal of some males from the locality coincident with territorial establishment by other males. As in domestic cocks it probably takes more male hormone to stimulate copulation than to stimulate crowing and male display; this helps account for the relative lag in onset of copulations as compared with crowing and display.

The rapid and large change in behavior indirectly induced by the relatively slow and small increase in day-length is noteworthy as illustrating the principle of adaptive amplification, which is one characteristic of living organisms. This contrasts with unfavorable environmental fluctuations, the effects of which are customarily damped by the adaptations of living things.

Reproductive behavior within the breeding season can be divided into sexual and parental phases, controlled respectively in birds by at least two types of secretions from the anterior pituitary, gonad-stimulating hormone, and prolactin. In addition to stimulating parental behavior in hens that have been laying eggs, prolactin has a strong inhibitory influence on the ovaries and causes egg laying to cease. Figure 2 illustrates the record of one individual domestic hen during a change from sexual to parental phase and back to the sexual phase. Copulations were observed during standard time-limited observation periods and are indicated by long vertical lines on the graph. Short vertical lines indicate observation periods when the hen did not copulate. Female hormone, but not male hormone, stimulates copulation by ovariectomized hens. When a hen becomes broody, she incubates persistently, ceases to lay eggs, clucks, and cares

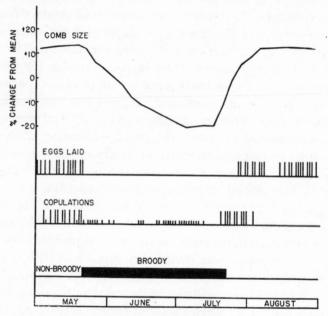

Fig. 2. Records for One Individual Hen Illustrating the Inverse Relationship Between Sexual and Parental Phases of Endocrine Control of Reproductive Behavior (see text).

for and defends chicks. The graph of broodiness in Fig. 2 refers specifically to clucking, which is a good indicator of broodiness. The inverse relationship between the sexual and parental phases of the reproductive cycle is clearly evident. Each phase is governed by a complex interplay between social and endocrine factors (20).

The nervous system and social behavior

The neural basis of social integration is a tremendously complex problem that is far from being solved at the present time. A little progress has been made in the anatomical localization of the neural basis for certain social behavior patterns; much more needs to be learned in a dynamic sense about the neural mechanisms of social control. These mechanisms may operate not only over anatomically set nerve pathways that excite or inhibit other nerve pathways, but they may also involve masses of excitation and inhibition more directly mediated by intercellular electric currents (31). In either case it is of fundamental interest that in both the anatomical and physiological sense, neural mechanisms, like behavior mechanisms, are organized into progressively more inclusive levels of organization.

Various cerebral operations, particularly in birds and mammals, have indicated that the social behavior mechanisms that are directly concerned with integration of an individual into its social environment are probably organized in the cerebral hemispheres. For example, the frequency of mating behavior in male rats can be decreased by lesions of the cerebral cortex, and breeding behavior in pigeons is abolished by removal of the upper part of the corpus striatum. Specific patterns of sensory stimulation produce specific and repeatable electrical patterns in the sensory areas of the cerebral cortex. A rhesus monkey with its temporal lobes removed shows difficulties of social comprehension and seems "psychically blind," although discrimination tests indicate that the elementary visual abilities are intact. For example, such a monkey, after being attacked and bitten by a normal animal, may approach the latter again and again in an attempt to examine it. Another function of the cerebral cortex is the inhibition and direction of aggressive and antisocial impulses; the excessive and uncontrolled aggressiveness of decerebrated cats has often been cited.

The basic motor patterns of aggressiveness and fear behavior are organized in the hypothalamus in cats, as indicated by the results of decerebration and by precisely localized electrical stimulation. The hypothalamus probably helps to integrate somatic motor and autonomic impulses. Some of the anatomical pathways integrating cerebral and hypothalamic activity have been described by Papez (49) in relation to a proposed theory of the mechanism of emotion.

The autonomic accompaniments of social behavior are conveniently and delicately demonstrated by certain fish. The darkening of an aggressive fish is mediated by cholinergic nerve fibers, and the paling of a frightened fish by adrenergic fibers (Parker 50, 1948). One can watch a territorial cichlid gradually turn pale as it swims out of its territory and again gradually darken when it returns.

Social Behavior and Evolution

Trends in social evolution of animals

In this section some of the major problems and trends in social evolution will be mentioned. For more details, the reader is referred to reviews by Allee (1, 2, 3), Collias (17, 18), and Emerson (3).

The origin of multicellular organisms is a problem in social evolution. One-celled organisms are known to cooperate in a number of ways which have been summarized by Allee. A variety of colony types have evolved in protozoa, some of which illustrate how metazoan organisms might have arisen. Interdependence between cells increases as one ascends the phylogenetic scale from more primitive to more complex metazoans, as indicated by a parallel decrease in regenerative capacity after injury. In such primitive multicellular types as sponges, cells can be separated mechanically and reconstitute multicellular organisms if enough of the cells come together.

The evolution of sex is a complex problem with many ramifications. Its importance is indicated by its universal occurrence. The essential feature of sex is the coming together and exchanging of character factors of two parents in the making of a new individual, and as such, sex has recently been demonstrated in viruses and bacteria (23). Sex has long been known to occur in all animal phyla. The presence of multiple mating types in *Paramecium* may indicate a trial-and-error period in evolution before the standard number of two sexes became stabilized. The evolution of separate male and female individuals is associated with motility. For example most plants and sessile animals are hermaphroditic, whereas most motile animals have the sexes in separate individuals. Sex is quite labile in some of the lower animals and the same individual may be first one sex and then another; such consecutive sexuality has been reported for certain species among echinoderms, molluscs, annelids, crustaceans, lampreys, and sea perch. The change from femaleness to maleness is likely to occur when individuals are crowded and there is a food shortage. In view of the lability of sex in more primitive vertebrates it is not surprising that many of the higher vertebrates show a considerable degree of ambisexuality in behavior. Parthenogenesis occurs in many groups of invertebrates and functions to make possible rapid multiplication under favorable conditions by eliminating the problems involved in the meeting of two individuals for sexual reproduction.

Predator-prey relations, cannibalism, and aggressive-submissive behavior all have essentially similar motor patterns. The widespread occurrence of cannibalism in the invertebrates and lower vertebrates suggests that aggressive-submissive behavior may have had its inception in the predator-prey relations that arose coincidently with animal motility and animal nutrition, and was subsequently applied to competition for territories and mates. Fighting between males for females and incipient territoriality have been observed in the lake lamprey, which is near the bottom of the vertebrate evolutionary scale. Aggressive competition for mates is absent or poorly developed where the chances of fertilization by a given male seem relatively small, for example, in school-breeding fish that scatter their eggs widely. Aggressive competition for mates is well developed in fish whose mating habits permit a high degree of selective fertilization by one male, for example, in many freshwater fishes that are viviparous or that have external fertilization of grouped eggs. The evolution of adhesive eggs grouped in nests was probably facilitated in the remote ancestors of vertebrates by adoption of a freshwater habitat, since streams would tend continually to wash floating or nonadhesive eggs out to sea. The evolution of terrestrial life led to internal fertilization, which in turn favored aggressive competition for mates, as seen in many lizards, birds, and most mammals. Threat is often used in place of direct fighting, and aggressive color displays are best developed among small diurnal species such as freshwater fishes, lizards, and birds, whereas nocturnal species rely more on auditory and olfactory signals, as do alligators and many mammals.

Defense of the nest and its vicinity may have originated in relation to egg masses as competition for a food supply as suggested by Smith (57). He observed that a primitive salamander, the hellbender, in addition to eating some of the eggs, would aggressively defend its large egg mass from other hellbenders. Smith believed that only a few of the eggs were needed to satisfy the hunger of the guardian. In general, territorial defense is best developed among vertebrates with nests and eggs like certain fish, lizards, and birds, and is often extended to include defense of the young. Most mammals are viviparous, and often have extensive overlapping between their home ranges.

Viviparity occurs in a number of species of lizards and is associated with a relatively cold habitat compared with that of oviparous lizards (62). Such unfavorable environmental conditions as cold sometimes result in retention of the eggs, which may then hatch in the uterus of the mother. Similar conditions may have been responsible for the evolution of the viviparous trait in mammals. It is of interest in this connection that the great adaptive radiation of the placental mammals began with the cool Paleocene epoch which followed the Mesozoic, or "Age of Reptiles." In birds the necessity for lightness in flight has apparently precluded the evolution of viviparity.

Many factors have influenced the evolution of family size and duration. Excessive mortality of the young is associated with the production of large numbers of young that receive little or no parental care, including most of the lower invertebrates, school-breeding fishes, and amphibians. As compared with most lower vertebrates, birds and mammals produce much fewer young, and these young receive much more parental care and protection. Within the various taxonomic groups of mammals the general evolutionary trend toward increased size is accompanied by an increase in the time required for the young to mature (42). This trend reaches its climax in the higher primates, where evolution seems to have favored a prolonged period of immaturity, apparently in association with increased opportunities for education. Increase in size of the group results when the young continue to remain with the parents after a new generation is born, as in a beaver colony and among some of the primates.

The stages in evolution of parental care among insects as outlined by W. M. Wheeler show many similarities to that described above for vertebrates: (a) the female merely lays eggs in a place favorable for the development of the young; (b) she provides a protective covering for the eggs; (c) she remains with the eggs and young larvae and protects them; (d) she feeds the young; and (e) the young cooperate with the mother in rearing subsequent broods, leading to increased size of the group.

Very large groups have often evolved among animals, and something is known of the conditions under which they have evolved. An abundant food supply is needed and makes it necessary for very large groups often to be on the move as in large migrating flocks of birds, the nomadic legions of army ants, and migrating swarms of locusts and lemmings; or else to scatter out very widely when feeding, as in the case of large breeding colonies of seabirds or of large crow roosts. Vegetarian animals generally form larger aggregations than do predators; the large herds of bison and of various antelopes in rich grassland are examples. The hunting, pastoral, and agricultural stages of human history made possible progressively larger population concentrations. The same three stages occur in the phylogenetic history of ants, and it is generally the vegetarian ants, particularly those that cultivate fungi for their food that have the largest colonies. The primitive ants are carnivorous, and, with the exception of the army ants, generally have small colonies (63).

According to Montagu (43) the small noctural lemurs live either in pairs or in single families, while the larger diurnal lemurs tend to live in small groups that contain the members of at least one other family. Montagu suggests that increase in body size may have been a potent factor in releasing the early primates from their nocturnal or crepuscular habits by enabling them to hold their own against most aggressors, and that diurnal life favored more extended social relations.

Increased tolerance within small, well organized groups of birds and mammals probably makes it possible for them to compete more effectively as aggressive units (17). The size and stability of groups organized into a dominance hierarchy in birds and mammals is much greater than in fishes, and depend on such things as greater capacity for recognizing and remembering other individuals. The formation of large compound groups that function as units for intraspecific attack or defense is common in man, but seems to be uncommon in nonhuman animals. Honeybees sometimes take honey from other colonies, particularly when there is a scarcity of nectar in the fields, and, according to Cale (15), when robbing occurs between two apiaries that are some distance apart, every colony in the robbing apiary may participate in the destruction of the colonies being robbed.

No completely asocial animal has been described. Allee (1, 2, 3) has given many illustrations that indicate that some degree of aggregation is associated with beneficial effects for the aggregated individuals among many primitive types of animals not ordinarily considered as social animals. Such instances of primitive mutualism have been demonstrated in all major groups of the animal kingdom, and Allee suggests that the more advanced or specialized types of social evolution arose from a basic tendency to sociality present in all animals. Such major social advances as multicellularity, parental care, viviparity, gregariousness, and extensive overlap of generations have evolved independently, many times, and in different taxonomic groups. Degenerative social specialization also occurs, as is evident from the parasitic cowbirds which have lost the nest-building and territorial instincts, or as in the case of certain slave-making ants which starve in an abundance of food if their slaves be taken from them.

Social life and the mechanisms of evolution

Evolution of nonhuman animals depends on genetic variations, some degree of isolation, and natural selection. The interrelations between these principles of evolution and social life will be illustrated by a few selected examples. A great wealth of examples with emphasis on the ecological aspects of evolution has been summarized by Emerson (3).

To be of continuing significance in social evolution of nonhuman animals differences in adaptive reactions must basically be genetic, since animal traditions characteristically differ from human traditions in not being accumulative. Among domestic animals a genetic basis for social differences is well known, for example, variation in litter size in different families of guinea pigs. Various breeds of domestic fowl are known to differ in aggressiveness, copulatory frequency, rate of egg-laying, and broodiness.

Divergence of local populations in social characteristics may take place with local inbreeding, even before the establishment of the complete reproductive isolation that results in new species. Differences in songs of subspecies of certain song birds and crickets are known. Differences in social habits themselves may influence the amount of local inbreeding. The greater permanence of the sex pair and of the family in geese favors local inbreeding more than do the loose pairs of ducks, and the formation of local races or subspecies is much more common in geese than in ducks (41).

Reproductive isolation of related species may be maintained by various social mechanisms. For example, closely related species may be interfertile but interbreed only rarely in nature because of distinctive vocalizations, colors, or displays. The eastern and western species of meadowlark are almost identical in appearance but have very different songs; hybrids have been produced in the laboratory, but occur rarely, if at all, in the field. The mallard (*Anas platyrhyn-*

chus) and the black duck (*Anas rubripes*), which occasionally produce fertile hybrids in nature, have practically identical voices, but distinctive flight patterns. In addition, the male of the mallard has a very distinctive plumage which is associated with a special courtship display.

Evidence of a fairly direct sort for natural selection in relation to a social trait has been presented by Lack (39) for family size in certain birds. Mortality rate of the young rises in the starling and in the alpine swift as soon as brood size exceeds the commonest size found in nature. The number of young produced starts to fall off with abnormally large broods, and this limits the size of the family in an evolutionary sense. Details of the mechanism seem to be that in large broods as compared with small broods the nestlings get less food per bird, weigh less on the average, suffer greater nest mortality, as in the swift, or else leave the nest in such poor condition that they suffer greater mortality during the first two months after leaving the nest, as in the starling.

As pointed out by Darwin the adaptive evolution of sterile castes among the social insects can be explained by the assumption that natural selection has operated not on separate individuals but on the colony as a whole. Worker honeybees, like the soldiers of ants and termites, are often killed in defense of their colony; such behavior benefits only the group and not the individuals that die. Emerson has reviewed many other examples where natural selection has apparently operated on the group rather than on the individual, including the evolution of mammary glands in mammals, and of different life forms in the complex life cycles of various parasites, such as malarial protozoans, flukes, and tapeworms. Adult may-flies have vestigial mouthparts, eat nothing, and serve only the social function of reproduction.

The normal existence of an individual animal depends not only on the proper integration of its component cells, tissues, organs, and organ systems, but also upon the proper functioning of that individual as a unit in a social system. The competition between individuals is often with respect to degree of social adjustment. The normal existence of social groups in turn depends on their proper functioning as units within ecological systems of a higher order. This viewpoint has been elaborated elsewhere (17). The hierarchial pattern of organization of living things indicates that natural selection must be operating at all levels to produce harmonious adjust-ments within the entire community, or indeed the whole biosphere.

The best conditions for social evolution are the same as for evolution in general, and these are much the same as the general conditions that have proved best for continued progress in livestock breeding: the establishment of many different inbred lines to fix, or at least multiply, various genotypes, selection between these dif-ferent strains, followed by crossbreeding of the favored types to restore variability and thereby provide a basis for further progress. The whole process is then repeated indefinitely (64, 65, 67). The method depends particularly on the maintenance of a great variety of more or less homogeneous populations without undue weight being placed on any one type at the expense of all the others.

The breeding structure of many natural populations provides likely parallels to the conditions of this theory (66). Animal species in nature are generally distributed in many partially isolated popula-tions whose effective breeding densities are usually much smaller than indicated by the actual numbers of animals present.

Social behavior exerts a reciprocal influence on evolutionary mechanisms, because social behavior plays an important role in regu-lating the breeding structure of natural populations. The nonrandom distribution of animals in nature is regulated largely by their social habits. Habitat selection, traditional locality fixation, local aggrega-tion, parthenogenesis, restriction of reproduction to certain indi-viduals, family life, dispersal to peripheral habitats, and restriction of population density by intraspecific mechanisms all tend to favor the establishment of *local genetic types* within the species, and all depend to an important extent on social behavior. Factors tending to reduce genetic variability are balanced against sex, which is the prime source of variability among living organisms and essentially a social phenomenon.

Bibliography

1. Allee, W. C., *Animal Aggregations: a Study in General Sociology.* Chicago: University of Chicago Press, 1931.
2. ———— *Approaches to National Unity* (L. Bryson, L. Finkelstein, and R. M. MacIver, Eds.), Chapter 20, pp. 321-367. New York: Harper and Brothers, 1945.
3. ———— Emerson, Alfred E., Park, Orlando, Park, Thomas, and Schmidt, Karl P., *Principles of Animal Ecology.* Philadelphia and London: W. B. Saunders Company, 1949.

4. ———— Greenberg, B., Rosenthal, G. M., and Frank, P., Some Effects of Social Organization on Growth in the Green Sunfish, *J. Exper. Zoöl.*, 1948, **108**, 1-19.

5. Austin, Oliver L., Site Tenacity, a Behavior Trait of the Common Tern (*Sterna Hirundo*, Linn.), *Bird-banding*, 1949, **20**, 1-39.

6. Beach, Frank A., Current Concepts of Play in Animals, *Amer. Naturalist*, **79**, 523-541.

7. ———— *Hormones and Behavior*. New York: Paul B. Hoeber, 1948.

8. ———— and Gilmore, Robert W., Response of Male Dogs to Urine from Females in Heat. *J. Mammalogy*, 1949, **30**, 391-392.

9. Bowen, Edith S., The Role of the Sense Organs in Aggregations of *Ameiurus melas*, *Ecological Monographs*, 1931, **1**, 1-35.

10. Braddock, James C., The Effect of Prior Residence upon Dominance in the Fish, *Platypoecilus maculatus*, *Physiol. Zoöl.*, 1949, **22**, 161-169.

11. Bradt, Glenn W., A Study of Beaver Colonies in Michigan, *J. Mammalogy*, 1938, **19**, 135-162.

12. Breder, C. M., Jr., An Experimental Study of the Reproductive Habits and Life History of the Cichlid Fish *Aequidens latifrons* (Steindachner), *Zoologica*, 1934, **18**, 1-42.

13. ———— and Halpern, Florence, Innate and Acquired Behavior Affecting the Aggregation of Fishes, *Physiol. Zoöl.*, **19**, 154-190.

14. Brian, Anne D., Dominance in the Great Tit, *Parus major*, *The Scottish Naturalist*, 1949, **61**, 144-155.

15. Cale, G. H., *The Hive and the Honeybee* (Roy A. Grout, Ed.), Chapter 15, 313-383. Hamilton, Illinois: Dadant and Sons, 1946.

16. Collias, Nicholas, Statistical Analysis of Factors Which Make for Success in Initial Encounters between Hens, *Amer. Naturalist*, 1943, **77**, 519-538.

17. ———— Aggressive Behavior Among Vertebrate Animals, *Physiol. Zoöl.*, 1944, **17**, 83-123.

18. ———— Social Life and the Individual Among Vertebrate Animals, *Annals of the New York Academy of Science*, 1950, **51**, 6, 1074-1092.

19. ———— Some Variations in Grouping and Dominance Patterns among Birds and Mammals, *Zoologica*, 1951, **35**, 97-119.

20. ———— Hormones and Behavior with Special Reference to Birds and to the Mechanisms of Hormone Action, *Symposium on Steroid Hormones* (E. Gordon, Editor), Madison: University of Wisconsin Press, 1950, pp. 277-329.

21. ———— Development of Social Behavior in Birds, *The Auk* (in press).

22. Darwin, Charles, *The Expression of the Emotions in Man and Animals*, 2nd ed. London: James Murray, 1890.

23. Delbrück, Max, and Delbrück, Mary Bruce, Bacterial Viruses and Sex, *Scientific American*, 1948, **179**, 46-51.

24. Diebschlag, E., Psychologische Beobachtungen über die Rangordnung bei der Haustaube, *Zeitschrift für Tierpsychologie*, 1941, **4**, 12-188.

25. Douglis, Marjorie B., Social Factors Influencing the Hierarchies of Small Flocks of the Domestic Hen: Interactions Between Resident and Part-time Members of Organized Flocks, *Physiol. Zoöl.,* 1948, **21,** 147-182.

26. Fabre, J. Henri, *The Sacred Beetle and Others.* New York: Dodd, Mead and Company, 1918.

27. Fennell, R. A., The Relation between Heredity, Sexual Activity, and Training to Dominance-subordination in Game Cocks, *Amer. Naturalist,* 1945, **79,** 143-159.

28. Fisher, James, and Waterston, George, The Breeding Distribution, History and Population of the Fulmar *(Fulmarus glacialis)* in the British Isles, *J. Animal Ecology,* 1941, **10,** 204-272.

29. Fitch, Henry S., Ecology of the California Ground Squirrel on Grazing Lands, *Amer. Midland Naturalist,* 1948, **39,** 513-596.

30. Frisch, Karl von, Die Bedeutung des Geruchsinnes im Leben der Fische, *Die Naturwissenschaften,* 1941, **29,** 321-333.

31. Gerard, R. W., The Interactions of Nerones, *Ohio State J. Science,* 1941, **41,** 160-172.

32. Gordon, Kenneth, The Natural History and Behavior of the Western Chipmunk and the Mantled Ground Squirrel, *Oregon State Monogr.,* 1943, No. 5, pp. 104.

33. Göz, Hans, Uber den Art-und individual Geruck bei Fischen, *Zeitschrift für Vergleichende Physiologie,* 1941, **29,** 1-45.

34. Greeley, F. (in press).

35. Greenberg, B., and Noble, G. K., Social Behavior of the American Chameleon *(Anolis carolinensis* Voight), *Physiol. Zoöl.,* 1944, **17,** 392-439.

36. ———— Some Relations between Territory, Social Hierarchy, and Leadership in the Green Sunfish *(Lepomis syanellus),* *Physiol. Zoöl.,* 1947, **20,** 267-299.

37. Hediger, H., Die Bedeutung von Miktion und Defäkation bei Wildtieren, *Schweizerische Zeitschrift für Psychologie,* 1944, **3,** 170-182.

38. Kendeigh, S. C., Territorial and Mating Behavior of the House Wren, *Illinois Biological Monogr.,* 1941, **18,** 1-120.

39. Lack, David, Natural Selection and Family Size in the Starling, *Evolution,* **2,** 95-110.

40. Lutz, F. E., Invisible Colors of Flowers and Butterflies, *Natural History* (Journal of the American Museum of Natural History), 1933, **33,** 565-576.

41. Mayr, Ernst, *Systematics and the Origin of Species.* New York: Oxford University Press, 1942.

42. Mitchell, P. Chalmers, *The Childhood of Animals.* London: William Heinemann, 1912.

43. Montagu, M. F. Ashley, On the Relation between Body Size, Waking Activity, and the Origin of Social Life in the Primates, *American Anthropologist,* 1944, **46,** 141-145.

44. Morrison, Frank B., *Feeds and Feeding, Abridged.* Ithaca, New York: Morrison Publishing Company, 1949.
45. Mowrer, O. H., Animal Studies in the Genesis of Personality, *Transactions New York Acad. Sci., Series II,* 1941, **3**, 1-4.
46. Nice, Margaret Morse, Studies in the Life History of the Song Sparrow. II. The Behavior of the Song Sparrow and Other Passerines, *Transact. Linnaean Soc. of New York,* 1943, **6**, 1-329.
47. Noble, G. K., and Curtis, B., The Social Behavior of the Jewelfish, *Hemichromis bimaculatus, Bulletin of the American Museum of Natural History,* 1939, **76**, 1-76.
48. Palmer, Ralph S., A Behavior Study of the Common Tern, *Proc. Boston Soc. Nat. History,* 1941, **42**, 1-119.
49. Papez, J. W., A Proposed Mechanism of Emotion, *Archiv. Neurol. and Psychiat.,* 1937, **38**, 725-743.
50. Parker, G. H., *Animal Colour Changes and Their Neurohumours.* Cambridge: The University Press, 1948.
51. Pierce, George W., *The Songs of Insects.* Cambridge, Massachusetts. Harvard University Press, 1948.
52. Potter, Jane Huntington, Dominance Relations between Different Breeds of Hens, *Physiol Zoöl.,* 1949, **22**, 261-280.
53. Riess, Bernard F., Freezing Behavior in Rats and Its Social Causation, *J. Soc. Psychol.,* 1946, **24**, 249-251.
54. Schmid, Bastian, Uber die Ermittlung des menschlichen und tieri-schen Individualgeruchs durch den Hund, *Zeitschrift für Vergleichenede Physiologie,* 1935, **22**, 524-538.
55. Schneirla, T. C., Problems in the Biopsychology of Social Organizations, *J. Abnor. Soc. Psychol.,* 1946, **41**, 385-402.
56. Skinner, M. P., *The American Antelope in Yellowstone National Park.* Syracuse, New York: Roosevelt Wild Life Forest Experiment Station, 1924.
57. Smith, Bertram G., The Life History and Habits of *Cryptobranchus Alleghaniensis, Biol. Bull.,* 1907, **13**, 5-39.
58. Taber, Richard D., Observations on the Breeding Behavior of the Ring-necked Pheasant *(Phasianus torquatus), Condor,* 1949, **51**, 153-175.
59. Tinbergen, N., Social Releasors and the Experimental Method Required for their Study, *Wilson Bulletin,* 1948, **60**, 6-51.
60. ———— Wat prikkelt een Scholekster tot broeden?, *De Levende Natur,* 1948, **51**, 65-69.
61. ———— and Perdeck, A. C., On the Stimulus Situation Releasing the Begging Response in the Newly Hatched Herring Gull Chick, *(Larus a. argenatus* Pontopp.), *Behaviour,* 1950, **2**, (in press).
62. Weekes, H. C., A Review of Placentation Among Reptiles with Particular Regard to the Function and Evolution of the Placenta, *Proc. Zool. Soc. London,* 1935, II, 625-645.
63. Wheeler, William Morton, *Social Life Among the Insects.* New York: Harcourt, Brace and Company, 1923.

64. Wright, Sewall, Evolution in Mendelian Populations, *Genetics*, 1931, **16**, 97-159.

65. ———— Genetic Principles Governing the Rate of Progress of Livestock Breeding, *32nd Annual Proceedings of the American Society of Animal Production*, 1939, 18-26.

66. ———— Breeding Structure of Populations in Relation to Speciation, *Amer. Naturalist*, 1940, **74**, 232-248.

67. ———— Tempo and Mode in Evolution: a Critical Review, *Ecology*, 1945, **26**, 415-419.

CHAPTER 13

Social Behavior in Primates

HENRY W. NISSEN

Yale University and
Yerkes Laboratories
of Primate Biology

The longer I study man, the more interested I become in apes and monkeys, because human physique, temperament, and behavior are rooted in the lower primates.—*Earnest Hooton*

The monkeys, and even more obviously the great apes, are incomparably more like man socially than is any other existing creature.... Strategically important lines of sociobiological research, ... although impracticable for one reason or another with human subjects, are eminently feasible with chimpanzee, other anthropoid ape, or monkey.—*Robert M. Yerkes and Ada W. Yerkes*

A ccording to morphological criteria the order of primates includes man, along with the anthropoid apes, Old and New World monkeys, tarsiers, and lemurs. A psychologist, depending mainly on behavioral criteria, might have arranged things differently; he probably would have put man into a class or phylum all to himself. He might have decided, also, that some of the carnivores and cetaceans, perhaps even some of the birds, resembled man more closely, psychologically, than do the tarsiers and some of the lemurs. But we shall not here try to reform taxonomic classification. For obvious, practical reasons, however, this chapter will be restricted largely to the nonhuman primates. Our interests and approach, our interpretations, and even our terminology will be colored by knowledge of human society, but the factual discussion will center on the monkeys and apes.

Values, Aims, and Methods

Social stimuli and objects

What is social behavior, and how is it to be distinguished from asocial or nonsocial behavior? We usually designate as social those activities that are elicited by other members of the same species and that have some effect on other individuals. Behavior is an interaction; stimulus and response aspects imply each other, and both enter into the definition. We might, in like manner, speak of "visual" or "olfactory" behavior as being stimulated by, and directed toward, objects with visual or olfactory characteristics. There would then be partial overlap between social psychology and the psychology of vision, of motivation, of learning; some learning, some drives, and some visual activities are elicited by and are aimed at social objects, whereas others, involving the same sense organs and the same kind of central processes, have no social reference.

Occasionally the train of events is more devious. The initiating source of stimulation and the acted-upon object may be different. In social interactions particularly we sometimes find that the overt response is not directed at the object that provided the precipitating stimulus, but rather at some other feature of the environment. Among chimpanzees, for instance, the anger aroused by one cagemate may find its outlet in attack on a second cagemate, on the human observer, or even in self-mortification.

Social stimuli and objects have certain characteristics or properties that distinguish them in degree, if not in kind, from those of the inanimate world. What follows will make this statement more explicit.

1. The social environment is relatively more variable and unpredictable. Given a push, a stone moves, or does not move according to laws that are known.[1] The same push applied to a social object, on the other hand, may have consequences ranging from flight—a gross exaggeration of the reaction of the billiard ball—to a vicious attack. The effects of manipulating the social environment are less foreseeable; they change from time to time and with different partners.

2. Even when only two individuals are involved, determinants of the interaction are complex and often subtle. How each reacts to the other depends not only on what is done, but also on how it is done. The phrase, "it's not what you say, but how you say it," applies to the nonverbalized behavior of chimpanzees as well as to human interchanges. The whole past history of each participant, the "conditionings" that each has undergone, and the generalization or identification resulting from similarities between the present and past situations,

---

[1] Certainly the howling monkey "knows" the law of gravity, even though he cannot articulate it verbally or in a precise mathematical equation. "I would be sitting quietly observing the animals as they were in the trees above me. Either seen or unseen, an individual would slowly approach to a place directly above me or as near-by as possible, and then would release excrement, either urine or fecal matter or both. When the act was completed, the individual would usually quickly withdraw." (2, p. 27).

enter as critical factors. This is true also of fluctuating physiological conditions: current mood, attitude, and level of fatigue and irritability, as determined by immediately preceding circumstances; phase of the sex cycle; general state of health; and contextual background of concurrent social and physical stimulation. As the number of participants in the situation increases to three, four, five, or more, the complexity of the interrelated determinants becomes very great indeed.

3. It is clear that occurrence of certain behavior patterns is dependent on the social environment. Two of these, at least, subserve functions that are vital for preservation of the species: mating and care of the young. Others, perhaps equally indispensable for the individual and the species, include a variety of activities that may be labeled "mutual aid," for example cooperative problem solving, concerted defense or attack in respect to a common enemy, care of the sick, wounded, or aged, mutual grooming, and so on. Interindividual conflict, such as competition, rivalry, bluffing, and fighting, likewise presupposes the social environment.

4. Introspection, as well as observation of man and animals "from outside," reveals that social stimuli and objects are usually involved in emotion. We may be afraid of high places and loud noises, but most of our fears are of people and of what they may do; most of our words denoting strong feelings imply social factors: love, hate, anger, jealousy, envy, resentment, pity, and so on. When we study social behavior, therefore, we become intimately concerned with the emotions; when we investigate emotions, we find them primarily in a social setting.

5. The preceding point may be repeated, substituting "communication" for "emotion." The precise role of communication in the development of language and other forms of symbolism is abstruse in the extreme. But that there have been interactive relationships between the growth of communicative functions and of the symbolic processes that mediate thought, seems highly probable. In attempting to analyze and to trace the origins of human reasoning, therefore, we are again involved in a phylogenetic study of social behavior.

Although, as we have seen, social stimuli and objects have definite characteristics that distinguish them from those of the inanimate and vegetal environment, they retain all characteristics of the latter. Social psychology emphasizes what is peculiar to the social situation, but it is not necessarily an incomplete psychology. All aspects of behavioral adjustment—the cognitive as well as the motivational and emotional—appear in the social situation. Discrimination and generalization, reflexes and automatisms, learning, insight, and problem solving generally, are as much a part of interaction with other individuals as with forces and objects of the physical world.

Phylogenetic significance of primate social behavior

The study of social behavior in primates has unique importance for the field of comparative psychology, and especially for an understanding of the psychological status of man in the phylogenetic scale. In respect to behavior, a survey of the animal kingdom reveals differences mainly in degree (30). The later evolutionary stages show more (sometimes less) of the same *kind* of thing as may be seen in earlier stages. Thresholds become lower, more sensory inlets are provided, the ratio of individually acquired to innately determined behavior increases, the number of elements contributing to response-determination becomes larger, the speed of reaction and the role of learning may increase. Even comparisons of those major groupings called phyla, manifest only such quantitative differences. The underlying structures may vary radically and details of the movements may differ conspicuously, but the resultant behaviors are often quite similar. Nature has found many ways of skinning the cat.[2]

It may be that future research, with more refined methods of measurement and analysis, will reveal qualitative changes, behavioral "emergents" at various points along the phylogenetic scale. The evidence presently available, however, does not seriously challenge the view proposed above: that with one notable exception the phylogenetic course of behavioral development has been gradual; that it has been a continuous affair, proceeding by quantitative rather than qualitative changes. The one exception is that which marks the transition from the highest nonhuman primates to man (that is, "modern man"). At this point a new "dimension" or mode of development emerges: culture or "social heredity." The processes of phylogenetic and ontogenetic development are now supplemented by the transmission of cumulative individual experience. Evolution (cumulative mutation and selection) produces new patterns of inherited structures and capacities. Ontogeny (growth and experience), building on these innate potentialities, provides for individual development in which each new situation and response is integrated with and is a function of earlier events in the life history. Social heredity, building on both phylogeny and ontogeny, is mediated by

---

[2] This argument obviously hinges on the "level of description" employed. In gross teleological terms, all behavior may be subsumed under a few rubrics, whereas in terms of individual muscular contractions almost every bit of behavior is different from any other. We are here trying to maintain a middle position in which the terms used correspond to the units with which psychology typically deals.

communication as well as by material (buildings, roads, engines) and immaterial (knowledge of facts and methods) accretions; it provides each new generation with a changed—usually a richer and more complex—environment, with which members of the later generation may, can, and must interact.

It is in the interindividual relations among the higher primates, therefore, that we may expect to find either the *Anlagen* of, or the jumping-off point to, that realm or dimension of accelerated behavioral development that characterizes man.[3] Competition and cooperation, the longer life span and the greater period of relative helplessness, acquisition of directive communication and of symbolic tools of thought, are all involved in that transition (although which are causes and which are effects is not always clear). Insofar as an understanding of social behavior among the primates gives insight into the origins and nature of human relations, it offers the opportunity for more intelligent control of the direction in which this latest mode of development may lead us.

Human intelligence has been analyzed into a number of vectors or dimensions. We speak, for instance, of mechanical, verbal, and social intelligence. Most of our tests of animal intelligence are still quite crude and nonanalytical. There are no formal tests—and certainly none that would permit comparison with man—of social intelligence in primates. Nevertheless it is the impression of almost everyone who has worked with chimpanzees that their social intelligence is relatively closer to that of man than is their intelligence in the conventional problem-solving situation.[4] The bulk of the evidence supporting this impression consists in a long series of incidental observations ("anecdotes," but recorded by more or less trained and critical observers). It is certain that the social perceptiveness of these apes is very keen; they respond to very subtle shades of posture, gesture, movement, and vocalization. It might be suggested that a

---

[3] This is not to say that we may extrapolate from modern-day monkey or anthropoid societies, assuming that they give us a picture of primitive human social organization. The marked differences existing today between the social life of catarrhine and of platyrrhine monkeys should alone be enough to warn us against such rashness. Social organization is a pattern, the resultant of many simultaneously operative factors. The same set of elements may produce very different results by emphasis or intensification of some at the expense of others. When a new factor, such as language, is added, the picture may change unrecognizably.

[4] Perhaps it would be more accurate to say that whereas man's control over the physical world has advanced by leaps and bounds, human social intelligence is still at the anthropoid level.

high degree of social responsiveness—of attention to social stimuli— may be a prerequisite for those developments, listed above, which have led to the complex social organization characteristic of modern civilization.

Methods and materials

Behavior may be studied in the field or in the laboratory. Field studies are usually qualitative, and tell us *what* animals do in their native habitat, whereas controlled laboratory experiments are designed to show, quantitatively, what animals *can* do. These are rough distinctions, and there are many exceptions. C. R. Carpenter (4) made recordings of gibbon vocalizations in the field that certainly are quantitative. (Incidentally, it would not be surprising if gibbons *can* and do make some sounds in their Siam homeland that they never make in captivity.) Some behaviors, on the other hand, may be observed with the aid of laboratory apparatus that might escape detection in the field. Finally, we may not uncritically assume that the native habitat in which we now find a given species is ideally or optimally suited for it, or that the present environment is very similar to the one in which this animal form began and initially survived. Conditions of captivity are usually different from those of the native habitat, but that is not to say that they are less well suited to the species or even that they are necessarily more "artificial." Judging from physical appearance, reproductive and survival rates, it seems probable that chimpanzees are better adapted to ecological conditions prevailing at a laboratory in Florida than to some of the disease-ridden and hot areas of Africa where they were captured.

The literature on social relations among primates is surprisingly small in volume (37, 39, 46), and much of that is unreliable. Casual observations by travelers, explorers, collectors, traders, and missionaries, are one source of information. Some reports by zoo keepers and animal trainers, and by enthusiastic but scientifically naive amateur observers, are excellent, but many are biased and uncritically interpretative. The number of well-trained students of behavior who have studied primate groups in the field is very small. There have been only a few laboratory investigations having social behavior of monkeys and apes as the focus of interest, and the number of different primate species experimentally studied is much smaller still. Of all subhuman primate behavior, that of the chimpanzee is probably best known. There is almost no material on the orangutan and very little on the gorilla. Most of what we know about the gibbon comes from one excellent field study (4). Only a fraction of the many species of Old World and American monkeys is represented by adequate field or laboratory studies.

Social Structures

A social structure is in a sense the result or end product of individual interactions. It will be useful, nevertheless, to begin our discussion with a brief survey of groupings as they exist in the wild today. This information will indicate what it is that needs to be explained and will provide some basis for evaluating and interpreting social responses observed in the field and in the laboratory.

The lower primates

The least human-like of the primates are the lemurs. (One authority, indeed, excludes them from this order and classifies them with the insectivores.) The true lemurs, the indrises, and the aye-ayes are found in Madagascar, the galagos and pottos in Africa, the lorises in Southeastern Asia and Africa. Little is known of their social organizations in the wild; small family groups rather than large troops appear to be the rule. The aye-aye travels in pairs; bush babies (galagos) are found in family groups of from three to six. The avahis are solitary or in pairs, whereas the related sifakis are said to go about in groups of from six to eight. Some of the lemurs, together with the American marmoset, are the only primates that commonly bear more than one offspring at a birth. The relatively rare tarsiers of the East Indies apparently never form large groupings; they are found singly or in twos. Marmosets, most primitive (or most degenerated) of the New World monkeys, are said to be found in "small groups."

Monkeys

Social organization among the Old and New World monkeys often involves larger groupings. Where sex identification has been possible, a preponderance of females over males seems to be the rule. Carpenter (5) found macaques living in groups of two, three, and up to 150 individuals. In Thailand, a typical group of *Macaca asamensis* consisted of two adult males, six adult females, and four youngsters. In 1938, about 400 rhesus monkeys from India were released on a small island off the coast of Puerto Rico. Fifteen months later Carpenter (6) made a detailed survey of the surviving 350 (which number included some 110 infants born on the island). He found that most of them had organized themselves into five hetero-sexual groups ranging in size from 13 to 147 individuals, an average of about 70 animals per group. In addition, there were 12 sub-adult males that lived in unisexual groupings. Among the adults, there were six females to each male. The baboons of Africa are found in troops of from 25 to several hundred; one count of about 500 is recorded. These troops also comprise more adult females than adult males. Various species of langurs in Asia have been reported in "family parties of less than 30" and in "large hordes." There are some 80 species or races of guenons in Africa; some of these have been found in groups of a dozen or less, each led by an adult male. Colobus and proboscis monkeys are said to be organized in "small troops."

Exact group-counts of two New World monkeys have been made by Carpenter. On Barro Colorado Island (2) he found howler mon-keys in groups varying from 4 to 35 individuals and averaging about 17. Of the adults, 30 per cent were males and 70 per cent were females. Red spider monkeys of Central America assembled at night in groups comprising up to 40 individuals, but during the day these tended to split up into sub-groups of 3 to 17 animals (3). Among the spider monkeys, also, females were in the majority. Except for the sakis of Guiana and the Amazon valley, which are said to live in pairs, most other American monkeys apparently are organized in larger groups.

Anthropoid apes

In a total population of 93 gibbons, Carpenter (4) found 21 groups, comprising two to six animals. Adults were evenly divided as to sex. The typical family group thus consisted of an adult male, an adult female, and two youngsters. Little is known about the social struc-tures of the orangutan; the forests of Borneo and Sumatra are not favorable for observation in the field. It seems certain, however, that the orangutan does not live in any large groupings. It has been reported that several females and their young live together and are joined only at the mating season by the male who otherwise leads a solitary existence. Other reports have it that the orangs live in family groups like those of gibbons.

A field study (28) made in French Guinea indicates that chimpanzees in that part of Africa live in groups of from 4 to 14 animals, averaging 8.5. There were apparently more females (65 per cent) than males. (In this connection it may be reported that of 87 chimpanzee births at the Yerkes Laboratories from 1930 to 1950, males slightly outnumbered females.) In a few instances it was established that a group contained more than one adult male or more than one adult female; perhaps these were grown children that had not yet broken home ties to form their own families. Earlier reports from other parts of Africa are conflicting; some speak of much larger bands and there are repeated stories of solitary males.

Zuckerman (47) states that gorillas are found in "small bands" of from 4 to 50 individuals. The larger numbers perhaps represent temporary associations of smaller family groups. One field worker (cited by Hooton, 18) reports that the maximum number of nests found in close proximity was 14. Again there are reports of solitary males.

The Problem of Gregariousness

The fact that animals live in spatial proximity, rather than being randomly distributed over a fairly homogeneous environment, indicates the influence of cohesive factors that bring the individuals together. If the environment is not homogeneous, if some parts are more favorable than others, a concentration of animals in the former would be expected. Such an *extrinsic* factor is, no doubt, responsible for many of the aggregations among lower organisms. Its influence may be augmented by the fact that certain by-products of physical proximity—chemical or thermal conditions, for instance—result in a more favorable environment. Variations in climate, terrain, flora, and fauna are very probably responsible also for the geographical distribution of the various species of primates. They are only incidental, however, for "social organization" in the usual sense. Social behavior is largely a function of factors *intrinsic* to the individuals of the species, and it is with these that we shall be mainly concerned in the following.

Many observations attest to the need for companionship among chimpanzees. In his book, *The Mentality of Apes,* Köhler made the now-famous statement that "a chimpanzee kept in solitude is not a real chimpanzee at all." In saying this, Köhler evidently had two points in mind: (*a*) a large fraction of typical chimpanzee behavior is elicited only by stimulation emanating from other chimpanzees; and (*b*) the chimpanzee in solitude is lonesome and unhappy. Both of these points are doubtless correct, but one important qualification should be made explicit: Members of other species, and especially man, can substitute quite effectively (though not in all respects), both as sources of stimulation and as companions. Even the reflex-like, highly specific components of the copulatory pattern are occasionally elicited by presence of the human observer.

Fig. 1. Unrestrained Hilarity. Such mutually facilitated emotion is the product of thorough confidence, achieved only through prolonged acquaintance and interaction. Viki, here about three years old, has lived with the Hayes family since birth. See text. (Courtesy of Dr. and Mrs. Keith J. Hayes and the Yerkes Laboratories.)

The chimpanzee Fin was raised for the first two and one-half years of his life in the home of Dr. and Mrs. Glen Finch, and during this time had practically no contact with other members of his species (14). Fin could not give verbal reports about his feelings (and even if he could, of course had no basis of comparison). But in his behavior he gave every indication of being just as happy as his laboratory "cousins" living in groups of from two to six. He was unhappy when left alone and overjoyed at the return of his human companions. Reports of other chimpanzees living in a human social environment—Toto (20), Meshie (35, 36), Alpha (19), Gua (21), Joni (23), and most recently, Viki (16)—are very similar in this respect. When the Finches could no longer keep Fin at home, he was brought to the Laboratory and was caged with other chimpanzees of his age. For months he was an unhappy little fellow; he did not mix with the others and sat looking longingly at people who were visible on the grounds. His "in-group" consisted of people, not chimpanzees.[5]

Laboratory chimpanzees usually have contact with people and with other chimpanzees. Most of them tend to be rather friendly toward the people they know well, but occasionally they may resent something we do, or have a dislike for some particular person. A few animals appear essentially indifferent or neutral toward their human contacts—they can take them (especially if they are carrying a pan of food), or leave them. Still others seem to prefer people to chimpanzees; they are tractable and cooperative, manifest rather extreme friendliness towards human beings, and seem to feel quite dependent on us. Among the latter group are found most of the individuals who do not get along well with others of their kind, and also most of those who are either slow in becoming good breeding animals or who never mate at all. A strong "fixation" on man is correlated with inadequacies or abnormalities of intraspecies relationships.[6] There is, again, a positive relation between the extremes of friendliness to man and a history of prolonged exposure to human contacts and little opportunity for chimpanzee company.

In biology, however, and especially in respect to behavior, the rule is that every rule has exceptions. Moos, the most friendly, trusting, and cooperative animal we have ever had at these Laboratories, was captured in Africa at the estimated age of three years. He showed these characteristics from the very first day of capture. Moos got along well enough with his cage companions but died before reaching maturity. On the other hand, Bula, born in captivity, consistently

---

[5] It is interesting to speculate on whether other primates or even other orders of mammals would be as adequate as man in substituting for chimpanzee companions. There are several cases on record indicating that young chimpanzees, gorillas, and orangs have successfully provided each other with companionship. Dogs, cats, and other animals have served as companions-in-play. Great difference in size is perhaps incompatible with most social relationships other than the parental kind. Man, of course, has some marked advantages over animals in establishing extra-species relationships: he usually has better physical control over the situation, he can impose dependence on himself (for example, for food), and perhaps he has a better understanding of other species. (Some people, indeed, seem to understand their dogs better than they do their wives and neighbors.)

[6] Perhaps the reader should be reminded at this point that these observations are based on a population well under a hundred, so that caution must be observed in making generalizations.

has been our most misanthropic chimpanzee; several people have scars attesting to that fact. Bula has always been rather popular with other chimpanzees, shows normal mating behavior, and by the age of 19 years has given birth to six infants.

At the Yerkes Laboratories, approximately sixty chimpanzees live in roomy cages, one to four animals in a cage. In addition there are two large enclosures in each of which as many as six or more apes may live together. Usually animals of similar age and size are selected as cagemates. Combinations are chosen on the basis of compatibility, experimental requirements, and the breeding program. For various reasons certain individuals are never put together. There may be too much fighting and risk of bodily injury. Even without fighting, one of the partners may appropriate most of the food. Sometimes, although there is no obvious hostility, the animals do not "take to each other" and one or both may become depressed, lose their appetite, or become ill. It should be stressed, however, that such incompatibilities are the exception rather than the rule. Especially among individuals who have grown up together or have known each other for a long time, there is usually a considerable degree of friendliness. Nowlis' study (32) shows that there is a hierarchy of preferences, by each animal, for others in a group, and that this order remains constant over a period of time. With the possible exception of a young castrate (who was low in popularity), there was no indication that certain individuals were generally or consistently preferred or not preferred by others in the group. More recent work at the Yerkes Laboratories by E. F. Kinder, however, suggests that some animals regularly elicit more social interchanges from their partners than do others.

When two animals known to each other, but recently caged apart, are again brought together, there is usually much social interaction between them during the first hours or days. As the novelty wears off, the amount of interaction usually decreases, and this occurs more quickly and certainly in the case of adults than with youngsters. Boredom sets in; each animal goes his own way, or he may engage in repetitive actions such as grooming. There are occasions, however, when the opposite holds true; the partners find each other increasingly stimulating; they may invent more games and other ways of amusing each other; or irritation may gradually mount until there is overt conflict.

Extreme instances of friendship are quite impressive. Wendy and Josie, two adult females, who did not become acquainted until they were adults, got along well and so were often caged together. Over the years a strong friendship and dependence grew up between them. They groomed each other a great deal, and play-wrestled and tickled each other (which is common among young animals, much rarer among adults). When one got into a vocal-gestural dispute with an animal in the adjacent cage, the other one invariably took sides with her friend. They never competed for food. When Josie was ill and was given medicine daily, in two cups of grape juice, Wendy also wanted some. So Josie swallowed the first cupful, but the second one she held in her mouth and then "poured" it from her lips into Wendy's mouth. When it became necessary to separate these two animals, each became restless and apparently unhappy. Providing an acceptable substitute companion helped some, but even then Wendy became nervous and tense; she picked at her anus until it bled profusely, lost her appetite and became generally irritable.[7]

The foregoing discussion indicates the critical importance of gregariousness as a determinant of primate behavior. The need for social interaction is evidently one of the more powerful motivating forces among chimpanzees and probably among other apes and most monkeys as well. But whether gregariousness is a primary, innately-determined drive, or whether it is secondarily derived from the asso-

---

[7] The reader who is acquainted with Hebb's *Organization of Behavior* (17) will recognize how well much of the behavior described in this section fits the psychoneurological mechanisms hypothecated in that volume. The stranger, having enough in common with known animals (or humans) to activate an organized perception or phase sequence that yet is at variance with the familiar pattern in some details, produces excitement. According to past and present circumstances this excitement may express itself in flight (fear), aggression (anger), disorganized activity or "freezing" (panic), or in exploration (curiosity). In general, the social situation provokes interest and activity—more in the young than in the old—because when two or more animals are together there is a constantly shifting pattern of stimulation and so enough novelty "feeding" into the cortex to keep the established phase sequences "alive." Older animals, in general less active in the unchanging physical environment and very thoroughly used to each other, get less "new" stimulation, become bored and less active. But obviously this is not the whole story. New caretakers, new staff members, new animal neighbors, do appear from time to time. Sex interest waxes and wanes in relation to physiological rhythms. There is probably, a recurrent impulse to muscular activity, and this must express itself in behavior that may stimulate other animals. Finally, the continuing, active friendships, such as that of Wendy and Josie, plus the fact that young as well as older individuals deprived of all social contacts become listless, depressed, and even ill, suggests an innate organization that demands the sensory patterns provided by living primates.

ciation of social stimuli with the satisfaction of nutritional, sexual, and other primary needs, remains a problem for future research.[8] The helplessness of the primate infant has thus far discouraged attempts to raise an individual in a completely nonsocial situation that would avoid opportunities for the relevant associations to be formed.

Cohesive Aspects of Social Behavior

Other than providing companionship, what do individuals of a group do for each other? What rewards and satisfactions derive from the social environment; how does it contribute to the attainment of individual goals, the reduction of individual needs? And finally, how does social organization contribute to survival of the individual and of the species?

Care of the young

All primates are quite helpless at birth and perpetuation of the species requires a considerable amount of care by older animals. In subhuman societies most of this burden is assumed by the mother, who provides nourishment, warmth, protection from physical injury, transportation, and probably a certain amount of education. As we shall see, some of these duties may be shared, especially as the infant grows into childhood, by other members of the group.

Dependence of the young is of course not an exclusive characteristic of the primates. It is found to some degree in all mammals, in most birds, in many of the lower vertebrate classes, and among some invertebrates. In general, the duration of dependency increases, in absolute amount and in relation to life span, at the later phylogenetic levels. In man, at least 15 years—a good fifth of the life span—are devoted to attainment of adult capacities. For the great apes these values are probably similar; for monkeys they are lower. (Information on length of life span and ontogenetic development is too incomplete to permit of a more definite statement.)[9]

---

8 Practically, the question is of little importance since the effect is the same whatever its cause, but theoretically it has very considerable interest.

9 Lashley and Watson (24) observed the development of a rhesus monkey born in captivity. In respect to sensory-motor development they remark that "by the 10th week the young monkey had become mature in all but the sexual activities. He was lacking chiefly in muscular control." See also Foley (15).

The captive chimpanzee mother gives birth to her infant about 228 days after conception. Parturition itself usually appears to occur easily and without prolonged discomfort. Initial reactions to the infant vary widely. Most captive mothers show an immediate, intense solicitude for the young and great skill in caring for it. There is an occasional female, however, who shows only mild interest and little aptitude for maternal duties. There have been a few primipara who have been terrified at seeing this new, wriggling, squalling object, and have run away from it. If the infant is taken away soon after birth, the mother gives few or no signs of missing it. But if the separation occurs some weeks or months later, the female often expresses her distress for many days following.

For the first six months of life mother's milk is the infant's sole source of nourishment. During this time mother and infant are never separated; usually the infant clings with hands and feet to the hair or skin-folds of the mother's ventral trunk. Nursing at the breast occurs at frequent intervals. Occasionally the mother may hold the infant away from herself, suspended by one or two hands or feet. Gradually the youngster is allowed to supplement its diet with available items of food. Suckling, however, continues well into the second year of life and may persist to the end of the second year. Gradually, also, the youngster wanders away from the mother, more often and for greater distances. At the slightest sign of danger, however, it scampers back to mother, sometimes after she gives a sharp, low vocalization.

In the wild, the chimpanzee father, or at any rate an adult male of the group, contributes to the care of the young. When a high tree is to be climbed, or a long branch-to-branch jump has to be made, he may temporarily take over the problem of transporting the youngster. Adults, and especially juveniles of the group, participate in playing with the baby, bringing twigs within its grasping reach, and, at a later age, playing mild games of tag or wrestling. In captivity, an adult male and female have been caged together during the gestational period and for months after birth of a male infant. Even under these artificial conditions all was peaceful; the female behaved rather protectively towards her baby, but the male made no attempt to injure it (42).

Among the Old World monkeys, baboons and macaques in particular, the situation appears to be a less happy one. The males are aggressively dominant over females, and in the course of sexual relations this overt aggressiveness often results in bodily injury to the female and to the infant which may be with her at the time. Zuckerman paints a dismal picture indeed of social relations among captive baboons in the London zoo. One gets the impression of strong, sex-obsessed males ruthlessly attacking females and young in bloody slaughter. Zuckerman states that "the pattern of socio-sexual adjustments in captive colonies is identical with that observed among wild animals" (47, p. 216). He believes that these adjustments in the zoo "are determined by the mutual responses of the animals, and not by environmental influences" (p. 217). The view that the "pattern" is similar receives support from the repeated observation of male dominance and aggressiveness in these animals, which has led Hooton to name them the "totalitarian monkeys of the Old World." But there is still room for questioning whether the intensity, the degree of this behavior, and the frequency of its fatal consequences may not be exaggerated by the conditions of captivity. Regarding his own field studies, Zuckerman remarks that "the extent to which fighting occurs is unknown" (p. 198).

Sex behavior

Chimpanzees raised in captivity, separated by sexes during adolescence, and having had no opportunity for close-range observation of mating behavior by other animals, do not copulate when first given the opportunity. Left together for a few months, they will eventually do so. The possible importance of imitation and tuition in facilitating the behavior, is not known. Perhaps it is largely a matter of statistical probability—a chance concatenation of component postures and movements by the two animals. That there is at least an innate "readiness" for certain, specific action-patterning is suggested by the fact that, once the behavior has been established, it is quite uniform for all members of the species, particularly so for the females. Furthermore, there is on record one observation of immediate, complete, species-specific copulatory behavior by a female chimpanzee the first time she was caged with an adult male. In this case, the male was experienced, and exhibited the typical male "invitational" posture and gestures..

There is considerable interindividual variability in the intensity and expression of the sex drive. Some males are rather fussy about their sex partners, preferring some females to others, and copulating only during the period of maximal tumescence.[10] Others copulate promptly with any female in swelling. A detumescent female may "present" in response to threat of attack (by a male or by another female) but this rarely eventuates in actual mounting or penetration. Penetration of a female not in swelling is physically difficult and probably not satisfying to either the male or the female. (Occasionally a male will punish his partner for refusal or delay in presenting, but, equally infrequently, the male may attack, rather than mate with, a female in estrus who has presented.) Females also vary considerably in intensity of the sex drive. Some definitely solicit the male until he is sexually exhausted, whereas others respond, apparently with reluctance, after repeated and insistent demands of the male. The chimpanzee male may bully the female into acceptance and cooperation, but rape, in the sense of direct physical coercion, is probably impossible.

In captivity aberrations of sex behavior are fairly common. Masturbation, in both males and females, is frequent when the "normal" sex object is absent, rare when congenial mates are caged together. At moments of danger or other excitement, chimpanzees of any age and regardless of sex, rush towards each other and often embrace in a ventro-dorsal position resembling that of copulation. There may even be some pelvic thrusts by the one in the "male position." To designate this unqualifiedly as sex behavior does not seem justified. At feeding time, erection and rubbing against any convenient object is almost invariable among males of all ages. To call this "sexual" is unwarranted. It would be equally justifiable to interpret all instances of mouth-opening as eating or drinking, and any manipulation of sticks as nest-building. The anticipation of food often precipitates copulation when a male and a female in estrus are caged together. Tinklepaugh (38) has interpreted such phenomena as the "overflow" of emotional excitement into motor outlets that already have a low threshold.

Sex plays a relatively more conspicuous role in the social life of the Old World monkeys than in the case of the apes and some of the American monkeys. Even more prominent is the male dominance and overt aggressiveness that accompanies sexuality in the catarrhine

---

[10] The sexual cycle of the female chimpanzee is clearly marked, externally, by a period of swelling, followed by detumescence, of the perineal region. The animal is sexually receptive during the tumescent phase; menstruation occurs at about the middle of the detumescent phase. The complete cycle recurs at intervals of approximately 35 days.

monkeys. Whether these variations should be ascribed to differences in absolute or relative strength of the sex drive, in amount of "sublimation," in the interplay of sexual and other motivations, or in intelligence, are at present matters of speculation.

Grooming

More than any other spatially and temporally organized series of movements to be seen in chimpanzees, "grooming" conforms to the usual conception of an instinct—an innately-determined pattern of response. Bright, shiny objects often evoke it the first time. (Self-

Fig. 2. Social Grooming. Wendy submits with pleasure to the ministrations of her friend, Josie. Both are adult female chimpanzees. See text, pages 435 and 441. (From Yerkes (45); photograph by R. K. Helmle.)

grooming usually comes later than grooming of objects and of other animals.) The motor pattern, including close, intense visual regard, coordinated movements of an extended finger, and lip-smacking, may be complete on first appearance, and before there has been opportunity for tuition by, or imitation of, older animals. Frequency of the behavior, the most effective stimuli, relative prominence of the several components, and details of the movements involved vary among individuals, but essentials of the pattern are universally present. Self-grooming and grooming of other chimpanzees are the main forms in older animals. Mutual grooming is always a sign of friendly relations. No other activity commands a like degree of long-continued, concentrated attention. Especially in relation to man, some chimpanzees definitely prefer to do the grooming, whereas others prefer the passive role of being groomed. A clinical psychologist might find this a good projective test of personality types.

The biological utility of the behavior is obvious: it keeps the animals clear of ectoparasites (fleas, ticks, lice), and is really the only way chimpanzees have of cleaning their skin. Often, however, grooming continues long beyond the demands of such practical ends; perhaps it is a cause-and-effect link in a chain of social interaction analogous to social games and small talk. Yerkes (41) has suggested that grooming may be the phylogenetic forerunner of various human social services, such as barbering, nursing, and surgery. Social grooming is found among many or most primate species. It has been observed in gorillas, gibbons, spider monkeys, macaques, baboons, and several of the lemuroids.

Play; communication

Playful activity is characteristic of young animals. In general, the amount of time and energy devoted to play is greater in species having a relatively long period of infancy and childhood than in those (for example, the insects) whose ultimate capacities are present soon after birth takes place. As would be expected from this relation, the apes exceed all other animals except man in the variety and extent of their play behavior. Descriptive accounts have been provided by a number of authors (for example, 22, 29, 45). Some forms of play have no social reference: acrobatics, digging holes in the ground, and looking at objects through a perforation in a leaf, may involve only the individual and his physical environment. But even these activities seem often to be facilitated by a social milieu. Among primates—and probably most of all in man—play increasingly involves interaction between two or more individuals, as in games of tag, wrestling, sex-play, and so on. It has been pointed out (30) that play behavior gives opportunity not only for muscular exercise and for increasing motor skills, but also for acquiring knowledge of the world through perceptual development. It may be that exploratory and playful activities, like perception, are largely functions of what Woodworth (40) has termed "a direct, inherent motive which might be called the will to perceive."

There is, so far, no good evidence that any of the living, nonhuman primates have spontaneously developed modes or systems of communication that are superior to those found among some of the lower mammals and birds. Most of the monkeys and apes vocalize a good deal, and the sounds evoked by each of a number of situations are differentiable; other individuals apparently understand them and respond appropriately. For example, the "alarm cry" alerts them to danger, and the "food bark" elicits the same reactions anticipatory to eating as does the sight of food. But, in general, the vocalizations themselves appear to have no specifying or directive function; they merely express an emotion or attitude of the animal making them. Recent observations by Dr. and Mrs. K. Hayes indicate that it is most difficult for the chimpanzee to bring his vocal sounds under voluntary control and to use them in a purposeful manner. Usually the particular movements or actions required are indicated (if at all) by other aspects of the situation, including, sometimes, postures and gestures of the vocalizing individual. [See, for instance (29), page 552.]

Facilitation, imitation, teamwork

In human society, the concepts of cooperation, division of labor, and teamwork imply a deliberate, intentional, and planned working together, usually for the direct or indirect good of all participants. There seems to be very little of this sort of thing among the subhuman primates. At any rate, most known instances of joint action by several individuals may be nothing more than a simultaneity of individual actions set off by the same stimulus. That would be the most economical explanation, for instance, of mass attack on an enemy. Literature on the subject contains many anecdotal accounts of two or several monkeys or apes contriving a cunning attack, one perhaps acting as decoy while another makes a surprise rush from behind. As a matter of fact, there are more (and better) anecdotes of this sort about dogs, foxes, and other animals than about primates. The simians are opportunists, no doubt, and as one engages the enemy's attention from the north another will attack from the south. The effect is the same as that of planned teamwork, but psychologically the cooperation may be an "accident."

Social facilitation may appear when the males of a monkey band are defending or expanding territorial boundaries. What one animal alone will not venture, a number will dare to undertake. The response-tendencies of the individual are reinforced by presence of other members of the group; they give each other "moral support." In dealing with captive chimpanzees, it is a great deal safer for the human observer to enter a cage with one animal than with two or more. Not so much because two apes can do more damage than one, but because the probability of attack is so much greater. If one of the animals becomes frightened or angry, it gives a particular cry that acts like a trigger to bring about an immediate attack by the entire group. Although social facilitation does not meet the usual criteria of "teamwork," it may well be a prerequisite for the development of genuine cooperation.

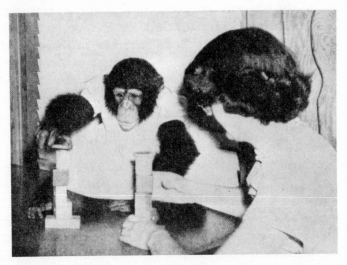

Fig. 3. Viki Makes a Copy of a Tower, Using the Same Sequence of Blocks as Appears in the Model. This three-year-old, home-reared chimpanzee has had much practice in imitating human activities. See text page 444. (Courtesy of Dr. and Mrs. Keith J. Hayes and the Yerkes Laboratories.)

Comparative psychologists of the post-Darwinian period were much concerned with the problem of imitation. In more recent literature, however, one finds little mention of it. Like "instinct," the term is considered by many a bit disreputable, or at least out of fashion. One reason for this state of affairs may be that psychologists have thought of imitation as a single process or mechanism, whereas actually there may be many degrees or kinds of imitation, not all conforming to the same criteria. Aping of "motor acts"—operating a water faucet, spitting, using keys, scribbling with pencil on paper, looking where others are looking, and so on—is very frequently seen in monkeys and apes. On the other hand, it is extremely difficult or impossible for a chimpanzee to learn, purely by observation of another animal, that response to triangle is correct, response to square incorrect (12). Imitating hand-clapping is easy; imitating certain human vocal sounds (which are within the capacity of the animal) is very difficult (16). Imitation is obviously of critical importance in human learning; its limitations and potentialities in anthropoid behavior remain to be explored.

In a laboratory experiment, Crawford (8) first trained young chimpanzees individually to pull in a weighted box, by means of an attached rope, in order to obtain the food reward on the box. Then the weight of the box was increased (so that one animal could not move it); next, two ropes were attached, the box was baited with two portions of reward, and two animals were put in the cage. At first each chimpanzee pulled without any reference to his partner's actions; only by chance did the two pull at the same time and so move the box. It was necessary for the experimenter to give a signal, which the partners had individually associated with initiating the pull, to get them to pull together. Once the temporal coordination of effort had been established in this way, the extraneous signal could be omitted. One of the partners, *A*, usually watched the other one, *B*, and was ready to add her pull as soon as *B* started heaving on the rope. Sometimes it was arranged that *B* was satiated when the experiment began; *A* would then urge and direct *B* to pull. Eventually *B* would pull, although she had no desire for the food reward. Under these circumstances *A* often reaped the entire material benefits of the teamwork.

In a later experiment by Crawford (10) one animal was trained to push against four colored plaques, arranged around the sides of a cage, in a certain order. The cage was then divided into two sections by a partition of bars; the colors to be pushed first and third were on one side, the colors to be pushed second and fourth were in the other part of the cage. The trained animal was then put on one side, and her partner, who knew the mechanics of pushing the plaques but not the correct order, was put on the other side of the partition. The trained animal *X* watched her partner's actions and pushed the color available to her after *Y* had pushed the color preceding it in the sequence; *X* sometimes solicited her partner, using begging gestures (see below) that were spatially directed toward the particular color on her partner's side that was the next one in order.

Reciprocity and "prostitution"

The results of the cooperative weight-pulling experiment, described above, bring up the question of how animal B benefited, when it neither wanted nor got any of the food reward. Conceivably it was returning past favors by A, or was anticipating favors in the future. It seems more probable, however, that B's contribution was in part a well-ingrained habit, and in part a means of putting a stop to A's solicitation. The human observer gets the impression that solicitation or begging is both unpleasant and a very compelling stimulus for the second animal. Such compulsiveness appears also in a food-sharing experiment (31). Two friendly chimpanzees are caged next to each other, with only bars separating them. When a quantity of food is given to one of them, the other individual may get as much as half of it. The "rich" animal may just hand over some of his store, or may move it near the bars where his "poor" friend can reach it. Or, the poor animal may beg, using rapid flexions of the upturned hand and vocalizing in an unhappy manner. Often it appears that the rich animal cannot tolerate this; reluctantly or even with some show of irritation or anger, he hands over some of the food, or throws it violently at the beggar.

Evidence has been cited (28) indicating that a sick or injured chimpanzee, unable to climb a fruit-bearing tree, is fed by others of the group who toss fruit down to it. Just what, if anything, the sick animal may have done (earlier or later) in reciprocation is, of course, not known. The concept of reciprocity, operationally defined, may be applicable also to social grooming, and to some features of the mother-child relationship.

Among chimpanzees and some of the Old World monkeys "presentation" is a frequent response to attack or threat of attack. The presenting animal turns its back and crouches down low, almost prone. In this position it may glance over its shoulder, give a short high-pitched scream, and move backwards, towards the other animal. The picture is one of complete and abject submission. Sometimes this behavior pattern occurs not as a response to attack but as an obvious "bid" for food. The subordinate (usually the smaller) animal is afraid to take its share of the food, or wants some that is already in possession of the dominant partner. When the attacking or dominant individual is a male, the presenting animal a female, this behavior has been interpreted as prostitution: the female offers sexual favors in return for exemption from attack or for food. But, although the attack may have been successfully avoided, or the food may have been obtained by the subordinate animal, frequently copulation does not follow. Furthermore, this sort of interaction may occur between two females, two young males, or when a larger female attacks a smaller male. It may be argued that these latter instances represent a generalization from sexual prostitution. Especially since the pattern is seen in very young individuals, however, it is more plausible to assume that presentation is a primary response with a largely innate basis of organization. Attack is presumably the unlearned stimulus. Young chimpanzees, incidentally, often exhibit the pattern toward the human aggressor. Occurrence of the behavior in a competitive food situation may involve a learned anticipation of aggression.

Disruptive Aspects of Social Behavior

Within a wide range of variability, some interindividual conflict is universal in animal and human societies. The interests of one individual, or of one group, are incompatible with those of another. In the present section we shall consider social interactions to which are applied terms such as rivalry, competition, precedence, prestige, dominance, submission, jealousy, teasing, bluffing, and fighting.

Response to frustration

Finch (13) has classified chimpanzee responses to frustration as follows: (a) aggression—actual or threatened attack on the human observer, on objects in the cage, or on other animals in the same or adjacent cage; also self-aggression—clawing at the face and ventral trunk or banging the head against the wall; (b) withdrawal from the situation; (c) satisfying other drives, seeking other objects; and (d) emotional activity—temper tantrums and screaming. Finch points out that "Age is a factor.... Characteristically young chimpanzees tend to show a relatively much higher incidence and much more violent kind of response." (p. 250.)

Food, sex, and dominance

Competition for food and females is a conspicuous feature of many primate societies. The general rule is that the bigger animal gets most of the food, the stronger male most of the females. Scarcity of either increases the intensity of the competitive struggle, other things being equal. For Old World monkeys, Hooton describes the situation thus: "In these baboon and macaque societies dominant individuals are ruthless in their cruelty and apparently devoid of any of the tenderer emotions and of the least semblance of altruism. There is such utter selfishness that the animal which has the ascendency will nearly starve to death subordinate animals, even when the overlord has stuffed himself to utter repletion." [(18), p. 325.] The gibbons, on the other hand, and the American monkeys that Carpenter observed in the field, rarely have violent disagreements about food. As far as we know, food competition is the exception among wild gorillas and chimpanzees, also.

In a colony of captive chimpanzees, equitable division of the food supply among two or more individuals caged together becomes a problem under certain conditions. Some individuals do not like certain other animals; when such unfriendly pairs are caged together, and especially if there is a marked disparity in size, the larger one may get most of the food. If cagemates are strangers to each other, they are almost sure to dispute about food—unless one is clearly afraid of the other, in which case the latter gets it all, without argument. Occasionally one animal eats much more slowly than the others; if it has a large amount left over when the others have finished their shares, they may try to take some of the remaining supply. If the food is merely thrown into the cage (instead of a portion being handed to each animal) each will scramble for the largest share; the distribution is then usually in proportion to the agility and quickness of the individuals.

Maslow and Flanzbaum (27) devised a simple but accurate technique for testing relative dominance of two or more animals. A limited supply of food (usually one piece at a time) was made available and a record kept of the number of pieces obtained by each animal. In a variety of primate types, these scores were found to be related to a number of other measures of dominance: sexuality, leadership, and activity. The results led Maslow to the hypothesis that sexual behavior "may roughly be divided into two types, that motivated mainly by the sexual drive, and that motivated mainly by the dominance drive." The "dominance drive" is thus conceived of as an independent, primary source of motivation, which "may be used as a power weapon" [(25), p. 336]. It is presumably the approximate equivalent of what other writers have called the "self-regard-ing," the "mastery," or the "ego-motive."

In a later paper, Maslow theorized that three types of primate social organization, exemplified by catarrhine monkeys, platyrrhine monkeys, and chimpanzees, respectively, are correlated with the "quality or type of dominance" shown in these three groups. "Catar-rhine dominance is rough, brutal and aggressive" [(26), p. 316]. The platyrrhines "are generally low in expression" and "use vocaliza-tions as an expression of dominance" (p. 317); furthermore they "rarely show anything that may be called friendship, or protection or dependence on each other, but neither do they bother each other very much." [11] Chimpanzees, he suggests, have a more closely knit organization, and manifest more social interdependence and inter-action; dominance relations are present but are "mostly of a friendly kind." These interpretations are, of course, quite speculative, and introducing the concept of "friendly dominance" really begs the main question. However, the distinctions as summarized above are generally consistent with the available evidence and probably indi-cate basic differences in social organization within the order of primates.

The one-piece-of-food-at-a-time dominance test has been employed extensively with chimpanzees by Yerkes (43, 44), Crawford (9, 11), and Nowlis (33, 34). Since the two animals show considerable "in-ertia" in respect to the positions that they assume on the very first trial—that is, the individual who obtains the first piece stays by the food chute, while the other one remains at a distance—Nowlis intro-duced two modifications of technique: (a) successive trials of a series are separated by a considerable interval of time, or (b) position at the chute is systematically alternated by intervention of the experi-menter. These procedures tend to make successive trials independent of each other and to give scores that reflect more accurately quanti-tative gradations of dominance (instead of all-or-none scores).

The distribution of food between two animals of a pair was little affected by merely making the subordinate member more hungry, but it was changed significantly, in favor of the subordinate, when the

---

[11] This account probably exaggerates the *laissez-faire* attitude of platyrrhine monkeys. In his account of red spider monkeys in Panama, Carpenter [(3), p. 180] says: "Several specimens have been collected that show large scars on the hands, shoulders and head; some had their ears torn." This author thinks it is possible that "the seriousness of the fight helps to determine the short duration of encounters and the infrequency of their occurrence."

latter was starved and the dominant one was satiated before the tests. Nowlis interprets this result as reflecting the "punishment-value" of the partners for each other; that is, satiation of the dominant animal reduced the likelihood of his punishing his partner for taking the food. The results also suggest that the dominant chimpanzee takes most of the food because he wants it and can enforce his wants, not merely in order to demonstrate his prestige and to show who is boss.

A number of studies with chimpanzees show the relation between food dominance and sex hormones. The proportion of food obtained by the female, paired with a male, is significantly higher during her period of estrus than when she is detumescent. Partly on the basis of qualitative aspects of the behavior, Yerkes speaks of the male as "granting privilege" to the female when she is in condition to grant him sexual favors. Roughly the same shift in food distribution during the sex cycle of a normal female occurs when the partner is a castrated female, rather than a male. Food dominance of the castrate females was raised by administration of alpha estradiol (the female hormone), which induces tumescence of the sex skin, and also by giving the male hormone, methyl testosterone, which does not cause tumescence (1). In a male castrate chimpanzee the index of dominance was raised by testosterone, and was lowered by estradiol (7).

Fighting and bluffing

The expression of feelings and attitudes differs enormously in various human cultures, and even in different "classes" of the same culture. In some, it is direct, uninhibited, and demonstrative; in others it is restrained and indirect. The differences are especially conspicuous in respect to antagonisms, which may express themselves in immediate, physical assault, in a verbal lashing, or in delayed and devious ways. The subhuman primates in general favor a prompt and direct outlet. Once an attitude has been established, however, it may persist over a long time, and express itself whenever opportunity offers.

As we have seen, among Old World monkeys antagonism usually shows itself in a vicious physical attack on the smaller, subordinate individual. Among the New World monkeys, on the other hand, the antagonists often give vent to their feelings in vocalizations. The one who howls the loudest wins. It is the chimpanzee which most closely approximates the variety and subtlety of human emotional expression, and it is to this primate that we shall devote most of the following discussion.

If the provocation reaches a threshold value, the chimpanzee's response is lightning-fast, intense, and usually brief. In a few seconds he inflicts heavy damage, almost always with his teeth. In other circumstances he may flee, or practically "freeze" in immobility. Occasionally these forms of expression alternate in quick succession. Ordinarily the flare-up burns itself out quickly. The overt signs of fear or anger (by the loser) persist much longer, as a rule, than does the aggression of the winning animal. We might say that the latter has had closure, the former has unfinished business that continues to rankle. If the injury has been inflicted on an individual (man or chimpanzee) with whom the animal has in general friendly relations, the attack may be followed very shortly by most amicable behavior; almost immediately the animals may start grooming each other.

Even between animals that hold chronic grudges against each other (and there are such), fighting is intermittent rather than continuous. They stay apart, leave each other alone most of the time, until some minor incident triggers the antagonism and a violent fight ensues. There is an armed truce during the long intervals between fighting.

In a laboratory situation, man has certain advantages over chimpanzee. With partitions and doors, water hoses and blank cartridges, regulation of food and water supply, he has considerable physical control. Some of these controls, and the uses to which they are put, the chimpanzee accepts (in the sense of apparently not resenting them); others provoke violent and sometimes persistent antagonism. The acceptance is often as difficult for us to understand as the resentment. Taking a newborn infant away from its mother is more often followed by increased friendliness on the part of the female than by the opposite. If antagonism is somehow established, the chimpanzee may show it by sulking and negativism or by repeated efforts at retaliation—biting, scratching, throwing feces, spitting regurgitated material, and so on.

The chimpanzee is a great bluffer, and often bluffing is a substitute for fighting. A corollary of this, of course, is that chimpanzees themselves are susceptible to threat and a show of aggressiveness. The adult male may intimidate his fellows by swaggering and stomping or, most impressively, by a violent sort of dance in upright position.

This dance is initiated by a crescendo of deafening vocalization, and is accompanied by hand-clapping and by pounding, with hands and feet, on any animate or inanimate object that happens to be handy.[12] (In Africa, hollow logs and tree buttresses are favorite forms of drum.) The chimpanzee's auditory threshold is similar to ours, but unless given a special "set" for attending to sounds, he does not ordinarily make much use of auditory cues of moderate intensity. Nevertheless, he is easily and greatly frightened by loud noises. As a substitute for fighting and means of indicating dominance, milder and less dramatic forms of display are more frequent; often a posture or slight gesture, and perhaps a low grunt, suffices.

In captivity, at least, the rather awe-inspiring dance just described sometimes appears to be a form of exhibitionism. At any rate, it is often performed when human visitors, effectively protected by a wire partition and probably not mistaken for sex rivals, are present. Tricks and acrobatic feats, such as forward and backward somersaults, pirouettes, tumbling, and so on, are also exhibited when there is an audience. As visitors approach, one chimpanzee runs to the water faucet, fills his mouth, and then spits a pint or so at the strangers with deadly accuracy. Is all this just a matter of intense stimulation that sets off the available repertoire of movements? Or do the animals like to show off, to be admired, to enhance their ego-feeling by getting back at people and exercising the few ways they have of controlling the environment? Perhaps there is pleasure in seeing people jump and run, in hearing them laugh or scream.

Territoriality

Up to this point we have confined ourselves largely to consideration of interindividual relations. In the study of human society, social psychologists and especially sociologists are often more interested in a different level of interaction, namely in the relations of various intraspecies *groups*. They may be concerned with the interrelations of large groupings classified according to economic, political, racial, national, religious, geographic, or educational distinctions; or of in-groups and out-groups, minorities and majorities. Such a multiplicity of large, interlocking, and overlapping groups is possible only at the human level. In the territoriality of many monkey species as well as of various phylogenetically-earlier animal forms, we have a

---

[12] Younger animals, and females, also exhibit such behavior, but usually in milder and abbreviated form.

simple analogue of this phenomenon. A large band or horde establishes itself within a certain region, ordinarily confining its activities
to that area and stoutly defending the boundaries against encroach-
ment by neighboring bands of the same species. As the size of one
horde grows, or its food supply diminishes, it may seek to expand its
Lebensraum and may come into conflict with adjacent groups. Such
disputes, however, are more in the nature of border incidents than
of total war.

What determines whether individual *a* shall be a member of group
A and not of *B*? It is probably not a matter of differing ideologies,
nor of economic or educational status. Perhaps the accident of being
born into a group, plus the apparently deep-seated and almost universal preference for the familiar over the nonfamiliar, is a major
factor. The individuals of group *A* are "accustomed to" each other
and are strangers to the members of *B*. The inbreeding that would
thus ensue would gradually produce minor physical and behavioral
distinctions between members of the two groups that in turn would
heighten or intensify the influence of strangeness.

Determinants of Social Organization

Sex and dominance

In summarizing his careful and detailed account of infra-human
social relations, Hooton [(18), p. 324] says: "The most important
aspects of the social behavior of primates are included under the
categories of sexual relations and dominance. Topics of subsidiary
interest are altruism and food-sharing, play activities, parent-young
relations, group co-ordination, and 'territoriality.' The subject of
individuality or personality is perhaps more important than any of
the others except sex and dominance."

This is an evaluative judgment pertaining to the *description* of
behavior. Zuckerman [(47), p. 3] goes a step further by reducing the
behavior to an underlying physiological process: "Reproductive
physiology is the fundamental mechanism of society. Individual
responses within a group are both limited by it and adapted to it,
so that the most profitable classification of the societies of mammals
involves the classification of their sexual mechanisms."

Hormones are essential determinants of reproductive behavior, but
obviously they are not the only determinants. What effect a given

hormone has depends very much on the sex and species characteristics of the nervous system that it affects, as well as on the sensory
and motor equipment of the individual. Quite aside from such
quibbling, the question may be raised whether these authorities—
and many others who would agree with them—are essentially correct
in their conviction that sex (or reproductive processes in general) is
the factor in subhuman primate organization.

A definite answer to this question is as impossible as a final affirma-
tion or denial of the Freudian contention that "sex" is *the* motivation
in human affairs. The unrestrained sexuality and ferocious aggressiveness of the catarrhine male are indeed spectacular, but that is
not necessarily an accurate gauge of their relative importance. That
the relations between mates and between mother and young are of
far-reaching social significance, among apes as well as monkeys, is
beyond argument. But that is not to say that all or most other
social interactions are derived from the sexual and maternal. Nor
does it deny that, among some primate species, there may be other
motives (perhaps something like "gregariousness" or "companionship-
need") that are independently effective in maintaining some form
of social organization. These problems are amenable to experimental
investigation, but so far the necessary experiments have not been
done.

Significant variables

The effective variables in social interactions may be typed or classified in different ways, and some of these we have already touched
upon. The physical environment, which determines, among other
things, the scarcity or abundance of food and the presence or absence
of natural enemies, has obviously important consequences for social
behavior. So too have individual anatomical and physiological factors, such as sex, age, size, health, strength of drives, and hormonal
conditions regulating activity level and the sex cycle. When we add
to the foregoing such "sociological" factors as population density
and sex ratio, we probably have covered the most important influences operative in a society of Old or New World monkeys. Among
gorillas and chimpanzees, individual differences in such "psychological" factors as intelligence, skills, past experience, temperament, and
personality presumably play an increasingly important role in determining the nature of the social organization.

Instinct and intent

In evaluating social responses of man and animals, comparison is often attempted in terms of instinctive versus intentional, voluntary versus involuntary, or reflective versus impulsive behavior. Such distinctions, difficult enough to make when we are dealing with human beings who are capable of verbal report, become extremely hazardous when applied to animal behavior. In addition to implying consciousness or its absence, the terms have an ethical connotation. The self-determined, deliberate act is somehow a "higher-level" response. One author, after saying that selfless, altruistic behavior may occur in monkeys, adds that "we ought to exclude from this category the activities of mothers relative to their offspring, which are directed by some instinct or drive which removes from them any element of free will" [(18), p. 329].

One way to resolve the difficulty is to adopt a strict determinism; since an organism can do only what it must, or wants to do, the problem of free will is irrelevant. But psychologically, the distinctions have relevance and validity. The difficulty is in defining the criteria and in identifying the particular instance. The words "sadism" and "altruism," for instance, clearly imply free will, volition, and intent; "cooperation" and "prostitution" may or may not; "parturition" definitely does not. Evidently we are dealing with a continuum that has no clearly marked divisions. We may still differentiate between extremes, but, in reference to animal behavior at least, even such rough distinctions must be made with great caution.

Integration of positive and negative factors

The essence of social organization is interaction. Usually both negative (disruptive) and positive (cohesive) factors are involved. Members of the society attract and repel each other; their interests coincide or are incompatible. Some conflict between individuals is almost as characteristic of a society as is cohesion. Society offers rewards, but it also makes demands. Even from a biological-teleological point of view, it cannot be said that in an ideal society only the positive factors would be operative. In the principle of sexual selection, Darwin recognized the function of interindividual competitive struggle in evolution. It is clear, on the other hand, that if individuals only repelled each other, there eventually would be no interaction, no society, and no individuals. Social organization, therefore, is an integration of positive and negative factors, a patterned succession of interactions. It may be "loosely organized" or "closely knit"; it may result in small groupings (mateships, families), large ones (bands, troops), or in a hierarchy of smaller-within-larger groupings. Social psychology is a study of the nature of those interactions in terms of the behavior mechanisms of the individual.

Bibliography

1. Birch, H. G., and Clark, George, Hormonal Modifications of Social Behavior. II. The Effects of Sex-hormone Administration on the Social Dominance Status of the Female-castrate Chimpanzee, *Psychosom. Med.,* 1946, **8,** 320-331.
2. Carpenter, C. R., A Field Study of the Behavior and Social Relations of Howling Monkeys, *Comp. Psychol. Monogr.,* 1934, **10,** No. 2, pp. 1-168.
3. ——— Behavior of Red Spider Monkeys in Panama, *J. Mammalogy,* 1935, **16,** 171-180.
4. ——— A Field Study in Siam of the Behavior and Social Relations of the Gibbon (*Hylobates Lar*), *Comp. Psychol. Monogr.,* 1940, **16,** No. 5, pp. 1-212.
5. ——— Societies of Monkeys and Apes, *Biological Symposia,* 1942, **8,** 177-204.
6. ——— Sexual Behavior of Free Ranging Rhesus Monkeys (*Macaca mulatta*). I. Specimens, Procedures and Behavioral Characteristics of Estrus, *J. Comp. Psychol.,* 1942, **33,** 113-142.
7. Clark, George, and Birch, H. G., Hormonal Modifications of Social Behavior. I. The Effect of Sex-hormone Administration on the Social Status of a Male-castrate Chimpanzee, *Psychosomat. Med.,* 1945, **7,** 321-329.
8. Crawford, M. P., The Cooperative Solving of Problems by Young Chimpanzees, *Comp. Psychol. Monogr.,* 1937, **14,** 1-88.
9. ——— The Relation Between Social Dominance and the Menstrual Cycle in Female Chimpanzees, *J. Comp. Psychol.,* 1940, **30,** 483-513.
10. ——— The Cooperative Solving by Chimpanzees of Problems Requiring Serial Responses to Color Cues, *J. Soc. Psychol.,* 1941, **13,** 259-280.
11. ——— Dominance and Social Behavior, for Chimpanzees, in a Noncompetitive Situation, *J. Comp. Psychol.,* 1942, **33,** 267-277.
12. ——— and Spence, K. W., Observational Learning of Discrimination Problems by Chimpanzees, *J. Comp. Psychol.,* 1939, **27,** 133-147.
13. Finch, G., Chimpanzee Frustration Responses, *Psychosom. Med.,* 1942, **4,** 233-251.
14. ——— Unpublished manuscript, 1942.
15. Foley, J. P. Jr., First Year Development of a Rhesus Monkey (*Macaca mulatta*) Reared in Isolation, *J. Genet. Psychol.,* 1934, **45,** 39-105.

16. Hayes,. Cathy, *The Ape in Our House*. New York: Harper & Bros., 1951.
17. Hebb, D. O., *Organization of Behavior: A Neuropsychological Theory*. New York: John Wiley & Sons, Inc., 1949.
18. Hooton, E. A., *Man's Poor Relations*. New York: Doubleday, Doran & Co., 1942.
19. Jacobsen, C. F., Jacobsen, M. M., and Yoshioka, J. G., Development of an Infant Chimpanzee During her First Year, *Comp. Psychol. Monogr.*, 1932, **9**, No. 1, pp. 1-94.
20. Kearton, C., *My Friend Toto. The Adventures of a Chimpanzee and the Story of His Journey from the Congo to London*. London: Arrowsmith, 1925.
21. Kellogg, W. N., and Kellogg, L. A., *The Ape and the Child*. New York: McGraw-Hill Book Company, 1933.
22. Köhler, W., *The Mentality of Apes*. New York: Harcourt, Brace & Co., 1925.
23. Kohts, N., *Infant Ape and Human Child. (Instincts, Emotions, Play, Habits)*. Moscow: *Sci. Mem. Mus. Darwinianum*, 1935. (Russian with English abstract. Reviewed in *J. Genet. Psychol.*, 1937, **50**, 465-467.)
24. Lashley, K. S., and Watson, J. B., Notes on the Development of a Young Monkey, *J. Anim. Behav.*, 1913, **3**, 114-139.
25. Maslow, A. H., The Role of Dominance in the Social and Sexual Behavior of Infra-human Primates. III. A Theory of Sexual Behavior of Infra-human Primates, *J. Genet. Psychol.*, 1936, **48**, 310-338.
26. ——— Dominance-quality and Social Behavior in Infra-human Primates, *J. Soc. Psychol.*, 1940, **11**, 313-324.
27. ——— and Flanzbaum, S., The Role of Dominance in the Social and Sexual Behavior of Infra-human Primates. II. An Experimental Determination of the Behavior Syndrome of Dominance, *J. Genet. Psychol.*, 1936, **48**, 278-309.
28. Nissen, H. W., A Field Study of the Chimpanzee: Observations of Chimpanzee Behavior and Environment in Western French Guinea, *Comp. Psychol. Monogr.*, 1931, **8**, No. 1, p. 1-122.
29. ——— Primate Psychology. In *Encyclopedia of Psychology* (P. L. Harriman, Ed.), New York: Philosophical Library, 1946, pp. 546-570.
30. ——— Phylogenetic Comparisons. In *Handbook of Experimental Psychology* (S. S. Stevens, Ed.), New York: John Wiley & Sons, 1951.
31. ——— and Crawford, M. P., A Preliminary Study of Foodsharing Behavior in Young Chimpanzees, *J. Comp. Psychol.*, 1936, **22**, 383-419.
32. Nowlis, V., Companionship Preference and Dominance in the Social Interaction of Young Chimpanzees, *Comp. Psychol. Monogr.*, 1941, **17**, No. 1, 1-57.

33. ——— The Relation of Degree of Hunger to Competitive Interaction in Chimpanzee, *J. Comp. Psychol.*, 1941, **32**, 91-115.

34. ——— Sexual Status and Degree of Hunger in Chimpanzee Competitive Interaction, *J. Comp. Psychol.*, 1942, **34**, 185-194.

35. Raven, H. C., Meshie, the Child of a Chimpanzee, *Natural History*, 1932, **32**, 158-166.

36. ——— Further Adventures of Meshie, *Natural History*, 1933, **33**, 606-617.

37. Ruch, T. C., *Bibliographia Primatologica. A Classified Bibliography of Primates Other Than Man* (Part I). Springfield, Illinois: Chas. C. Thomas, 1941.

38. Tinklepaugh, O. L., Le comportement sexuel chez les chimpanzes et les singes inferieurs, considere comme une reaction de substitution consecutive a des troubles emotionnels, *J. Psychol. Norm. Path.*, 1933, **30**, 930-954.

39. ——— Social Behavior of Animals, *Comparative Psychology*, Rev. Ed., (F. A. Moss, Ed.). New York: Prentice-Hall, Inc., 1942, pp. 366-393.

40. Woodworth, R. S., Reenforcement of Perception, *Amer. J. Psychol.*, 1947, **60**, 119-124.

41. Yerkes, R. M., Genetic Aspects of Grooming, a Socially Important Primate Behavior Pattern, *J. Soc. Psychol.*, 1933, **4**, 3-25.

42. ——— A Chimpanzee Family, *J. Genet. Psychol.*, 1936, **48**, 362-370.

43. ——— Social Dominance and Sexual Status in the Chimpanzee, *Quart. Rev. Biol.*, 1939, **14**, 115-136.

44. ——— Social Behavior of Chimpanzees: Dominance Between Mates, in Relation to Sexual Status, *J. Comp. Psychol.*, 1940, **30**, 147-186.

45. ——— *Chimpanzees: A Laboratory Colony.* New Haven: Yale University Press, 1943.

46. ——— and Yerkes, A. W., *Social Behavior in Infrahuman Primates* (C. Murchison, Ed.). Worcester: Clark University Press, 1935, pp. 973-1033.

47. Zuckerman, S., *The Social Life of Monkeys and Apes.* New York: Harcourt, Brace & Co., 1932.

CHAPTER 14

Abnormal Behavior in Animals

University of Pittsburgh,
Western Psychiatric
Institute and Clinic

Introduction

Claude Bernard has been widely recognized as the father of experimental medicine. His work long ago laid the physiological basis for Cannon's concept of homeostasis and, more recently, for Selye's General Adaptation Syndrome. In 1865, he had this to say regarding the contributions of comparative studies to a science of behavior:

> To sum up, I not only conclude that experiments made on animals from the physiological, pathological and therapeutic points of view have results that are applicable to theoretic medicine, but I think that without such comparative study of animals, practical medicine can never acquire a scientific character. In this connection I shall finish with the works of Buffon, to which we might ascribe a different philosophic meaning, but which are scientifically very true for this occasion: "If animals did not exist, man's nature would be still more incomprehensible." [(7), p. 126.]

One of the basic assumptions of comparative psychology is that similar fundamental principles of behavior are operating in human and infrahuman behavior. If this is true, studies of experimental methods of producing behavior abnormalities in animals will contribute much to an understanding of human mental disorders. A few examples of experimental psychopathology in animals will be discussed in this chapter.[1]

Scientific advances have often resulted from the ability of an investigator to grasp the importance of unexpected results occurring during an experiment. It has now been more than 35 years since

---

[1] Theoretical discussions of this field of research together with an outline of projected problem areas may be found in two National Research Council Monographs (110, 111).

Shenger-Krestovnikova observed violently disordered behavior in a dog during a conditioning experiment carried out in Pavlov's laboratory [(123), p. 291-ff]. A recognition of the possible importance that these observations might have for experimental psychopathology led Pavlov to a considerable reorganization of subsequent research in his laboratory.

In this experiment a dog was trained to salivate when a luminous circle was presented, as evidence of discrimination between a circle and an ellipse. Such a discrimination between circle and ellipse could be quickly established with a ratio between the semiaxes of 2:1. However, as the training proceeded and as the ratio between the semiaxes became 9:8, the discrimination broke down. At the same time the behavior of the animal underwent an abrupt and lasting change. During the subsequent three weeks the animal's discrimination did not improve and the description of its violent emotional behavior in the experimental room has become one of the classic accounts of animal psychopathology. Pavlov called these behavior disturbances experimental neuroses. His work has been the basis for many subsequent experiments in which the effect of experimental "conflict" upon behavior has been investigated. The behavioral symptoms observed during this and subsequent experiments from Pavlov's laboratory have been described by a number of authors (38, 61, 123, 124). Since that time abnormal behavior has been produced by comparable methods in many animals, including the dog, goat, sheep, chimpanzee, cat, pig, pigeon, rat, and human child (18).

It is of considerable interest that in this country the work of Liddell and his associates on experimental neurosis also began as the result of an unexpected laboratory event. These experimenters were surprised to find that thyroidectomized sheep and goats could equal the maze-learning scores of their normal twins. Although there were some increased time scores, the learning of the operated animals was as efficient as that of the controls, even on unsolvable problems. It seemed to the investigators that the maze might be an inadequate instrument for the precise measurement of certain types of adaptive behavior. These observations led to the adoption of conditioning methods similar to those used previously by Pavlov. The use of such methods, in turn, quickly led to the production of acutely disturbed behavior in sheep that was descriptively similar to the neurotic behavior of Pavlov's dogs (81). In this way, Pavlovian conditioning methods have become the prototype for most of the studies on experimental neurosis in this country. A few of the ways in which these basic conditioning methods have been amplified and applied will now be considered.[2]

Pavlov himself never attempted systematically to outline and compare the methods he utilized for producing abnormal behavior in the dog. A careful survey of his methods has been made by Cook (18). Behavioral deviations developed at some stage of the following procedures: (a) continued presentation of a conditioned stimulus which not only had the effect of establishing a new association but also resulted in the inhibition of a strong inborn reflex; (b) presentation to the animal of similar conditioned stimuli to mutually exclusive behavior; (c) delay of reinforcement of positive conditioned reflexes for a given period of time after the beginning of the conditioned stimuli; (d) rapid transition from one conditioned stimulus to another, the two stimuli being conditioned to evoke antagonistic behavior; (e) reinforcement of a conditioned stimulus that had previously had an inhibitory effect; and (f) occurrence of very strong or unusual stimuli.

In the case of the above situations, the disturbed behavior was somewhat different from animal to animal although running through the descriptive accounts of these experiments there were certain common symptoms that have been outlined by Cook [(18), p. 1266].

These symptoms are, in general, very similar to those since observed by Liddell (73) and Anderson and Liddell (2) in other animal species. The varied behavior that different investigators have described in animal studies of experimental neuroses may be classified under three general headings: (a) an impairment of discrimination or learning as well as disturbed behavior in the training situation; (b) recorded or overt behavioral evidence of autonomic disturbance during training—cardiac, respiratory, sexual, and secretory abnormalities have been observed together with fear or rage responses; (c) behavioral changes *outside* the training situation, such as hyper-

---

[2] Although it is now firmly entrenched in the literature, the term "experimental neurosis" is perhaps an unfortunate one. It raises immediately the question of the relationships that the behavioral disturbances in animals bear to so-called neurotic conditions in man. Although these relationships are by no means clear, this question will be considered later in the chapter. In the discussion that follows, the term "experimental neurosis" will refer to the syndrome of disturbed behavior typically produced by Pavlovian conditioning methods.

activity, antisocial behavior, or long-term abnormalities in autonomic functions mentioned above.

Experimental Neurosis in Different Animal Species

Sheep and goats

Liddell's experiments at the Cornell Behavior Farm afford a number of examples of a truly comparative approach to the study of abnormal behavior in several different animal species. This work has utilized conditioned motor responses based upon the defensive reaction of an animal's foreleg to a mild electric shock (76). Such a procedure does not differ fundamentally from that used in Pavlov's laboratory.

After confining the animal by a Pavlov conditioning frame, mild electric shocks are applied to its foreleg. The animal must then learn to anticipate the shock by raising its leg when certain conditioning signals are presented in advance of this shock. During early training, the startling but weak shocks evoke escape behavior. Increased head movements, running responses, heartbeat and respiration are all recorded. As the training progresses, however, these disturbances begin to assume a more deliberate and restricted pattern. Only localized and momentary forelimb movements are seen and the disturbances of autonomic functions are transient. As the time for forelimb response approaches, the flexions increase in magnitude. After the shock, however, respiration and pulse return to normal in a matter of seconds. The animal now comes willingly to the laboratory and, when well trained, will maintain a state of quiet for as long as two hours.

Liddell especially emphasized the importance of the restraining harness and the prevention of escape. This apparatus, which in many of Pavlov's experiments was exceedingly cumbersome, has been reduced to its simplest components as shown in Fig. 1. In recent experiments, to prevent escape, only a web strap has been placed around the animal's chest and attached to the wall. After preliminary trials the animal assumes a pose of quiet watchfulness during the hour's experimental period. There is also an element of coercion in the situation that consists of forcing the animal into a predetermined mode of action at the experimenter's convenience. Thus, if a metronome or telegraph sounder begins sounding twice a second and is followed by a mild and brief electric shock to the forelimb, after nine or ten such episodes, the animal alerts at the first click and, in from two to four seconds, lowers its head and flexes the forelimb one or more times before the shock. There is a decisive flexion to the shock itself, after which the animal returns again to its usual state of tense and alert behavior. This is the basic procedure for the establishment of what has been termed a *positive* conditioned reflex. A *negative* conditioned reflex can then be developed as follows: if the telegraph sounder or metronome clicks four times a second for ten seconds but is not followed by shock, the animal abandons its flexion response with repeated trials. During the early

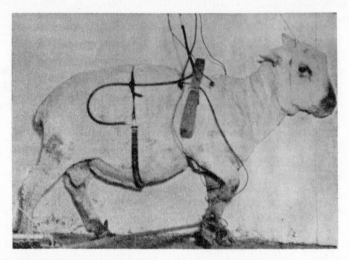

Fig. 1. Simple Restraining Harness for Motor Conditioning. The sheep is flexing the foreleg at the clicking of a telegraph sounder in anticipation of an electric shock to this foreleg. [From Liddell (78).]

stages of the development of such a negative conditioned reflex there may be a more vigorous reaction to the signal for no shock than there is to the signal for shock. The animal may forcibly extend the forelimb at the negative signal.

In summary, animals subjected to the restriction of movement and brief episodes of forced conditioned and unconditioned activity may find themselves under different degrees of stress. If such stress is not unduly severe, the animal is able to maintain a high level of conditioned activity over long periods of time. There is evidence, however, to show that there is a mounting tension during the hour's experimental period in an animal, such as a sheep or a goat, that has been positively and negatively conditioned for mild shock. As only one instance of the increasing tension, an animal was observed to show a respiratory rate increase from 36 per minute after the second signal to 139 per minute 15 minutes after the last (18th signal) for the day. The breathing became deeper and more audible and was accompanied by clicking of the teeth, yawning, and apnoeic pauses of greater frequency and longer duration. The animal was increasingly reactive to the onset of each signal but remained quiet at the intervals between each signal. The conditioned forelimb remained immobile with brief tremors appearing, however, toward the end of the test period. It is important to remember also that in well-trained sheep or goats, the level of tension or "vigilance" seemed to increase in intensity during test periods when no signals or shocks were given. Liddell concluded that this evident stress imposed by the restraint of movement in the conditioning harness is derived from the residuals of previous periodic alerting reactions elicited by training stimuli. Stress, then, is a function of the intensity, duration, and temporal spacing of alerting reactions aroused by positive and negative conditioned stimuli when each positive signal is inevitably terminated by shock and negative signals by no shock. It is also affected in a cumulative fashion by the after-effects of previous test periods.

During the course of this work it became apparent that many of the long-continued and exceedingly cumbersome experimental situations that Pavlov described might not be necessary in inducing behavioral breakdowns.

Recent experiments by Liddell (74, 75, 76, 77) have described some interesting abberant symptoms in sheep and goats that occurred in a much simplified conditioning situation. In these experiments the ten-second signals for shock were separated by pauses of only two minutes, instead of the six-minute intervals used in a previous experiment (3). Twenty signals a day were given. In interesting contrast to the marked agitation that resulted when the shock signals were six minutes apart, the shorter pauses seemed to lead to a chronic state of tonic immobility. Such tonic immobility bore a strong resemblance to descriptions of conversion hysteria. The foreleg of the animal to which the electrode was attached was rigidly extended rather than flexed, and the heartbeat showed little or no increase before the shock. Such animals limped from the laboratory on a stiffened foreleg but seemed to run freely when turned out to pasture. Again, as in previous experiments, the animal avoided the experimenter and animal-room attendant, and resisted vigorously being brought to the laboratory. Thus, even in a simple conditioning setup it seemed that the temporal interval between the signals indicating shock bore a precise relationship to the type of symptomatology of the experimental animal. It has been found possible to select at random a sheep or a goat and predict the type of symptom that would develop when it was subjected to rigid temporal conditioning [(77), p. 576]. With longer intervals, severe agitation resulted, and, with short intervals, tonic immobility. These symptoms persisted in some animals for as long as nine years, reappearing with their former intensity whenever the animals were again placed in the conditioning situation.

The pig

The production of behavioral breakdowns in the pig has been complicated by the extremely tedious and long-continued training that is necessary to accustom them to the conditioning situation. The havoc that a 425-lb. animal could create in an experimental situation often proved to be traumatic to both experimenter and apparatus (94). In one of these experiments (82), a pig was taught to lift the cover of a box to secure food to a particular signal. The next day, however, the signal was followed by electroshock to the animal's foreleg. The temporal pattern of signals was similar each day. Conflict was inherent in the alternate feeding and punishment that made the experimental situation an unpredictable place in which either punishment or reward might be expected. The alternation of the signals was effective in producing great emotional upset.

The dog

Extending the work with the dog by Pavlov, Gantt (36, 38), in the Pavlovian laboratory at Johns Hopkins, has conducted the most thorough and long-continued study of a single case history of experimental neurosis on record. The dog, Nick, was, for over 12 years, a subject of continuous observation and experiment. Gantt has recorded over 1,500 conditioned responses in one subject. His work, which in general followed the methods of Pavlov has attempted to extend the latter's studies along three main lines:

(a) As already indicated, considerable attention has been paid to the long-continued study of a single case history.

(*b*) Considerable attention was paid to the early detection of behavioral breakdowns. Controlled measurements of cardiac, respiratory, sexual, and secretory mechanisms revealed disturbance long before the animal's overt behavior showed a demonstrable change.

(*c*) Specific attention was paid to the effects of prolonged stress not only upon the conditioned responses but also upon the way in which the extension of the behavioral disorder would involve, in sequence, various physiological systems. These important findings would have escaped notice in a short-term experiment.

A rather detailed description of the physiological changes observed during previous studies has been given by Gantt. These involved significant alterations in the functions of digestive, circulatory, sexual, urinary, and respiratory mechanisms, as well as changes in social relationships. Among these changes, it was found that heart rate was a far more sensitive indicator of central nervous excitation than either bodily activity or salivary secretion (37). The cardiac conditioned reflexes, although formed more quickly than salivary or motor, were generally far more difficult to extinguish. An important contribution of the study was the establishment of norms of conditioning performance in various autonomic functions (for example, heart rate). This permitted a more objective definition of abnormal states in terms of a certain deviation from the normal range of activity. Visceral conditioned reactions, as represented by heart rate, may persist for years after the external situation no longer demands excessive activity. In the case of Nick, mentioned above, the heart rate was nearer normal in the presence of real danger, such as an attacking cat, than it was in the situation of conflict.

The gradual spread of the neurotic disturbance over several years involved the following general sequence: first came changes in activity, restlessness, and inhibition of food-conditioned reflexes; then came disturbed respiration, frequent micturition, and finally pathological sexual erections—all initiated by the clicking of the metronome.

The cat

Masserman (96) has investigated the behavior of cats exposed to various types of conflict situations. Cats were trained to approach a food box, raise the lid, and eat, when visual or auditory signals were given. After such responses were established, the situation was made conflictful by blowing a blast of air into the cat's face. There was then established a conflict between the opposing behavioral tendencies of eating and retreat from a fear-producing stimulus. Three general types of behavioral deviations appeared: (a) phobic responses (fear and escape reactions); (b) anxiety responses, as shown by crouching, trembling, restlessness, and, in many animals, food refusal; and (c) other symptoms such as excessive grooming and compulsive head hiding in the food box.

Complex habit patterns were also established in the same situation. In some instances, the animals operated a switch, which in turn produced the signal for food. In other cases, the animals had to pass a barrier to reach the food. The abnormal behavior was attributed to animals showing food refusal that seemed to accentuate the behavioral symptoms.

Masserman's work has made contributions toward the therapy of conflict-induced behavior disorders. Various methods were utilized. Working-through of the conflict by the animal itself seemed most effective. This method involved training the animal to activate its own signals and rewards. The abnormal symptoms were diminished if the animal gained some manipulative control over the situation. Rest periods, reduction in drives, and simplifying the problem were not found to be so effective.

The rat

There have been few attempts to utilize Pavlovian techniques for producing behavioral breakdowns in the rat. Perhaps the best known experiment has been that of Cook (18). A conditioning frame was used and the animals were strapped to it. The rats were required to flex a forelimb for a bright light and inhibit flexion to a dim light. When the preliminary conditioning was accomplished, the brightness difference between the lights was reduced. In this situation, three out of six animals showed alteration in behavior. The symptoms observed consisted of loss of the acquired flexion habit, food refusal, reduced activity, and fear responses.

Bijou (8) observed lack of responsivity, rigidity, and molding in one animal during a difficult brightness discrimination. In another experiment (9), various problems of spatial arrangement or brightness discrimination of lights were presented to a confined animal. Some changes in behavior were observed such as defecation and urination in the apparatus, squealing and struggling, biting, and resistance. These fear responses were intensified by electroshock to the leg. A new apparatus has since been designed (10). The number of rats utilized for "experimental neurosis" experiments has thus far been few.

Factors Affecting Stress Tolerance

Liddell's method of attack upon the problems of inducing experimental neurosis in different animal species has enabled him to attack two fundamental problems at once. First, a method is available whereby the investigator may discover specific and reproduceable factors in the conditioning situation that impose stress to the point of breakdown. In the second place, the investigator has a means of isolating specific factors in the procedure itself or in the animal which can significantly change its tolerance for environmental stress. One of the most important areas that Liddell has investigated concerns the factors that can modify an experimental animal's tolerance to stress (78).

Increasing the conditioned stimulus load

Earlier studies showed that when the number of conditioned stimuli given during a test period was increased from 10 five-second *positive* signals to 20 signals, a behavioral breakdown resulted (81). In more recent experiments with sheep and goats, it has been found that such a drastic increase in the stimulus load may also lead to breakdown when 30 or more *negative* (no-shock) conditioned stimuli of 10-seconds duration are given at one-minute intervals in the same test period on two or more successive occasions.

Timing of stimuli

Another method for increasing stress in the training situation has been to utilize a monotonous sequence of 10-second conditioned stimuli separated by constant intervals of two to seven minutes. During earlier experiments, positive and negative conditioned stimuli were alternated (2), but it was later found that a series of 10-second positive signals followed by shock and separated by constant intervals led to the same pathological outcome. During these experiments, it was also found that when single shocks without preceding conditioning signals were repeated at regular intervals, they did not lead to neurosis. Apparently the shock alone was insufficient to lead to marked behavioral deviations unless preceded by conditioned stimuli.

Regular alternation of positive and negative conditioned stimuli

The regular alternation of positive and negative signals separated by five- to seven-minute intervals has been found to lead to the sudden appearance of an agitated type of experimental neurosis. One of the distinguishing signs of the behavioral disruption is the appearance of frequent flexions of the trained foreleg in the absence of stimulation. These animals exhibit tic-like foreleg movements again and again. The records of some of these may be seen in Figs. 2 and 3. In one of these experiments, a very interesting phe-

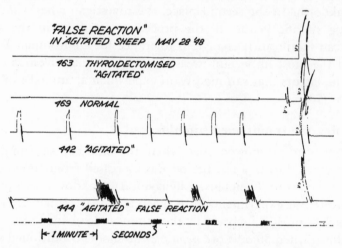

Fig. 2. Simultaneous Records of the Movements of the Conditioned Foreleg in Four Sheep. Sheep 463, 442, and 444 have developed experimental neurosis of the agitated type. Thyroidectomy was performed on sheep 463 after the onset of the experimental neurosis. A conditioned reflex to the telegraph sounder clicking once a second for ten seconds followed by shock to the foreleg is shown at the right of the tracing. [From Liddell (78).]

nomenon was observed. Sheep were subjected to a total of 10 signals per day; these were alternately positive and negative and were separated by six-minute intervals. The clicking of a telegraph sounder at 60 to 120 per minute served as *positive* and *negative* conditioned stimuli.

It was found that if a faint shock accompanied the positive stimulus, a previously traumatic conditioning routine failed to produce neurotic symptoms. If, however, the faint premonitory shocks were discontinued, acutely disturbed behavior suddenly appeared in all animals after only 30 additional signals. This meant that behavioral disruptions appeared after only 30 signals had been given, 15 positive alternating with 15 negative, spaced 15 minutes apart. Unlike the normal animals, which showed progressively greater relaxation in the harness when brought to the laboratory day after day, these experimental animals exhibited agitation for long periods of time in the absence of the usual conditioned and unconditioned stimuli. The importance of this experiment is inherent in some of the questions that it raised. One might ask why the weak preliminary shocks protected the animals from the stress usually imposed

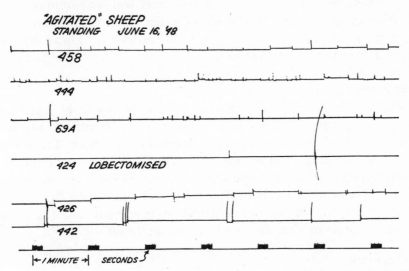

Fig. 3. **Simultaneous Records of the Movements of the Conditioned Foreleg in Six Neurotic Sheep Confined by Restraining Harness as Shown in Fig. 1.** All sheep are confined in the same room. Neurotic sheep 424 has had a bilateral frontal lobectomy. No signals or shocks have been given during this test. [From Liddell (78).]

by the rigid time schedule of alternating conditioned rates of clicking. In some important manner, they afforded a means for an important reduction in the sheep's stimulus load. When the clicking was accompanied by weak shock, it was thus robbed of its expectancy value for the final shock, which was only a little stronger. The second question concerns the influence of temperament or breed in the tolerance for environmental stress. It is interesting in this regard that these animals were of different breeds, age, and previous training. A possible answer is that the factor of temperament, which Pavlov stressed in earlier writings, may have a negligible influence on the outcome of certain stress-producing procedures in sheep and goats.[3]

Endocrine relationships

In the earlier investigations mentioned previously, it was found that thyroidectomized animals seemed to show a greater tolerance for stress-producing situations than normal twin controls. An interesting follow-up to this has been the recent discovery that thyroidectomy in the neurotic animal is accompanied by a cessation of neurotic manifestations that, however, may promptly reappear following injections of thyroxine. Thus, sheep 463 (Fig. 2) showed an aberrant pattern of foreleg movement before thyroidectomy. This record is similar to that of sheep 444 (Fig. 3). However, after thyroidectomy, there was a complete disappearance of such "neurotic" foreleg movements.

Earlier studies (79, 80) reported a favorable effect of cortin in diminishing anxiety symptoms in neurotic sheep. Gantt (38) utilized intraperitoneal injections of cortin with the dog, Nick. Little evidence of any helpful effect was observed. The question of the endocrine relationships in experimental neuroses has been raised by Selye (133) in his discussions of the General Adaptation Syndrome. The relationships of experimental neurosis to adrenal cortical activity present a problem that merits additional attention.

Lobectomy

Bilateral frontal lobectomy has also been found to lead to a virtual disappearance of experimental neurosis in some animals. Abnormal foreleg movements in an experimentally neurotic animal disappeared entirely after the removal of both frontal lobes. This animal became

---

[3] The pronounced variability in the reactions that various animals show to stressful conditioning procedures indicates that there is considerable individual difference in susceptibility. Pavlov noted that certain dogs were more excitable than others and that some appeared to be more inhibitable. A careful summary of Pavlov's generalizations about the types of dogs and their typical reactions during conditioning experiments can be found in Hilgard and Marquis [(61), p. 300]. James (65) has done some exceedingly important work in attempting to classify dogs on the basis of various types of conditioned behavior. These studies represent a careful basis for later work in which it will be possible to set up a scale on which all animals may be classified. It will be necessary to coordinate the various dimensions of behavior with many other behavioral measurements before a specific trait can be said to have much significance. So far, there is no satisfactory type theory of conditioning that is satisfactorily established. This area of research is an exceedingly important one, since genetic and constitutional variables probably account for many of the wide individual differences observed during conditioning experiments.

as quiet in the harness as a normal animal, as may be seen in the tracing of foreleg movement in Fig. 3.

Age and maternal protection

In recent investigations of the effect of age and maternal protection on the tolerance of environmental stress, four pairs of twin kids between one and two months of age were utilized. An ingenious mechanism fastened to the animal's body allowed the presentation of the shock and also gave a record of locomotion in the young goat

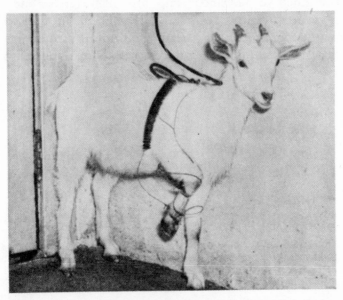

Fig. 4. Young Goat Showing Conditioned Reflex to Darkness. It is flexing the fore-limb that will receive a shock when the light in the room is turned on after ten seconds. (Flash-bulb photograph.) The flexible suspension which records the animal's locomotion and through which the shock is administered is shown attached to the goat's back. [From Liddell (78).]

that was free to run in the room. The stress routine for the young animals and their mothers was arranged as follows: one twin and its mother occupied one laboratory room with the mother free but with the cable for recording movement and delivering shock to the leg attached to the young animal's back, as shown in Fig. 4; the other twin was placed in the adjoining room for training and isolation. The signal employed was darkness, since these animals maintained a constant alertness under such conditions. The lights were turned out for 10 seconds and as they came on again both animals received a mild shock on the foreleg. Twenty "lights-out" signals were given, separated by two-minute intervals. Preliminary tests have shown definitely that the presence of the mother has a protective effect on the young animal subjected to stress when the behavior of isolated animals and those conditioned with their mothers was contrasted. In these experiments, the mothers showed indifference to the young animal. Some evidence of the relative freedom from stress in the goat with the mother during training is shown in the locomotion records during the test (Fig. 5). The isolated animals were progressively more restrained in movement, and, after 260 signals, one of these animals spent the entire hour standing close to the wall with very little movement. In addition, being conditioned in isolation proved to be traumatic for all four animals, with the youngest giving up

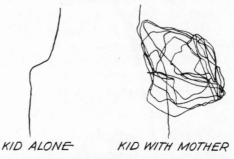

KID ALONE   KID WITH MOTHER

Fig. 5. **Simultaneous Tracings of the Movements of Twin Goats During a One-hour Test of 20 Signals.** Both goats had been given 260 previous signals, each followed by shock. The tracing at the left records the locomotion of the twin alone. The record at the right is from the twin in the adjoining room with its mother. [From Liddell (78).]

sucking entirely and dying after the sixth hour of training. The other three animals showed signs of experimental neurosis after 100 signals at 20 per day. One may contrast this with the usual duration of exposure to this routine in the adult that is necessary to precipitate behavioral disorder. Since the number of signals with older animals is about 1,000, it was inferred that the stress tolerance is much less in younger animals.

Behavioral Abnormalities in Primates

There are several recorded instances of marked behavioral abnormalities in primates. Most of these have been emotional outbursts observed during tests of learning or discrimination. Systematic attempts to produce experimental neurosis with conditioning techniques have not yet been published. Hebb (59) has given very interesting descriptions of neurosis arising *spontaneously* in two chimpanzees in the Yerkes Laboratories at Orange Park, Florida. There was the advantage in these two cases of knowing considerably more of the previous history of the animals than is usually possible with human patients in the clinic. These animals had been under daily observation by trained observers who carefully recorded illness, unusual experiences or peculiarities of behavior. It also happened that control subjects were available. Four chimpanzees had been reared together under similar circumstances for the larger portion of their developmental period. Alpha and Bula were born in captivity, while Kambi and Bimba were captured at about nine months of age. There was no evidence in the case histories of these animals that could account for the great difference in the adult personalities. By the time of adolescence, Kambi was behaviorally a hypochondriac and the other, Alpha, at full maturity, suddenly developed an extreme phobia. Alpha, at the age of 12, without previous neurotic history or ascribable cause, refused solid food although she would accept the food if it were cut in pieces. Four months later, Alpha showed a strong tendency to avoid the attendant, but no other persons, and became viciously aggressive toward this person for the first time in her life. After punishment (soaking with a hose) she again became friendly, but the fear of food persisted for two years, disappeared, and recurred again at the end of three years.

The second animal, Kambi, was brought to the laboratory at nine months of age. The menarche occurred at nine. The animal was spayed at 12. The behavior of the animal was characterized by depression that was judged from the following evidence: (a) long-term inconstancy of behavioral base line; (b) periods of extreme lack of spontaneous activity or responsiveness; (c) an exceptional emotional instability and ease of frustration; and (d) a marked sexual abnormality (59). The behavior of these animals indicated that the chimpanzee can show behavioral disturbances that parallel human neurotic conditions to a surprising degree. The first animal simulated phobic behavior while the second suggested the objective picture of human depression. In recent work, Hebb (57, 58, 59, 60) has laid the basis for an objective study of the emotional behavior of primates.

Finch (30) and Haslerud (55) have attempted to identify frustration responses in the chimpanzee and isolate the factors that determine their incidence. Jacobsen, Wolfe, and Jackson (64) described emotional behavior in a chimpanzee being trained on a delayed response problem. During prolonged training the animal showed temper tantrums, rolling on the floor, defecating, and urinating after failures in problem solving. It was necessary to drag the animal to the testing room where it had formerly been willing to come. Emotional outbursts of a similar nature have been observed by Crawford (19), Galt (35), and Yerkes (148). Wendt (144), in investigations of the auditory acuity of monkeys, observed a generalized inhibition that resulted when he immobilized his animals completely.

Studies of Fixated and Regressive Behavior

The development of position habits or persistent nonadaptive responses during early experiments on learning usually resulted in the animal being discarded by a frustrated experimenter. In experiments utilizing shock or punishment, such stereotyped behavior patterns or *fixations* often persist despite the availability of more efficient modes or response. In *regression* behavior, the animal reverts to a previously established mode of behavior and persists in it despite the fact that it is inefficient in solving the problem. Defined this way, regression is a special case of fixated behavior. Fixations are usually considered as primitive analogues of compulsive disorders in the mentally ill, and regression may be related to Freudian concepts as the stimulating experiments of Mowrer (107) and Whiting and Mowrer (145) have shown. Miller (99) has made a comprehensive theoretical and experimental analysis of conflict behavior in the rat and its relationships to learning principles. Hamilton (53) gave one of the earliest descriptions of fixations in 1916 when he observed that where efficient learning was made impossible, repetitive behavior patterns tended to be adopted by several animal species.

Maier, Glaser, and Klee (91) and Klee (69); on the basis of several experiments, have distinguished between fixations appearing during normal learning and outwardly similar behavioral tendencies produced under conditions of conflict. From these and other studies, the authors concluded that the abnormal behavior fixations produced under conditions of frustration were fundamentally different from similar behavior patterns appearing during the course of motivated learning. Some of the animals in Klee's experiment developed fixations so persistent that the animals starved to death rather than alter the fixations in order to obtain readily available food. It was felt that such fixations were qualitatively different from habits, and that present learning theory does not apply to these behavior patterns appearing under conditions of frustration.

It seems possible, however, that the concept of anxiety-reduction as a secondary reinforcing state may be of help in explaining fixated behavior. If so, it would not be necessary to consider the abnormal phenomenon as a problem independent of present learning theory. This concept has been elaborated in a number of papers by Mowrer (106, 108) and by Miller (100). Miller's study indicates clearly that fear may be objectively studied as a motivating factor and fear-reduction may reinforce the learning of new responses by the rat. If so, his findings are directly applicable to the explanation of abnormal fixations as well as having wider applications in experimental psychopathology. In these experiments, the apparatus consisted of two compartments separated by a door. A white compartment was equipped with an electric grid; the black compartment was without a grid. When animals were placed in the white compartment, they could escape through an open door to the black compartment when shocked. The animals subsequently ran from the white compartment without shock being present. The essence of this study was that a new drive (fear or anxiety) had been acquired. This acquired drive was then demonstrated to have the property of motivating an entirely new habit without further shock. This was demonstrated by closing the door between compartments which could then be opened by the animals when they turned a small wheel or pressed a bar. Thus, motivating conditions were set up that led to the learning of new habits that were dependent upon electric shocks given only during early stages of training. Hypotheses supported by the study were:

... that responses which produce strong stimuli are the basis for acquired drives; that such responses may be the basis for certain of the phenomena of learning which have been labeled "expectancy," thus reducing this from the status of a primary to a secondary principle, and that neurotic symptoms, such as compulsions, may be motivated by anxiety and reinforced by anxiety-reduction like the two new responses learned in this experiment. (p. 100)

It seems probable that bizarre and unadaptive responses, such as the fixation or "abortive" jumps, might be reinforced because of anxiety-reduction. It is also possible that when an animal is repeatedly tested in a conflict situation an originally prepotent hunger drive would not continue to play a major role. Klee's experiment, already mentioned, lends some support to this. As the result of a review of earlier work with fixation and a series of experiments, Farber (25) concluded: "On the basis of these considerations, the inference has been drawn that fixation resulting from shock may be the result of the operation of secondary reinforcement resulting from anxiety reduction, and therefore due to factors operating in ordinary learning situations." [(25), p. 131]

A number of experimental situations involving painful stimuli such as shock have been found to produce an analogue of what is called regression in human subjects. In the usual regression experiment an animal learns to select a particular pathway to a goal. The response is then extinguished by delay of reward or failure. A second habit in the apparatus is then established. When the animal is shocked (by electric grid) and reverts to the original habit, regression is said to occur. In Hamilton and Krechevsky's experiment (54) the rats subjected to shock in the maze either fixated on the earlier response (regression) or the one in progress. Regression was found in 11 of 18 animals studied. Variability or "plasticity" of behavior was reduced almost to zero in the shocked animals. Fixation occurred even when no possibility for regression was permitted. The weight of evidence [see Farber (25); Kleemeier (70)] indicates that regression is directly related to the relative strength of the on-going response. All the studies that have investigated regressive behavior in a two-choice situation have found that animals, when shocked, either fixated the habit being developed (preservation) or returned to an earlier response (regression).

Theoretical Considerations

What are the factors inherent in conditioned-response techniques that can exceed an organism's stress tolerance? Pavlov's theory of experimental neurosis was based upon his concept of a collision between processes of excitation and inhibition in the cerebral cortex. Recent experimental work, however, has dealt harshly with these concepts (61) and subsequent investigators have usually preferred to define more precisely the conditions under which breakdowns occur.

Liddell is of the opinion that certain characteristics of the conditioned-reflex method are of fundamental importance as etiological factors in subsequent behavioral breakdowns. One significant feature of this method is the repetitive nature of the animal's conditioned activity within the confining environment of the Pavlov frame and the laboratory room. The concept of "stimulus vigilance" has been used to describe the recurrent alerting reactions to each positive and negative conditioned stimulus. Another characteristic that is now of obvious importance is the relationship that may develop during months and years of conditioning between the animal and the experimenter. As behavior moves toward a pathological terminus, the animal's responses toward the investigator change from dependence to hostility and avoidance. It is probable that daily training in self-imposed restraint, together with giving up certain types of spontaneous behavior, lays the basis for the pathological outcome of long conditioning. This, however, is in and of itself not enough. Something more seems necessary, and it is Liddell's belief that the something more is in its most elementary form provided by monotonous repetition of certain patterns of stimulation within the confines of the experimental situation.

Another question that is of importance is why conditioned response techniques are singularly effective in precipitating experimental neuroses. Liddell has stated, "When an animal is called upon to anticipate food or shock at certain signals but not at others it cannot escape the issue as it can in the maze or discrimination box." [(73), p. 1038]. Maier and Schneirla (93) also expressed doubt about the effectiveness of discrimination-box techniques for producing conflict because of the opportunities they presented the animal for alternative responses. Many workers share the opinion that conflict that is effective in precipitating experimental neurosis is best produced by conditioned-response techniques. However, there is certainly evidence that other types of conflictful learning may produce abnormal emotional manifestations in animals. Karn (66) has reviewed a number of cases of disturbed behavior produced in animals by maze or discrimination-box techniques. It is his feeling that any situation in which the organism is attempting to choose between several courses of action may elicit a neurosis if the decision is difficult and the organism highly motivated. There seems to be no doubt but that the conditions for conflictful learning can be imposed upon animals by discrimination-box or maze techniques. The weight of present evidence, however, indicates that the most clear-cut and lasting behavioral abnormalities have been produced in restrained animals with conditioned-response techniques.

However, there is another reason why acute behavioral disturbances have been observed less often under free conditions. It will be recalled that under punishment an animal may show fixated or regressive behavior. There is some evidence also that these behavioral abnormalities are retained because they are reinforced by anxiety-reduction. It is possible then that an animal's relative freedom in a discrimination box or maze may facilitate the development of certain behavioral symptoms, which, although nonadaptive, serve to protect the organism against further stress. Perhaps the condition that distinguishes various techniques is the opportunity they allow for behavioral patterns that may be developed and fixated because they are anxiety-reducing. Thus some of the less severe abnormalities observed during studies of conflictful learning may actually be adaptive in the sense that they protect the animal against the symptoms of acute behavioral breakdown. The nature of conditioned-response techniques reduces alternative behavioral possibilities to a minimum.

Still another question that was raised at the beginning of the chapter concerns the relationship of behavioral disturbances in animals with neurotic conditions observed clinically in human subjects. Hebb (59) has expressed the opinion that the abnormalities he observed in the chimpanzees presented a truer picture of neurosis as it appears clinically in humans than the many other instances of abnormal behavior observed in conditioning or learning situations. It was pointed out that in human neuroses the condition is simultaneously generalized and that its emotional components persist after the cessation of the exciting cause. He failed to find the analogue of this condition in the reports of neuroses in animals such as the dog, cat, or sheep. While these animals developed striking abnormalities of emotional behavior, it was abnormal behavior that developed mainly in *specific training situations*. It did not seem to be a generalized anxiety nor one that persisted after the situational threat was removed. In other words, it is Hebb's opinion that the evidence that situationally-determined emotion or anxiety persists for prolonged periods in animals is thus far inconclusive. For example, the pieces of apparatus that investigators have used to make periodic checks on persistent vascular abnormalities or breathing, and so forth, might themselves have become conditioned stimuli for pain reactions.

Several investigators [(61), p. 281; (23); (94)] have indicated that it is extremely difficult to distinguish between normal emotional expression and neurosis. Temper tantrums are much too usual to be designated as neuroses. Frequently only the whim of the experimenter seems to designate behavior as neurotic, and evidence for a carry-over of abnormality to situations other than the training situation is entirely lacking. At the present time, it must be said that additional work is necessary in developing criteria for the definition of experimental neurosis in animals. It is therefore premature to evaluate many of the findings on animal neuroses with respect to their explanatory value for clinical disorders in man.

Hebb (57, 58, 59, 60), in a series of studies, has laid a promising objective basis for the study of emotional states in primates. There is evidence that certain complex modes of human emotional behavior do occur in animals, and it is toward the recognition and quantification of these states that his work is directed. This, in turn, will be a means of classifying deviations from a habitual behavioral baseline. This makes necessary a knowledge of the organism's past and present behavior so that the direction of the deviation can be defined. These methods will greatly increase the range of symptoms that can be measured as a function of stress. In addition to the behavioral deviations that have been defined by Liddell and others, social behavior and specific emotional states can be identified and measured. Hebb's work indicates clearly that, with primates, it is possible to use frankly anthropomorphic categories of emotion and discover by analysis what behavioral relationships they are based on. The extension of this work promises to provide additional information about emotional states in animals and their relationships with normal and abnormal affective states in humans.

Convulsive Behavior in the Rat

Epilepsy is a general term referring to a tendency to recurrent convulsive seizures. A convulsive seizure is manifested by an explosive electrochemical disturbance within the nervous system, by autonomic changes, and by tonic or clonic muscular contractions. Seizures have been observed in many animal species and may be induced by a variety of techniques. A convulsion is a response of the whole organism, and many of the neurophysiological events leading up to it have already transpired at the time the muscular contractions are observed. There is not the slightest reason to speak of it as a disease entity. Properly speaking, it is a *symptom* that may be common to a great many etiological factors. Cobb (16) has listed 56 clinical factors and 13 physiological mechanisms of causal importance for convulsions. There are probably more.

Finger (33) in reviewing the extensive literature on convulsions in the rat has discussed them as produced under conditions of electrical stimulation, drug injection, auditory stimulation, "conflict," and dietary deficiency. Although we shall not be able to discuss all of these, it is important to realize, when considering convulsive behavior in any animal species, that many diverse factors may enter into its etiology. The goal of the researcher is to discover the basic principles that govern the manifestations of a given convulsive syndrome. A knowledge of the principles in animals can then be tested at the human level. As the mechanism of a fit is as yet unexplained, any controlled approach to the problem of the convulsive disorders will eventually be found to contribute to what is still an unsolved problem.

In 1924, Donaldson, in discussing behavior abnormalities in the rat, made a brief reference to maniacal running, jumping, and exhaustion in some rats subjected to the sound of jingling keys [(21), p. 134]. This isolated observation seems to be the first reference to an abnormal pattern of convulsive behavior in the rat. It has now been widely observed that some rats exhibit violent convulsive seizures when tested under various conditions of auditory stimulation.

The first extensive report on these convulsive seizures was given during the 1938 meetings of the American Association for the Advancement of Science. In these experiments (84), an air-blast was used to force rats to respond to a difficult discrimination problem. "Conflict" imposed by forced reaction in an unsolvable problem situation was at first thought to be a necessary determinant of the abnormal behavior. Studies soon appeared that demonstrated that auditory stimulation alone (5, 52, 104, 105) was an effective means of eliciting convulsions in susceptible animals. Primarily, as the result of the research of Morgan and his collaborators, the convulsions are now generally referred to as "audiogenic seizures," although a variety of descriptive terms has been applied to them by other investigators.

The "neurotic pattern" described by Maier (84) has been found to have little in common with the "experimental neurosis" described by Pavlov, Liddell, and others. Thus, experiments dealing with the conflict hypothesis as it may relate to problems of human neurotic behavior have become, in time, an extensive body of research dealing with audiogenic seizures as such and their relationship with other convulsive disorders. In a long series of studies (87), Maier and his colleagues have continued to emphasize the effects of conflict in their interpretation of seizures. Other investigators, notably Morgan and his group, paid particular attention to the acoustic determinants of the convulsions, while a great number of others have made observations on constitutional and dietary factors that affect the response.

Conflict and Audiogenic Seizures [4]

In the research by Maier and his collaborators (84), a modified Lashley jumping apparatus was used to train rats to discriminate between circular patterns differing in brightness and background. Such a problem is easy for rats to learn, and no disturbances in behavior were observed. The conflict (opposing behavioral tendencies) was introduced by making the problem unsolvable for the animal in various ways. For example, a card that the animal had previously been trained to avoid was presented alone in a one-window situation. The animal was then forced to jump by electrifying the jumping platform or applying a blast of air. No disturbance was observed in some of the animals, while others developed "abortive" jumping that missed the pattern entirely, the animal leaping out toward the side of the apparatus. A few of the animals showed an unusual and pathological response in which they would leap to the floor, and, after a period of great hyperactivity, exhibit convulsive seizures followed by an unresponsive or stuporous condition.

The seizures appeared only in the situation involving the air-blast, and although Maier recognized this fact, he emphasized the conflict interpretation without adequate controls over the effect that the air-blast alone might have. When it was found by a number of other investigators that sound alone was an effective way of eliciting these convulsive responses in untrained animals, a controversy arose over the relative role that conflict and sound stimuli play in inducing the attacks. Morgan and Waldman (105) dealt a telling blow at the

---

[4] The nature of the seizure as well as the violent controversy stirred up by its interpretations stimulated great interest in the field of comparative psychology. These researches have been capably reviewed by Finger in 1944 and 1947 (32, 33). Maier's point of view may be obtained by contrasting his early conclusions (84) with those expressed in a recent publication (92). An objective and comprehensive account of the studies on convulsive behavior in the rat is in the recent book by Munn (109). The extent of these bibliographies attest to the research effort expended on seizures in the rat.

conflict hypothesis in their investigations relating the intensity and frequency of auditory stimulus to the incidence of seizures. They found that the frequency of seizures varied with the distance of the sound source from the animal and thus was a function of sound intensity. It was here pointed out that in testing the effects of sound alone in Maier's original experiment, the rats were about eight feet from the source of sound, whereas when they were tested with "conflict-plus-sound," the animals were only a few inches away from the sound source. Consequently, the conclusions drawn from that experiment, that more seizures were obtained when the conflict situation was used, might be explained simply in terms of a difference in the intensity of sound situation.

In other early experiments, Maier and Glaser (91) found significantly more seizures when animals were confined in a small box than in a large one, and more in an opaque box than in a transparent one. These findings were interpreted in terms of "trapping" the animal more effectively in the small and in the opaque boxes. In another study, Maier (85) found that rats that had developed the abortive "jumps" had fewer seizures than those animals that failed to show these responses. These abortive responses removed the animal from the immediate proximity of the air-blast and included jumping too high, too far to the side, or jumping down into the net below. Maier felt that these and other studies (88) lent support to his original contention that seizures associated with sound stimulation are conflict induced. Sounds were thought to induce seizures by not providing any localized escape reaction. They function primarily by being irritants that furnish no release and build up tension in the organism that it is unable to resolve except by a catastrophic type of reaction [(88), p. 286].

The above mentioned study of Morgan and Waldman pointed out that without controls the acoustical conditions could vary importantly with the type and size of enclosure and with the distance of the experimental animal from the source of sound. With this in mind, Maier and Longhurst (92) undertook a repetition of some of their earlier experiments with certain additional controls over sound stimulation. This article also recapitulated the arguments in support of the conflict interpretation. In these experiments, animals were again taught to discriminate between cards with a small black circle on a white background and a small white circle on a black background. No air blast was used during the training. At that time, the one-window situation was introduced, which, in random frequency, contained the negative and positive stimuli. If the animals failed to jump within 30 seconds, the air-blast was applied and a jump was required regardless of the nature of the stimulus confronting the animal. The air blast was stated to be "below the seizure-producing threshold for most rats." During this time, littermate controls for the experimental animals were handled daily but received no discrimination training. This group was then tested in the one-window situation without the learned conflict associated with a forced jump to a negative stimulus. It was thought in this way that these animals would be affected only by the air-blast. These animals received a slightly greater duration of air exposure than the experimental group. These groups were then compared carefully on their convulsive responses in a situation that was a "negative card situation" only for the experimental group. The percentage of tests that were associated with seizures was 20.3 in the experimental group and 7.6 in the control group. Likewise, 37.8 per cent of the experimental rats had seizures as compared with 9.1 per cent in control animals. With respect to the litter comparisons, the experimental group had a significantly greater number of seizures per animal. Three times as many animals had seizures to the negative card plus the air-blast situation as in the air-blast situation alone. This is, according to Maier and Longhurst, contrary to the view that makes auditory stimulation the sole cause of the seizure and makes necessary the recognition of the importance of conflict in this type of abnormality [(92), p. 409].

The great majority of investigators have either opposed the conflict hypothesis because of other interpretations of the data or simply found it unnecessary. Their interpretations of conflict *vs.* audiogenic factors have usually stressed the following points:

1. The seizures have been found to have little in common with "experimental neuroses" as described by Pavlov. Although certain behavioral abberations were noted in three of Cook's rats in a conditioning situation (18), nothing resembling convulsive seizures was described. Most investigators regard the seizures as a special instance of epileptoid phenomena.

2. A wide range of sound stimuli has been found effective in eliciting seizures in susceptible, untrained animals. The intensity of acoustic stimulation is particularly important (105). The seizures are not of the nature of a reflex, as studies on the latency and vari-

ability of attacks have shown. Sound happens to be the most efficient "triggering off" stimulus known now. Sound itself, however, is probably neither a necessary nor a sufficient condition as, for example, the controlled studies of dietary deficiency have shown.

3. There is little evidence that a "soundless conflict" can play any part in eliciting seizures. A report by Griffiths (49) describes seizures in *a rat* when electric shock was used as a forcing agent in a conflict situation. Lazovik and Patton (71), beginning with normal, unsusceptible rats, induced susceptibility to convulsions by maintaining them on purified diets deficient in a mineral, magnesium. Although extremely sensitive to sound-induced convulsions, no seizure sensitivity was apparent when shock (instead of sound) was used to force the animals to respond in the Lashley jumping apparatus. A conflict interpretation seemed superfluous, as in the other experiments on dietary deficiency, because control animals on a diet containing magnesium were subjected to the same testing procedures without developing seizures.

As additional information on seizures has become available, Maier has changed his interpretation considerably from his earlier position where auditory stimulation was all but disregarded. His present position is that conflict is the basic factor even when a confined animal is stimulated with auditory stimulation alone. Maier and Longhurst have also shown, as described above, that conflict plus sound can elicit more seizures in susceptible animals than sound alone.

Further consideration of the controversy is pointless if one may not separate sound from the conflict said to be caused by it. An investigator interested in the controversy *per se* would now seem to be facing an unsolvable problem. The controversy has some historical interest for those who have participated in the work. Some of the interest in the seizures may have been due to a vague uneasiness on the part of many investigators. The widespread convulsive sensitivity of the laboratory rat may have involved a heretofore unrecognized type of pathology. It may well have influenced the course and interpretation of many other previous researches on discrimination, conditioning, or other behavioral problems. It is possible that the controversy's main positive value has been the fact that it introduced the study of convulsive phenomena as an additional area for research in comparative psychology.

The Effect of Different Variables on the Incidence of Audiogenic Seizures

The seizure

Audiogenic seizures have a general pattern that is not unlike that of convulsions induced by a wide variety of other procedures. Individual animals differ in susceptibility from day to day and there are also variations in severity from one animal to another. In general, seizures consist of: (a) rotary pivoting and bursts of hyperactivity after variable periods of auditory stimulation; (b) a generalized convulsion in which a cephalo-caudad progression of clonic contractions may be evident; and (c) a stage of tonic immobility during which an animal can be molded into various positions and is unresponsive to strong sensory stimulation. The latter stage is sometimes characterized by cyanosis, exopthalmos, excessive salivation, and impairment of reflexes.

The convulsive seizures that were described above have been found to appear in varied proportions of animal colonies in different parts of the country. A detailed description of audiogenic seizures as observed by a number of different investigators has been given by Finger (33).

Stimulus characteristics

Morgan and his collaborators devoted a very considerable amount of work in attempting to evaluate the role of auditory stimuli so that the role of other variables would become more clear. The earlier work on conflict indicated to them that most of the studies would remain in question because acoustical conditions had not been controlled. For this reason they investigated the effect of the intensity and frequency of the auditory stimulus on the incidence of audiogenic seizures. The general findings of this important study by Morgan and Waldman have already been mentioned. Morgan and Gould (103) varied the frequency of a Galton whistle and also of an oscillator and found that the frequency of seizures increased as the frequency of the sound stimulus was increased from approximately 10,000 to 20,000 cycles per second. There was the suggestion that the most important aspect of auditory stimulation was the loudness of the sound above the rat's threshold for a given frequency. In later studies by Morgan and Galambos (101, 102, 34) some of these factors were subjected to intensive study. It was found that the rat's hearing had an audiogram that was displaced upward from that of man with the region of maximum sensitivity between 15,000 and 60,000 cycles per second. This upper level could only be estimated. The work indicated that some of the high frequencies, particularly those inaudible to man, were most effective in producing seizures. Sensation levels of 100 decibels were sufficient to induce seizures in susceptible animals regardless of the frequency that was used. Galambos and Morgan produced seizures with an apparatus that could produce a continuous or interrupted 4,000 cycle tone at an intensity level of around 134 decibels. The duration of the sound-silence cycle was varied systematically. When a sound-to-silence ratio of 1:1 was utilized, the stimulus became more effective as the silence cycle decreased from 10 seconds (five seconds on and five seconds off) to one second ($\frac{1}{2}$ second on and $\frac{1}{2}$ second off). Shorter cycles were just as effective as a steady tone in eliciting seizures. In all these seizures the latent period was approximately the same with different types of stimuli.

These studies made it clear that the most effective sound stimuli were high frequencies, but that seizures also resulted if the loudness level of low frequencies was increased. These were important findings and indicated very clearly that the characteristics of the stimulus, particularly frequency and intensity, must be controlled in seizure studies that investigated the effect of other conditions. They also clarified one reason for the disagreements and confusion in the early interpretations of the seizures in showing that the differences in the sound stimuli used by the many different investigators might themselves be responsible for discrepancies in the results and hence in the interpretation of the results.

Age and sex

As evidence that the number and the severity of seizures in groups of rats is in part a function of the age at which the animals were tested, Smith (137) and Maier and Glaser (90) reported an increase in the number of susceptible animals with repeated stimulation as the animals grew older. Farris and Yeakel (26) showed that in Wistar albino rats, younger animals were more susceptible, with a decrease in frequency in both sexes after the age of 240 days. Metabolic changes associated with age seemed important and there was the suggestion that the effect of possible food deficiencies would be more acute during a period of rapid growth. It also seemed that age rather than adaptation was responsible for the decrease in the sensitivity of older animals. These results were confirmed in later studies by Finger (31), who found the highest incidence of first seizures from 30 to 60 days of age with an increase in general susceptibility up to 150 days.

Finger, in 1947 (33), as the result of a review of the literature, concluded that susceptibility may vary markedly with age, and that, therefore, a particular effort should be made to control this factor in investigations where other variables are utilized and where a wide age range is to be covered. In most of the studies that have appeared, data on sex differences have been mentioned incidentally to other experimental findings. There is little clear-cut evidence at the present of reliable sex differences in sensitivity.

Genetic factors

On the basis of the early experiments, Maier and Glaser (89) suggested an all or nothing inheritance of susceptibility transmitted according to a Mendelian dominant trait. Most of the subsequent studies have indicated that hereditary determinants of susceptibility are of a more complex nature. Griffiths (47), by selective breeding of susceptible parents, varied the percentage of abnormally responding animals; however the crossing of normals invariably produced some convulsive offspring. These two studies utilized animals of different age and genetic stock. A further study by Finger (31) utilized a greater number of cases, and the age factor was more adequately controlled by testing the animals over longer periods. In this study, it was found that susceptible parents yielded a proportion of susceptible offspring no greater than that found in litters from crossings between two nonsusceptible parents or one susceptible and one nonsusceptible parent. The fact that from 66 to 73 per cent of all of the young animals tested, no matter which apparent genetic cross, showed seizures at some time during their life, seemed to rule out susceptibility as the inheritance of a simple dominant trait. That genetic factors are extremely important, however, is evident from the findings af Maier, Glaser, and Griffiths. A later study by Maier (86) reported that inheritance in two different strains of rats did not follow a simple Mendelian pattern. Both the strain and the individual reactiveness influenced the transmission. It seemed to indicate that susceptibility could be transmitted more readily in the unstable animals than in the stable strain.

Farris and Yeakel (27) have found greater susceptibility in gray Norway rats than in tame Wistar albinos. It is interesting to compare these results with the findings of Griffiths (50) that wild Norway and Alexandrine rats did not show any tendency to seizures. Dietary deficiency and endocrine changes were suggested by Farris and Yeakel as possible factors influencing sensitivity shown by domesticated rats. It is an interesting example of behavioral differences associated with domestication. Wide variations in susceptibility have been reported in different laboratories with different strains of animals. Martin and Hall (95) found that their nonemotional strain of animals had more frequent and more severe seizures than rats of the emotional strain.

Before final conclusions may be drawn concerning the importance of hereditary factors in audiogenic seizures, larger samples must be employed and the significance of age recognized by a testing program extended over relatively long periods of time. The development of strains differing in sensitivity would also be an advantage.

Audiogenic seizures that are descriptively similar to the seizures observed in the rat have also been described in mice (51). These seizures were elicited by an electric bell, and two different strains of mice were found to differ markedly in their susceptibility to seizures. In the case of the *DBA* strain, a high proportion had seizures and died following the convulsion. In contrast, the *C*-57 strain showed very little evidence of susceptibility. There is considerable evidence (42, 43) that the tendency to develop these seizures has a genetic basis that offers interesting possibilities in the testing of various genetic hypotheses with another kind of animal. In these investigations, genetically homogenous mice were used. These animals were the result of more than 50 generations of brother-sister matings and have been shown to have a definitely predictable susceptibility to sound-induced seizures when they are given standardized sound tests for a two-minute period. A more complete discussion of this work is given in Chapter 11.

The effect of previous seizures

There are contradictory results concerning the effects of seizures on subsequent sensitivity. Available evidence indicates that the seizure threshold rises immediately after an audiogenic seizure and this general finding has support from a number of studies on other types of seizures, such as those induced by electrical stimuli or by the injection of drugs. The conclusions of studies that have investigated the problem of adaptation over periods longer than 24 hours do not permit any definite conclusions about the question at the present. The probability of response (32) depends on many factors, including age, the intervals between tests, characteristics of stimulation, and the physiological condition of the animals. It is possible that varying amounts of irreparable damage may result from the repeated seizures themselves. Differences in the findings from different laboratories probably reflect varying degrees of control over these variables.

Dietary deficiency

A detailed consideration of dietary deficiency as a factor of possible importance in the rat's sensitivity to convulsions was necessitated by many references to similar syndromes in the literature of biochemistry and nutrition. Another consideration prompting the investigation of dietary deficiency was the fact that early experiments on seizures could be criticized because it was so difficult to control the initial sensitivity of rats selected for experimental and control groups. Usually only those animals in various colonies showing the behavior abnormality in question were selected. The classification of seizures in terms of their objective similarity seemed hazardous in view of the marked variability of the attacks. It seemed desirable to attempt to produce such seizures experimentally in normal animals, that is, in animals showing no convulsive sensitivity during preliminary sound tests. With some degree of control exercised over the origin and severity of the symptoms, one can be more sure of the effect that other variables have on their appearance.

The nutritional studies to be described below utilized the split-litter technique with normal weanlings divided into matched groups. In this way the incidence of observed seizures associated with a given nutritional deficiency could be compared with that occurring in normally-growing young animals of the same strain. Purified diets were used which gave control over the nutritional substances known to be necessary for good growth in the rat. A resonator buzzer with a constant duration and intensity in a soundproof box was used as a sound source for these experiments. The possible complicating effects of stress or conflict were in some measure controlled by maintaining normal control animals subjected to similar tests throughout.

The first experiment that suggested a relationship between audiogenic seizures and nutritional deficiencies was that of Patton (113). In a later series of studies (117, 118), it was found that sound-induced seizures appeared when normal young rats were maintained for extended periods on purified diets deficient in vitamin B_1. These studies, however, indicated clearly that the observed sensitivity could not be directly associated with vitamin B_1 deficiency *per se,* but rather seemed a function of the inanition that invariably accompanies such deprivations. In further studies of prolonged food restriction, it was found that the resulting high level of seizures was not suppressed by high daily supplements of vitamin B_1. This seemed to indicate that low caloric intake (and the associated deficiencies of the essential food substances) played a basic role in sensitivity to seizures. Additional evidence that this was true was obtained in the experiment on different levels of vitamin B_1 intake. The factor of food intake was held constant for all experimental groups that were subjected to a gradual decrease in daily food intake as controlled by the voluntary consumption of the group receiving the lowest vitamin B_1 supplement. Under these conditions, an almost parallel rise in sensitivity occurred in all the groups despite differential levels of vitamin B_1 intake. Control animals maintained throughout this time on an adequate dietary regime showed no evidence of sensitivity. The most interesting aspect of this experiment was the evidence that increased sensitivity associated with low food intake and persisting despite adequate vitamin B_1 supplements might be quickly reduced by the addition of a group of ten vitamin and mineral supplements without increasing the caloric intake. This indicated that protection was afforded by the supplements *per se* or that they permitted a more efficient utilization of food substances already present in the reduced food allowance.

The extension of these studies gave evidence that was well supported by other studies in the field of biochemistry to the effect that two of these substances were closely associated with sound-induced seizures. The incidence of sensitivity to sound and to spontaneous convulsions without known sound stimulation could be observed to develop in normal young animals maintained on purified diets deficient in pyridoxin and magnesium. Patton, Karn, and Longenecker (119) observed that spontaneous convulsions appeared toward the end of lactation in young rats born of mothers maintained since parturition on pyridoxin-deficient diets. These seizures developed in the animals while they were in their cages and in the absence of known auditory stimulation. Pyridoxin supplements (50 gammas) quickly alleviated or prevented the spontaneous seizures. It should be emphasized, however, that they failed to offer continued protection against a latent sensitivity that appeared when these animals were later exposed to systematic auditory tests. The observed fits were similar to those previously studied and descriptively similar to those observed during previous biochemical studies of pyridoxin-deficient animals (15, 20). A later experiment by Pilgrim and Patton (125) confirmed these findings and made the important additional observation that when endemic middle-ear infection is controlled, sensitivity to sound can be reversed or entirely prevented in almost all the young animals by the administration of pyridoxin. Later experiments (116) indicated that it was possible to protect rats against the appearance of seizures by the addition of a B-complex concentrate early in the animal's development. While a high degree of sensitivity could be prevented by the inclusion of such concentrates, they were not found effective if added to the diet of young animals after the seizures had developed. This may indicate irreversible damage. On the other hand, it may simply mean that the group of vitamin supplements does not exercise a specific protective function but permits better-nourished young animals to adjust more adequately to a yet unknown pathological condition of which the convulsion is one symptom.

Patton and Longenecker (120) [5] have studied the sensitivity to seizures that developed swiftly in young rats deprived of magnesium. Dependent upon the duration of the deficiency, normal animals subjected to regular sound tests could be observed to pass through a uniform sequence of convulsive reactivity. Animals first showed hyperactivity to sound. As the deficiency progressed, they developed clonic seizures and finally, later, a severe tonic seizure in which the hyperactivity and tonic movements were brief. During the terminal stages of such a deficiency, spontaneous seizures appeared without known stimulation, in which young animals usually died. The type of seizure response was clearly a function of the stage of deficiency, further stimulation becoming unnecessary in the terminal stages.

---

[5] Other nutritional factors involved in the development of convulsive reactivity in the rat have been studied by Greenberg, Boelter, and Knopf (45).

Patton (115) observed a similar picture of sound-induced seizures associated with a magnesium deficiency in the hamster. These experiments gave additional information· on the manifestations of magnesium deficiency in a different animal species. There is no present experimental work that clarifies the possible relationships between pyridoxin and magnesium deficiency. It seems quite apparent that both substances are related in some way to physiological mechanisms underlying the rat's sensitivity to seizures.

These experiments seemed to offer a high degree of control over the origin and the severity of convulsive responses. They made no attempt, however, to explain a complex bit of animal behavior in terms of a single variable. It was quite clear that audiogenic seizures were dependent in several important ways upon the nutritional state of the animals. Controlled alterations in the diets made it possible to produce or alleviate such sensitivity to seizures in a high percentage of normal animals. In a manner not yet understood, sound appeared to function as a most effective manner of inducing attacks. It did not, however, seem to be a necessary condition for the appearance of seizures in acutely deficient animals.

Middle-ear infection

Patton (114) called attention to middle-ear infection as a factor of possible importance in the rat's sensitivity to sound-induced convulsions. A high degree of association was found between the infection and susceptibility in groups of young animals. In contrast, mature animals, although showing a high incidence of infection were not nearly so sensitive to seizures. In a later study, Patton and Zabarenko (122) extended these observations to include groups of young animals raised under different laboratory conditions. Over 355 young animals were tested for seizures and for observable signs of ear infection. This latter study (see also Kenshalo and Kryter, 67) found some animals sensitive to seizures but without observable signs of infection. The great majority of sensitive animals, however, were infected. As Kenshalo and Kryter pointed out, the sensitivity in noninfected animals indicates that the observed infection is not a necessary condition for audiogenic seizures. There was the definite indication, however, that the infection made susceptible animals more sensitive to seizures than noninfected animals also showing sensitivity.

The high percentage of middle-ear infection in laboratory rats is astonishing. Quite aside from the bearing that infection may have on sensitivity is the complicating effect it may have had on animals used in other experimental investigations. Its role in sensitivity to seizures is not clear from the few findings now reported. It may play no causal role whatever. It may augment sensitivity in animals already susceptible from another cause entirely. It may be a residual of an earlier pathological condition that is related to the sensitivity to seizures. Finally, it may account for the lessened sensitivity that several investigators have observed in older rats. Perhaps these animals had suffered a permanent impairment in the auditory receptor mechanism. Certainly the condition is a widespread one and its presence in animal colonies makes autopsy procedures necessary. A check on the condition may clarify in retrospect ambiguous findings during other types of experimental study of the laboratory rat.

Neurophysiological Factors

Some investigations of audiogenic seizures have been oriented toward the discovery of the neurophysiological mechanisms involved. These have been in general of three different types: (a) those investigating electrocortical activity, (b) those investigating the effects of various drugs known to have an effect on neural mechanisms, and (c) those investigating the effect of brain injury on seizures.

Electrocortical activity

An isolated but extremely stimulating research by Lindsley, Finger and Henry (83) showed that audiogenic seizures were accompanied by changes in the electroencephalogram that were very similar to those associated with convulsive disorders in man. They found that the nature of the activity varied with the phase of the attack. Large, slow waves or spike and slow waves of from two to four per second were found to be associated with clonus, and there were series of spike or fast waves of low amplitude during tonic periods. Similar to the EEG patterns of human epileptic patients, it was found that there was a great decrease in electrocortical activity while the animal was in the comatose recovery phase of the seizure. A marked variability of heart rate was also associated with the period just before seizures. Heart rate increased markedly during the seizure and fell to a low level during the comatose state. These effects are illustrated in Fig. 6.

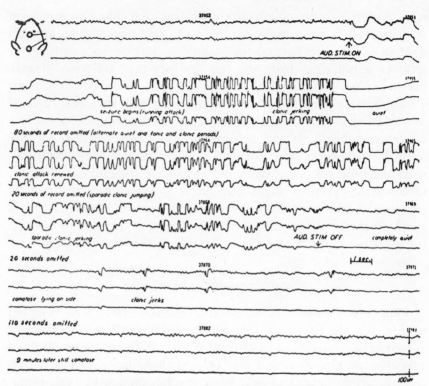

Fig. 6. The Electroencephalogram of a Rat During an Audiogenic Seizure. Three tracings of different amplification. [From Lindsley, Finger, and Henry (83, p. 188). Used by permission of the *Journal of Neurophysiology* and Charles C. Thomas, Publisher.]

The effect of drugs

Studies on the effects of drugs have resulted from the fact that certain drugs and hormonal substances have known effects on neural mechanisms. So far, although there has been much careful work, these experiments have not clarified the specific neuromechanism involved in audiogenic seizures. Humphrey, in two studies (62, 63), tested a number of parasympathetic drugs. In particular, atropin and eserine were found to have opposite effects. Atropin diminished the frequency of seizure and eserine was found to increase the number of attacks. Mecholyl and benzyl benzoate were found to have no appreciable effect, and nicotine was found to increase the frequency of seizures. A consideration of the effects of these various drugs indicated that one must look elsewhere than in the parasympathetic nervous system for the explanation of the effect of these substances on seizures.

Arnold (4) observed that adrenalin injections reduced the incidence of seizures in susceptible rats as well as in animals rendered susceptible by injections of strychnine. Many of the drugs reported used in these and other studies have the general effect of increasing the irritability of the nervous system, and a number of investigators have tested out the effect of such drugs to see whether seizure incidence is increased by their use. A number of these studies (33) have shown that metrazol, coramine, strychnine-sulphate and caffein-sodium-benzoate markedly increase the susceptibility to seizure when given in subconvulsive doses. There is a definite indication that these drugs, as well as other procedures that are known to increase the irritability of nervous tissue, result in an increased susceptibility to seizures.

On the other hand, a number of drugs that are effective in reducing the incidence of epileptic seizures in human subjects have been shown to exert similar effects on audiogenic seizures in rats. Griffiths (46) and Cohen and Karn (17) thus observed that dilantin reduces the incidence of convulsions. Shohl (134) found similar results when the dilantin was mixed with the animals' food. Adams and Griffiths (1) have recently found that tridione gave no clear effect on the incidence of seizures. This is one of the newer drugs used for the symptomatic treatment of *petit mal* epilepsy. Its effect upon *grand mal* seizures in humans has been found to result in equivocal or negative results.

The effect of brain lesions

Maier (84) suggested that there might be a difference in susceptibility in animals subjected to brain lesions, and there was the strong suggestion from the study of Lindsley, Finger, and Henry that cortical mechanisms were directly involved in various phases of the attack. This question has received attention in two studies, one by Beach and Weaver (6) and one by Weiner and Morgan (143). The results of these studies, however, are not easily interpreted at the moment because the findings are diametrically opposed. The former study found that nearly complete decortication increased susceptibility but exerted no effect upon duration of attack. There is some indication that the severity of the seizures was increased. The latter study of Weiner and Morgan showed in general a marked reduction in the frequency of seizures. This was particularly prominent in the group subjected to prefrontal lobectomy. In these animals, the convulsive aspects of the seizures were greatly reduced.

The Mechanism

What are the possible mechanisms involved in convulsive seizures elicited by sound stimulation? Despite the great volume of work that has been done, no adequate explanation has yet been advanced. Questions that remain to be asked and answered are many. It is agreed that seizures are definitely not of the nature of a reflex response to sound; they involve the whole organism and can probably be influenced by any change in environmental factors that can affect the excitability of the neural tissue. Usually in the theoretical explanations of epilepsy, a basic constitutional abnormality is postulated. In addition to this *continuous* abnormality, it is always necessary to postulate *discontinuous* environmental factors that may recurrently elicit neuronal discharge seen overtly in the form of clinical symptoms. It seems quite probable that a similar interaction of conditions has made the problem of audiogenic seizures such a difficult one to solve.

There have been certain trends that the experimental work has taken that are suggestive of the nature of the neurophysiological mechanisms involved. Some of the most stimulating of these hypotheses emerged from the early study of Lindsley, Finger, and Henry (83). Some of the ideas in this report have been amplified in certain ways by research studies that have appeared since that time, as the review by Finger (33) has indicated. Certain additional hints as to the mechanisms involved have resulted from the studies of the characteristics that effective auditory stimuli have, and still other suggestions have come from studies of drug effects and dietary deficiency.

There is evidence that an overstimulation of the auditory projection pathways initiates certain underlying conditions for audiogenic seizures. These, in the order of their probable sequence are: (*a*) a widespread autonomic discharge of both sympathetic and parasympathetic nature, but with the former system tending to predominate, and (*b*) a marked electrocortical discharge. In cases where the autonomic discharge occurs without the electrocortical discharge, a convulsive seizure may not be observed. Seizures may be in some way obviated in this case when the animals show a form of "substitute behavior," such as motor activity, grooming, or teeth-chattering. The stimulus seems to act as a trigger for autonomic reactions, during which the diencephalon discharges both centrally and peripherally. Thus, it is possible that the effects of central bombardment of the motor cortex may be altered or reinforced by feedback from peripheral autonomic activity. If confirmed, the findings reported in the study of Lindsley, Finger, and Henry that seizure responses were lacking in vagotomized animals will have important implications for this point of view.

The manner in which the auditory stimulus induces the autonomic changes is not clear. It may, as the above authors have indicated, directly stimulate the auricular branch of the vagus, which supplies part of the tympanic membrane and has reflex connections with the sympathetic nervous system through the superior ganglion of the vagus. It may act on the auditory receptor mechanism as a pain-producing stimulus.

In addition to these possibilities, one might postulate a lowering of central neural threshold conditions that could facilitate a spread of excitation shown overtly in the form of the generalized convulsive attack. The symptoms associated with magnesium deficiency offer only one example of conditions of this kind. There is evidence that magnesium tetany involves preliminary midbrain centers. An ionic imbalance in the tissues might be expected to affect the nervous system in accordance with its vulnerability or functional demands. It is of interest that hypothalamic nuclei are served by a vascular supply much more extensive per square millimeter of tissue than the cerebral cortex. The neurons of the anterior regions are especially sensitive to chemical or thermal changes in the blood. In this specific deficiency, there would be the possibility that increased metabolic demands and/or circulatory changes attendant upon sudden sensory stimulation could precipitate a seizure by making acute an already hypersensitive condition of nervous tissue. Gibbs and Gibbs (41) have shown that the region anterior to the thalamus has a lower convulsive threshold than the motor cortex. A functional proximity of this region to the central connections of the auditory projection system may well have some bearing upon the effectiveness of sound in precipitating seizures.

Any condition that can affect neural thresholds should affect seizures in a similar manner. Perhaps the many diverse conditions that culminate in convulsive seizures do so because of a common effect upon basic biochemical processes of neural transmission, for example, the cortical synthesis and destruction of acetylcholine. If such processes are severe enough, a seizure may result without sensory stimulation. If less severe, external stimuli may be effective in facilitating a spread of excitation from a critical focal point.

These ideas are, for the most part, speculations that continued work may prove false. They do offer, however, some leads for future research. In any event, it seems certain that when the tale is finally told, much will have been learned about the fundamental nature of the convulsive disorders.

The Effects of Electroconvulsive Shock on Animal Behavior

In 1938, Bini (11) reported studies of epileptic attacks induced in dogs by means of electric current. This research with infra-human animals marked the beginning of a form of treatment that has since had extensive clinical use in the field of human mental disorders. Insulin shock treatment introduced by Sakel and Metrazol injections, first used by Meduna, have also been used as forms of psychiatric therapy. Electroshock treatment, however, has received the most extensive attention, possibly because of the control that is possible in its administration. Despite this wide use, little is known of the precise manner in which electroconvulsive shock treatment exerts its therapeutic effects.

In the following section, a few of the basic principles that the animal work on electroshock has suggested will be discussed. There are several reasons for including a consideration of these studies in the present chapter. For one thing, they have an important bearing upon the understanding of "convulsive mechanisms." An additional reason would be the fact that, for the efficient clinical use of this technique, it is very important to know its effects on behavior other than that which is being specifically treated. Animal subjects can and have been used profitably in this kind of research.

Instrumental variables

Many different electroshock machines are commercially available for clinical use. Some of them, however, are not satisfactory to the researcher because they do not exert adequate control over various aspects of the electroshock stimulus. Amperage, duration, impedance, voltage, current frequency, current intensity, and wave form are all important variables that the experimenter must control. New apparatus for administering electroshock convulsions has been described by Russell, Pierce, Rohrer, and Townsend (130).

The nature of electroshock convulsions

Detailed descriptions of electroshock convulsions have been given by Page (112), Stainbrook (138), Stainbrook and deJong (139), Golub and Morgan (44), Siegel and Lacy (135) and Braun, Russell, and Patton (13).

1. **The seizure.** The stages of the electroshock convulsions and the method of applying the electrodes are shown in Fig. 7. This seizure

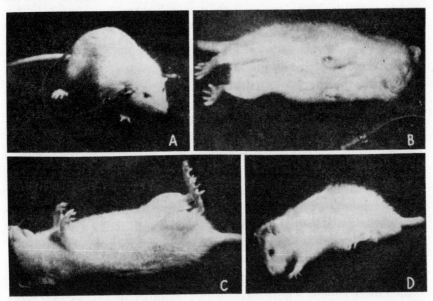

Fig. 7. **Stages of Electrically Induced Convulsive Seizures in the Rat.** See text. [From Braun, Russell, and Patton (13, p. 96). Used by permission of the *Journal of Comparative and Physiological Psychology* and the American Psychological Association.]

was induced in a mature male albino rat by a current of 20 milliamperes passing for one second. The description of these seizures from Braun, Russell and Patton (13) is as follows:

With the application of the current, the rat gave a start, with the spine flexed ventrally, and fell on its side with the hind legs drawn up and the front legs brought down. After two to four seconds, the animal passed into a state of "tonic contraction" of all of the bodily musculature, the extensors predominating (Fig. 7B). The eyes were closed, the ears laid back, the fore paws were held rigidly to the sides, while the hind limbs were in extension. Such rigidity seemed similar to that shown by a decerebrate preparation. During the tonic phase the pupils were dilated and un-responsive to light. There was also a brief cessation of breathing, and usually ejaculation, defecation, and urination were observed as well as an occasional appearance of reddish material from the orbit (probably protoporphyrin from the Harderian gland). Approximately 15 to 20 seconds following application of the current the tonic state gave way to clonic movements, which involved principally the hind legs but which affected the whole skeletal musculature (Fig. 7C). This clonic stage lasted for an additional 20-25 seconds, following which there appeared a cata-tonic stage characterized by waxy flexibility and an impairment of placing and righting reflexes (Fig. 7D). This state was in evidence for approxi-mately 120 to 150 seconds (after the application of the current) from the first to the fifth shocks, but grew shorter with succeeding shocks, so that by the twentieth shock the animal could stand when so placed 90 seconds after the shock. (Pp. 96-97)

2. Convulsive thresholds. The "convulsive mechanism" in com-mon with threshold mechanisms of other neuromuscular systems seems to obey an "all-or-none" course. While there are some inter-individual differences in convulsive thresholds, it has been found that thresholds for single subjects as measured in terms of amperage remain rather constant from one convulsion to the next (98). There is also a great deal of evidence that the threshold may be influenced by various drugs (141) as well as by other characteristics of the electro-shock impulse, such as frequency (72), wave form (126), and sensory stimulation (121), or other physiological conditions. There is also evidence that neither the intensity nor the duration of supraliminal stimulation seemed closely related to the duration of the various convulsive phases.

3. Other effects. There have been a number of studies that have dealt with the physiological or structural changes accompanying the convulsions. These changes may be of a reversible or irreversible nature. Winder and Stone (146), as well as others, have indicated that electroconvulsive shocks reduce the rat's activity level. Observa-tions of weight changes have been made in two studies by Braun, Russell, and Patton (14). Twenty-five electroshock convulsions were accompanied by a weight loss during the first half of the series. This impairment, despite continued shocks, appeared to be reversible. During the second half of the shock series the animals gained weight and surpassed the control animals after the convulsive series was terminated. Russell, Pierce, and Townsend (131) have shown that tissue impedance is altered as a function of stimulus intensity as well as the number of convulsions. Impedance decreases initially and then gradually returns to its original level.

Alteration of brain tissue has been reported by Wortis, *et al.* (147), Merrit and Putnam (98), Ferraro, *et al.* (29), and Ferraro and Roizin (28), and compression fractures of the spinal cord have been described by Russell, Townsend, Braun, and Patton (132).

It is not certain that there are definite histopathologic changes in the brain within the usual range of electroshock dosages (Siekert, Williams, and Windle, 136). However, the foregoing work, as well as many additional studies suggests strongly that, if damage to the organism is to be minimized, only supraliminal shock values should be used. A careful control of the stimulus during any experimental work is emphasized.

Behavioral effects

1. **Learning.** One of the areas of greatest interest in the field of electroshock phenomena has been the effect of repeated convulsions on learning. A group of important studies has been performed by Stone (140), Porter, Stone, and Erickson (128), and Erickson, Porter, and Stone (24). The latter investigators studied the effects of 10 electroconvulsive shocks that were administered before training on a multiple T-maze. These shocks were administered to young animals between the ages of 20 and 29 days. Ten shocks were given with a current intensity of 50 milliamperes. All of these experiments showed an increase in trial and error scores in the shocked animals. Braun, Russell, and Patton (13), with a fairly complex water maze (Lashley III pattern), showed that decrements in the learning of a new habit followed a series of 25 electroshocks administered under controlled conditions. Learning was tested after the series of shocks had been terminated. There was evidence in this experiment that the decrement in learning was of a transitory nature disappearing within thirty days following the final convulsion. Hayes (56) found that decrements were also apparent when the shocks were given concurrently with learning trials. The decrements that he observed were most apparent on the second trial.

Certain studies have given an indication that the effect of electroshock on learning would be a function of the complexity of the task confronting the experimental animals. Russell (129), and Braun, Russell, and Patton (13) conducted a series of experiments in which all conditions were constant except that the level of difficulty of the task was varied from a simple straightaway to a single-choice-point maze and finally to the five-choice-point (Lashley III) maze. These experiments did not show any decrement in learning the first two of these problems, which were fairly easy for the animals. A significant decrement, however, was found when the convulsions preceded the five-choice-point maze.

2. Retention. In addition to learning, there has been a considerable amount of work on the effects of shocks on retention of maze habits. In all the experiments on retention in which complex tasks have been used, the shocked animals have shown much poorer retention and relearning than the control animals. Duncan, in 1945 (22), found that shocked animals were significantly inferior to control groups in relearning a Lashley III maze. Duncan added a second control group that was given comparable shocks to the hind legs to test for the effects of cutaneous shock alone. In addition to the demonstration that the electroshock convulsions impaired the animal's performance, it was shown that shock alone with its emotional components was not responsible for the impaired retention. Porter and Stone (127) performed an experiment in which etherization prevented convulsions during cerebral shocks. These authors found that the group receiving convulsions showed poorer performance during and following the shock treatments. Where etherization eliminated a convulsion, the electroshock had but a mild effect which did not impair maze performance in measurable degree. Townsend, Russell, and Patton (142) investigated differences in performance where the strength of current was systematically varied. Convulsions were induced by current strengths of 20, 25, and 30 milliamperes per second. Again, retention in shocked groups was significantly inferior to the control group, although there was no relation between the degree of impairment and the current intensity used. As in the case of learning, it has been found (129, 13, 14) that the effects of electroshock on retention are functions of the difficulty of the tasks originally learned. In the experiments that have been previously mentioned, no decrement appeared in the retention of relatively simple habits such as a straightaway or a single-choice-point maze. Significant decrements, however, did appear in the retention of a more difficult five-choice-point maze. Since these were noted as long as 90 days after the convulsive series, and since there was an accentuation of the impairment rather than a recovery, the retention decrements were regarded as permanent.

In addition to the investigations of the effect of electroshock on the retention of a single maze habit, work has been carried out on the retention of diverse habit systems. Duncan (22) trained animals to go first to the left on a single-choice-point T-maze, and, after this habit was established, he taught them to go to the right. A single electroshock convulsion produced a significant return to the older habit on the first postshock maze trial. In a similar investigation, Braun and Patton (12) studied habit reversal as a function of the difficulty of the tasks involved. They concluded that under the conditions of their experiment "a series of 12 electroshock convulsions can disorganize a recently acquired habit and reinstate a previously learned habit only when the recent habit is relatively more difficult ... a simple habit is not disrupted to the extent that previously learned habits (simple or complex) supersede it."

3. **Conditioned Responses.** A number of stimulating papers have dealt with the effects of electroshock convulsions on conditioned responses. The findings here are similar to the results of the habit-reversal studies. There is now a considerable amount of evidence that indicates (68) that conditioned responses that have undergone experimental extinction show a considerable amount of recovery after convulsive-shock treatments. Gellhorn (39) showed that the degree of recovery is a function of its stability before extinction and that a temporal sequence of conditioned responses may recover simultaneously following the treatments. The duration of these recoveries seems to be variable and to depend, in an as yet undefined manner, upon the number of convulsions and the type of convulsing agent (40). On the other hand, McGinnes and Schlosberg (97) presented evidence that convulsive shocks may result in the complete inhibition of a conditioned response.

One may conclude from these and other studies that electroshock convulsions can impair maze learning and alter retention for as long as 90 days after the shock series is over. Its effects are most pronounced in the loss of retention of complex tasks. It can impair maternal behavior. When convulsions are prevented by anesthesia the electric current itself does not produce marked behavioral impairment.

Conclusions

In this chapter, we have considered many diverse behavioral abnormalities. Some attempt was made to summarize the main findings at the end of individual sections. The symptoms considered ranged from experimental neuroses in sheep to convulsive phenomena in rats. Etiological factors as diverse as monotonous conditioned stimuli and dietary deficiencies were discussed. Is there at the present time any inclusive theory under which all these factors can be grouped and integrated? The answer is simple. As yet there is not! If we are dealing with regressive behavior in a rat, do we know whether it is similar to psychoneurotic regression in a patient? Again the answer is simple. We do not! These questions, however, raise another more fundamental question, which is: How may we tell whether a resemblance between two behavioral phenomena is the same? It is possible to answer this question. If the mechanisms underlying the two cases are the *same*, the phenomena are the same despite superficial differences. If the mechanisms are different, then the cases are different despite apparent similarities.

Thus, in neurotic and convulsive symptoms alike, many diverse etiological factors may result in apparently similar symptoms. Certain conditions of electrical stimulation may simulate an audiogenic convulsion. Similar "neurotic" symptoms may appear as the result of a thyroid condition or dietary deficiency. They may also appear, however, as the result of learned, "psychogenic" factors. It may be as Hebb has suggested that a major advance can be made by treating such apparently diverse factors as *remote* rather than *immediate* causes of neurosis. In this way, conflict and malnutrition could exert the same end-effect on behavior. As in the cases of the chimpanzees, Kambi and Alpha, certain neurotic behavior could occur without any known traumatic event in the animal's past. Experience and constitutional factors both play a role in the behavior disorders. A knowledge of underlying mechanisms will show that superficially similar behavior symptoms have different causes and hence different cures. The definition of experimental conditions under which objectively measurable behavioral deviations appear marks the great contribution of the foregoing studies.

Bibliography

1. Adams, J. S. and Griffiths, W. J., Jr., The Effects of Tridione on Audiogenic Fits in Albino Rats, *J. Compar. and Physiol. Psychol.* 1948, **41**, 319-326.

2. Anderson, O. D., and Liddell, H. S., Observations on Experimental Neurosis in Sheep, *Archiv. Neurol. and Psychiat.* 1935, **34**, 330-354.

3. Anderson, O. D. and Parmenter, R., A Long-term Study of the Experimental Neurosis in the Sheep and Dog, *Psychosom. Medi. Monogr.*, 1941, **2**, 1-150.

4. Arnold, M. B., Emotional Factors in Experimental Neuroses, *J. Exper. Psychol,* 1944, **34**, 257-281.

5. Auer, E. T., and Smith, K. U., Characteristics of Epileptoid Convulsive Reactions Produced in Rats by Auditory Stimulation, *J. Compar. Psychol.*, 1940, **30**, 255-259.

6. Beach, F. A., and Weaver, T., Noise-Induced Seizures in the Rat and Their Modification by Cerebral Injury, *J. Compar. Neurol.*, 1943, **79**, 379-392.

7. Bernard, C., *An Introduction to the Study of Experimental Medicine* (Translated by Henry C. Greene and L. J. Henderson). U.S.A.: Henry Schuman, Inc., 1949 (1949 reprinting).

8. Bijou, S. W., The Development of a Conditioning Methodology for Studying Experimental Neurosis in the Rat, *J. Compar. Psychol.*, 1942, **34**, 91-106.

9. ———— A Study of "Experimental Neurosis" in the Rat by Conditioned Response Technique, *J. Compar. Psychol.*, 1943, **36**, 1-20.

10. ———— A New Conditioned Response Technique to Investigate "Experimental Neurosis" in the Rat, *Amer. Psychol.*, 1947, **2**, 319.

11. Bini, L., Experimental Researches on Epileptic Attacks Induced by the Electric Current, *Amer. J. Psychiat.*, 1938, **94**, 172-174.

12. Braun, H. W., and Patton, R. A., Habit Reversal After Electroshock Convulsions as a Function of the Difficulty of the Tasks, *J. Compar. and Physiol. Psychol.*, 1950, **43**, 252-263.

13. Braun, H. W., Russell, R. W. and Patton, R. A., Duration of Decrements in Learning and Retention Following Electroshock Convulsions in the White Rat, *J. Compar. and Physiol. Psychol.*, 1949, **42**, 87-106.

14. ———— Duration of Effects of Electroshock Convulsions on Retention of a Maze Habit in White Rats, *J. Compar. and Physiol. Psychol.*, 1949, **42**, 332-337.

15. Chick, H., el Sadr, M. M., and Warden, A. N., Occurrence of Fits of an Epileptiform Nature in Rats Maintained for Long Periods on a Diet Deprived of Vitamin B, *Biochem. Jour.*, 1940, **34**, 595-600.

16. Cobb, S., Causes of Epilepsy, *Archiv. Neurol. Psychiat.*, 1932, **27**, 1245-1256.

17. Cohen, L. M., and Karn, H. W., The Anti-Convulsant Action of Dilantin on Sound-Induced Seizures in the Rat, *J. Compar. Psychol.*, 1943, **35**, 307-310.

18. Cook, S. W., A Survey of Methods Used to Produce Experimental Neurosis, *Amer. J. Psychiat.*, 1939, **95**, 1259-1276.

19. Crawford, M. P., *et al.*, Frontal Lobe Ablation in Chimpanzee: A Resumé of "Becky" and "Lucy," pp. 3-58, in *The Frontal Lobes*, A.R.N.M.D., 1947, **27**.

20. Daniel, E., Kline, O. L. and Tolle, D., A Convulsive Syndrome in Young Rats Associated with Pyridoxine Deficiency, *Jour. Nutrit.*, 1942, **23**, 205-216.

21. Donaldson, H. H., *The Rat: Data and Reference Tables* (2nd Edition), Philadelphia: Wistar Institute of Anatomy, 1924.

22. Duncan, C. P., The Effect of Electroshock Convulsions on the Maze Habit in the White Rat, *J. Exper. Psychol.*, 1945, **35**, 267-278.

23. Dworkin, S., Conditioning Neuroses in Dog and Cat, *Psychosom. Med.*, 1939, **1**, 388-396.

24. Ericksen, C. W., Porter, P. B., and Stone, C. P., Learning Ability in Rats Given Electroconvulsive Shocks in Late Infancy. Part I., *J. Compar. and Physiol. Psychol.*, 1948, **41**, 144-154.

25. Farber, I. E., Response Fixation Under Anxiety and Non-Anxiety Conditions, *J. Exper. Psychol.*, 1948, **38**, 111-131.

26. Farris, E. J. and Yeakel, E., The Effect of Age Upon Susceptibility to Audiogenic Seizures in Albino Rats, *J. Compar. Psychol.*, 1942, **33**, 249-251.

27. ———— The Susceptibility of Albino and Gray Norway Rats to Audiogenic Seizures, *J. Compar. Psychol.*, 1943, **35**, 73-80.

28. Ferraro, A., and Roizin, L., Cerebral Morphologic Changes in Monkeys Subjected to a Large Number of Electrically Induced Convulsions, *Amer. J. Psychiat.*, 1949, **106**, 278-284.

29. ———— and Helfand, M., Morphologic Changes in the Brain of Monkeys Following Convulsions Electrically Induced, *J. Neuropathol. Exper. Neurol.*, 1946, **5**, 285-308.

30. Finch, G., Chimpanzee Frustration Responses, *Psychosom. Med.*, 1942, **4**, 233-251.

31. Finger, F. W., Factors Influencing Audiogenic Seizures in the Rat: Heredity and Age, *J. Compar. Psychol.*, 1943, **35**, 227-232.

32. ———— Experimental Behavior Disorders in the Rat, pp. 413-430, in *Personality and the Behavior Disorders* (J. McV. Hunt, Ed.). New York: Ronald Press Co., 1944.

33. ———— Convulsive Behavior in the Rat, *Psychol. Bull.*, 1947, **44**, 201-248.

34. Galambos, R., and Morgan, C. T., The Production of Audiogenic Seizures by Interrupted Tones, *J. Exper. Psychol.*, 1943, **32**, 435-442.

35. Galt, W. E., The Capacity of the Rhesus and Cebus Monkey and

the Gibbon to Acquire Differential Response to Complex Visual Stimuli, *Genet. Psychol. Monogr.*, 1939, **21**, 387-457.

36. Gantt, W. H., The Origin and Development of Nervous Disturbances Experimentally Produced, *Amer. J. Psychiat.*, 1942, **98**, 475-581.

37. ———— Measures of Susceptibility to Nervous Breakdown, *Amer. J. Psychiat.*, 1943, **99**, 839-849.

38. ———— *Experimental Basis for Neurotic Behavior.* New York: Paul B. Hoeber, Inc., 1944.

39. Gellhorn, E., Further Investigations on the Recovery of Inhibited Conditioned Reactions, *Proc. Soc. Exper. Biol. and Med.*, 1945, **59**, 155-161.

40. ———— Kessler, M., and Minatoya, H., Influence of Metrazol, Insulin Hypoglycemia, and Electrically Induced Convulsions on Reestablishment of Inhibited Conditioned Reflexes, *Proc. Soc. Exper. Biol. and Med.*, 1942, **50**, 260-262.

41. Gibbs, F. A., and Gibbs, E. L., The Convulsion Threshold of Various Parts of the Cat's Brain, *Arch. Neurol. Psychiat.*, 1936, **35**, 109-116.

42. Ginsburg, B. E., and Hovda, R. B., On the Physiology of Gene Controlled Audiogenic Seizures in Mice, *Anat. Rec.*, 1947, **99**, 621 (Abstract).

43. Ginsburg, B. E., and Huth, E., Some Aspects of the Physiology of Gene Controlled Audiogenic Seizures in Inbred Strains of Mice, *Genetics*, 1947, **32**, 87 (Abstract).

44. Golub, L. M., and Morgan, C. T., Patterns of Electrogenic Seizures in Rats: Their Relation to Stimulus-Intensity and to Audiogenic Seizures, *J. Compar. Psychol.*, 1945, **38**, 239-245.

45. Greenberg, D. M., Boelter, M. D. D., and Knopf, B. W., Factors Concerned in the Development of Tetany by the Rat, *Amer. J. Physiol.*, 1942, **137**, 459-467.

46. Griffiths, W. J., The Effects of Dilantin on Convulsive Seizures in the White Rat, *J. Compar. Psychol.*, 1942, **33**, 291-295.

47. ———— Transmission of Convulsions in the White Rat, *J. Compar. Psychol.*, 1942, **34**, 263-277.

48. ———— The Persistence of Convulsions in the White Rat, *J. Compar. Psychol.*, 1942, **34**, 279-283.

49. ———— The Production of Convulsions in the White Rat, *Compar. Psychol. Monogr.*, 1942, **17**, No. 8, 29 pp.

50. ———— Absence of Audiogenic Seizures in Wild Norway and Alexandrine Rats, *Science*, 1944, **99**, 62-63.

51. Hall, Calvin S., Genetic Differences in Fatal Audiogenic Seizures Between Two Inbred Strains of House Mice, *J. Hered.*, 1947, **38**, 3-6.

52. ———— and Martin, R. F., A Standard Experimental Situation for the Study of Abnormal Behavior in the Rat, *J. Psychol.*, 1940, **10**, 207-210.

53. Hamilton, G. V., A Study of Perseverance Reaction in Primates and Rodents, *Behav. Monogr.,* 1916, **3**, No. 13, 65 pp.

54. Hamilton, J. A., and Krechevsky, I., Studies in the Effect of Shock Upon Behavior Plasticity in the Rat, *J. Compar. Psychol.,* 1933, **16**, 237-253.

55. Haslerud, G. M., Some Interrelations of Behavioral Measures of Frustration in Chimpanzees, *Character and Personality,* 1938, **7**, 136-139.

56. Hayes, K. J., Cognitive and Emotional Effects of Electro-Convulsive Shock in Rats, *J. Compar. and Physiol. Psychol.,* 1948, **41**, 40-61.

57. Hebb, D. O., Emotion in Man and Animal: An Analysis of the Intuitive Processes of Recognition, *Psychol. Rev.,* 1946, **53**, 88-106.

58. ———— On the Nature of Fear, *Psychol. Rev.,* 1946, **53**, 259-276.

59. ———— Spontaneous Neurosis in Chimpanzees: Theoretical Relations With Clinical and Experimental Phenomena, *Psychosom. Med.,* 1947, **9**, 3-16.

60. ———— Temperament in Chimpanzees: I. Methods of Analysis, *J. Compar. and Physiol. Psychol.,* 1949, **42**, 192-206.

61. Hilgard, E. R., and Marquis, D. G., *Conditioning and Learning,* New York: Appleton-Century, 1940.

62. Humphrey, G., Experiments on the Physiological Mechanism of Noise-Induced Seizures in the Albino Rat. II. The Site of Action of the Para-Sympathetic Drugs, *J. Compar. Psychol.,* 1942, **33**, 325-342.

63. ———— Noise Induced Seizures and the Peripheral Theory of Emotion. *Bull. of the Canadian Psychol. Association,* 1942, **2**, 24.

64. Jacobsen, C. F., Wolfe, J. B., and Jackson, T. A., An Experimental Analysis of the Frontal Association Areas in Primates, *J. Nerv. Ment. Dis.,* 1935, **82**, 1-14.

65. James, W. T., Morphological Form and its Relation to Behavior, In *The Genetic and Endocrine Basis for Differences in Form and Behavior,* (C. R. Stockard, Ed.). Philadelphia: Wistar Institute, 1941.

66. Karn, H. W., The Experimental Study of Neurotic Behavior in Infra-Human Animals, *J. General Psychol.,* 1940, **22**, 431-436.

67. Kenshalo, D. R., and Kryter, K. D., Middle Ear Infection and Sound Induced Seizures in Rats, *J. Compar. and Physiol. Psychol.,* 1949, **42**, 328-331.

68. Kessler, M., and Gellhorn, E., The Effect of Electrically and Chemically Induced Convulsions on Conditioned Reflexes, *Amer. J. Psychiat.,* 1943, **99**, 687-691.

69. Klee, J. B., The Relation of Frustration and Motivation to the Production of Abnormal Fixations in the Rat, *Psychol. Monogr.,* 1944, **56**, 1-45.

70. Kleemeier, R. W., Fixation and Regression in the Rat, *Psychol. Monogr.,* 1942, **54**, No. 4, 34 pp.

71. Lazovik, A. D., and Patton, R. A., The Relative Effectiveness of

"Conflict" and Auditory Stimulation in Precipitating Magnesium Tetany, *J. Compar. and Physiol. Psychol.*, 1947, **40**, 191-202.

72. Liberson, W. T., Time Factors in Electric Convulsive Therapy, *Yale J. of Biol. Med.*, 1945, **17**, 571-578.

73. Liddell, H. S., The Experimental Neurosis and the Problem of Mental Disorder, *Amer. J. Psychiat.*, 1938, **94**, 1035-1043.

74. —— The Alteration of Instinctual Processes Through the Influence of Conditioned Reflexes, *Psychosom. Med.*, 1942, **4**, 390-395.

75. —— Animal Behavior Studies Bearing on the Problem of Pain, *Psychosom. Med.*, 1944, **6**, 261-263.

76. —— Conditioned Reflex Method and Experimental Neurosis, pp. 389-412, in Personality and the Behavior Disorders (J. McV. Hunt, Ed.). New York: Ronald Press Co., 1944.

77. —— Chapter in *Annual Review of Physiology* (V. E. Hall, Ed.). Stanford: Annual Reviews, Inc., 1947, pp. 569-579.

78. —— Specific Factors that Modify Tolerance for Environmental Stress. To be published, 1951.

79. —— Anderson, O. D., Kotyuka, E. and Hartman, F. A., The Effect of Cortin Upon the Experimental Neurosis in Sheep, *Amer. J. Physiol.*, 1935, **113**, 87-88.

80. —— Effect of Extract of Adrenal Cortex on Experimental Neurosis in Sheep, *Archiv. Neurol. and Psychiat.*, 1935, **34**, 973-993.

81. —— and Bayne, T. L., Auditory Conditioned Reflexes in the Thyroidectomized Sheep and Goat, *Proc. Soc. Exper. Biol. and Med.*, 1927, **24**, 289-291.

82. Liddell, H. S., James, W. T., and Anderson, O. D., The Comparative Physiology of the Conditioned Motor Reflex Based on Experiments with the Pig, Dog, Sheep, Goat and Rabbit, *Compar. Psychol. Monogr.*, 1934, **11**, 89.

83. Lindsley, D. B., Finger, F. W., and Henry, C. E., Some Physiological Aspects of Audiogenic Seizures in Rats, *J. Neurophysiology*, 1942, **5**, 185-198.

84. Maier, N. R. F., *Studies of Abnormal Behavior in the Rat: The Neurotic Pattern and an Analysis of the Situation Which Produces It*. New York: Harper, 1939.

85. —— Studies of Abnormal Behavior in the Rat. IV. Abortive Behavior and its Relation to the Neurotic Attack, *J. Exper. Psychol.*, 1940, **27**, 369-393.

86. —— Studies of Abnormal Behavior in the Rat. XIV. Strain Differences in the Inheritance of Susceptibility to Convulsions, *J. Compar. Psychol.*, 1943, **35**, 327-333.

87. —— *Frustration*. New York: McGraw-Hill Book Co., 1949.

88. —— and Feldman, R. S., Studies of Abnormal Behavior in the Rat; Water Spray as a Means of Inducing Seizures, *J. Compar. Psychol.*, 1946, **39**, 275-286.

89. Maier, N. R. F., and Glaser, N. M., Studies of Abnormal Behavior in the Rat. V. The Inheritance of the "Neurotic Pattern," *J. Compar. Psychol.*, 1940, **30**, 413-418.

90. ———— Studies of Abnormal Behavior in the Rat. X. The Influence of Age and Sex on the Susceptibility to Seizure$ During Auditory Stimulation, *J. Compar. Psychol.*, 1942, **34**, 23-28.

91. ———— and Klee, J. B., Studies of Abnormal Behavior in the Rat. III. The Development of Behavior Fixations Through Frustration, *J. Exper. Psychol.* 1940, **26**, 521-546.

92. Maier, N. R. F., and Longhurst, J. U., Studies of Abnormal Behavior in the Rat. XVIII. Conflict and "Audiogenic" Seizures, *J. Compar. and Physiol. Psychol.*, 1947, **40**, 397-412.

93. Maier, N. R. F., and Schneirla, T. C., *Principles of Animal Psychology*, New York: McGraw-Hill, 1935.

94. Marcuse, F. L., and Moore, A. U., Tantrum Behavior in the Pig, *J. Compar. Psychol.*, 1944, **37**, 235-247.

95. Martin, R. F., and Hall, C. S., Emotional Behavior in the Rat. V. The Incidence of Behavior Derangements Resulting From Air-Blast Stimulations in Emotional and Non-Emotional Strains of Rats, *J. Compar. Psychol.*, 1941, **32**, 191-204.

96. Masserman, J. H., *Behavior and Neurosis*, Chicago: University of Chicago Press, 1943.

97. McGinnes, E., and Schlosberg, H., The Effects of Electroshock Convulsions on Double Alternation Lever-Pressing in the White Rat, *J. Exper. Psychol.*, 1945, **35**, 361-373.

98. Merritt, H. H., and Putnam, T. J., A New Series of Anticonvulsant Drugs Tested by Experiments on Animals, *Arch. Neurol. and Psychiat.*, 1938, **39**, 1003-1015.

99. Miller, N. E., Experimental Studies in Conflict, in *Personality and the Behavior Disorders*, (J. McV. Hunt. Ed.). New York: Ronald Press Co., 1944.

100. ———— Studies of Fear as an Acquireable Drive: I. Fear as Motivation and Fear-Reduction as Reinforcement in the Learning of New Processes, *J. Exper. Psychol.*, 1948, **38**, 89-101.

101. Morgan, C. T. and Galambos, R., Production of Audiogenic Seizures by Tones of Low Frequency, *Amer. J. Psychol.*, 1942, **55**, 555-559.

102. ———— Audiogenic Seizures Elicited in Rats by Tones of Low Frequency, *Psychol. Bull.*, 1942, **39**, 510-511.

103. Morgan, C. T. and Gould, J., Acoustical Determinants of the "Neurotic Pattern" in Rats, *Psychol. Rec.*, 1941, **4**, 258-268.

104. Morgan, C. T., and Morgan, Jane D., Auditory Induction of An Abnormal Pattern of Behavior in Rats, *J. Compar. Psychol.*, 1939. **27**, 505-508.

105. Morgan, C. T., and Waldman, H., "Conflict" and Audiogenic Seizures, *J. Compar. Psychol.*, 1941, **31**, 1-11.

106. Mowrer, O. H., Anxiety-Reduction and Learning, *J. Exper. Psychol.*, 1940, **27**, 497-516.

107. —— Animal Studies in the Genesis of Personality, *Transactions of the New York Academy of Science,* 1940, **3**, 8-11.

108. —— An Experimental Analogue of "Regression" With Incidental Observations on "Reaction Formation," *J. Abnor. and Soc. Psychol.,* 1940, **35**, 56-87.

109. Munn, N. L., *Handbook of Psychological Research on the Rat,* Boston: Houghton-Mifflin Co., 1950.

110. National Research Council, Conference on Experimental Neuroses and Allied Problems. Washington, D. C.: April 17 and 18, 1937 (Mimeographed).

111. National Research Council, *Problems of Neurotic Behavior.* Washington, D. C.: 1938 (Mimeographed).

112. Page, J. D., Studies in Electrically Induced Convulsions in Animals, *J. Compar. Psychol.,* 1941, **31**, 181-194.

113. Patton, R. A., The Effect of Vitamins on Convulsive Seizures in Rats Subjected to Auditory Stimulation, *J. Compar. Psychol.,* 1941, **31**, 215-221.

114. —— Purulent Otitis Media in Albino Rats Susceptible to Sound-Induced Seizures, *J. Psychol.,* 1947, **24**, 313-317.

115. —— Sound-Induced Convulsions in the Hamster Associated With Magnesium Deficiency, *J. Compar. and Physiol. Psychol.,* 1947, **40**, 283-289.

116. —— Vitamin B-Complex Concentrates and the Incidence of Sound-Induced Seizures in Young Albino Rats Maintained on Purified Diets, *J. Compar. and Physiol. Psychol.,* 1947, **40**, 323-332.

117. —— Karn, H. W., and King, C. G., Studies on the Nutritional Basis of Abnormal Behavior in Albino Rats. I. The Effect of Vitamin B_1 and Vitamin B-Complex Deficiency on Convulsive Seizures, *J. Compar. Psychol.,* 1941, **32**, 543-550.

118. —— Studies on the Nutritional Basis of Abnormal Behavior in Albino Rats. III. The Effect of Different Levels of Vitamin B_1 Intake on Convulsive Seizures; the Effect of Other Vitamins in the B-Complex and Mineral Supplements on Convulsive Seizures, *J. Compar. Psychol.,* 1942, **34**, 85-89.

119. Patton, R. A., Karn, H. W., and Longenecker, H. E., Studies on the Nutritional Basis of Abnormal Behavior in Albino Rats. IV. Convulsive Seizures Associated with Pyridoxine Deficiency, *J. Biol. Chem.,* 1944, **152**, 181-191.

120. Patton, R. A., and Longenecker, H. E., Studies on the Nutritional Basis of Abnormal Behavior in Albino Rats. V. The Effect of Pyridoxine Deficiency Upon Sound-Induced Magnesium Tetany, *J. Compar. Psychol.,* 1945, **38**, 319-334.

121. Patton, R. A., Russell, R. W., and Pierce, J. F., The Effects of Auditory Stimulation on the Electroconvulsive Threshold, *Amer. Psychol.,* 1949, **4**, 233 (Abstract).

122. Patton, R. A., and Zabarenko, L. M., Further Observations on the Incidence of Middle-ear Infection and Sensitivity to Sound-

Induced Convulsive Seizures in Young Albino Rats. To be published.

123. Pavlov, I. P., *Conditioned Reflexes,* (Translated by G. V. Anrep). London: Oxford University Press, 1927.

124. ———— *Lectures on Conditioned Reflexes,* (Translated by W. H. Gantt). New York: International Publishers, 1928.

125. Pilgrim, F. J., and Patton, R. A., Production and Reversal of Sensitivity to Sound-Induced Convulsions Associated with a Pyridoxin Deficiency, *J. Compar. and Physiol. Psychol.,* 1949, **42,** 422-426.

126. Pierce, J. F., Russell, R. W., and Patton, R. A., Electroconvulsive Thresholds in Rats as Functions of Various Types of Stimulating Currents, *J. Psychol.,* 1950, **30,** 157-170.

127. Porter, P. B., and Stone, C. P., Electroconvulsive Shock in Rats Under Ether Anesthesia, *J. Compar. and Physiol. Psychol.,* 1947, **40,** 441-456.

128. ———— and Eriksen, C. W., Learning Ability in Rats Given Electroconvulsive Shocks in Late Infancy, *J. Compar. and Physiol. Psychol.,* 1948, **41,** 423-431.

129. Russell, R. W., Effects of Electroshock Convulsions on Learning and Retention in Rats as Functions of Difficulty of the Task, *J. Compar. and Physiol. Psychol.,* 1949, **42,** 137-142.

130. ———— Pierce, J. F., Rohrer, W. M. and Townsend, J. C., A New Apparatus for the Controlled Administration of Electroconvulsive Shock, *J. Psychol.,* 1948, **26,** 71-82.

131. Russell, R. W., Pierce, J. F., and Townsend, J. C., Characteristics of Tissue Impedance in the Rat Under Conditions of Electroconvulsive Shock Stimulation, *Amer. J. Physiol.,* 1949, **156,** 317-321.

132. Russell, R. W., Townsend, J. C., Braun, H. W., and Patton, R. A., The Relationships of Certain Instrumental Variables to the Occurrence of Spinal Lesions in Rats Subjected to Controlled Electroshock Convulsions, *Amer. Psychol.,* 1948, **3,** 359-360.

133. Selye, H., *Stress.* Montreal: Acta, Inc., 1950.

134. Shohl, J., Effects of Oral Administration of Dilantin Sodium on Abnormal Behavior in the Rat, *J. Compar. Psychol.,* 1944, **37,** 243-250.

135. Siegel, P. S., and Lacey, O. L., A Further Observation of Electrically-Induced "Audiogenic" Seizures in the Rat, *J. Compar. Psychol.,* 1946, **39,** 319-320.

136. Siekert, R. G., Williams, S. C., and Windle, W. F., Histologic Study of the Brains of Monkeys After Experimental Electroshock, *Archiv. Neurol. and Psychiat.,* 1950, **63,** 79-86.

137. Smith, K. U., Quantitative Analysis of the Pattern of Activity in Audio-epileptic Seizures in the Rats, *J. Compar. Psychol.,* 1941, **32,** 311-328.

138. Stainbrook, E. J., Shock Therapy: Psychologic Theory and Research, *Psychol. Bull.,* 1946, **43,** 21-60.

139. ———— and de Jong, H., Symptoms of Experimental Catatonia in the Audiogenic and Electroshock Reactions of Rats, *J. Compar. Psychol.*, 1943, **36**, 75-78.

140. Stone, C. P., Deficits in Maze Learning by Rats Tested From Two and One-Half to Three Months After a Course of Electroconvulsive Shocks," *Amer. Psychol.*, 1948, **3**, 237 (Abstract).

141. Tainter, M. L., Tainter, E. G., Lawrence, W. S., Neuru, E. N., Lackey, R. W., Luduena, F. P., Kirtland, H. B., and Gonzalez, R. I., Influence of Various Drugs on Threshold for Electric Convulsions, *J. Pharmacol.*, 1943, **79**, 42-54.

142. Townsend, J. C., Russell, R. W., and Patton, R. A., Effects of Electroshock Convulsions on Retention in Rats as Functions of Intensity of Electroshock Stimulus, *J. Compar. and Physiol. Psychol.*, 1949, **42**, 148-155.

143. Weiner, H. M., and Morgan, C. T., Effects of Cortical Lesions Upon Audiogenic Seizures, *J. Compar. Psychol.*, 1945, **38**, 199-208.

144. Wendt, G. R., Auditory Acuity of Monkeys, *Compar. Psychol. Monogr.*, 1934, **10**, 51 pp.

145. Whiting, J. W. M., and Mowrer, O. H., Habit Progression and Regression—A Laboratory Study of Some Factors Relevant to Human Socialization, *J. Compar. Psychol.*, 1943, **36**, 229-253.

146. Winder, C. L., and Stone, C. P., Reduction of General Activity in Male Albino Rats From Electroconvulsive Shock, *Proc. Soc. Exper. Biol. and Med.*, 1946, **61**, 63-92.

147. Wortis, S. B., Shaskan, D., Impastato, D. J., and Almanski, R., Brain Metabolism: VIII. The Effects of Electric Shock and Some Newer Drugs, *Amer. Jour. Psychiat.*, 1941, **98**, 354-359.

148. Yerkes, R. M., *Chimpanzees: A Laboratory Colony*, New Haven: Yale University Press, 1943.

Author Index

515

Subject Index

A

Abiogenesis, 11-12
Abnormal behavior in animals, 458-504
  effect of endocrine glands on, 470
  study of, 458-461
  theories on, 476-479
Activity, level of, 63-68
  cycles, 63
  measurement of, 63-68
Aggregation:
  and reproduction, 397-398
  ecological aspects of, 396-398
  necessary for survival, 397-398
Amphibia:
  correlated neuromuscular development
    and behavior in, 35-36
  hastening metamorphosis in, 37-38
    effect of thyroid on, 37-38
Animal behavior, and electroconvulsive
    shock, 498-503
  behavioral effects, 501-504
    conditioned responses, 503
    on learning, 501-502
    on retention, 502-503
  effect of instrumental variables on, 498-
    499
  nature of convulsion, 499-501
    convulsive thresholds, 500
    the seizure, 499-500
Animal mind, 2-3
Animal sociology, 388-418
Aristotle, theory of evolution of, 14-15
Association-reinforcement (S-R) theory,
    247-256
  habit strength, 250-251
  inhibitory factors, 253-255
  need, drive, drive stimulus, 249, 250
  nonassociative factors, 251-253
  reinforcement, 249, 250
  response measure, related to interven-
    ing variables, 255-256
  secondary motivation, 250
  stimulus trace (s), 249

B

Bacon, Francis, natural science of, 16
Behavior:
  "insightful," 216
  instinctive, 54-58
Behavior, abnormal, in primates, 472-474
  effect of spaying on, 473
  in chimpanzees, 473-474
Behavior, animal, motivation of (See
    Motivation)
Behavior, direct effect of hormones on,
    116-127
  in the female, 121-128
    effect of estradiol, estrone, and pro-
      gesten on, 122-217
  in the male, 116-121
    effect of testosterone on, 117-119, 121
    effect of thyroid on, 120
Behavior, environmental controls of, 90-94
  emergency reactions, 93-94

Audiogenic seizures, 480, 481-496
  and conflict, 481-485
  effect of variables on, 485-493
  mechanism of, 496-498
  neurophysiological factors in, 493-496
Audiogenic seizures, effect of variables on:
  áge and sex, 486-487
  dietary deficiency, 489-492
  genetic factors, 487-488
  middle-ear infection, 429-439
  nature of seizure, 485
  previous seizures, 488-489
  stimulus characteristics, 485-486
Audiogenic seizures, mechanism of:
  theories on, 496-498
Audiogenic seizures, neurophysiological
    factors in:
  effect of brain lesions on, 495-496
  effect of drugs on, 494-495
  electrocortical activity, 493
Auditory discrimination, in bats, 323-325